D1306894

UNDERSTANDING
RESEARCH

W. Lawrence Neuman

University of Wisconsin at Whitewater

PEARSON

Boston • New York • San Francisco
Mexico City • Montreal • Toronto • London • Madrid • Munich • Paris
Hong Kong • Singapore • Tokyo • Cape Town • Sydney

U18402 9722247

Executive Editor: *Jeff Lasser*
Development Editor: *Jennifer Albanese*
Series Editorial Assistant: *Lauren Macey*
Senior Marketing Manager: *Kelly May*
Production Editor: *Claudine Bellanton*
Editorial Production Service: *Pine Tree Composition*
Manufacturing Buyer: *Debbie Rossi*
Electronic Composition: *Pine Tree Composition*
Interior Design: *Ellen Pettengell*
Photo Researcher: *Kate Cebik*
Cover Administrator/Designer: *Joel Gendron*

For related titles and support materials, visit our online catalog at www.pearsonhighered.com.

Copyright © 2009 Pearson Education, Inc.

All rights reserved. No part of the material protected by this copyright notice may be reproduced or utilized in any form or by any means, electronic or mechanical, including photocopying, recording, or by any information storage and retrieval system, without written permission from the copyright owner.

To obtain permission(s) to use material from this work, please submit a written request to Pearson Education, Rights and Contracts Department, 501 Boylston Street, Suite 900, Boston, MA 02116 or fax your request to 617-671-3447.

Between the time website information is gathered and then published, it is not unusual for some sites to have closed. Also, the transcription of URLs can result in typographical errors. The publisher would appreciate notification where these errors occur so that they may be corrected in subsequent editions.

Library of Congress Cataloging-in-Publication Data
Neuman, William Lawrence
  Understanding research / W. Lawrence Neuman. — 1st ed.
    p. cm.
  ISBN-13: 978-0-205-47153-9
  ISBN-10: 0-205-47153-6
  1. Social sciences—Research. 2. Social sciences—Methodology. 3. Sociology—Research. 4. Sociology—Methodology. I. Title.
  H62.N3882 2009
  300.72—dc22

                                                                              2008015369

Printed in Canada

6 7 8 9 10   WEB   16 15 14 13

Brief Contents

Contents

Part 1 Beginning the Research Process

Part 2 Quantitative Data Collection and Analysis

Chapter 9 Making Sense of the Numbers 230

Part 3 Qualitative Data Collection and Analysis

Chapter 10 Observing People in Natural Settings 262

Chapter 11 Looking at the Past and Across Cultures 292

Part 4 Research Report

Appendices

Preface

TO THE STUDENT

Welcome to *Understanding Research*. Learning about how to do social research is a lot of fun, but many students feel they know only a little about this topic or feel intimidated by it. You have already encountered the results of research studies. You've heard about them during your years of schooling, and you've read the findings from numerous research studies in textbooks or elsewhere. Each time you read a book for a college class, you are reading about the findings of research studies. Newspapers, Internet sources and news programs often mention research studies. Professional work settings and organizations in a wide range of fields use studies all the time. While you may have encountered the results of research, this book helps you look at the process of doing a research study that produces the results.

Any book has many ideas. Here are three basic ideas about social research to keep in mind as you read this book:

- Research is a process.
- Research is relevant.
- You can understand and do research.

First, to say that social research is a process means that doing a study is an ongoing activity that takes time. Someone has to engage in a set of specific actions to produce the results. It does not happen by itself; it is not a static thing or something you put on a shelf to gather dust. Doing a study is not something passive, in which people simply sit back and watch it happen. As a process or activity, it involves real people who must take action, make decisions, take risks, engage in various steps, write things down, and think seriously about what is going on. The process of doing a study comes from many hundreds of researchers who worked over many decades to iron out difficulties and who found the best ways to learn new things about the social world. As you learn about doing research, you will develop an understanding of the process by which we acquire knowledge about the social life around us.

Second, the results of research and the process of doing research are both relevant. At times, some findings may seem obscure or esoteric, but most findings have very real consequences. They are relevant to everyday life and to being a citizen, a friend, a parent, a professional, an employee, or a business owner. While it is not always immediately apparent, most research has real implications and practical consequences for someone. You may have to think about it and draw out connections, but more often than not, research has relevance. Some people, out of ignorance, say it is "just research" or "only a study" because they do not see how research connects to their lives and to the lives of people, organizations, and events around them.

Third, you can understand and do research. Yes, college professors, high-powered research scientists and others with years of advanced schooling and training do many of the research studies. This does not mean that research is beyond you, the beginning student. You have the ability to think, to collect evidence, and to see connections or implications—these are the requirements for doing research. A beginning student may not grasp or do the most highly sophisticated research study, but the basic principles and procedures, the overall process and implications are accessible with just modest amounts of time and effort. Once you understand the fundamentals of the research process, it is a short distance to beginning to do small-scale studies of your own. Understanding and doing research can open an entire world of studies, findings, and new insights.

TO THE INSTRUCTOR

Whether you are a new instructor teaching social research or a veteran of many decades, you are probably aware that many students approach a course on research methods with feelings of fear and dread. Often it is one of a few required courses in the curriculum, and it creates unnecessary angst and anxiety. I say unnecessary because learning how to do research does not have to be unpleasant, difficult, or fraught with stress. At its core, doing research can be fun and exciting because students can explore and learn new things, examine features of social life in new ways, and be empowered to create new findings or knowledge. While a degree of self-awareness, rigor, and discipline is necessary to do social research—these are not necessarily unpleasant attributes. Students who are interested in a sport or hobby, or who develop an intense curiosity in a topic, accept and embrace the need for self-awareness, rigor, and discipline.

My passion and approach to teaching about social research comes from experience. I say passion because I genuinely enjoy seeing students learn—and specifically, learn about the process of discovery and knowledge creation called social research. I have been teaching social research methods to undergraduates and some graduate students for roughly thirty years. I have not been redoing the same thing across those thirty years but constantly reflecting, adjusting, learning, and hopefully improving. In addition, this book builds on my past textbooks on research that have been around for over a decade. I never tried to please with the textbooks, I only expressed what I thought was important to know and did so in a manner that students could grasp. This meant breaking core research ideas or techniques into their basics, providing students with both simple examples and specific, published studies as examples. I respect good pedagogy but dislike fads and never tried to mimic any other author. I have always presented what I believe is most important and tried to do it in a way that students find accessible. Instead of just fulfilling an academic requirement, I hope students can become truly excited about the research process.

Social research is a broad topic area. A vast array of professions, applied fields, and academic disciplines use the findings and techniques of social science. My own background has been as a rather eclectic and wide-ranging sociologist. My goal in this book is to make accessible the principles, process, and procedures of social research. In so doing, I want to avoid the danger of "mono-method." The scientific-research community has produced diverse approaches and techniques for conducting social scientific research. I believe it is a serious error to become fixed on a single research approach—be it the experiment or survey, quantitative methods in general, or qualitative ethnographic research. I believe it is a serious error both for expanding our understanding of a complex, changing social world and for how we teach beginning students about research. My commitment to a broad, ecumenical approach to social scientific inquiry comes from experience. For over thirty years, I have waded in the waters of philosophical debate over social science's foundations, conducted studies by applying the many techniques and methods outlined in this book, and become an avid reader of studies across academic fields that use different research methods. I believe we collectively learn much more by being inclusive with regard to diverse social science research approaches than by closing our eyes and ears to everything beyond a single research method, or jumping on the bandwagon of the latest research technique to the exclusion of past research methods.

Authors write books for many reasons. Some seek fame, fortune, or tenure. None of these applies to me. Ultimately, I wrote this book based on two strongly held beliefs. First, applying the principles, process, and results of social research is exceedingly valuable and consequential for the choices and decisions we make in our daily lives and in organizational settings. In the end, better choices and decisions are likely to result if an open-ended understanding of the logic and results of social research inform them. Second, students can benefit and improve their lives and the life conditions of people around them if they understand the research process. The corollary of this point is that the next generation is more likely to fall behind, make bad decisions, and contribute to forms of harm to themselves or others if they fail to understand the principles of the research process. Most students who learn about social research do not go on to become full-time professional research scientists, but they do become parents, friends, professional workers, citizen-voters, and community members. Understanding the research process and appreciating how it informs us about social life can improve how they fulfill those life-long roles. In short, I personally believe a great deal is at stake when we teach students about the research process.

CHAPTER CONTENT

Each chapter of the book follows a similar format and mixes the practical-applied aspects of research with the foundational principles and techniques of doing a study. After a brief introductory study, students learn about a specific aspect of the research process. Throughout the book, students will see many cross-references to material in other chapters. This is to help students see the interconnections among the various parts of the research process.

Chapter 1 outlines the basics of what social research entails. It explains why a student will find it beneficial to understand the research process. Students learn that research involves critical thinking and applying specific techniques to gather empirical evidence in a careful, systematic way. They see the steps in conducting a research study and learn about some of the purposes for doing a research study.

Chapter 2 is about getting started on a study. Students learn about the literature of empirical research studies in scholarly journals. The chapter aims to make students better consumers of research findings and teaches them how to access the literature. They learn the basics of finding and documenting sources, and of preparing a literature review. In addition, the chapter explains the process of refining a broad, general topic into a focused research question for a specific study, with some discussion of the theory-method connection. There is also some advice on how to prepare a research proposal. A discussion of the research proposal will reappear in the last chapter after students have learned about all the techniques and parts of social research process.

Chapter 3 discusses the ethics of doing social research and their importance. This chapter reviews the principles that distinguish ethical from unethical social research and covers requirements for conducting ethical studies. It also describes some of the ethical controversies in the history of social research. Students also learn about the ideas of value-free or objective research, and the issues/tensions that can arise with sponsored research or external pressures on the research enterprise.

Chapter 4 is about why we sample in many studies and the principle of generalizing from a small number of cases to a larger population. Students learn the logic, reasons for, and techniques of random sampling. They also learn about several non-random sampling methods. The chapter presents both practical issues and some more abstract ideas, including the concept of confidence intervals.

Chapter 5 primarily teaches students about quantitative measurement. The reason for measurement is to allow us to make aspects of the social word visible for research purposes. The chapter includes a brief discussion of quantitative versus qualitative forms of measuring that reinforces the quantitative–qualitative balance found throughout the book. Students learn about measurement reliability and validity, as well as how to create an index. They also learn the basis of scaling in social research and see illustrations of a few widely used social science scales.

Chapter 6 describes how to conduct a survey. Students see how to write good survey questions, organize a questionnaire, and conduct a survey interview. They learn about several types of survey questions and survey formats. As with other chapters, there is a mix of a practical "hands on" application of how to conduct a survey with a discussion of the principles and methodological issues involved in survey research.

Chapter 7 is on the logic and method of the experiment. I present the experiment as the "gold standard" for demonstrating causal relations in a research study. Besides being a rigorous method in its own right, the experimental method has principles that extend to other research techniques. Thus, the experimental logic of making comparisons in a research design and in looking at results has wider implications. The issue of research ethics that students first learned about in Chapter 3 reappears in several other chapters, including this one on the experiment.

Chapter 8 discusses an array of research techniques and quantitative data sources. Students see how we can learn from techniques such as content analysis and the creative examination of nonreactive or unobtrusive forms of evidence. The chapter also describes research that does not involve direct data collection. Students learn that they can address research questions by locating and reorganizing data collected by others. These sources include existing statistical sources, usually in government or organizational documents, as well as secondary data sources, such as survey data.

Chapter 9 is a brief foray into statistics. There are many ways to approach the relationship between research methods and statistics. Sometimes students take a statistics course prior to learning about research, sometimes it is afterwards, and sometimes students learn about quantitative data analysis integrated with learning about research. Obviously, one chapter cannot substitute for a full statistics course, and this chapter emphasizes understanding the principles of quantitative data analysis. It offers students a foundation for quantitative data analysis and introduces basic statistical ideas that may be a review for students who have had a statistics course, a preparation for those who will later take a statistics course, or a quick, pragmatic, and accessible "crash course" for students for whom this will be their only learning about statistics.

Chapter 10 discusses the principles and practice of ethnography. Qualitative field research offers an alternative approach to learning about social life from the many quantitative techniques of the previous chapters. As with other chapters, students see a mix of a practical "hands on" application of how to conduct an ethnographic study with a discussion of the core principles and methodological issues of qualitative field research. In addition, students learn about focus group research. This increasingly popular technique is not ethnography or participant observation, but the data it produces is qualitative and often is closer to field notes.

Chapter 11 is about a type of social research often omitted in books about social research methodology but that is widely used by researchers in many fields to examine important questions. Historical and comparative studies have been the basis of a great deal of our knowledge about many macro-level issues. Like research that requires advanced statistical training, few students will have the background, time, or resources to conduct a study in another culture. While a few students may be interested in questions that involve historical evidence, serious historical research differs from social research on historical issues. Nonetheless, the principles, logic, and process of conducting historical and comparative research has profound implications for social research generally. It also offers us a research method for examining a type of question about social events with serious thought and evidence that the other research techniques are not capable of addressing. By learning about historical-comparative research, students acquire an understanding both of the core principles found in social research generally and how scholars approach and answer large-scale questions about social life that would otherwise go unanswered or be answered by ideology instead of serious research.

Chapter 12 explains how to prepare a research report. In also reviews the fundamentals of writing that students learned in English courses in high school and college, and applies them to writing about research. In addition to writing basics and the organization of a report on research, this chapter discusses how to seek grant funding for conducting a research study.

Appendices

This book has three appendices. The first has two examples of research proposals: a quantitative-survey study, and a qualitative-ethnographic study. These are to show students what a research proposal looks like. The second appendix is a list of journal publications and online sources of published research across many disciplines. The last appendix contains excerpts of journal articles that demonstrate attributes of a published study.

PEDAGOGICAL FEATURES

Understanding Research contains a number of pedagogical features to allow students to view research through its application to their fields of study, its connection to classic studies of the past, and its usefulness when interpreting the bits of information students consume in their daily lives.

Chapter Opening Application: Each chapter opens with a research topic, drawn from a variety of fields. Some of these topics are fast food advertising directed at children (Chapter 1), measuring the quality of life of the elderly (Chapter 5), and occupations that require "emotional work" (Chapter 10).

Making It Practical: These boxes give students a glimpse into the researcher's toolbox so they can understand how practitioners use research methods in their work. Making It Practical serves as a "quick start" guide for those students conducting their own research, or seeking to understand others' research. Examples include *Using Article Search Tools* (Chapter 2), *Improving Unclear Questions* (Chapter 6), and *Recommendations for Taking Field Notes* (Chapter 10).

Example Study: Example Study boxes use findings from real research studies to exemplify research concepts. The research used in Example Study boxes comes from a range of disciplines. The topics in this feature include *Evaluating D.A.R.E* (Chapter 1), *Social Distance and People with Disabilities* (Chapter 5), *Magazine Covers and Cultural Messages* (Chapter 8), and *College Students Selling Door-to-Door* (Chapter 10).

Summary Review: Throughout the text, the exposition pauses to break information down for students in a list or outline form. Summary Review boxes consolidate preceding sections into an outline. The Summary Review boxes include *Basic Principles of Ethical Research* (Chapter 3), *Steps in Conducting an Experiment* (Chapter 7), and *Steps in the Writing Process* (Chapter 12).

Learning from History: Learning from History boxes provide examples from important studies, considered to be the cornerstones of social science. These boxes show students that research ideas are tied to established theory. These studies include *The Famous Literary Digest Mistake* (Chapter 4), *Who Is Poor?* (Chapter 5), and *The Galton-Tyler Discovery* (Chapter 11).

Tips for the Wise Consumer: A major theme of this text is understanding that students are daily consumers of research, and that they can develop a critical approach to understanding research. Tips for the Wise Consumer lists questions that students should consider when reading research studies, helping to dispel common misconceptions and encouraging a thoughtful approach to reading study results. Some of these boxes are *Using the Internet for Social Research* (Chapter 2), *Who Paid for the Study?* (Chapter 3), and *Intimidation and Quantitative Research Results* (Chapter 9).

Chapter Review: Each chapter provides materials to assist students in reviewing the content of the chapter, and applying their learning in various settings. The end of each chapter includes

- **What Have You Learned?**—a summary of the chapter
- **Key Terms:**—a list of the important terms defined in the chapter
- **Applying What You Know**—numerous hands-on activities that help students apply what they have just learned. Some activites are presented in workbook style, so students can write directly in the book.

SUPPLEMENTS

Instructor's Manual

For each chapter in the text, the Instructor's Manual, written by Stephen Kandeh, University of Science and Arts of Oklahoma, provides chapter summaries and outlines, learning objectives, key terms with definitions, online resources, suggested readings, class exercises and activities, and video resources.

Test Bank

The Test Bank, written by Chris Wells, Gateway Community College, contains approximately 70 questions per chapter in multiple choice, true-false, short answer, and essay formats. All questions are labeled and scaled according to Bloom's Taxonomy and the correct answer is provided for each.

Computerized Test Bank

The printed Test Bank is also available through Pearson's computerized testing system, TestGen EQ. This fully networkable test-generating software is available on a multi-platform CD-ROM for Windows and Macintosh. The user-friendly interface allows you to view, edit, and add questions, transfer questions to tests, and print tests in a variety of fonts. Search and sort features allow you to locate questions quickly and to arrange them in whatever order you prefer.

PowerPoints

The PowerPoint slides, prepared by Annette Taylor, University of San Diego and available online, were created especially for *Understanding Research*. They feature lecture outlines for every chapter and many of the tables and charts from the text.

MyResearchKit (www.myresearchkit.com)

Created by Dominic Little, California State University–Northridge, this online supplement offers chapter summaries; multiple-choice practice tests; flashcards for learning glossary terms; video clips and animations; research exercises; an SPSS tutorial; tips on writing research reports and documenting sources; a regular "Research in the News" blog; and access to a searchable database of scholarly articles in the humanities and social sciences. Free when a MyResearchKit access code card is packaged with the text upon request.

ACKNOWLEDGMENTS

Many thanks go out to the reviewers who gave thoughtful feedback on all or parts of this text:

Ken Baker, Gardner-Webb University
Karen Benton, Urbana University
Nina Coppens, University of Massachusetts
Elizabeth Easter, University of Kentucky
Molly George, University of California, Santa Barbara
Phyllis Kuehn, California State University, Fresno
John Lewis, University of Southern Mississippi
Angus McCartney, Troy University
Andrew Supple, University of North Carolina, Greensboro
Annette Taylor, University of San Diego

I would like to dedicate this text to Diane, for all her understanding.

W. Lawrence Neuman

CHAPTER 1

Why Do Research?

Christina Kennedy/PhotoEdit Inc.

Perhaps you have young children, or siblings or nieces/nephews, or maybe you will have children in the future. Any parent will tell you that the eating habits of children are a major concern. In the United States, the rapid increase in childhood obesity and diabetes is a public health issue. Children are greatly influenced by advertising, and one-half of all advertising for children is for food. Research (Gantz, et al. 2007) found that children ages 2 through 7 see an average of 12 food ads per day on TV (30 hours per year) whereas those ages 8 to 12 see an average of 21 food ads per day (50 hours per year). The study found that most of the advertised food is snacks, candy, or fast food. Only 4 percent of ads are for dairy products, 1 percent is for fruit juices, and no ads are for fruits or vegetables. Perhaps this is why several nations ban advertising that targets children. One well-known fast food chain has been especially successful in using branding to attract children (or their parents) as customers. "Branding" is when a company or other organization actively attaches its name, usually with a logo, to products or services and aggressively promotes them to the public. This is to create a strong mental and emotional connection within potential consumers. As of 2007, McDonald's had more than 30,000 restaurants serving 50 million people in more than 119 countries each day. Researchers (Robinson et al. 2007) looked at the impact of McDonald's on the food choices made by young children (ages 3 to 5). They placed two sets of food items in front of the children; one food item (milk, French fries, hamburger, chicken nuggets, and baby carrots) was in a McDonald's wrapper, and the other was not. They asked, "Can you tell me which is from McDonald's?" to make certain the children saw the difference. They next asked the children to take one bite and taste each food item, then tell the researchers whether the food was the same or one tasted better than the other. In fact, the food was identical. The researchers also asked parents about television viewing habits and fast food restaurant visits. Results (see Figures 1.1 and 1.2) showed that more children said that the item in the McDonald's package tasted better for all five food items. Note that McDonald's did not sell baby carrots at the time of this study. In addition, children whose parents had taken them to McDonald's were most likely to prefer McDonald's. The researchers concluded that by the age of 5, children internalized the McDonald's brand as an

■ **Figure 1.1   Bar Chart from Robinson Study**

Number of television sets in the household as a moderator of taste preferences. Total preference scores may range from -1 (preferred the unbranded
food in all comparisons) to 1 (preferred the McDonald's branded food in all
comparisons).

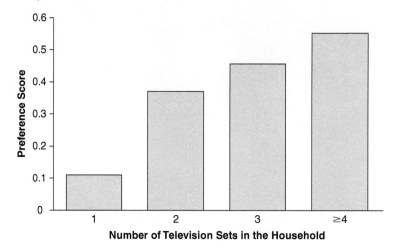

Source: **"Effects of Fast Food Branding on Young Children's Taste Preferences."**
Thomas N. Robinson, MD, MPH; Dina L. G. Borzekowski, EdD; Donna M. Matheson,
PhD, Helena C. Kraemer, PhD. *Archives of Pediatric and Adolescent Medicine* 2007;
161 (8):792–797.

■ **Figure 1.2   Bar Chart from Robinson Study**

Frequency of eating at McDonald's as a moderator of taste preferences.
Total preference scores may range from -1 (preferred the unbranded food
in all comparisons) to 1 (preferred the McDonald's branded food in all
comparisons).

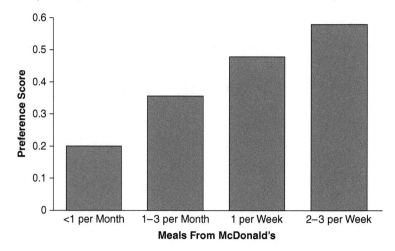

Source: **"Effects of Fast Food Branding on Young Children's Taste Preferences."**
Thomas N. Robinson, MD, MPH; Dina L. G. Borzekowski, EdD; Donna M. Matheson,
PhD, Helena C. Kraemer, PhD. *Archives of Pediatric and Adolescent Medicine* 2007;
161 (8):792–797.

indicator of superior food taste. These two studies help us understand how young children in the United States make food choices. We can conduct studies on many topics, such as children's food choices, to understand what is happening in the social world. We may or may not use study findings to make improvements in our daily lives or society—doing so requires taking social-political action. By learning how researchers conduct such studies, you will be in a better position to make decisions and choices for yourself, your family, and community.

ON WHAT BASIS DO YOU MAKE DECISIONS?

You make thousands of choices and decisions every day. Most are trivial, such as what to have for breakfast; when to call a friend; whether to purchase pink, white, or blue facial tissue; and which TV show to watch. Other decisions are important and have consequences for your personal and family life, your role as a citizen and community member, or your career. Studies suggest that most of us make decisions by using a mix of common sense; advice from experts, friends, and family; past experiences; cultural literacy; and school knowledge. Some of us also use religious faith, personal prejudice and values, horoscopes and lucky numbers, guesswork, or folklore.

You might ask, how will a book on social research help me make decisions? Although social research does not have all the answers, often it can help you to

- Make better decisions about your daily life (such as, What type of person should I marry? What is the best way to raise my child? Why are many people getting divorced?).
- Understand events in the larger world around you (such as, Why do students shoot their teachers? Do drug courts really work?).
- Decide professional issues (such as, Which product is likely to sell the most? How do I find out whether my employees are happy? Which children's reading program is most effective?).

Research is a process in which people use specific principles and techniques to create knowledge. It also refers to a body of knowledge (i.e., information, ideas, or theories) built up over time, and a way to look at information, questions, or issues. You have probably heard of people doing research, or you may have read research findings or done some research. The various aspects of research are interrelated.

Making It Practical **Looking at the Word** *Research*

What do you think of when you hear the word *research*?

_____ *It is fun and exciting.* Yes, research allows you to exercise your creativity and discover new things, which is almost always fun.

_____ *It is difficult and mysterious.* Yes, research has some difficult parts that may seem mysterious until you learn about them, but most aspects of research are easy to grasp.

_____ *It is practical and relevant.* Yes, it can yield results you can use and make a difference in real life.

_____ *It is valuable and rewarding.* This is usually true. Properly conducted research can have a big payoff for life decisions you make, workplace effectiveness, and job prospects.

_____ *It is a waste of time and effort.* Not exactly. Research can take time and effort, but it is rarely a waste if done properly.

_____ *It is always correct.* No, it is not always right, but it is more likely to be right than the alternatives, such as relying on tradition, authority or your personal experience. It is useful to distinguish between better and worse research.

HOW DO WE KNOW WHAT WE KNOW?

Ways of Knowing Without Research

As just mentioned, most people make decisions without doing research, checking out research results, or looking at issues with a research orientation. Most of the time, this turns out fine, especially for trivial decisions. Yet many psychological studies suggest that few of us are great decision makers. We often misjudge or use distorted thinking and are not even aware of our misjudgment or bias. This is where research comes in. Research reduces misjudgment, bias, and distorted thinking.

Research produces valuable information and expands understanding, but it is not 100 percent foolproof. It does not guarantee perfect results every time or yield "absolute truth." However, in a head-to-head comparison with all the other ways we reach decisions, research wins hands down. This is why professional organizations, highly educated people, and most leaders rely on research when they make important decisions. Centuries ago, people went to oracles, looked at the leaves at bottom of a teacup, or consulted the stars to make major decisions. Today, people in all fields—medicine, business, education, law enforcement, public policy—instead look to research publications or study findings.

Relying on research is not always simple. You may have heard the dozens of contradictory and confusing research-based recommendations about health and diet in the mass media. You may ask, What is so great about research if there is so much disagreement? In reality, a lot of what fills the mass media using the terms *research* or *scientific* does not involve scientific research. Unfortunately, it is legal to use the word *research* in the media when technically no real research backs a statement. Some of what you hear may be research backed, but it could be selective or incomplete, overstated or distorted. The media "noise machine" jumbles together many different types of statements. It is little wonder that many people are skeptical of research. Media distortion of research or social issues can be confusing. You may hear of a terrible problem in the mass media, but closer inspection and a little research may reveal that it was seriously distorted (see Tips for the Wise Consumer).

By the time you read this book, you have already had many years of schooling. You have undoubtedly heard about research and science during the many years you sat in classrooms, did homework, and read textbooks. Unless you had talented, enthusiastic teachers, you might have had an unpleasant experience or developed "research phobia." Maybe it was smelly science labs or challenging math tests without enough preparation time. In many schools, only about 10 percent of students (the brains, eggheads, nerds, or geeks) really get into research and science. Many other students see it as being irrelevant or strange at best. Some are frightened or intimidated by the idea of scientific research. Perhaps when you hear "scientific research" you have images of the fictional mad scientist from science fiction stories or horror movies.

Many people believe that only college professors, people with medical or Ph.D. degrees, and high-powered professional scientists can do research. Maybe you watched a famous researcher being interviewed on television or picked up an obscure research publication filled with incomprehensible jargon, statistics, and exotic formulas. You may feel that research is beyond you and that it has little relevance for your daily life or career. Yet many students, after just one class in doing research, can use the techniques, insights, and information-gathering skills to improve decision making.

One purpose of this book is to show you that empirical social research is not frightening, is not beyond you, and can be relevant. Yes, doing research can be hard

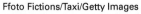
Ffoto Fictions/Taxi/Getty Images

Tips for the Wise Consumer   Media Reports Are Not Always Accurate

Have you seen the missing children photos on milk cartons or posters? Most people are very concerned about abducted and missing children. They believe it is a huge and growing problem. President Ronald Reagan brought it to national attention and called it the nation's most dire problem, based on statistics showing that 1.5 million children are abducted and 50,000 are never found. Numerous television news shows repeated this "fact." The TV show *America's Most Wanted* repeated the numbers and claimed, "This country is littered with mutilated, decapitated, raped and strangled children" (Glassner 1999:63). But is this true? An official Justice Department report (1999) shows that caretakers (parent, guardian, babysitter, etc.) thought 1.3 million children were missing, but they only reported 800,000 cases to an official agency or the police. Of the 800,000, only 115 fit the stereotypical kidnapping by a stranger (Department of Justice 2002). Although 115 missing children is a serious issue, it is dramatically different from claims of over 1 million missing children. Horror stories in the media shape the public's attention and have intense emotional appeal. Most people accept such stories as true and base their actions on them. Few take the time to look calmly and carefully at the research-backed evidence to determine the actual situation. Before you make decisions, it may be wise to do some independent investigation and find out whether the horror stories are true or not.

PA / Topham/The Image Works

work. It allows little room for being sloppy, lazy, "spaced out," or careless. Research takes concentration, serious thinking, rigor, and self-discipline. In this respect, it is not unique. Making great music or art, cooking fantastic food, growing an outstanding garden, starting up a new business, providing excellent health care, being a star athlete, or repairing highly complex machinery all take concentration, serious thinking, rigor, and self-discipline. Doing research takes rigor, but it is also a creative, exciting, and fun process.

If research is better than the alternative ways to get answers such as asking a friend, relying on some supposed expert, or guessing, you may well ask, Why don't more people learn to do research and use it in their lives? A simple answer is ignorance. If you do not know it, you cannot use it. However, people may also reject the results or method of research not from ignorance, but because the results, or how people got to the results, contradict a deep-held belief, a traditional way of doing things, or because it goes against peer pressure or "what everybody knows."

Some people turn away from research because it does not guarantee 100 percent perfect answers all the time. They misunderstand a key feature of research: **Research is an ongoing process of searching and working toward the truth.** Knowledge from research slowly accumulates over time. Although it is not perfect, it still beats the alternative ways of producing knowledge. If you want to find best answers in real life, then research is for you.

Large numbers of people, even in the United States in the twenty-first century,[1] continue to believe in things that research repeatedly demonstrates to be false, such as the following:

- UFOs and ESP (extrasensory perception)
- Horoscopes and astrology
- Unscientific thinking about age of the earth or basic forces of nature
- Goblins, demons, witches, evil spirits, and devils

Although the average level of schooling in the population has risen, many people cling to invented stories or magical-fantasy thinking. Studies suggest that average reading comprehension, critical thinking skills, basic social-geographic knowledge, and understanding of scientific research in the public have changed little (Pew Research Center Report 2007). Why? Part of the answer is that not everyone continues to practice and apply the knowledge, skills, or thinking acquired in their school years later in their daily life or job decisions. Another part of the answer is a simple matter of numbers. Imagine that 25,000 educated people want to be better informed. They read a book written by an expert who carefully researched a topic for six years. At the same time, 100 million people, who are just a little lazy, go out to watch an entertaining, glitzy 90-minute movie on the same topic. The movie contains inaccurate and distorted information. Most people's views and thinking are based on inaccurate and distorted information from the movie. Just because most people believe something is true does not make it true. A good reason for you to learn to think critically and to conduct research properly is so you do not follow what most other people think when it is wrong.

Developing Critical Thinking Skills

The word *critical* has three common meanings: (1) being very important, or being an urgent need; (2) being highly negative or antagonistic and looking for flaws; and (3) being very aware, judging carefully, and questioning by not accepting just anything that comes along. The *critical* in critical thinking refers to the last meaning, although the first one also fits. **Critical thinking** is a way to think and see things. Psychologists and others who study how we think have cataloged a long list of common misperceptions or logical fallacies. Just as we can become misled when we look into a distorted mirror, we can fall for these fallacies. Here are two common ones for the sake of illustration.

- Gambler's fallacy—We tend to think that if something has not occurred for a long time, it will soon happen. If you flip a fair coin six times and get heads, the odds that the next flip will result in tails is actually no greater than the odds for heads.
- Attribution error—We tend to attribute or assign blame for negative outcomes to others or outside forces, but believe we are personally responsible for positive outcomes.

Critical thinking helps us avoid common fallacies. It also discourages us from rushing to arrive at a fixed, closed or set answer. Many people feel uncomfortable with ambiguity or an open-ended process of searching. They want the absolute correct answer, here and now. Critical thinking warns us that there is rarely one quick, simple correct answer.

Critical thinking points to the value of looking at a question, issue, or evidence from more than one point of view. It tells us that adopting a single perspective or point of view often blinds us to important aspects of a question, issue, or problem.

Critical thinking leads us to uncover hidden assumptions. Assumptions—unstated premises or untested starting points—are necessary, and we use them all the time. There is nothing wrong with having assumptions. However, assumptions tend to block off certain avenues of inquiry while favoring others. Problems can arise when we fail to recognize or examine our assumptions. Critical thinking tells us to notice assumptions and see that they can limit choices. If we adopt alternative assumptions, the outcome may be very different. Here is a simple example (see Making It Practical: Recognizing Assumptions).

critical thinking a highly aware perspective that tries to avoid fallacies, reveal assumptions, adopt multiple viewpoints, and keep an open mind while questioning simple solutions.

Making It Practical   Recognizing Assumptions

Often debates or disagreements reach an impasse because participants are using different assumptions. Revealing hidden assumptions can shift the discussion and allow a resolution or at least clarify the real issue. For example, two executives, Mark and Susan, disagree over whether to advance product X or product Y. Product X costs less to produce, has a three-year life expectancy, and yields a $10 profit for each item sold. Product Y has slightly higher production costs but is of higher quality. It lasts six years and yields an $8 profit per item. Mark favors item X. He projects that it will sell 10,000 units to produce $100,000 in total profits. Susan favors item Y. She projects that it will sell 15,000 units for $120,000 in total profits. Their disagreement is not over cost or profits, but over time horizon and customer loyalty. Mark assumes a two-year time frame and thinks that retaining customers and building brand loyalty are minor concerns. Susan assumes a longer time frame and that building brand loyalty among customers is important.

Here is another example: A school district creates two charter schools. The new principals of each try to create a high-quality learning environment. After the schools were operational for ten years, 75 percent of students from both charter schools entered a four-year college and equal numbers went on to highly successful careers. However, the principals of each school recruited students differently. Whereas Principal A assumed that academics alone were important, Principal B assumed that having a socially diverse classroom and student cooperation skills were equally as important as academic test scores. Principal A recruited based on academic test scores alone, taking top-scoring students. Principal B recruited half the students based on academics and half based on other talents (art, athletics, drama, music, or volunteering) or strong motivation. In Principal A's school, 85 percent of students entering came from one section of town, Eliteville, where high-income, well-educated people lived. Principal B's charter school had only 30 percent of its students from Eliteville; 70 percent came from all over the community.

Social research uses critical thinking and a particular form of argument. The word *argument* here does not mean shouting down another person. It means a set of logically connected statements that start simple and end with a clear conclusion that pulls everything together. We use two major types of arguments in discussions and descriptions about how things are now, why social events or behaviors happen, and what might be the best way to resolve an issue or problem based on likely consequences. One type uses moral, religious, or ideological reasoning, and the other uses critical thinking and systematic **empirical evidence**.

Many students in my classes and much of the public confuse the two types of argument. They do not easily recognize a key distinction between the two types: Research arguments greatly rely on systematic empirical evidence, whereas arguments based on a moral position, religious doctrine, or ideological values do not. We examine this distinction in the next section.

empirical evidence evidence of actual events occurring in the world that come from direct or indirect observations.

Summary Review   Four Features of Critical Thinking

- Avoid logical fallacies; practice careful thinking using "cold logic."
- Maintain an open mind and look at all aspects of an issue; be cautious about simple, fast and easy solutions offered for serious issues.
- Do not get locked into a single point of view; look at issues from multiple perspectives.
- Examine hidden assumptions; be aware of your assumptions and their implications.

Learning from History **Religion and Research**

Mary Evans Picture Library/The
Image Works

Research usually wins out over horoscopes, lucky numbers, or superstition, but organized religion is a more sensitive subject. Most people, especially in the United States, profess a belief in God and feel attached to a specific religion (usually Judeo-Christian). Scientific research and religion, including non-Judeo-Christian religious beliefs like Islam and Buddhism, can disagree. This is nothing new. In fact, it has been going on at least since Galileo Galilei (1564–1642). Although he tried to remain loyal to his religion, Galileo was committed to research, honesty, and truth. These caused him to reject a blind allegiance to philosophical and religious authority. Based on careful research and systematic empirical evidence, he changed his views on how the world works. He insisted the earth went around the sun and not vice versa, as religious authorities at the time held. Because he opposed established doctrine, authorities placed him under house arrest and banned his books. Today we recognize that Galileo was right, and in time religious authorities relaxed their views and changed their position.

The science versus religion conflict is easily overdrawn. At one extreme are some highly devout people who reject all science and believe only in religious faith. Whether it is gravity, age of the earth, medical care, causes of crime, or whatever, they believe that religion alone has the only true answers. At the other extreme are some nonreligious people who think all religion is false and believe in science alone. Whether it is social justice, moral decisions of right or wrong, life after death, or whatever, they feel that only science has the true answers. Most people, including most scientists, fall in between the extremes. Religious extremists of any religion (Christianity, Islam, Hinduism, or others) and science extremists each think they have all the answers, but most people think that both sides have value and each side addresses certain issues better than the other.

Science-based research is better at providing answers for some questions whereas religion may be better for others.

Science cannot tell moral right from wrong, whether there is a God, whether we have a soul, or what happens after death. In the past, religious authorities made rather foolish statements about astronomy, biology, and many social issues (such as supporting slavery). The line between what belongs to religion or to science is always shifting. At one time, science only dealt with the physical world (planets, chemistry, or plants) and religious thinking dominated all social issues. As research techniques and scientific thinking advanced, people applied them to social issues—such as why crime rates rise and whether children raised in certain ways are better adjusted. Over time, people were less likely to accept the old answers, such as that errant behavior is caused by the devil or original sin. Increasingly, they looked to research-based answers such as increased economic distress, child rearing without strong, clear values, or a breakdown of community ties.

Research answers many questions that overlap with religious-moral issues. Research cannot answer questions such as, Should I marry John? Is abortion immoral? Is the death penalty right or wrong? Should same-sex marriage be allowed? Will prayer help cure my mother's cancer? However, it can answer related questions: If one marries someone with a background of emotional instability and excessive alcohol or illegal drug use, is one likely to experience physical abuse and divorce? Do women who have an abortion experience less or more social, educational, and economic success? Does having a death penalty lower murder rates? Do children raised by same-sex couples grow up to be as well adjusted as those raised by opposite-sex couples? Does praying for a person end the spread of cancer? Answers to these questions may help you make decisions about moral and religious concerns but do not provide a fixed moral answer.

Suppose you found that the death penalty has no effect on reducing murder rates. You may still want to keep it for other reasons (e.g., revenge or religious beliefs). At least if you know the research findings, you can choose to base your decision on the facts or something else (e.g., moral or religious belief). Suppose studies showed that praying for a seriously ill person has no impact on recovery rates. You may still want to pray for other reasons. Perhaps it makes you feel better and gives your life focus, or it may help give the ill person a feeling of hope, and that may indirectly aid in recovery. In short, research and other moral-religious reasoning differ, but they are often compatible.

WHAT IS EMPIRICAL SOCIAL RESEARCH?

Research takes many forms. For example, I want to purchase a new car. I "research" by reading several magazine articles about features of the various autos, I visit the showroom and test drive cars, I go online to examine reports on crash test safety or mechanical reliability, I compare specifications such as leg room length or tire size. The topic of this book, empirical social research, involves gathering information, but it is much more than that.

We use the word *research* in the following four ways:

1. Research is closely reading and studying specific documents. You identify certain documents and then read and reread the documents (religious texts such as the Bible or Koran, legal texts such as the Constitution or court decisions, literary texts such as novels, artistic texts such as paintings or music scores) to attain a deeper understanding, to reveal patterns and themes, or to find ultimate truth.
2. Research is gathering preexisting information from academic journals or official government reports and making sense of it. You first search for and collect information, then evaluate what you found, and finally synthesize the findings. During the process, you do not treat all information equally. You may weigh some evidence (your friend says a car looks cool) differently than other evidence (test driving the car or reading about its rate of mechanical failure).
3. Research is a process of applying accepted techniques and principles. The process is to ask questions in certain ways, gather information systematically, observe in detail, measure precisely, draw a sample, analyze using statistics, or perform experiments.
4. Research is applying critical thinking and adopting an orientation. You adopt a critical thinking attitude and skeptical perspective. You examine assumptions, consider alternatives, and do not accept what you see at face value. You reflect on how you and others arrived at decisions.

Empirical social research can involve all four of these activities. It is also an ongoing process of accumulating information, with results stated in terms of likelihood or probabilities and not as fixed absolutes. Because it is evidence based, findings change over time as the accumulated evidence reveals new insights and understandings. These features of research can create frustration. You may ask, What is the use of doing research if it does not give me an answer now? It may give an answer, but a provisional one. Leading professionals rely on research because it is better than the alternatives, and its answers tend to improve over time. What we, as a society or all humanity, knew last year may differ little from this year. However, what research tells us today differs quite a bit from what we knew 20 years ago for many questions and issues.

Some people get frustrated because research findings are not fixed and unchanging. Because research relies on empirical evidence, its statements or theories[2] about events can change if there is new or better evidence. All research-based statements, findings, or theories are provisional. They only stand as long as most of the evidence backs them. Moreover, the quality and amount of evidence determines the amount of confidence we place in a statement, idea, or theory.

Some people get frustrated because research findings are in the form of chance-like statements. They want a more definitive answer than "teacher attention is likely to affect a child's learning"; "providing flexible benefits or work hours increases the likelihood of high employee satisfaction"; or "being overweight increases the chances you will develop diabetes." People may like 100 percent certainty, but most research findings are stated in chance terms. Despite the comfort of simple, fixed answers, as an adult you probably already learned that such answers are extremely rare for complex issues in the real world. Although research does not offer us 100 percent certainty, it is better than the alternatives and it improves our understanding over time. Studies suggest that few of us are good at evaluating the risks and probabilities of things we do every day: the risk of getting injured or killed, the probability of winning the lottery, the likelihood that we will make a profit in the stock market, and so forth. Moreover, we tend to resist learning quickly from our misjudgments. Luckily, research has built-in features to improve the evaluation of risk and probabilities of events occurring.

What Evidence?

As stated previously, social research relies on systematic empirical evidence. We use evidence all the time and evaluate it in daily life. Would you accept a third-hand rumor as good evidence? Would you trust a written statement witnessed and co-signed by two neutral observers as evidence over an oral statement made without any witnesses? Courts of law have rules of evidence that outline what is acceptable and what is not. In many areas of life, we adopt standards of what counts as good, legitimate evidence. We have rules about how to interpret or assign meaning to evidence. Without a set of standards and rules, different people might look at the same evidence but arrive at different conclusions. For this reason, social research provides rules of evidence—how to collect it, what counts as good evidence, and how to interpret it. We can have more confidence in research when we have a lot of strong evidence versus scanty or very weak evidence.

Research requires you to look at empirical evidence (i.e., data or evidence that ultimately can be tied to something empirical—it can be seen, touched, smelled, heard, etc.). Moreover, we must collect the empirical evidence carefully and systematically according to generally accepted rules or standards. The standards of evidence are key. Suppose a person is in a boat going down the Colorado River in the Grand Canyon. An artist looks at the rock formations and sees beauty based on aesthetic standards. An environmentalist sees serious erosion based on standards of water flow and soil/rock removal. A geologist sees evidence of ancient geological shifts or volcanic action based on standards from the field of geology. A Native American sees evidence of messages from the Great Spirit based on standards from religious beliefs and folklore. Someone else sees evidence of UFO visits based on standards from reading lots of science fiction or fantasy literature. It is not enough to simply say *evidence*; standards for specific types of evidence are also needed.

This book discusses what constitutes stronger empirical evidence when doing social research. You may ask, Where do the standards come from? Over several decades, thousands of people have conducted many research studies, and other people have examined the studies looking for flaws. The standards we have today developed slowly as people evaluated, critiqued, and suggested areas for improvement in studies. A shorthand way to talk about the standards-creating process is to say that it comes from the operation of the scientific community.

Many standards for research evidence follow common sense. Suppose you have two samples of all the students at a large university. One sample contains 100 students and another contains 1000. Everything else about the samples is identical. Common sense says you should use the one with 1000 students. Suppose you want to find out a person's attitude about a subject. You can ask that person once in one way with a single question, or you can ask him or her in more than one way, with multiple questions and at multiple time points. Common sense tells you that asking with multiple ways, questions, and times is the better way to learn someone's true attitude on a subject. Other standards in research can get more technical or may not agree with common-sense thinking.

Evidence in social research takes two forms: **quantitative data** and **qualitative data**. Some people confuse the idea of strong evidence with the form of evidence. They hold the false notion that quantitative data are always stronger and qualitative data are always weaker. The standards are what determine whether evidence is strong, not whether the data come in a quantitative or qualitative form. Strong, solid evidence has less to do with being either quantitative or qualitative than with how carefully and systematically a researcher gathered the evidence.

Joy Stein/Shutterstock.com

quantitative data evidence in the form of numbers.

qualitative data evidence in the form of visual images, words, or sounds.

Research Is a Process that Results in a Product

As stated previously, research is less a single thing than an ongoing process. The process has multiple parts or steps and adheres to guidelines. The parts come together and ultimately yield a product. The product of the research process is knowledge or information. In other words, research results are answers to questions. The outcome of the research process is the answer to a research question. Good research also stimulates new thinking and raises new questions, questions that you would not have imagined until you did the research. The research process's specific form will vary by topic area, form of evidence, and type of research question.

Varieties of Social Research

To conduct a study, you need to collect data using one or more specific techniques. This section gives you a brief overview of the major techniques. In later chapters, you will read about these techniques in detail and learn how to use them. Some techniques are more effective when addressing specific questions or topics. It takes skill, practice, and creativity to match a research question to an appropriate data collection technique.

Some people get locked into using one technique (such as questionnaire) and use it all the time, even when it is not as effective as other techniques. A good researcher is aware of the full range of techniques as well as their strengths and limitations. We can divide research techniques based on whether the data you are gathering are quantitative or qualitative. Of course, we can blend the various types as needed.

Quantitative Data Collection Techniques

Experiments. Experimental research closely follows the logic and principles found in natural science research. To conduct an experiment, you create a situation and examine its effects on study participants. You can conduct an experiment in laboratories or in real life with a relatively small number of people. Experiments require a well-focused research question. In the typical experiment, you divide the people being studied into two or more groups. Next, you treat both groups identically, except you do something with one group (but not the other): the "treatment." You measure the reactions of both groups precisely. By controlling the setting for both groups and giving only one group the treatment, you can conclude that any differences in the reactions of the groups are due to the treatment alone. The chapter opening study of young children presented with food in a McDonald's package or not used the experimental technique. Instead of treating the children differently, the researchers altered the food package.

Surveys. In survey research, you ask people questions in a written questionnaire (e-mailed or handed to people) or during an interview and then record their answers. Unlike the experiment, you do not manipulate a situation or condition. You simply ask many people numerous questions in a short time period. Typically, you later summarize answers to questions in percentages, tables, or graphs. Surveys give you a picture of what many people think or report doing. Often, a sample or a smaller group of selected people (e.g., 150 students) is used in survey research. If properly conducted, you can generalize results to a larger group (e.g., 5000 students) from which the smaller group was selected. Example studies 1 and 2 later in this chapter used survey research.

Content Analysis. Content analysis is a technique for examining information, or content, in written or symbolic material (e.g., pictures, movies, song lyrics, etc.). In content analysis, you first identify a body of material to analyze (e.g., books, newspapers, films, etc.). Next, you create a system for recording specific aspects of it. The system might include counting how often certain words or themes occur. Finally,

Summary Review **Quantitative and Qualitative Data Collection Techniques**

Quantitative Data Collection Techniques	**Qualitative Data Collection Techniques**
• Experiments	• Ethnographic field research
• Surveys	• Historical-comparative research
• Content analyses	
• Existing statistics	

you record what was found in the material. Often you measure information in the content as numbers and present it as tables or graphs. This technique lets you discover features in the content of large amounts of material that might otherwise go unnoticed. The study cited earlier on children's television viewing habits is an example of a content analysis study.

Existing Statistical Sources. In existing statistics research, you first locate previously collected information. Often it is in the form of public documents, government reports, or previously conducted surveys. Next, you reorganize the information in new ways to address a research question. Locating sources can be very time consuming. You may not even know whether the information for your research question is available when you start a study. When you reexamine existing quantitative information, you may use various statistical procedures.

Qualitative Data Collection Techniques

Ethnographic Field Research. To conduct a field research study, you closely observe a small group of people over a length of time (e.g., weeks, months, years). Usually you begin with a loosely formulated idea or topic, not a fixed theory or hypothesis. You select a social group or natural setting for study, gain access and adopt a social role in the setting, and observe in great detail. You will get to know personally the people being studied and may conduct open-ended and informal interviews. In field research, it is important to take very detailed notes on a daily basis. After leaving the field site, you will reread the notes and prepare a written report. Part of Example Study 2, page 14, later in this chapter, used the ethnographic field research technique.

Historical-Comparative Research. In historical-comparative research, you examine aspects of social life in a past historical era or across different cultures. You may focus on one historical period or several, compare one or more cultures, or mix historical periods and cultures. As in field research, you combine theory building/ testing with data collection. You begin with a loosely formulated question that you refine during the research process. In this type of study, you gather a wide array of evidence. Evidence often includes existing statistics and documents (e.g., novels, official reports, books, newspapers, diaries, photographs, and maps). In addition, you may make direct observations or conduct interviews.

FIT THE QUESTION YOU WANT TO ANSWER WITH A TYPE OF SOCIAL RESEARCH

Newcomers to research struggle to connect a specific research question with a particular research technique. Often, you will need to reformulate or rephrase the question. Even then, it is not easy to match your question to a type of research. First, you should clarify the purpose of the research.

People conduct research with different goals or purposes. If you ask someone why he or she is conducting a study, you might get a range of responses: "My boss told me to"; "It was a class assignment"; "I was curious"; "My roommate thought it would be a good idea." There are nearly as many reasons to do research as there are researchers. We can organize the purposes of research based on what you are trying to accomplish—explore a new topic, describe a social phenomenon, explain why something occurs, or evaluate an outcome. Studies may have multiple purposes (e.g., both to explore and to describe), but one major purpose is usually dominant.

The four major purposes of research are as follows:

- Exploring a previously unknown, brand-new issue
- Describing in depth some issue, situation, or relationship
- Explaining why an event or situation happens or occurs in specific ways
- Evaluating whether a program/policy works

Exploring

In **exploratory research**, you examine a new area that no one has studied. Your goal is to formulate precise questions for future research. Exploratory research is often a first stage in a sequence of studies. You may need to conduct an exploratory study to find out enough to design and execute a second, more systematic and extensive study. Exploratory research addresses the "what?" question: "What is this social activity really about?"

Exploratory researchers tend to use qualitative data. They are not wedded to a specific theory or research question. Exploratory research adds focus but rarely yields definitive answers. If you conduct an exploratory study, you may get frustrated and feel it is difficult because there are few guidelines to follow. Everything is potentially important, the steps are not well defined, and the direction of inquiry changes frequently. You need to be creative, open minded; and flexible; adopt an investigative stance; and explore all sources of information.

Describing

Perhaps you may have an idea or question about a topic—a new marketing plan, a way to improve patient care, a way to deliver a client service, a way to help a group of new students, and so forth. Often, someone studied a similar topic somewhere at some time, but you want to learn about it in a specific place. The goal of **descriptive research** is to present a picture of the specific details of a situation, social setting, or relationship. It focuses on the "how?" and "who?" questions ("How did it happen?" "Who is involved? Which group is increasing faster?"). A great deal of social research is descriptive. Much of the social research found in scholarly journals or used for making policy decisions is descriptive.

exploratory research research into a new topic to develop a general understanding and refining ideas for future research.

descriptive research research that presents a quantitative or qualitative picture of an event, activity, or group.

Example Study Box 1 **Social Bonds and Internet Pornography Use**

Stack, Wasserman, and Kern (2004) conducted a descriptive study on pornography use on the Internet among Americans. Based on survey data from 531 people, they found that the greatest users were people with weak social bonds. Social bonds include religious, marital, and political ties. Heavy adult users of pornography tended to be males in unhappy marriages and who had few ties to organized religion. Pornography users were also more likely to have engaged in nonconventional sexual behavior (i.e., had an extramarital affair or engaged in paid sex) but not other forms of social deviance, such as illegal drug use.

Descriptive and exploratory research can blend together in practice. For a descriptive study, you begin with a well-defined subject and conduct a study to describe it accurately. The outcome is a detailed picture of the subject. It may indicate the percentage of people who hold a particular view or engage in specific behaviors—for example, that 8 percent of parents physically or sexually abuse their children. A descriptive study can also tell you which types of people engage in which activities (such as finding out that young males really enjoy one type of music whereas older females really dislike it).

Explaining

When you have a well-recognized issue and already have a description of it, you might wonder why things are the way they are (why do younger males like this type of music but not older females?) **Explanatory research** identifies the sources of social behaviors, beliefs, conditions, and events; it documents causes, tests theories, and provides reasons. It builds on exploratory and descriptive research. For example, an exploratory study discovers a new type of child abuse by parents; a descriptive study documents that 10 percent of parents abuse their children in this new way and describes the kinds of parents and conditions for which it is most frequent; an explanatory study

explanatory research research that attempts to test a theory or develop a new accounting of why activities, events, or relations occur as they do.

Example Study Box 2   Abuse and Marriage

Cherlin, Burton, Hurt, and Purvin (2004) conducted an explanatory study to learn why some women have difficulty forming stable marriages or cohabitation relationships. The researchers surveyed a random sample of 2402 women and gathered ethnographic field qualitative data in low-income neighborhoods in three cities, Boston, Chicago, and San Antonio. They considered many factors, including experience with sexual or physical abuse. The researchers tested the hypothesis that women with a history of abuse, as children or adults, are less likely to marry than those without such histories. They found that abused women have fewer social supports and resources to resist or avoid abusive partners. Also, previously abused women tend to harbor feelings of self-blame, guilt, and low self-esteem that inhibit the formation of a healthy romantic relationship. An abusive experience creates emotional distance and a hesitancy to make long-term commitments. The researchers found that adult women who had experienced abuse were less likely to be married and tended to enter into a series of unstable, transitory relations. The 1996 welfare reform law, the Personal Responsibility and Work Opportunity Reconciliation Act, emphasizes marriage and presents it as a fundamental good. When the U.S. Congressional debates discussed rules to encourage marriage for all unmarried women who received welfare payments, this study's findings were introduced. Rather than always encouraging marriage as a simplistic solution, the findings suggest reducing sexual/physical abuse while encouraging healthy and stable marriages. Despite the study's general implications, the mass media ignored the study results and did not report them (see American Sociological Association, *Footnotes*, May/June 2005).

Bonnie Kamin/PhotoEdit Inc.

may focus on why certain parents are abusing their children in this manner. It may test two competing theories about why some people become abusive parents.

Evaluating

Researchers design an **evaluation research** study to find out whether a program, a new way of doing something, a marketing campaign, a policy, and so forth is effective—in other words, "Does it work?" Large bureaucratic organizations (e.g., businesses, schools, hospitals, government, large nonprofit agencies) often conduct evaluation studies to demonstrate the effectiveness of what they are doing. The specific research techniques in an evaluation study are no different from other kinds of research. The difference lies in the purpose of the research, which is typically to use evaluation results in a practical situation (although there are exceptions, as Example Study Box 3: Evaluating D.A.R.E. suggests).

An evaluation study might ask questions such as, Does a Socratic teaching technique improve learning over the lecture method? Does a law-enforcement program of mandatory arrest reduce spouse abuse? Does a flextime program raise employee productivity? Evaluation researchers usually measure the effectiveness of a program, policy, or way of doing something and often by using multiple research techniques (e.g., a survey and field research). If they can, many evaluation researchers like to use the experiment technique. Practitioners involved with a policy or program may conduct evaluation research on their own or do so at the request of outside decision makers. Outside decision makers sometimes place limits on the research, fix boundaries on what a study can look at, or pressure for a particular finding. This may create ethical dilemmas for a researcher.

evaluation research applied research that is designed to learn whether a program, product, or policy does what it claims to do.

Even if an evaluation study yields clear evidence about a program's effectiveness, people may not use the results. At times, people ignore solid empirical evidence

Example Study Box 3 **Evaluating D.A.R.E.**

Perhaps you have participated in a Drug Abuse Resistance Education (D.A.R.E.) program. Established in 1983, D.A.R.E. operates in about 80 percent of all U.S. school districts. It focuses on elementary schools, with middle and high school curricula reinforcing the early lessons. The D.A.R.E. elementary school curriculum, usually in the fifth or sixth grade, consists of 17 lessons taught by trained uniformed police officers. The lessons teach students about various drugs and provide decision-making and peer pressure resistance skills. Many evaluation studies[3] have followed students who participated in D.A.R.E. programs and compared them to students who did not; the studies have looked at the five to seven years after program participation. The studies suggest that drug use differs little between the two sets of students. In short, participation in the program does not achieve its primary goal, to reduce illegal drug use among teens. Despite repeated evidence that it does not work, the program continues to be popular among parents, school officials, local businesses, and police. After 25 years and several billion dollars, the ineffective program continues, for social and political reasons, because of a strong desire to reduce drug use, and because there are few other accepted drug abuse education alternatives.

Rachel Epstein/PhotoEdit Inc.

■ **Figure 1.3**   Selection from General Accounting Office Letter on Evaluations of the D.A.R.E. Program

United States General Accounting Office
Washington, DC 20548

January 15, 2003

The Honorable Richard J. Durbin
United States Senate

Subject: Youth Illicit Drug Use Prevention: DARE Long-Term Evaluations and Federal Efforts to Identify Effective
       Programs

Dear Senator Durbin:

The use of illicit drugs, particularly marijuana, is a problem among our nation's youth. The adverse effects of illicit drug use play a role in school failure, violence, and antisocial and self-destructive behavior. A recent national survey[1] showed that for 1996 through 2002, more than 30 percent of tenth and twelfth grade students reported using marijuana in the past year. Further, about 20 percent of high school seniors reported using marijuana within the past 30 days. In fiscal year 2000, the federal government spent over $2.1 billion on illicit drug use prevention activities for youth, according to the Office of National Drug Control Policy (ONDCP).

Many programs are designed to help prevent and reduce illicit drug use among youth. Often, these programs also address the use of other substances, such as alcohol and tobacco. Youth drug abuse prevention programs are implemented in school, family, and community settings. School-based prevention programs are the most prevalent because schools provide easy access to children and adolescents. The most widely used school-based substance abuse prevention program in the United States is the Drug Abuse Resistance Education (DARE) program,[2] which is funded by a variety of sources, including private, federal, and other public entities. DARE's primary mission is to provide children with the information and skills they need to live drug- and violence-free lives through programs at the elementary school, middle school, and high school levels. The DARE program is usually introduced to children in the fifth or sixth grade. According to research literature, concerns have been raised about the effectiveness of the DARE fifth and sixth grade curriculum in preventing illicit drug use among youth. As agreed with your staff, this report contains information you requested on (1) the results of evaluations on the long-term effectiveness of the DARE elementary school curriculum in preventing illicit drug use among children and (2) federal efforts to identify programs that are effective in preventing illicit drug use among children.

To identify evaluations on the effectiveness of DARE at preventing illicit drug use among children, we searched social science, business, and education databases, which included the Department of Health and Human Services' (HHS) National Institutes of Health's (NIH) National Library of Medicine, for evaluations of DARE published in professional journals. We identified articles published in the 1990s on six evaluations of the DARE elementary school curriculum that included illicit drug use as an outcome measure and that also met key methodological criteria for our review, such as a long-term evaluation design and the use of intervention and control groups for comparisons. The six long-term evaluations that we discuss in this report were conducted at different times up to 10 years after student participants were initially surveyed. The six evaluations are based on three separate studies in three states. We reviewed each of the six evaluations and summarized the results of our review. We also held discussions with the researchers who conducted the evaluations. We did not independently validate the research designs or verify the results of evaluations on the effectiveness of the DARE program. (Enclosure I contains citations for the articles on evaluations of the DARE elementary school curriculum that we reviewed and enclosure II describes the methodology we used to select the evaluations).

To determine federal efforts to identify programs that are effective in preventing youth illicit drug use, we interviewed federal officials and reviewed documentation on efforts by HHS and the Department of Education (Education) to recognize programs that demonstrate success in reducing illicit drug use among children and adolescents. We did not independently verify the results of prevention programs recognized by the federal agencies. We conducted our work from January through December 2002 in accordance with generally accepted government auditing standards.

---

[1]Lloyd D. Johnston, Patrick M. O'Malley, and Jerald G. Bachman, Monitoring the Future National Results on Adolescent Drug Use: Overview of Key Findings, 2001, NIH Publication No. 02-5105 (Bethesda, Md.: National Institute on Drug Abuse, 2002).
[2]The DARE program is administered by DARE America—a nonprofit foundation.

■ Figure 1.3   *Continued*

In brief, the six long-term evaluations of the DARE elementary school curriculum that we reviewed found no significant differences in illicit drug use between students who received DARE in the fifth or sixth grade (the intervention group) and students who did not (the control group). Three of the evaluations reported that the control groups of students were provided other drug use prevention education. All of the evaluations suggested that DARE had no statistically significant long-term effect on preventing youth illicit drug use. Of the six evaluations we reviewed, five also reported on students' attitudes toward illicit drug use and resistance to peer pressure and found no significant differences between the intervention and control groups over the long term. Two of these evaluations found that the DARE students showed stronger negative attitudes about illicit drug use and improved social skills about illicit drug use about 1 year after receiving the program. These positive effects diminished over time.

We are sending copies of this report to the Secretary of HHS, the Secretary of Education, the Director of the Office of National Drug Control Policy, and others who are interested. We will also make copies available to others upon request. In addition, the report is available at no charge on GAO's Web site at http://www.gao.gov.

If you or your staff have questions about this report, please contact me at (202) 512-7119 or James O. McClyde at (202) 512-7152. Darryl W. Joyce and David W. Bieritz made key contributions to this report.

Sincerely yours,

Marjorie Kanof

Marjorie E. Kanof
Director, Health Care—Clinical and Military Health Care Issues

and make decisions based on other factors—such as moral, political, and personal reasons. Despite clear evidence, they will continue programs found to be ineffective or end highly effective ones (see Example Study Box 2: Abuse and Marriage).

Your research topic and interest often determine the purpose of a study, and the purposes of a study tend to go hand in hand with specific research techniques. Experiments are most effective for explanatory purposes and popular for evaluation research. Researchers use survey techniques in descriptive or explanatory purposes. They can use content analysis for exploratory and explanatory purposes but primarily use it for descriptive purposes. Researchers use existing statistics research for all three purposes, but they most frequently use it for a descriptive purpose.

Summary Review   **Purposes of Research**

Type of Study	Purpose	Stage in Learning Process	Question	Main Audience	Outcome
Exploratory	Learn about something entirely new and unknown	Earliest	What?	Varies; usually a researcher	General ideas and research questions
Descriptive	Provide details on something known	Middle	Who? When? How?	Varies	Factual details and descriptions
Explanatory	Build a new or test an existing explanation	Late	Why?	Professional researchers	Test a theory; compare explanations
Evaluation	Determine the effectiveness of a program or policy	Late	Does it work?	Practitioners and policy makers	Practical recommendations

Researchers use field research most often for exploratory and descriptive purposes. Historical-comparative research can be use for all three purposes separately or together.

Ethical and political conflicts tend to arise in evaluation research because people may have opposing interests in the findings. Research findings can affect who gets or keeps a job, they can build political popularity, or they may help promote an alternative program. If you conduct a serious evaluation study of a program and find it to be ineffective and a waste of time and money, people who make a living carrying out that program may become unhappy with you. They may express their displeasure by attacking you personally or criticizing your methods of research. This teaches us something else about research: Research produces knowledge, and knowledge can be powerful. New knowledge can aid decision making; it can also upset people who are benefiting from ignorance.

HOW TO USE RESEARCH

Research has two orientations. Some researchers adopt a detached, purely scientific, and academic orientation; they try to advance general knowledge over the long term. Others are more activist, pragmatic, and interventionist oriented; they try to solve specific, immediate problems. This is not a rigid separation. Researchers in both orientations cooperate and maintain friendly relations, and some individuals move from one orientation to another over time.

Basic Research

Basic social research advances fundamental knowledge. Basic researchers focus on refuting or supporting theories that explain how the social world operates, what makes things happen, why social relations are a certain way, and why society changes. Basic research is the source of most new scientific ideas and ways of thinking about the world. It is also the source of most new and advanced research techniques.

Many nonscientists criticize basic research and ask, "What good is it?" They consider it a waste of time and money. Although basic research often lacks a practical short-term application, it provides a foundation for knowledge that advances understanding in many policy areas, problems, or areas of study. Also, basic research is the source of most of the tools, methods, theories, and ideas about underlying causes of how people act or think used by applied researchers. It provides the major breakthroughs that lead to significant advances in knowledge; it is the painstaking study of broad questions that has the potential to shift how we think about a wide range of issues. It may have an impact for the next 50 to 100 years.

Frequently, the usefulness of basic research appears years or decades later. Practical applications may be apparent only after many accumulated advances in basic knowledge build up over time. For example, in 1984 Alec Jeffreys, a geneticist at the University of Leicester in England, was engaged in basic research studying the evolution of genes. As an indirect accidental side effect of a new technique he developed, he discovered how to produce what is now called human DNA "fingerprints" or unique markings of the DNA of individuals. This was not his intent. He even said he would have never thought of the technique if DNA fingerprints had been his goal. Others created applied uses of the technique and now DNA analysis is widely used technique by criminal investigators. Today's standard crime investigation technique was an unintended outcome of basic research into a different issue over two decades ago.

Applied Research

Applied social research addresses a specific concern or offers solutions to a problem identified by an employer, club, agency, social movement, or organization. Applied social researchers rarely worry about building, testing, or connecting findings

basic research research to extend basic understanding and fundamental knowledge about the world by creating and testing theories.

applied research research to answer a specific practical question and give usable answers in the short term.

to a larger theory, developing a long-term general understanding, or carrying out a large-scale investigation that might span years. Instead, they conduct a quick, small-scale study that provides practical results for immediate use. Although applied research can be of any type, most often it is descriptive or evaluative.

People employed in businesses, government offices, health care facilities, social service agencies, political organizations, and educational institutions often conduct applied research and use the results in decision making. Applied research affects decisions such as the following: Should an agency start a new program to reduce the wait time before a client receives benefits? Should a police force adopt a new type of response to reduce spousal abuse? Should a political candidate emphasize his or her stand on the environment instead of the economy? Should a company market a skin care product to mature adults instead of teenagers?

Researchers are the primary consumers of basic research. The consumers of applied research findings are practitioners—such as teachers, counselors, and social workers—or decision makers—such as managers, agency administrators, and public officials. Often, someone other than the researcher who conducted the study uses the results for his or her own purposes. The decision makers using the results may or may not use them wisely. Because applied research has immediate implications or involves controversial issues, such as teen sexuality or drug use, it is more likely than basic research to generate conflict and ignite social controversy (see Example Study Box 4: Teenage Sex Education).

Your primary goal when doing research is to find out what is really happening, but many practitioners who use applied research findings have other interests or priorities. For example, a famous social researcher, William Whyte (1984), conducted applied research in a factory in Oklahoma and in restaurants in Chicago. In both cases, he found that the practitioners were uninterested in his findings or wanted to suppress them. In the first case, the management was interested only in defeating a union, not in learning anything about employment relations. In the second case,

Example Study Box 4 Teenage Sex Education

Peter Dench/Corbis

Teen pregnancy rates in the United States are among the highest in the developed world. By their eighteenth birthday, 6 in 10 teen girls and 5 in 10 teen boys have had sexual intercourse, usually without birth control. Nearly 80 percent of the fathers of babies born to teen mothers do not marry their babies' mothers. Sexual activity among young teens is a concern of parents, health officials, religious leaders, educators, and politicians. There is a broad consensus that a problem exists, but people differ on solutions. Almost everyone favors some type of sex education. They differ over its content. Most health care professionals and educators favor comprehensive sex education (also called abstinence-plus). It teaches teens about the social and biological aspects of adult sexuality, sexual diseases, and forms of birth control. Conservative politicians and some religious organizations favor abstinence-only education. It promotes chastity until marriage and does not teach about birth control. Perhaps you have participated in a sex education program that promoted abstinence. Even if you have not participated, you may have heard of such programs. In 1996, the

■ **Figure 1.4**   Teen Sex Education

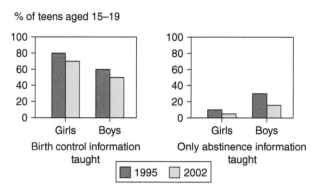

(*Facts on Sex Education in the United States,* Guttmacher Institute, December 2006)

U.S. Congress authorized $50 million per year for abstinence-only programs. States added matching money, and all states created such programs. Today, over $128 million of federal money goes to abstinence-only programs each year. By 2002, one in four teens had received abstinence-only education. What has been its effect? From 1995 to 2002, as more teens received abstinence-only education, fewer of them knew about birth control (Guttmacher Institute 2006). After years of abstinence-only programs, many of them faith based, some people began to ask, Do these programs work? Several studies provided consistent answers: Abstinence-only programs showed no lasting impact on reducing teen sexual activity, and teens in them know less about sexual diseases than teens in other programs (http://www.advocatesforyouth.org/publications/stateevalua-tions/index.htm, March 26, 2008). After these studies, most health organizations (such as the American Medical Association, the American Academy of Pediatrics, the National Institutes of Health, the Institute of Medicine, and the Office of National AIDS Policy) backed comprehensive sex education. They are not alone, 82 percent of the U.S. public support comprehensive sex education (*Archives of Pediatric and Adolescent Medicine*, November 2006). In April 2007, an independent research company, Mathematica Policy Research, Inc., released the most rigorous large-scale study on abstinence-only education (Mathematica Policy Research 2007). Again, it showed that the programs do not work. Some people called for ending the programs. Nonetheless, others reaffirmed their support for abstinence-only programs, largely for moral or other reasons. Proponents of abstinence-only programs say study results that show no effect actually mean that the programs have not been intense or long enough. Rejecting the evidence, they favor even more abstinence-only programs. What do you think? Has the U.S. government wasted nearly $1 billion on a failed program, or is abstinence-only the best way to address issues of teen sexual behavior and pregnancy? As you learn more about the process of social research, you will be better prepared to answer such questions.

restaurant owners only wanted to make their industry look good and did not want any findings about the nitty-gritty of the industry's operations to appear in public.

STEPS IN THE RESEARCH PROCESS

Social research proceeds in a sequence of steps. There is some minor variation, but most studies follow the seven steps discussed here. First, you begin the research process by selecting a topic. This is a general area of study or issue, such as improving elder care, marketing to a new customer base, reducing injuries on an athletic field, reducing domestic abuse, or identifying corrupt corporate elites. Most topics are too broad for conducting a study. This makes the second step crucial: You must narrow the topic, or focus it into a specific research question (e.g., "Are people who marry younger more likely to engage in physical abuse of a spouse under conditions of high stress than those who marry older?"). As you learn more about a topic, you can better narrow its focus. This means you need to look at past studies, or "the literature," on a topic or question. You will also want to develop a possible answer, or hypothesis, and testable theory to explain the process can be important at this stage.

Third, after specifying a research question, you develop a detailed plan on how to carry out the study. This step requires you to make decisions about the practical details of doing research (e.g., whether to use a survey or qualitative observing in the field, how many subjects to use, etc.). To prepare a design, you need to be familiar with various research techniques and their strengths or limitations. Only after completing the design stage can you gather the data (e.g., ask people the questions, record answers, etc.), which is step 4 is the process. After you have carefully collected the data, the fifth step is to analyze the data. This helps you see patterns in data. Data analysis enables you to give meaning to, or to interpret, the data, which is step 6 (e.g., "People who marry young and grew up in families with abuse have higher rates of physical domestic abuse than those with different family histories"). Lastly, in step 7 you must prepare a report that describes the study's background, how you conducted it, and what you discovered. An essential final step in the research process is telling other people what you discovered and how you conducted the study.

The seven-step process shown in Figure 1.5 is oversimplified. In practice, you rarely complete one step and then leave it behind to move to the next step. Rather, it is an interactive process and the steps blend into each other. What you do in a later step might stimulate you to reconsider and slightly adjust your thinking in a previous one. The process allows some flowing back and forth before reaching an end. The seven steps are followed for each research project.

Research is an ongoing enterprise. It builds on past research and contributes a larger, collectively created body of knowledge and understanding. One specific study is only a small part of the larger whole. Except for a very narrow applied question, we rarely end at just one study. The research process requires a constant addition of new studies and findings. A single researcher might work on multiple research projects at once, or several researchers may collaborate on one project. Likewise, one research project may result in one research report or several, and sometimes several smaller projects are described in a single report.

■ Figure 1.5   Steps in the Research Process

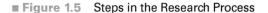

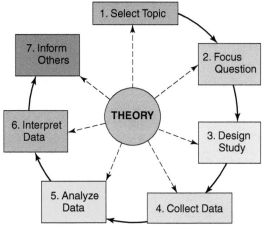

Source: Neuman, W. Lawrence 2007. *Basics of Social Research,* 2nd ed. Allyn & Bacon.

WHAT HAVE YOU LEARNED?

In this chapter, you learned that research is a powerful way to improve decision making. Research is not 100 percent foolproof, but it is better than the alternatives. It reduces misjudgment, bias, and distorted thinking. Research is often rigorous and time-consuming. Research uses critical thinking. Critical thinking is a perspective and a way to see things. By using critical reasoning skills, you will be more careful about what you accept as true. Critical reasoning will help you to be a better consumer of research: it rejects putting "blind faith" in research. It encourages you to understand how research works and to develop an ability to evaluate the quality of research. Many students, after just one basic class in doing research, can use the techniques, insights, and information-gathering skills to improve their decision making.

There are many kinds of research. Empirical social research is an ongoing process of accumulating information. Its findings are stated in terms of probabilities, not as fixed absolutes. It is based on carefully gathered evidence that meets certain standards. The standards have been developed over many years of studies by many researchers who critiqued one another's research, so there is improvement over time.

Research is about answering questions. One way to fit research with a question is to consider the purpose of the research. There are four main purposes in doing research: exploring a previously unknown, brand-new issue; describing in depth some issue, situation, or relationship; explaining why an event or situation happens or occurs in specific ways; and evaluating whether a program/policy works. The evidence or data for research can be in a quantitative (numbers) or qualitative (words, images) form. The care and detail of gathering data, not its form (numbers versus word), determines whether the data are solid and trustworthy. Research is used both to build new knowledge (basic) and to address practical issues (applied). In either case, a research study generally follows a similar sequence of steps: You begin with a topic that is narrowed to a focused question. Next, you decide on details of a study design and how data collection will proceed. You analyze data for patterns, which are interpreted to address the original question. The final step is to communicate what you learned in the study and how you conducted the study. In the next chapter, we will examine how to plan and design a study.

KEY TERMS

applied research *18*
basic research *18*
critical thinking *6*
descriptive research *13*
empirical evidence *7*

evaluation research *15*
explanatory research *14*
exploratory research *13*
qualitative data *10*
quantitative data *10*

APPLY WHAT YOU'VE LEARNED

Activity 1

Go to the Web site Advocates for Youth, which provides a list of publications on the Web, both research studies showing that the programs do not work and reports by abstinence-only advocates.

The Web site is http://www.advocatesforyouth.org/abstinenceonly/index.htm

Look through the sources. Now create two columns, one for abstinence-only programs and one for alterna-

tive programs. Under each column, list types of reasons and evidence given. Now explain on what basis each side is making its case.

Activity 2

Contact your local police department or a local elementary school to see whether it has a D.A.R.E. program. Now locate a police officer who conducts D.A.R.E. sessions and a school official (principal, vice principal, teacher) where the program operates. Without telling them about all the research findings that show the program to be ineffective, ask what they think and whether they find the program valuable. Do they find it worthwhile? How do you reconcile the feelings and beliefs of local participants with the many studies and official reports?

Activity 3

Contact management of any major company (that employs over 1000 people), any large hospital (with over 250 beds), or a large city government (a city of over 250,000), and identify a policy or decision area. Ask the organization's management how they use research results in decision making.

REFERENCES

American Sociological Association. 2005.

Brown, Joel H., and Ita G. G. Kreft. 1998. "Zero Effects of Drug Prevention Programs: Issues and Solutions." *Evaluation Review.* 22:3–14.

Cherlin, Andrew, Linda Burton, Tera Hurt, and Diane Purvin. 2004. "The Influence of Physical and Sexual Abuse on Marriage and Cohabitation." *American Sociological Review* 69:768–789.

Gantz, Walter, Nancy Schwartz, James R. Angelini, and Victoria Rideout. 2007. *Food for Thought, Television Food Advertising to Children in the United States.* Menlo Park, CA. Henry J. Kaiser Family Foundation (March 2007).

Glassner, Barry. 1999. *The Culture of Fear: Why Americans Are Afraid of the Wrong Things.* New York: Basic Books.

Guttmacher Institute. 2006. "Facts on Sex Education" *In Brief* (online publication). December 2006. http://www.guttmacher.org/pubs/fb_sexEd2006.html

Mathematica Policy Research, Inc. 2007. *Impacts of Four Title V, Section 510 Abstinence Education Programs, Final Report.* Princeton, NJ: Mathematica Policy Research, Inc.

Pew Research Center Report. 2007. "Public Knowledge of Current Affairs Little Changed by News and Information Revolutions" http://people-press.org/reports/display.php3?ReportID=319

Robinson, Thomas N., Dina Borzekowski, Donna Mutheson, and Helena Kraemer. 2007. "Effects of Fast Food Branding on Young Children's Taste Preference." *Archives of Pediatrics and Adolescent Medicine* 161:792–796.

Stack, Steven, Ira Wasserman, and Roger Kern. 2004. "Adult Social Bonds and Use of Internet Pornography." *Social Science Quarterly* 85:75–88.

Tobler, Nancy, and Howard H. Stratton. 1997. "Effectiveness of School-Based Drug Prevention Programs: A Meta-Analysis of the Research." *Journal of Primary Prevention* 18: 71–128.

United States Department of Justice. 2002. *National Incidence Studies of Missing, Abducted, Runaway and Throwaway Children: National Estimates on Missing Children, an Overview* (October 2002). U.S. Department of Justice, Office of Justice Programs, Office of Juvenile Justice and Delinquency Prevention. http://www.missingkids.com/en_US/documents/nismart2_overview.pdf

Whyte, William. 1984. *Learning from the Field.* Beverly Hills, CA: Sage.

Wysong, E., et al. 1994 "Truth and DARE: Tracking drug education to graduation and as symbolic politics." *Social Problems* 41:448–472.

Zagumny, M. J. and M. K. Thompson. 1997. "Does D.A.R.E. Work? An Evaluation in Rural Tennessee." *Journal of Alcohol and Drug Education* 42:32–41.

ENDNOTES

1. See Harris Poll of 889 Americans conducted in November 2005 at http://www.harrisinteractive.com/harris_poll/index.asp?PID=618
2. Theories are systematic, abstract, general explanations about why events occur or how some aspect of the world operates. They contain assumptions, arguments, and a set of interconnected ideas.
3. For some of the many studies showing the ineffectiveness of D.A.R.E., see Brown, Joel H., and Ita G. G. Kreft (1998),Tobler and Stratton (1997), Wysong et al. (1994), and Zagumny and Thompson (1997).

CHAPTER

2

Planning a Study

Rick Friedman/Corbis

Do you have a tattoo? Have you ever wondered why people get tattoos? Your curiosity about tattoos can be the start of a research study. You might begin by looking at the several books and 25 social research articles on tattooing published in the past five years. This may help you turn the broad topic of tattoos into a research question for a study. You might ask, Why are tattoos popular for people in certain cultures or times? This question directs you to look at the cultural and historical development of tattoos—their use to brand people or in religious rituals. You might learn that the word *tattoo* originated from the Tahitian word *tatau*. Tattoos were used thousands of years ago in what is today Japan, Siberia, India, Peru, and Egypt. Certain peoples, such as the Maori in New Zealand, some Amazon tribes, and certain subcultures, such as Japanese crime gangs or Neo-Nazi skinheads, regularly tattoo. Alternatively, you might ask, How many people in the United States today have tattoos and what types of people get them? To answer these questions you might conduct survey research. One 2003 survey found that 16 percent of the U.S. population has a tattoo. This rises to 28 percent of people under the age of 25. There is no difference in the male–female tattoo rate. Democrats are slightly (18 percent) more likely to get them than Republicans (14 percent) and gay-lesbian-bisexuals (31 percent) more than straights and so forth (Harris Interactive 2003). Maybe you want to ask, How do others think about people who have tattoos? To answer this question, you might conduct an experiment similar to that by Hawkes, Senn, and Thorn (2004). They looked at people's reactions to college females with a tattoo. Participants in the study read about women. The researchers varied details about each woman's characteristics and her tattoo (its size and location). They also measured related factors, such as how people view gender roles. If your question is about tattoos on people in music videos, you could conduct a content analysis study of music videos to see what tattoos are shown and who has them. Maybe you are curious about the business of tattooing. You could examine existing statistics and records to find the number of tattooing businesses, suppliers, and tattoo artists. If you are curious about subjective beliefs of people who get tattoos, you could conduct a qualitative field research study like that by Atkinson (2004). He spent a lot of time with tattooed people and tattoo artists and got to know them very well. Alternatively, you might focus on field research with a specific subgroup, such as gang members or Neo-Nazis, to see whether they see their tattoos differently. Many young people in North America today who get a tattoo say that it signals a rejection of authority, is a statement about control over their body, indicates group membership, or is a form of spiritual-artistic self-expression. Of course, once top celebrities or most of your friends get a tattoo, you may get one to mimic an idol or to conform to peer pressure. This example of tattoos shows how to turn a topic into the start of a research study. In this chapter, we will look at how to take a topic and design a research study to examine that topic in depth.[1]

In Chapter 1, you learned about principles and types of social research. You are now ready to look at the specifics of study design. Recall the steps of the research process: Begin with a general topic, narrow it into a specific research question, and then decide how to conduct a study that can address the research question. Before gathering data, you might prepare a **research proposal**, which is written a detailed plan for doing a study.

PICKING A STUDY TOPIC

Topics arise from many sources: past studies, television or film, personal reactions or experiences, discussions with friends and family, or ideas from a book, magazine, or newspaper. A topic may be something that arouses your curiosity, something about which you hold deep commitments, or something you believe is wrong and want to change. A topic appropriate for social research is one that you *generalize* about social *patterns* that operate in *aggregates* and are *empirically observable*. Let us look at these four features briefly:

- *Generalize.* The topic is beyond one isolated unique instance; it is likely to reappear and applies to a broad scope of people, places, times, or events.
- *Social pattern.* The topic has regularity or some kind of structure/form that describes interconnections among a set of events, situations, or relationships in a condensed way.
- *Aggregates.* The topic applies to a collection of people or other units (e.g., families, businesses, schools, hospitals, or neighborhoods). The people/units do not have to be connected to one another or even be aware of the others. There could be as few as ten or as many as hundreds of millions.
- *Empirically observable.* The topic appears in the observable world in a way that we can detect and observe it using our senses (sight, sound, touch, smell) directly or indirectly.

These four features rule out some topics. They eliminate particularistic situations (e.g., why your boy/girlfriend dumped you yesterday, why your friend's little sister hates her third grade teacher) and a single case (e.g., your own family). Nonetheless, patterns (boyfriends of this type tend to act in this way, children often dislike third grade teachers for one of four main reasons) help us understand particular situations. Also ruled out are things impossible to observe, even indirectly (e.g., unicorns, alien space creatures, or ghosts with supernatural powers). We cannot study imaginary objects, but we can study people's beliefs about them (e.g., what types of people tend to believe in ghosts and why).

research proposal a detailed plan for conducting a study on a specific research question, that includes a literature review and specific techniques to be used.

CONDUCTING A REVIEW OF PAST STUDIES

An early step when doing study is to read past studies, or to conduct a **literature review**. The "literature" refers to past research reports on a topic. Reading the literature serves several functions.

- It helps you to narrow down a broad topic by showing you how others conducted their studies. You can use other studies as a model of how narrowly focused your research question should be.
- It provides you with examples of research designs, measures, and techniques that you might use.
- It informs you about what is known about a topic. Past studies teach you the key ideas, factors, terms, and issues surrounding a topic. You may wish to replicate, test, or extend what others already found.
- It presents you with examples of what final research reports look like, their parts, form, and writing style.
- It can help you to improve writing skills and learn subtle elements of conducting a good research study.
- It is often fun and may stimulate your creativity and curiosity.

Before you go off to search for the published reports of studies, it is essential to be organized. To prepare a well-written, complete literature review, you have to schedule your time and develop a search plan. The ideal literature review is a carefully crafted summary of the recent studies on a topic. It discusses both study findings and how researchers reached the findings. In the review, you must carefully document all sources.

Doing a literature review is rooted in an assumption that knowledge accumulates. We build on what others have done. Recall that research is the collective effort of many people who share their results with one another. We pursue knowledge as a community. This is why researchers constantly compare, replicate, or criticize other studies. Certain studies may be especially important and a few individual researchers may become famous, but each research project is just one small part of the larger, collective process of expanding what we know. The study you do today builds on those of the past, and studies you or others conduct in the future will build on the studies being conducted today. As Sir Isaac Newton put it, "If I have seen further it is by standing on the shoulders of giants."[2] Every research achievement builds on those who came before.

Where Do You Find the Research Literature?

You can find research reports in several locations. This section briefly discusses each type and provides you with a simple road map for how to access them.

Periodicals. You can learn about social research in newspapers, in popular magazines, on television or radio broadcasts, and in Internet news summaries. They can be the start of a topic or research question, but they are not sufficient for preparing a literature review. They are not the full, complete reports of a study that you need for a literature review. Media reports are selected and highly condensed summaries journalists prepare for a general audience. They lack many essential details required to evaluate a study. Textbooks and encyclopedias contain condensed summaries of studies to introduce readers to a topic. They are also inadequate for a literature review because essential details are absent. To conduct a literature review, you must locate the complete report of a study. The full reports first appear in specialized periodicals.

A periodical (or "serial," in librarian terminology) is any publication (print or electronic) that appears regularly over time (such as daily, weekly, monthly, quarterly, or annually). There are thousands of periodicals and they come in a vast array

literature review a summary of previously conducted studies on the same topic or research question.

Making It Practical A Literature Review Search Plan

Evaluate resources: How much time can you devote to the search? Do you have access to a college or university library? Do you know what computerized literature search tools are available at the library and how to use them? Do you want to locate a minimum number of studies? Can you easily distinguish an empirical research study from other articles? After answering these questions, you may wish to start preparing a time schedule with benchmarks or self-created deadlines for each step. The more practice you have in published studies, the faster it will go. A first-time search by a novice can take three or more times longer than one by an experienced person.

Select and narrow the topic: You search a specific question, not a general topic. The faster you can focus on a specific research question, the quicker you can proceed. Some people devote days or weeks to focusing on a research question; this is not always necessary. The question you begin with is preliminary because you can adjust and refine it as you learn more from reading past studies.

Learn to use literature search tools: Use computerized search tools (discussed later in this chapter) to search the literature. The tools require that you convert your research question's central ideas and terms into keywords. It takes time and practice to become skilled at using specific tools. Librarians can help or may offer workshops that teach about the tools. If you have never used a tool, expect to spend an hour or more to learning to use it.

Plan to locate and scan read articles: The search tools yield a list of articles with your keywords, but they can-

not determine the true relevance of the articles for your research question. You must decide their relevance by scanning the articles' titles, abstracts (to be discussed later), or first few paragraphs. Based on a quick scan-read, you decide what is relevant. If the search tool locates 35 articles, it may take two hours to scan-read all of them and decide their relevance. You may end with 10 relevant, useful studies to read in depth.

Allow time to extract the major findings: Reading a scholarly research study is a skill that improves with practice. Most have a sophisticated vocabulary and technical information. It takes time to know what to look for. As you read, ask three questions: What was this study really about? How did researchers conduct the study (i.e., gather data), and What is the study's main finding or outcome? You want to extract the essential elements from a research report and write them as notes. Plan how to take notes and record all key source details (discussed later in this chapter). You might spend one hour reading and taking notes on each relevant article.

Final stage—synthesize: Once you have enough articles (because there are no more, you are learning nothing new with additional ones, or you ran out of time), you must pull together and integrate what they said. You might use a few quotes, but you mostly want to paraphrase (put in your own words). Integrating different studies and synthesizing what they really say in combination is a difficult thinking and writing task. Plan to reread what each study said more than once and return to the full article for clarification and verification.

■ **Figure 2.1** Advancing Knowledge

of types. It is easy to be confused about the types of periodicals. With skill, you can learn to distinguish among the following five types:

- Peer-reviewed scholarly journals in which researchers present reports of studies
- Popularized social science magazines for an educated general audience
- Practitioner advice/opinion/news-technical publications, newsletters, and magazines
- Opinion magazines in which scholars and experts debate and express their views
- "Mass market" or "trade" newspapers and magazines that are written for the general public

You want to locate scholarly journals because that is where full reports of empirical research appear. Articles in the other types of periodicals may discuss study findings, but they lack essential details about the study. Popularized social science magazines offer the interested, educated public a simplified version of study findings without all the details. Most professions have news/communication newsletters for working professionals in which you may find discussions of a research study or its implications, but they lack full study details. Experts and scholars write articles for serious opinion/public issue magazines about topics on which they may also conduct empirical research (e.g., welfare reform, prison expansion, voter turnout, new marketing techniques). These publications differ in purpose, look, and scope from scholarly journals. They are an arena for debates about issues, not where researchers present a full report of their studies. Mass market publications provide the general public with news, opinion, and entertainment. You can find them at large newsstands, public libraries, or bookstores. They are source for many current events, but they do not contain reports of research studies.

You can find full reports of research studies in the following six outlets:

- *Scholarly journals.* The main place to look; they are stored for long periods in many locations and have a well-developed system to help you locate relevant articles;
- *Books.* In-depth and valuable for some topics, but difficult to find and time-consuming to read;
- *Government documents.* Only some are relevant and access may be limited, difficult to find;
- *Ph.D. dissertations.* Can be very valuable for an extensive review but difficult to find and access;

PhotoAlto/James Hardy/Getty Images Royalty Free

Summary Review   **Different Types of Periodicals**

Periodical Type	Example	Authors	Purpose	Strength	Weakness
Peer-reviewed scholarly journal	*Social Science Quarterly, American Educational Research Journal, Journal of Applied Psychology, Social Forces*	Professors and professional researchers	Report on empirical research studies to professionals and build scientific knowledge	Highest quality, most accurate and most objective with complete details	Technical, difficult to read, requires background knowledge or training, not always about current issues
Semischolarly professional publication	*American Prospect, Society, Psychology Today, American Demographics*	Professors, professional policy makers, politicians	Disseminate and discuss new findings and their implications for professionals and the educated public	Generally accurate, somewhat easy to read	Lacks full detail and explanation, often includes opinion mixed in with discussion
Practitioner magazine or newsletter	*Coach & Athletic Director, Military Police, Retail Merchandiser, Mental Health Weekly*	Working professionals and some professors or "experts"	Provide a communication forum for working professionals	Current news and debates on relevant issues	Narrow focus and rarely builds general knowledge
Opinion magazine	*Nation, Human Events, Public Interest, Commentary*	Professors, professional policy makers, politicians	Present value-based ideas and opinions for professionals and educated public	Carefully written and reasoned	One-sided view and highly value based
Mass market magazines for the public	*Time, Esquire, Ebony, Redbook, Forbes, Fortune*	Professional journalists and other writers	Entertain, present, and discuss current events for lay public	Easy to read, easy to locate	Often inaccurate and incomplete

- *Policy reports.* Often relevant but are difficult to locate and only available for short periods of time; and
- *Presented papers.* Very difficult to locate, many are later published in scholarly journals.

A Special Type of Periodical: Scholarly Journals. The primary place where researchers disseminate information about studies is in scholarly journals (e.g., *Advances in Nursing Science, American Educational Research Journal, American Political Science Review, Journal of Marketing, American Journal of Sociology, Criminology, Nursing Research,* and *Social Science Quarterly*). Scholarly journals are essential to a literature review because they have the complete reports of research. You rarely find them outside of college and university libraries (or an online service connected with a college library). Many have *journal* or *review* in their title but not all do. They have the following features:

1. Most if not all of the articles are reports about original research studies.
2. Articles are peer-reviewed (see discussion in next section).
3. The articles have a reference or bibliography section that lists sources in detail.
4. Articles are part of an indexing location system accessible with **article search tools** (discussed later).

Peer review is a type of quality assurance system for the publication of research. After a researcher completes a study and writes a report about it, he or she presents it in several forums. The most frequently used and respected forum is a scholarly journal. It demands the highest level of rigor and is widely read by knowledgeable professional researchers. A critical feature of scholarly journal is that articles are **peer reviewed**. This means a study report went through the following peer review process:

1. A researcher prepares the detailed report of a study in a specific format and sends it (in pre-publication form it is called a manuscript) to the editor of a scholarly journal for consideration for possible publication.
2. The editor (a respected, experienced researcher with a deep knowledge of the field) looks at the manuscript and makes certain it meets minimal standards and is relevant for the specific journal.
3. The editor selects several (two to six) respected peer researchers to be volunteer reviewers. Each reviewer independently reads and evaluates the manuscript. He or she looks for a study's contribution to advancing knowledge, its originality, the quality of research design and execution, and the technical correctness of the research procedures. The editor also evaluates the report's completeness, organization, use of sources, and writing quality.
4. Each peer reviewer returns to the editor a written evaluation with criticisms, comments, and suggestions.
5. The editor examines all the evaluations from the reviewers and then decides to accept the manuscript as is and publish it; to ask the researcher to revise and resubmit the report for a second round of evaluation; or to reject the manuscript.

Most scholarly journals use a "blind review" version of the peer review process. In it, a researcher does not know the identity of the peer reviewers who evaluate the manuscript, and reviewers do not know who conducted the study. A blind review ensures that reviewers judge the manuscript solely on its own merits. Personal relationships with the author and his or her reputation do not influence decision making.

Many scholarly journals accept one-half to one-fourth of what they receive for consideration. Some highly prestigious and widely read journals publish 10 percent of the submitted manuscripts. That is, they turn down 90 percent of what researchers have sent to them. When you read articles in the high-prestige journals, you are seeing the top 10 percent of current research.

article search tool an online service or publication that provides an index, abstract list, or database with which you can quickly search for articles in numerous scholarly journals by title, topic, author, or subject area.

peer reviewed a scholarly publication that has been independently evaluated for its quality and merits by several knowledgeable professional researchers and found acceptable.

Scholarly journals feature more than reports of research. They also contain letters to the editor, theoretical essays, book reviews, legal case analysis, and comments on other published studies. Some specialized journals have only have book reviews; others only have literature review essays *(e.g., Annual Review of Psychology, Annual Review of Nursing Research, Annual Review of Law and Social Science, Annual Review of Public Health)* in which a researcher gives a "current state of the field" essay.

Except for peer review, there is no simple "seal of approval" to distinguish scholarly journals from other periodicals. Once you find a peer-reviewed scholarly journal, you need to distinguish an empirical research study from other types of articles. This takes judgment skills or the advice of experienced researchers or professional librarians. The best way to learn to distinguish among types of publications and articles is to read many articles in scholarly journals.

The Internet has a full copy of some, but not all, scholarly journal articles. Most journals charge a fee to access articles over the Internet; your college library may allow you free access (because the library paid the fee). Internet services sometimes provide a full, exact copy of the article, but some may only provide a short summary. Many services feature articles for a limited number of years and only from certain scholarly journals. Someday the Internet may replace print versions. For now, 99.5 percent of full scholarly journal articles are available in print, and about one-half of those from the past decade are available on the Internet in full form.

You need to use an online library service to find articles. Once you locate a scholarly journal (see Making It Practical: Locating Scholarly Journals), you need to check that it is an article with study results and not another type (e.g., opinion essay, book

Photo Courtesy of Annie Pickert, Permission granted by Wiley-Blackwell for reproduction of *Social Science Quarterly*, March 2008, Volume 89, Number 1

abstract short summary, usually on the first page of a scholarly journal article.

Making It Practical **Locating Scholarly Journals**

Your college library has a section for scholarly journals and magazines, or, in some cases, it mixes them with books. Look at a map of library facilities or ask a librarian to find this section. Many libraries place the most recent issues, which look like thin paperbacks or thick magazines, in a "current periodicals" section. The library stores them temporarily until it receives all the issues of a volume. After the library has an entire volume, staff members bind all issues together and place the volume in the library's collection. They place scholarly journals from different fields together with other periodicals or serials. Libraries post a list of the periodicals to which they subscribe.

Scholarly journals are published as rarely as once a year or as frequently as weekly. Most appear four to six times a year. For example, *Sociological Quarterly* appears four times a year, where as the *Annual Review of Nursing Research* appears once a year. Librarians and scholars created a system for tracking articles in scholarly journals. Every scholarly journal has a year, volume number, and issue number. When a journal begins, it is with volume 1, issue 1, and the numbers increase thereafter. The volume is a year of articles, and an issue is a part of the volume with several articles. Each issue has a table of contents with the title, author(s), and pages of articles. Most journals number pages by volume, not by issue or article. Page 1 is the first issue of a volume. Not all journals begin their publishing cycle in January. Issue 1 might begin in July or September. Page numbering continues throughout the entire volume and articles on consecutive pages. One issue may have from 1 to 50 articles, but most have 8 to 18 articles. Articles are 5 to 50 pages long. Because one volume is one year, a journal issue with volume 52 usually means that it has been operating for 52 years.

To locate an article, we use journal name, volume, year, issue, author, article title, and page numbers. These details are the **"citation"** of a source in the reference section of an article or literature review. Most journal articles have an **abstract**. A good abstract tells you the topic, research question, method, and findings. There are hundreds of scholarly journals in most fields. Each journal charges an annual subscription fee ($100 to $3000). For this reason, only the largest research libraries subscribe to most of them. If an article is not available on the Internet or at your local library, you can often obtain a copy from a distant library through an interlibrary loan service, a system by which libraries lend materials to other libraries.

review). It is easier to identify quantitative studies because most have a methods or data section and charts, statistical formulas, and tables of numbers. Qualitative research articles are easy to confuse with theoretical essays, literature review articles, idea-discussion essays, policy recommendations, book reviews, and legal case analyses.

Books. Books communicate information, provoke thought, and entertain. There are many types of books: picture books, textbooks, short story books, novels, popular fiction or nonfiction, religious books, children's books, and others. Some books report on original research or are collections of research articles. Libraries shelve and assign call numbers to them as with other types of books. You can find information on them (e.g., title, author, and publisher) in the library's catalog system. Only college or university libraries have books that report on research. It is difficult to distinguish them from other books. Some publishers, such as university presses, specialize in publishing them. Qualitative types of research are more likely to appear in a book format, as are the results of long, complex studies that may also be published in scholarly journal articles. Because they are not in the article search tool system, finding studies in books is difficult. Three types of books can contain research reports:

- *Monographs.* Contain the details of a long complex study or a set of interconnected studies.
- *Readers.* Contain articles on a topic, original or gathered from journals. Often the editor of the book has modified the research (i.e., shortened and simplified it) to make it easier for nonexperts to read.
- *Edited collection.* A collection of new research reports, articles reprinted from scholarly journals, or a mixture of both on a common topic.

Dissertations. All graduate students who receive the Ph.D. degree are required to do original research. They write the study as a dissertation thesis. Dissertations are in the library of the university that granted the Ph.D. About one-third of dissertation results are published later as books or articles. Because dissertations report on original research, they can be valuable sources of information. Specialized indexes list dissertations. *Dissertation Abstracts International* (online and print version) lists dissertations with their authors, titles, and universities (see Figure 2.2). To get a copy of the dissertation, you must borrow it via interlibrary loan from the degree-granting university, if that university permits this, or purchase a photocopy of it.

Government Documents. The U.S. federal government, the governments of other nations, state- or provincial-level governments, the United Nations, and international agencies such as the World Bank, all sponsor research studies and publish research reports. Many college and university libraries have some of these documents in their holdings, often in a special government documents section. Most libraries hold only the most frequently requested documents and reports. You can use specialized lists of publications and indexes to search for them, but usually you will need the help of a librarian. Some are also available online.

Policy Reports. Research institutes and policy centers (e.g. Brookings Institute, Rand Corporation) publish papers and reports (see Example Study Box 1: Sexual Harassment). An organization might list its reports on its Internet site and make copies available on the Internet. To find all of them, you need to contact the organization and request a list of reports. Sometimes organizations charge a fee for their reports.

Presented Papers. Each year, the professional associations in various fields (e.g., criminal justice, education, marketing, nursing, political science, psychology, recreation, sociology) hold annual meetings. At them hundreds of researchers gather to deliver, listen to, or discuss oral reports of recent research, with many

■ **Figure 2.2** Example Dissertation Abstract

Title: Learning English in a midwestern urban high school: A case study of an ELL Vietnamese student
Author(s): Fan, Yanan
Degree: Ph.D.
Year: 2006
Pages: 00179
Institution: Michigan State University; 0128
Advisor: Adviser Anne Haas Dyson
Source: DAI, 67, no. 10A (2006): p. 3686
Standard No: **ISBN:** 978-0-542-90694-7

Abstract: The goal of this ethnographic case study is to examine what it means to learn English within the sociocultural contexts of a mid-sized Midwestern urban high school, focusing on a Vietnamese teenager. The data set consists of fieldnotes from key educational sites; interviews of students, teachers, and a first language aide; and collected artifacts (e.g., photocopies of student's written work, class handouts and syllabi, audio-taped interactions of the student in classrooms, visual images of sites, and site documents). Based on an inductive analysis of the data set, I asserted that the student's learning experiences are embedded in and influenced by the sociopolitical assumptions of a larger educational system that defines second-language learning. The student was lost in the institution's inconsistent vision of literacy while negotiating expectations and opportunities for participation in varied classrooms with little support and resources. In the meantime, the student's language proficiency, immigrant history, ethnicity, race, gender, and the model minority rhetoric all figure into her identity formation in the peer self-segregation of her school. This study extends the understanding of the complexities of second language learning, of the challenges adolescent immigrant students face in secondary schools, and of the cultural construction of the model minority rhetoric. It also contributes to the methodological discussion on conducting ethnographical studies by offering a reflection of the researcher's own negotiation of her relationship with the participants, considering issues of membership, reciprocity, and power.

Source: Copy of an abstract from *Dissertation Abstracts,* International.

Example Study Box 1 Sexual Harassment

In December 2005 the AAUW (American Association of University Women) Educational Foundation released a 72-page report, "Drawing the Line: Sexual Harassment on Campus." It is an advocacy policy report that describes an applied research study on sexual harassment. Instead of an abstract, as in a scholarly journal, it contains a three-page executive summary, and research methods are described in an appendix. Data for the study came from a stratified random sample (discussed in Chapter 4) and an online survey. A professional survey organization sent people in its national database password-protected e-mail invitations to participate in a survey. Organization employees randomly selected a sample of students enrolled in public and private postsecondary schools that offered two- and four-year degrees. In total, they interviewed 2036 U.S. residents ages 18 to 24 enrolled in college in 2005. The average interview lasted 17 minutes.

The executive summary shows you that this was a descriptive study. Its research questions were as follows: How common is sexual harassment, who is being harassed, who is doing the harassing, how are students being affected by harassment, and what do students think should be done about it? Key findings are that one-third of students experience sexual harassment in their first year of college. Most harassment is verbal, but about one in three of the harassed students also experienced physical harassment. Men and women are both likely to be harassed but in different ways. Harassed students feel upset, embarrassed, angry, less confident, afraid, worried, and confused. They are likely to be disappointed in their college experience. Lesbian, gay, bisexual, or transgender (LGBT) students are more likely than heterosexual students to experience sexual harassment. Males harass more than females, with nearly one-half of male college students saying that they sexually harassed someone. The harassing men thought it was funny or thought the victim wanted attention. They did not consider it serious or think about the consequences. Less than 10 percent of harassed students file a report with university officials. The study report contains charts and statistics. It also contains quotes from individual students about their ideas on and experiences with sexual harassment. A hard copy of the report is for sale from the AAUW for $12, 1111 Sixteenth Street NW, Washington, DC, 20036, helpline@aauw.org, or you can download a free copy if you complete an information form at. http://www.aauw.org/research/dtl.cfm.

also in written form. People who attend can pick up a copy. If you do not attend, you can obtain a meeting program with a list of each paper with its title, author, and author's place of employment. You can write directly to the author to request a copy.

How to Conduct a Literature Review: A Six-Step Process

In this section, we examine six steps (see Figure 2.3) in locating research reports and preparing a literature review.

STEP 1. Refine the topic. Your search begins with a research question, not a topic. It is impossible to examine a broad topic with any depth or seriousness. A topic such as "divorce" or "crime" or "patient care" is too broad. Narrow the topic to something such as, "the stability of families with stepchildren" or "economic inequality and crime rates across 50 nations" or "long-term care of elderly patients with a heart condition." You further narrow this into a research question by adding conditions and limiting the range of cases/situations to which it applies (see discussion later in this chapter). Searching the literature itself also helps you focus a research question.

STEP 2. Design your search. (1) Decide on the review's extensiveness by fixing parameters for your search: how much time can you devote to it, how many years back will you look, what is the minimum number of reports you will examine, how many libraries you can visit, if you will look at both articles and books or only articles, and so forth. Expect to make multiple visits to a library (online or physically). If you have 15 hours to do a literature review, do not expect to locate and include

■ **Figure 2.3**   **The Six Step Process**

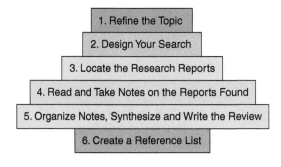

more than 10 to 12 research reports. (2) Decide which article search tools to use (discussed later in this chapter). (3) Decide how you will record the bibliographic information for each source and how to take notes (e.g., in a notebook, on 3 × 5 cards, in a computer document).

STEP 3. Locate the research reports. Searching varies by type of research report (article, book, or dissertation). Scholarly journal articles are usually the most valuable and least time-consuming to find. Locating a full copy of the reports can take time. After you find a full copy, you must read and take notes on it.

Articles in Scholarly Journals. Most studies are reported in scholarly journals. However, there are hundreds of journals, most go back several decades, and each may have over a hundred articles each year. Luckily, article search tools (sometimes called indexes or research literature services) make the task easier (See Making It Practical: Using Article Search Tools).

Many article search tools only provide author, titles—and abstract, not the full text of an article. Once you get search results, you can scan the titles and abstracts for relevant articles. Articles usually contain reference sections with leads to additional sources. For example, the article discussed in Figure 2.4 on a content analysis study of the media contained 53 references. The article on sexual harassment of college women listed 93 items, including journal articles, books, and other research reports. Reading the reference section can point you to relevant sources that you might not find using an article search tool.

Making It Practical Using Article Search Tools

Until about 10 years ago, a search for scholarly journal articles meant many hours reading through specialized books or magazines available only in college libraries. Today, you use such article search tools via online services. There are about 50 of them, some general and some specialized. Most only have articles from scholarly journals, although some also include papers from professional conferences, dissertations, and policy reports. Libraries pay to access the services.

To locate an article you use keywords or search by author name. Many article search tools are titled *abstracts* or *indexes* (e.g., *Psychological Abstracts*, *Social Sciences Index*, and *Gerontological Abstracts*). For education-related topics, the Educational Resources Information Center (ERIC) system is valuable; for medicine, MEDLINE is widely used. The name *abstract* is from an article's "abstract" or a short summary, usually placed at the beginning of an article. It does not contain all the findings or details of a study, but you can use abstracts to screen articles for relevance. Some are highly organized and contain specific details whereas others are less structured (see Figure 2.4).

You can search by author, subject, or keyword. Search tool subjects are limited to a few popular ones. Unless you

know that a specific researcher did a study or you are at a late stage in searching, you probably will not use the author name for a search. For most searches, you will use keywords. You must develop key terms for your research question. The question *Are illegal drugs more common in urban than rural high schools?* might include keywords such as *drug abuse*, *substance abuse*, *drug laws*, *illegal drugs*. You can combine these with keywords as *high schools*, *high school students*, *rural schools*, *urban schools*, and *secondary schools*.

You should consider several synonyms for keywords. For example, a search with the keyword *homicide* may not find articles that use the word *murder*, so you want to try both. Most search tools look for a keyword in a title or the abstract. Often you can use multiple keywords using the connectors *or* or *and*. If you choose very board keywords or many connected by *or* you will get a huge number of irrelevant articles. Narrow keywords or several keywords connected with *and* may yield zero articles. To learn what works best, try experimenting with alternatives. The best search tools are only available to students or employees through a college library.

■ **Figure 2.4**   Examples of Two Abstracts from Scholarly Articles

Example abstract of journal article: Highly Structured

Article title: Measuring Media Bias: A Content Analysis of Time and Newsweek Coverage of
Domestic Social Issues, 1975–2000
Authors: Tawnya J. Adkins Covert and Philo C. Wasburn
Publication Information: *Social Science Quarterly* Vol. 88 (3), pp. 690–706 [September 2007].

Abstract

Objective. This study is an effort to produce a more systematic, empirically-based, historical-comparative understanding of media bias than generally is found in previous works. **Methods.** The research employs a quantitative
measure of ideological bias in a formal content analysis of the United States' two largest circulation news magazines,
Time and Newsweek. Findings are compared with the results of an identical examination of two of the nation's leading partisan journals, the conservative National Review and the liberal Progressive. **Results.** Bias scores reveal stark
differences between the mainstream and the partisan news magazines' coverage of four issue areas: crime, the environment, gender, and poverty. **Conclusion.** Data provide little support for those claiming significant media bias in either ideological direction.

Example abstract of journal article: Less Structured

Article title: The Moderating Roles of Race and Gender-Role Attitudes in the Relationship Between Sexual Harass-
ment And Psychological Well-Being
Authors: Juliette C. Rederstorff, Nicole T. Buchanan, and Isis H. Settles
Publication Information: *Psychology of Women Quarterly* Vol. 31 (1), pp 50–61 [March 2007]

Abstract

Although previous research has linked sexual harassment to negative psychological outcomes, few studies have focused on moderators of these relationships. The present study surveyed Black (n = 88) and White (n = 170) female undergraduates who endorsed experiences of sexual harassment to examine whether traditional gender attitudes
differentially moderated the relationship between sexual harassment and three outcomes: posttraumatic stress symptoms, general clinical symptoms, and satisfaction with life. We replicated past findings that sexual harassment is related to negative outcomes. Further, the results supported our hypothesis that less traditional gender attitudes (i.e.,
more feminist attitudes) would buffer the negative effects of sexual harassment for White women, whereas the same
attitudes would exacerbate its negative effects for Black women. We discuss reasons for these differences, including
Black women's double consciousness and differences in the meaning of feminist and traditional gender attitudes for
Black and White women.

Example Study Box 2   Sexual Harassment, Literature Search

Here is a search I conducted using article search tools. My general topic was "sexual
harassment." I narrowed the topic to "sexual harassment of female college students." I looked for peer-reviewed articles published from 2001 to 2006. I started
with the article search tool called "EBSCO-Host Academic Elite." This tool examines 1500 peer-reviewed journals for all academic fields back to the late 1990s for
most journals. Other article search tools contain information from different journals or cover different time spans. My first keywords were *sexual harassment* and
university. The search located 199 articles. I found that many were not about college
students. The search tool had picked up the word *university* from where the author
worked. A search with *sexual harassment* and *student* yielded 80 articles. Some were
about high school students and some were about males being harassed by females,
but many were relevant. I narrowed my search further to *sexual harassment* and
college female and got 28 articles. Not all were on my topic of interest. I noticed that

"gender-related harassment" and "unwanted sexual encounters" appeared in some articles. This gave me the idea to use them as alternative keywords for sexual harassment. I next used three other article search tools with the same restrictions and used the same keywords as before. I found that the four article search tools located many of the same articles, but at times one search tool found articles not located by a different article search tool. This suggests that is usually best to use more than one search tool.

Number of Articles Found Using Different Article Search Tools (peer reviewed articles, 2001–2006)

Keywords Used	Article Search Tool			
	EBSCO-Host	Wilson-Web	Pro-quest	CSA-Illumina
Sexual harassment & university	199	24	35	321
Sexual harassment & student	80	27	39	115
Sexual harassment & college & female	28	6	11	79

Specific article databases within each Article Search Tool: EBSCO-Host: Academic Elite; Wilson Web: Social Sciences, Education; Pro-quest: Criminal Justice, Gender Watch; CSA-Illumina: Social Services Abstracts & Sociological Abstracts.

Books. It is very difficult to find studies in books. The subject lists in library catalog systems are broad and not very useful. Moreover, they list only books in a particular library system. Professional librarians can help you locate books from other libraries. There is no sure-fire way to locate relevant books. Use multiple search methods, including a look at journals that contain book reviews and the bibliographies of articles.

Other Outlets. (Government documents, Ph.D. dissertations, Policy Reports, and Presented Papers) Locating studies in other outlets is far more difficult and time-consuming. A specific study might be highly relevant to your question, but few beginning researchers have the time or skills to search other outlets systematically.

STEP 4. Read and take notes on the reports found. It is easy to feel overwhelmed as you gather studies. To help, develop a system for taking notes. The old-fashioned approach is to write notes onto index cards. You then shift and sort the note cards, placing them in piles, then look for connections among them. This method still works. Today, most people use word-processing software and gather photocopies or printed versions of many articles.

Create Source and Content Files. Several strategies are used in literature searches and article reading. My strategy is to create two kinds of files: a *source file* and a *content file*. I recommend that you adopt a similar strategy.

In the source file, I record *all* the bibliographic information for each source, even if I may not use some of the articles. This includes journal name, full article title, date, volume and issue number, starting and ending page numbers, and the full names of all authors. It is easier to erase an unused source than to try to locate bibliographic information later when needed. The source file allows me to create a list of complete references very quickly.

I put substantive details in the content file. This file contains major findings, details of methodology (such as if it was a survey or experiment, the number of

■ Figure 2.5   Web Page from EBSCO-Host Academic Elite Advanced Search

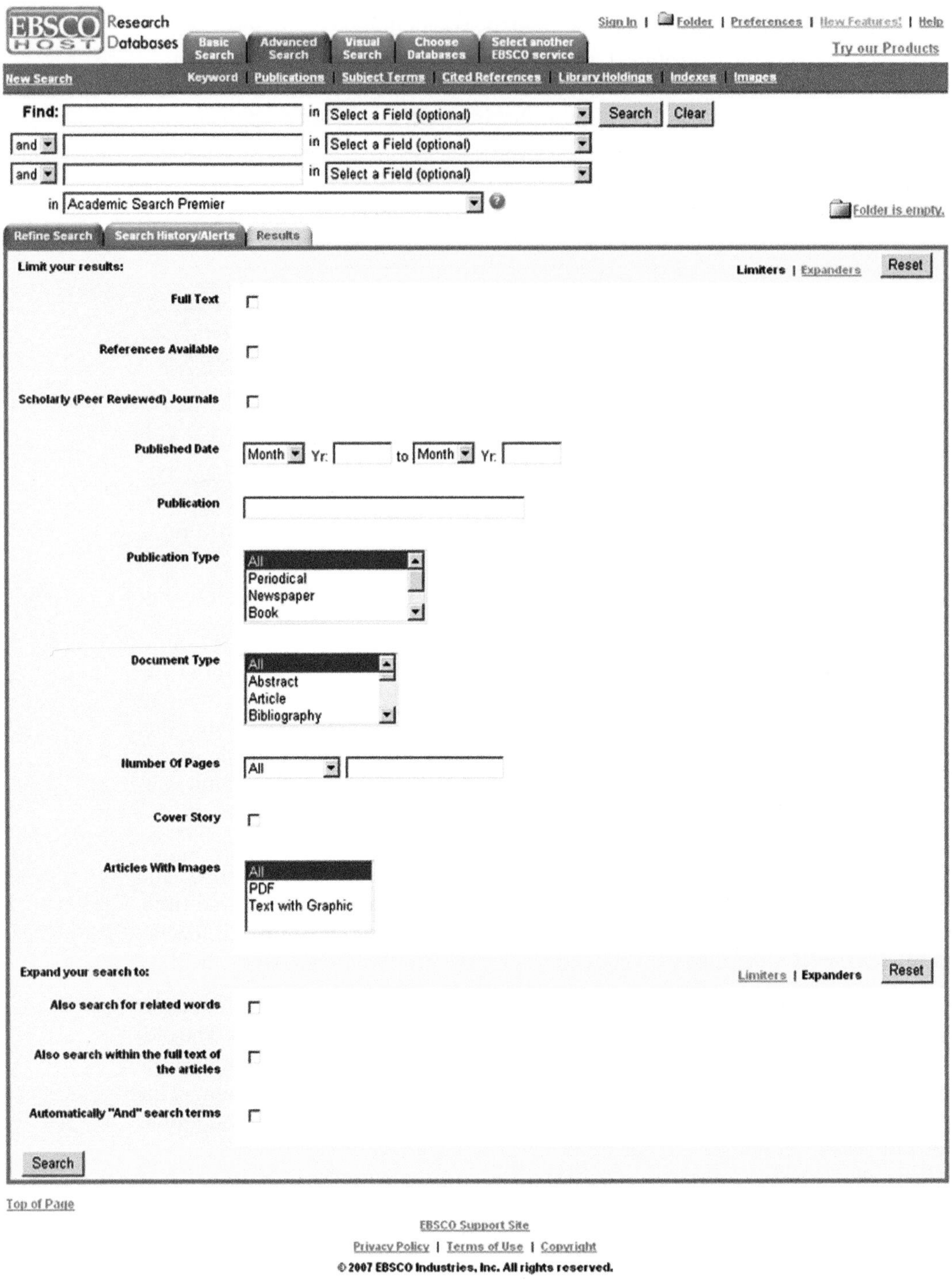

Making It Practical **How to Read a Scholarly Journal Article**

1. Read with a clear purpose in mind. Are you reading to gain background knowledge on a broad topic or to find information for a very specific research question?
2. First read the title and abstract for an article's relevance and general content. Next, quickly scan subheadings and the introduction and conclusion sections.
3. Form a mental image of the article's topic, major findings, method, and general conclusion.
4. Consider your own opinion about or bias toward the topic, the method, the publication source. How might your own opinion color how you read and evaluate the study?

5. Marshal external knowledge. What do you know about the topic and the research methods used?
6. As you read the entire article, evaluate. What errors might be present? Does the discussion of findings follow the data? Is the article's conclusion consistent with its approach?
7. Summarize. Prepare your own abstract. Include the topic, the methods used, and the main findings. Next, take notes, including quotation from the article and page numbers for quotes or ideas.
8. Review the reference section or bibliography for additional sources.

participants), definitions of major concepts, how concepts were measured, and interesting quotes. When quoting, I *always* record the specific page number(s) on which the quote appears. On each content note, I put the author's last name and the publication year, which allows me to link multiple cards or computer notes in the content file to a specific source in the source file.

What to Record in Notes. It is best to be consistent when writing notes—use all computer files or all note cards of the same size. As you decide what to record about an article, book, or other source, it is better to err by writing a little too much rather than not enough. Your notes should answer the following questions:

• What is study's basic topic and question? Does it state expectations of what the data will show based on a theory? Often a study will look at multiple questions, but only one is of interest to you.
• How did the authors define and measure their major ideas?
• What is the study's basic design? What procedures and techniques did the author use (e.g., was it an experiment, a survey, a field research study, and so forth)?
• What is the data, group, or sample? What units were examined (individuals, families, companies, towns, or nations). How many were examined (5 or 5000)? How were units chosen?
• What findings are relevant to your research question? Studies often have multiple findings, and the findings most relevant for your research could be buried deep inside an article.

Critically reading research reports is a skill that takes time and practice to develop. Despite a peer review procedure, errors and sloppy logic can slip into research reports. Sometimes titles, abstracts, and the introduction are misleading; they may not fully explain the study's method and results. A good article is logically tight, and all its parts fit together. Weak articles make huge leaps in logic or omit transitional steps.

As you read for details and take notes, you develop a mental image of how researchers conducted a study. This is why reading many studies will expand your research design skills. If you read a study in which the authors were disorganized or did not clearly provide all the details, you will see quickly the importance of good organization and clearly specifying all details. As mentioned earlier, look at the reference section to find new sources.

You may encounter unfamiliar terms, new theoretical ideas, advanced technical vocabulary, or sophisticated statistical charts, graphs, and results beyond your back-

■ **Figure 2.6   Example of Notes on an Article**

ENTRY IN SOURCE FILE

Bearman, Peter, and Hannah Bückner. 2001. "Promising the Future: Virginity Pledges and First Intercourse." *American Journal of Sociology* Volume 106, pages 859–912, January, issue number 4.

CONTENT FILE

Bearman and Bückner 2001

Background: Since 1993, the Southern Baptist Church sponsored a movement among teens. Teens make a public pledge to remain virgins until marriage. Over 2.5 million teens have made the pledge. This study looks at whether the pledge influenced the timing of first sexual intercourse and whether pledging teens differ from those who did not pledge. Critics say the pledge supporters often reject sex education, hold an unrealistic and overly romanticized view of marriage, and push teens to follow to traditional gender roles.

Questions/expectations: Adolescents try to engage in behaviors that adults enjoy but that are forbidden to them. When social controls are high, adolescent opportunities to engage in forbidden behavior is limited. Expectation 1: Teens from nontraditional families will have fewer social controls, more freedom and less supervision. They are more likely to engage in forbidden behavior (sexual intercourse) than those from traditional families and close to their parents. Teens from traditional families experience greater social control and delay sexual activity. Expectation 2: Teens closely tied to an "identity movement" outside the family will modify their behaviors based on the norms taught by the movement. As a result, family influence on them will not be as strong.

Definitions and measures: Identity movement is a social movement that emphasizes a self-identity separate from the larger society and being the member of a select group. Movements recruit members who modify their identity. The abstinence pledge movement recruits through the Internet, church groups, and Christian music and rallies. A person sustains his or her movement-pledge identity by repeated interactions with other pledging members. Pledge—A public shift in identity. The study measured it by asking unmarried teens if they have "ever taken a public or written pledge to remain a virgin until marriage." Family type—The study measured three types: living with both biological parents; living with only a mother or father; and living with two adults one or both of whom are step- or foster parents Religiosity—Measured with three behavioral items: frequency of praying, church attendance, and self-report of the importance of religion in the person's life.

Research Design: U.S. teens who were in randomly sampled public or private schools in 1994–1995 completed a questionnaire on a single day within one 45-60-minute class period. About 80 percent of students in a school completed it. Researchers also interviewed a subset of the students at home for 90 minutes. All students were asked about their parent's educational and occupational background, household structure, risk behaviors, visions of the future, self-esteem, health status, contacts with friends, and the sports and extracurricular activities in which they participated. The in-home interview measured sensitive health risk behaviors, such as drug and alcohol use, sexual behavior, criminal activities and family dynamics.

Data or Subjects: 90,000 students in grades 7–12 in 141 schools. Schools varied from under 100 to more than 3,000 students. 20,000 of the 90,000 students completed a second questionnaire.

Findings: Teens who pledged substantially delayed the timing of first sexual intercourse. However, pledging teens were largely in social contexts where abstinence was already a social norm. Pledging teens were more religious, less developed physically, and from traditional family backgrounds. Once social context is considered, the pledging itself had little effect on the delay of sexual activity compared to teens who did not pledge. In short, teens from traditional social backgrounds, strong religious beliefs and close family ties were less likely to engage in early sexual activity whether or not they pledged. Teens from non-traditional backgrounds, weak religious beliefs and few family ties are more likely to engage in early sexual activity whether or not they pledged. Another finding was that pledging teens who engaged in sexual intercourse were less likely to use contraceptives than non-pledgers.

ground. This is because professional researchers are the primary audience for research reports. The technical terms and results communicate important information to this audience. Do not be overly concerned if you cannot follow everything. As a novice researcher and consumer of studies, you should not expect to have the sophisticated knowledge of an expert researcher. A lack of knowledge might prevent you from fully evaluating all aspects of a study, but you can still learn from and build on the studies. Even if parts are over your head now, you can improve and expand your understanding over time. Be prepared to read an article more than once.

Photocopying all the relevant articles can save time in recording notes, and you will have the entire report and can write on the photocopy. Although photocopying sounds like the easy route, it has several downsides:

- The time and cost of photocopying can add up (30 articles of 20 pages = 600 pages, at 7 cents = $42, at 10 minutes to copy each article = 300 minutes).
- Be aware of copyright laws. U.S. copyright laws permit photocopying for personal research use.
- Be certain to include all citation details (title, page numbers, volume, etc.) of each article.
- Organizing many articles can be cumbersome. Plus, you may use several parts of a single article for different ideas or purposes.
- You may have to reread articles more than once unless you highlight carefully or take good notes.

STEP 5. Organize notes, synthesize, and write the review. Synthesizing and discussing findings with clear writing is the most difficult step in preparing a literature review. After gathering information, you need to organize specific findings to create a mental map of how they fit together. Your organizing method depends on the purpose of the review. Usually, it is best to organize findings around your research question or around a few core shared findings. Most professionals try several organizing schemes before they settle on a final one. Organizing is a skill that improves with practice. Some people place notes into several piles, each representing a common theme. Others draw charts or diagrams to show the connections among different findings. Others create lists of how the many study findings agree and disagree. Organizing notes is a process. Often you will find that some references and notes are no longer relevant, and you will discard them. You may discover gaps or new areas that you did not consider previously. This may require return visits to the library to refine your search.

A common error when writing a first literature review is to list summaries of articles, one study after another. This indicates an incomplete process that stopped before synthesis. To synthesize means to combine parts or elements into an integrated whole. You want to blend the findings, methods, or statements from separate studies and end up with a coherent whole in which the studies fit together as one integrated picture. Like fitting together the pieces of a jigsaw puzzle, all the parts fit to present an overall picture. However, with jigsaw puzzles someone started with the picture and then cut it up. In a literature review, there is no preexisting picture. You create one out of the many studies. It is more like weaving cloth from many separate threads. The threads start separate and different but end up as one piece of cloth or clothing tightly held together.

You use all the skills of good writing to produce a literature review. Your goal is to produce a compact document that clearly summarizes what many studies say about a research question. A literature review is a neutral summary-description. It does not include your personal opinion or conjecture. The rules of good writing (e.g., clear organizational structure, an introduction and conclusion, transitions between sections, etc.) apply.

A good literature review communicates its purpose to the reader by its organization. If you write a review by listing a series of summaries, you to communicate a sense of purpose; your review reads as notes strung together. You want to organize

Making It Practical What a Good Literature Review Looks Like

EXAMPLE OF WEAK REVIEW

Sexual harassment has many consequences. Adams, Kottke, and Padgitt (1983) found that some women students said they avoided taking a class or working with certain professors because of the risk of harassment. They also found that men and women students reacted differently. Their research was a survey of 1000 men and women graduate and undergraduate students. Benson and Thomson's study in *Social Problems* (1982) lists many problems created by sexual harassment. In their excellent book *The Lecherous Professor*, Dziech and Weiner (1990) give a long list of difficulties that victims have suffered.

Researchers study the topic in different ways. Hunter and McClelland (1991) conducted a study of undergraduates at a small liberal arts college. They had a sample of 300 students, and students were given multiple vignettes that varied by the reaction of the victim and the situation. Jaschik and Fretz (1991) showed 90 women students at a mideastern university a videotape with a classic example of sexual harassment by a teaching assistant. Before it was labeled as *sexual harassment,* few women called it that. When asked whether it was sexual harassment, 98 percent agreed. Weber-Burdin and Rossi (1982) replicated a previous study on sexual harassment, but they used students at the University of Massachusetts. They had 59 students rate 40 hypothetical situations. Reilley, Carpenter, Dull, and Bartlett (1982) conducted a study of 250 female and 150 male undergraduates at the University of California at Santa Barbara. They also had a sample of 52 faculty. Both samples completed a questionnaire in which respondents were presented vignettes of sexual-harassing situations that they were to rate. Popovich et al. (1986) created a nine-item scale of sexual harassment. They studied 209 undergraduates at a medium-sized university in groups of 15 to 25. They found disagreement and confusion among students.

EXAMPLE OF BETTER REVIEW

The victims of sexual harassment suffer a range of consequences, from lowered self-esteem and loss of self-confidence to withdrawal from social interaction, changed career goals, and depression (Adams, Kottke, and Padgitt, 1983; Benson and Thomson, 1982; Dziech and Weiner, 1990). For example, Adams, Kottke, and Padgitt (1983) noted that 13 percent of women students said they avoided taking a class or working with certain professors because of the risk of harassment.

Research into campus sexual harassment has taken several approaches. In addition to survey research, many have experimented with vignettes or presented hypothetical scenarios (Hunter and McClelland, 1991; Jaschik and Fretz, 1991; Popovich et al., 1987; Reilley, Carpenter, Dull, and Barlett, 1982; Rossi and Anderson, 1982; Valentine-French and Radtke, 1989; Weber-Burdin and Rossi, 1982). Victim verbal responses and situational factors appear to affect whether observers label a behavior as harassment. There is confusion over the application of a sexual harassment label for inappropriate behavior. For example, Jaschik and Fretz (1991) found that only 3 percent of the women students shown a videotape with a classic example of sexual harassment by a teaching assistant initially labeled it as *sexual harassment.* Instead, they called it "sexist," "rude," "unprofessional," or "demeaning." When asked whether it was sexual harassment, 98 percent agreed. Roscoe et al. (1987) reported similar labeling difficulties.

common findings or arguments together, address the most important ideas first, logically link findings, and note discrepancies or weaknesses in the research (see Making It Practical: What a Good Literature Review Looks Like for an example).

STEP 6. Create the Reference List. The last step is to create a reference list, works cited list, or bibliography. Works cited and reference list are the same thing—an alphabetical list of sources cited or to which you referred. They differ from a bibliography, which is an alphabetical list of all the materials you consulted, whether or not you cited them. For a literature review, use a reference list of sources you discussed in the review.

How you indicate sources in the text of your review and in the reference list is very important. There are several format styles, each with separate rules. Different fields (e.g., psychology, history) use specific formats. In the text of a review itself, an in-text citation format in most common. It has the author or authors' last name and year of publication for a general statement, with page numbers for specific details or quotes. To discuss an article on abstinence pledges, I might say, *Bearman and*

Brückner (2001) studied the identity movement in which teens pledge to stay virgins until marriage. Alternatively, I could state, *In a study of the identity movement, teens pledged to stay virgins until marriage (Bearman and Brückner 2001).* A quote from a specific page might look like this: *The movement has been successful in organizing mass rallies in which speakers extol the benefits of abstinence to stadiums full of eager adolescents. Its growth rate has been phenomenal, and with it, the movement has spawned a whole new subculture in which it is "cool" to say no to sex (Bearman and Brückner 2001: 860).*

The order and format of source **citation** information can vary greatly. You need to learn which format style an instructor or publication requires. The citation format style precisely specifies how to organize details of source information in a reference list. Two reference books on the topic in social science are the *Chicago Manual of Style*, which contains nearly 80 pages on bibliographies and reference formats, and the *American Psychological Association Publication Manual*, which devotes about 60 pages to the topic.

The entry for a book is shorter and simpler than for an article. It has the following: author's name, book title, year of publication, place of publication, publisher's name. Article entries are more complex than book entries. They require the names of all authors, article title, journal name, and volume and page numbers. Some formats require the authors' complete first names whereas others use initials only. Some require the issue or month of publication; others do not (see Figure 2.7 for four styles, MLA [Modern Language Association], ASA [American Sociological Association], APA [American Psychological Association] and Chicago [*Chicago Manual of Style*]).

citation documenting a source of information in a standardized format.

■ **Figure 2.7** Different Reference Citations for a Book and a Journal Article

Style	Book with One Author in Reference List
MLA	Pillow, Wanda S. Unfit Subjects: Educational Policy and the Teen Mother. New York: Routledge, 2004.
ASA	Pillow, Wanda S. 2004. *Unfit Subjects: Educational Policy and the Teen Mother*. New York: Routledge.
APA	Pillow, W.S. (2004). *Unfit subjects: Educational policy and the teen mother*. New York: Routledge.
Chicago	'Same as MLA for the arts, literature or history. Same as ASA for science fields.

Style	Journal Article with Two Authors in Reference List (Journal Pagination by Volume)
MLA	Bearman, Peter and Hannah Bückner. "Promising the future: Virginity pledges and first intercourse." American Journal of Sociology 106 (2001) 859–912.
ASA	Bearman, Peter and Hannah Bückner. 2001. "Promising the Future: Virginity Pledges and First Intercourse." *American Journal of Sociology* 106:859–912.
APA	Bearman, P., and Bückner, H. (2001). Promising the future: Virginity pledges and first intercourse. *American Journal of Sociology* 106, 859–912.
Chicago	Same as APA for science fields. Same as MLA for arts, literature and history.
Others	Bearman, Peter and Hannah Bückner, 2001. "Promising the future: Virginity pledges and first Intercourse." *Am. J. of Sociol.* 106:859–912.
	Bearman, P. and Bückner, H. (2001). "Promising the Future: Virginity Pledges and First Intercourse." *American Journal of Sociology* 106 (January): 859–912.
	Bearman, Peter and Hannah Bückner. 2001. "Promising the future: Virginity pledges and first intercourse." *American Journal of Sociology* 106 (4):859–912.
	Bearman, P. and H. Bückner. (2001). "Promising the future: Virginity pledges and first intercourse." American Journal of Sociology *106, 859–912.*
	Peter Bearman and Hannah Bückner, "Promising the Future: Virginity Pledges and First Intercourse," American Journal of Sociology 106, no. 4 (2001): 859–912.

Format styles for sources in a reference list.

Tips for the Wise Consumer Using the Internet for Social Research

The Internet has revolutionized research. Only fifteen years ago, few people used it. Today, researchers and others use it Internet regularly to review the literature, to communicate with others, and to search for information. The Internet has been a mixed blessing. It has not proved to be the panacea that some people first thought it might be. It is an important way to find information, but it remains one tool among others. It is a supplement rather than a replacement for traditional library research. On the positive side, it is easy, fast, and cheap. On the negative side, there is no quality control over what gets on the Internet. Unlike standard academic publications, there is no peer review process, or any review at all. Anyone can put almost anything on a Web site. It may be poor quality, undocumented, highly biased, totally made up, or fraudulent.

Many excellent sources and important resource materials for social research are not available on the Internet. Most information is available only through library subscription services. Contrary to popular belief, the Internet has not made all information free and accessible to everyone. Internet sources can be "unstable" and difficult to document. After you conduct a search on the Internet and locate Web sites, note the specific URL (uniform record locater) or "address" (usually it starts http://) where it resides and the date you saw it. This address refers to an electronic file sitting in a computer somewhere. If the computer file moves, it may not be at the same address two days later. Unlike a journal article stored on a shelf in hundreds of libraries for many decades and available for anyone to read, Web sites can quickly vanish. This means it may not be possible to check Web references easily, verify a quote, or go back to original materials. It is easy to copy, modify, or distort and then reproduce copies of a Web source, so you may find several variations on the same material. A few rules can help you locate the best sites on the Internet—ones that have useful and truthful information. Sources that originate at universities, research institutes, or government agencies usually are more trustworthy. Many Web sites fail to provide complete information to make citation easy. Better sources will provide complete information about the author, date, location, and so on.

FOCUSING ON A RESEARCH QUESTION

By now you know that before you conduct a literature review or develop a proposal for a study, you need to focus on a research question that is much narrower than a topic. The way you do this varies depending on whether your study follows one of two general approaches to research, an inductive or deductive approach. A study that is **inductive** starts with by evidence and then slowly builds toward generalizations, patterns, or summary ideas. A **deductive** study starts with a summary idea or an "educated guess" of what you think might occur and then moves toward specific, observable evidence to test or verify the ideas.

Many studies are not strictly inductive or deductive, but most emphasize one approach over the other. There is no rigid rule; however, the type of data and purpose of a study is a guide. Most often, an inductive approach goes with qualitative data and the deductive approach with quantitative data. Most exploratory studies use the inductive approach, explanatory studies use the deductive approach, and descriptive studies use both.

If you follow a deductive approach with quantitative data, you will need to devote significant time early in a research study to specifying the research question precisely and planning most study details. Once you design the study, the other steps (i.e., collecting and analyzing data) can proceed in a fairly straightforward way. By contrast, if you follow an inductive approach with qualitative data, you can devote less time to developing a research question and planning study details in advance. However, you must spend far more time and effort during the subsequent stages of a study (i.e., collecting and analyzing data).

It takes time to develop the judgment skills to decide whether a deductive-quantitative or an inductive-qualitative study works best for a research question. Three things can help you pick most effective type:

- Reading many past studies
- Appreciating the specific features of qualitative and quantitative data

inductive research in which you start many specific observations and move toward general ideas or theory to capture what they show.

deductive research in which you start with a general idea or theory and test it by looking at specific observations.

■ Figure 2.8   Inductive or Deductive Approach

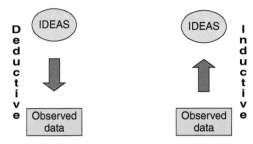

Making It Practical   **Narrowing a Topic into a Research Question**

You want the research question to be empirically testable and specific. Here are four ways to do this:

Examine the research literature. From a literature review, you may decide to replicate a past study exactly or with slight variations. You can also explore unexpected findings discovered in past research. In many reports, authors offer suggestions for future research that you can follow. You can also extend an existing explanation to a new topic or setting. For example, a study of workplace relations in a hospital found that nurses and other staff cooperate and are more productive under certain arrangements. You might conduct a study to see whether the same arrangements have the same outcome in a nonmedical setting (e.g., a large legal office). You can examine the intervening process. For example, a study found that increased police foot patrols produced more calls to police when trouble occurred. You might examine exactly how this occurred—did the foot patrols increase familiarity, feelings of trust, and belief in the honesty in police?

Talk over ideas with others. Ask people who are knowledgeable about the topic for questions. It is often useful to seek out those who hold opinions that differ from yours on the topic and discuss possible research questions with them. A research question might help resolve different positions on an issue.

Specify the context. Apply a finding or topic a specific time, society, geographic unit, or category of people. Let us say you want to study divorce. Your research question might examine divorce in a particular era (divorce in the 1950s versus the early 2000s), location (Southwest versus New England states), or category of people (among people of different religions versus a shared religion).

Specify the purpose of your study. Do you want the study to be an exploratory, descriptive, explanatory, or evaluation study? Tailor your research question to one or another purpose.

COMPARING GOOD AND NOT-SO-GOOD RESEARCH QUESTIONS

Not-So-Good Research Questions

Not empirically testable, nonscientific questions. Should abortion be legal? Is it right to have capital punishment?

General topics, not research questions. Treatment of alcohol and drug abuse. Sexuality and aging.

Set of variables, not questions. Capital punishment and racial discrimination. Urban decay and gangs

Too vague, ambiguous. Do police affect delinquency? What can be done to prevent child abuse? How does poverty affect children?

Good Research Questions for Parallel Structure

Exploratory questions. Has the actual incidence of child abuse changed in California in the past 10 years? Is a new type of abuse occurring?

Descriptive questions. Is child abuse, violent or sexual, more common in families that have experienced a divorce than in intact, never-divorced families? Are children raised in impoverished households more likely to have medical, learning, and social-emotional adjustment difficulties than children raised in nonimpoverished households?

Explanatory Questions. Does the emotional instability created by experiencing a divorce increase the chances that divorced parents will physically abuse their children? Is a lack of sufficient funds for preventive treatment a major cause of more serious medical problems among children raised in families in impoverished?

Evaluative Questions. Has the new patient tracking system produced higher satisfaction ratings? Does the automatic arrest of abusive males in domestic violence calls to police reduce later violent domestic abuse incidents? Will third-grade children's readings scores show larger improvements under the new program than the existing reading program? Does calling customers to remind them of their appointment a day in advance reduce the percent of customer no-shows at the service center?

- Understanding how to use various research techniques and recognizing their strengths and limitations

You need a specific research question to make decisions about study design, although you adjust the research question as the study progresses. If you adopt a deductive-quantitative approach, you must be very specific before you can proceed. If you adopt the inductive-qualitative approach, you can begin with a general a research question that you narrow further during the data collection process.

THE RESEARCH PROPOSAL

As stated at the start of this chapter, the research proposal is a written document in which you review the literature and provide a detailed plan for research study. Your proposal will vary depending on whether the approach and research evidence is primarily deductive-quantitative or inductive-qualitative. A mixed approach with both types of data is also possible and has many advantages.

A Proposal for Quantitative or Qualitative Research

In all empirical research studies, you systematically collect and analyze data. If your data are qualitative in the form of words, sentences, photos, symbols, and so forth, you must use different strategies and data collection techniques than if the data are numbers. Techniques appropriate for qualitative data may be wholly inappropriate for quantitative data, and vice versa. One data form is not always superior; rather, each has strengths. Your goal is to fit the form of data to a specific research question and situation in a way that utilizes its strengths. The form of data affects how to conduct a study and influences your research proposal as follows:

1. When and how you do focus the research question?
2. To what universe can you generalize from a study's findings?
3. Will you follow a linear or nonlinear path when doing research?
4. Do you examine variables and hypotheses or cases and contexts?
5. How will you analyze patterns in the data that you gather?
6. What type of explanation will you use to give meaning to the patterns in the data?
7. What are your units of analysis in your study?
8. What is the level of analysis of your study?

1. When Do You Focus the Research Question? If you plan to conduct research gathering quantitative data, you need to develop a specific focus early in the process, before gathering any data. The research question directs you to the particular data you will need to gather. Past studies, theories, or a few discussions might help you focus. For example, your question tells you to collect data about the attendance of students in specific grades, and to measure their learning (using test scores, course grades, teacher notes) in specific subject areas. If you intend to gather qualitative data, you proceed slowly and focus on a research question after you gather data. You will need a topic, such as how do high school students actually learn course material, but do not have to focus on a specific question at first. You may spend many hours gathering data by talking with, observing, and interacting with students, teachers, and parents. After examining the data, you develop a specific question to direct later stages of data collection. The research question emerges slowly, in an ongoing, interactive process of data gathering.

universe a broad category of cases or units to which the study findings apply.

2. To What Universe Can You Generalize from a Study's Findings? As you move to focus on a research question, you will also specify the **universe** to which you can generalize an answer to the question. Only rarely do you want to restrict findings to the specific units or cases you happened to study. Instead, you want to extend them to a broader category of people, organizations, and other units. For example, your research question is, Does a new attendance policy help high school students learn more? You plan to study three high schools in one U.S. city in 2008. The universe, in this case, is all high school students. You want to generalize what you learn beyond the specific students in three high schools of one U.S. city in 2008 to all high school students, or at least all U.S. high school students in the early twenty-first century.

3. Which Type of Research Path Do You Follow? A path is a metaphor for the sequence of activities you do. It is a way of thinking and a way of looking at issues. In general, with quantitative data you will follow a **linear path**. You follow a relatively fixed sequence of steps in one direction. It is like a staircase, a straight pathway that moves upward without deviation and takes you to a single location. When gathering qualitative data, the pathway is less a straight line or fixed sequence; the set of steps is somewhat flexible, multidirectional, and nonlinear. A **nonlinear path** makes successive passes through steps and moves sideways before going forward. You advance slowly but not directly. It is more of a spiral. At each cycle or repetition, you collect data and gain new insights, then move ahead.

If you are accustomed to the direct, linear approach with fixed steps, the nonlinear path may look inefficient and sloppy. A nonlinear approach does not have to be disorganized and is never an excuse for doing poor-quality research. It has its own discipline and rigor. It can be highly effective when adjusting to a fast-changing, fluid situation. It can create a feeling for the whole, allow grasping subtle shades of meaning, pull together divergent information, and permit switching perspectives. If you are used to a nondirect approach, the linear approach may appear to be rigid and artificial. It may look so set, fixed, and standardized as to miss what is most interesting and important in dynamic human relations. The linear path can offer a highly efficient, disciplined, and simple-to-follow sequence that makes it easy to spot a mistake and to repeat a past study.

linear path a relatively fixed sequence of steps in one forward direction, with little repeating, moving directly to a conclusion.

nonlinear path advancing without fixed order that often requires successive passes through previous steps and moves toward a conclusion indirectly.

Making It Practical **Practical Limitations on Study Design**

Designing a perfect research project is an interesting academic exercise, but if you actually carry out a study, practical limitations have an impact on its design. You need to ask the following questions:

- How much time you can devote to the study?
- What is the cost of conducting the study and do you have the required funds?
- Can you gain access to needed resources, people, and locations?
- Do you have required approval of authorities or officials?
- Have you addressed all ethical concerns?
- Do you have the needed skills, expertise, and knowledge?

If you can devote 10 hours a week for five weeks to a study but answering a research question requires a five-year study, narrow the research question. It is difficult to

estimate accurately how much time you will need to conduct a study. The research question, research technique you use, and the amount and types of data you collect will all have an impact. Consulting with experienced researchers is the best way to get a good estimate.

Access to resources is a common limitation on a study. Beyond money and time, required resources include the expertise of others, special equipment, and information. For example, you have a research question about burglary rates and family income in the 20 largest nations. This is almost impossible to answer because information on burglary and income is not available for most countries. Some questions require the approval of authorities (e.g., to see medical records) or involve violating basic ethical principles (discussed in the next chapter). Your expertise or lack of it can be a limitation. Answering some research questions may require knowledge of research techniques, a statistical ability, or foreign language skills that you do not yet have.

4. What Do You Examine? The **variable** is a central idea in quantitative research. Simply defined, a variable is a concept that varies. Research with quantitative data uses a language of variables and emphasizes relationships among variables. Once you begin to look for them, you will see variables everywhere. For example, gender is a variable; it can take on two values: male or female. Marital status is a variable; it has the values of never married single, married, divorced, or widowed. Type of crime is a variable; it can take on values of robbery, burglary, theft, murder, and so forth. Family income is a variable; it can take on values from zero to billions of dollars. A person's attitude toward abortion is a variable; it ranges from strongly supporting the right to a legal abortion to strongly opposing abortion.

It is easy to confuse a variable with the categories or values of variables. Confusion arises because a category in one variable can itself become a separate variable with a slight change in definition. "Male" is not a variable; it describes a category of the variable gender. A related idea, "degree of masculinity," is a variable. It describes the intensity or strength of attachment to attitudes, beliefs, and behaviors associated with being masculine within the broader idea of gender. "Married" is a category of the variable "marital status." Related ideas such as "number of years married" or "depth of commitment to a marriage" are variables. If you wish to gather quantitative data, you must convert most of your ideas into the language of variables.

Types of Variables. We can classify variables into three basic types, depending on their location in a cause-effect statement. The cause variable is the **independent variable**. The result or effect variable is the **dependent variable**. The independent variable is "independent of" prior causes that act on it. The dependent variable "depends on" the cause.

It is not always easy to determine whether a variable is independent or dependent. Two questions help identify the independent variable:

- Does it come earlier in time? Independent variables always come before any other type.
- Does it have an impact on another variable? Independent variables have an impact on other variables.

You can reword most research questions in terms of the dependent variables because dependent variable is what you will explain. If your research question is about reasons for an increase in the crime rate in Dallas, Texas, then your dependent variable is the Dallas crime rate.

A simple cause-effect relationship requires only an independent and a dependent variable. A third type of variable, the **intervening variable**, appears in complex relations. It shows the link or mechanism between the independent and dependent variable. To advance knowledge, we both document simple cause-and-effect relationships and try to specify the mechanisms within a causal relation. In a sense, the intervening variable acts as a dependent variable with respect to the independent variable and as an independent variable toward the dependent variable.

Here is a three-variable example. The famous French sociologist Emile Durkheim developed a theory about a causal relationship between marital status and suicide rates. He found that married people are less likely to commit suicide than single people and believed it was because married people were more socially integrated (i.e., had feelings of belonging to a group or family). We can restate his theory as the following: Being married (independent variable) increases social integration (intervening variable), which in turn reduces the suicide rate (dependent variable).

Specifying the chain of variables clarifies the linkages in a causal explanation. Complex theories have multiple independent, intervening, and dependent variables. They link together a string of intervening variables. You notice that people from disruptive family settings have lower incomes as adults. Why? Family disruption causes lower self-esteem among children, which causes greater psychological depres-

variable a feature of a case or unit that represents multiple types, values, or levels.

independent variable the variable of factors, forces, or conditions acting on another variable to produce an effect or change in it.

dependent variable the variable influenced by and changes as an outcome of another variable.

intervening variable a variable that comes between the independent and dependent variable in a causal relationship.

■ **Figure 2.9**   Chain of Variables

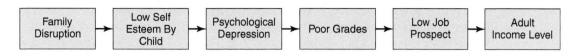

| Family Disruption | → | Low Self Esteem By Child | → | Psychological Depression | → | Poor Grades | → | Low Job Prospect | → | Adult Income Level |

sion, which causes poor grades in school, which causes reduced prospects for getting a good job, which causes a lower adult income (see Figure 2.9).

Family disruption is the independent variable. Adult income level is the dependent variable. All the rest are intervening variables. Two explanations of the same dependent variable may use different independent variables, or agree about the independent and dependent variables but differ on the intervening variable. Both may say that family disruption causes lower adult income. One holds that disruption encourages children to join deviant peer groups that are not socialized to norms of work and thrift. Another emphasizes the impact of the disruption on childhood depression and poor academic performance.

In a single study, you usually test only a part of a complex causal explanation. Even though you might test one small part, you want to link it to a larger explanation. In a study, you connect independent and dependent variables with the hypothesis. A **hypothesis** is a tentative statement of a relationship between two variables. It is a guess about how the world works and can be restated as a prediction about what you expect to find. A causal hypothesis has the following five characteristics:

- It has at least two variables.
- It specifies how the variables are connected, which is the cause, and which is the effect.
- It includes a time order assumption (what comes first).
- You can restate it as a prediction or expected finding.
- You can show that it is supported or false with empirical data.

   Example: The more a couple attends religious services together, the lower the chances that they will divorce.

- Two variables: (1) attendance at religious services, (2) probability of divorce.
- Connection: Lower attendance causes higher chance of divorce, and vice versa.
- Time order: attendance is earlier and divorce comes later.
- Prediction: Couples who attend religious services together very often will have fewer divorces than couples who never or rarely attend religious services together.
- Testable with empirical data: We can look at 1000 couples and ask how often they attend religious services together, then see how many of them are still married to one another 10 years later.

Knowledge cannot advance far with one test of a single hypothesis. In fact, you may get a distorted picture of the research process if you focus too much on a single study that tests one hypothesis. Knowledge develops over time as many researchers test many hypotheses. It grows out of the shifting and winnowing of many findings about hypotheses. If data fail to support some hypotheses, researchers gradually drop them from consideration. If data support a hypothesis, they keep it in contention. Researchers constantly create new hypotheses that challenge existing ones that have received support. Over time, if a hypothesis continues to receive empirical support in test after test and it stands up as better than alternative hypotheses, we can begin to accept it as likely to be true. To gain acceptance, the hypothesis needs multiple tests with consistent and repeated empirical support.

The Null Hypothesis.   Our confidence in the truthfulness of a hypothesis grows as it defeats its competitors in repeated tests. A curious aspect of hypothesis testing is that we treat evidence in support of a hypothesis differently than evidence that

hypothesis a statement about the relationship of two (or more) variables yet to be tested with empirical data.

negates it. We give the negative evidence greater importance. Technically, researchers never say that they have proved a hypothesis true; however, they do say it is rejected.

If your evidence supports a hypothesis, the hypothesis is a possibility; it is still in the running and the case is not closed. When evidence fails to support a hypothesis, it is tarnished and falls out of the running. This is because a hypothesis makes a prediction. Negative evidence shows that the prediction is wrong. Positive evidence is less critical, because alternative hypotheses may make the same prediction. Confirming evidence may reinforce your belief in a hypothesis, but it does not automatically beat out the alternative hypotheses making the same prediction. Whereas negative evidence seriously weakens a hypothesis, piling up more and more evidence in favor of a hypothesis is not as significant.

Researchers test hypotheses in two ways: a straightforward way and by using the **null hypothesis**. Most of us talk about a hypothesis as a way to predict a relationship between two variables. The null hypothesis does the opposite; it predicts no relationship. Many quantitative researchers, especially experimenters, use a null hypothesis. They look for evidence that will let them accept or reject the null hypothesis. For example, Sarah believes that students who live on campus in dormitories get better grades than students who live off campus and commute. Her null hypothesis is that residence and grades are unrelated. She matches the null hypothesis with a corresponding alternative hypothesis. It is that a relationship exists; more specifically that a student's on-campus residence has a positive effect on grades.

null hypothesis a hypothesis that there is no relationship between two variables, that they do not influence one another.

Making It Practical   From the Research Question to Hypotheses

Going from a well-formulated research question to a hypothesis is a short step. A good research question has hints about the hypothesis. The hypothesis is a tentative answer to the research question. Consider the research question, "Is age at marriage associated with chances of divorce?" It has two variables: "age at marriage" and "chances of divorce." Age at marriage is the independent variable because marriage must logically come before divorce. Beyond stating that two variables are connected, you need to decide the direction of the relationship. You have two choices: (1) The lower the age at time of marriage, the greater the chances that of divorce; (2) the higher the age at time of marriage, the greater the chances of divorce. A hypothesis makes a prediction, with choice (1) it says that people who marry younger are more likely to divorce. This may help you to better focus the research question, "Are couples who marry younger more likely to divorce?"

You can create several hypotheses from one research question. The question was, "Is age at marriage associated with chances of divorce?" Here is another hypothesis from it: "The smaller the difference between the ages of the marriage partners at the time of marriage, the lower the chances of divorce." Here age at marriage is specified differently. You can also specify conditions under which a relationship works. For example, "The lower the age at time of marriage, the greater the chances that the marriage will

end in divorce, unless it is a marriage between two members of a tight-knit traditional religious community in which early marriage is the norm."

Besides answering a research question, a hypothesis can be an untested proposition from a theory. You can express a hypothesis at two levels: (1) an abstract, conceptual level of general theory; and (2) a concrete, measurable level that you actually test in a study. The theory explains why the prediction in your hypothesis is true. We can continue with the same example but now put it in the form of a theoretical statement.

Adults stabilize their self-identity and develop mature coping abilities as they move from their late teens to their late twenties. A stable self-identity and mature coping abilities help people to sustain a long-term committed intimate relationship, such as marriage. If two adults enter into a marriage relationship before they have a stable a self-identity and mature coping abilities, the marriage is unlikely to last many years.

Now let us look at the same hypothesis but phrased as empirically testable statement with specific measures:

The rate of divorce within the first 10 years of a marriage is much higher when both partners are 21 years old or younger at the time of a marriage than when both marriage partners are 28 years old or older.

You may feel that the null hypothesis is a backward way of hypothesis testing. It rests on the assumption that hypothesis testing should make finding a relationship between variables very demanding. With the null hypothesis approach, you directly test the null hypothesis. If evidence supports the null hypothesis (technically—you accept it as true), you are forced to conclude that the alternative hypothesis is false. On the other hand, if the evidence rejects the null hypothesis, then the alternative hypothesis remains as a possibility. You keep it in contention. As you repeatedly test and reject the null hypothesis, the alterative hypothesis looks stronger over time. Researchers use the null hypothesis because they are extremely cautious. They hesitate to say that a relationship exists until they have mountains of evidence. This is similar to the Anglo-American legal idea of innocent until proved guilty. Assume that the null hypothesis is correct until reasonable doubt suggests otherwise.

Quantitative data studies emphasize variables. By contrast, studies with qualitative data examine cases and contexts. A researcher who uses qualitative data may not think in terms of variables or testing hypotheses. He or she sees many areas of social life, human relations, and social activities as being intrinsically qualitative. Rather than try to convert fluid qualitative social life into variables or precise numbers, he or she retains the loose images or ideas that people use in natural social contexts.

Qualitative researchers usually examine a limited number of cases in depth. The cases are usually the same as a unit of analysis (discussed later). Instead of precise numerical measures of a very large number of cases, as in quantitative data analysis, in a qualitative study you examine in detail many aspects of a few cases. The rich detail and astute insight into the cases replace precise measures across numerous cases. Because you closely examine the same case or a few over time, you can see an issue evolve, a conflict emerge, or a social relationship develop. This places you in a good position to detect and observe processes. In historical research, the passage of time may involve years or decades. In field research, it may be days, weeks, or months. In both, you observe what unfolds and can quickly notice when something unusual or important occurs.

The social context is very important for studies with qualitative data. This is because an event, social action, or statement's meaning depends, in an important way, on the context in which it appears. When you remove an event, social action, or conversation from its social context, or ignore the context, you can seriously distort its meaning. Without the context, its real importance or significance is often lost. This requires you to pay close attention to what surrounds an action, event, or statement. It also implies that the same actions, events, or statements can have different meanings in different situations, cultures, or historical eras.

Let us say you studied voting. Instead of simply counting votes across time or cultures, you might ask, What does voting mean in the context? The same action (e.g., voting for a presidential candidate) may differ depending on the context, such as intense argument and competition among several parties, no difference among candidates, or a situation of total one-party dominance. Until you place the parts of social life into a larger whole, you may not grasp the part's meaning. It is hard to understand a baseball glove without knowing about the game of baseball. If you look at it as a glove, like a mitten for cold weather, a pair of driving gloves, or gloves to use for working in the garden, the baseball glove has little meaning. The glove's meaning comes from its use and placement within the flow of a baseball game. The whole of the game—innings, bats, curve balls, hits—gives meaning to each of the parts. Each part without the whole has little meaning.

5. How Do You Look for Patterns in the Data? Researches look for patterns in both the quantitative and qualitative data but do so differently. With quantitative data you rearrange, examine, and discuss numbers by using charts, tables, and statistics to see patterns. They reveal patterns in the numerical data. You connect the patterns with your research question. In a way, the hypothesis is both an answer to the research question and a prediction about what will appear in your charts, tables, and statistics.

With qualitative data, you look for patterns by rearranging, examining, and discussing textual or visual data. You do this in a way that conveys an authentic voice, or that remains true to the original understandings of the people and situations that you studied. Instead of relying on charts, statistics, and displays of numbers, you identify patterns (i.e., sequences, cycles, contrasts) in the data, (i.e., observed events, conversations, or situations) as they appear in a specific context. You might discuss the patterns in terms of themes or as narratives. A narrative is a story that has a beginning and ending and major actors or forces that pull the reader from start to finish. Qualitative data are often more complex and filled with specific meaning than numbers. Essentially, you must translate, or make understandable, the data for people who lack a direct experience with the specific research setting. For example, you describe a 30-second social interaction in which no one spoke.

> A middle-aged man in a business suit rushes into a coffee shop, opens his wallet, and puts a five-dollar bill on the counter. Without a word, the clerk at the shop quickly pours a cup of coffee into a take-away container and adds cream for the man. The man picks up the container, turns, and quickly walks out the door.

You create a translation based on observations, conservations, and the context. The man is a regular patron of the coffee shop near a train station. He has been coming each morning for five years. Today he is in a rush to catch a commuter train to his office downtown. He will drink the coffee while on the train. The clerk knows the man and knows what he wants. The man orders the same thing every day. In return, the clerk rushes to take care of the man each time. When the man is very rushed, he just puts down a five-dollar bill. The coffee only costs $1.50; the money covers the cost of the coffee, $1.50 for the newspaper that the man took from outside the front of the coffee shop before entering, and a $2.00 tip. On the days that he has time, the man sits and chats with the clerk about baseball and current events.

 Summary Review **Quantitative versus Qualitative Research**

Overall Type of Study	Quantitative Research	Qualitative Research
Approach	Approach is usually deductive.	Approach is usually inductive.
Research Question	Developed and refined before gathering data	Developed and refined while gathering data
Path	Path is linear.	Path is non-linear.
Main goal	Test a hypothesis that you started with.	Discover/capture the meaning of a social setting.
Concepts and Ideas	Are expressed in the form of distinct variables	Are expressed in the form of themes and motifs
Measurement	Plan precise measurements before data collection	Create measures ad hoc as gathering data
Data	In the form of numbers	In the form of words and images
Theory	Theory is largely causal.	Can be causal or other.
Data Analysis	Data analysis includes statistics, tables, or charts with relationships among numbers.	Often includes narrative story with a detailed description of a social setting.

6. What Type of Explanation Will You Use? We use the word *explanation* in two ways. One is an everyday type, in which *explanation* means making something clear or comprehensible to another person with examples or everyday reasons. The other is a research study type that means answering the why question and making something comprehensible by placing it within a relevant structure of theory, ideas, or set of circumstances.

When doing explanatory research, you create a research explanation. There are several research explanations, but the most common one is a **causal explanation** In it you explain by finding one or more causes for an effect or outcome. The cause in the explanation corresponds to your independent variable and the effect to your dependent variable. A causal explanation is usually inside a larger theory or idea framework and has the following three elements:

- *Time order:* The cause must come earlier in time than the effect or the result it produces.
- *Association:* The cause and effect are associated or they go together and vary with one another. Some people call it correlation, although technically correlation is a specific measure of association.
- *Alternative causes ruled out:* There is no better or stronger cause than the one you identified.

To be a cause (an independent variable), something must happen first. Usually you can observe or logically determine time order. Two factors that occur together are associated: that is, when one factor is present or at a high level, the other one is also present or at a high level. Several statistics measure an association. The most well known is the correlation. The last item in the list is the most difficult one to document or observe. If you claim that one factor causes another, there should not be any stronger, truer, or better cause present that you are not including. This is an important element because there can be multiple causal factors, some obvious and some hidden. If you say that a factor causes another but an unacknowledged and stronger cause is present, it is misleading. You try to rule out other possible causes (see the discussion of spuriousness later in this chapter).

In a causal explanation, you make a generalization and specific instance of it, as follows:

A causes B generally.
This situation is A, therefore, we expect to find B.
Example: People who spent many years in prison have difficultly finding stable, well-paid work after their release. Joe Brown was imprisoned for many years; he is having difficulty finding stable, well-paid work after his release.

You fit a specific observable instance within the more general rule or pattern. You can covert a causal explanation into independent and dependent variables.

Independent variable: Whether a person was previously imprisoned for many years
Dependent variable: Amount of difficulty in finding stable, well-paid work

Sometimes researchers who use qualitative data use causal explanation. At other times they do not but instead develop ideas or theories during the data collection process. They build up from specific data to general ideas. Instead of a causal connection between two variables, their explanation is in the form of motifs, themes, or distinctions. Many explanations with qualitative data take the form of **grounded theory**. In a grounded theory explanation you build the explanation by making comparisons. For example, you observe an event (e.g., a police officer confronting a speeding motorist). You look for similarities and differences. You ask, Does the police officer always radio in the car's license number before proceeding? After radioing the car's location, does the officer ask the motorist to get out of the car sometimes but at other times casually walk up to the car and talk to the seated driver? When data collection and theorizing are interspersed, theoretical questions arise that

causal explanation a type of research explanation in which you identify one or more causes for an outcome, and place cause and effect in a larger framework.

grounded theory ideas and themes that are built up from data observation.

■ Figure 2.10   Quick Checklist of Study Design Issues in a Research Proposal

When do you focus the research question?	Very early or it emerges later
What is the universe of your study?	The broad set of units to which you can generalize
What is your research path?	Linear or nonlinear
What do you examine?	Variables and hypotheses or cases and contexts
How do you interpret patterns in the data?	Statistics and charts or themes and narratives
What type of explanation do you use?	Causal explanation or grounded theory
What are your units of analysis?	The cases or units you measure
What is your level of analysis?	Micro to macro

suggest future observations. You collect new data so they can answer theoretical questions that came from thinking about previous data.

7. What Are the Units of Analysis in Your Study? Every study contains units of analysis. They are critical for clearly thinking through and planning a research study. Few researchers explicitly identify units of analysis as such. Your research question shapes the unit of analysis, which in turn influences study design, so being aware of them will help you to design a better study and to avoid errors. The **unit of analysis** is the unit on which you measure variables and gather data. Common units are the individual, the group (e.g., family, friendship group), the organization (e.g., corporation, university), the social category (e.g., social class, gender, race), the social institution (e.g., religion, education, the family), and the society (e.g., a nation, a tribe). Say you want to conduct a descriptive study to find out whether colleges in the North spend more on their football programs than do colleges in the South. Your variables are college location and amount of spending for football, and the unit of analysis in this situation is the college. It flows from the research question.

In social research the individual is the most commonly used unit of analysis, but it is by no means the only one. Different questions imply one or another unit of analysis, and different research techniques work best for specific units. For example, the individual is the unit of analysis in the survey of students about sexual harassment (see Example Study Box 1: Sexual Harassment, page 33). On the other hand, you might conduct a study to compare the level of sexual harassment at 20 different colleges. Perhaps you think harassment is greater at colleges with more alcohol-related problems. You could measure the number of alcohol-related behavior problems/arrests at the colleges and measure degree of harassment by the number of harassment reports filed and amount of hours counselors devote to sexual harassment at the colleges. Your unit of analysis would be the organization, or specifically the college. This is because you are comparing characteristics of the colleges. Units of analysis influence how to gather data and the level of analysis (see below).

8. What Is the Level of Analysis of Your Study? The social world operates on a continuum from small scale or micro level (e.g., a few friends, a small group) to large scale or macro level (e.g., entire civilizations or a major structure of a society). The **level of analysis** is the level of reality you examine. It is a mix of the number of people, the expanse of geographic space, the scope of the activity, and the length of time. A micro-level study might involve 30 minutes of interaction among five people in a small room. A macro-level study could involve a billion people on three continents across a century. The level of analysis delimits the kinds of assumptions, concepts, and theories you will use. It also influences the appropriate units of analysis. Let us look at examples at each end of the continuum.

unit of analysis the case or unit on which you measure variables or other characteristics.

level of analysis the level of reality to which explanations refer, micro to macro.

Micro Level: Suppose you want to study the topic of dating among college students. A micro-level analysis uses ideas such as interpersonal contact, mutual friendships, and common interests among individual students. Suppose you believe that students tend to date someone with whom they have had personal contact in a class, share friends in common, and share common interests. You might gather data from 100 students on their friends, contacts, and relationships. The individual student is your unit of analysis.

Macro Level: Suppose you want to learn how social-economic inequality affects violent behavior in a society. You may be interested in the degree of inequality (e.g., the distribution of wealth, property, income, and other resources) throughout a society. Likewise, you may look at patterns of societal violence (e.g., aggression against other societies, level of violent crime, violent feuds between families, organized crime with gangs, bandits, and warlords, religious-racial-based conflicts). You develop a macro-level explanation because of the topic and the level of social reality. You gather data on the level of inequality in each of 50 countries for 20 years, as well as data on how many acts of violence occurred in each country. The country is your unit of analysis.

Warning: Avoid Spuriousness. As you design a study with a causal explanation, you need to be aware of an issue that may totally upset your explanation. As you learned previously, you need three things for a causal explanation: time order, association, and ruling out of alternative causal factors. You can observe or test the first two, but the third element can be tricky. It involves making certain that there are no alternative causes. The alternative cause may not be obvious. If an unseen alternative cause strongly affects your dependent variable, then claims you make about the cause (independent variable) could be false. Having time order and a strong association between two variables does not mean you can relax. It could be an illusion, just like the mirage that resembles a pool of water on a road during a hot day.

Spuriousness is an illusionary relationship due to an unacknowledged other variable that is a cause of both the independent and the dependent variable. You could have a strong correlation between the two variables, but the two variables may be not really be cause and effect. You must also check for spuriousness to claim causality.

Spuriousness may seem complicated, but it uses common-sense logic. You already know that there is an association between the use of air conditioners and ice cream cone consumption. If you measured the number of air conditioners in use and the number of ice cream cones sold each day, you would find a strong correlation. More cones are sold on the same days when more air conditioners being used. However, you know that eating ice cream cones does not cause people to turn on air conditioners, or turning on an air conditions does not produce a craving for ice cream. Instead, a third factor causes both variables: hot days.

spuriousness when two variables appear to be causally connected but in reality, they are not because an unseen third factor is the true cause.

Learning from History   Night-Lights and Spuriousness

For many years, researchers observed a strong positive association between the use of a night-light and children who were nearsighted. Medical professionals thought that the night-light somehow caused children to develop vision problems and advised parents against using a night-light for their children. Other researchers could find no good reason for night-light use causing nearsightedness. A 1999 study provided the answer. It found that nearsighted parents are more likely to use night-lights. Parents also genetically pass on their vision deficiency to their children. The study found no link between night-light use and nearsightedness once the effect of parental vision was considered. Thus, the initial causal link was misleading or spurious once the previously unrecognized impact of parental vision impairment and night-time behavior was considered (see *New York Times,* May 22, 2001).

You may ask, How can you tell whether a relationship is spurious? How do you discover the mysterious third factor? As you prepare a research proposal, how can you build in a safeguard against spuriousness? You can deal with spuriousness in different ways using different research techniques. The internal design of an experiment helps to control for spuriousness. In survey data and existing statistical sources, you must decide on control variables that measure possible alternative causes. You then use statistical techniques (discussed later in this book) to test whether an association is spurious. In all situations, including qualitative data analysis, you need a theory, or at least a good guess, about what alternative causes might influence what you see as the cause and effect, and then take them into consideration. One way to grasp the idea of spuriousness is with an example (see Learning from History: Night-Lights and Spuriousness).

Let us look a spurious relationship. Does taking illegal drugs cause more suicide, school dropouts, and violent acts? Many people point to positive correlations between taking drugs and being suicidal, dropping out of school, and engaging in violence. They argue that ending drug use will end such problems. A second position argues that many people turn to drugs to cope with their emotional problems or high levels of disorder in their communities (e.g., high unemployment, unstable families, high crime, few community services, and lack of civility). At the same time, people with emotional problems or who live in disordered communities are often in such straits that they are more likely to commit suicide, drop out of school, and engage in violence. It may be that reducing emotional problems and community disorder will end both drug use and the other problems. Reducing drug taking alone will have a limited effect because it does not address the root causes (i.e., emotional problems and community disorder). If the second position is correct, the apparent relationship between illegal drugs and the problems stated is spurious and misleading. This is because emotional problems and community disorder are the true and initially unacknowledged alternative causes (see Figure 2.11).

■ **Figure 2.11**   Spuriousness Example—Relationship Between Illegal Drugs and Suicide

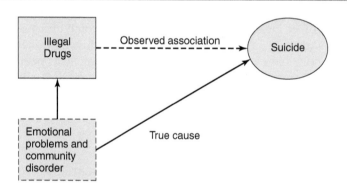

WHAT HAVE YOU LEARNED?

In this chapter, you encountered the groundwork to begin a study. You saw how to conduct a literature search, narrow a topic into a focused research question, and identify units and levels of analysis. The decision to use qualitative or quantitative data suggests a different sequence of decision making as you get started. Choosing a qualitative or quantitative approach (or a mix of both) depends on your topic, your purpose and intended use of study results, as well as your own assumptions.

If you decide that quantitative data are best, you take a linear path and emphasize objectivity and use explicit, standardized procedures and a causal explanation. You use the language of variables and hypotheses testing. The process is a set of discrete steps that precede data collection: Narrow the topic to a more focused question, transform concepts into variables, and develop hypotheses to test. In actual practice, you move back and forth, but the general process flows in a single, linear direction. Your explanations usually take a cause-effect form.

If you decide that qualitative data are best, you follow a nonlinear path that emphasizes becoming intimate with the details of a natural setting or a particular con-

text. You use fewer standardized procedures or explicit steps, and you must devise on-the-spot techniques. You use a language of cases and contexts that directs you to examine particular cases or processes in detail. You do not separate planning and design decisions into a distinct pre–data collection stage, but you continue to develop the study design throughout early data collection. You slowly evolve toward a specific focus based on what you learn from the data. As you reflect on the data, you can develop a grounded theory explanation.

The qualitative and quantitative distinction is overdrawn and is not a rigid dichotomy. You can mix the two types. Before you mix the data types, you need to understand each and appreciate each on its own terms. You should recognize that quantitative and qualitative data each have strengths and limitations. Your ultimate goal is to better understand and explain events in the social world, and the best way to do so is to appreciate the value of each style of data collections has to offer.

Studying people and doing a research study about human relations also has an ethical-moral dimension. In the next chapter, we examine that aspect of doing research.

KEY TERMS

article search tool *30*
abstract *31*
causal explanation *53*
citation *43*
deductive *44*
dependent variable *48*
grounded theory *53*
hypothesis *49*
independent variable *48*
inductive *44*
intervening variable *48*

level of analysis *54*
linear path *47*
literature review *27*
nonlinear path *47*
null hypothesis *50*
peer reviewed *30*
research proposal *26*
spuriousness *55*
unit of analysis *54*
universe *46*
variable *48*

APPLY WHAT YOU'VE LEARNED

Activity 1

Go to your college library (physically or via its Web site) and locate article search tools. You may have to ask your librarian about which specific services at available at the library; some common ones are **JSTOR, EBSCO, WilsonWeb,** and **Proquest.** Pick one of the article search

tools and conduct a search using the term *tattoo*. Restrict your search to peer-reviewed scholarly publications. Then answer the following:

• How many total studies have been conducted on the topic of tattoos during the past 10 years? _____

- How many total studies have been conducted on the topic of tattoos during the past 5 years? _____
- Based on the article title or abstract, what percent of studies in the past 5 years appear to be about medical issues (e.g., infection, etc.)? _____

Activity 2

Repeat Activity 1 but with a different article search tool. What differences did you discover? What accounts for the differences?

Activity 3

Take the five most recent scholarly journal articles you found in Activity 1 or 2. Prepare a reference/bibliography using the ASA (American Sociological Association) format. Be sure to put the articles in alphabetical order by the last name of the first author. Note that in a scholarly journal article that has more than one author, the first listed author usually did more work on the study than the others, so you want to retain name order.

If you Google "American Sociological Association style" you will find many college library sites that have additional help on how to organize the references. You can also find information on the ASA format at the following Web site: http://www.asanet.org/page.ww?name=Quick+Style+Guide&section=Sociology+Depts

Activity 4

Design the first part a study using quantitative data on a topic of interest to you. Complete each of the following parts of the design:

Topic: _____

Research question: _____

Hypothesis: _____

Your independent variable of the hypothesis above:

_____

Your dependent variable of the hypothesis: _____

The unit of analysis for your study: _____

Activity 5

Identify the unit of analysis, Universe, and dependent variable in each of the three articles from the scholarly journal *Social Science Quarterly* listed below.

1. "The Effects of Visual Images in Political Ads: Experimental Testing of Distortions and Visual Literacy" (*Social Science Quarterly*, 2000, 81:913–27) by Gary Noggle and Lynda Kaid.
2. "The Politics of Bilingual Education Expenditures in Urban Districts" (*Social Science Quarterly*, 2000, 81:1064–72) by David Leal and Fred Hess.
3. "Symbolic Racism in the 1995 Louisiana Gubernatorial Election" (*Social Science Quarterly*, 2000, 81:1027–35) by Jon Knuckey and Byron Orey.

REFERENCES

Atkinson. Michael. 2003. *Tattooed: The Sociogenesis of a Body Art*. Toronto: University of Toronto Press.

Atkinson, Michael. 2004. "Tattooing and Civilizing Processes: Body Modification as Self-control." *Canadian Review of Sociology & Anthropology* 41(2):125–146.

Caplan, Jane (editor). 2000. *Written on the Body*. Princeton NJ: Princeton University Press.

DeMello, Margo. 2000. *Bodies of Inscription*. Durham NC: Duke University Press.

Fisher, Jill A. 2002. Tattooing the Body, Marking Culture. *Body & Society* 8 (4):91–107.

Harris Interactive. 2003 "A Third of Americans With Tattoos Say They Make Them Feel More Sexy" http://www. harrisinteractive.com/harris_poll/index.asp?PID=407 (downloaded 3/25/08).

Hawkes, Daina, Charlene Seen and Chantal Thorn 2004. Factors That Influence Attitudes Toward Women With Tattoos. *Sex Roles* 50 (9/10):593–604.

Horne, Jenn, David Knox, Jane Zusman, and Marty Zusman, 2007. "Tattoos And Piercings: Attitudes, Behaviors, and Interpretations of College Students." *College Student Journal* 41 (4):1011–1020.

Kang, Miliann, and Katherine Jones. 2007. "Why do people get tattoos." *Contexts* 6(1):42–47.

ENDNOTES

1. For more on the topic of tattoos see Atkinson (2003, 2004), Caplan (2000), DeMello (2000), Fischer (2002), Horne, Knox, Zusman, and Zusman (2007) and Kang and Jones (2007).

2. Sir Isaac Newton in letter to Robert Horne, Feb. 5, 1676. http://en.wikiquote.org/wiki/Isaac_Newton

3

Becoming an Ethical Researcher

THE ETHICAL IMPERATIVE

Scientific Misconduct
Unethical but Legal

ETHICAL ISSUES INVOLVING RESEARCH PARTICIPANTS

The Origin of Ethical Principles for Research with Humans
Protect Research Participants from Harm
Participation Must Be Voluntary and Informed
Limits to Using Deception in Research
Privacy, Anonymity, and Confidentiality
Extra Protections for Special Populations
Formal Protections for Research Participants

ETHICS AND THE SPONSORS OF RESEARCH

Arriving at Particular Findings

POLITICAL INFLUENCES ON RESEARCH

VALUE-FREE AND OBJECTIVE RESEARCH

WHAT HAVE YOU LEARNED?

APPLY WHAT YOU'VE LEARNED

Corbis Sygma

I n 1932, the U.S. Public Health Service began a study on how the disease syphilis progressed. The goal was to improve treatment programs for infected African Americans. Six hundred low-income black men in Macon County, Alabama participated in the "Tuskegee Study of Untreated Syphilis in the Negro Male." Of participants, 399 had syphilis and 201 did not have the disease. Researchers never told the participants that the study was on syphilis or that they had syphilis. Instead, they told the participants that they were being treated for "bad blood," a local term for many ailments, including syphilis, anemia, and fatigue. In exchange for participating in the study, the men received free medical exams, free meals, and burial insurance. Researchers instructed local physicians not to treat participants for syphilis. Although the study was supposed to be six months long, it continued for 40 years. Researchers never treated the participants for syphilis, even after a highly effective treatment, penicillin, became available in 1947. They followed the men until death. Untreated syphilis goes through several stages. Second stage syphilis develops three months to three years after onset. It causes fever, swollen lymph glands, sore throat, patchy hair loss, headaches, weight loss, muscle aches, and fatigue. If untreated, it becomes late stage syphilis. This stage damages the victim's heart, eyes, brain, nervous system, bones, and joints. It can produce mental illness, blindness, deafness, memory loss, serious neurological problems, heart disease, and death.

The "Tuskegee Study of Untreated Syphilis in the Negro Male" ended in 1972 because of an exposé by a news reporter. By the time it ended, 28 participants had died of untreated syphilis. One hundred others died due to syphilis-related complications. Participants had infected 40 wives, and 19 children had contracted the disease at birth. The reporter who wrote the story that ended the study had talked to a research interviewer working for the study. The interviewer had been trying to raise ethical concerns with the U.S. Public Health Service for five years, but he could not get top research officials to end the study and provide proper medical care for the participants.

With the media exposé, a national scandal erupted over the study in 1973. After the U.S. Congress held public hearings, the federal rules on ethics in research with humans were overhauled. Eventually, the surviving research participants sued the U.S. government and were awarded $10 million in an out-of-court settlement. Even after the 1974 settlement, it took another 23 years before the President of the United States officially apologized to the surviving research participants.

The Tuskegee syphilis study is one of the most outrageous instances of a disregard of basic ethical principles in research with humans in the United States. Two books, a play, and a dramatic movie, *Miss Evers' Boys* (1997), document this incident. This unethical research and the publicity surrounding it illustrate that research with humans has limits. When you study people, you must follow ethical principles. In this chapter, you will learn about ethical issues that arise when doing social research.

When you conduct research with humans, you do more than simply gather data according to certain procedures; you must do so in an ethical manner. We conduct a study to create knowledge, answer questions, solve problems, or help humanity, but we must always do this in a morally responsible manner. Research ethics includes the concerns, dilemmas, and conflicts over the proper way to conduct a study. Ethics defines what is or is not morally legitimate. This is not as simple as it may appear at first. There are few clear ethical absolutes, but many general ethical principles or guidelines require that you apply judgment. Some principles may conflict with others in practice or ask you to balance competing priorities (see Figure 3.1).

You must balance potential benefits from research—such as advancing understanding and improving decision making—against its potential costs—such as loss of dignity, self-esteem, privacy, or democratic freedoms.

THE ETHICAL IMPERATIVE

You should think of ethics early in the research process, as you plan a study or prepare a research proposal. While conducting a study, you may confront ethical issues and must quickly decide how to act. It is difficult to appreciate ethical issues fully until you actually begin to conduct a study, but waiting until you are in the middle of doing research is too late. You need to prepare ahead of time and consider ethical concerns. By being familiar with ethical concerns, you can build sound ethical practices into a study's design and be alert to potential ethical concerns that may arise. An ethical awareness also will help you to understand the research process.

Researchers have a strong moral and professional obligation to act ethically *at all times and in all situations.* This holds even if research participants are unaware of or are unconcerned about ethics. It holds even if an employer or the sponsor of a study cares little for ethics or asks you to engage in unethical research acts. "The research participants did not care" or "my boss told me to do it" are never acceptable reasons for engaging in unethical behavior.

Most professions (e.g., journalists, law enforcement, medicine, accounting, etc.) have ethical standards. The ethical standards for doing research with humans may be more rigorous than standards in other areas. Being ethical is not always easy. For

■ Figure 3.1   Balancing Two Priorities When Doing Research

Gaining knowledge and finding a clear answer to a research question

Protecting research participants and upholding broader human rights.

centuries, moral, legal, and political philosophers debated the issues that a researcher may face. Ultimately, ethical behavior begins and ends with you, the individual researcher. The best defense against unethical behavior is a strong personal code of moral behavior. Before, during, and after conducting a study, you will have opportunities to, and *should,* reflect on the ethics of research actions and consult your conscience. Ultimately, doing ethical research rests on your personal integrity.

Given that most people who do research are genuinely concerned about other people, you might ask, Why would anyone act in an ethically irresponsible manner? The most common cause of unethical behavior is a lack of awareness and pressures to take ethical shortcuts. People feel pressures to build a career, publish new findings, advance knowledge, gain prestige, impress family and friends, satisfy job requirements, and so forth. Doing ethical research usually takes longer, is more costly, and is more complex to complete. In addition, there are many opportunities to act unethically, and the odds of being caught are small. Written ethical standards are in the form of vague principles that may not be simple to apply.

If you act ethically all the time, few people will rush to praise you. This is because ethical behavior is expected. However, if you act unethically and are caught doing so, expect public humiliation, a ruined career, and possible legal action against you. To prepare yourself to act ethically, internalize a sensitivity to ethical concerns, adopt a serious professional role, and maintain contact with others who are doing research studies.

Scientific Misconduct

Professional researchers, research centers, and government agencies that fund research all have rules against **scientific misconduct** (see Example Study Box 1: Scientific Misconduct and the Miracle Study). Two major types of scientific misconduct are research fraud and plagiarism. Both are serious ethical violations for which there is never an excuse.

Research fraud is serious deception or lying about data or a study. It happens when a researcher invents data that he or she did not really collect and fails to disclose honestly and fully how he or she conducted a study. Fraud in research is rare but includes significant, unjustified departures from the generally accepted practices for doing and reporting on research. If anyone conducts a study that sharply differs from generally accepted research practice, other people will suspect either incompetence or possible fraud.

Plagiarism is "stealing" someone else's ideas or writings and then using them without citing the source. It is misrepresenting what someone else wrote or thought as your own. If you copy two sentences from someone's research report or use another researcher's questionnaire but fail to report the source, you committed plagiarism. You must put very serious effort into keeping track of sources and properly citing them. Good documentation always allows others to track a source back to its origin.

scientific misconduct violating basic and generally accepted standards of honest scientific research, for example, research fraud and plagiarism.

research fraud to invent, falsify or distort study data or to lie about how a study was conducted.

plagiarism using another person's words or ideas without giving them proper credit and instead passing them off as your own.

Example Study Box 1 Scientific Misconduct and the Miracle Study

In October 2001, a peer-reviewed publication, the *Journal of Reproductive Medicine,* published a study by three Columbia University medical school researchers. Lobo, Cha, and Wirth claimed to have demonstrated that infertile women who had people pray for them became pregnant twice as often as women for whom no one said prayers. The researchers reported that 199 women undergoing in vitro fertilization in Korea, and who had Christian groups in Australia, Canada, and the United States pray for them, conceived at twice the rate as women who did not receive prayer. Researchers never told patients they were part of a study or that anyone was praying for them. Articles touting the findings appeared in newspapers worldwide, and television news programs announced the miracle study.

Serious readers of the study quickly became suspicions due to a lack of details and the use of an unusual and extremely complex study design. Suspicions increased when the researchers refused to share data or to answer questions. Dr. Rogerio Lobo, the lead author, first failed respond to inquiries; next said he did not know about the study until 12 months after it was finished. He then removed his name from the study and stepped down as chairman of the Obstetrics and Gynecology Department. Dr. Lobo had connections with the journal and might have influenced the peer review process. The second author, Dr. Cha, refused to answer questions and left Columbia University shortly after the study appeared. A few years later, another scholarly journal found him guilty of plagiarism. Shortly after the study appeared, Daniel Wirth (a lawyer without a medical degree who had used a series of false identities over the years) pleaded guilty to conspiracy to commit fraud in shady business dealings. Soon it was learned that researchers had failed to get informed consent from participants. Informed consent means a research participant "consents," or voluntarily agrees to be part of a study, and is "informed," i.e., he or she knows something about the study to which he or she is agreeing to participate. This triggered an official investigation by the United States Department of Health and Human Services. Over time, suspicions grew that researchers faked study data and that the study was a case of scientific fraud. The reputations of all the authors, of the sponsoring university, and of the scholarly journal in which it appeared have been irreparably tarnished.

Another study on the healing power of prayer was conducted by Mitchell Krucoff of Duke University and others. It appeared in 2005 in the scholarly journal *Lancet*. In this study, 700 heart patients received prayers by Buddhist, Muslim, Jewish, and Christian congregations around the world. The authors fully disclosed all study details, answered all questions, and obeyed all ethical guidelines. The study design was straightforward, and there was no evidence of fraud. However, this study found that prayer had no effect on healing. The study authors stated that until more research is conducted, we do not know whether prayer has any effect on medical recovery.

Unethical but Legal

Do not confuse being ethical with acting legally. A research action can be fully legal (i.e., not breaking any law) but clearly unethical (i.e., violate accepted standards of ethical research). This happens in other areas of life. You might be a dishonest, deceptive, and untrustworthy person who fails to keep your word and often lies. This makes you an immoral person, but you are not violating a law (unless you engage in deceptive business practices or lie while under a sworn oath). You may not have friends and few people will trust you, but you will not be sent to jail. (See Figure 3.2 for relations between legal and moral actions.)

As shown in Figure 3.2, most research actions are both moral and legal. People can quickly recognize actions that are both illegal and immoral. A few rare instances occur when a research action is illegal but ethical (see Example Study Box 5: Not

■ Figure 3.2   Typology of Legal and Ethical Actions in Research

Legal	Ethical	
	Yes	No
Yes	Moral and Legal	Legal but Immoral
No	Illegal but Moral	Immoral and Illegal

Breaking the Confidence Guarantee later in this chapter). More common are legal research actions that violate ethical standards, because ethics are broader than the law. Acting within the law does not guarantee that you are acting ethically in research. You may want to seek guidance about ethics in research. Luckily, there are several resources: colleagues, ethical advisory committees, institutional review boards (discussed later in this chapter), professional codes of ethics (discussed later in this chapter), and published discussions of research ethics.

ETHICAL ISSUES INVOLVING RESEARCH PARTICIPANTS

Have you ever been a participant in a research study? If so, how were you treated? More than any other ethical issue, most attention in research ethics focuses on possible negative effects on the research participants. This is because of past situations of abuse and because total protection for research participants with absolute rights of noninterference would make research impossible. It is important to protect participants in research while still involving them in research studies.

Learning from History **Nazi Doctors**

The Hippocratic Oath that physicians take pertains to the ethical practice of medicine. It says, "Never to do deliberate harm to anyone." During the 1940s, respected scientific and medical experts in Germany violated this Oath. They conducted horrible acts on innocent men, women, and children for the purpose of studying them. The researchers used high research standards and carefully gathered data. They even published results in scholarly journals. Nonetheless, they acted unethically and failed to protect the research participants.

Using the large populations in concentration camps, German researchers gased, poisoned, and froze research participants to death. They injected participants with typhus and malaria to study the diseases. Researchers purposely exposed people to mustard gas and incendiary bombs to study how they caused injury, and they starved people to death to study the starvation process. At the same time that German research was occurring, the Japanese conducted similar horrific studies on humans at research Unit 731 to improve bacteriological warfare. As many as ten thousand people were research participants, both civilians and prisoners of war. Physicians performed vivisections (opening the body and cutting flesh) and infected prisoners with various diseases and then removed organs to study disease. These procedures were conducted while the patients were alive. Vivisected prisoners included men, women, children, and infants. Prisoners had limbs amputated in order to study blood loss. Researchers froze the limbs (hands, arms, legs) and amputated them for study, or froze intact limbs and then thawed them to study the effects of untreated gangrene and rotting. Researchers

also used humans as targets to test grenades, flamethrowers, germ-releasing bombs, chemical weapons, and explosive bombs. Other researchers looked at how long it took a person hung upside down to choke to death.

When World War II ended, the Allies (mostly British, French, and American) brought Nazi doctors before a war crimes tribunal in Nuremburg, Germany. They found many of the researchers to be guilty of "crimes against humanity." The trials resulted in the creation of an international set of ethical standards for conducting research with humans. Postwar trials charged few Japanese researchers with war crimes, and the events of Unit 731 received less publicity. This was because the Pacific War ended later, European involvement was less, and most of the victims were Asians subject to racist views that treated them as less important.

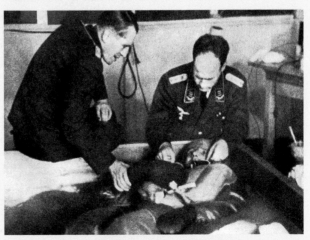

Scherl/Sueddeutsche Zeitung Photo/The Image Works

There are many gray areas in ethics in which you must balance competing values; however, the community of researchers, codes of ethics, and sometimes the law recognize a few clear prohibitions:

- Never cause unnecessary or irreversible harm to research participants.
- Always get voluntary consent from research participants before a study begins.
- Never unnecessarily humiliate or degrade research participants.
- Never release harmful information about specific individuals collected for research purposes.

If you wish to act ethically, follow a simple rule: Always show respect for the research participant. As the person conducting a study, you have a clear ethical responsibility to provide research participants with basic protections.

The Origin of Ethical Principles for Research with Humans

We can trace concerns over the treatment of research participants to medical studies in the early 1900s. This concern expanded after the public learned of gross violations of basic human rights in the name of research. The most notorious violations were "medical experiments" in Nazi Germany and Japan in the 1940s (see Learning from History: Nazi Doctors). Despite the mistreatment of people in the name of research, such as the Tuskegee syphilis study, each exposure of these incidents helped to extend and advance the discussion of ethical principles.

In the syphilis study and in horrific medical experiments during World War II, vulnerable, powerless people suffered in the name of scientific research and advancing knowledge. No one voluntarily agreed to participate in the study, and no one was told what would happen to them. This situation gave rise to the principle of voluntary participation (see discussion later in this chapter). It would be wonderful to report that all such abuse ended in the 1940s. However, incidents of unethical research have reappeared.

Until the 1970s, U.S. medical researchers did not always provide full ethical protection. For example, in 1940 U.S. researchers injected 400 prisoners with malaria to study the disease. They did not tell inmates about the nature of the experiment. Similar studies on malaria continued through 1946. As the U.S. military developed atomic weapons, researchers conducted studies on the effects of radioactive substances on people from the 1940s and the 1960s. In addition to prison inmates, researchers often used U.S. soldiers, hospital patients, or children with mental disabilities as research participants. In one case, researchers put radioactive material in the breakfast cereal of children. In other studies, the U.S. military gave unsuspecting people hallucinogenic drugs, such as LSD, to study their effects. During the 1960s, medical researchers injected patients at the Jewish Chronic Disease Hospital with live cancer cells and injected the hepatitis virus into children with developmental disabilities institutionalized at the New York Willowbrook School. Through the 1970s, researchers tested over 90 percent of new pharmaceuticals on prison inmates, despite increased questions about ethical protections.

Protect Research Participants from Harm

Most discussions about not harming people in research focuses on medical research, but social research can also cause harm in several ways:

- Physical harm or bodily injury
- Great emotional distress or psychological harm
- Legal harm and damage to a person's career, reputation, or income

Certain types of harm are more likely in certain types of research (e.g., in experiments versus field research). As a researcher, you have a responsibility to be aware of potential harm and to take precautions that will minimize the risk of harm to participants. The guiding ethical principle is that no person should experience harm as the direct result of his or her participating in a research study.

Physical Harm. Physical harm is rare in social research studies. The ethical rule is simple: Never—under any circumstance—purposely cause physical harm to a research participant. To be ethical, you must anticipate risks, including basic safety concerns (e.g., safe buildings, furniture, and equipment). This means screening out high-risk participants (those with heart conditions, mental breakdown, seizures, etc.) if you will subject them to great stress. A researcher accepts moral and legal responsibility for injury due to participation in research. You should terminate a project immediately if you can no longer guarantee the physical safety of those involved (see Example Study Box 3: Zimbardo Prison Experiment). Of course, if you do research in a dangerous situation, you also want to protect yourself from harm.

Psychological Abuse, Stress, or Loss of Self-Esteem. Some social research studies place participants in stressful, embarrassing, anxiety-producing, or unpleasant situations. By placing participants in realistic situations with psychological distress, we can learn about people's responses in real-life, high-anxiety situations. However, is it unethical to cause discomfort? Researchers still debate the ethics of the famous Milgram obedience study (see Example Study Box 2: The Milgram Obedience Study). Some say that the precautions Milgram undertook and the great knowledge gained outweighed the potential psychological harm to participants. Others believe that the extreme stress and the risk of permanent harm were too great. Today, no one would conduct such an experiment due to a heightened sensitivity to the ethical issues involved.

Social psychologists who study helping behavior often place participants in stressful, emergency situations to see whether they will lend assistance. For example, Piliavin and associates (1969) studied helping behavior in subways by faking a person's collapse onto the floor. In the field experiment, the riders in the subway car were unaware of the experiment and did not volunteer to participate in it. The study's findings were valuable, but the lack of informed consent (see later in this chapter) and anxiety created were ethically controversial.

Only experienced researchers should consider conducting a study in which they purposely induce great stress or anxiety. They must take all necessary precautions before inducing anxiety or discomfort. This includes consulting with others who have conducted similar studies as well as with mental health professionals. They should screen out high-risk populations, arrange for emergency interventions, and be prepared to end the study immediately if a dangerous situation arises. They must always obtain written informed consent (discussed later in this chapter) and always debrief participants (explained later). Even with these safeguards, they can never create unnecessary stress. *Unnecessary* means beyond the minimal amount required for the desired effect. Any discomfort they create must have a very clear, legitimate research purpose. Knowing what *minimal amount* means comes with experience. It is best to begin with too little stress, risking a finding of no effect, than to create too much. Also, it is best to work in collaboration with other researchers, because involving several sensitive researchers reduces the chance of making an ethical misjudgment.

Legal Harm. A researcher is responsible for protecting research participants from an increased risk of arrest simply because they are in a study. If a risk of arrest is associated with research participation, the willingness of people to participate in research will decline. Potential legal harm is one criticism of the study by Humphreys (1973) (see Example Study Box 4: Humphreys Tearoom Study). A related ethical issue occurs if you learn of illegal activity when collecting data. You must weigh the value of protecting the researcher-participant relationship against potential harm to innocent people if you do not report what you discover. In the end, you, as the researcher, alone are morally and legally responsible.

In field research on police, Van Maanen (1982:114–115) reported seeing police beat people and witnessing illegal acts and irregular procedures but said, "On and following these troublesome incidents I followed police custom: I kept my mouth shut."

Field researchers who study the "seamy side" of society can face difficult ethical decisions. For example, when studying a mental institution, Taylor (1987) discovered the mistreatment and abuse of inmates by the staff. He had two choices: Abandon the study and call for an immediate investigation, or keep quiet and continue with the study for several months, publicize the findings afterward, and then become an advocate to end the abuse. After weighing the situation, he followed the latter course and is now an activist for the rights of mental institution inmates. In some studies, observing illegal behavior may be central to the research project. A researcher who closely works with law-enforcement officials must face the question, Are you an independent professional who ethically protects participants to advance knowledge in the long term, or are you freelance undercover informant who is working for the police and is trying to catch criminals now?

   Example Study Box 2   The Milgram Obedience Study

Courtesy of Alexandra Milgram. Copyright 1968 by Stanley Milgram. Copyright renewed 1993 by Alexandra Milgram. From the film OBEDIENCE, distributed by Penn State Media Sales

Stanley Milgram's studies on obedience (Milgram, 1963, 1965, 1974) are widely discussed. He wanted to learn how ordinary people could have carried out the horrors of the Holocaust under the Nazis. The study examined the impact of social pressure on people obeying authority figures. After signing informed consent forms, he assigned a volunteer-participant, in rigged random selection, to be a "teacher" while a confederate working for him was the "pupil." The pupil was located in a nearby room, where the research participant could hear but not see the pupil. The pupil was connected to electrical wires. Milgram told the participant to test the pupil's memory of word lists and to increase the electric shock level if the pupil made mistakes. The shock apparatus was clearly labeled with increasing voltage that indicated its danger. As the pupil increasingly made mistakes and the teacher-participant turned switches, the pupil would make noises as if in severe pain. The researcher was always present and made quiet comments such as, "You must go on" to the participant. As the voltage levels got higher, Milgram reported, "Subjects were observed to sweat, tremble, stutter, bite their lips, groan and dig their fingernails into their flesh. These were characteristic rather than exceptional responses to the experiment" (Milgram, 1963:375). At the end, he told participants what really took place. The "pupil" was actually a confederate who was acting, and no one was shocked. The percentage of "teacher" participants who applied electrical shocks to very dangerous levels was dramatically higher than Milgram expected; 65 percent gave shocks at 450 volts. This study raised ethical concerns over using deception and about the extreme emotional stress participants experienced. Despite the precautions, many people believe that the degree of distress and risk of long-term emotional problems among the participants was too great.

■ **Figure 3.3**   Diagram of Milgram Study Layout

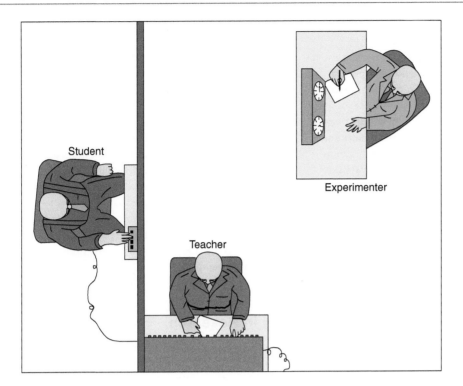

Participation Must Be Voluntary and Informed

A fundamental ethical principle is, Never coerce anyone into participating; participation *must* be voluntary at all times. This is the ethical **principle of voluntary consent**. Permission is not enough. To make an informed decision, people need to know what they are being asked to participate in. Researchers need to make participants aware of their rights. To do this they provide participants with a statement about the study and ask participants to sign it. This is **informed consent**. Government agencies require informed consent in most studies involving people, with a few exceptions. You should get informed consent unless there are good reasons for not obtaining it (e.g., covert field research, use of secondary data, etc.).

An informed consent statement gives a research participant specific information (see Making It Practical: Obtaining Informed Consent) about research procedures and the uses of the data. For survey research, we know that participants who receive a full informed consent statement respond the same as those who do not. If anything, people who refuse to sign the statement are likely to guess or say "no response" to survey questions.

A formal, signed informed consent statement is optional for most survey, field, existing statistics, and secondary data research, but it is mandatory for most experimental research. The general rule is, the greater the risk of causing possible harm to a research participant, the greater the need to obtain a written informed consent statement. There are many sound reasons to get informed consent and very few reasons not to get it.

Informed consent that discloses research details along with the researcher's identification helps to protect research participants against fraudulent research and to protect legitimate research. It lessens the chances that a con artist can use a bogus identity to defraud or abuse research participants, market products, or obtain personal information for unethical purposes.

principle of voluntary consent never force anyone to participate in a research study, participants should explicitly and voluntarily agree to participate.

informed consent an agreement in which participants state they are willing to be in a study and know what the research procedure will involve.

Making It Practical   **Obtaining Informed Consent**

You must get informed consent for most research on humans. Consent upholds the principle of voluntary participation and is mandated in various laws, regulations, and codes of ethics. There are a few exceptions to the use of consent, such as field research observation in a large public setting. In situations such as a survey questionnaire that do not ask for highly personal information, consent can be a short oral statement. Consent must always be in written form with a signature for research that involves physical discomfort, induced stress, or the collection of highly personal information. Informed consent statements contain the following eight elements:

1. A brief description of the purpose and research procedure, including how long the study will last

2. A statement of any risks or discomfort associated with participation
3. A guarantee of anonymity and the confidentiality of data records
4. Identification of who the researcher is and contact information for more information about the study
5. A statement that participation is voluntary and participants can withdraw at any time without penalty.
6. A statement of any alternative procedures that may be used
7. A statement of any benefits or compensation that research participants may receive
8. An offer to provide a summary of the findings when the study is completed

Limits to Using Deception in Research

Has anyone ever told you a half-truth or lie to get you to do something? How did you feel about it? Deception is a mild type of harm to participants; it harms the sense of trust and honesty in human relations. When a study uses deception, voluntary participation and a person's right not to participate can be a critical issue.

Example Study Box 3   **Zimbardo Prison Experiment**

PG Zimbardo, Inc.

Philip Zimbardo (Zimbardo 1972) designed an experiment on prison conditions. Before the experiment, he gave male volunteer students personality tests and only included those in the "normal" range. He randomly divided the volunteers into two role-playing groups: guards and prisoners. The study took place in a simulated prison in the basement of a Stanford University building. Zimbardo informed participants assigned to play prisoner that they would be under surveillance and would have some civil rights suspended, but that no physical abuse was allowed. He deindividualized (dressed in standard uniforms and called only by their numbers) the prisoners, and militarized (given uniforms, nightsticks, and reflective sunglasses) the guards to make the simulation feel real. He told guards to maintain a reasonable degree of order. Guards served 8-hour shifts while he had prisoners locked up 24 hours per day. The study was to last two weeks. Unexpectedly, participants got very caught up in their roles. The prisoners became passive, depressed, and disorganized. The guards became aggressive, arbitrary, and dehumanizing. By the sixth day, Zimbardo called off the experiment for ethical reasons. The risk of permanent psychological harm, and even physical harm, was too great.

Researchers debate whether using deception is ethically acceptable. Some say it is never acceptable. Others say it is ethical, but only for specific purposes and with strict conditions.

Sometimes an experimental researcher deceives participants or uses misrepresentation for legitimate methodological reasons. The most common use of deception is when you expect that participants would modify their behavior or statements if they knew the study's true purpose. For example, you want to study body posture. If you tell participants you are studying their body posture, they might adjust how they stand or sit because they know this is something you were observing. This could make it impossible for you to learn about their real body posture. Another use of deception is in covert field research. For example, you could not gain access to a research site if you told the truth, so you lie or hide your identity as a researcher. Say you want to conduct a field study on teens who use illegal drugs and commit minor crimes. If you told the teens when you first approached them you were going to carefully observe and study them, they might not cooperate or reveal all their actions.

In any type of study, deception is *never preferable* if you can accomplish the same thing without using it. It is a last resort. Deception is acceptable only within strict limits, if you do following:

- Show that it has a clear, specific methodological purpose.
- Use it only to the minimal degree necessary and for the shortest time.
- Obtain informed consent and do not misrepresent any risks.
- Always debrief (i.e., explain the actual conditions to participants afterward).

It is possible to obtain prior informed consent and use deception if you describe the basic procedures involved but conceal limited information about specific details. You could inform participants that they will sit alone in a room for 10 minutes, chat with one other participant for 5 minutes, and then complete a 15-item questionnaire, but not tell them your hypotheses or that the other participant in the room is secretly working for you. Experimental researchers often invent stories about the purpose of a study to distract participants from the true purpose of a study (see Chapter 7). For example, a researcher studying male-female eye contact might tell participants the study is about college student opinions on current affairs.

Some field researchers use covert observation to gain entry to a field research setting. In studies of cults, small extremist political sects, and illegal or deviant behavior, it may be impossible to conduct research if you disclose your purpose. *If a covert stance is not essential, the ethical rule is very clear: Do not use it.* If you are unsure of whether covert access is necessary, then use a strategy of gradual disclosure. Begin with limited disclosure, then reveal more as you learn more about a setting and participants. When in doubt, it is best to err in the direction of disclosing your true identity and purpose.

Covert field research is controversial among researchers. Many feel that all covert research is unethical. Even researchers who accept covert research in certain situations place limits on its use. It is only acceptable when overt observation is impossible. If you use covert research, you must inform participants of the covert observation immediately afterward and give them an opportunity to express concerns.

A downside to deception and covert research are that they increase mistrust and cynicism and lower public respect for doing research. Secretly spying on people without their permission and lying to get information carry real dangers. They are analogous to being an undercover government informer in a nondemocratic society.

Avoid Coercion. Coercion is another issue that creates difficulty in obtaining informed consent. Coercion can be physical, social, legal, professional, financial, or other pressure put on people to agree to participate in a study. The general rule is clear: Never coerce people to participate. This includes offering people a special benefit that they cannot attain other than through participation in a study. For example, it is unethical for a commanding officer to order a soldier to participate in a study, for a professor to require a student to be a research participant to pass a course, or for an employer to expect an employee to complete a survey as a condition of continued employment.

The rule against coercing people to participate in a study can become tricky in specific situations. For example, a convicted criminal faces the alternative of two years' imprisonment or participation in an experimental rehabilitation program. The convicted criminal does not believe in the benefits of the program, but the researcher believes that it will help the criminal. The criminal is being coerced to participate; the alternative is two years in prison. In such a case, the researcher and others must honestly decide whether the benefits to the criminal and to society clearly and far outweigh the ethical prohibition on coercion. Plus, the coercion must be limited. Even so, such decisions are risky. History shows many cases in which researchers forced powerless participants to be in a study allegedly to help them, but later it turned out that the research participants received few benefits but experienced great harm (see the discussion of the Tuskegee syphilis study at the beginning of this chapter).

Perhaps you have been in a social science class in which a teacher required you to participate in a research project. This is a special case of coercion. Usually, it is ethical. The legitimate justification for it is that students learn more about research when they experience it directly in a realistic situation. Such minor, limited coercion is acceptable as long as the teacher meets three conditions:

- The participation in research is attached to a clear educational objective of the specific course.
- Students have a choice of the research experience or an alternative activity of equal difficulty.
- The teacher follows all other ethical principles of conducting research.

 Example Study Box 4 Humphreys Tearoom Study

Kelly Redinger/Design Pics/Corbis
Royalty Free

Laud Humphreys studied male homosexual behavior (Humphreys 1973). He focused on "tearooms"—places where anonymous sexual encounters occur. He observed about 100 men engaging in sexual acts in a public restroom in a park. To do this, Humphreys pretended to be a "watchqueen" (a voyeur and lookout). He also followed research participants to their cars and secretly recorded their license numbers. He next obtained the names and addresses of participants from law enforcement registers by posing as a market researcher. One year later, in disguise, Humphreys used a deceptive story about conducting a health survey to interview the men in their homes. Humphreys kept names in safety deposit boxes and took precautions. He significantly advanced knowledge about the men who frequent "tearooms" and overturned previous false beliefs about them. He learned that most of the men were married and had stable jobs. They were not isolated loners without stable relationships or jobs, as was previously thought. The study generated an ethical controversy. It was covert research based on deception. None of the participants voluntarily agreed to be in the study. Despite precautions, Humphreys put participants at risk of great legal and personal harm. Had he lost control of the names, someone might have used them to blackmail participants, destroy their marriages and careers, or initiate criminal prosecution against them.

Privacy, Anonymity, and Confidentiality

How would you feel if someone learned private details about your personal life and shared them with the public without your permission or knowledge? Because researchers sometimes learn intimate details about participants, they must take precautions to protect research participants' privacy.

Privacy. When you study people, you may learn private details about them. As survey research probes into beliefs, backgrounds, and behaviors, it often reveals intimate, private details. Experimental researchers sometimes use two-way mirrors or hidden microphones to "spy" on a person's behavior. Even if research participants are aware they are in a study, they may not know what a researcher is looking for. Field researchers observe private aspects of behavior or eavesdrop on personal conversations. They have studied people in public places (e.g., in waiting rooms, walking down the street, in classrooms, etc.), but some "public" places are more private than others (consider, for example, the use of periscopes to observe people who thought they were alone in a public toilet stall). Eavesdropping on conversations and observing people in quasi-private areas raises ethical concerns.

When you conduct research, you need to protect the privacy of participants. To be ethical, you can only violate a participant's privacy to the minimum degree necessary and collect private information only for a legitimate research purpose. In addition, you must take several steps to protect the information you have learned about participants from public disclosure. This takes two forms that many people confuse: anonymity and confidentiality.

Anonymity. **Anonymity** means to remain anonymous or nameless. No one can trace information back to a specific individual. You can protect anonymity differently in different research techniques. In survey and experimental research, you do not collect names or addresses of participants and refer to them by a code number. If you use a mail survey and include a code on the questionnaire to determine which respondents failed to respond, you are not keeping respondents anonymous during that phase of the study. If you collect completed questionnaires from individuals on which they do not provide their names but you are able to narrow down which person submitted a particular questionnaire based on details about them and a list of name, your questionnaire is not anonymous. You might breach a promise of anonymity unknowingly in small samples. For example, you survey students at a small college of 250 students and ask questions including age, sex, religion, hobbies, and hometown. You notice answers from a 22-year-old Jewish male born in Stratford, Ontario whose hobby is to be on the football team. Such information among a small group allows you to learn who the specific individual is, even if you did not ask his name. This violates a promise of anonymity.

Protecting anonymity in field research is difficult. You learn details about research participants and their names. You can disguise some details and give false names, but even this does not always work. In one community study, researchers invented a false town name, "Springdale," and altered facts to protect the anonymity of the people studied, but they did not do enough. As a result, readers could identify the town and particular individuals when the study appeared as a book, *Small Town in Mass Society* (Vidich and Bensman 1968). Town residents became very upset about how the researchers portrayed them. They even staged a parade mocking the researchers. An additional issue is that when you use fictitious information, the gap between what you studied and what you report may raise questions about what you found and what you made up.

anonymity not connecting a participant's name or identifying details to information collected about him or her.

Confidentiality. Even if you cannot protect anonymity, you should always protect participant confidentiality. Anonymity means that no one can learn the identity of specific individuals. **Confidentiality** allows you to attach the information to particular

confidentiality holding information in confidence or not making it known to the public.

■ **Figure 3.4**   Anonymity and Confidentiality

	Anonymity	
Confidentiality	**YES**	**NO**
YES	Gather data so it is impossible for anyone to link it to any name and release findings in aggregate form.	Privately link details about a specific participant to a name, but only publicly release findings in aggregate form.
NO	Release details about a specific participant to the public, but withhold the name and details that might allow someone to trace back to the person.	**Unethical** Reveal publicly details about a person with his/her name.

individuals, but you keep it secret from public disclosure. You only release data in a way that does not permit anyone else to link specific individuals to information. To do this, you present data publicly only in an aggregate form (e.g., as percentages, statistical means, etc.). It is possible for you to provide anonymity without confidentiality, or vice versa, although they usually go together (see Figure 3.4).

Here is an example of each situation listed in Figure 3.4:

- **Anonymity with confidentiality** You conduct a survey of 100 people but do not know names of any of the participants and only release data as percentages of the total.
- **Anonymity without confidentiality** You conduct a field research study and learn a lot about person X but never learn the person's name. You report all the details about the person publicly but alter only a few details to make it impossible for anyone to track down the person to discover the name.
- **Confidentiality without anonymity** You conduct a survey of 100 people and have each person's name listed on his or her questionnaire but only publicly release the data as percentages of the total.
- **Neither anonymity nor confidentiality (this is unethical)** You conduct a survey of 100 people and have each person's name on his or her questionnaire. You publicly release a person's answers with the name, or with enough details to allow easy discovery of the person's name.

Anonymity and confidentiality become more complicated if you study "special populations" (see the discussion later in this chapter). In many large bureaucracies, people in positions of authority may restrict research access unless you violate confidentiality and give them information about participants. For example, you want to study drug use and sexual activity among high school students. School authorities only agree if you give them the names of all drug users and sexually active students. They might say they want to assist the students with counseling and to inform the students' parents. An ethical researcher must refuse to continue. If the school officials really wanted to assist the students and not use researchers as spies, they could develop their own outreach program. Another example is a survey of a company. A company manager asks to see all employee complaints and names of who complained. The supposed reason is to address the complaining individual's concerns. The ethical researcher protects participant privacy and only releases findings without names to protect the employees from potential retaliation.

Privacy rules operate with those to protect participants from legal or physical harm. Draus and associates (2005) protected the participants in a study of illegal drug users in rural Ohio. They conducted interviews in large multiuse buildings, avoided any reference to illegal drugs in their written documents, did not include the names of drug dealers and locations, and did not affiliate with drug rehabilitation services. This is because the rehabilitation services had ties to law enforcement. They (2005:169) noted, "We intentionally avoided contact with local police,

Example Study Box 5 Not Breaking the Confidence Guarantee

Social researchers can pay a high personal cost for being ethical. Washington State University Professor Rik Scarce went to jail. Professor Scarce had studied extremist social-political movements using accepted field research techniques. He introduced himself, slowly gained access and won trust, explained his research interests, and guaranteed confidentiality. He attended a local group's meetings, talked with activists and leaders, and spent time observing. In a second study of extremist groups, Dr. Scarce was studying a radical animal liberation group when police suspected the group leader of breaking into at nearby animal facility, releasing the research animals, and causing $150,000 in vandalism damage. Although some past court rulings appeared to offer social researchers protection, other rulings have not upheld confidentiality protections for social research data. When police asked for all of Dr. Scarce research notes, he followed professional ethical rules and principles. He refused to break the research confidentiality guarantee and hand over his notes or testify to a grand jury about his observations. As a result, he spent 159 days in a Spokane, Washington jail for contempt of court.

Petre Buzoianu/Corbis

prosecutors, or parole officers" and "surveillance of the project by local law enforcement was a source of concern."

In a few, rare situations, other principles overrule the principle of protecting research participant privacy. One exception is a clear, immediate danger to a person's safety, such as learning that a participant is considering suicide or plans to injure or kill another person. For example, you study parents, and during an interview with a father, you learn that he is abusing his child physically or sexually. In this case, you weigh protecting participant privacy against harm that the child would experience. The ethical course of action is to protect the child from imminent harm and notify the authorities.

Extra Protection for Special Populations

Some research participants may not be able to give true voluntary informed consent. **Special populations** such as students, prison inmates, employees, military personnel, the homeless, welfare recipients, children, or the developmentally disabled may not be fully capable of giving consent freely. Some may agree because it is a way to a desired good—such as higher grades, early parole, promotions, or additional

special populations people lacking the cognitive competency or full freedom to give true informed consent.

services; others may not understand what research means. If you wish to have "incompetent" people (e.g., children, mentally disabled, etc.) participate in a research study, you must meet two minimal conditions:

- The person's legal guardian/parent grants written informed consent permission.
- You closely follow all standard ethical rules to protect participants from any form of harm.

For example, you want to survey high school students to learn about their sexual behavior and drug or alcohol use. If you wish to conduct the survey on school property, you must obtain permission from school officials and get informed consent from the parent/legal guardian of any student who is a legal minor (usually under 18 years old) as well. You should also obtain informed consent from the research participant. High schools students are a special population that requires extra protections.

Formal Protections for Research Participants

In the United States, the U.S. Department of Health and Human Services Office for the Protection from Research Risks issues regulations to protect research participants. Federal regulations follow a biomedical model and protect participants from physical harm. It is one federal government agency, and technically its rules apply to when federal money is involved, but all other government agencies and most researchers follow its guidance. Most local governments, hospitals, universities, and private companies model their internal policies on the federal rules. Other U.S. government rules require the creation of institutional review boards at all research institutes, medical facilities, colleges, and universities where research with humans occurs. An **institutional review board (IRB)** applies ethical guidelines by reviewing research procedures at a proposal or preliminary stage. Some forms of research are exempt from a formal, full review by the IRB. These include educational tests, normal educational practice, most nonsensitive survey questionnaires, observation of public behavior, and studies of existing public data in which individuals cannot be identified. Submitting a proposal to an IRB for review requires a little extra time and planning. Most IRB members are concerned with upholding ethical protections of research participants. They are an "extra set of eyes" looking at a research design to ensure that participants will be fully protected.

Most professionals (such as physicians, attorneys, family counselors, social workers, and others) have organizations that developed a written code of ethics, peer review boards, or licensing regulations. A **code of ethics** is a written statement of ethical rules that identify proper and improper behavior. Most professional social science associations have codes of ethics that represent a consensus of professionals on ethics. Although not all researchers may agree on every ethical issue, they uphold ethical standards as members of a profession.

We can trace formal codes of research ethics to the Nuremberg Code adopted during the Nuremberg Military Tribunal on Nazi war crimes immediately after World War II. It was a direct response to the cruelty of concentration camp experiments, and it outlines ethical principles and rights of human research participants. These include the following:

institutional review board (IRB) a committee of researchers and community members that oversees, monitors, and reviews the impact of research procedures on human participants.

code of ethics a written, formal set of professional standards that provides guidance when ethical questions arise in practice.

- Ensure that participants have voluntarily consented to be in the study.
- Avoid unnecessary physical and mental suffering.
- Avoid any research where death or disabling injury to participants is likely.
- End a research study immediately if its continuation is likely to cause injury, disability, or death.
- Highly qualified people using the highest levels of skill and care should conduct research studies.
- Study results should be for the good of society and unattainable by any other method.

Making It Practical **Codes of Ethics**

Professional associations promote codes of ethics and hear about possible violations, but there is no formal policing of the codes. The penalty for a minor ethical violation rarely goes past public embarrassment and a letter of complaint. Those who commit a serious ethical violation, even if they violated no law, will face loss of reputation, loss of employment, a ban on the research findings being published, or restrictions from future jobs. Besides making explicit the beliefs of the research community and providing individual researchers with guidance, codes of ethics help universities and other institutions defend legitimate, ethical research against outside political or other pressures. If researchers receive unjustified demands to stop legitimate research or to reveal protected details about research participants, they look to written codes of ethics on websites. If you review the codes of ethics of several professional organizations, such as nursing, social work, public opinion research, psychology, or sociology, you will discover that they are not identical but they do overlap a great deal.

■ **Figure 3.5**   Code of Professional Ethics and Practices

We, the members of the American Association for Public Opinion Research, subscribe to the principles expressed in the following code. Our goals are to support sound and ethical practice in the conduct of public opinion research and in the use of such research for policy- and decision-making in the public and private sectors, as well as to improve public understanding of public opinion and survey research methods and the proper use of public opinion and survey research results.

We pledge ourselves to maintain high standards of scientific competence and integrity in conducting, analyzing, and reporting our work; in our relations with survey respondents; with our clients; with those who eventually use the research for decision-making purposes; and with the general public. We further pledge ourselves to reject all tasks or assignments that would require activities inconsistent with the principles of this code.

THE CODE

I. Principles of Professional Practice in the Conduct of Our Work
   A. We shall exercise due care in developing research designs and survey instruments, and in collecting, processing, and analyzing data, taking all reasonable steps to assure the reliability and validity of results.
      1. We shall recommend and employ only those tools and methods of analysis that, in our professional judgment, are well suited to the research problem at hand.
      2. We shall not knowingly select research tools and methods of analysis that yield misleading conclusions.
      3. We shall not knowingly make interpretations of research results that are inconsistent with the data available, nor shall we tacitly permit such interpretations.
      4. We shall not knowingly imply that interpretations should be accorded greater confidence than the data actually warrant.
   B. We shall describe our methods and findings accurately and in appropriate detail in all research reports, adhering to the standards for minimal disclosure specified in Section III.
   C. If any of our work becomes the subject of a formal investigation of an alleged violation of this Code, undertaken with the approval of the AAPOR Executive Council, we shall provide additional information on the survey in such detail that a fellow survey practitioner would be able to conduct a professional evaluation of the survey.
II. Principles of Professional Responsibility in Our Dealings with People
   A. The Public:
      1. When preparing a report for public release we shall ensure that the findings are a balanced and accurate portrayal of the survey results.
      2. If we become aware of the appearance in public of serious inaccuracies or distortions regarding our research, we shall publicly disclose what is required to correct these inaccuracies or distortions, including, as appropriate, a statement to the public media, legislative body, regulatory agency, or other appropriate group, to which the inaccuracies or distortions were presented.
      3. We shall inform those for whom we conduct publicly released surveys that AAPOR standards require members to release minimal information about such surveys, and we shall make all reasonable efforts to encourage clients to subscribe to our standards for minimal disclosure in their releases.

(continued)

■ **Figure 3.5** *Continued*

B. Clients or Sponsors:
1. When undertaking work for a private client, we shall hold confidential all proprietary information obtained about the client and about the conduct and findings of the research undertaken for the client, except when the dissemination of the information is expressly authorized by the client, or when disclosure becomes necessary under the terms of Section I-C or II-A of this Code.
2. We shall be mindful of the limitations of our techniques and capabilities and shall accept only those research assignments that we can reasonably expect to accomplish within these limitations.
C. The Profession:
1. We recognize our responsibility to the science of survey research to disseminate as freely as possible the ideas and findings that emerge from our research.
2. We shall not cite our membership in the Association as evidence of professional competence, since the Association does not so certify any persons or organizations.
D. The Respondent:
1. We shall avoid practices or methods that may harm, humiliate, or seriously mislead survey respondents.
2. We shall respect respondents' concerns about their privacy.
3. Aside from the decennial census and a few other surveys, participation in surveys is voluntary. We shall provide all persons selected for inclusion with a description of the survey sufficient to permit them to make an informed and free decision about their participation.
4. We shall not misrepresent our research or conduct other activities (such as sales, fund raising, or political campaigning) under the guise of conducting research.
5. Unless the respondent waives confidentiality for specified uses, we shall hold as privileged and confidential all information that might identify a respondent with his or her responses. We also shall not disclose or use the names of respondents for non-research purposes unless the respondents grant us permission to do so.
6. We understand that the use of our survey results in a legal proceeding does not relieve us of our ethical obligation to keep confidential all respondent identifiable information or lessen the importance of respondent anonymity.

III. Standards for Minimal Disclosure
Good professional practice imposes the obligation upon all public opinion researchers to include, in any report of research results, or to make available when that report is released, certain essential information about how the research was conducted. At a minimum, the following items should be disclosed.
1. Who sponsored the survey, and who conducted it.
2. The exact wording of questions asked, including the text of any preceding instruction or explanation to the interviewer or respondents that might reasonably be expected to affect the response.
3. A definition of the population under study, and a description of the sampling frame used to identify this population.
4. A description of the sample design, giving a clear indication of the method by which the respondents were selected by the researcher, or whether the respondents were entirely self-selected.
5. Sample sizes and, where appropriate, eligibility criteria, screening procedures, and response rates computed according to AAPOR Standard Definitions. At a minimum, a summary of disposition of sample cases should be provided so that response rates could be computed.
6. A discussion of the precision of the findings, including estimates of sampling error, and a description of any weighting or estimating procedures used.
7. Which results are based on parts of the sample, rather than on the total sample, and the size of such parts.
8. Method, location, and dates of data collection.
From time to time, AAPOR Council may issue guidelines and recommendations on best practices with regard to the release, design and conduct of surveys.

Copy of American Association of Public Opinion Research of Code of Professional Ethics (a pdf file) as revised in 2005.

Summary Review   Basic Principles of Ethical Research

- Accept responsibility for all ethical decisions and the protection of research participants.
- Use the research techniques that are most appropriate for a topic or situation.
- Follow accepted methodological standards and strive for high accuracy.
- Detect and remove any threats of harm to research participants.
- Never exploit research participants for personal gain.
- Get informed consent from the research participants before beginning.
- Treat the research participants with dignity and respect at all times.

- Only use deception if absolutely needed, and always debrief participants afterward.
- Honor all guarantees of privacy, confidentiality, and anonymity you make to participants.
- Be candid and honest when interpreting and reporting study results.
- Identify the sponsors of funded research to participants and to the public.
- Release all details of the study procedures with the results.
- Act with integrity and adhere to the behaviors outlined in professional codes of ethics.

The principles of the Nuremberg Code focused on medical experimentation, but they became the basis for the ethical codes for all research with humans.

ETHICS AND THE SPONSORS OF RESEARCH

You might find a job in which you are assigned to conduct research for a sponsor— an employer, a government agency, or a private firm. Special ethical issues can arise when a sponsor pays for research, especially applied research. Some sponsors ask researchers to compromise ethical or professional research standards as a condition for continued employment. If a sponsor makes an illegitimate demand, you have three basic choices: be loyal to an organization and cave in to the sponsor, exit from the situation by quitting, or voice opposition and become a whistle-blower (see the discussion later in this chapter). You need to set ethical boundaries beyond which you refuse a sponsor's demands and choose your own course of action. Whatever the case, it is best to consider ethical issues early in a relationship with a sponsor and to express your concerns up front.

Arriving at Particular Findings

A sponsor might tell you, directly or indirectly, what results you should come up with before you conduct a study. The ethical choice is to refuse to continue if told you must reach specific findings as a precondition for doing research. Legitimate research does not have restrictions on the possible findings. In an ethical, legitimate study, you will not know the findings for certain until after you have gathered the data and completed the study.

Limits on How to Conduct Studies. Sponsors can legitimately set some conditions on research techniques used (e.g., survey versus experiment) and limit costs for research. However, as a researcher, you must follow generally accepted research standards. Often there is a trade-off between research quality and cost. You should give a realistic appraisal of what you can accomplish for a given level of funding. If you cannot uphold generally accepted standards of research, refuse to do the research.

Unfortunately, some sponsors care little for the actual results or truth. They have little respect for research or its ethical principles. To them research is only "a cover" that legitimates a predetermined decision or only a way to deflect criticism. They are abusing the reputation of research and its integrity to advance their own narrow goals. If a sponsor asks you to use illegitimate research techniques (such as a biased sample or leading survey questions), the ethical choice is a refusal to cooperate. In the long run, ethical violations harm the sponsor, researchers, the scientific community, and society in general. You need to decide whether to prostitute your skills and give sponsors whatever they want, even if it is unethical, or be a professional who is obligated to teach, guide, or even oppose sponsors based on higher principles.

Suppressing Findings. Perhaps you conduct a study, and the findings make the sponsor look bad. The sponsor decides to suppress the study's results. This kind of situation happens fairly often in applied research. In one case, a state government created a lottery commission to examine starting a government-sponsored lottery. Some politicians and members of the public asked for a study on the likely effects of a state lottery, so the commission hired a sociologist with expertise in that area. After she completed the study, but before releasing the report to the public, the commission asked her to remove sections of the report that discussed the negative social effects of gambling. They tried to eliminate sections of the report that predicted that the lottery would cause a large increase in compulsive gamblers and the recommendation that the state create social services to help them. The commission ordered and paid for the study, but the researcher felt a professional ethical obligation to show the public the full, uncensored report. Unless she went beyond the commission and released the complete report, the public would see a distorted, biased picture of study findings.

Unfortunately, even the U.S. federal government has a record of suppressing research findings that contradict the political goals of high officials. In 2004, many leading scientists, including Nobel laureates, medical experts, former federal agency directors, and university presidents, voiced their concern over the dramatic increase in the government's misuse of research. A major complaint was that government officials had suppressed important research findings that disagreed with their political goals. In addition, they suppressed findings on the poor safety or pollution records of industries that just happened to be major political campaign contributions. Researchers working for government agencies said that their politically appointed managers had suppressed findings or omitted important technical information to advance nonscientific, political goals that the findings had contradicted.

In sponsored research, you want to negotiate conditions for releasing findings *prior to beginning* the study or signing a contract. It is best to begin with an explicit guarantee that you will only conduct ethical research. It is legitimate to delay the release of findings to protect the identity of informants, to maintain access to a research site, or to protect your personal safety. It is not legitimate to censor findings because a sponsor does not want to look bad or wants to protect its reputation. The researcher directly involved and knowledgeable about a study shoulders a responsibility for both conducting the research and to making its findings public.

Whistle-blowing occurs when a researcher informs an external audience of a serious ethical problem that is being ignored. It is never a first step; rather it occurs after the researcher has repeatedly attempted to inform superiors and fix the problem internally. The whistle-blowing researcher must believe that the situation is a serious breach of ethics and the organization will not end it without public pressure. Whistle-blowing is risky in several ways:

whistle-blowing when a researcher sees unethical behavior and, after unsuccessful attempts to get superiors to end it, goes public to expose the wrongdoing.

- Outsiders may not be interested in the ethical abuse and simply ignore it.
- Outsiders might not care about ending unethical behavior instead use the exposure of unethical behavior to advance their own goals.

Tips for the Wise Consumer Who Paid for a Study?

It is unethical to hide the identity of research sponsor. You should tell study participants who the sponsor is and inform the readers of research reports. Participants in a study have a right to know the sponsor. Telling participants is rarely controversial, but it becomes tricky in a few instances. For example, a pro-choice organization sponsors a study to look at the attitudes of members of religious groups opposed to abortion. The organization asks that you not reveal the sponsor to participants. You must balance the ethical rule to reveal a sponsor's identity against the sponsor's desire for confidentiality and possible bias or reduced cooperation by study participants. In general, unless you have a very clear, strong methodological reason for not doing so (such as reduced cooperation and strong bias), tell participants of the sponsor of a study. If telling participants of the sponsor will create a bias or noncooperation, then wait until after you have gathered the data.

When reporting study results, the ethical mandate is unambiguous: You must always reveal sponsors who fund a study. One study can have multiple sponsors, especially if it is a large one; you should list all the sponsors. Government agencies, foundations, or nonprofit organizations fund most research studies. Here is the sponsor information from the footnote of an article (Kane 2005: 463): "This research was conducted in part under National Institute of Justice grant #1996IJCX0053. Neither the NIJ nor any agencies mentioned in the manuscript bear responsibility for the analyses and interpretations of the data contained herein."

If you see no funding source listed, the study was probably part of the researcher's professional duties or supported by an employer. As you read more research reports, you may notice that certain organizations regularly sponsor studies on a topic.

- Managers will try to protect the organization and discredit the whistle-blower.
- The whistle-blower often experiences emotional distress and strained relations, and even lawsuits.
- Future employers may not trust the whistle-blower and may avoid hiring him or her.

A whistle-blower needs to be prepared to make sacrifices—loss of a job or no promotions, lowered pay, an undesirable transfer, abandonment by friends at work, or legal costs. There is no guarantee that doing the ethical-moral thing will end the unethical behavior or protect an honest researcher from retaliation.

POLITICAL INFLUENCES ON RESEARCH

The ideals of a free, open, and democratic society include advancing and sharing knowledge. People have a right to study and inquire into any question and to share their findings publicly. Ethical issues largely address moral concerns and standards of professional conduct. Most of the time, these are under the researcher's control. Political concerns can also influence and interfere with the research process. Organized advocacy groups, powerful interests, government officials, or politicians may try to restrict or control the direction of research.

In the past, powerful political interests and groups have tried to stop research or the spread of legitimate research findings. They did this to advance their own narrow political goals. They have used their political power to threaten researchers or their employers, to cut off research funds, to harass individual researchers and ruin their careers, and to censor publication of findings that they disliked.

Politically powerful groups have directed research funds away from studying questions that researchers see as important and toward studies of policy positions that favored their own political views. Members of the U.S. Congress targeted and removed funds for individual research projects that panels of independent scientists evaluated as being well designed and critical to advanced knowledge. Why? The politicians personally disliked the study topics (such as sexual behavior of teens, illegal drug users, voting behavior). Politicians are not the only ones interfering with

Example Study Box 6 Political Influence on Crime Research

Savelsberg, King, and Cleveland (2002) conducted a content analysis study on shifts in U.S. criminal justice policy during the last the thirty years of the twentieth century. They looked at articles in leading scholarly journals between 1951 and 1993 to see whether politicians changed how the federal government awards research funds to increase the politicization of criminal justice research. More specifically, they asked whether the government money went to studies that supported specific crime policy ideas advocated by powerful politicians rather than to purely science-based ideas. For example, they asked whether funds directed research away from looking at certain ways to fight crime (altering social conditions, using informal community controls, and emphasizing rehabilitation) and toward others (imposing more formal, coercive police actions and emphasizing punishment). They found that politics had influenced crime research. If the head of a government agency with research funds was politically appointed or funds only were for a crime-fighting policy that was closely tied to political ideology, they called it "political funding." They found that the proportion of research articles listing sponsors classified as "political funding" grew from 3 percent to 31 percent over the nearly 40-year time period they examined. They documented a large-scale shift in research, away from examining the sociological conditions of crime and the effects of rehabilitation and toward a focus on control and punishment (Savelsberg, King, and Cleveland 2002 and Savelsberg, Cleveland and Ryan 2004). This study illustrated how politicians and political movements gained control of government research funding and then politicized it and used the money to redirect the type of research that was conducted.

the free flow of knowledge. Large corporations have threatened individual researchers with lawsuits for delivering expert testimony in public about research findings that revealed to the public the corporation's bad conduct (for many examples, see Mooney 2005).

The powerful in society try to control or censor research out of fear that free, unbiased research might uncover something damaging to their interests. They put a higher value on protecting and advancing their political or economic interests than on the open pursuit of truth. This shows the tight connection between unimpeded, open scientific inquiry and the ideals of open public debate, democracy, and freedom of expression. Censoring and controlling research has always been the practice in dictatorships and totalitarian regimes.

VALUE-FREE AND OBJECTIVE RESEARCH

You have undoubtedly heard about "value-free" research and the importance of being "objective" in research. This is not as simple at it might first appear for the following three reasons:

- The terms *value free* and *objective* have multiple meanings.
- Researchers have alternative ultimate goals for doing research.
- Doing value-free, objective research does not mean that individual researchers are devoid of all values.

Multiple Meanings. *Value free* has two meanings: (1) research without any prior assumptions or theory; and (2) research free of influence from an individual researcher's personal prejudices/beliefs. The first meaning is rarely possible. It means "just facts" without theory or assumptions. Assumptions and theory are in virtually every research study. The best thing is to acknowledge them and make them explicit. Having theoretical assumptions does not prevent study findings from reversing or overturning them. The second meaning is standard practice. It means that an individual person doing the research temporarily "locks up" his or her personal beliefs, values, and prejudices during the research process (i.e., design, data collection, data interpretation). Your personal beliefs should not distort using standard research procedures but can still influence the choice of a study topic or research question or how to publicize or use findings.

Objective has two meanings as well: (1) focus only on what is external or visible; and (2) follow clear and publicly accepted research procedures and not haphazard, invented personal ones. The first meaning is not accurate. We conduct empirical research based on direct or indirect evidence. Although some evidence is not directly visible, such as a person's personality or opinion, you can create measures to make it visible. The second meaning is standard practice. You should always conduct research in an open, public manner that fits with widely accepted procedures.

Alternative Goals. Some professional researchers say they reject value-free research. They mean that they maintain personal values in certain parts of the research process, not that they embrace sloppy and haphazard research or research procedures that follow personal whims. They believe that a researcher should be explicit about his or her values, not that a study has foregone conclusions and automatically supports a specific value position. You should reflect carefully on reasons for doing a study and the procedures used. In this way, other researchers see the values and judge for themselves whether the values unfairly influenced a study's findings.

Devoid of Values. Even researchers who strongly advocate value-free and objective studies admit a place for personal, moral values. Personal, moral views can enter select parts of the process: when choosing a topic to study and how to publicize the findings. Although you must follow standard procedures and contain personal views and values in some parts of the research process, you can still study the questions you believe to be important and make extra efforts to publicize the findings among specific interest groups.

WHAT HAVE YOU LEARNED?

We conduct research to gain knowledge about the social world. The perspectives and techniques of social research can be powerful tools for understanding the world. Nevertheless, with that power to discover comes the responsibility to be ethical. It is a responsibility to yourself, a responsibility to your sponsors, a responsibility to the community of researchers, and a responsibility to the larger society.

The responsibilities of research can conflict with each other. As Rik Scarce (1999:984–985) observed,

"Ethics are morality—fundamental rights and wrongs—in practice. They are not . . . legally acceptable statements. . . . They are standards higher than any law." Ultimately, you personally must decide to conduct research in an ethical manner. Research is not automatically moral. Individual researchers must uphold ethical-moral research and demand ethical conduct by others. The truthfulness and use/misuse of the knowledge we gain from research depends on individual researchers like you.

KEY TERMS

anonymity *73*
code of ethics *76*
confidentiality *73*
informed consent *69*
institutional review board (IRB) *76*
plagiarism *63*

principle of voluntary consent *69*
research fraud *63*
scientific misconduct *63*
special populations *75*
whistle-blowing *80*

APPLY WHAT YOU'VE LEARNED

Activity 1

To better understand possible sponsors of research, locate 30 scholarly journal articles on two topics of your choice. For each article, look to see whether there is a sponsor other than the author's employer. You can find this in a footnote at the beginning or the end of an article saying that there was a grant that provided funding. How many of the 30 articles you located had an outside sponsor? For some topics, you may find no article with sponsors. For other topics, a large majority might have sponsors.

Activity 2

Social science fields and related practitioners have professional organizations with a code of ethics. Figure 3.5 provided an example of the ethical code of the American Association for Public Opinion Research. Here is a list of 14 other U.S.-based professional organizations that have such codes:

Select five associations from the list above and look up what their code of ethics says about conducting research. In what areas do they all agree or say the same thing? In what areas do you see differences among them?

Professional Organization	Web Site for Code of Ethics
1. Academy of Criminal Justice Sciences	http://www.acjs.org/pubs/167_671_2922.cfm
2. American Anthropological Association	http://www.aaanet.org/committees/ethics/ethics.htm
3. American Counseling Association	http://www.counseling.org/Resources/CodeOfEthics/TP/Home/CT2.aspx
4. American Educational Research Association	http://www.aera.net/aboutaera/?id=717
5. American Nurses Association	http://www.med.howard.edu/ethics/handouts/american_nurses_association_code.htm
6. American Planning Association	http://www.planning.org/ethics/
7. American Political Science Association	http://www.apsanet.org/513.cfm
8. American Psychological Association	http://www.apa.org/ethics/code2002.html
9. American Society for Public Administration	http://ethics.iit.edu/codes/coe/amer.soc.public.admin.d.html
10. American Sociological Association	http://www.asanet.org/page.ww?section=Ethics&name=Ethics
11. Association for Institutional Research	http://www.airweb.org/?page=140
12. Association of American Geographers	http://www.aag.org/Publications/EthicsStatement.html
13. Marketing Research Association	http://www.mra-net.org/
14. National Association of Social Workers	http://www.socialworkers.org/pubs/code/code.asp

Activity 3

Find out about your college's or university's IRB. If it does not have one, ask your teacher to explain why it does not. If it does, find out who the members are and ask to attend a meeting as an observer when a "nonexempt" social research project is being discussed. Obtain a copy of the informed consent form used and write a short description of the meeting and issues discussed at it.

Activity 4

A whistle-blower can be in any professional field (such as accounting, banking, education, engineering, or medicine), not just doing research. What is common among whistle-blowers is that a professional identifies repeated improper-unethical conduct and, after unsuccessful attempts to remedy the issues, goes public with a revelation about it. What protections, legal, career, or otherwise, does a researcher have if he or she becomes a whistle-blower? Also, what consequences have past whistle-blowers experienced? To address these questions, you may wish to examine laws protecting whistle-blowers or the U.S. government's Office of Research Integrity statement on the issue: http://ori.hhs.gov/misconduct/nprm_reg.shtml. You may also wish to look at a book on the topic, such as Alford, C. Fred (2001). *Whistleblowers: Broken Lives and Organizational Power.* Ithaca, NY: Cornell University Press.

REFERENCES

Draus, Paul J., Harvey Siegal, Rober Carlson, Russel Falck, and Jichuan Wang, Jichuan. 2005. "Cracking the Cornfields." *Sociological Quarterly* 46:165–189.

Humphreys, Laud. 1973. *Tearoom Trade.* Chicago: Aldine.

Kane, Robert J. 2005. "Compromised Police Legitimacy as a Predictor of Violent Crime in Structurally Disadvantaged Communities." *Criminology* 43:469–498.

Milgram, Stanley. 1963. "Behavioral Study of Obedience." *Journal of Abnormal and Social Psychology* 6:371–378.

Milgram, Stanley 1965. "Some Conditions of Obedience and Disobedience to Authority." *Human Relations* 18:57–76.

Milgram, Stanley. 1974. *Obedience to Authority.* New York: Harper and Row.

Mooney, Chris. 2005. *The Republican War on Science.* New York: Perseus Books.

Piliavin, Irving, J. Rodin, and Jane Piliavin. 1969. "Good Samaritanism: An Underground Phenomenon?" *Journal of Personality and Social Psychology* 13:289–299.

Savelsberg, Joachim, Lara Cleveland, and Ryan King. 2004. "Institutional Environments and Scholarly Work: American Criminology, 1951–1993." *Social Forces* 82:1275–1302.

Savelsberg, Joachim, Ryan King, and Lara Cleveland. 2002. "Politicized Scholarship? Science on Crime and the State." *Social Problems* 49:327–349.

Scarce, Rik. 1994. "(No) Trial (But) Tribulations: When Courts and Ethnography Conflict." *Journal of Contemporary Ethnography* 23:123–149.

Scarce, Rik. 1999. "Good Faith, Bad Ethics: When Scholars Go the Distance and Scholarly Associations Do Not"*Law & Social Inquiry* 24:977–986.

Taylor, Steven. 1987. "Observing abuse." *Qualitative Sociology* 10:288–302.

Van Maanen, John. 1982. "Fieldwork on the Beat." *Varieties of Qualitative Research.* Edited by J. Van Mannen, J. Dabbs, Jr., and R. Raulkner (pp. 102–151). Beverly Hills, CA: Sage.

Vidich, Arthur, and Joseph Bensman. 1968. *Small Town in Mass Society*, rev. ed. Princeton, NJ: Princeton University Press.

Zimbardo, Philip. 1972. "The Pathology of Imprisonment." *Society* 9:4–6.

Sampling: How to Select a Few to Represent the Many

Philip Wallick/Corbis

Firearms are the third leading cause of death for American children aged 5 to 16. A gun in the home is the primary source of unintentional firearm injuries to children, as well as youth suicides and school-associated homicides. Some surveys suggest that about 40 percent of all American homes contain guns, but gun ownership varies by rural versus urban area. Although intentional gun deaths are highest in poor, inner-city areas, low-income urban minorities have the lowest reported rates of gun ownership. Guns in the home can be dangerous. Gun safety advocates recommend making guns at home inaccessible by using trigger locks or storing them in locked safes, drawers, or cabinets, whether or not children are present.

Susan M. Connor (2005) wanted to study of whether adults followed safety recommendations when children were in the home in rural and urban areas. She could not examine all gun owners in America, so she focused on northeast Ohio and drew a sample. From a market research firm, she obtained lists of northeast Ohio telephone numbers of rural homes either likely or unlikely to have children under 16, and similar lists for urban homes. Next, she called every tenth name on the four lists. She conducted two surveys: one of 400 urban and 400 rural households with children, and another of 400 urban and 400 rural households without children. Interviewers asked adults in the 1600 homes about gun ownership, gun storage, and other factors.

Dr. Connor found firearms to be more common in rural households (31 percent) than in urban households (13 percent). Households with children were generally less likely to have guns (20 percent with children reported having at least one firearm versus 29 percent without children). Only 22 percent followed gun safety recommendations (trigger locks and stored in a locked place unloaded). Homes with children were equally unlikely to use safe gun storage than those without children present.

It was difficult to call 1600 people, but we do not want to limit findings to them. By using careful sampling methods, we can generalize the findings to larger groups. A well-developed sample of 1600 allows us to estimate what is occurring across the United States. In this chapter, we examine why and how to sample in a research study.

HOW AND WHY DO SAMPLES WORK?

Researchers use samples in many types of studies. Whether you have quantitative or qualitative data, and the purpose of your study will influence the particulars of sampling. Quantitative researchers devote a lot of effort to sampling. They want to get a genuinely representative **sample**, (i.e., a sample that has all the features of the **population** from which it came). A proper sample allows you to study features of the sample and produce highly accurate generalizations about the entire population. The most representative samples use a random selection process. The random process allows us to build on mathematical theories about probability. Probability sampling enables us to use mathematics of probability. Due to their use of random selection, we also call probability samples **random samples**.

Random samples can be highly efficient in terms of time and cost. A properly conducted sample can yield results at 1/1000th the cost and time of contacting and gathering data on a population. In the study that opens this chapter, Dr. Connor drew a sample of 1600. Her findings based on the 1600 interviews will be almost identical to what she would have gotten if she had interviewed all 300 million Americans. Later in this chapter, you will see exactly how to draw a random sample.

A well-designed, carefully executed random sample can give you results that are equally and sometimes more accurate than if you tried to reach everyone in the population. You probably heard of the census. A census is an official government count carried out at periodic intervals. It provides information on things such as sex, age, job, and so forth. In the United States, there is an official count of the population every 10 years. For the 2000 census, all the leading scientists advised the government to use specialized statistical sampling to get the most accurate measure of the population rather than trying to count everyone, as was the case in the past. Unfortunately, due to political considerations, factors other than solid scientific advice prevailed, and the government used the less accurate method of trying to count everyone.

Qualitative researchers often have different goals than to get a representative sample of a large population, so they rarely use random sampling. Instead, they usually want to learn how a small collection of cases, units, or activities, can illuminate key features of an area of social life. They use sampling less to represent a population than to highlight informative cases, events, or actions. Their goal is to clarify and deepen understanding based what they learn from the highlighted cases.

FOCUSING ON A SPECIFIC GROUP: FOUR TYPES OF NONRANDOM SAMPLES

Random samples are best to get an accurate representation of a population, but they are difficult to conduct. Researchers who cannot draw a random sample or who have difficult goals use nonprobability samples. We next look at four nonprobability sampling techniques.

Convenience Sampling

Convenience sampling (also called accidental or haphazard sampling) is easy, cheap, and fast but of limited use. Its biggest problem is that it can produce very unrepresentative samples. It also lacks the depth and context demanded by qualitative research. If you haphazardly select any convenient cases, you can easily get a nonrepresentative sample of what is in the population (see Figure 4.1).

With caution, you can use a convenience sample for the preliminary phase of an exploratory study, but otherwise they are of limited use. The person-on-the-street interview conducted by television programs is a convenience sample. Television interviewers go out on the street with a camera to talk to a few people who are convenient

sample a small collection of units taken from a larger collection.

population a larger collection of units from which a sample is taken.

random sample a sample drawn in which a random process is used to select units from a population.

convenience sampling a nonrandom sample in which you use an nonsystematic selection method that often produces samples very unlike the population.

■ Figure 4.1   Representative and Nonrepresentative Samples of 6 out of 18

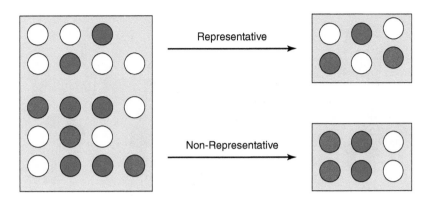

to interview. The people walking past a television studio in the middle of the day do not represent everyone. Likewise, the interviewers pick people who look "normal" to them and avoid unattractive, very busy, or inarticulate people. Have you watched a television show that asks you to call in your opinion? These too are convenience samples. Only some people who are watching television will call. Even if the number who do so is large (e.g., 500,000), the sample can not be generalized accurately to the population. Such samples may have entertainment value, but they can seriously misrepresent the population. Do not confuse them with a true representative sample.

In sampling, the terms *haphazard* and *random* have very different meanings. *Haphazard* means without being systematic; a carefree "anything goes" selection method. *Random* follows a systematic, mathematically based meaning of a true random process (discussed later).

Quota Sampling

Quota sampling is not as accurate as a random sample for a representative sample, but it is much easier and faster. It is a major improvement over convenience sampling. In quota sampling,

- First identify several relevant categories of people or units (e.g., male and female; or under age 30, ages 30 to 60, over age 60, etc.). The categories should reflect aspects of diversity in the population that you believe to be important.
- Next, decide how many units to get for each category. For example, you are interested in a sample of 80 shoppers at a grocery store. You think gender and age are important aspects of diversity. You select 10 males and 10 females under age 30, 10 of each gender aged 30–40, 10 of each gender aged 40–50, and 10 of each gender over age 60.
- After you fix the categories and number of units in each category, select units by any method. For example, you might interview the first 12 males who walk into the store, asking each his age. Once you have 10 who are under 30 years of age, you have to skip all other males in that age group because you have filled your quota.

Quota sampling is better than convenience sampling because with it you ensure that major differences in the population also appear in your sample. In convenience sampling, everyone interviewed might be of the same age, gender, or race. However, it has limitations and can give you a nonrepresentative sample. (See Figure 4.2).

One limitation comes from using a convenience selection process for the quota categories. You might only select people who "act friendly" or who want you to

quota sampling nonrandom sample in which you use any means to fill preset categories that are characteristics of the population.

■ **Figure 4.2**   Quota Sampling

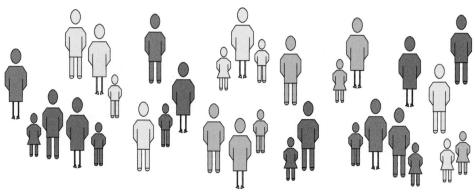

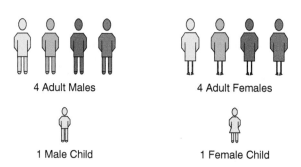

Of 32 adults and children in the street scene, select 10 for the sample:

4 Adult Males   4 Adult Females

1 Male Child   1 Female Child

Popperfoto/Getty Images

interview them. Another limitation is that you only capture the diversity of a few pre-determined population characteristics. A population might differ in 20 ways, but quota samples rarely include more than three characteristics. It is difficult to conduct a quota sample with more than three characteristics. Let us say your quota sample has combinations of gender (male/female), age (over/under 50), race (white/nonwhite), and shopping companion (none/with others). For the sample you must find enough people in each combination, such as over-50-year-old nonwhite males who shop alone. A last limitation is that you arbitrarily fix the size of a quota for each category. You must often do this without having prior knowledge of the population. If you set a quota of 10 percent of the sample of grocery shoppers to be people under age 30, but they actually make up 18 percent of the grocery shopping population, your sample will not accurately represent the population.

An interesting historical case illustrates the limitations of quota sampling. George Gallup's American Institute of Public Opinion used quota sampling. It successfully predicted the outcomes of the 1936, 1940, and 1944 U.S. presidential elections. However, in 1948, Gallup predicted wrong and said Thomas Dewey would win over Harry Truman. The incorrect prediction had several causes (e.g., many voters were undecided, interviewing stopped early), but the main reason was that quota sampling categories did not represent all geographical areas and all types of people who actually voted.

Purposive or Judgmental Sampling

purposive sampling a nonrandom sample in which you use many diverse means to select units that fit very specific characteristics.

Purposive sampling is a widely accepted special technique appropriate when your goal is other than getting a representative sample of an entire population. In purposive sampling, you use judgment to select cases and have a very specific purpose in mind. In a way, it is convenience sampling for a highly targeted, narrowly defined population. You can use it in two types of situations:

- To select especially informative cases. You want to pick cases that have richer information. For example, you want to examine magazine content for cultural themes. You select two specific popular women's magazines to study because they are trend setting rather than select a representative sample of all women's magazines.
- To select cases from a specific, difficult-to-reach population. To study a targeted group, you may use many diverse methods to identify as many cases as possible. For example, you want to study people under 30 who use wheelchairs in the Seattle metropolitan area. Without a list of wheelchair users, you cannot use a random sampling method. To use purposive sampling, you use many diverse forms of information to get a sizable collection (maybe of 60 names). To get the names, you may go to locations where wheelchairs are sold and repaired or ask knowledgeable local experts (e.g., health workers, other wheelchair users, or disability advocate groups).

Snowball Sampling

Snowball sampling (also called network, chain-referral, or reputational sampling) is a special technique in which your goal is to capture an already-existing network. The name is based on the selection process and is an analogy to the way a snowball increases in size: It begins small but gets larger as you roll it and it picks up additional snow. It is a multistage technique. You begin with one or a few cases, then spread out based on direct or indirect links to the initial case.

You may wish to use snowball sampling if you want to sample a social network of people or linked organizations. Networks for which researcher used snowball sampling include

- Scientists around the world who are investigating the same issue
- The elites of a medium-sized city who consult with one another
- Drug dealers and suppliers who work together for form a distribution network
- People on a college campus who have had sexual relations with one another

The crucial feature is that each person or case has a connection with the others. The linkage can be either direct or indirect. Members of the network may not directly know or interact with all others in the network. Rather, taken as a whole, each is part of a larger linked web.

snowball sampling a nonrandom sample in which selection is based on connections in a preexisting network.

Example Study Box 1 **A Snowball Sample of Golfers**

In 2002 a group of five Augusta State University students used snowball sampling to conduct a study of African American golfers in Georgia. For generations, legal and later social practices of racial segregation barred African Americans from playing on private and public golf courses. At one time, they could only be caddies for white golfers. Slowly, they were able to participate in a sport once closed to them. The students began with two local African American men who their professor knew. A snowball sample was appropriate in this situation because the golfers formed a community. They often interacted with each other, both on and off the golf course. The students' sample grew to 20 based on recommendations from the golfers they had first contacted. They interviewed the 20 African American golfers, aged mid-twenties to 91. Based on the interviews, the students learned that the sport provided the players with important business contacts and as well as being a form of recreation. (For more information, see http://www.aug.edu/sociology/StudentWork/masters.htm.)

Jeff Greenberg/PhotoEdit Inc.

COMING TO CONCLUSIONS ABOUT LARGE POPULATIONS

For an accurate small collection of cases that can most accurately represent a far larger population, you should use a random sampling method (see Figure 4.3). We already covered the basics: You draw a sample (a small subset) from a population (a large pool of cases).

Random sampling has a specialized vocabulary (see Summary Review: Ten Terms in Random Sampling). You are already familiar with three of the terms, *population*, *sample*, and *universe*. The case or unit of analysis in the population is a **sampling element**. It can be a person, a group, an organization, a written document or symbolic message, or even a social action (e.g., an arrest, a divorce, or a kiss). Three terms with very similar meanings can be a source of confusion, but actually they are related by degree of specificity. You learned the first term in Chapter 2.

- *Universe*—The broad group to whom you wish to generalize your theoretical results (e.g., all people in Florida)
- *Population*—A collection of elements from which you draw a sample (e.g., all adults in the Miami metro area)
- *Target population*—The specific population that you used (e.g., people aged 18–88 who had a permanent address in Dade County, Florida in September 2007, and who spoke English, Spanish or Haitian Creole).

The population is more an idea than it is something concrete. Except for small or specialized populations (e.g., all the students in a classroom, all employees currently working the second shift at factory number three of Tom's shoe company on March 30 of this year), you have to refine the population to be very specific (i.e., the target population) before you can draw a sample.

Once you have a target population, you must create a list of all its sampling elements, your **sampling frame**. There are many types of sampling frames: telephone directories, tax records, driver's license records, and so on. In the study about gun owners in Ohio that opened this chapter, Dr. Connor had four sampling frames that she obtained from a marketing research company; each was a list of phone numbers for specific types of households (urban or rural, with or without children). Listing the elements is often difficult because no good list of the elements in a population exists. A good sampling frame is crucial to accurate sampling. If there is a mismatch between the sampling frame and the population, it can create major errors and cause invalid sampling.

Any statistical characteristic of an entire population (e.g., the percentage of city residents who smoke cigarettes, the average height of all women over the age of 21, the percent of people who believe in UFOs) is a **population parameter**. If you have all the elements in a population, you accurately compute a parameter with absolute

sampling element a case or unit of analysis of the population that can be selected for a sample.

target population a population specified in very concrete terms.

sampling frame a specific list of sampling elements in the target population.

population parameter any characteristic of the entire population that you estimate from a sample.

■ **Figure 4.3**   A Model of the Logic of Sampling

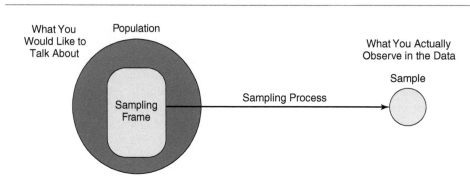

Learning from History The Famous *Literary Digest* Mistake

The *Literary Digest* was a major U.S. magazine that predicted presidential elections in the 1920s and 1930s. The magazine sent postcards to people before the U.S. presidential elections. The magazine staff created a sampling frame by taking names from automobile registration and telephone directories. People returned the postcards indicating the candidate they supported. The magazine correctly predicted election outcomes in 1920, 1924, 1928, and 1932. The magazine's success with predictions was well known. In 1936, the magazine increased its sample size to 10 million. The magazine predicted a huge victory for Alf Landon over Franklin D. Roosevelt. In this election, the *Literary Digest* was very wrong; Franklin D. Roosevelt won by a landslide. The prediction was wrong because the sampling frame did not accurately represent all voters. It excluded people without telephones or automobiles, a sizable

percentage of the population in 1936, during the worst of the Great Depression of the 1930s. The frame excluded as much as 65 percent of the population. More importantly, this segment of the voting population (lower income) tended to favor Roosevelt. The magazine had been accurate in earlier elections because people with higher and lower incomes did not differ in how they voted. In addition, before the Depression, more lower-income people could afford telephones and automobiles. We can learn two lessons from the *Literary Digest* mistake. First, the sampling frame is crucial. Second, the size of a sample is less important than whether or not it accurately represents the population. An excellent sample of 2500 will produce more accurate predications about the nearly 300 million in the U.S. population than a nonrepresentative sample of 10 million people.

accuracy. For very large populations (e.g., an entire nation), you never have all elements so you use information in a sample to estimate the population parameter. If you end up taking a statistics class and hear about "parameter estimation," this is where it comes from.

The sample is smaller than a target population. You can compute a **sampling ratio** to indicate what percent of the target population is in your sample. You simply divide sample size by target population. For example, a target population has 50,000 people and you draw a sample of 150 from it. Your sampling ratio is 150/50,000 = 0.003, or 0.3 percent. If the target population is 500 hospitals and you sample 100 of them, your sampling ratio is 100/500 = 0.20, or 20 percent.

Why Use a Random Sample?

Random samples are most likely to produce a sample that truly represents the population. However, sampling with a random selection processes requires a lot more work than nonrandom ones. In statistics, the word *random* refers to a random selection process, one that gives each element in a population an equal (or known) probability of being selected. Two critical features of true random processes are (1) they are purely mechanical or mathematical without human involvement, and (2) they allow us to calculate the probability of outcomes with great precision.

A random process makes it possible for us to estimate mathematically the degree of match between the sample and the population, or **sampling error.** Whenever you sample and do not have the entire population, the sample might deviate from the entire population. Sampling error indicates the size of this deviation or mismatch. Later in this chapter, we will look at how to minimize the sampling error.

The several kinds of random samples all have three key features:

- You must begin with an accurate sampling frame or list of elements in the target population.
- You must use a random selection process without subjective human decisions (e.g., a computer program, random number table).
- You must identify and pick a particular sampling element, rarely using substitutions.

sampling ratio the ratio of the sample size to the size of the target population.

sampling error the degree to which a sample deviates from a population.

For example, if you use a telephone directory as your sampling frame (actually is it inaccurate, as you will see later) and sample names for a telephone survey, you must reach the specific sampled household or person. This means calling back many times before giving up and going to a substitute randomly selected alternative. In the opening study by Dr. Connor, she called back seven times (different days, different times) before going to a substitute phone number in her sampling frame.

Types of Random Samples

1. Simple Random Samples. The simple random sample is the one on which other types of random samples are modeled. In simple random sampling, you

- First develop an accurate sampling frame,
- Next select elements from the frame based on to a mathematically random selection procedure,
- Then locate the exact selected elements to be in your sample.

In all random samples, you start by numbering each element in your sampling frame from 1 to the last element. Next, obtain a set of randomly generated numbers, from 1 to the largest number in your sampling frame. Most people do this with a special computer program that asks you to enter the size of sampling frame and the size of the sample; then the program produces a list of random numbers. Dozens of such programs are on the market; some are very inexpensive. Notice that you must decide the sample size before you can select elements. How large should your sample be? This is not simple to answer, so we will postpone answering it until later in this chapter. At this stage, the most important thing to remember is that using a bigger sample is not always better. The selection process you use is usually more important than sample size if you want a representative sample.

You may ask, After I select an element from the sampling frame, should I then return it to the sampling frame or do I keep it separate? You usually do not return it, or sample without replacement. Pure unrestricted random sampling is random sampling with replacement—that is, replacing an element after sampling it so you can selected again. In most situations with people as the unit, this makes no sense.

We can see the logic of simple random sampling with a favorite example of statisticians—sampling marbles from a jar. Let us say you have a large jar full of 5000 marbles, some blue and some white. The 5000 marbles are your target population. You want to estimate a population parameter, the percentage of blue marbles. You randomly select 100 marbles (you close your eyes, shake the jar, pick one marble, and repeat the procedure 100 times). You now have a random sample of marbles. Count the number of blue marbles in the sample to estimate the percentage of blue versus white marbles in the population. This is a lot easier than counting all 5000 marbles. Your sample has 52 white and 48 blue marbles. Does this mean that the population parameter is 48 percent blue marbles? Maybe or maybe not. Because of random chance, a specific sample might be off. You can check the results by dumping the 100 marbles back in the jar, mixing the marbles, and drawing a second random sample of 100 marbles. On the second try, your sample has 49 white marbles and 51 blue ones. Which is correct? You may ask, How good is this random sampling business if different samples from the same population can yield different results? You repeat the procedure over and over until you have drawn 130 different samples of 100 marbles each (see Figure 4.4 for results). Most people might empty the jar and count all 5000, but you want to see what is going on. The results of your 130 different samples reveal a clear pattern. The most common mix of blue and white marbles is 50/50. Samples that are close to that split are more frequent than those with uneven splits. The population parameter looks like 50 percent white and 50 percent blue marbles.

Mathematical proofs and tests like the one above both show that the pattern in Figure 4.4 is something that *always* happens when we draw many sample. The **sampling distribution** shows the same bell-shaped pattern whether your sample size is 1000 instead of 100; if there are 10 colors of marbles instead of 2; if the population has 100 mar-

sampling distribution a plot of many random samples, with a sample characteristic across the bottom and the number of samples indicated along the side.

■ **Figure 4.4**   Example of Sampling Distribution

Blue	White	Number of Samples
42	58	1
43	57	1
45	55	2
46	54	4
47	53	8
48	52	12
49	51	21
50	50	31
51	49	20
52	48	13
53	47	9
54	46	5
55	45	2
57	43	1
	Total	130

Number of blue and white marbles that were randomly drawn from a jar of 5,000 marbles with 100 drawn each time, repeated 130 times for 130 independent random samples.

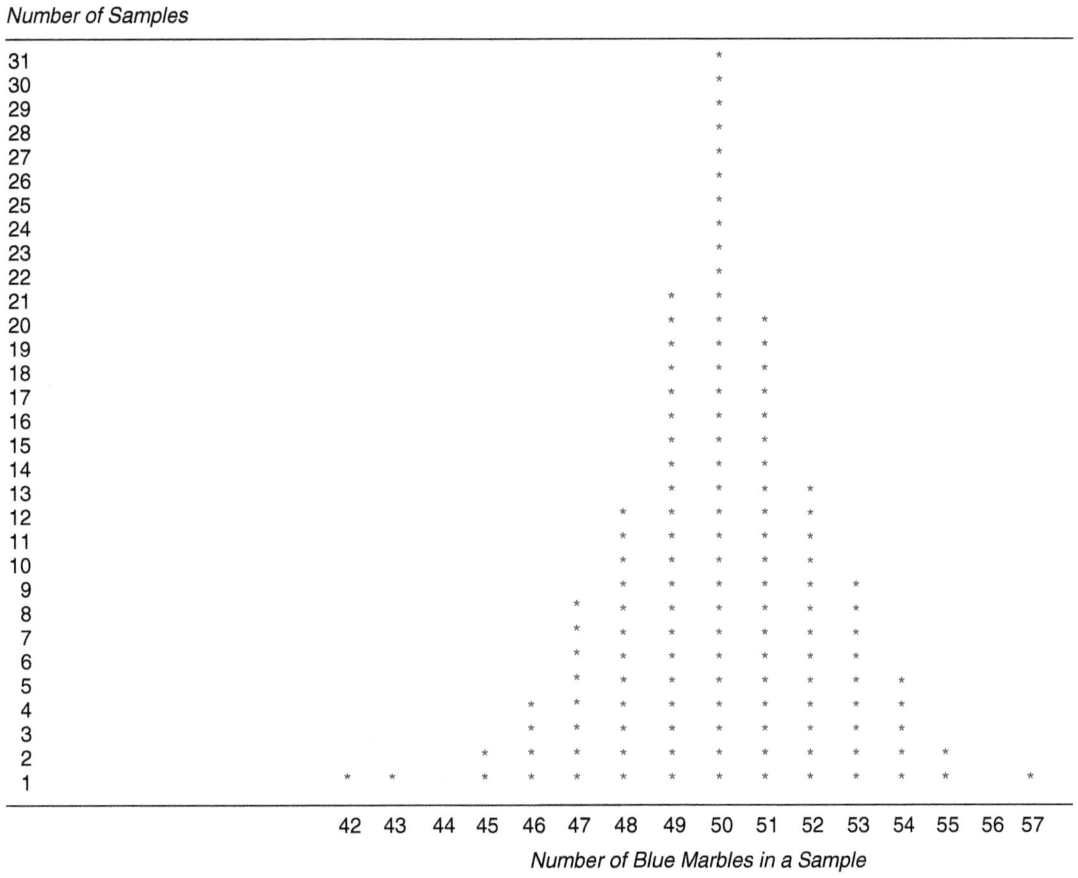

Number of Samples

Number of Blue Marbles in a Sample

bles or 10 million marbles instead of 5000; and if the population of interest is people, automobiles, or colleges instead of marbles. In fact, the more random samples you draw, the clearer the pattern becomes. The sampling distribution shows that over many separate samples, the true population parameter (i.e., the 50/50 split in the preceding example) is the most frequent result. Some samples deviate from it, but they are less common. Perhaps you heard of the bell-shaped or normal curve. If you plot many different random samples in the graph in Figure 4.4, you will see the bell-shaped curve in the sampling distribution (Figure 4.5). This curve is widely used in probability theory.

Mathematical proofs tell us that as we increase the number of random samples in a sampling distribution toward infinity, the bell-curve pattern and the population

■ Figure 4.5   Sampling Distribution with Bell-Shaped Curve Shown

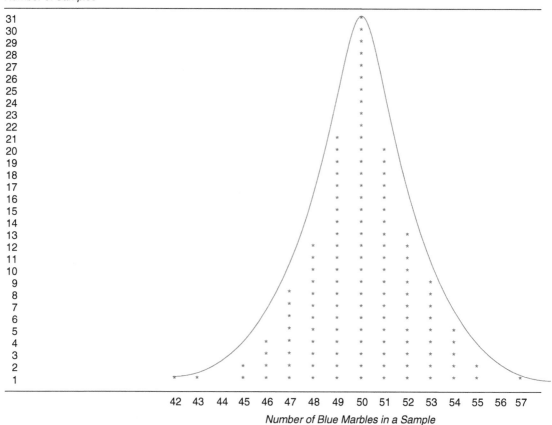

Number of Samples

Number of Blue Marbles in a Sample

parameter become more predictable. The sampling distribution forms a normal curve, and its midpoint will be the population parameter.

You may say, I only need one sample and do not have the time or energy to draw many different samples. You are not alone. Researchers rarely draw numerous samples. They use knowledge of what always happens to generalize from one sample to the population. The mathematical proof is about many samples, but it also allows us to calculate the probability of a particular sample being off from the population parameter. This is because we know that any one sample is somewhere in the bell-curve pattern of all possible samples that make up the sampling distribution. The

Summary Review   Ten Terms in Random Sampling

1. Population
2. Population parameter
3. Sample
4. Sampling distribution
5. Sampling element

6. Sampling error
7. Sampling ratio
8. Sampling frame
9. Target population
10. Universe

mathematics of bell-shaped curves lets us estimate the odds that one particular sample is near the bell center or off in one of its tails.

Random sampling does not guarantee that every random sample you pick perfectly represents the population. It means is that most times, a proper random sample yields results that are close to the population parameter. Moreover, the mathematics behind all this lets us estimate how close to the population parameter it may be. We use this same type of logic to calculate sampling errors and estimate the probability that a particular sample is unrepresentative. In short, we can use information from one sample to estimate what the sampling distribution is like. We can combine it with the mathematics about sampling distributions to estimate the chances of being far off from the true population parameter.

A central idea in random sampling, and many related areas of statistics, is that we do not have 100 percent accuracy 100 percent of the time. In reality, such accuracy is almost impossible in most endeavors. Life is full of risk and chance. Some activities have a high risk of serious mishap or death, such as skydiving, speeding while driving drunk, or being in a combat zone defusing a bomb. Other activities have a very low risk of serious mishap or death, such going to the local store, sitting in a classroom, or eating you lunch. We cannot predict an outcome with 100 percent accuracy, but we have a sense that that the probability of a specific outcome varies by type of activity.

We do not have 100 percent accuracy in random sampling, but we have is something extremely powerful. We can express our results precisely in terms of odds or probabilities. If we find that the odds of our results being off are very small, we place a high level of confidence in stating that what we learned from a sample is highly likely to be true in the entire population. As other studies with high levels of confidence find the same results, our belief that we have a true picture gets stronger. Later in the chapter, we will look at using these ideas to create a zone of confidence.

2. Systematic Sampling. If you cannot locate a computerized random number generator to create a pure random sample, there is a quasi-random method, **systematic sampling**. It was used in the past before computer number generations became widely available. You still must number each element in the sampling frame as in a simple random sample, but instead of using a pure random process to create a list of random numbers, you calculate a **sampling interval**. It tells you how many elements to skip in the sampling frame before you pick one for your sample. To calculate the sampling interval, divide the total number of elements in the frame by the sample size, and round to the nearest whole number. For instance, a sampling frame has 1800 names of clients for a social service agency, and you want to sample 300. To calculate a sampling interval, divide the number of clients by the sample size, or 1,800/300 = 6. This tells you to skip five names then pick the sixth one for your sample. You repeat this until you have the 300 names in the sample.

3. Stratified Sampling. In some situations, you want to make certain to include specific kinds of diversity in your sample. For example, you learn that people with four physical disabilities (walking, seeing, hearing, and speaking) are 8 percent of

systematic sampling an approximation to random sampling in which you select one in a certain number of sample elements; the number is from the sampling interval.

sampling interval the size of the sample frame over the sample size, used in systematic sampling to select units.

Making It Practical   How to Draw Simple Random and Systematic Samples

1. Number each case in the sampling frame in sequence. The list of 40 names is in alphabetical order, numbered from 1 to 40.
2. Decide on a sample size. We will draw two 25 percent (10-name) samples.
3. For a *simple random sample*, locate a random-number table (see excerpt). Before using random-number table, count the largest number of digits needed for the sample (e.g., with 40 names, two digits are needed; for 100 to 999, three digits; for 1,000 to 9,999, four digits). Begin anywhere on the random number table (we will begin in the upper left) and take a set of digits (we will take the last two). Mark the number on the sampling frame that corresponds to the chosen random number to indicate that the case is in the sample. If the number is too large (over 40), ignore it. If the number appears more than

once (10 and 21 occurred twice in the example), ignore the second occurrence. Continue until the number of cases in the sample (10 in our example) is reached.
4. For a *systematic sample*, begin with a random start. The easiest way to do this is to point blindly at the random number table, then take the closest number that appears on the sampling frame. In the example, 18 was chosen. Start with the random number, then count the sampling interval, or 4 in our example, to come to the first number. Mark it, and then count the sampling interval for the next number. Continue to the end of the list. Continue counting the sampling interval as if the beginning of the list was attached to the end of the list (like a circle). Keep counting until ending close to the start, or on the start if the sampling interval divides evenly into the total of the sampling frame.

No.	Name (Gender)	Simple Random	Systematic	No.	Name(Gender)	Simple Random	Systematic
01	Abrams, J. (M)			21	Hjelmhaug, N. (M)	Yes	
02	Adams, H. (F)	Yes	Yes (6)	22	Huang, J. (F)	Yes	Yes (1)
03	Anderson, H. (M)			23	Ivono, V. (F)		
04	Arminond, L. (M)			24	Jaquees, J. (M)		
05	Boorstein, A. (M)			25	Johnson, A. (F)		
06	Breitsprecher, P. (M)	Yes	Yes (7)	26	Kennedy, M. (F)		Yes (2)
07	Brown, D. (F)			27	Koschoreck, L. (F)		
08	Cattelino, J. (F)			28	Koykkar, J. (M)		
09	Cidoni, S. (M)			29	Kozlowski, C. (F)	Yes	
10	Davis, L. (F)	Yes*	Yes (8)	30	Laurent, J. (M)		Yes (3)
11	Droullard, C. (M)	Yes		31	Lee, R. (F)		
12	Durette, R. (F)			32	Ling, C. (M)		
13	Elsnau, K. (F)	Yes		33	McKinnon, K. (F)		
14	Falconer, T. (M)		Yes (9)	34	Min, H. (F)	Yes	Yes (4)
15	Fuerstenberg, J. (M)			35	Moini, A. (F)		
16	Fulton, P. (F)			36	Navarre, H. (M)		
17	Gnewuch, S. (F)			37	O'Sullivan, C. (M)		
18	Green, C. (M)		START, Yes (10)	38	Oh, J. (M)		Yes (5)
19	Goodwanda, T. (F)	Yes		39	Olson, J. (M)		
20	Harris, B. (M)			40	Ortiz y Garcia, L. (F)		

Excerpt from a Random-Number Table (for Simple Random Sample)

15010	18590	00102	42210	94174	22099
90122	38221	21529	00013	04734	60457
67256	13887	94119	11077	01061	27779
13761	23390	12947	21280	44506	36457
81994	66611	16597	44457	07621	51949
79180	25992	46178	23992	62108	43232
07984	47169	88094	82752	15318	11921

* Numbers that appeared twice in random numbers selected.

Tips for the Wise Researcher Drawing Systematic Samples

You do not want to start systematic sampling at the beginning of the list. If everyone always started at the beginning, names at the very beginning would never be in a sample. This violates the principle of being mathematically random—each element has an equal probability of being selected. There is a simple solution: First pick a random staring place, then start using your sampling interval. Once you get to the end of the list, just treat the list as if it were a loop. Continue counting off based on the sampling interval until you have your sample. You should be back where you began. In most cases, a simple random sample and a systematic sample yield virtually equivalent results. Dr. Connor used systematic sampling the study on guns and children that opened this chapter. She selected every tenth name from her four sampling frames (urban and rural households, without and without children).

You can usually substitute systematic sampling for a simple random method, but there is a situation when you should not use it. Do not use it in a situation when the elements in a sampling frame are in a cycle or repeated pattern. For example, your list is of people who got married in the past four years. The list is by couple, with the male name first and the female second (see Table 4.1). You will get a nonrepresentative sample if you use systematic sampling. Let us say you used systematic sampling with a sam-

■ **Table 4.1**   Problems with Systematic Sampling of Cyclical Data

Case	
1	Husband
2[a]	Wife
3	Husband
4	Wife
5	Husband
6[a]	Wife
7	Husband
8	Wife
9	Husband
10[a]	Wife
11	Husband
12	Wife

Random start = 2; Sampling interval = 4.
[a] Selected into sample.

pling interval of six. By taking every fourth name, your sample would include only females. The easiest solution is to use a simple random sample instead.

population you want to study. You want to be certain to include them as that same percent in your sample. **Stratified sampling** addresses this situation. In stratified sampling, you first divide the population into subpopulations (strata). To use stratified sampling, you must to have information about strata in the population and this can be a limitation. Next you create multiple sampling frames, one for each subpopulation. For example, you might have two sampling frames, one with the 8 percent with physical disabilities and another for the 92 percent who do not. Next, draw random samples, one from each sampling frame. Because you control the relative size of each stratum rather than letting random processes control it, your sample will be representative of the strata. In general, stratified sampling gives you a slightly more representative sample than simple random sampling (see Figure 4.6).

Here is a simple example. Let us say your population is all employees who work at Specialized Consulting Services, Inc. The Human Resources Department tells you that 8 percent of the 10,000 employees have the four above listed disabilities; 92 percent do not. You want a sample of 200. If you use simple random sampling, you might get the true 8 percent of employees with disabilities, or, due to random chance, you could get 7.5 percent, 9.2 percent, or 8.4 percent. Because you know the population parameter of employees with the four disabilities is exactly 8 percent and can create two sampling frames, you use a stratified sample. First, create two sampling frames for the 10,000 employees. One has the 800 employees with disabilities, and one has 9200 employees without the disabilities. You want a sample of 200, and 8 percent of 200 is 16, so you draw one random sample of 16 from the disabilities sampling frame. You then take the remaining 184 randomly from the sampling frame of employees

stratified sampling a type of random sampling in which a random sample is draw from multiple sampling frames, each for a part of the population.

■ **Figure 4.6**   Stratified Sampling

Step 1: Divide the population into subpopulations or strata

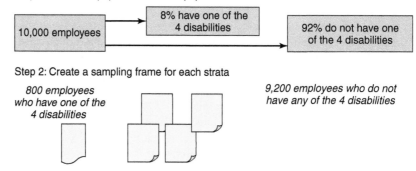

Step 2: Create a sampling frame for each strata

800 employees who have one of the 4 disabilities

9,200 employees who do not have any of the 4 disabilities

Step 3: Decide on a sample size and randomly select from each sampling frame

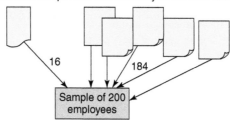

16   184

Sample of 200 employees

without disabilities. After you put the two samples of 16 and 184 together, your entire sample accurately represents the population with regard to this key feature.

4. Cluster Sampling. In many situations, there is no good sampling frame. Let us say you want to sample all teachers employed at colleges with over 500 students in North America. For a simple random sample, you need a sampling frame, but there is no list of all teachers. Instead of using a single sampling frame, you can use multiple-stage sampling with clusters (See Figure 4.7). A cluster is a grouping of the elements in the final sample that you are interested in. You treat the cluster as temporary sampling element itself. Maybe you cannot get a list of all teachers, but you can get an accurate list of all colleges that have a least 500 students. This is

cluster sampling a multistage sampling method in which clusters are randomly sampled, and then a random sample of elements is taken from sampled clusters.

Learning from History   General Social Survey Oversample

In most situations, you want each subgroup of a sample to be the exact same proportion as in the population. However, at times researchers select a proportion different from what it is in the population. This happens when a subgroup that is not a large proportion in the population and you wish to analyze it in depth. Let us say a subgroup is 10 percent of the population, and your sample is 200. You would only have 20 of the subgroup in the sample to analyze. If you wanted to look at details such as the education of divorced people with children in the subgroup, you might only have a small handful to examine. For this reason, researchers sometimes purposely oversample, or sample a larger percent of a subgroup than its size in the population, so they can analyze details of the subgroup. The General Social Survey, a sample of all adult Ameri-

cans (discussed in a later chapter), in 1987 and 2006 oversampled African Americans. A purely random sample of the U.S. population yielded 191 blacks, about 13 percent of the sample and the percent of African Americans in the U.S. adult population. Because researchers wanted to analyze details about African Americans, they conducted a separate sample of African Americans to increase the total number of blacks to 544. The 544 blacks are 30 percent of the disproportionate sample. The oversample allowed a more in-depth study of African Americans than using a sample of only 191. The larger sample of 544 better reflected the diversity in the African American subpopulation. When researchers wanted to look at the entire U.S. population, they only used the 191 African Americans in the pure random sample.

■ **Figure 4.7** Cluster Sampling Example

Step 1: Randomly select a county among the 3,143 counties and similar units in the United States.

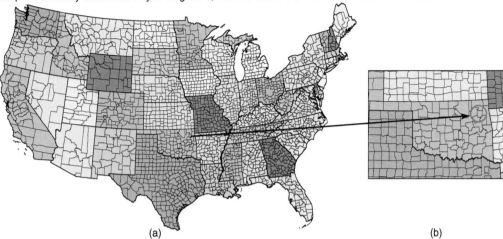

(a)   (b)

Step 2: Randomly select a city block or section of the county.

Step 3: Randomly select a household within the block or section.

Step 4: Randomly select an individual within the household.

Source: (city skyline) Frank Siteman/PhotoEdit Inc.; (aerial, homes) Bill Aron/PhotoEdit Inc.; (family) David Bacon/The Image Works.

your cluster. First, you sample clusters. In this case, the college is a cluster. You have a sampling frame of all two- and four-year colleges in North America. You might randomly pick 150 out of the 5000 colleges in your cluster sampling frame. Each college maintains a list of its teachers. You then draw a second sample of five teachers from each selected cluster, or college in this case. You would have a sample of 5 × 150 = 750 teachers. This has a big practical advantage. You can have a good sampling frame of clusters, even if it is impossible to create one for sampling elements. Once you have a sample of clusters, creating a sampling frame for the elements within each cluster is manageable. You can use more than two stages and have a set of larger clusters that contain small clusters, which in turn contain elements.

Cluster sampling has practical advantages and is less expensive than simple random sampling, but it is slightly less accurate. Each stage in cluster sampling introduces sampling errors. Generally, a multistage cluster sample will have more sampling errors than a single-stage random sample.

In cluster sampling, each cluster may not have the same number of elements. This requires you to make adjustments. For example, if all colleges in the North America had the exact same number of teachers, you could follow the procedure outlined above and take five from each college. However, some colleges have 50 teachers whereas others have over 2000. When the number of final elements for each cluster is of unequal size, you violate the principle that each element has an equal change of being in your sample unless you make an adjustment. To show you why, let us say you took five teachers from each sampled college. After sampling colleges, the probability of selecting a teacher from a college with 50 would be 5/50 or 10 percent. This not equal to selecting one of the 5 teachers from a college with 2000. The chances are 5 in 2000, or 0.25 percent. You need to adjust so that the number you sample from each cluster (or college, in this example) has an equal chance of being selected.

Details for adjusting samples with unequal clusters are beyond in this book, but the principle is easy to see. To create a representative cluster sample, you adjust the number of teachers your from a small versus a large college so that the probability of being selected is equal for all teachers. Let us say you sample 1 teacher from a college that has 50. The chances of selecting a teacher from that college are 1 in 50, or 2 percent. You want to sample the same percent for the large college. If

Example Study Box 2   Cluster Sample Example

Vaquera and Kao (2005) studied displays of affection among adolescent couples in which the couple were either from the same or different racial groups. Their data were from a national longitudinal study of adolescent health given to students in grades 7 through 12 in 80 randomly selected U.S. high schools. There were over 90,000 students in these schools. After the schools were sampled, approximately 200 students were sampled for interviews from within those schools. Thus, the first cluster was the school, and students were sampled from within the school. Because the schools were not of the same size, ranging from 100 to 3,000 students, the authors adjusted using probabilities proportionate to size (PPS). They found that 53 percent of respondents had a relationship with someone of the opposite sex in the previous 18 months. Whites and Blacks were more likely to have same-race relationships (90 percent) compared to Asians and Hispanics (70 percent). The authors found that same- and mixed-race couples differed little in showing intimate affection, but the interracial couples were less likely to do so in public than the same-race couples.

one of the sampled colleges has 2000 teachers, you take 2 percent of 2000 or 40 teachers. This means that after you sample the clusters (or colleges), to find out how many elements (teachers) each has, you must adjust your sample size from each cluster so that it is proportionate to the cluster's size. You take a few from small clusters and more from larger clusters. See Example Study: Cluster Sample Example for another application of cluster sampling.

THREE SPECIALIZED SAMPLING SITUATIONS

Random-Digit Dialing

Sometimes you want to interview members of the public or a large, spread-out collection by telephone. One difficulty is that a published telephone directory is a bad sampling frame. You miss four kinds of people if you use a telephone directory as the sampling frame:

- People without telephones
- People who have recently moved
- People with unlisted numbers
- People who only use a cell phone

Any telephone interview study will miss people without phones (e.g., poor, uneducated, and transient people), but this is usually not a big problem since nearly 97 percent of people in advanced industrialized nations have phones. As more people got phones, the percentage of them with unlisted numbers also grew. In some urban areas, over 50 percent of phone numbers are unlisted. In addition, people change their residences, so directories often have numbers for people who have left and do not include those who have recently moved into an area.

Random-digit dialing (RDD) avoids the problems of telephone directories by randomly sampling possible telephone numbers, not a list of people with telephones. This avoids the bias of using listed numbers. RDD is not difficult, and there are several specialized computer programs designed to make the calls. However, it takes time and can frustrate the person doing the calling. Many of the numbers may not be operating or may have been disconnected. As with any sampling that uses the telephone, you must retry reaching a selected, working number many times before giving up on it.

random-digit dialing computer based random sampling of telephone numbers.

Making It Practical   How RDD Works

In the United States, a telephone number has three parts: a three-digit area code, a three-digit exchange number or central office code, and a four-digit number. It is easy to create a list of all possible phone numbers by getting a list of active area codes and three-digit phone exchanges in the area code. Possible phone numbers in an exchange go from 0000 to 9999. In RDD, a computer randomly selects a number (0000 to 9999) in an exchange and makes the call. Some selected numbers are out of service, disconnected, pay phones, or numbers for businesses. Only some numbers are what you want—a working residential phone

number. Until you call, it is not possible to know whether the number is a working residential number. This means spending a lot of time getting phone disconnected numbers, numbers for businesses, and so forth.

The sampling element in RDD is the phone number, not the person or the household. Several families or individuals can share the same phone number, or each person may have a separate phone number or more than one number. This means that after contacting a person at a residential phone, a second stage is necessary, within-household sampling, to select the person that you will interview.

Within-Household Sampling

In many situations, it is difficult to create a sampling frame of individuals, but easy to create one of households. You may be able to get a list of households (i.e., a home, apartment, or other residential location in which one or more people reside). In a way, the household is a cluster in which there can be multiple sampling elements or individuals. Instead of picking the first person who answers the door, or a telephone, or who happens to read the mail first, you sample individuals within a household. For within-household sampling, you first determine the number of eligible members (such as adults over a certain age). If there is only one person, you choose that person. If there are two people or more, you randomly pick one. Let us say you want to consider all adults over 18 years old who reside in a household. At one house, you learn that there are three eligible people: a 50-year-old woman, a 53-year-old man, and a 20-year-old woman. To select a person randomly, you create selection rules, such as the following:

- if the last sampled person you interviewed was male, select a female (or vice versa).
- if there is one male or one female, interview that person.
- if there are two females/males, select the oldest one first, next time select the youngest.

Sampling Hidden Populations

hidden population a group that is very difficult to locate and may not want to be found and therefore is difficult to sample.

Sometimes a particular type of person is very difficult to locate, making sampling more complicated. A **hidden population** includes people who engage in concealed activities. They are often central in the studies of deviant or stigmatized behavior. Examples of hidden populations include users of illegal drugs, prostitutes, homosexuals, people with HIV/AIDS, people on parole, or homeless people. You will need

 Example Study Box 3   Finding Drug Users in a Small Midwestern Town

Draus and associates (2005) sampled a hidden population in a field research study of illicit drug users in four rural Ohio counties. They used a special technique, respondent-driven sampling (RDS). It is a version of snowball sampling and appropriate when members of a hidden population are likely to maintain contact with one another. RDS begins by identifying an eligible case or participant. The researchers give this person, called a "seed," referral coupons to distribute among other eligible people who engage in the same activity. For each successful referral, the "seed" receives some money. This process is repeated with several waves of new recruits until a point of saturation (no new people). Draus and associates interviewed a drug-using participant who was paid $50 for an initial two-hour interview and $35 for an hour-long follow-up interview. The participants received three referral coupons at the end of the initial interview. They got $10 for each eligible participant they referred who completed an initial interview. No participant received more than three referral coupons. Sometimes this yielded no new participants, but at other times more than the three people were recruited. In one case, a young man heard about the study at a local tattoo parlor. He called the study office in July 2003. He (participant 157) had been a powder cocaine user. During his interview, he said that he knew many other drug users. He referred two new participants (participants 161 and 146), who came in about one month later. Participant 161 did not refer anyone new, but participant 146 referred four new people, and two of the four (154 and 148) referred still others. Participant 154 referred four new people and 146 referred one new person, and that one person (participant 158) referred four others. Between June 2002 and February 2004, the researchers were able to interview 249 users of cocaine or methamphetamine with this sampling process.

Summary Review Types of Samples

Nonrandom Samples

1. Convenience	Select any element that is convenient.
2. Quota	Select nonrandomly a fixed number of elements into preset categories of the population.
3. Purposive	Use diverse methods to select elements that match narrowly defined criteria.
4. Snowball	Select based on direct or indirect connections to a few elements.

Random Samples

1. Simple Random	Select from a sampling frame using a pure random process.
2. Systematic	Select from a sampling frame using a sampling interval.
3. Stratified	Select randomly from multiple sampling frames that are preset categories in the population.
4. Cluster	Multiple samples, first randomly select clusters, then randomly select elements within each cluster.

Special Techniques

1. Random-Digit Dialing	Randomly select phone numbers out of all possible phone numbers.
2. Within Household	Randomly select individuals, usually by gender and age order, within a sampled household.
3. Hidden Populations	Use purposive or snowball methods to select elements.

to make adjustments for a hidden population because they are more difficult to sample than the general population of visible and accessible people. To sample hidden populations, you need to be creative with sampling principles. Sometimes you may use nonprobability sample techniques, such as purposive or snowball sampling (see Example Study Box 3: Finding Drug Users in a Small Midwestern Town).

INFERENCES FROM SAMPLE TO POPULATION

A probability sample allows you to make valid inferences from the sample to the population. You directly observe variables using the units from the sample, not all units in the population. You may have information on 750 sampled teachers, not the hundreds of thousands of North American teachers, or on 200 sampled employees, not all 10,000 who work for Specialized Consulting Services, Inc. In the chapter opening study, Dr. Connor had data on 1600 households in northern Ohio, not all households in the United States. The sample stands in for, or represents, the entire population. You are not interested in a sample in itself. Rather, you want to talk about the population, so you use the data on the sample to do this. When you draw a random sample, you want to minimize any gap between the sample and population, or sampling error, to make inferences. Next, we will look at what affects sample error size.

How to Reduce Sampling Errors

The detailed mathematics to calculate the sampling error are beyond this book, but we can look at a conceptual picture so you understand what is happening. Imagine you are the manager of XYZ department store. Last year, 90,000 shoppers visited the department store. You do not know it, but exactly 69 percent were female (population parameter). For your sample, you picked 10 days at random. The store has only four entrances, and you position cameras and station observers at each entrance. During the 10 days, 800 shoppers entered and you determined how many were male and how many were female. Purely by random chance, you might get 66 percent female in any 10-day sample. If I estimate the population parameter to be 66 percent female, I will be off from what is true in the total population. This is sampling error; it is the 3 percent difference between the 69 percent population parameter and 66 percent in your sample.

Sampling error assumes random sampling and is influenced by two factors: the sample size and the diversity of cases in the sample:

- The larger the sample size, the smaller the sampling error.
- The greater the homogeneity (or the less the diversity), the smaller its sampling error.

If you have a large sample (8000 randomly selected from 80,000) and there is very little diversity among cases, the sampling error will be tiny. If you have a small sample (80 randomly selected from 80,000) and there is great diversity among cases, the sampling error will be very large and your sample may not accurately represent the population.

How Large Should My Sample Be?

A large sample size alone does not guarantee a representative sample. A large sample without random sampling or with a poor sampling frame will be less representative than a smaller one with random sampling and an excellent sampling frame.

Calculating sample size mathematically requires making sophisticated assumptions, estimating population size and diversity, knowing how many variables you plan to examine, determining how confident you want to be, and determining the degree of accuracy you require. The mathematics and calculations are beyond the level of this book. Most people just use "rules of thumb." These are rough approximations based on target population size, assuming one or a few variables, moderate population diversity, and medium accuracy (such as getting within 3 percent of the population parameter). Table 4.2 provides sample sizes for a range of target population sizes (50 to 100 million).

Notice from Table 4.2 that the sampling ratio is very large when the target population is small. When your population is under 500, you will need over one-half the population in your sample to be highly confident and accurate. If your population

■ **Table 4.2**   Sample Sizes for Two Levels of Confidence and Various Population Sizes

Target Population Size	95 Percent Confident	99 Percent Confident
50	48	49
200	168	180
500	340	393
1,000	516	648
5,000	879	1347
25,000	1023	1717
100,000	1056	1810
250,000	1063	1830
1,000,000	1066	1840
100,000,000	1067	1843

is under 100, you might as well take everyone in the sample. However, if your population is 25,000, you need less than 10 percent. This percentage gets smaller as the population grows in size. Without getting into the complexity of this, three simple principles can help you make sense of what is important:

1. For small populations (less than 500), you need over half or more in your sample, and the required sample size grows very fast as the population size gets smaller.
2. For target populations over 5000, you need 17.5 percent or 27 percent of the population, depending on confidence. Sample size changes very little as the population size grows larger.
3. Once your target population is over 250,000, the sample size hardly changes at all.

Practically, this means that if you want to sample a very small target population, such as the 50 employees of the local fast food outlet, you might as well include everyone, or a sample ratio of close to 100 percent. However, to sample a city of 250,000 people, you can be equally accurate with a sample of 1063 in your sample, or a sampling ratio of 0.4 percent. The main idea about sample sizes is that *the smaller the population, the bigger the sampling ratio must be for an accurate sample.* Larger populations permit smaller sampling ratios for equally good samples because as the population get bigger, returns in accuracy for sample size quickly shrink. This is why random sampling is so powerful and efficient when you want estimates about large populations.

How to Create a Zone of Confidence

The term **confidence interval** expresses an idea that you may be familiar with already. When reporters discuss poll results, they say, "the margin of error being plus or minus 2 percentage points." They are using a simple version of confidence intervals. After you draw a random sample, you may look at a characteristic or measure you get from the sample, such as the average income percent saying "agree" to a question. From the above discussion of sampling error, you know this does not mean that the sample measure is identical to what is in the population, or the population parameter. You use the sample results to estimate the population parameter.

The mathematics around a sampling distribution helps us estimate a zone or range around what we find in a sample within which the population parameter will be. *Interval* in confidence interval is this zone or range around what you found in sample. *Confidence* in confidence interval refers to the probability that the population parameter falls within the interval. A typical level of confidence is 95 percent. It means you can be 95 confident that the true population parameter falls within the interval. As you saw in Table 4.2, a higher level of confidence (99 percent) requires you to have a slightly larger sample size, everything else being identical. Sample size affects the confidence interval. Everything else being the same, as your sample size gets bigger, the interval gets narrower.

The mathematical calculations for sampling errors or confidence intervals build on the ideas of the sampling distribution. For example, you cannot say, "There are precisely 2500 red marbles in the jar based on a random sample." You can say, "I am 95 percent certain that the population parameter of red marbles is between 2450 and 2550." You can combine characteristics of the sample (e.g., its size and variation) to set up an interval and level of confidence. Let us say you have two identical samples except that one is larger. A larger sample will have a smaller sampling error and a narrower confidence interval. A narrow confidence interval lets you be more precise when estimating the population parameter.

We will not go into the mathematics involved but illustrate the basic ideas with an example to show how sample size reduces the sample error, which in turn can change the confidence interval. Let us say you want to know how many people are

confidence interval a zone, above and below the estimate from a sample, within which a population parameter is likely to be.

■ **Figure 4.8**   Confidence Interval with Sample Size of 100. 99% Confidence

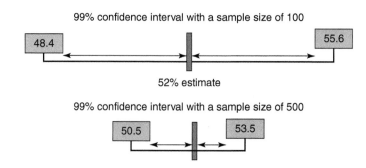

99% confidence interval with a sample size of 100

48.4 ◀————————————▶ 55.6

52% estimate

99% confidence interval with a sample size of 500

50.5 ◀——▶ 53.5

likely to support a referendum to add a tax for a new school in a city with 5000 eligible voters (target population). You want to be 99 percent confident. You get a good sampling frame and use simple random sampling. At first, you draw a sample of 100 people and find that 52 percent support the referendum. Your confidence interval is 3.6 percent above or below that number, or 48.4 to 55.6 percent support. In other words, you can be 99 percent certain that the population parameter (true vote intention in the population) lies somewhere between 48.4 and 55.6. It is too close to call, and it could easily go either way. You want to be more certain, so you draw a second sample. This time you increase it to 500 eligible voters. Again you find that 51 percent support the referendum, but your confidence interval with this larger sample size is narrower. It is 1.5 percent above or below, or from 50.5 to 53.5 percent. It now looks as if it will be close, but the referendum is likely to pass (see Figure 4.8).

WHAT HAVE YOU LEARNED?

You learned about sampling in this chapter. Sampling is widely used in social research. You learned about types of sampling that are, and that are not, based on random processes. Only some nonrandom types of samples are acceptable. Qualitative research is most likely to use nonrandom sampling. In general, random or probability sampling yields the most representative sample. It is widely used by quantitative researchers because they often wanted to generalize from a small number of cases to a much larger collection. Random sampling can produce samples that represent the population accurately. Random samples also enable you to use powerful statistical techniques.

In addition to simple random sampling, you learned about systematic, stratified, and cluster sampling. This book does not cover the statistical theory used in random sampling. However, from the discussion of sampling error and sample size, you saw that random sampling produces more accurate and precise sampling. You may wish to express the results from a sample as confidence interval.

Before moving on to the next chapter, it may be useful to restate a fundamental principle of social research: Do not compartmentalize the steps of the research process; rather, learn to see the interconnections between the steps. Research design, measurement, sampling, and specific research techniques are interdependent. Unfortunately, the constraints of presenting information in a textbook necessitate presenting the parts separately, in sequence. In practice, researchers think about data collection when they design research and develop measures for variables. Likewise, sampling issues influence research design, measurement of variables, and data collection strategies. As you will see in future chapters, good social research depends on simultaneously controlling quality at several different steps—research design, conceptualization, measurement, sampling, and data collection and handling. The researcher who makes major errors at any one stage may make an entire research project worthless.

KEY TERMS

APPLY WHAT YOU'VE LEARNED

Activity 1: Sociogram and Snowball Sampling

Snowball samples use social networks. Researchers represent a social network by drawing a sociogram—a diagram of circles connected with lines. For example, Sally and Tim do not know each other directly, but each has a good friend, Susan, so they have an indirect connection. All three are part of the same friendship network. The circles represent each person or case, and the lines represent friendship or other linkages (see Figure 4.9).

■ **Figure 4.9   Sociogram of Friendship Relations**

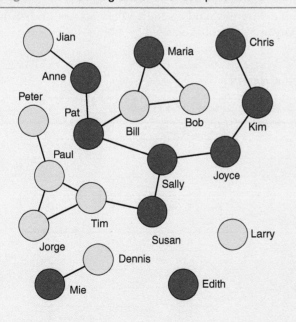

What to do:

Identity two people who you know but who are not your best friends, and who may or may not know one another. Ask each to name three of his/her close friends. Contact those six people, Ask them to name their three closest friends. Repeat a third time. Now draw a sociogram or map of interconnections. Show when more than one person named another person in the same network. This could be the basis for a snowball sample of this network (or two networks, if they do not overlap).

Name 1 you started with

_____   Name 2 _____

Name 1's 3 Friends   Name 2's 3 Friends

1A_____   2A_____

1B_____   2B_____

1C_____   2C_____

1A's 3 Friends   2A's 3 Friends

_____   _____

_____   _____

_____   _____

1B's 3 Friends   2B's 3 Friends

_____   _____

_____   _____

_____   _____

1C's 3 Friends   2C's 3 Friends

_____   _____

_____   _____

_____   _____

Draw the sociogram of the 26 people you identified.

Activity 2: Sampling Frame

Let us say you would like to sample all people in a region of the United States. You could try to get a list of everyone with a driver's license. Some people do not have a driver's license, and the lists of those with licenses, even if updated regularly, quickly go out of date. You could try income tax records. But not everyone pays taxes; some people cheat and do not pay, others have no income and do not have to file, others have died or have not begun to pay taxes, and still others have entered or left the area since the last time taxes were due. You could try telephone directories, but they are not much better; some people are not listed in a telephone directory, some people have unlisted numbers, and others have recently moved. With a few exceptions (e.g., a list of all students enrolled at a university), sampling frames are frequently inaccurate. A sampling frame can include some of those outside the target population (e.g., a telephone directory that lists people who have moved away) or might omit some of those inside it (e.g., those without telephones).

What to do:

Compare three possible sampling frames for overlap. First, contact a local government official in charge of voter lists (usually an elections official) for a local voting district. Ask if you could have a list of registered voters (this is generally public information). Next, get a published telephone directory that includes the same area. Lastly, get either a list of property tax records from a county clerk for the district or contact the department of motor vehicles for driver's license holders. Begin with voter registration list. Take 100 names from the list. How many of these names do not appear in the published telephone directory? How many of these names do not appear in the property tax or the driver license records?

Develop a chart the following for recordkeeping.

Voter Registration Name	Phone Directory		Driver's License		Tax Record	
_____	Y	N	Y	N	Y	N
_____	Y	N	Y	N	Y	N
_____	Y	N	Y	N	Y	N
_____	Y	N	Y	N	Y	N

Activity 3: Simple Random versus Systematic Sampling

Making it Practical Box 1 illustrates simple random sampling and systematic sampling. Notice that I picked different names in each sample. For example, H. Adams is in both samples, but C. Droullard is only in the simple random sample. In fact, it is rare for any two random samples to be identical. My sampling frame had 20 males and 20 females (gender is in parenthesis after each name).

My simple random sample yielded 3 males and 7 females. My systematic sample yielded 5 males and 5 females.

What to do:

Use different random numbers; try taking the first two digits and beginning at the end (e.g., 11 from 11921, then 43 from 43232). Draw a random sample of 10 names. Now draw a new systematic sample of 10 names with a different random start. What did you find? How many are there of each sex?

A RANDOM SAMPLE OF 10 NAMES

Random Number	Name Picked	Systematic Sample Name Picked
1. _____	_____	_____
2. _____	_____	_____
3. _____	_____	_____
4. _____	_____	_____
5. _____	_____	_____
6. _____	_____	_____
7. _____	_____	_____
8. _____	_____	_____
9. _____	_____	_____
10. _____	_____	_____

Activity 4: Sampling Details Reported in the Media

Locate five newspaper articles or magazine stories that discuss using a sample to get study results. Answer the following four questions to see how sampling was used.

1. What was the population examined in the study?
2. Did the researchers use probability or nonprobability sampling? Which sample type did they use?
3. How large was the sample? Do you also have the size of the population so you can estimate the sampling ratio, or is the sampling ratio given?
4. Was a margin of error or confidence interval given? How large is it? Are you told both the interval size (margin of error) and level of confidence (e.g., 95 percent)?

REFERENCES

Connor, Susan D. 2005. "The Association Between Presence of Children in the Home and Firearm-Ownership and Storage Practices." *Pediatrics* 115:38–43.

Draus, Paul J., Harvey Siegal, Robert Carlson, Russell Falck, and Jichuan Wang. 2005. "Cracking in the heartland." *Sociological Quarterly* 46:165–189.

Vaquera, Elizabeth and Grace Kao. 2005. "Private and public displays of affection among interracial and intraracial adolescent couples." *Social Science Quarterly* 86:484–508.

CHAPTER 5

Measuring Social Life

Sonda Dawes/The Image Works

A chronic disease or condition is one that does not end or that keeps returning. For people with a chronic condition, medical professionals look beyond a patient's immediate physical pain or problems to consider how medical treatments affect his or her quality of life. When a person will live for years with a condition such as diabetes, eyesight loss, serious walking problems, cancer, cognitive impairment, or liver malfunction, quality of life becomes a serious concern. Medical professionals must define quality of life and measure it before they can suggest ways to improve and/or sustain patient quality of life. Quality of life is defined as a person's physical, psychological, and social well-being. Measures of it include a person's subjective experience, physical ability, emotional condition (contented or depressed), ability to complete daily and social activities, overall health functions, and pain. The medical community has measured quality of life by combining survey questionnaires with direct physical measures (e.g., the ability to lift a certain weight or to stand unassisted). Medical professionals combine ratings from the patient, close family members, and nursing staff and use these measures to monitor a person across time and to evaluate alternative treatments. About 5 to 7 percent of the U.S. and Canadian populations have the chronic disease diabetes. One study (Smith 2004) matched 42,154 diabetics to a nondiabetic person on age, sex, race, ethnicity, marital status, and health care access. Both groups completed a quality of life survey. The diabetics showed lower quality of life on every measure. Compared to nondiabetics, people with diabetes reported more days per month that they were impaired by physical health, poor mental health and depression, limited activity, pain, stress, inadequate sleep, and low energy. However, not all diabetics were equal. Diabetics who had trouble paying for health care, who had attained a lower level of education, and who lacked regular employment reported a much lower a quality of life. Our ability to measure ideas like quality of life helps us to understand conditions and make decisions. This chapter examines how to create measures of features in social life in the research process.

In the previous chapter, you learned about sampling. Sampling and measurement share a similar logic: Connect specifics you observe in the empirical world to an abstract idea that you cannot see directly. You infer from the specific observed data, in a sample or in a measure, to an entire population or to abstract ideas about the operations in the world.

WHY MEASURE?

You may have heard of the Stanford Binet IQ test to measure intelligence, the Index of Dissimilarity to indicate racial segregation in a city, the J. D. Powers customer satisfaction measure for new cars, the poverty line to determine whether someone is poor, and uniform crime reports to assess crime trends. We measure for many reasons: to evaluate an explanation, test a hypothesis, provide empirical support for a theory, make a decision about medical treatment, or study an applied issue. Measurement is a critical task in doing research. It transforms our ideas and general observations into specific and concrete data. Measuring helps you share thoughts and observations with other people more effectively.

In research, measurement issues are more central for quantitative than qualitative data. In a quantitative data study, you create the measures early in the research process before you collect any data. To do this, you begin with a clearly thought out idea or concept. Next, you create a way to capture it precisely and accurately as numbers. In a qualitative data study, you also want to capture ideas or concepts but do so without numbers. This often involves an inductive approach (see Chapter 2 on inductive versus deductive approaches to research). In all social research, you will want to measure types, amounts, frequency, intensity, duration, location, and so forth about the concepts you wish to study.

Measures can profoundly shape both research outcomes and larger social issues. Consider intelligence. Psychologists debate what intelligence means and how to measure it. Most intelligence tests used in schools, on job applications, or in statements about racial or other inherited superiority measure only one type of intelligence, analytic reasoning (i.e., a capacity to think abstractly and to infer logically). Most experts agree that we have several types of intelligence in addition to the analytic type. Some have identified practical, creative intelligence, social-interpersonal, emotional, body-kinesthetic, musical, or spatial intelligences. If we have many types of intelligence but schools and businesses are only measuring and using one type, then schools and businesses are limited in how they evaluate, promote, and recognize people's contributions. The ways we measure intelligence influence the ability to value diverse human abilities.

Here is another example. Human service agencies allocate assistance from social programs (e.g., subsidized housing, food aid, health care, child care, etc.) to people identified as being poor. Government agencies shift funding to an area based on the number of poor people living there. Politicians and economists argue over rising and falling poverty rates. Who is poor? Some say a person is poor if he or she cannot afford essential food required to prevent malnutrition. Others say a person is poor if his or her annual income is less than one-half of the average (median) income of everyone else. Still others say that someone is poor if he or she earns less than a "living wage." A living wage is the income required to meet minimal community standards for health, safety, hygiene, housing, clothing, diet, transportation, and so forth. How we define and measure poverty greatly influences agency decision making and the daily living conditions of millions of people. Measuring poverty is controversial (see Learning from History: Who Is Poor?), but without a measure of it, we cannot make decisions.

Cleve Bryant/PhotoEdit Inc.

Learning from History Who Is Poor?

There are many definitions of poverty and ways to measure it. Most studies examine relative poverty (i.e., comparing people to others) and absolute poverty (i.e., requirement for bare physical survival). The most common measure internationally is a certain percentage (e.g., 50 percent) below the average income (i.e., median or midpoint) level of a society, and social scientists agree that it is the most accurate method. The United States created its official "poverty line" in the 1960s. The poverty line was a temporary measure with an arbitrary dollar amount created for the bureaucratic purpose of estimating the size of the poor population. The line was based on a preexisting study of the U.S. Department of Agriculture on the amount a family would need to spend on food to meet its minimal nutritional needs. To estimate minimal living costs, officials multiplied minimal food costs by three. This is because in the 1950s most poor people devoted roughly one-third of their incomes to buying food. Ever since, the poverty line has become a permanent fixture for official reports and the delivery of a range of social programs in the U.S. It has not been updated except for inflation increases and adjustments for the number of family members. Experts agree that the current measure is inadequate and have repeatedly made recommendations to recalculate the poverty line. They note changes in living conditions, new services provided to people, and that few people spend one-third of their income on food. Every attempt at a change has become embroiled in political controversies. This is because almost every suggestion for an improvement in measurement accuracy would classify far more people as being poor than by the current poverty line. Few politicians want the publicity or cost of suddenly having many more people officially called poor, so a poverty measure widely acknowledged to have serious flaws continues.

MAKING ASPECTS OF THE SOCIAL WORLD VISIBLE

You use many measures in daily life. For example, this morning I woke up and hopped onto a bathroom scale to see how well my diet is working. I glanced at a thermometer to find out whether to wear a coat. Next, I got into my car and checked the gas gauge to be sure I could make it to campus. As I drove, I watched the speedometer so I would not get a speeding ticket. By 8:00 A.M., I had measured weight, temperature, gasoline volume, and speed—all measures of the physical world. Such precise, well-developed measures in daily life are fundamental in the natural sciences. We also measure the social world, but usually in less exact terms. We measure when we say that a restaurant is excellent, that Pablo is smart, that Karen has a negative attitude toward life, that Johnson is prejudiced, that children in Sunny Valley School perform at below average levels, or that the real estate market in East River City is hot. However, such everyday judgments as "really prejudiced" or "hot market" are imprecise, vague intuitive measures.

Measurement extends the range of our senses. You know that the astronomer or biologist uses a telescope or the microscope to extend his or her natural vision. In addition to extending our senses, scientific measurement produces a more exact measure than ordinary experience, and it varies less with the specific observer. A thermometer gives you more specific, precise communicable information about temperature than touch can. Likewise, a good scale gives you more specific, constant, and precise information about the weight of a 5-year-old girl than you get by lifting her and calling her "heavy" or "light." Social scientific measures provide precise information about features of the social world.

Measures make visible ideas that otherwise are unseen. This happens in social and physical worlds. For example, you cannot see a magnetic field with your natural senses. Scientists had the idea that magnetism existed as a physical force but they could not see it directly, so they developed ways to observe the effects of invisible magnetic fields indirectly. For instance, metal flecks move near a magnet. The magnet lets us "see" or measure invisible magnetic fields that at first we could only imagine. Natural scientists have invented thousands of measures to "see" very tiny things (molecules or insect organs) or very large things (huge geological landmasses or planets) that are not observable through ordinary senses. By extending the reach of our senses, measurement extends our range of knowledge.

We can easily see some of what we want to measure (e.g., age, sex, skin tone, eye shape, etc.), but we cannot directly observe many other things of interest (e.g., employee satisfaction, poverty, a child's self-esteem, sex roles, desire to purchase, or quality of life). Just as natural scientists invent indirect measures to observe the "invisible" forces of the physical world, social researchers create measures to reveal difficult-to-see aspects of the social world.

MEASURING WITH NUMBERS OR WORDS

In all research, we collect data using careful, systematic methods. Depending on whether your data are quantitative or qualitative, this process differs in four ways: timing, direction, form, and linkages.

1. *Timing.* In a quantitative data study, first think about concepts as variables. Convert them into specific measurement actions at the planning stage before and separate from gathering or analyzing data. In a qualitative data study, create measures of concepts as you collect the data. The processes of thinking about concepts, collecting data, and starting to analyze qualitative data all blur together. Measurement is integrated with other research activities and not a separate stage.

2. *Direction.* You learned about the inductive and deductive directions in Chapter 2. Most quantitative data research follows a deductive route: Start with the abstract idea and end with visible empirical data. Most qualitative data research follows an inductive route: Start with empirical data and end with a mix of ideas and data. In both, the process is interactive, with measuring affecting ideas and vice versa.

3. *Data form.* In quantitative data study, measures produce data in the form of numbers. You go from an abstract idea to a data collection technique that will yield precise numerical information. In a qualitative data study, data might in the form of numbers, but more often, they are written or spoken words, actions, sounds, symbols, physical objects, or visual images (e.g., maps, photographs, videos, etc.). Instead of converting all observations into a single medium, numbers, you leave the data in many diverse shapes, sizes, and forms. They stay as words, images, quotes, and descriptions instead of all becoming numbers.

4. *Linkages.* In all research, you link ideas to observable empirical data. In a quantitative data study, you reflect on and refine ideas and then create specific measurement techniques (such as a questionnaire) to capture the ideas. Logic links ideas to the measures that you use to gather empirical evidence. You may begin with a very abstract idea ("quality of life"), link it to a less abstract idea ("being socially engaged"), then link it to a specific measurement act (answers to a survey question, "How often do you see friends socially?"). In a qualitative data study, you try to make sense of data by actively creating new, or adapting existing, concepts. You simultaneously gather data and try to link data to ideas that can clarify the data's meaning. You may first develop an idea (such as "dining in isolation") only as you gather the data (observe many people eating silently alone at a nursing home). The idea, once developed, may influence your subsequent observations.

Two Parts of the Measurement Process

conceptualization refining an idea by giving it a very clear, explicit definition.

All measurement builds on two processes: conceptualization and operationalization. **Conceptualization** is refining thoughts about an idea and putting your thinking into words so that other people can better understand the idea. As you put ideas into words, you provide a **conceptual definition**. There is no magical way to create a definition. You must think carefully, be observant, consult with others, read what others have said, and try out several possible definitions.

Let us say you want develop a conceptual definition of *discrimination*. Perhaps you think it means a "negative action." To begin conceptualization, you consider multiple sources: personal experience, deep thought, discussions with other people, and the scholarly literature. You reflect on what you already know, ask others what they think about it, and look up its definitions. As you think about it, the core idea should get clearer and you may need to sort out many alternative definitions.

Let us say that you settle on, "Discrimination is the act of treating people unequally simply because they belong to a social category or group." You conclude that discrimination involves the treatment of a kind of people, and it refers to "others" or to an outgroup (a group to which a person does not belong). You expand your thinking to consider types of discrimination based on various types of groups that a person may treat unequally—racial, religious, age, gender, and so forth.

As you conceptualize, you also need to consider the unit of analysis (see Chapter 2 on units of analysis) and develop a measure with a unit of analysis that fits your conceptual definition. For example, discrimination is an action by individuals, so the individual could be the unit of analysis. However, groups and organizations (e.g., families, clubs, churches, companies, or media outlets) may also treat outgroups unequally (such as not talking to a person, not hiring someone), so you could make the group or organization the unit of analysis. To conceptualize and develop a measure, you must decide on a unit of analysis. Do you want to look at discrimination only as individual actions or as actions by groups, organizations, and institutions?

Part of the conceptualization process is to distinguish your concept from closely related ones. Often ideas overlap with others and blur into one another. Good measurement requires that you separate the concept you want to study from others. For example, How are prejudice, racism and stereotypes similar to or different from discrimination?

Conceptualization requires you to think carefully about your concept. You might define *discrimination* as "a negative action of unequal treatment by a person directed toward an outgroup member based on stereotypes." This is more precise than your initial idea, "negative action," and it is now linked to other ideas, such as outgroup and stereotype. You reevaluate each part of your definition, such as "negative action." Can a positive action be a kind of discrimination? Can there be positive discrimination, or unequal treatment in favor of a group based on stereotypes? As you see, the process of conceptualization requires you to state ideas clearly and in explicit terms for others to see.

Operationalization links your conceptual definition to a specific set of measurement procedures, or its **operational definition.** An operational definition might be one or more survey questions, a method of observing events in a field setting, or a way to count symbols in the mass media. It is a specific activity to observe, document, or represent a conceptual definition. For example, Gee, Spencer, Chen, and Takeuchi (2007) wanted to see whether Asian Americans who experienced more everyday discrimination suffered worse health. Their operational definition of "everyday discrimination" was how people answered nine survey questions about routine unfair treatment:

1. You are treated with less courtesy than other people.
2. You are treated with less respect than other people.
3. You receive poorer service than other people at restaurants or stores.
4. People act as if they think you are not smart.
5. People act as if they are afraid of you.
6. People act as if they think you are dishonest.

conceptual definition defining a variable or concept in theoretical terms with assumptions and references to other concepts.

operationalization the process of linking a conceptual definition with specific of measures.

operational definition defining a concept as specific operations or actions that you carry out to measure it.

Learning from History Measuring Social Distance

The famous sociologist Emory Borgadus (1882–1973) wrote 275 books and articles. Twenty-seven dealt with the idea of social distance. In a 1925 article ("Social Distance and Its Origins," *Journal of Applied Sociology* 9:216–226), he outlined the concept of social distance. He saw social distance as a force that influenced most social relationships and indicated social-emotional closeness and trust in others. He tried to capture how close or distant people felt toward people of different racial and ethnic categories. Researchers still use variations of it today. Borgadus measured social distance by asking people whether they were willing to interact and establish relationships with members of racial and ethnic groups other than their own by using seven statements. He asked people how they would feel to have a member of group X

a. in close kinship marriage
b. in my club as a personal chum

c. in my street as a neighbor
d. as a fellow employee in my occupation
e. as a fellow citizen in my country
f. as a visitor only in my country
g. I would exclude all members of X from my country.

In the original list, X stood for 30 racial-nationality groups. After people rated how they felt toward each group, Borgadus developed a picture of social distance among groups. The results showed that the dominant white majority felt very socially distant from some groups and socially close to others. Borgadus created an average distance score for each of the 30 groups. In subsequent years, other researchers replicated the study and found slight changes in how distant social groups feel from one another. Others extended the idea of social distance to issues beyond racial-ethnic relations.

Tips for the Wise Researcher Creating a Good Measure

1. Remember the conceptual definition. You must match the measure to a specific conceptual definition of the idea or concept. Without a clear conceptual definition, you cannot develop a good measure.
2. Keep an open mind. Do not get locked into a single measure or type of measure. Be creative and constantly look for better measures.
3. Borrow from others. Do not be afraid to borrow from other researchers, as long as you give them credit. You can find good ideas for measures in other studies or modify the measures of others.

4. Anticipate difficulties. Logical and practical problems often arise when you try to measure. Sometimes you can anticipate a problem and avoid it with careful forethought and planning. Other times, you only can adjust and modify the measure based on experiences with using it.
5. Do not forget your unit of analysis. Tailor a measure to the units of analysis of a study. You will want a measure that can generalize to the universe of interest. (See the discussion of universe in Chapter 2.)

7. People act as if you are not as good as they are.
8. You are called names or insulted.
9. You are threatened or harassed.

If a person's answers indicated that many of these actions occurred to him or her on a regular basis, the researchers considered it as empirical evidence of routine discrimination.

Quantitative Conceptualization and Operationalization

Measuring of quantitative data flows in a three-part sequence:

1. *Conceptualization* Think through the idea and create a conceptual definition of it.

2. *Operationalization* Link the conceptual definition to specific measurement procedures.
3. *Measurement* Apply the operational definition to collect the data.

The process connects three levels of reality. The three levels, from the most abstract to the most concrete, are conceptual, operational, and empirical.

Starting with the most abstract level of ideas, you can specify the relationship between two concepts to form a **conceptual hypothesis.** After you develop a conceptual definition of each variable and conceptual hypothesis, you create measures or operationalize the variables. Using the operational definitions of variables, you can create an **empirical hypothesis.** It is a restatement of the conceptual hypothesis in operational terms. Lastly, at the level of the visible, concrete empirical world, you use operational definitions of variables to gather data. Often called indicators, these measures indicate the presence and degree of variables. You can use statistics such as correlations to determine the degree of empirical association among the indicators. Findings of empirical associations among indicators test the empirical hypothesis that connects logically back to the conceptual hypothesis.

Mikael Karlsson/Arresting Images

To see an application of these ideas let us look at the causal hypothesis (discussed in Chapter 2) tested by Weitzer and Tuch (see Appendix C). They began with four concepts:

1. Whether a person is a member of the dominant or nondominant racial group,
2. A person's belief that the police are or are not racially biased,
3. Number and type of experiences with the local police, and
4. Amount of exposure media reports about police actions of corruption or brutality.

In this study the unit of analysis is the individual. The researchers conceptualized the primary independent variable, racial group, with three categories: white, black, and Hispanic. They said that white represented the dominant group. They conceptualized the primary dependent variable, racially biased policing, as a person's belief that the police treated whites and nonwhites unequally. They considered two other variables, experience with police and media exposure. They conceptualized experience with police as a person's direct or indirect interactions with local police officers, and exposure to media as a person hearing about police brutality or corruption in the mass media. They had two related conceptual hypotheses:

1. Nondominant racial group members are more likely to believe that policing is racially biased than dominant group members.
2. The perception of racial bias by nondominant group members grows with both (a) their experience with police and (b) with their exposure to media reports about police racial bias or corruption.

The researchers' operational definition of the independent variable was asking people to self-identify in a survey question about race. They operationalized the main dependent variable (perception of racial bias by police) with four sets of survey questions:

1. Questions about whether police treat blacks better than, the same as, or worse than whites, and the same question with Hispanics substituted for blacks
2. Questions about whether police treat black neighborhoods better than, the same as, or worse than whites, with the same question asked for Hispanic neighborhoods

conceptual hypothesis stating a hypothesis with the variables as abstract concepts.

empirical hypothesis the hypothesis stated in terms of specific measures of variables.

3. A question about whether there is racial-ethnic prejudice among police officers in the city
4. A question about whether police were more likely to stop some drivers just because they were black or Hispanic

Weitzer and Tuch gathered survey data for each variable. After they had the data, they conducted statistical tests and looked at charts and tables for associations to test their hypothesis.

Figure 5.1 illustrates how the measurement process links the three levels (abstract theoretical, operational, and concrete empirical). It shows the measurement process for two variables linked together with a hypothesis. You need to consider all three levels together.

Look at Figure 5.1 for a quick review. In a study with quantitative data, you usually move from the abstract concept toward a concrete measure. First, conceptualize by creating a clear conceptual definition for each variable. Next, operationalize by giving each an operational definition. Finally, gather empirical data with the measurement operations of the operational definition. You test the hypothesis empirically with the data. The empirical tests connect to the abstract concepts. In this way, empirical tests provide evidence to support or refute a conceptual hypothesis that flows into broad theoretical statements.

Qualitative Conceptualization and Operationalization

As stated above, you refine abstract ideas into a conceptual definition early in research with quantitative data. By contrast, in qualitative data research you use rudimentary working ideas during the data collection process. As you gather and analyze qualitative data (i.e., field notes, photos and maps, historical documents, etc.), you rethink old ideas and develop new ones based on your observations. You try to make sense of the data by creating clearer definitions of the ideas. Eventually, you will connect the ideas and they become theoretical relationships. Often this is the grounded theory that you learned about in Chapter 2. The process requires you to be self-aware and reflect continuously on how you are doing the research while you are in the midst of doing it. You must simultaneously document both the actual data as well as the process of how you gathered the data.

■ **Figure 5.1**   Conceptualization and Operationalization: Abstract Construct to Concrete Measure

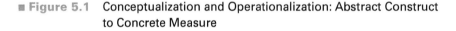

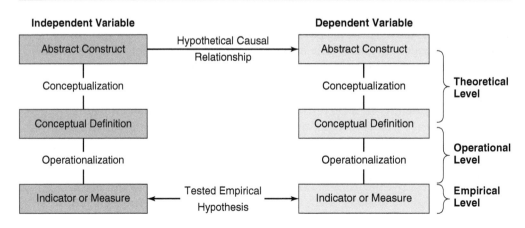

During conceptualization, you ask theoretical questions about the data (e.g., Is this a case of idea Z? What is the sequence of events and could it be different? Why did this happen here and not somewhere else?). As in research with quantitative data, you conceptualize by developing clear, explicit definitions. These definitions are more abstract than your direct observations, but you tie them to specific data. You anchor the conceptual definitions in the specific words, events, or actions of the people you are studying. Because qualitative measurement is integrated with other parts of a study and not a set of separate steps, it may be more difficult to carry out.

Ed Kashi/Corbis

To help you understand the measurement process, let us look at the qualitative field research study of two California high schools in Appendix C. In the study Perry (2001) used the concept "naturalization of white culture," a very abstract idea that is difficult to see or measure. She conceptualized it by building on past studies and by what she observed in the schools. *Naturalization* means that a culture—set of values, outlooks, and assumptions—is so fully taken-for-granted, accepted, and embraced that it becomes invisible and people treat it as being "natural." *White culture* is a culture—set of values, outlooks, and assumptions—associated with the white racial group. Perry anchored the concept by contrasting the two high schools she studied.

In research using quantitative data, you operationalize by linking your idea to a preplanned technique of measuring. You might write a survey questionnaire or create a scoring sheet for counting observations (how many males or females entered the store). You do this before you collect any data. In a study with qualitative data, you operationalize by describing in detail how you gathered data. In almost a reverse process from quantitative data, you operationalize after-the-fact. You describe how you discovered or created a concept and found it useful during your observation and data gathering.

In the white-majority Valley Grove School, Perry operationalized "naturalized white culture" by providing readers of the study with a description of how she did the study and with many quotes from white students. The students are shown talking about themselves as being "just American" or "normal." At the same time, they describe the nonwhite students at the school as "being ethnic" or "having culture." School events (sports, dances, etc.) do not highlight or draw attention to ethnic-cultural diversity. At Clavey, a school that has few white students, white students said the "school is like a foreign country" and major school events were multicultural assemblies.

Perry operationalized concepts by describing her specific experiences at the schools. She tells us what she saw and offers quotes of what she heard. She grounded her concepts in what she saw or heard as student comments about food, clothing, music, speech, and leisure-time activities. In doing this, Perry shows us that in a white-dominant environment, students "live" white culture but are unable to name it. This is because to them, white culture is simply a normal life. By contrast, in the school where whites were the numerical minority, the white students easily recognized and quickly distinguished their white culture.

The discussion above emphasizes quantitative-qualitative differences. In practice, neither follows a rigid process. For both types of data, ideas and data mutually influence one another. For both, you draw on ideas from beyond the data of a specific research setting, and blend preexisting techniques and concepts with ones that emerge during data collection. In this way, ideas and evidence are mutually interdependent. Remember, the heart of all operationalization is a process of connecting ideas with data.

Summary Review Steps in Quantitative and Qualitative Conceptualization and Operationalization

QUANTITATIVE	QUALITATIVE
1. Conceptualize variables by developing a clear, complete written conceptual definition for the core idea of each. You want build on past theories, consider definitions others have used, and be very logical.	1. Gather empirical data and simultaneously think about concepts to organize and make sense of the data. Develop a clear definitions for each idea that you use. They may be ones you have read about, new ideas you create, or ones that the people you are studying use.
2. Operationalize variables by creating specific activities to measure each. This is your operational definition that will closely match how you have defined the variable in its conceptual definition.	2. As you gather data, be very aware of processes you use to make sense of the data and your own thinking. Reflect on and describe this process of linking ideas to specific observations in the data.
3. Gather empirical data using the specific measurement activities of your operational definition; this links data to the conceptual definition.	3. Review and refine your definitions and the descriptions of how you gathered data and made sense of it.

HOW TO CREATE GOOD MEASURES: RELIABILITY AND VALIDITY

Reliability and Validity in Quantitative Research

The terms *reliability* and *validity* have multiple meanings. Here, they refer to desirable aspects of scientific measurement. They tie the unobservable idea "in your head" to specific actions in the visible world. You can never achieve perfect reliability and validity. Rather, they are ideals toward which you want to strive. We want measures to be reliable and valid because it leads to truthfulness, credibility, or believability.

Reliability means that a measurement does not vary because of characteristics of how you measured (or the measurement instrument itself). Measurement reliability is easier to see in the physical world. Let us say you get on a bathroom scale and measure your weight. Now you get off and get on repeatedly. A reliable scale gives the same weight each time—assuming, of course, that you are not eating, drinking, changing clothing, and so forth. An unreliable scale registers different weights over time, even when your true weight is unchanged. The analogy of weight on a bathroom scale carries over to all other kinds of measures. Reliability means that the method or instrument (bathroom scale) you use to make measurements is consistent and dependable.

Validity suggests truthfulness and indicates how well your mental picture of an idea fits with what you do to measure it in empirical reality. In simple terms, validity addresses, how well the aspect of reality you measure matches up with the ideas you use to understand that aspect of reality.

Validity is an overused term meaning "true" or "correct." There are several kinds of validity. Here, we are concerned with **measurement validity**. Measurement validity is the fit between conceptual and operational definitions—the better the fit, the greater the validity. A measure can be valid for one purpose (i.e., a research question with units of analysis and universe) but invalid for others. For example, a

reliability a feature of measures—the method of measuring is dependable and consistent.

validity a feature of measures; the concept of interest closely matches the method used to measure it.

measurement validity the fit between a concept and how it is measured.

Making It Practical **How to Improve Reliability**

You can improve a measure's reliability in four ways:

1. **Clearly conceptualize.** Sloppy, loose, or fuzzy thinking weakens reliability. It allows other issues that may or may not be connected with your core idea to get into a measure, making it less dependable. Reliability improves when you have clear and unambiguous definitions of concepts. It is better when you define a concept to eliminate "noise" (i.e., distracting or interfering information) that spills over from other concepts. Make certain that each measure indicates one and only one idea. Otherwise, it is impossible to determine exactly what concept your measure is indicating.

2. **Increase the level of measurement.** We will discuss levels of measurement later in this chapter. At this point, you only need to know that a higher or more precise level of measurement is more reliable than a less precise one. This is because the imprecise measures pick up less detailed information. If you do not measure very specific information, you may pick up things other than the concept of interest. The general principle is to try to measure at the most precise level possible.

3. **Use multiple indicators.** You can improve reliability by using **multiple indicators,** because two (or more) indicators of the same concept are better than one. Using more than one measure is a widely accepted principle of good measurement. For example, I create three indicators of

employee satisfaction. My first indicator is an attitude question on a survey. I ask research participants their beliefs and feelings about different job areas. For a second indicator, I observe research participants at work. I note whether they smile, appear to be happy, maintain good relationships with coworkers and customers, or appear stressed, complain, and act gruff. Lastly, I examine employment records for absenteeism, disciplinary actions, length of service, and rates of turnover. I can use three separate indicators—survey, observation, and written records—to tell me about satisfaction. If all three show high consistent satisfaction (high or low), I am more confident that I have a dependable measure. Multiple indicators let you measure different aspects of the concept (such as employee satisfaction with pay, with workplace conditions, with supervision) each with its own indicator. In addition, one may be imperfect or unstable, but several indicators are unlikely to have the same (systematic) error.

4. **Use pilot studies and replication.** Trying pilot versions of a measure can improve its reliability. Develop one or more draft or preliminary versions of a measure and try them out before using the final version. Of course, this takes more time and effort. You can also replicate the measures other researchers have used. If you find measures from past research, you can build on and use them, citing the source, of course.

measure of job satisfaction might be valid for measuring job satisfaction among retail clerks in a clothing store but invalid for measuring it among police officers.

Validity is more difficult to achieve than reliability. We never achieve absolute validity because it links invisible, abstract ideas with specific empirical observations. A gap always exists between our mental images about the world and the concrete reality we experience. Nonetheless, some measures are more valid than others are.

In the previous chapter, you learned about sampling error. Measurement validity and sampling error are similar. In sampling, you want minimal sampling error—that is, you want a specific sample, for which you have data, to represent accurately the population that you cannot directly observe. A sample with little sampling error allows you to estimate accurately the population parameter. In measurement, you want specific empirical measures that represent accurately abstract concepts that you cannot directly observe. If you have a valid measure, it deviates very little from the concept it represents.

Three Types of Measurement Validity

1. *Face validity.* This is easiest to achieve and the most basic kind of validity. It is a judgment by knowledgeable people that the indicator really measures the concept it purports to measure. It addresses the question, On the face of it, do people believe that conceptual definition and measurement fit? For example, few

multiple indicators having several different specific measures that to indicate the same concept.

Summary Review   Summary of Measurement Validity Types

Validity (True Measure)

Face—in the judgment of others

Content—captures the entire meaning

Criterion—agrees with an external source

people would accept a measure of college student math ability using a question that asked students 2 + 2 = ?. This is not valid on the face of it.

2. *Content validity.* Content validity is a special type of face validity. A conceptual definition is "space" that contains ideas, and measures that capture all areas in the conceptual space have high content validity. For example, your concept of discrimination has three aspects. A measure that captures all three aspects has content validity.

3. *Criterion validity.* Criterion validity uses a standard or criterion to indicate a concept. An indicator's validity depends on comparing it with another measure of the same construct in which you have strong confidence.

Example Study Box 1   Content Validity and Measuring Stress

Do you feel stress? How can we measure it? Bell and Lee (2002) noted that stress has both physical and subjective forms. They defined subjective stress as a discrepancy between the demands of a person's life and the physical, emotional, and other resources to cope with such demands. Stress has several dimensions, so Bell and Lee developed measures for each dimension to ensure *content validity*. These included a person's subjective feeling of stress, specific stressful life events, health issues that cause stress, behaviors associated with stress, and physical symptoms of stress. They gathered survey data from 14,700 Australian women aged 18–23 by asking 94 questions, on all five dimensions, about the following:

Dion Ogust/The Image Works

1. Twelve life areas that the women rated 1–6, from not at all to highly stressed (e.g., relationship with boyfriends, exams, work)
2. Thirty-five life event questions (e.g., loss of job, break-up in a long-term relationship, major health problem)
3. Medical conditions such as cancer, diabetes, heart condition, plus general physical and mental health questions

4. Three stress-related behaviors: (a) smoking status, from 1, never smoked, to 5, smoke 20 or more cigarettes per day; (b) binge drinking of alcohol, defined as 5 or more drinks at one occasion, rated from 1 never to 5 more than once a week; (c) exercise status, from 1 inactive to 5, highly active
5. Questions about common physical symptoms of stress (e.g., migraines, back pain)

Reliability and Validity in Qualitative Research

You want reliable and valid measures of qualitative data; however, these measurement principles operate differently for qualitative than with quantitative data. Reliable qualitative data means you collected the data consistently. Although qualitative data techniques emphasize being flexible and adaptive to changing conditions, you do not want to be vacillating and erratic over time. In qualitative studies, you frequently interact with and develop deep social relations with people. You may treat the relationships as a growing, evolving process. Thus, how you gather data, observe, and interact with others may evolve over time, but it is not sloppy, erratic, or inconsistent. To reliably measure qualitative data, you measure it in a thoughtful and consistent manner so that it is dependable. For example, observing a field setting on the first day may differ from how you observe after you have been in the field site for six weeks. This difference does not mean unreliable or inconsistent observing; rather, you carefully and consistently monitor how you are observing over time.

In a qualitative data study, you consider a wide range of data sources and measure in many diverse ways. The interactive and situational nature of qualitative data means that two different researchers may not always get identical results. One researcher may use a unique mix of measures that another researcher does not use. The diverse measures and differences among researchers illuminate the many facets or dimensions of an issue or setting. Different measures or specific researchers can yield reliable measurement—It is not as reliable as with quantitative data by creating a single, fixed, standard, and unchanging measure, but reliable by observing and measuring in a consistent and self-conscious way. You must develop self-conscious, consistent ways to measure that you adjust to fit a specific research situation.

Recall that validity is linking a concept to empirical measures. Valid measures of qualitative data validity have authenticity. Authenticity means a fair, honest, and balanced account of social life from the standpoint of a person who lives in a specific social world. It means that you capture what is "real" for particular people living in a specific time and place. The emphasis is less on trying to match an abstract concept with a single, fixed, standard version of reality. Instead, your goal is to capture social life in a manner that is rings true to the experiences of people who are being studied. Valid qualitative data get an inside view. You capture and offer to others a detailed account of how the people you study see, feel about, and understand events. In one sense, authenticity substitutes for quantitative measurement validity. In another sense, it is the same, because both adhere to the core of validity—truthfulness (i.e., avoid false or distorted accounts). For both qualitative and quantitative data, you want to create a tight fit between ideas and statements you make about the social world and what is actually occurring in it.

Putting Reliability and Validity Together

Reliability is necessary for validity and is easier to achieve than validity. Although reliability is necessary for a valid measure, it does not guarantee that a measure is valid. It is not a sufficient condition for validity. A measure can produce the same result over and over, but what it measures may not match the definition of the construct (i.e., validity). You can have a reliable measure that is invalid.

Here is a simple example: You get on a scale to get weighed. The weight registered by the scale is the same each time you get on and off. Your scale is reliable. Then you go to another scale—an "official" one that measures true weight—and it says that your weight is much heavier. The first scale yielded reliable (i.e., dependable and consistent) results, but it did not give a valid measure of weight. A diagram (Figure 5.2) might help you see the relationship between reliability and validity. Figure 5.2 illustrates the relationship between the concepts by using the analogy of a target. The bull's-eye represents a fit between a measure and the definition of the construct.

■ **Figure 5.2**   Illustration of Relationship Between Reliability and Validity

A Bull's-Eye = A Perfect Measure

 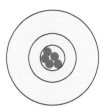

| Low Reliability
and Low Validity | High Reliability
but Low Validity | High Reliability
and High Validity |

Source: Adapted from Babbie (2004:145).

A GUIDE TO QUANTITATIVE MEASUREMENT

Thus far, you have learned measurement principles, including reliability and validity. Quantitative researchers developed many specialized measures using levels of measurement. This section is a brief guide to levels of measurement and a few of the widely used measures.

Levels of Measurement

Levels of measurement vary from a highly refined level with great precision to rougher or less precise levels. The level of measurement depends on your assumptions about characteristics of the concept you are measuring. The way in which you conceptualize a variable limits the levels of measurement you can use, and it will influence how statistical analysis can proceed.

Continuous and Discrete Variables. We can begin by thinking of all variables as being either continuous or discrete. A **continuous variable** has an infinite number of values that flow along a continuum. You can subdivide the variable into smaller and smaller increments; the number of increments can be infinite. Such variables include temperature, age, income, crime rate, and amount of schooling. A **discrete variable** has a fixed set of separate values or categories. Instead of a smooth continuum of many values, discrete variables have two or a few separate, distinct categories. Examples include gender (male or female), religion (Protestant, Catholic, Jew, Muslim, atheist), and marital status (never married single, married, divorced or separated, widowed). Whether a variable is continuous or discrete affects its level of measurement.

Four Levels of Measurement. Levels of measurement expand on the difference between continuous and discrete variables. The four levels organize the degree of measurement precision. You may not find it easy to decide on the appropriate level for a concept at first. The appropriate level of measurement depends on inherent features of the variable and the ways you conceptualize a variable.

Some concepts and variables can only be discrete and have a few distinct categories. In the social world, martial status has just a few basic categories. Marital status is either married or not married, and not married is subdivided into never married, divorced, separated, or widowed. You can conceptualize other of the variables as either continuous or discrete. Age can be continuous, indicating how old a person is in years, months, days, hours, and minutes. You can also treat it as a set of discrete categories, such as infancy, childhood, adolescence, young adulthood, middle age, and old age. Education can be continuous, indicating years of schooling. You can also treat it as a set of discrete categories by degree/diploma, such

levels of measurement the degree a measure is refined or precise.

continuous variable a variable that can be measured with numbers that can be subdivided into smaller increments.

discrete variable a variable measured with a limited number of fixed categories.

as less than high school, high school diploma, more than high school but less than four-year college degree, four-year college degree, and graduate degree.

You can collapse most continuous variables into a few discrete categories, but you cannot turn a discrete variable into continuous measures. For example, sex, religion, and marital status cannot be conceptualized as continuous. Nevertheless, you can shift to related concepts that you can conceptualize as being continuous. Sex is discrete, but "degree of femininity" or "degree of masculinity" are continuous variables. A specific religion (e.g., Catholic, Lutheran, or Baptist) may be discrete, but degree of commitment to religion is continuous. Marital status is discrete, but number of years a person has been married is continuous.

The four levels of measurement, from lowest (discrete and least precise) to highest precision, are nominal, ordinal, interval, and ratio. Each level provides different types of information (see Making It Practical: Levels of Measurement Examples). Discrete variables are at the nominal and ordinal levels, whereas you can measure continuous variables at the interval or ratio levels.

Making It Practical   **Levels of Measurement Examples**

Nominal measures only indicate a difference among categories. Examples include gender: male or female; religion: Protestant, Catholic, Jew, Muslim, or other; racial heritage: African, Asian, Caucasian, Latino, other; state/province or region of residence: Illinois, Ontario, New York, Texas, or Midwest, Northeast, and so on.

Ordinal measures indicate a difference among categories, and the categories can be ordered or ranked. Examples include letter grades: A, B, C, D, F; opinion measures: Strongly Agree, Agree, Disagree, Strongly Disagree; quality ratings: Excellent, Very Good, Good, Fair, Poor.

Interval measures do everything the first two do, plus they specify the distance between categories. Examples include Fahrenheit or Celsius temperature: 5°, 45°, 90°; and IQ scores: 95, 110, 125.

Ratio measures do everything all the other levels do, plus they have true zero. A true zero means a score of zero really indicates a value of zero or nothing. A true zero makes it possible to talk about relationships in terms of proportion or ratios, such as twice as much. Examples include money income: $10, $100, $500; years of formal schooling: 1 year, 10 years, 13 years; age: 18 years, 32 years, 64 years. In most situations, the distinction between interval and ratio levels makes little difference. The arbitrary zeros in some interval measures can lead to mistakes. For example, a rise in temperature from 30 to 60 degrees is not a doubling of the temperature, although it may appear to be the numbers double, because zero degrees is not the absence of all heat.

Summary Review   **Levels of Measurement Features**

Characteristics of the Four Levels of Measurement

Level	Different Categories	Ranked	Distance between Categories Measured	True Zero
Nominal	Yes			
Ordinal	Yes	Yes		
Interval	Yes	Yes	Yes	
Ratio	Yes	Yes	Yes	Yes

There are good practical reasons to conceptualize and measure variables at higher levels of measurement. You can always collapse a high level of measurement to a low

level, but the reverse is not true. If you measure a concept very precisely, you can decide later to "throw away" or ignore some of the precision. But you cannot measure a concept with little precision and then make it more precise later. You can turn a ratio-level measure (annual family income) into ordinal level (High, Medium, or Low income) or nominal level (same as or different from others). However, the process does not work in the opposite way. You cannot measure something at the nominal level and then reorganize it to be ordinal, interval, or ratio.

When you use an ordinal measure, try to have at least five ordinal categories and obtain multiple observations for each. Interval measures can be confusing because a few measures, like temperature, use arbitrary zeros, not true zeros. As mentioned in Making It Practical, many people get confused by the arbitrary zeros used in interval measures; they are "arbitrary" or just there to help keep score and do not indicate a real zero, or nothing. The temperature can be zero, or below zero, but zero is an arbitrary number when it is assigned to temperature. Compare zero degrees Celsius with zero degrees Fahrenheit—they are different temperatures. In addition, doubling the degrees in one system does not double the degrees in the other. Unless we are fooled by the arbitrary numbers, it makes no sense to say that it is "twice as warm" if the temperature rises from 2 to 4 degrees, from 15 to 30 degrees, or from 40 to 80 degrees, as is possible with ratio measurement. Examples of the four levels of measurement are shown in Table 5.1.

■ **Table 5.1**   Example of Levels of Measurement

Nominal Level

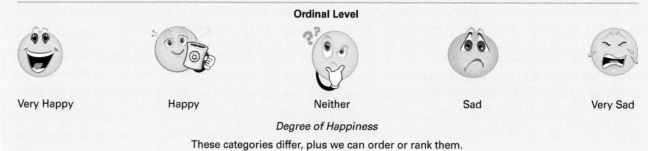

| Protestant | Catholic | Muslim | Jewish |

Religious Faith
The categories differ, but we do not assume that one is "better/high" or "worse/lower" than others.

Ordinal Level

| Very Happy | Happy | Neither | Sad | Very Sad |

Degree of Happiness
These categories differ, plus we can order or rank them.

Interval Level

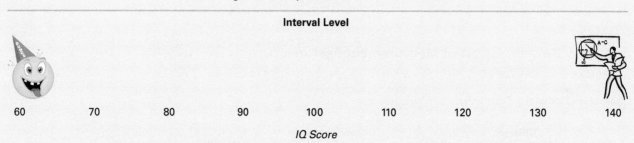

60   70   80   90   100   110   120   130   140

IQ Score
We can precisely determine the size of differences among score, but there is no absolute zero.

Ratio Level

2 4 6 8 10 12 14 16 18 20 22 24 26 28 30 32 34 36 38 40 42 44 46 48 50 52 54 56 58 60 62 64 66 68 70 72 74 76 78

Age
We can precisely determine the size of differences among scores, plus a true or absolute zero exists.

Specialized Measures: Scales and Indexes

Scales and indexes are sophisticated, information-filled measures for quantitative data that researchers created to measure variables. Researchers created hundreds of indexes and scales to measure the prestige of occupations, the adjustment of people to a marriage, the intensity of group interaction, the level of social activity in a community, the degree to which a state's sexual assault laws reflect feminist values, the level of socioeconomic development of a nation, and much more. You can borrow already created scales/indexes or create your own. We will look at the principles of scale and index construction and explore a few major types. Before we begin, keep two things in mind:

1. We can develop a measure of every social phenomenon. Some concepts may be measured directly and produce precise numerical values (e.g., family income) whereas others use proxies that indirectly measure a variable and may not be as precise (e.g., predisposition to commit a crime).
2. You can learn a great deal by looking at measures created by other researchers. You do not have to start from scratch but can use a previously used scale or index, or you can modify it.

The terms *index* and *scale* are used interchangeably because they have overlapping features and people are not always careful with labels. Social researchers do not use a consistent nomenclature to distinguish between them. One person's scale can be another's index. Both produce ordinal- or interval-level measures. You can combine scale and index techniques to create a single measure. Both scales and indexes give you more information about variables, increase measurement reliability and validity, and organize or condense the information collected. For most purposes, you can treat scales and indexes as interchangeable.

A **scale** creates an ordinal measure of intensity, direction, level, or potency by arranging responses or observations on a continuum. It can be a single indicator or multiple indicators. An **index** combines information from separate indicators into a one score, often a sum of their values. In most indexes, you add together the numerical values of several items for a score at the interval level of measurement. You can combine several indicators measured using scales into a single composite index measure.

Mutually Exclusive and Exhaustive Attributes. Two features of good measurement affect indexes and scales and all measures. The categories of your variables should be mutually exclusive and exhaustive. **Mutually exclusive** means that a unit goes into one and only one variable category. For example, a variable measuring type of religion—with the attributes Christian, non-Christian, and Jewish—is not mutually exclusive. Judaism is both a non-Christian religion and a Jewish religion. A Jewish person fits into both the non-Christian and the Jewish category. Likewise, type of city as river port city, state capital, and interstate exit lacks mutually exclusive attributes. One city could be all three (a river port state capital with an interstate exit), any one of the three, or none of the three. For numerical data, you do not want any overlap. The following question about years of school is *not* mutually exclusive (it is exhaustive):

How much schooling did you complete?

_____ 0–6 years	_____ 6–10 years	_____ 11–12 years
_____ 12–15 years	_____ 16–18 years	_____ 18 or more years

Exhaustive means all possibilities are included in how you measure a variable. If you measure religion and ask whether a person is Catholic, Protestant, or Jewish, it is not exclusive. A Buddhist, a Muslim, or an agnostic does not fit anywhere. You need to develop variable categories to include every possible situation. For example, Catholic, Protestant, Jewish, or other is both exclusive and mutually exclusive. The following question about years of schooling is mutually exclusive but it is *not* exhaustive:

scale a measure that captures a concept's intensity, direction, or level at the ordinal level of measurement.

index a composite measure that combines several indicators into a single score.

mutually exclusive each unit fits into one, and only one, category of a variable.

exhaustive all units fit into some category of a variable.

How much schooling did you complete?

_____ 6–10 years _____ 11–12 years _____ 13–15 years _____ 16–18 years _____19 years

People with less than 6 years or more than 19 years of schooling are not included.

Unidimensionality. In addition to being mutually exclusive and exhaustive, scales and indexes should be unidimensional or have one dimension. **Unidimensionality** means that all the items in a scale or index fit together. They all measure a single concept. Unidimensionality says that if you combine several specific pieces of information into a single score or measure, all the parts should act alike and measure the same core concept.

Many indexes combine subparts of a concept into a single measure. This appears to contradict the principle of unidimensionality. It does not because you can define concepts at different levels of abstraction. You can define a general, abstract concept (e.g., happiness) as having subparts (happiness with health, with job, with marriage). Each subpart is an aspect of the concept's content. Yet one subpart, marital happiness, is a concept at a lower level of abstraction. It too may have subparts (e.g., happiness with communication in marriage) and so forth.

It is easy to become confused: A measure can indicate a unidimensional construct in one situation but measure a part of a different concept in another situation. This is possible because concepts are at different levels of abstraction. General happiness is more abstract than marital happiness, which is more abstract than happiness with communication in the marriage.

ADDING MEASURES TO GET A SCORE: INDEX CONSTRUCTION

If you watch the news or read newspapers in the United States, you will hear reports of the Federal Bureau of Investigation (FBI) crime index, the consumer price index (CPI), the index of leading economic indicators, and the consumer confidence index. The FBI index is the sum of police reports on seven so-called index crimes (criminal homicide, aggravated assault, forcible rape, robbery, burglary, larceny of $50 or more, and auto theft). It began with the Uniform Crime Report in 1930. The CPI, which is a measure of inflation, is created by totaling the cost of buying a list of goods and services (e.g., food, rent, and utilities) and comparing the total to the cost of buying the same list in the previous year. The U.S. Bureau of Labor Statistics has used a consumer price index since 1919; wage increases, union contracts, and social security payments are based on it. The index of leading economic indicators and the consumer confidence index are created by private companies. The leading indicators index tries to predict economic conditions in the near future by adding scores on 11 items. The 11 items include average hours in employee work weeks, new unemployment claims, new orders for consumer goods, new equipment orders, building permits, stock prices (S&P 500), and so forth. The consumer confidence index is based on a monthly survey of a random sample of 5000 households that has been conducted since 1985. It contains questions about the current situation and about future expectations. It is the sum of respondents' appraisal of current business conditions, current employment conditions, and expectations six months hence regarding respondents' employment conditions, total family income, and business conditions. Respondent answers are scored positive, negative, or neutral.

To create an index, you combine two or more items into a single numerical score. Indexes measure the most desirable place to live (based on unemployment, commuting time, crime rate, recreation opportunities, weather, and so on), the degree of crime (based on combining the occurrence of different specific crimes), and a person's mental health (based on the person's adjustment in various areas of life). Also called a summative or composite index, you add several specific numerical measures that represent parts of one concept.

unidimensionality all items of an index or scale measure the same concept or have a common dimension.

Two Complications in Index Construction

1. Count Items Equally or Weigh Them? If you find an index, unless it is otherwise stated, assume that each item in an index is weighted the same, or it is an unweighted index. Add up the items without modification, as if each were multiplied by 1 (or −1 for items that are negative). Unless you have a very good reason to do otherwise, this is usually best. In a weighted index, you value or weight items differently. The size of the weights comes from your conceptualization, assumptions, conceptual definition, or specialized statistical techniques. Weighting can produce different scores than an unweighted index. For example, in a weighted index of a

---

Learning from History **Index of Dissimilarity**

Racial segregation in the United States is an issue discussed by activists, social scientists, educators, and policy officials, and it is connected to numerous other social issues. How much residential racial segregation is there? Duncan and Duncan (1955) invented the Index of Dissimilarity, or D index, to measure the integration or separation of groups across all neighborhoods of a city or metropolitan area. The D index helps us evaluate the degree of segregation in cities. It only compares two groups and is based on city blocks. A D score of zero means no segregation, whereas a score of 1.0 means total segregation. If a city's white-black dissimilarity index were 65, then 65 percent of white people would need to move to another neighborhood to make an equal balance of whites and blacks across all neighborhoods. The basic formula for the index of dissimilarity is

$$.5 \times \text{sum of } (bi/B - wi/W)$$

bi = the black population of the ith area, (e.g. a city block)

B = the total black population of the large geographic entity (e.g., the entire city)

wi = the white population of the ith area

W = the total white population of the large geographic entity

The measure of dissimilarity helps to reveal historical patterns of segregation. For example, the black-white D index times 100 for Saint Louis was 39.1 in 1900, it rose to 54.3 by 1910, and to 92.6 in 1940. It dropped to 89.3 in 1970 and to 74.3 by 2000 (DeRango 2001). Researchers modified the measure and extended it to other topics (e.g., gender segregation in occupations). The D indexes for racial relations in ten U.S. cities based on the 2000 census are as follows:

City/Metro Area	White vs. Black	White vs. Asian	White vs. Hispanic
Boston	68.8	50.4	56.8
Chicago	83.6	50.9	64.8
Denver	66.2	37.7	51.8
Detroit	86.7	53.4	48.3
Houston	71.8	53.9	48.3
Milwaukee	84.4	48.1	60.6
New York City	84.3	55.1	69.3
Philadelphia	76.9	51.6	63.3
San Francisco	65.6	52.0	55.2
Seattle	57.9	42.9	38.6

The table shows the index of dissimilarity scores multiplied by 100 for easier interpretation and that black-white segregation was highest in Detroit and lowest in Seattle, that Asian-white segregation was lower than black-white segregation in all ten cities, and white-Hispanic segregation was highest in New York City.

desirable place to live, the percent of days with sunshine might be weighted one-half the importance of a low crime rate or quality of public schools but the same as amount of park land or number of museums.

2. Missing Data. Missing data can become an issue when constructing an index, threatening validity and reliability. For example, you construct an index of the degree of societal development for 50 nations using United Nations statistics. You sum four items:

- Average life expectancy
- Percentage of homes with indoor plumbing
- Percentage of population that is literate
- Number of telephones per 100 people

As you gather data, you discover that literacy data are available for only 47 of the 50 countries. The remaining three countries did not collect the data. You may drop down to comparing only 47 nations, or you can substitute weaker measures.

CAPTURING INTENSITY: SCALE CONSTRUCTION

You can use scales to create an ordinal or less commonly, interval, or ratio measure of a variable. Most scales help us measure the intensity, hardness, or extremity of a person's feelings/opinion at the ordinal level. The simplest scale is a visual rating. It is easy to construct and use. You ask participants to indicate their feelings or rating by checking a point on a line that runs from one extreme to another. This conveys the idea of a continuum, and numbers on the line can help people think about quantities. When using a scale, you assume that people with the same subjective feeling mark the visual line at the same place. Figure 5.3 is an example of a "feeling

■ Figure 5.3   "Feeling Thermometer" Graphic Rating Scale

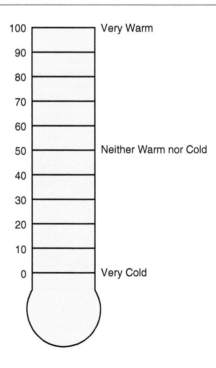

thermometer" scale. Researchers used it to learn how people feel about various groups in society (e.g., the National Organization of Women, the Ku Klux Klan, labor unions, physicians, etc.). Political scientists have used it since 1964 in the National Election Study to measure people's feelings toward political candidates, social groups, and public issues.

Commonly Used Scales

We look at four commonly used scales of the hundreds that researchers use: the Likert, social distance, semantic differential, and Guttman scales.

Likert Scale. You have probably used a Likert scale even if you did not know its name. Survey researchers often use Likert scales to measure opinions or ratings at the ordinal level. The Likert scale offers a statement or questions, and participants indicate their response with a set of answer choices, such as strongly agree, agree, disagree, or strongly disagree. Other answer categories are possible—approve or disapprove; support or oppose; believe the statement is always true, almost always true, almost never true, or never true; do something frequently, sometimes, rarely, never. Answers in Likert scales need a minimum of two categories. However, using only two choices creates a crude measure and cannot capture complex distinctions. Usually you want to use four to six answer categories. If you use six categories, you can reduce to four or two categories after you collect the data. But if you collect data with just two categories, you cannot make your data more precise later. Keep the number of answer choices to under nine. More distinctions than that are rarely meaningful, and people may become confused. Always balance the answer choices (e.g., "strongly agree," "agree" with "strongly disagree," "disagree").

Should you use a "don't know," "undecided," "unsure," "no opinion" category in addition to the directional categories (e.g., "disagree," "agree") in a Likert scale? Researchers are somewhat divided on this issue, but in most situations it is best to include the "don't know" category. It is usually better to have people who are really uncertain or without an opinion indicate that than to force them to guess.

Another issue arises when you have a long set of Likert scale questions on the same issue. If answer choices are set up such that answering one way (such as "strongly agree") always indicates the same position on the issue, it can create problems. For example, you ask nine questions about the issue of right to a legal abortion. If you word all nine such that the response "strongly oppose" means strong opposition to abortion, you may create a "response set" problem. Some people stop listening closely after four or five similar questions or have a tendency always to agree or disagree to many similar Likert scale questions. The solution is to reverse the wording of some questions. You might word three questions so that "strongly oppose" indicates opposition to legal abortion, and word six so that "strongly oppose" indicates support for legal abortion. Then mix the questions. For example, after the question "Do you oppose or support a woman's choice for legal abortion if she is pregnant due to rape?" you ask, "Do you support or oppose laws that restrict a woman's access to abortion clinics?" A person with a strong antiabortion view must switch from saying "strongly disagree" to "strongly agree" if when indicating a consistent viewpoint.

You can easily to combine several Likert-scaled items into an index if they all measure a single concept. Consider the Self-Esteem Index (see Making It Practical). Combining a Likert scale and index construction improves reliability and validity. This is because the index uses multiple indicators, a feature that improves reliability. When the multiple indicators measure various aspects of one concept, content validity is improved. In addition, an index score can give you a more precise quantitative measure of a person's opinion, raising the level of measurement from ordinal to interval. For example, you create an index that has nine questions with five Likert scale answer categories. You assign a numerical score to each answer choice

Making It Practical Self-Esteem Measure

You have heard about self-esteem and may have also heard that certain social problems or personal issues stem form a lack of self-esteem. Morris Rosenberg operationalized the idea into a widely used measure in 1965. In the measure, people read a list of ten statements dealing with general feelings and then answer using a Likert scale from strongly agree to strongly disagree. Below is the scale. Take this opportunity to measure you own self-esteem with it.

Statements	Strongly Agree (SA)	Agree (A)	Disagree (D)	Strongly Disagree (SD)
1. On the whole, I am satisfied with myself.	____	____	____	____
2.*At times, I think I am no good at all.	____	____	____	____
3. I feel that I have a number of good qualities.	____	____	____	____
4. I am able to do things as well as most other people.	____	____	____	____
5.*I feel I do not have much to be proud of.	____	____	____	____
6.*I certainly feel useless at times.	____	____	____	____
7. I feel that I'm a person of worth, at least on an equal plane with others.	____	____	____	____
8.*I wish I could have more respect for myself.	____	____	____	____
9.*All in all, I am inclined to feel that I am a failure.	____	____	____	____
10. I take a positive attitude toward myself.	____	____	____	____

Scoring: SA = 3, A = 2, D = 1, SD = 0. Items marked with an asterisk (*) are reverse scored: SA = 0, A = 1, D = 2, SD = 3. Sum the scores for the 10 items. The higher your score, the higher your self-esteem.

(0 = strongly agree, 1 = agree, 2 = neutral, 3 = disagree, 4 = strongly disagree). An index lets you composite measure a person's opinion on the nine questions combined. It creates a score for each person, ranging from 0 (strongly disagree to all) to 36 (strongly agree to all nine).

Likert scale answer categories are ordinal and indicate rank. If you number the categories, it does not change the scale into a ratio level of measurement. It makes no difference whether Strongly Agree, Agree, Disagree, Strongly Disagree, and Don't Know are score from 1 to 5, −2 to +2, or 10, 20, 30, 40, 90. The basic scale is at the ordinal level of measurement. If you carefully assign numbers to categories (Strongly Disagree = 1, Agree = 2, Disagree = 3, Strongly Disagree = 4) and assume equal distance among each category, you can have interval but not ratio-level measurement.

Measuring Social Distance. Social distance is a widely used sociological concept (see Learning from History on page 118). The Borgadus social distance scale measures the amount of social distance separating groups. Here is how it works: People respond to a series of ordered statements; from most socially distant to most socially intimate. For example, people from Group X are entering your country, are in your town, work at your place of employment, live in your neighborhood, become your personal friends, and marry your brother, sister, son, or daughter to become part of your extended family. People indicate their comfort with each statement. Starting with the most distant statement, people indicate the point at which they no longer

Example Study Box 2 Social Distance and Disabilities

The social distance scale is a convenient way to determine how close people feel toward a social group to which they do not belong. The social distance scale has two limitations. First, you need to tailor the categories to a specific outgroup and social setting. Second, it is not easy to compare how people feel toward several different groups unless a research participant completes a similar social distance scale for all outgroups at the same time. Gordon and associates (2004) used the social distance scale to measure how much social distance college students felt toward people with various disabilities. They found large differences depending on the disability. Over 95 percent of students said they would be a friend with someone with arthritis, cancer, diabetes, or a heart condition, whereas under 70 percent would consider being a friend to someone with mental retardation.

feel comfortable. The scale assumes that a person who refuses contact or is uncomfortable with a distant item will refuse the socially closer items (see Example Study Box 2). The original scale measured social distance among racial-ethnic groups, but researchers extended the scale to measure social distance in many other social relations, such as doctor-patient distance and social distance toward ex-convicts, toward people with HIV-AIDS, or toward people with disabilities.

Semantic Differential. We communicate our evaluations with adjectives in spoken and written language. Many adjectives have polar opposites (e.g., *light/dark*, *hard/soft*, *slow/fast*). The semantic differential measures a person's subjective feelings about a concept, object, or other person indirectly by using sets of polar opposite adjectives to create a rating scale.

By using general adjectives, the semantic differential scale captures connotations that people associate with a rating. Instead of asking a person directly, "Do you feel positive or negative toward Joan Jones a candidate for mayor?" you ask him or her to rate Joan Jones with general adjectives. You might ask, "Do you feel that Joan Jones is warm or cool, happy or sad, active or passive?" and so forth on a rating from zero to seven for each. Researchers use the semantic differential for many purposes. Marketing researchers use it to learn how consumers feel about a product. Political advisers use it to discover what voters think about a candidate or issue. Therapists use it to determine how a client feels about relations with other people. For example, you might discover that younger voters perceive Joan Jones as traditional, weak, and slow and as halfway between good and bad. Elderly voters perceive her as leaning toward strong, fast, and good and as halfway between traditional and modern. The pattern of responses illustrates how the research participant feels overall.

To use the semantic differential, you present research participants with a list of about a dozen paired opposite adjectives on a visual continuum showing 7 to 11 points between them. Participants then mark the place on the continuum that expresses their inner feelings. The adjectives can be very diverse and include opposite positive and negative items mixed on each side. The analysis of semantic differential results is difficult. You will need to learn rather complex statistical procedures to analyze the data (see Heise 1970).

Guttman Scaling. The Guttman scale differs from the previous scales or indexes because you use it to evaluate the data after you collected them. This means you must

Example Study Box 3 The Semantic Differential and Tattoos

In Chapter 2, you read about tattoos and the study on attitudes toward women with tattoos (Hawkes, Senn, and Thorn 2004). The researchers asked 268 students at a medium-sized Canadian university to complete a semantic differential form in response to several scenarios about a 22-year-old female college student with a tattoo. They varied the size of the tattoo (small versus large) and whether the tattoo was visible or not. Other features of the scenario that varied were weight problem or not; part-time job at restaurant, clothing store, or grocery store; boyfriend or not; average grades or failing grades. In addition, participants completed

Camille Tokerud/Photographer's Choice/Getty Images Royalty Free

Feminist and Women's Movement and Neosexisms scales. The semantic differential indicated three factors: evaluative, activity, and potency (strong/weak). The 19 adjectives that the researchers used in the semantic differential scale are listed below.

Good	___ ___ ___ ___ ___ ___ ___	Bad*
Beautiful	___ ___ ___ ___ ___ ___ ___	Ugly
Clean	___ ___ ___ ___ ___ ___ ___	Dirty
Kind	___ ___ ___ ___ ___ ___ ___	Cruel*
Rich	___ ___ ___ ___ ___ ___ ___	Poor*
Honest	___ ___ ___ ___ ___ ___ ___	Dishonest*
Pleasant	___ ___ ___ ___ ___ ___ ___	Unpleasant*
Successful	___ ___ ___ ___ ___ ___ ___	Unsuccessful
Reputable	___ ___ ___ ___ ___ ___ ___	Disreputable
Safe	___ ___ ___ ___ ___ ___ ___	Dangerous
Gentle	___ ___ ___ ___ ___ ___ ___	Violent*
Feminine	___ ___ ___ ___ ___ ___ ___	Masculine
Weak	___ ___ ___ ___ ___ ___ ___	Powerful*
Passive	___ ___ ___ ___ ___ ___ ___	Active*
Cautious	___ ___ ___ ___ ___ ___ ___	Rash*
Soft	___ ___ ___ ___ ___ ___ ___	Hard
Weak	___ ___ ___ ___ ___ ___ ___	Strong
Mild	___ ___ ___ ___ ___ ___ ___	Intense
Delicate	___ ___ ___ ___ ___ ___ ___	Rugged*

*These items were presented in reverse order.

design a study with the Guttman scaling technique in mind. Guttman scaling is a powerful technique that tells you whether a particular structured pattern holds among a set of items. It has been applied to many phenomena (e.g., opinions on public issues, patterns of crime or drug use, characteristics of societies or organizations, voting or political participation, psychological disorders). The structured pattern is hierarchical such that certain items are basic, lower, or easier, whereas others are advanced, higher, or difficult. You order items from lower to higher, then see whether the data you gather fit that structured pattern. In opinion studies, the structure is that almost everyone may agree with lower items, but few agree with higher items. Almost all who agree with the lower items also agree higher ones too, but the opposite is not the case.

Here is an example. You have four items about what a five-year old child knows. She knows her age, her telephone number, whether her teacher is married, and the mayor's name. The little girl may know her age but no other answer, or all three, or only her age and telephone number. In fact, for four items there are sixteen possible combinations of answers or patterns of responses. Each item is yes or no for whether the child knows the answer.

16 Possible Combinations for Four Items

	Age	Phone Number	Teacher Marriage	Mayor's Name
1	YES	YES	YES	YES
2	YES	YES	YES	NO
3	YES	YES	NO	YES
4	YES	YES	NO	NO
5	YES	NO	YES	YES
6	YES	NO	YES	NO
7	YES	NO	NO	YES
8	YES	NO	NO	NO
9	NO	YES	YES	YES
10	NO	YES	YES	NO
11	NO	YES	NO	YES
12	NO	YES	NO	NO
13	NO	NO	YES	YES
14	NO	NO	YES	NO
15	NO	NO	NO	YES
16	NO	NO	NO	NO

At one extreme (sequence 1) is the child who knows all the four items. At the opposite extreme (sequence 16) is the child who knows none of the four. With a Guttman scale you hypothesize combinations that will be frequent and fit a structured pattern. Let us say you might think the pattern is the following order: age, phone number, teacher marital status, and mayor's name. Most children know their age even if nothing else, but few who know the mayor's name do not also know the lower or "easier" questions. With a Guttman scale you can measure how well the data form a hierarchical pattern. To do this, you look at how many people answer the predicted pattern and how many answer some other way. Various statistical measures can tell you how "scalable" the data are (i.e., how well they fit the hierarchical pattern among items that you hypothesized).

With a Guttman scale, you can measure the degree to which an item answered fit a scale, ranging from zero to 100 percent. A score of zero indicates a random pattern of answer, or no hierarchical pattern. A score of 100 percent indicates that everyone's answer fit the hierarchical or scaled pattern.

Example Study Box 4 Guttman Scaling and Political Protest

Crozat (1998) examined survey data on the public's acceptance of forms of protest in Great Britain, Germany, Italy, the Netherlands, and the United States in 1974 and 1990. He found that the pattern of the public's acceptance fit the hierarchal pattern of a Guttman scale. People who accepted more intense forms of protest (e.g., strikes and sit-ins) almost always accepted mild forms (e.g., petitions or demonstrations). However, not all those who accepted mild forms accepted the more intense forms. In addition to demonstrating the Guttman scale pattern, Crozat found that people in different nations saw protest similarly and the pattern increased over time. Thus, the pattern of acceptance of protest activities was Guttman "scalable" in both time periods, but it more closely followed the pattern in 1990 than in 1974.

Guttman Scalable Patterns

Form of Protest

Petition	Demonstration	Boycott	Strike	Sit-In
N	N	N	N	N
Y	N	N	N	N
Y	Y	N	N	N
Y	Y	Y	N	N
Y	Y	Y	Y	N
Y	Y	Y	Y	Y

Other Nonscalable Patterns (examples only)

Form of Protest

Petition	Demonstration	Boycott	Strike	Sit In
N	Y	N	N	N
Y	N	Y	N	N
Y	N	N	Y	N
N	Y	Y	N	Y
Y	N	Y	Y	N
Y	Y	N	N	Y

Summary Review Major Scales

Likert—General Attitude Measure. Indicates attitude using ranked answers showing degree of agreement/support.

Borgadus—Social Distance Measure. Indicates acceptance of various levels of social intimacy with out-groups.

Semantic Differential—Indirect Evaluation Measure. Indicates subjective feelings using connotations in adjective sets.

Guttman—Structural of Response Measure. Indicates whether a set of items corresponds to a hierarchical pattern.

WHAT HAVE YOU LEARNED?

In this chapter, you learned about the principles of measurement in quantitative and qualitative data studies. You learned that a vital measure task is conceptualizing the ideas you use. This means refining and clarifying them with explicit conceptual definitions. Another task is operationalizing. You must develop a set of techniques that can link your conceptual definition to specific operations or measurement procedures. In quantitative data, you generally take a deductive path, whereas for qualitative data you use a more inductive path. The goal remains the same: to establish unambiguous links among your abstract ideas and the empirical data you collect.

You also learned about the principles of reliability and validity. Reliability refers to the dependability or consistency of a measure. Validity refers to a measure's truthfulness; how well an idea and the measure for it fit together. These principles are applied somewhat differently for quantitative and qualitative data. Nonetheless, in both you want to measure in a consistent and truthful manner. In both you want to create a good fit between the abstract ideas you use to understand social world and what is occurring in the observable empirical world.

You also learned some of the ways that quantitative researchers apply measurement principles to indexes and scales. There are hundreds or different scales and ways to use indexes. You read about a few of the major ones.

Two fundamental principles of all good measurement are to have clear definitions for concepts and to use multiple measures or indicators. These principles hold across all fields of study and across the many research techniques (e.g., experiments, surveys, etc.). As you are probably beginning to realize, research involves doing a good job in each phase of a study. Even if you conduct one or two phases of the research project in a flawless manner, serious mistakes or sloppiness in another phase can do irreparable damage to the results. You must be careful and vigilant at each phase; the overall quality of the study will depend on how well you conduct all phases.

KEY TERMS

conceptual definition *117*
conceptual hypothesis *119*
conceptualization *116*
continuous variables *126*
discrete variables *126*
empirical hypothesis *119*
exhaustive attributes *129*
index *129*

level of measurement *126*
measurement validity *122*
multiple indicators *123*
mutually exclusive attributes *129*
reliability *122*
scale *129*
unidimensionality *130*
validity *122*

APPLYING WHAT YOU'VE LEARNED

Activity 1: Index of a Good Job

Consider the following six occupations:

Long-distance truck driver
Registered nurse
School janitor

Financial accountant
Airplane mechanic
Musician (in a local rock band)

Answer the following seven questions on the characteristics of each occupation. For each, 2 = Definitely Yes, 1 = Sometimes/Somewhat, 0 = No.

1. Does it pay a good salary?
2. Is the job secure from layoffs or unemployment?
3. Is the work interesting and challenging?
4. Does it offer good working conditions (e.g., hours, safety, time away from home)?
5. Are there opportunities for career advancement and promotion?
6. Is it prestigious or looked up to by others?
7. Does it permit self-direction and the freedom to make decisions?

Total the seven answers for each of the occupations. Each occupation will have a score of zero to 14. Which had the highest and which had the lowest score? The seven questions are my operational definition of the construct "good occupation." Each question represents a subpart of a theoretical definition. A different theoretical definition would result in different questions, perhaps more than seven. Creating indexes is so easy that you must be careful that every item in the index has face validity. Items without face validity should be excluded. Each part of the construct should be measured with at least one indicator. Of course, it is better to measure the parts of a construct with multiple indicators.

Activity 2: Measuring Social Dominance

You can replicate part of a study of college roommates and racial-ethnic groups. Van Laar and colleagues (2005) measured social dominance, which is a feeling that groups are fundamentally unequal, with the following four-item index that used a Likert scale, from 1 Strongly Disagree to 7 Strongly Agree.

1. It is probably a good thing that certain groups are at the top and other groups are at the bottom.
2. Inferior groups should stay in their place.
3. We should do all we can to equalize the conditions of different groups.
4. We should increase social equality.*

You may need the approval of your campus Institutional Review Board (IRB) (see Chapter 3) to conduct this activity. Write a questionnaire containing the preceding four questions and using Likert scoring. Distribute the questionnaire to 35 students. Take the scores of the Likert scale answers (1 to 7) for items 1 to 4 and add to yield an index that ranges from 4 to 28 for each student. What was the average score for your 35 students? Read the article by van Laar and colleagues (2005) and compare your findings with what they discovered.

Activity 3: Social Distance

Complete an updated version of the Borgadus social distance scale created by Kleg and Yamamoto (1998). In addition to yourself, you can ask your friends and family members to complete it. Exclude the in-group that you (or your friends or family) belong to.

I would desire with members of each group listed

1. To marry into that group
2. To have a group member as my best friend
3. To have as next-door neighbors members of that group
4. To work in the same office as members of that group
5. To have as speaking acquaintances only members of that group
6. To have as visitors to my country members of that group
7. To keep out of my country members of that group

Degree of association (1–7): Use the numbers 1 to 7 above to indicate how you feel about each group listed here.

Arab _____	Greek _____	Native American _____
Black American _____	Irish _____	Norwegian _____
Chinese _____	Italian _____	Polish _____
Danish _____	Japanese _____	Russian _____
Dutch _____	Jewish _____	Scottish _____
English _____	Korean _____	Spanish _____
French _____	Mexican _____	Swedish _____
German _____		

*This item was reverse scored.

REFERENCES

Babbie, Earl. 2004. *The Practice of Social Research*, 10 ed. Belmont CA: Wadsworth.

Bell, S., and C. Lee, C. 2002. "Development of the Perceived Stress Questionnaire for Young Women." *Psychology, Health and Medicine* 7:189–201.

Crozat, Matthew. 1998. "Are the Times-a-Changing? Assessing the Acceptance of Protest in Western Democracies." In *The Movement Society*, edited by D. Meyer and S. Tarrow, pp. 59–81. Totowa, NJ: Rowman and Littlefield.

DeRango, Kelly. 2001. "Discrimination and Segregation in Housing" Employment Research, paper of the W.E. Upjohn Institute for Employment Research. http://www.upjohninst.org/publications/newsletter/kd_701.pdf Downloaded March 25, 2008.

Duncan, Otis Dudley, and Beverly Duncan. 1955. "A Methodological Analysis of Segregation Indexes." *American Sociological Review* 20:210–217.

Gee, Gilbert C., Michael S. Spencer, Juan Chen, and David Takeuchi. 2007. "A Nationwide Study of Discrimination and Chronic Health Conditions Among Asian Americans." *American Journal of Public Health* 97:1275–1282.

Gordon, Phyllis A., Jennifer Chiraboga Tantillo, David Feldman, and Kristin Perrone. 2004. "Attitudes Regarding Interpersonal Relationship with Persons with Mental Illness and Mental Retardation." *Journal of Rehabilitation* 70:50–56.

Hawkes, Daina, Charlene Seen, and Chantal Thorn. 2004. "Factors That Influence Attitudes Toward Women With Tattoos." *Sex Roles* 50(9/10):593–604.

Heise, David R. 1970. "The Semantic Differential and Attitude Research" In *Attitude Measurement*, edited by Gene F. Summers. Chicago: Rand McNally, pp. 235–253.

Perry, Pamela. 2001. "White Means Never Having to Say You're Ethnic: White Youth and the Construction of 'Cultureless' Identities." *Journal of Contemporary Ethnography* 30(1):56–91.

Kleg, Milton, and Kaoru Yamamoto. 1998. "As the world turns." *Social Science Journal* 35: 183–190.

Rosenberg, Morris. 1965. *Society and the adolescent self-image.* Princeton, NJ: Princeton University Press (also see http://www.bsos.umd.edu/socy/Research/rosenberg.htm).

Smith, David W. 2004. "The Population Perspective on Quality of Life among Americans with Diabetes." *Quality of Life Research*. 13:1391–1400.

Van Laar, Colette, Shana Levin, and Shana and Stacey Sinclair. 2005. "The Effect of University Roommate Contact on Ethnic Attitudes and Behavior." *Journal of Experimental Social Psychology* 41:329–345.

Weitzer, Ronald, and Steven Tuch. 2005. "Racially biased policing." *Social Forces* 83:1009–1030.

CHAPTER 6

The Survey: Asking People Questions

Rick Friedman/Corbis

M any nations (Canada, Belgium, the Netherlands, South Africa, and Spain) recognize marriages between people of the same sex. Most of Europe, Argentina, Australia, Brazil, and New Zealand recognize same-sex civil unions that offer benefits similar to marriage. In the United States, this is a heated, divisive political issue. The issue surfaced in 1996 when the United States Congress passed, and President Bill Clinton signed, the Defense of Marriage Act. Since then, many states passed laws banning same-sex marriage. In November 2003, the issue exploded in the media. The Massachusetts Supreme Court just ruled in *Goodridge v. Department of Public Health* that it was unconstitutional to ban same-sex marriages in that state. In the 2004 Presidential election, social-religious conservatives made same-sex marriage a forefront issue that displaced the abortion issue. Beyond the court battles, advocacy campaigns, and political rhetoric, you may ask, What do ordinary Americans think about the issue? Dozens of polls and surveys tell us that 40 to 60 percent of the public opposes legal same-sex marriage, 30 to 50 percent would allow it, and 1 to 15 percent is uncertain. The data suggest that the most ardent opponents tend to be men, older people, those who say religion is central in their lives, people with less schooling, those with strong antiabortion views, and people who want to deny atheists basic legal rights. Results vary somewhat by how a survey asked the question. Did it ask about same sex-marriage, gay marriage, homosexual marriage, or the marriage of gay men and lesbians? Did it ask about permitting or banning such marriages? Did it place the issue at the federal level as a constitutional amendment or as a state law, or did it ask about a personal moral position? Did it ask about civil unions, specific legal rights for gay people, or only about marriage? With this issue, as with many others, you must first understand how the survey research method operates if you want to know what people think and try to find out why (see Brewer and Wilcox 2005).

WHAT IS A SOCIAL SURVEY?

Most people have some experience with surveys. Surveys are the most widely used data-gathering technique in the social sciences and other fields. They may be *too* popular. Many people say "do a survey" to get information when they should ask, "What is the most appropriate research technique for learning about this issue?" Despite its popularity, it is easy to create a survey that produces misleading or worthless results. A good survey that produces accurate data requires serious thought and effort. In this chapter, you will learn about what makes a quality social survey, limitations of the survey method, and the basics of how to do your own survey.

The survey technique gives us data based on self-reports. You use the survey method when you can phrase the research question, issue, and variables you want to learn about as questions that people are willing and able to answer without great difficulty. These include questions such as how much schooling a person completed or whether a person favors or opposes same-sex marriage. Surveys are not very useful for learning about things people are unaware of or are unwilling to self-report on, such as illegal behaviors.

In a social survey, a large number of people (called respondents because they respond to a query) hear and give an answer to the exact same questions. They may answer questions about their past behaviors, experiences, opinions, and characteristics. You can use one survey to measure many variables and test multiple hypotheses at the same time. After you gathered the data, you can test hypotheses by looking for patterns among the answers given. For example, you might hypothesize that a person's view on the abortion issue is related to how he or she feels about same-sex marriage. In short, you predict one attitude by the other. You use statistical techniques to find the association between these two variables, abortion views and same-sex marriage, measured in a social survey (statistical techniques are discussed in Chapter 9).

You may wonder, Does an opinion poll differ from a survey? The difference is minor. An opinion poll is a type of survey; it is a short survey about opinions on current issues. Most polls look at a sample of the public over a short time period, such as one or two weeks. Many polling organizations (Roper, Gallup), media organizations (ABC/*Washington Post*, *Newsweek*, Fox News), political organizations, and research centers (Pew Research Center) regularly conduct polls on current issues, such as same-sex marriage. Most reputable polling organizations use techniques very similar to those used by professional academic survey researchers. In addition to polls, there are many other types of surveys. Some surveys use samples, others do not; some survey the public, and others focus on a specific group. Beyond asking about opinions on current issues, a survey may ask about knowledge, social background and characteristics, general beliefs, or behaviors. For example, a business may use a survey to measure employee job satisfaction or customer preferences for a product; and a medical clinic may conduct a survey to learn about patient health behaviors. Polls rarely have more than a dozen questions, but surveys can have over a hundred detailed questions. Survey researchers ask about many things at once to measure many variables simultaneously and to test multiple hypotheses. After they collect survey data, researchers analyze them to test theories, explore relationships among variables, and develop a picture of people's thoughts and actions.

A cause-effect explanation based on survey data differs somewhat from other research techniques, such as the experiment. Recall from Chapter 2, that if you want to say that one variable causes another, you must meet three conditions: (1) The independent variable must come before the dependent in time; (2) the two variables must be associated, or correlated with one another; and (3) no alternative cause for the relation exists, or there is no spuriousness. Survey data are sometimes called **correlational,** because they are strongest at meeting the second condition of causality. Meeting the first condition, time order, is complicated with survey data because

correlational research any non-experimental study in which correlations in data are examined and cause-effect relations are shown indirectly.

(text continues on p. 153)

Example Study Box 1 **American Views on Same-Sex Marriage**

In December 2003, Greenberg Quinlan Rosner Research and Public Opinion Strategies conducted a national poll for National Public Radio (see Figure 6.1 for the questionnaire). All 1002 respondents were registered voters, voted in the 2000 presidential election or the 2002 congressional elections, and indicated that they would certainly vote in 2004. The sample was generated by random-digit dial methodology (which you learned about in Chapter 4). Telephone interviewers asked, *Do you favor or oppose a law that would allow homosexual couples to legally form civil unions, giving them some of the legal rights of married couples?* Among respondents, 42 percent favored and 49 percent opposed civil unions (the rest had no opinion). A gender gap appeared: 57 percent of men compared to 43 percent of women said they oppose civil unions. A related national survey by the National Opinion Research Center (NORC) several months later in 2004 asked a random sample of 1216 American adults the following: *Homosexual couples should have the right to marry one another; do you agree or disagree?* Answer choices were a Likert scale (you learned about Likert scales in Chapter 5). People could Strongly Agree, Agree, Disagree, Strongly Disagree, or say they cannot choose. Questions were from the General Social Survey (GSS) (which is discussed in Chapter 8). More people opposed the right to marriage than civil unions: 28.9 percent of respondents expressed agreement, 54.2 percent disagreement, and the rest said neither or could not choose. A similar gender gap also appeared for the marriage question; 62.7 percent of men and 50.2 percent of women said disagree. Researchers combined these data with other data from the same survey to examine in greater depth who agrees or disagrees on the issue and why.

■ **Figure 6.1**   NPR—Swing Districts Frequency Questionnaire

Greenburg Quinlan Rosner Research
July 19–23, 2006
1000 Likely Voters

Q.3 First of all, are you registered to vote at this address?

	Total
Yes	100
No	—
(Refused)	—
(ref:SCREEN1)	

Q.4 Many people weren't able to vote in the 2004 election for President between George Bush and John Kerry. How about you? Were you able to vote, or for some reason were you unable to vote?

	Total
Voted	100
Not registered in 2004/Ineligible/too young	0
Did not vote	—
(Can't remember/Don't know/Refused)	—
(Refused)	—
(ref:VOTE00)	

Q.5 As you know, there was an election for Congress and other offices in 2002. Many people weren't able to vote. How about you? Were you able to vote or for some reason were you unable to vote?

	Total
Voted	91
Did not vote	7
(Can't remember/Don't know)	2
(Refused)	—
(ref:VOTE02)	

(continued)

■ **Figure 6.1**   *Continued*

Q.6 I know it's a long way off, but what are the chances of your voting in the election for Congress this year: are you almost certain to vote, will you probably vote, are the chances 50-50, or don't you think you will vote?

	Total
Almost certain	84
Probably	16
50-50	—
Will not vote	—
(Don't know/refused)	—
(Refused)	—
(ref:CP3)	

Q.8 Generally speaking, do you think that things in this country are going in the right direction, or do you feel things have gotten pretty seriously off on the wrong track?

	Total
Right direction	31
Wrong track	61
(Don't know/refused)	7
Right–Wrong	**−30**
(ref:DIRECT)	

[615 Respondents]

Q.9 (IF WRONG TRACK) Why do you say things are going in the wrong direction?

	Total
The war	43
The economy/jobs	22
Negative Bush (general)	16
Gas prices	14
Wrong priorities/money should be spent at home	9
No leadership	7
Healthcare	7
Illegal immigration	6
Bush cares only about wealthy/rich getting richer	6
Things are generally bad	5
Education	5
Environmental issues	4
Deficit	4
Morality	3
Cost of living skyrocketing	3
High taxes	3
Middle East/Lebanon/Israel	3
Government regulation of morality/abortion/gay marriage/stem cell research	3
Social security	2
Poor handling of Katrina	1
Other	6
DK/refused	0
(ref:WTRACKOE)	

Q.10 Do you approve or disapprove of the way George Bush is handling his job as president?

	Total
Strongly approve	24
Somewhat approve	17
Somewhat disapprove	10
Strongly disapprove	45
(Don't know/Refused)	3
Total approve	**42**
Total disapprove	**55**
Approve–disapprove	**−14**
(ref:CANDAPP2)	

■ Figure 6.1   *Continued*

Q.11 And, on a scale of one to ten, with one meaning NOT AT ALL interested and ten meaning VERY INTERESTED, please tell me how interested you are in this year's elections?

	Total
10	58
9	8
8	12
7	7
6	3
5	8
4	1
3	1
2	0
1	1
Don't know	0
Mean	**8.7**
10	**58**
8–10	**78**
6–10	**88**
1–5	**11**
Don't know	**0**

(ref:INTEREST)

Q.12 I know it is far ahead, but thinking about this year's elections, if the election for U.S. Congress were held today, would you be voting for the Democratic candidate or the Republican candidate in your district where you live?

	Total
Democratic candidate	43
Lean Democratic candidate	5
Republican candidate	37
Lean Republican candidate	4
(Other candidate)	1
Lean (Other candidate)	0
(Undecided)	8
(Refused)	1
Total Democratic candidate	**48**
Total Republican candidate	**41**
Total (Other candidate)	**2**
Democratic candidate–Republican candidate	**7**

(ref:GC1)

[739 Respondents]

Q.14 (IF INCUMBENT IS RUNNING FOR RE-ELECTION) As you may know, there will also be an election for your Representative to Congress on the November ballot. Understanding that the election is a long way off, do you think you will definitely vote to re-elect (incumbent) to Congress, probably vote to re-elect (incumbent), probably vote for someone else, or definitely vote for someone else?[1]

	Total
Definitely re-elect incumbent	14
Probably re-elect incumbent	16
Probably vote for someone else	22
Definitely vote for someone else	24
(Depends on the person)	4
(Don't know/Refused)	20
Total Re-elect	**29**
Total Someone else	**46**
Re-elect incumbent–Someone else	**−17**

(ref: REELECT)

[1]For each district in which the incumbent is expected to run for reelection in 2006, the incumbent's actual name was inserted.

(continued)

■ **Figure 6.1** *Continued*

Q.15 I know it is far ahead, but thinking about the election for Congress this November, if the election for U.S. Congress were held today, would you be voting for (Democratic incumbent/candidate) or (Republican incumbent/candidate)?[2]

	Total
Democratic incumbent/candidate	47
Lean Democratic incumbent/candidate	3
Republican incumbent/candidate	40
Lean Republican incumbent/candidate	3
(Other candidate)	1
Lean (Other candidate)	0
(Undecided)	5
(Refused)	1
Total Democratic incumbent/candidate	**49**
Total Republican incumbent/candidate	**43**
Total (Other candidate)	**1**
Democratic candidate–Republican candidate	**6**
(ref:CONG06)	

Q.17 Even though you are not supporting (Democratic incumbent/candidate) now, what are the chances that you might support (Democratic incumbent/candidate) in the election for Congress this year—is there a fair chance that you might support that candidate, a small chance, just a very slight chance or no chance at all that you might support that candidate?

	Total
Fair chance	9
A small chance	9
Just a very slight chance	10
No chance at all	19
(Don't know/Refused)	3
Democratic candidate supporter	**49**
(ref:CONG06C)	

Q.18 Even though you are not supporting (Republican incumbent/candidate) now, what are the chances that you might support (Republican incumbent/candidate) in the election for Congress this year—is there a fair chance that you might support that candidate, a small chance, just a very slight chance or no chance at all that you might support that candidate?

	Total
Fair chance	8
A small chance	8
Just a very slight chance	10
No chance at all	28
(Don't know/Refused)	2
Republican candidate supporter	**43**
(ref:CONG06D)	

[2]For each district in which the incumbent is expected to run for reelection in 2006, the incumbent's actual name was inserted, and a generic candidate ("the Democratic candidate" or "the Republican candidate") was inserted for the opposition. For districts in which the incumbent is not expected to run for reelection, the actual name of each party's most likely candidate was inserted if one could be determined, and a generic candidate was inserted if a most likely candidate could not be determined.

■ **Figure 6.1**   *Continued*

Q.19/20 In deciding how to vote for Congress this year, which ONE of the following issue areas would be MOST important to you in deciding how to vote for a candidate for Congress? And which of the following issues would be the NEXT most important to you in deciding how to vote for Congress?

	Comb	**1st**	**2nd**
The war in Iraq	31	14	18
Jobs and economy	27	17	11
Taxes and spending	22	10	13
Health care	21	9	13
Terrorism and national security	20	10	11
Medicare and Social Security	18	9	10
Moral values	17	12	5
Illegal immigration	17	8	10
Corruption in Washington	15	7	9
(None of these)	3	2	1
(Don't know/Refused)	4	3	1
(ref:CONG06/CONC062)			

Q.21 Thinking about the congressional elections that will be held this November, compared to previous elections, are you more enthusiastic about voting than usual, or less enthusiastic?

	Total
More	54
Less	26
(No more/less)	18
(Don't know/refused)	2
More–less	**27**
(ref:ENTHUSIA)	

Q.22 I'm going to ask you about a number of issues that are being debated in the Congress and with the President. For each one, based on what you have heard recently, does it make you more likely to support the Democrats or the Republicans for Congress?

	Dems Strng	**Dems Smwt**	**Reps Smwt**	**Reps Strng**	**Both**	**Neither**	**DK/ Ref**	**Total Dems**	**Total Reps**	**Dems – Reps**
22 The illegal immigration issue	24	17	17	24	1	6	11	**41**	**41**	**0**
23 The war in Iraq	41	8	13	31	1	2	5	**49**	**44**	**5**
24 The state of the economy	35	14	13	30	0	3	5	**49**	**42**	**7**
25 The president's handling of detainees at Guantanamo and wiretapping of suspected terrorists	34	12	10	33	0	3	7	**46**	**44**	**2**
[500 Respondents] 26 (SPLIT A) The issue of stem cell research	39	12	11	22	1	3	12	**51**	**33**	**18**
[500 Respondents] 27 (SPLIT B) Values issues, like stem cell research, flag burning and gay marriage (ref:DEBISSUE)	38	12	10	28	0	3	8	**51**	**37**	**13**

(continued)

■ **Figure 6.1**   *Continued*

Q.28 Finally, I would like to ask you a few questions for statistical purposes. What is the last year of schooling that you have completed?

	Total
1–11th grade	2
High school graduate	25
Non-college post H.S.	1
Some college	25
College graduate	27
Post-graduate school	20
(Don't know/refused)	1
(ref:EDUC)	

Q.29 Are you a member of a labor union? (IF NO) Is any member of your household a union member?

	Total
Yes: Respondent belongs	12
Household member	9
No member belongs	78
(Don't know/refused)	1
(ref:UNION)	

Q.30 Are you married, single, separated, divorced, or widowed?

	Total
Married	64
Single	15
Separated/divorced	12
Widowed	8
(Don't know/refused)	1
(ref:MARITAL)	

Q.31 Generally speaking, do you think of yourself as a Democrat, a Republican, or what?

	Total
Strong Democrat	27
Weak Democrat	10
Independent-lean Democrat	12
Independent	6
Independent-lean Republican	9
Weak Republican	12
Strong Republican	24
(Don't know/refused)	1
(ref:PTYID1)	

Q.34 Thinking in political terms, would you say that you are Conservative, Moderate, or Liberal?

	Total
Liberal	20
Moderate	40
Conservative	36
(Don't know/refused)	3
(ref:IDEO1)	

Q.35 What is your religion?

	Total
Protestant	51
Catholic	26
Jewish	2
Muslim	–
(Other/none/refused)	22
(ref:RELIG1)	

■ **Figure 6.1**   *Continued*

[510 Respondents]

Q.36 (IF PROTESTANT) Which one of these words best describes your kind of Christianity—fundamentalist, evangelical, charismatic, Pentecostal, or moderate to liberal?

	Total
Fundamentalist	12
Evangelical	21
Charismatic/Pentecostal	10
Moderate to liberal	42
(Something else)	5
(Don't know/refused)	11
(ref:RELIG3)	

Q.37 How often do you attend church—every week, once or twice a month, several times a year, or hardly ever?

	Total
Every week	39
Once or twice a month	16
Several times a year	15
Hardly ever	20
(Never)	7
(Don't know/refused)	4
(ref:RELIG2)	

[996 Respondents]

Q.38 (IF VOTED IN 2004) In the 2004 election for President, did you vote for Democrat John Kerry or Republican George Bush?

	Total
Democrat John Kerry	46
Republican George Bush	49
(Ralph Nader)	0
(Other candidate)	2
(Don't know/refused)	4
Democrat John Kerry–Republican George Bush	**−3**
(ref:VOTE2004)	

Q.39 How many guns or rifles do you own?

	Total
None	57
1-2	15
3-9	14
10 or more	6
(Don't know/refused)	9
(ref:GUNS)	

Q.40 What racial or ethnic group best describes you?

	Total
White	83
African-American or Black	6
Hispanic or Latino	6
Native American	1
Asian	0
(Other)	1
(Don't know/refused)	2
(ref:RACETHN)	

[56 Respondents]

(continued)

■ **Figure 6.1**   *Continued*

Q.42 (IF HISPANIC OR LATINO) Would you describe your Hispanic origin as
Mexican, Puerto Rican, Cuban, Latin American, Central American, or Spanish?

	Total
Spanish	40
Mexican	22
Puerto Rican	12
Cuban	8
Latin American	8
Central American	7
(Other)	3
(Don't know/refused)	—
(ref:ORIGIN)	

Q.43 Last year, that is, in 2005, what was your total family income from all
sources, before taxes? Just stop me when I get to the right category.

	Total
Less than $10K	3
$10K to under $20K	5
$20K to under $30K	9
$30K to under $50K	18
$50K to under $75K	19
$75K to under $100K	14
$100K or more	13
(Refused)	15
(Don't know)	3
(ref:INCOME)	

Q.44 It is possible that a reporter for National Public Radio may do a news story
based on some of these topics and may want to ask a few follow-up questions of
some of the people we spoke to tonight. Would you be willing to allow an NPR
reporter to have your responses on the questions and then possibly call you for a
brief interview?

	Total
Yes	53
No	47
(ref:NPRFOLLOW)	

Q.2 Respondent's gender

	Total
Male	48
Female	52
(ref:GENDER)	

Q.7 In what year were you born?

	Total
18–24	3
25–29	5
30–34	9
35–39	7
40–44	8
45–49	11
50–54	11
55–59	12
60–64	9
Over 64	22
(No answer)	2
(ref:AGE)	

most survey data are collected at a single time point. Without data at multiple time points, you must logically show that information from one survey question (e.g., father's occupation while growing up) occurred earlier in time than information another question (the person's current income). To meet the third condition, no alternative cause, you must think of variables that are possible alternative causes and measure them in the survey. They are called **control variables**, because you can statistically control for, or take into account, their effects with statistics after you have collected the data. For example, you find that widowed people have more health problems than married people do. Before you say that being widowed itself is the cause, you need to consider alternative causes that might make the relationship spurious. If most widowed people are older than married people, then you must rule out the alternative of age as a cause of health problems before you can say that widowhood causes more health problems. When planning a survey about marital status and health, you will want to ask about age as well. As you plan a survey, you need to think about measuring variables from the main hypothesis (dependent and independent variables) and variables that represent potential alternative explanations.

HOW TO CONDUCT A SURVEY

Once you decide that the survey is an appropriate method for gathering data to test your hypothesis, you proceed through three stages. We can subdivide the stages into six steps (see Figure 6.2):

1. Start-up stage—Plan and prepare the survey questionnaire (steps 1, 2, and 3)
2. Execution stage—Collect and record data (step 4)
3. Data analysis stage—analyze and interpret the data, and report the final results (steps 5 and 6)

Start-Up Stage

In this stage, you address the following three questions:

Who will be the respondents of your survey?
What information do you want to learn from them?
How can you effectively get that information?

You first need to know about your respondents. The type of respondents will influence the topics you ask about and even how you word questions. Topics relevant in a survey of nursing home residents may not be relevant to one of college students. Survey questions about working for part-time workers at a fast food outlet may differ from questions on the same topic in a survey of medical doctors.

Second, you must be clear about exactly what you want to learn from a question. Survey questions are the operationalization of variables and depend on how well you conceptualized them (see Chapter 5 for a discussion of conceptualization and operationalization). Before you gather any data, consider how you intend to use the results. Without a picture of what possible results might look like, it is difficult to create a good survey that produces appropriate data. Newcomers to survey research are often disappointed when analyzing data because they find that their data do not allow them to answer their research question. This happens when they fail to think clearly about what the results might look like as they are designing their survey questionnaire. Too often they ask questions unrelated to their true concern or fail to ask specific enough questions.

To prepare a survey, follow the steps outlined in Figure 6.2. First, create an instrument—a survey questionnaire or interview schedule—to measure variables. Respondents may read the questions themselves and mark answers on a **questionnaire.** Alternatively, you may prepare an **interview schedule**—a set of

control variable a variable that represents a possible alternative explanation to the main hypothesis being tested; often control variables are measured in survey research with questions in addition to measures of the independent and dependent variables.

questionnaire a fixed collection of questions used in a social survey that respondents answer.

interview schedule a questionnaire specifically designed for an interviewer asking respondents the questions.

Control variables measure variables from alternative explanations that compete with the primary hypothesis you wish to test. Let us say you think that gender causes differences in opinion about same-sex marriage. An alternative explanation may be that age, or how religious a person feels, causes the opinion. Your survey should ask about gender, age, and strength of religious feeling. All three are possible causes of the dependent variable. In the data analysis stage, you can look at all three variables to evaluate the explanations. Multiple independent variables have an effect, but you usually want to know which one is strongest. You may believe that males oppose same-sex marriage because traditional males express greater antipathy toward homosexuality. Alternative explanations are that age and strength of religious feelings have bigger effects than gender, with older people or very religious people voicing opposition. You can look at all three variables to see which one has the greatest predictive power. If the gap in male-female opposition opinion is 12 percent with males more opposed, the age gap is 21 percent with older people more opposed, and the religiosity gap is 35 percent with highly religious people more opposed, then religiosity is the strongest independent variable (see the following table below).

View on Homosexual Marriage by Gender, Age, and Religosity

View on Gay Marriage	Gender of Respondent			
	Male	**Female**	**Total**	
Agree	24.0%	34.1%	29.6%	
Neither	13.3%	15.6%	14.6%	
Disagree	62.7%	50.2%	55.7%	Gender gap = 12.5%
Total (N)	525	659	1184	
	100.0%	100.0%	100.0%	

	Age of Respondent				
	under 35	**35–55**	**56+**	**Total**	
Agree	41.0%	25.9%	22.4%	29.7%	
Neither	14.6%	16.1%	2.1%	14.5%	
Disagree	44.5%	58.0%	65.4%	55.8%	Oldest/youngest gap = 20.9%
Total (N)	371	491	321	1183	
	100.0%	100.0%	100.0%	100.0%	

	How Religious?				
	Strongly	**Not Very Religious**	**Not Religious**	**Total**	
Agree	21.6%	30.9%	47.0%	29.5%	
Neither	10.4%	16.3%	20.2%	14.5%	
Disagree	68.0%	52.9%	32.7%	55.9%	Strong/no religion gap = 35.3%
Total (N)	462	541	168	1171	
	100.0%	100.0%	100.0%	100.0%	

Generated by author from General Social Survey 2004 data.

■ Figure 6.2   Steps in the Process of Survey Research

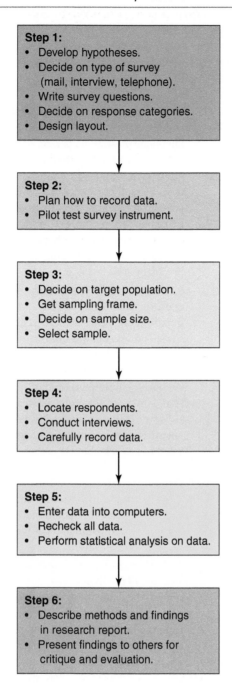

Step 1:
- Develop hypotheses.
- Decide on type of survey (mail, interview, telephone).
- Write survey questions.
- Decide on response categories.
- Design layout.

Step 2:
- Plan how to record data.
- Pilot test survey instrument.

Step 3:
- Decide on target population.
- Get sampling frame.
- Decide on sample size.
- Select sample.

Step 4:
- Locate respondents.
- Conduct interviews.
- Carefully record data.

Step 5:
- Enter data into computers.
- Recheck all data.
- Perform statistical analysis on data.

Step 6:
- Describe methods and findings in research report.
- Present findings to others for critique and evaluation.

survey questions designed so that an interviewer can read them to a respondent. The interview may be by phone or face-to-face. To simplify the discussion, I will use only the term *questionnaire*.

Once you decide on who the respondents will be, exactly what you want to measure, and a survey format, you can start writing questions. Expect to write and rewrite questions several times for clarity and completeness. It is also important to organize carefully the flow of questions on a questionnaire. You should base the organization on your research question, your respondents, and the type of survey. (Types of surveys are discussed later in this chapter.) When preparing a questionnaire, try to think ahead to how you will record and organize data for statistical analysis.

Tips for the Wise Researcher What to Avoid when You Write Survey Questions

1. **Avoid *jargon, slang, and abbreviations*.** Jargon and technical terms come in many forms. Plumbers talk about *snakes*, lawyers about a contract of *uberrima fides*, psychologists about the *Oedipus complex*. Slang is a kind of jargon within a subculture. Homeless people may talk about a *snowbird* and skiers about a *hotdog*. Abbreviations are problematic. *NATO* usually means North Atlantic Treaty Organization, but for a respondent, it might mean something else (National Auto Tourist Organization, Native Alaskan Trade Orbit, or North African Tea Office). Slang and jargon are only useful for surveying highly specialized populations. For the general public, aim at the language used on television. It is for someone with an eighth-grade reading level.

2. **Avoid *ambiguity, confusion, and vagueness*.**
Ambiguity and vagueness plague most question writers. You can easily make assumptions without thinking. You should be highly aware of the situations of all respondents. The question "What is your income?" seems simple. However, it could mean weekly, monthly, or annual; family or personal; before taxes or after taxes; for this year or last year; from salary or from all sources. The confusion can cause inconsistencies. Different respondents may assign diverse meanings and answer the question as they interpret it, not as you mean it. If you want before-tax annual family income for last year, ask for it. Ill-defined words or response categories create ambiguity. An answer to the question "Do you jog regularly? Yes _____ No _____" hinges on the word *regularly*. Some respondents may define *regularly* as "every day." Others may think it means "once a week." You want to be very specific to reduce respondent confusion and get more information.

3. **Avoid *highly emotional words*.** Many words have more than dictionary definitions and contain emotional content. Advocates or advertisers often try to manipulate the emotional aspects of language to persuade you, but when writing survey questions you want to use neutral words. Words with emotional "baggage" may cause respondents to react to the emotionally laden words rather than answer a question. Asking "What do you think about a policy to pay murderous terrorists who threaten to steal the freedoms of peace-loving people?" is full of emotional words—such as *murderous*, *freedoms*, *steal*, and *peace*. It is not always easy to know what words have emotional baggage or to avoid them. Survey questions refer to same-sex marriage as "gender-neutral marriage," "equal marriage," "gay marriage," "lesbian marriage," "homosexual marriage," and "same-gender marriage." More people oppose "homosexual marriage" than "gay marriage," and more oppose "gay marriage" than "same-gender marriage," and

more oppose it than "equal marriage." The phrase used can influence answers.

4. **Avoid *prestige bias*.** Titles or positions in society (e.g., president, expert, etc.) carry prestige or status. *Prestige bias* is linking a statement or position on an issue with a well-known or prestigious person or group. Many respondents will answer based on their feelings toward the person or group rather than addressing the issue. Consider the question, "President George Bush and Pope Benedict XVI oppose same-sex marriage. Do you favor or oppose a law to ban same-sex marriages?" With a question like this, you cannot distinguish whether a respondent is giving his or her own view or expressing his or her agreement with the President and the Pope.

5. **Avoid *writing double-barreled questions*.** Make each question about one and only one issue. A **double-barreled question** joins two or more questions together and makes a respondent's answer ambiguous. For example, consider the question, "Do you support marriage and civil unions for gay people?" A respondent who opposes marriage but supports civil unions could respond either yes or no. If respondents read the *and* very strictly, they would say no. However, if they interpret it weakly, more like *or*, they may answer yes. You would not know what they really felt. If you want to ask about two things—for example, gay marriage and civil unions—write two separate questions. Once you have the results, you can also look at the answers to both questions. You can then see whether respondents support one or the other position or neither or both. You will both avoid confusion and get more information by using two separate questions.

6. **Avoid *treating a respondent's belief about a hypothesis as a test of the hypothesis*.** People have beliefs about many things. They may think exercise causes people to have a positive attitude about life, or they may think having more education reduces the odds of a divorce. If you want to examine the hypothesis that educated people are more accepting of gay marriage, you need two questions, one about each variable (education, view on gay marriage). After you have the data, you can then see whether the two variables (education, gay marriage view) are related to one another. The *wrong way* to test the hypothesis between education and favoring gay marriage is to ask people, "Do you think less educated people oppose gay marriage more than highly educated people?" This asks people their opinion about the hypothesis rather than letting you actually test the hypothesis. Answers to this question will tell you about people's beliefs about variables but not about the actual relationship of the variables. The people's beliefs might be right or wrong about the actual relationship among variables.

Do not collect the data just yet. It is always best first to conduct a short pilot test or "dry run" of the survey questionnaire. Pilot tests can increase question clarity. Use a small set of respondents who are similar to those in the final survey. After they answer, ask pilot respondents whether questions were clear. You want to check whether their interpretations of your questions had the intended meaning and whether the answer choices offered were sufficient. Based on pilot test feedback, you may want to reword questions or answer choices and reorganize items in the questionnaire. If you plan to interview, you have several choices: Will you interview by phone or face-to-face? Will you personally do the interviews or have others conduct interviews for you? If you use other people, you need to train them with the questionnaire. In addition to proper survey interview behavior (discussed later in this chapter), interviewers must become very familiar with the wording and purpose of each question and practice following the flow of questionnaire items. In this stage, you also need to draw the sample of respondents, i.e., you pick people to be in your sample in a specific way.

Execution Stage

Finally, you are ready to collect data. Many newcomers are surprised that planning and preparation take so much time. You need to locate the sampled respondents in person, by telephone, over the Internet, or by mail. Provide respondents with information about the survey and instructions on how to complete it. Survey questions follow a simple stimulus/response or question/answer pattern. Record all responses clearly and accurately immediately after respondents give them. After a respondent finishes and you thank him or her, quickly look over responses for completeness and clarity of responses. Once all respondents have completed all questionnaires, you organize all the recorded data and prepare them for statistical analysis.

Large-scale survey research, such as with 1000 respondents over a large geographic area and 100 or more questions, can be very complex and expensive. It requires coordinating many people and dozens of detailed steps. Such a large survey research project requires excellent organization and accurate recordkeeping to keep track of each respondent, questionnaire, and interviewer. Similar procedures apply for a small-scale survey, such as 80 people in one location with 20 questions, but they are more manageable.

If you conduct a small-scale survey, assign each sampled respondent an identification number. Place the number on each questionnaire and then check completed questionnaires against a list of sampled respondents. You should review the responses on each questionnaire and transfer data from questionnaires to a format for statistical analysis (discussed in Chapter 9). Also, safely store the original questionnaires. Meticulous bookkeeping and labeling are essential. Otherwise, you may find that valuable data and your efforts are lost through sloppiness.

Data Analysis Stage

This stage (steps 5 and 6) will be discussed in Chapters 9 and 12. The analysis, interpretation, and reporting of survey data differ little from those of other quantitative data.

WRITING GOOD SURVEY QUESTIONS

Excellent communication is the foundation of writing quality survey questions. Two core principles guide good survey questions: *Avoid confusion, and keep the respondent's perspective in mind.* Good survey questions provide a valid and reliable measure of your variables. They also help respondents feel that they understand what you are asking in a question and that their answers are meaningful. When

double-barreled question a confusing survey question that includes two or more ideas.

survey questions do not mesh well with a respondent's viewpoint or respondents find them confusing, the questions will not produce high-quality data.

You face a bit of a dilemma in survey research. You want each respondent to hear the exact same question. This is because you want to measure the exact same thing across many people. On the other hand, if respondents have diverse backgrounds and frames of reference, the same wording may not have the same meaning for everyone. If you tailor question wording to each respondent, you cannot make comparisons and will not know whether the question wording or differences among the respondents account for various answers.

Writing good survey question takes a lot of practice, patience, and creativity, even for experienced and skilled professionals. You can get a sense of the principles of survey question writing by looking at the six things to avoid when you write survey questions. (See Tips for the Wise Researcher, page 156.) The list does not include every possible error, only the more frequent problems.

What Are Leading Questions?

leading question a survey question worded such that respondents are pushed to a specific answer or position.

You've probably heard about "leading questions," but what are they and should you put them in a survey? Let us address the second question first. You should never intentionally use leading questions in an honest, ethical survey. They are often in dishonest surveys, in which someone tries to manipulate results or mislead people, but you should avoid them. A **leading question** leads the respondent to pick one response over another. A good survey question is one in which respondents do not know which answer you expect, and they feel totally free to state what they really think or feel. There are many types of leading questions.

Making It Practical Improving Unclear Questions

Here are three survey questions written by experienced professional researchers. They revised the original wording after a pilot test revealed that 15 percent of respondents asked for clarification or gave inadequate answers (e.g., don't know). As you can see, question wording is an art that may improve with practice, patience, and pilot testing.

Original Question	Problem	Revised Question
Do you exercise or play sports regularly?	What counts as exercise?	Do you do any sports or hobbies, physical activities, or exercise, including walking, on a regular basis?
What is the average number of days each week you have butter?	Does margarine count as butter?	The next question is just about butter—not including margarine. How many days a week do you have butter?
[Following question on eggs] What is the number of servings in a typical day?	How many eggs is a serving? What is a typical day?	On days when you eat eggs, how many eggs do you usually have?

	Responses to Question		Percentage Asking for Clarification	
	Original	Revision	Original	Revision
Exercise question (% saying "yes")	48%	60%	5%	0%
Butter question (% saying "none")	33%	55%	18%	13%
Egg question (% saying "one")	80%	33%	33%	0%

Source: Adapted from Fowler (1992).

Summary Review   Summary of Survey Question Writing Pitfalls

Things to Avoid	Not Good	A Possible Improvement
1. Jargon, slang, abbreviations	Did you drown in brew until you were totally blasted last night?	Last night, about how much beer did you drink?
2. Vagueness	Do you eat out often?	In a typical week, about how many meals do you eat away from home, at a restaurant, cafeteria, or other eating establishment?
3. Emotional language 4. Prestige bias	"The respected Grace Commission documents that a staggering $350 BILLION of our tax dollars are being completely wasted through poor procurement practices, bad management, sloppy bookkeeping, `defective' contract management, personnel abuses and other wasteful practices. Is cutting pork barrel spending and eliminating government waste a top priority for you?"*	How important is it to you that Congress adopt measures to reduce government waste? Very Important Somewhat Important Neither Important or Unimportant Somewhat Unimportant Not Important at All
5. Double-barreled questions	Do you support or oppose raising social security benefits and increased spending for the military?	Do you support or oppose raising social security benefits? Do you support or oppose increasing spending on the military?
6. Beliefs as real	Do you think more educated people smoke less?	What is your education level? Do you smoke cigarettes?
7. Leading questions	Did you do your patriotic duty and vote in the last election for mayor?	Did you vote in last month's mayoral election?
8. Issues beyond respondent capabilities	Two years ago, how many hours did you watch TV every month?	In the past two weeks, about how many hours do you think you watched TV on a typical day?
9. False premises	When did you stop beating your girl/boyfriend?	Have you ever slapped, punched, or hit your girl/boyfriend?
10. Distant future intentions	After you graduate from college, get a job, and are settled, will you invest a lot of money in the stock market?	Do you have definite plans to put some money into the stock market within the coming two months?
11. Double negatives	Do you disagree with those who do not want to build a new city swimming pool?	There is a proposal to build a new city swimming pool. Do you agree or disagree with the proposal?
12. Unbalanced responses	Did you find the service at our hotel to be, Outstanding, Excellent, Superior, or Good?	Please rate the service at our hotel: Outstanding, Very Good, Adequate, or Poor.

*Actual question taken from a mail questionnaire that was sent to me in May 1998 by the National Republican Congressional Committee. It is also a double-barreled question.

Some Leading Questions. The question, "Stable gay and lesbian couples have same rights as any other law-abiding citizens. Do you agree that your fellow citizens who are gay or lesbian have the same right to the benefits and responsibilities of a legal marriage as anyone else?" may lead respondents to state that they favor gay marriage even if they are uncertain. This is because of the statement about the "same rights as other law-abiding citizens." You can state loaded questions to get a positive or a negative answer. For example, "Should we alter the law so that sexually deviant people get the privileges and benefits of a marriage, or should we uphold the natural basis of a marriage as between one man and one woman as it has been for centuries in custom, law, and religious teachings?" leads a respondent to disagree.

Getting Answers to Survey Questions

David Gould/Photographer's Choice/Getty Images Royalty Free

Should You Use an Open or Closed Answer Format? Survey experts have debated the pluses and minuses of using open-ended versus closed-ended survey question answers. In an **open-ended question format** (also called unstructured or free response), respondents can give any answer, whereas in the **closed-ended question format** (also called structured or fixed response), they must chose among fixed answer choices. Each format has advantages and disadvantages (see Summary Review on page 161). You must decide which format is most appropriate for the conditions or purpose of your particular survey. This depends on your study's goal and the practical limitations of your research project.

An open-ended answer format takes more time than a closed-ended format. It requires a respondent to have writing or verbal skills. It is easier for respondents to get off track and give a lot of unrelated information. Interviewers must write extensive verbatim answers. Coding open-ended responses to analyze the data is complex and time-consuming. An open-ended format is impractical for all but small-scale samples (under 200 people) with a few questions (under 20). Nonetheless, it is very useful for exploratory research, when you know little about an issue. It is also more effective when the goal is to capture a respondent's thinking process.

Writing closed-ended questions requires some decisions. How many response choices should you give? Should you offer a middle or neutral choice? How should you order answer choices? How should you measure the direction of answers? Making such decisions is not easy. For example, two response choices are too few, but more than five response choices can create confusion. You want to measure meaningful distinctions and not collapse them. Very specific answer choices yield more information, but too many specifics may create confusion. You can offer more choices and get more information without confusion if you rephrase a yes/no question, "Are you satisfied with your dentist?" by using a Likert scale format such as, "How satisfied are you with your dentist: very satisfied, somewhat satisfied, somewhat dissatisfied, or not satisfied at all?"

Large-scale samples or long questionnaires require you to use a closed-ended format. This format is much faster and easier for both respondents and the researcher. Yet you can lose something important by forcing an individual's beliefs and feelings into a few fixed categories. One way to reduce the disadvantages of an answer format is by mixing open-ended and closed-ended formats in a questionnaire or by using a partially open format. Mixing formats also changes the pace and helps interviewers establish rapport. Periodic probes (see the discussion later in this chapter) with closed-ended answers can reveal a respondent's reasoning. For large-scale surveys, you can use open questions in pilot tests, then develop closed question responses based on answers to the open questions. The partially open format is a closed format question with an open-ended "other" option. The following is a survey question used in CBS/*Newsweek*/*New York Times* polls that I modified to make partially open:

open-ended question format survey questions that allow respondents to give any answer.

closed-ended question format survey questions in which respondents must chose among fixed answer choices.

Which of the following comes closest to your view?
_____ *Gay couples should be allowed to marry, OR* _____ *form civil unions, OR* _____ *there should be no legal recognition of gay couple's relationship,* **OR some other arrangement, please specify** _____

Summary Review Threatening Questions and Sensitive Issues

Advantages of Closed	Disadvantages of Closed
• It is easier and quicker for respondents to answer. • The answers of different respondents are easier to compare. • Answers are easier to code and statistically analyze. • The response choices can clarify question meaning for respondents. • Respondents are more likely to answer about sensitive topics. • There are fewer irrelevant or confused answers to questions. • Less articulate or less literate respondents are not at a disadvantage. • Replication is easier	• They can suggest ideas that the respondent would not otherwise have. • Respondents with no opinion or knowledge can answer anyway. • Respondents can be frustrated because their desired answer is not a choice. • It is confusing if many (e.g., 20) response choices are offered. • Misinterpretation of a question can go unnoticed. • Distinctions between respondent answers may be blurred. • Clerical mistakes or marking the wrong response is possible. • They force respondents to give simplistic responses to complex issues • They force people to make choices they would not make in the real world.
Advantages of Open	**Disadvantages of Open**
• They permit an unlimited number of possible answers. • Respondents can answer in detail and can qualify and clarify responses. • Unanticipated findings can be discovered. • They permit adequate answers to complex issues. • They permit creativity, self-expression, and richness of detail. • They reveal a respondent's logic, thinking process, and frame of reference.	• Different respondents give different degrees of detail in answers. • Respondents may be irrelevant or buried in useless detail. • Comparisons and statistical analysis become very difficult. • Coding responses is difficult. • Articulate and highly literate respondents have an advantage. • Questions may be too general for respondents who lose direction. • Responses are written verbatim, which is difficult for interviewers. • A greater amount of respondent time, thought, and effort is necessary. • Respondents can be intimidated by questions. • Answers take up a lot of space in the questionnaire.

Writing Good Closed-Format Response Choices. Most surveys offer preset answers from which a respondent chooses. Writing good answer choices is just as important as writing a good question. The answer choices should have three features:

- *Mutually exclusive.* Response categories do not overlap. You can easily correct numerical ranges (e.g., 5–10, 10–20, 20–30) that overlap (e.g., 5–9, 10–19, 20–29). The ambiguous verbal choice is another type of overlapping response category—for example, "Are you satisfied with your job or are there things you don't like about it?" It is not clear how a person who is generally satisfied but has a few minor complaints would answer this. (You already learned about variables being mutually exclusive in Chapter 5.)
- *Exhaustive.* This means that that each respondent has a choice—a place to go. For example, asking respondents, "Are you working or unemployed?" leaves out respondents who are not working but do not consider themselves unemployed (e.g., full-time homemakers, people on vacation, students, people with disabilities, or retired people). When writing a question, first think about what you want to know and then consider the circumstances of all possible respondents. For example, if you ask about a respondent's employment, do you want information on the primary job or on all jobs? Do you want both full- and part-time work? Do you only want jobs for pay or also unpaid jobs and volunteer jobs as well? If someone is temporarily unemployed, do you want the last job he or she held?

- *Balanced.* This means you offer the favorable or unfavorable choices equally in a set of responses. A case of unbalanced choices is the question, "What kind of job is the mayor doing: outstanding, excellent, very good, or satisfactory?" It offers three favorable and one neutral response choice. Another type of unbalanced question omits information—for example, "Which of the five candidates running for mayor do you favor: Eugene Oswego or one of the others?" You can balance responses by offering bipolar opposites. Unless there is a specific purpose for doing otherwise, offer respondents equal polar opposites at each end of a continuum. Asking, "How you strongly support the ban on gay marriage? Do you strongly support it, somewhat support it, or just barely support it?" is a set of unbalanced answers. To make it balanced, you could ask, "How do you feel about the ban on gay marriage; do support it, oppose it, or neither?"

Should you offer a "Don't Know" or "No Opinion" Response Choice? Professional survey researchers debate whether to include choices for neutral, middle, and nonattitudes (e.g., "not sure," "don't know," "undecided," or "no opinion") in closed-ended questions. They want to avoid two errors:

a. Getting a "no opinion" or "don't know" response when a respondent actually holds a nonneutral opinion
b. Forcing a respondent to choose a position when he or she has no opinion on an issue or knows nothing about it.

 Example Study Box 2 Questionnaire Items from the National Public Radio Survey

This marital status question has **mutually exclusive** and **exhaustive** answer choices.

Are you married, single, separated, divorced, or widowed?
Married
Single
Separated/divorced
Widowed
Don't know/refused

This question reduces the **social desirability bias** (discussed later in this chapter) to say that a person voted by offering the out of "for some reason."

Many people weren't able to vote in the 2004 election for President between George W. Bush and John Kerry. How about you? Were you able to vote, or for some reason were you unable to vote?
Voted
Ineligible/too young
Did not vote
(Can't remember/don't know/refused)

This question on political views is a **quasi-filter question** that offers balanced answer choices

Thinking in political terms, would you say that you are conservative, moderate, or liberal?
Liberal
Somewhat liberal
Moderate
Somewhat conservative
Conservative
Don't know/refused

Studies who looked at the effect of offering a "don't know" choice on getting honest answers from respondents distinguish among three kinds of attitude questions: standard-format, quasi-filter, and full-filter questions (see Making It Practical). A **standard-format question** does not offer a "don't know" choice and respondents must volunteer their lack of knowledge or opinion. A **quasi-filter question** offers respondents a "don't know" or "not certain" answer alternative. A **full-filter question** is a special type of contingency question (contingency questions are discussed later). It is a type-part question that first asks if respondents have an opinion and then asks for the opinion among those who say that they have one.

Studies suggest that if a "no opinion" choice is missing, as in the standard question, many respondents will answer, even if they are very uncertain or wholly unaware of an issue. They may find saying "I don't know" or "no opinion" difficult to assert when it is not offered and feel embarrassed in doing so. With a quasi-filter question, most such respondents choose "don't know" because it appears to be a legitimate response. A full-filtered question takes "no opinion" or "don't know" options one step higher. You should use a full filter for issues about which many people may not be informed or have a firm opinion. An option is to ask about an opinion using a quasi-filter question, then follow up all those with an opinion with a second question about how strongly they feel. Here is a full filter example:

> *What is your opinion about the issue of global warming? Do you feel in the future it is going to be a major threat, a minor threat, or no real threat to how our society will be, or do you have no opinion?.*
>
> _____ *Major Threat*
> _____ *Minor Threat*
> _____ *No Real Threat*
> _____ *No opinion {Go directly to next question}*

standard-format question a closed-ended survey question that does not offer a "don't know" or "no opinion" option.

quasi-filter questions a closed-ended survey question that includes a choice for respondents who have no opinion or do not know about an issue.

full filter question a contingency survey question that first asks whether a respondent knows about an issue, then only asks those with knowledge about the issue.

Making It Practical Standard-Format, Quasi-Filter, and Full-Filter Questions

STANDARD FORMAT

Here is a question about another country. Do you agree or disagree with this statement? "The Russian leaders are basically trying to get along with America."

QUASI-FILTER

Here is a statement about another country: "The Russian leaders are basically trying to get along with America." Do you agree, disagree, or have no opinion on that?

FULL FILTER

Here is a statement about another country. Not everyone has an opinion on this. If you do not have an opinion, just say so. Here's the statement: "The Russian leaders are basically trying to get along with America." Do you have an opinion on that? If yes, do you agree or disagree?

Example of Results from Different Question Forms

	Standard Form (%)	Quasi-Filter (%)	Full Filter (%)
Agree	48.2	27.7	22.9
Disagree	38.2	29.5	20.9
No opinion	13.6*	42.8	56.3

* Volunteered
Source: Adapted from Schuman and Presser (1981:116–125). Standard format is from Fall 1978; quasi- and full-filter are from February 1977.

[ASK ONLY IF FIRST THREE ANSWERS ARE GIVEN]

How strongly do you hold that opinion?

Do you hold the opinion _____ very strongly, _____ somewhat strongly, or _____ not very strongly at all?

Helping Respondents Remember. Many survey questions ask about past events, such as when you last saw a doctor or when you last bought a camera. Recalling events accurately takes more time and effort than the few seconds respondents typically use when answering. Also, accurate answering declines over time. Most respondents can recall highly significant events that occurred in the past four to six weeks, but after that the accuracy of their recall erodes. The following might interfere with good recall:

- *A sensitive or threatening topic*—people often suppress a bad memory and forget unpleasant or embarrassing events.
- *Events that occurred simultaneously*—when several things occur at once, they can blur together in memory.
- *Events that occurred after that being recalled*—More recent events often overshadow the memory of what happened earlier.
- *An issue or event that was not significant*—People remember what was important for them but if they did not consider it important, they are likely to forget it.
- *A person's need to be consistent and not appear to contradict him/herself* People tend to selectively remember what is consistent and forget what is contradictory.

These influences on recall do not mean that you cannot ask about past events. You just need to customize survey questions and interpret results cautiously. Give respondents special instructions, extra thinking time, and recall aids. One recall aid is to use a fixed time frame or location. Rather than ask, "How often did you attend sporting events last year?" instead, ask it this way: "I want to know how many sporting events you attended last winter. Let's go month by month. Think back to December. Did you attend any sporting events for which you paid admission in December? Now, think back to January. Did you attend any sporting events in January?" If you want information about activities over a long period, ask about a short time frame that a respondent is likely to know about, and then do the math yourself afterward. Instead of asking, "How many hours did you watch TV in the past year?" instead ask, "In a typical weekday during the past year, about how long did you watch TV? What about in a typical weekend day, how often?" You can then multiply the respondent's answers by the number of weekdays and weekend days to create an estimate for annual TV watching.

Asking Respondents about Sensitive Issues. You may want to ask issues about which respondents feel sensitive or that may threaten their public image. These questions are difficult. Most respondents try to present a positive image of themselves. They may feel ashamed, embarrassed, or afraid to give truthful answers, or find it emotionally painful to confront their own actions honestly, let alone admit them to other people. They may underreport or self-censor reports of behavior or attitudes they wish to hide or believe to be in violation of social norms. Alternatively, they may overreport positive behaviors or generally accepted beliefs (a discussion of social desirability bias follows shortly).

People tend to underreport having an illness or disability (e.g., cancer, mental illness, venereal disease) or engaging in illegal or deviant behavior (e.g., evading taxes, taking drugs, engaging in uncommon sexual practices). They are often hesitant to reveal their financial status (e.g., income, savings, debts). Several techniques may increase truthful answers to sensitive issues. One is to alter the context and question wording. Only ask about sensitive issues after a warm-up, when an interviewer has developed rapport and trust with the respondents. Interviewers can emphasize to respondents that they want honest answers and reassure them of confidentiality. Another way is to provide a context that makes it easier for respondents to answer and appear less unusual. For example, rather than asking an outwardly heterosexual male, "Have you ever had sex with another male?" researchers may ask, "In past surveys, many men have reported that at some point in their lives they have had some type of sexual experience with another male. This could have happened before adolescence, during adolescence, or as an adult. Have you ever had sex with a male at some point in your life?" Another technique is first to ask about more serious activities, making the sensitive question issue appear less unusual. A respondent may hesitate to admit shoplifting. However, a question about shoplifting appears after several questions about armed robbery or burglary, respondents may admit to shoplifting because it appears to be less serious than the other crimes. Likewise, they are more likely give an honest answer to the question "Did you ever take anything from a store without paying for it?" than "Did you ever shoplift?" or "Did you ever engage in the crime of shoplifting?" because it has been worded to sound less threatening by avoiding implications of illegality.

Social desirability bias occurs when respondents distort answers to look good or to conform to social norms. Many people overreport being highly cultured (i.e., reading, attending high-culture events), giving money to charity, having a good marriage, loving their children, and so forth. For example, one study found that one-third of people who said they gave money to a local charity in a survey really did not. Because a norm says that one should vote in elections, some people say they voted when they did not. To reduce the social desirability bias, phrase questions to make norm violation appear less objectionable. You can present a wider range of behavior as acceptable or give respondents "face-saving" alternatives. The National Election Survey asked about voting in the following way to reduce the social desirability bias: "In talking to people about elections, we often find that a lot of people were not able to vote because they weren't registered, they were sick, or they just didn't have time. Which of the following best describes you?—One, I did not vote. Two, I thought about voting this time but didn't. Three—I usually vote, but didn't this time. Four—I am sure I voted.

Contingency Questions. A **contingency question** (also called screen or skip question) is a two-question sequence that increases relevance. A first question selects respondents for whom the second question is relevant. It screens in/out respondents who get the second part. The following example is a contingency question.

1. Did you vote in the mayoral election last April when Guo, Smith, and Lopez were candidates?
   [ ] Yes (GO TO QUESTION 2)
   [ ] No (SKIP TO QUESTION 3)
2. Which candidate did you vote for? _____ Guo _____ Smith _____ Lopez _____ Don't remember
3. What kind of overall job is the mayor doing in your opinion? _____ Excellent _____ Good _____ Fair _____ Poor

Wording Effects. Wording effects occur when a particular word evokes a response. Professional survey researchers recognize that particular words in a survey questions may trigger strong feelings or have connotations that color answers. Because respondents react to one word rather than thinking about the issue in a question, you want to avoid such words in survey questions. It is easier to write survey questions if you have a large vocabulary, know the connotations and meanings of many words, and are sensitive to the vocabulary of respondents. In general, you want to use simple vocabulary and grammar to minimize confusion. Another issue is the impact of specific words or phrases. Unfortunately, it is not possible to know in advance whether a word or phrase will affect responses (see Learning from History: The Power of Words).

social desirability bias a tendency for survey respondents to answer in a way that conforms to social expectations or makes them look good rather than to answer honestly.

contingency question a two-part question in which a first question screens who gets the second question.

Learning from History The Power of Words

Survey researchers have uncovered several powerful wording effects in surveys. One well-documented effect is the difference between *forbid* and *not allow*. Both terms mean the same thing, but many more people are willing to "not allow" something than to "forbid" it. In general, less educated respondents are most influenced by minor wording differences. Certain words trigger an emotional reaction or have significant connotations that we are just beginning to learn about. Smith (1987) found large differences (e.g., twice as much support) in U.S. survey responses depending on whether a question asked about spending "to help the poor" or "for welfare." Heated political attacks on welfare in the 1970s and 1980s changed connotations of the word *welfare*, and it took on negative connotations that it did not previously have. The word had come to imply lazy and immoral people as well as wasteful, ineffective, and expensive government programs. Today, it is best to avoid using it. Hurwitz and Peffley (2005) discovered that many Americans connected the term *inner city* with racial stereotypes about African Americans. Racially prejudiced whites gave negative responses when the phrase appeared in a survey question but neutral responses for the same issue when it did not appear. Respondents also get confused about the meaning or connotations of key words. In one survey, respondents were asked whether they thought television news was "impartial." *Impartial* is a ninth-grade vocabulary term, and researchers assumed everyone knew its meaning. They later learned that fewer than half of the respondents had interpreted the word with its proper meaning. Over one-fourth had ignored it or had no idea of its meaning. Others gave it unusual meanings, and one-tenth gave it a meaning directly opposite to its true meaning. You need to be cautious, because although a few wording effects (e.g., the difference between *forbid* and *not allow*) are known, we are just learning about the power of specific words to shape respondent answers (see Foddy 1993 and Presser 1990).

EFFECTIVE QUESTIONNAIRE DESIGN TIPS

Length of Survey or Questionnaire

The length of a questionnaire depends on the format of your survey (discussed later in this chapter) and on respondent characteristics. A 5-minute telephone interview is rarely a problem. You can usually extend it to 15 minutes. Web surveys vary but few people spend more than 10–15 minutes taking them. Mail questionnaires are more variable. A short (three- or four-page) questionnaire is appropriate for the general population. Some researchers used questionnaires as long as 10 pages (about 100 items) with the general public, but responses drop significantly for longer questionnaires. For highly educated respondents and a salient topic, using questionnaires of 15 pages may be possible. Many face-to-face interviews last a half-hour. In special situations, researchers have been able to conduct face-to-face interviews for as long as three to five hours.

Question Order or Sequence

You face three survey question sequence issues:

1. How to organize questions on a questionnaire
2. How to reduce question order effects
3. How to control context effects

A few years ago, my students conducted a telephone survey on two topics: concern about crime and attitudes toward a new anti-drunk-driving law. A random half of the respondents heard questions about the drunk-driving law first; the other half heard about crime first. I examined the results to see whether there was a context effect—a difference by topic order. I found that respondents asked about the drunk-driving law first expressed less fear about crime than did those asked about crime first. Likewise, those asked first about drunk drinking expressed more support for a tough new drunk-driving law than those who first heard about crime. Apparently, the first topic created a context influencing answers to the second topic. After hearing questions about crime in general and about violent crime, respondents may have considered drunk driving to be a less serious offense. By contrast, respondents asked about drunk driving first may have thought about it as criminal behavior. When asked about crime in general, they still are thinking of drunk driving as a kind of crime.

1. How to Organize Questions on a Questionnaire. Every questionnaire has opening, middle, and ending questions. You want to sequence questions in a way that minimizes discomfort and confusion for respondents. After an introduction that explains the survey, opening questions should be pleasant, interesting, and easy to answer. They should help a respondent to feel comfortable about the survey process. Demographic questions (age, education level, and so forth) should go toward the end. In addition, place questions on the same topic together and introduce the section with a short statement (e.g., "Now I would like to ask you questions about housing") to orient respondents. Question topics should flow smoothly and logically. Organize them to assist respondents' memory and comfort levels.

2. How to Reduce Question Order Effects. The order in which questions appear may influence a respondent's answers. **Order effects** are strongest for people who lack strong views, for less educated respondents, and for older respondents or those with memory loss. For example, support for a single woman's having an abortion predictably rises if it comes after a question about abortion being acceptable when a fetus has serious defects, but not when the question is by itself or it comes before a question about fetus defects.

3. How to Control Context Effects. Respondents tend to answer questions based on a context of preceding questions and the interview setting. Context effects are strongest for ambiguous or unclear questions. This is because respondents will draw on the context to understand the question. It is not always possible to control context effects. A first step is to be aware of them. You want to ask a more general question before a more specific one. It takes a bit more work, but making two versions of the questionnaire and altering topics to two random parts of a sample allows you to check whether context effects are operating.

order effects when the ordering of survey questions influences how respondents answer them.

Making It Practical **The Effect of Previous Questions**

Previous questions in a questionnaire influence later ones in two ways:

1. **Question content (i.e., the issue).** This occurred in the above example of my student's study about drinking driving and crime. In another case, researchers compared three forms to ask how much a respondent followed politics: the question alone, after asking what the respondent's elected representative recently did, and after asking about what the representative did and about the representative's "public relations work" in the area. The percent of respondents' reporting that they followed politics "now and then" or "hardly at all" was 21 percent, 39 percent, and 29 percent, respectively, for the three forms. The second form apparently

made respondent's feel they knew little, but the last form gave respondents an excuse for not knowing the first question—they could blame their representative for their ignorance.

2. **Respondent's response.** A respondent having already answered one part of an issue may assume no overlap. For example, a respondent is asked, "How are you doing in classes in your major?" The next question is, "How are you doing in school?" Most respondents will assume that the second question only means classes outside their major because they already answered about the major. If you wanted to ask about school overall, then you should place that question before the question about the classes in the major.

ADVANTAGES AND DISADVANTAGES OF DIFFERENT SURVEY FORMATS

The social survey comes in several formats, each with advantages or disadvantages: self-administered, mail, face-to-face-interview, phone interview, and Web survey.

Mail and Self-Administered Questionnaires

Advantages. Mail questionnaires are popular because they are easy and inexpensive. You give or mail questionnaires directly to respondents. Respondents read instructions and questions and then record their answers. If mail is used, you can cover a wide geographical area. A mail survey allows respondents to check personal records at home if necessary. Mail questionnaires offer anonymity and avoid interviewer bias. They can be effective, and response rates may be high for an educated target population that has a strong interest in the topic.

Disadvantages. Since people do not always complete and return questionnaires, the biggest problem with mail questionnaires is a low response rate. You might mail out 500 questionnaires but get back only 50. Increasing the number mailed out to 50,000 so you have 500 both becomes much more expensive and can create a bias. The 10 percent of people who respond are unlikely to be representative. Perhaps only people who are highly interested in the survey topic or who have a lot of free time (e.g., unemployed, retired, traditional homemakers) respond. The opinions, education, income, age, and other characteristics of those who respond may not adequately reflect the entire sample and may create serious distortions in your results.

Another limitation is that you do not control the conditions under which a person completes a mail questionnaire. A questionnaire completed during a drinking party by a dozen laughing people may be returned along with one filled out by an earnest respondent. With mail questionnaires, no one is present to clarify questions or to probe for more information when respondents give incomplete answers. Someone other than the sampled respondent (e.g., spouse, new resident, etc.) may open the mail and complete the questionnaire. Respondents can complete the questionnaire weeks apart or answer questions in an order different from that intended by researchers. Incomplete questionnaires can also be a serious problem.

A mail questionnaire format limits the kinds of questions that a researcher can use. Questions that require visual aids (e.g., look at this picture and tell me what you see), open-ended questions, many contingency questions, and complex questions do poorly in mail questionnaires. Likewise, mail questionnaires are ill suited for the illiterate or nearly-illiterate in English.

Telephone Interviews

Advantages. The telephone interview is a popular survey method because you can reach about 95 percent of the population by telephone. You call a respondent (usually at home), ask questions, and record answers. The sample of respondents can come from lists, telephone directories, or random-digit dialing (RDD; see Chapter 4) and can be from a wide geographical area. A staff of interviewers can interview 1500 respondents across a nation within a few days and, with 5 to 10 callbacks, get response rates of 85 percent. The telephone interview is a flexible method and has most of the strengths of face-to-face interviews. Interviewers pick a specific respondent, control the sequence of questions, and can use some probes. A specific respondent answers the questions alone. Interviewers can use contingency questions effectively, especially with computer-assisted telephone interviewing (CATI) (discussed later in this chapter). Also, supervisors can monitor interview quality by listening in.

Disadvantages. Higher cost and limited interview length are major disadvantages of telephone interviews. Respondents without telephones are impossible to reach, or the call may come at an inconvenient time. The use of an interviewer reduces anonymity and introduces potential interviewer bias. Open-ended questions are difficult to use, and questions that require visual aids are impossible. Interviewers can only note serious disruptions (e.g., background noise) and respondent tone of voice (e.g., anger or flippancy) or hesitancy. Over the past 30 years, respondent cooperation with telephone interviews has steadily declined, with more refusals and inability to reach people, even with 10 callbacks at different times.

Face-to-Face Interviews

Advantages. Face-to-face interviews have the highest response rates and permit the longest questionnaires. Interviewers also can observe the surroundings and can use nonverbal communication and visual aids. Well-trained interviewers can ask all types of questions, can ask complex questions, and can use extensive probes.

Bonnie Kamin/PhotoEdit Inc.

Disadvantages. The training, travel, supervision, and personnel costs for interviews can be very high. Interviewer bias is also greatest in face-to-face interviews. The appearance, tone of voice, question wording, and so forth of the interviewer may affect the respondent. In addition, interviewer supervision is less than for telephone interviews.

Web Surveys

Advantages. Web surveys came into widespread use over the past five years. They are now the lowest cost format and get answers the fastest. Two other advantages are that Web surveys can span geographic space and include visual materials as well as the survey questions.

Summary Review **Question Order Effects**

QUESTION 1

"Do you think that the United States should let Communist newspaper reporters from other countries come in here and send back to their papers the news as they see it?"

QUESTION 2

"Do you think a Communist country like Russia should let American newspaper reporters come in and send back to America the news as they see it?"

	Percentage Saying Yes	
Heard First	*Yes to #1* *(Communist Reporter)*	*Yes to #2* *(American Reporter)*
#1	54%	75%
#2	64%	82%

Source: Adapted from Schuman and Presser (1981:29).

The context created by answering the first question affects the answer to the second question.

Disadvantages. A drawback with Web surveys is that not everyone has Internet access and that low response rate inhibits getting a representative sample. As Internet use spreads and incentives for Web survey participation improve, these issues may become less important. Another disadvantage is that you cannot control the conditions under which a person completes a Web survey. Someone who is not serious or someone other than the selected respondent may complete the Web survey. Also, no one is present to clarify questions or to probe for more information when respondents give incomplete answers.

SURVEY INTERVIEWING

The Interviewer's Role

Interviews are a special type of social relation. One person asks questions and the other person mostly answers. Interviews take many forms. There are police interrogation interview and job or celebrity interviews. Survey research interviewing is specialized interview in which the primary goal is to obtain accurate information from another person. It is a social relationship with expectations, social roles, and norms. The survey interview is a short-term, social interaction between two strangers. Its explicit purpose is for one person to obtaining specific information from the other. The roles are those of the interviewer and the interviewee or respondent. The interviewer obtains information in a structured conversation by asking prearranged questions; the respondent answers, and responses are recorded.

Some respondents are unfamiliar with their role as a survey respondent. They substitute another role that may affect their responses. Some believe the interview is an intimate conversation or therapy session. Some see it as a bureaucratic exercise in completing forms. Others view it as a citizen referendum on policy choices or as a testing situation. Some people even treat it as a contest in which interviewers try to trick or entrap respondents. Respondents reinterpret survey questions so they apply to personal situations or so they are easy to answer. Misunderstanding the respondent role can produce a misunderstanding of the meaning of survey questions. One task of a survey interviewer is to clarify the roles in the social relationship and follow them consistently. An interviewer may need to explain the nature of survey research or give hints about social roles in an interview.

The interviewer's role is difficult. He or she needs to control the interview and its flow of interaction. Interviewers must obtain cooperation and build rapport yet remain neutral and objective. They encroach on the respondents' time and privacy for information that may not directly benefit the respondents. They try to reduce embarrassment, fear, and suspicion so that a respondent feels comfortable revealing information. A good interviewer constantly monitors the pace and direction of the social interaction as well as the answers and the behavior of respondents. He or she helps respondents to feel that they should give truthful answers.

A survey interviewer is nonjudgmental and never reveals his or her opinions, verbally or nonverbally (e.g., by a look of shock). If a respondent asks for an interviewer's opinion, the interviewer politely redirects the respondent. For example, if a respondent asks, "What do you think?" the interviewer may answer, "Here we are interested in what *you* think; what I think doesn't matter." Likewise, if the respondent gives a shocking answer (e.g., "I was arrested three times for beating my infant daughter and burning her with cigarettes"), an interviewer should not show shock, surprise, or disdain but treat the answer in a matter-of-fact manner.

You might ask, "If the survey interviewer must be neutral and objective, why not use a robot or machine?" Machine interviewing has not been successful. It lacks the human warmth, sense of trust, and rapport that a human interviewer creates.

The interviewer helps define the situation for respondents. He or she determines whether respondents have the information sought, understand what is expected, are motivated, and provide relevant and serious answers.

Interview Stages

A survey interview proceeds through three major stages: Introduction, main part, and exit.

1. *Introduction and entry.* The interviewer gains access, provides authorization, and reassures and secures cooperation from the respondent. He or she is prepared for reactions such as, "How did you pick me?" "What good will this do?" "I don't know about this," "What's this about, anyway?" The interviewer can explain why the specific respondent is interviewed and not a substitute. In this stage, the interviewer assumes control and sets proper role expectations. Informed consent and assurances of confidentiality occur in this stage (you learned about informed consent in Chapter 3).

2. *The main part of the interview.* The main part consists of asking questions and recording answers. The interviewer follows the exact wording on the questionnaire—no added or omitted words and no rephrasing. He or she asks all applicable questions in order, without returning to or skipping questions unless the directions specify this. It is important to set a comfortable pace and give nondirective feedback to maintain respondent interest. In addition to asking questions, the interviewer accurately records answers. This is easy for closed-ended questions, where interviewers just mark the correct box. For open-ended questions, the interviewer's job is more difficult. An interviewer listens carefully, has legible writing or good recording machine skills, and records what a respondent says verbatim without correcting grammar or slang. The interviewer does not summarize or paraphrase because doing so leads to lost information or distorted answers. For example, the respondent says, "I'm really concerned about my daughter's heart problem. She is only 10 years old and already she has trouble climbing stairs. I don't know what she'll do when she gets older. Heart surgery is too risky for her and it costs so much. I guess she'll have to learn to live with it." If the interviewer summarizes, "Respondent is concerned about daughter's health," much is lost.

A good interviewer knows how and when to use **probes**. Interviewers need to understand the survey to recognize an irrelevant or inaccurate answer and use probes as needed. There are many types of probes. A three- to five-second pause is often effective, as is nonverbal communication (e.g., tilt of head, raised eyebrows, or eye contact). The interviewer can repeat the question or the reply and then pause. He or she can ask a neutral question such as, "Any other reasons?" "Can you tell me more about that?" "How do you mean?" "Could you explain more for me?" (see Making It Practical: Example of Probes and Recording Full Responses to Closed Questions).

3. *The exit.* The last stage is the exit. The interviewer thanks the respondent and leaves. He or she then goes to a quiet, private place to edit the questionnaire and record other details. The details include the date, time, and place of the interview; a thumbnail sketch of the respondent and interview situation; the respondent's attitude (e.g., serious, angry, or laughing); and any unusual circumstances (e.g., "Telephone rang at question 27 and respondent talked for four minutes before the interview started again"). He or she notes anything disruptive that happened during the interview (e.g., "Teenage son entered room, sat at opposite end, turned on television with the volume loud, and watched a music video"). The interviewer also records his or her personal feelings and anything that was suspected (e.g., "Respondent became nervous and fidgeted, changed answers once each on questions 14, 15, and 16 about his marriage").

probe a neutral request made by an interviewer to clarify an ambiguous answer, complete an incomplete answer, or obtain a relevant response.

Making It Practical **Example of Probes and Recording Full Responses to Closed Questions**

Interviewer Question: What is your occupation?

Respondent Answer: I work at General Motors.

Probe: What is your job at General Motors? What type of work do you do there?

Interviewer Question: How long have you been unemployed?

Respondent Answer: A long time.

Probe: Could you tell me more specifically when your current period of unemployment began?

Interviewer Question: Considering the country as a whole, do you think we will have good times during the next year, or bad times, or what?

Respondent Answer: Maybe good, maybe bad, it depends, who knows?

Probe: What do you expect to happen?

RECORD RESPONSE TO A CLOSED QUESTION

Interviewer Question: On a scale of 1 to 7, how do you feel about capital punishment or the death penalty, where 1 is strongly in favor of the death penalty, and 7 is strongly opposed to it?

(Favor) 1 ___ 2 ___ 3 ___ 4 ___ 5 ___ 6 ___ 7 ___ (Oppose)

Respondent Answer: About a 4. I think that all murderers, rapists, and violent criminals should get death, but I don't favor it for minor crimes like stealing a car.

Training Interviewers

Perhaps someday you may get a job interviewing for a professional survey organization. A large-scale survey often requires many interviewers. Few people other than professional survey researchers appreciate the difficulty of the interviewer's job. A professional-quality interview requires carefully selected and trained interviewers. As with any employment situation, interviewers need adequate pay and good supervision for consistent high-quality performance. Good interviewers are pleasant, honest, accurate, mature, responsible, intelligent, stable, and motivated. They are patient and calm. They have experience with many types of people and possess poise and tact. Face-to-face interviewers must have a nonthreatening appearance. If the survey involves face-to-face interviewing in high-crime areas, the interviewers need to have proper "street smarts" and may require extra protection (e.g., a partner or assistant).

Researchers consider the interviewers' physical appearance, age, race, sex, languages spoken, and even the voice. Most training for professional interviewers requires full-time sessions lasting one to two weeks. It usually includes lectures and reading, observation of expert interviewers, mock interviews in the office and in the field that are recorded and critiqued, many practice interviews, and role playing. Interviewers are taught about survey research and the role of the interviewer. They become familiar with the questionnaire and the purpose of questions.

Using Probes

Interviewers use probes to clarify a respondent's ambiguous or irrelevant response. They also use them to check whether respondents understand the questions as intended. However, probes are not substitutes for writing clear questions or creating a framework of understanding for the respondent. Unless carefully stated, probes might shape the respondent's answers. Yet flexible or conversational interviewing, in which interviewers use many probes, can improve accuracy on questions about complex issues for which respondents do not clearly understand basic terms or about which they have difficulty expressing their thoughts. For example, to the question, "Did you do any work for money last week?" a respondent might hesitate and then reply, "Yes." An interviewer can probe, "Could you tell me exactly what work you did?" The respondent may reply, "On Tuesday and Wednesday, I spent a couple hours helping my buddy John move into his new apartment. For that he gave me $40, but I didn't have any other job or get paid for doing anything else." If the question intended only to get reports of regular employment, the probe revealed a misunderstanding.

Interviewer Bias

Survey researchers prescribe interviewer behavior to reduce bias. Ideally, the actions of a particular interviewer have no effect on how a respondent answers, and responses are the same as if asked by any other interviewer. Proper interviewer behavior and exact question reading are critical, but there is a larger issue.

An interviewer's uncontrolled visible characteristics, including race and gender, often affect interviews and respondent answers. This means you should note the race and gender of both interviewers and respondents. The effect especially occurs in questions about issues related to visible characteristics such as race or gender. For example, African American and Hispanic American respondents tend to express different policy positions on race- or ethnic-related issues depending on the apparent race or ethnicity of the interviewer. This occurs even with telephone interviews when a respondent has clues about the interviewer's race or ethnicity (see Example Study Box 3: Interviewer Race Effects Are Subtle and Pervasive). Gender also affects interviews both in terms of obvious issues, such as sexual behavior, as well as support for gender-related collective action or gender equality. In general, interviewers of the same gender or ethnic-racial group as the respondent get the most accurate answers.

Example Study Box 3 **Interviewer Race Effects Are Subtle and Pervasive**

Survey researchers have been long aware that an interviewer's race can influence how respondents answer racially sensitive questions. Other research documented that women or racial minorities tend do poorly on certain tests administered by outside groups (such as white males) because of a stereotype that they will do poorly. They feel great pressure to disconfirm the negative stereotype, but the pressure creates test anxiety that lowers their test score. By contrast, when a member of their same group administers the test, the stereotype threat is not activated, test anxiety is reduced, and they score higher on tests. Davis and Silver (2003) wondered whether the stereotype-triggered test anxiety also operates in survey interviews. They conducted a telephone survey of whites and African Americans in the Detroit area. They wanted to see whether a survey interviewer's race affected how a respondent answered. They asked, "Do African Americans score differently on survey knowledge questions depending on whether they think the telephone interviewer is white or African American?" Results showed that white respondents answered the same irrespective of interviewer race. However, African American respondents scored higher on the knowledge questions when they believed their interviewer was an African American. David and Silver concluded that beyond widely known social desirability and racial conformity issues in surveys, the race of an interviewer can create subtle anxiety based on negative stereotypes. The stereotype-based anxiety may influence how a respondent answers many survey questions.

Bloomimage/Corbis

Computer-Assisted Telephone Interviewing

Most professional survey organizations that do phone interviewing have installed **computer-assisted telephone interviewing** *(CATI)* systems. With CATI, the interviewer sits in front of a computer and makes calls. Wearing a headset and microphone, the interviewer reads the questions from a computer screen for the specific respondent, then enters the answer via the keyboard. Once he or she enters an answer, the computer shows the next question on the screen. CATI speeds interviewing and reduces interviewer errors. It also eliminates the separate step of entering information into a computer and speeds data processing. The CATI system works well for contingency questions because the computer can show the questions appropriate for a specific respondent; interviewers do not have to turn pages looking for the next question. In addition, the computer can check an answer immediately after the interviewer enters it. For example, the interviewer enters an answer that is impossible or clearly an error (e.g., an *H* instead of an *M* for "Male"). The computer catches the error immediately.

THE ETHICAL SURVEY

As in all social research, you can conduct surveys in ethical or unethical ways. A major ethical issue in survey research is the invasion of privacy. When you ask about intimate actions and personal beliefs, you may be invading privacy. People have a right to privacy. It is up to you to be careful and ask questions in a polite, respective manner, and to protect the information if you obtain. Respondents are most likely to provide information if you ask for it in a comfortable context with mutual trust, when they feel that serious answers are required from them for legitimate research purposes, and when they believe that answers will remain confidential. This means you should treat all respondents with dignity and reduce anxiety or discomfort. As the researcher, you are also responsible for protecting the confidentiality of data.

A second issue involves voluntary participation by respondents. You can never force anyone to answer a survey and must obtain informed consent (you read about this in Chapter 3). They can withhold information or refuse to participate at any time. Because you depend on voluntary cooperation, you need to ask well-developed questions in a sensitive way, treat respondents with respect, and be sensitive to confidentiality.

A third ethical issue is the misuse of surveys and pseudosurveys. Because surveys are so common, some people use the survey format for illegitimate purposes. A *pseudosurvey* is when someone uses a survey format not to obtain information but in an attempt to persuade others to do something. A charlatan may have no interest in learning information from a respondent but only use a survey to gain entry into homes, persuade a person to vote in a certain way, or "suggle" (try to sell in the guise of a survey).

The mass media report more on surveys than other types of social research; however, the way mass media report on surveys permits abuse. Few people who read poll results in a newspaper or hear them on television realize that ethical codes require including certain details about the survey method (see Making it Practical: Ten Items to Include When Reporting Survey Research). The purpose of the details is to avoid misuse of survey research. Researchers urge the media to include the information, but it is rarely included. Few media reports tell us who conducted the survey or provide critical details on how they conducted it. The mass media may report on weak, biased, and misleading surveys along with sound, rigorous, professional ones without distinction. This increases public confusion and a distrust of all surveys.

computer-assisted telephone interviewing telephone survey technology that integrates interviewing over the phone with a computer for the questionnaire and data entry.

Making It Practical **Ten Items to Include When Reporting Survey Research**

1. The sampling frame used (e.g., telephone directories)
2. The dates on which the survey was conducted
3. The population that the sample represents (e.g., U.S. adults, Australian college students, housewives in Singapore)
4. The size of the sample for which information was collected
5. The sampling method (e.g., random)
6. The exact wording of the questions asked
7. The method of the survey (e.g., face to face, telephone)
8. The organizations that sponsored the survey (paid for it and conducted it)
9. The response rate or percentage of those contacted who actually completed the questionnaire
10. Any missing information or "don't know" responses when results on specific questions are reported

WHAT HAVE YOU LEARNED?

In this chapter, you learned about survey research. You also learned some principles of writing good survey questions. There are many things to avoid and to include when writing questions. You learned about the advantages and disadvantages of different types of survey research: mail, Web surveys, telephone interviews, and face-to-face interviews. You saw that interviewing, especially face-to-face interviewing, can be difficult. Although this chapter focused on survey research, researchers use questionnaires to measure variables in other types of quantitative research (e.g., experiments). The survey, often called the sample survey because most involve random sampling, is a distinct technique. It is a process of asking many people the same questions and examining their answers. Survey researchers try to minimize errors, but survey data often contain them. Errors in surveys can compound each other. For example, errors can arise in sampling frames, from people not answering survey questions, from question wording or order, and from interviewer bias. Do not let the existence of errors discourage you from using the survey, however. Instead, learn to be very careful when designing survey research and cautious about generalizing from the results of surveys.

KEY TERMS

closed-ended question *160*
computer-assisted telephone interviewing (CATI) *174*
contingency question *165*
control variable *154*
correlational research *144*
double-barreled question *157*
full-filter question *163*
interview schedule *154*

leading question *158*
open-ended question *160*
order effects *167*
probe *171*
quasi-filter question *163*
questionnaire *154*
social desirability bias *165*
standard-format question *163*

APPLYING WHAT YOU'VE LEARNED

Activity 1: Design a Two-Page Mail Questionnaire.

The only way to learn in depth about how to write survey questions is to write some. It helps to look at the questions in existing surveys, but often they do not ask what you want to find out. So you need to write your own questions. Pick a topic and design your own 10- to 15-item questionnaire for a mail survey. Remember that in a mail survey you need to be very explicit and clear because the respondent cannot ask anyone for clarification. In total, your questionnaire should be two pages long. Include

1 contingency question
1 partially open question
1 open-ended question
5 or more quasi-filter questions
2–5 demographic questions (age, education, race, marital status)

Activity 2: Complete an Online Survey.

Go to the Allyn and Bacon Web site at and locate a survey designed for readers of this textbook. Complete the survey (it should not take more than 5 minutes). After you complete the survey, answer the following four questions:

1. Did you feel any questions had social desirability bias? If so, which ones?
2. Where there any closed-end answer formats that did not offer choices that fit you? If so, which ones?
3. Were all answer choices mutually exclusive and exhaustive? If not, which ones?
4. Were any questions too vague and ambiguous? If so, which ones?

Activity 3: Conduct Short Face-to-Face Interviews.

Locate five adults to interview; these can be friends, relatives, co-workers, neighbors, and so on. This is not an official study and you will not be interviewing strangers, so IRB approval probably is not needed. Pick questions from the surveys of official survey organizations (see Roper, Gallup, pollingreport.com for hundreds of questions. Include some demographic questions (e.g., age, years of schooling). The interview topic should be noncontroversial and not involve intimate personal information. Write out all your questions before you begin, and use closed-ended questions. The interview should last at least 10 minutes. Follow the stages of an interview and the role of a survey interview discussed in this chapter.

Activity 4

Find print media (newspapers, magazine) reports on the results of two different surveys. Find out how many details about the methodology are reported. Specifically focus on the following:

	Survey 1	Survey 2
Media report/source	_____	_____
Survey organization	_____	_____
Sample size	_____	_____
Method of survey	_____	_____
Date of survey	_____	_____

REFERENCES

Brewer, Paul, and Clyde Wilcox. 2005. "Trends: Same-Sex Marriage and Civil Unions" *Public Opinion Quarterly* 69:599–616.

Davis, Darren, and Brian Silver. 2003. "Stereotype Threat and Race of Interview Effects in a Survey on Political Knowledge." *American Journal of Political Science* 47:33–45.

Foddy, William. 1993. *Constructing questions for interviews and questionnaires*. New York: Cambridge University Press.

Hurwitz, Jon, and Mark Peffley. 2005 "Playing the Race Card in the Post-Willie Horton Era: The Impact of Racialized Code Words on Support for Punitive Crime Policy." *Public Opinion Quarterly* 69(1):99–112

Presser, Stanley. 1990. "Measurement Issues in the Study of Social Change." *Social Forces* 68:856–868.

Schuman, Howard, and Stanley Presser. 1981. *Questions and answers in attitude surveys: Experiments on question form, wording and content*. New York: Academic Press.

Smith, Tom W. 1987. "That which we call welfare by any other name would smell sweeter." *Public Opinion Quarterly* 51(1):75–83.

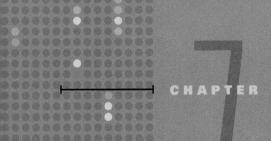

The Experiment

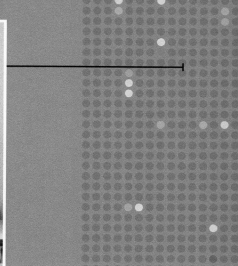

Sean Ellis/Photographer's Choice/Getty Images

Peers influence the views of adolescents and young adults, including college students. Does this include influence over their stereotypes about racial groups? To check this idea, some Washington State University (WSU) researchers conducted a social experiment. They asked for student volunteers in a public speaking course and included only white students. The volunteers first completed a short survey about their beliefs and views on racial and other issues. The experimenters told the students they were part of a study to evaluate news reports on public opinions on social issues. Next, they had the students read a booklet containing three news stories. The experimenters randomly divided the students into two groups. One group read a booklet with news stories titled "Parents Disturbed about TV Shows," "Poll Finds Voters Not in Favor of Impeachment," and "More Freshmen Appear Disengaged from Their Studies." A second group of students read a booklet with two of the same stories as the first group and a third made-up story created to look like a real news story. The made-up story reported that most WSU students held positive beliefs toward African Americans. It reported on a poll of WSU students that showed they rejected common negative stereotypes, including percentages of African Americans compared to whites who dropped out of school, engaged in crime, received welfare, and so forth. All the students then completed a second survey. The first survey asked students who they looked to when forming opinions. It confirmed that they rated peers highly. The second survey included items on racial attitude, other attitudes, and questions about stereotypes of whites, Mexican Americans, and African Americans. The researchers hypothesized that students who had read the booklet with the made-up story about their WSU peers would score differently. Results supported the hypothesis. The students who had read the made-up story were less likely to express negative stereotypes toward African Americans than those who had not read that story. The racial views of the two groups of students prior to reading the booklets had been the same. A simple social experiment like this one allows us to test targeted hypotheses about a specific social process. It gives us clear evidence about a particular causal relationship, in this case between the views of peers and maintaining racial stereotypes. (See Tan et. al. 2001.)

You may be familiar with experiments in the natural sciences (e.g., biology, chemistry, and physics) and related applied fields (e.g., agriculture, engineering, and medicine). Social experiments in education, criminal justice, journalism, marketing, nursing, political science, psychological social work, and sociology use the same basic logic that guides experiments to explain plant growth in biology or test a new metal in engineering. In this chapter, you will learn how to conduct social experiments.

DOING EXPERIMENTS IN EVERYDAY LIFE

In a way, a research experiment extends commonsense logic. Everyday experiments are less careful or systematic than scientific ones. In commonsense language, an *experiment* refers to two situations:

1. *Before-and-after comparison.* You modify something and then compare an outcome to what existed before the modification. One morning, you try to start your car. To your surprise, it does not start. You "experiment" by cleaning off the battery connections and then try to start it again. You modified something (cleaned the connections) and compared the outcome (whether the car started) to the prior situation (it did not start). You had a "hypothesis" that the car did not start because of a buildup of crud on the connections, and once the crud was removed, the car would start.
2. *Side-by-side comparison.* You have two similar things, and then you modify one but not the other and compare the two. You watch a young boy playing with a soft drink can. He vigorously shakes it. You hold one that is not shaken. You then open both cans for him. He laughs when the shaken can "explodes" with a fizzy mess, but the one you held does not explode. You began with two similar things (soft drink cans) and modified one (shook up a can) but not the other. Before you opened the cans, you hypothesized that the shaken can but not the other one would make a fizzy mess.

You do three things in an experiment:

1. Start with a cause-effect hypothesis.
2. Modify a situation or introduce a change.
3. Compare outcomes with and without the modification.

Compared to the other social research techniques, experimental research is the strongest for testing causal relationships. Experiments most clearly satisfy the three conditions needed to demonstrate causality—temporal order, association, and no alternative explanations (discussed in Chapter 2).

WHAT QUESTIONS CAN YOU ANSWER WITH THE EXPERIMENTAL METHOD?

Social researchers use different research techniques (e.g., experiments, surveys, field research) because certain techniques can better address some research questions than others do. A social survey is a good way to study issues about which people are aware and willing to answer direct questions. This makes it good for finding out many opinions about current issues among large collections of people. By looking at statistical relations in survey data, you can find evidence of connections among the variables. Experimental research is not suited to measure opinions held by many people. However, it offers a very powerful way to focus narrowly and demonstrate causal relations among a few variables when you can control a situation. Research questions most appropriate for an experiment fit its strengths and limitations, which include the following:

- The experiment has a clear and simple logic.
- It has the ability to isolate a causal mechanism.
- It is targeted on two or three variables and is narrow in scope.
- It is limited by the practical and ethical aspects of the situations you can impose on humans.

In general, the social experiment is better for narrowly targeted short-term micro-level concerns (e.g., individual or small-group phenomena) than for complex macro-level issues in which many factors work together. Experiments are usually not good for questions about many diverse influences that operate across an entire society or over decades, but they are excellent when you can isolate the impact of a few variables in a controlled, small-scale setting. Although they rarely help with issues across complex settings or numerous groups, experiments can provide insight into larger issues if you synthesize the results from many narrowly focused experiments.

Ethical and practical constraints limit what you can study with the experimental method. Let us say you want to know whether biracial children are more likely to develop an interest in a career in human services than single-race children are. You can study this issue using a survey or existing statistics research, but not the experimental method. For a true experiment, you would force some parents to have biracial children and not others, force all the parents to raise their children similarly, and then wait until the children grow up to examine their career choices. This is both unethical and impractical. Despite its great strength at demonstrating causal relations, the experiment is limited in the questions you can ask, the variables you can measure, and your ability to generalize from one experiment to larger society (see "External Validity and Field Experiments" later in this chapter).

The ideal solution is to study an issue using both experimental and a nonexperimental method and then combine what you learn from both. Maybe you are interested in attitudes toward people in wheelchairs. You could conduct an experiment asking participants to respond to photos of people in wheelchairs and not in wheelchairs, with the different research participants seeing the same person in or not in a wheelchair. You could ask them, Would you hire this person? How comfortable would you be if this person asked you for a date? and so forth. You could also conduct a social survey on attitudes about disability issues. In addition, you could do field research (see Chapter 10) and observe people's reactions to a person in a wheelchair in a natural setting, or you might be in a wheelchair and carefully note the reactions of others to you. Our greatest confidence in what we learn comes when we study the same issue using several different methods and numerous carefully conducted studies produce very similar results.

WHY ASSIGN PEOPLE RANDOMLY?

Comparison is at the core of experiments. The cliché, "Compare apples to apples, don't compare apples to oranges," is not about fruit; it is about making valid comparisons. In experimental social research, you want to compare things that are fundamentally alike. You can facilitate comparison by creating similar groups of research participants. To make valid a comparison, you want to compare participants who do not differ with regard to variables that could be alternative explanations to your hypothesis. Let us say you want to learn whether completing a college course affects a person's skill level. You have two groups of participants: One group completed the course whereas the other did not. To make a valid comparison, you want

Making It Practical **Random Assignment**

Random assignment is simple in practice. Start with a collection of people, such as 50 volunteers who show up to participate in a study. Next, divide them into two or more groups using a true random process, such as tossing a coin or throwing dice. If you toss a coin, you may assign all for whom heads appear in one group and the rest in another. You will probably have about 25 participants in each group. What if you have 80 people and want to assign them to four groups? You can use coin toss (every other toss goes to a group), dice, or another pure random process. The key feature of a random assignment process is that all have an equal, one-in-four chance of ending up in a group. Nothing about a specific participant or an experimenter's preference affects who goes to which group. It is entirely due to pure mathematical chance.

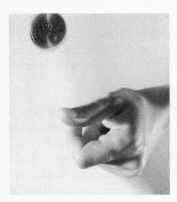

Thinkstock Images/Jupiter Images
Royalty Free

participants in the groups to be similar in every respect, except the one you are examining in the study—taking the course. If participants who completed the course are also two years older than those who did not, you could not know whether it was completing the course or being older that accounted for group differences in skill levels.

Many experiments use **random assignment,** also called randomization. To compare groups of participants, you do not assign them based on your feelings, their personal preference, or their specific features. Random assignment is unbiased because your desire to confirm a hypothesis or a participant's personal interests is not a part of the selection process. It is random in a statistical or mathematical sense, not in the everyday sense of unplanned, haphazard, or accidental. In probability theory, *random* is a process in which each case has a known and equal chance of selection. It obeys mathematical laws, which makes precise calculations possible (see Making It Practical: Random Assignment above).

Both random sampling and random assignment use mathematically random processes. When you randomly sample, you use a random process to select a smaller subset of people (sample) from a larger pool (population). When you randomly assign, you use a random process to sort a collection of participants into two or more groups (see Figure 7.1). You can both randomly sample and randomly assign. You can first sample to obtain a set of participants (e.g., 150 students out of 15,000), then randomly assign to divide the sampled participants into groups (e.g., divide the 150 people into three groups of 50 each). Combining random sampling and random assignment is the ideal; however, due to the extra effort required, we very rarely see it in social experiments.

If the purpose of random assignment is to create two (or more) equivalent groups, might it be simpler to match participants' characteristics in each group? Although professional researchers sometimes match participants on certain characteristics, such as age and sex, it is rare. Truly equal matching falls apart as the relevant characteristics expand and finding exact matches becomes impossible. Individuals differ in thousands of ways. You cannot know which traits are relevant and influence your variables. Let us say you compare two groups of 15 students. Group 1 has eight males. To match, group 2 must also have eight males. Two males in group 1 are only children; the rest have one or more siblings. Three are from a divorced family. One male is tall, slender, and Jewish; another is short, heavy, and Methodist, and so forth. To match groups, you have to find a tall Jewish male only child from

random assignment sort research participants into two or more groups in a mathematically random process.

■ **Figure 7.1**   Random Assignment and Random Sampling

Random Sampling

Population (Sampling Frame)   Sample

Random
Process

Random Assignment

Step 1: Begin with a collection of subjects.

Step 2: Devise a method to randomize that is purely mechanical (e.g., flip a coin).

Step 3: Assign subjects with "Heads" to one group   and "Tails" to the other group.

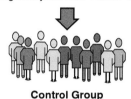

Control Group

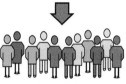

Experimental Group

a divorced home and a short Methodist male only child from an intact home. True matching on more than one or two characteristics is impossible. For this reason, randomization is preferred. By using a true random process, over the long run the odds are that people in the groups will be equal. If the groups are equal, it strengthens the internal logic of the experiment (see "Internal Validity" later in this chapter).

DO YOU SPEAK THE LANGUAGE OF EXPERIMENTAL DESIGN?

Experimental research has its own terms, concepts, and logic. We can divide an experiment into seven parts. Not all experiments have all these parts, and some have all seven parts and more.

1. Independent variable
2. Dependent variable
3. Pretest
4. Posttest
5. Experimental group
6. Control group
7. Random assignment

You already know the terms *independent variable* and *dependent variable*, but they operate a little differently here. In surveys you measure an independent variable by asking a question. In experiments, the independent variable is something a researcher does or introduces. It is a condition or situation you modify or alter. For this reason, it is also called the treatment, manipulation, stimulus, or intervention. In the experiment about student stereotypes that opened this chapter, the independent variable was whether students recceived the made-up news story. In the experiment described in Example Study Box 1: Was It a Gun or a Tool?, the

Example Study Box 1   Was It a Gun or a Tool?

f1 online/Alamy

In many situations, police officers must respond quickly and accurately to a potentially dangerous situation, such as trying to determine if an individual is holding a gun. In 1999, national outrage erupted after four white New York City police officers shot and killed an innocent unarmed black immigrant from West Africa who was holding out his wallet. The police mistakenly thought he was holding a gun. Payne (2001) created two experiments to learn whether racial stereotypes about people being dangerous interfere with the person's ability to make accurate split-second judgments. Payne built on past studies of "priming." The priming studies found that people link visual and other images to preexisting negative stereotypes. The images "prime" or "activate" a negative response, often automatically and unconsciously, in people who hold stereotypes. When revealing a negative racial stereotype is socially inappropriate, people try control-priming effects. This slows decision making as people reconsider responses to make them more acceptable or accurate. In his experiment, Payne had 31 white undergraduate students complete an attitude survey. Next, they looked at visual images on a computer. He told participants he was measuring their speed and accuracy of identifying visual images. Participants practiced using the equipment and classifying 48 photos. Payne then told them that they would see a pair of photos. The first one was a warning that the second would soon appear. The first photo was always the face of either a white or a black man. The second photo was of a handgun or a tool (hand drill or socket wrench). The first photo appeared for 200 milliseconds; the second photo appeared for 200 milliseconds. After a participant responded, the screen went blank. Participants did not have a fixed time by which they had to respond. After a response, the next pair of photos appeared. Participants identified 192 photos with the race of the first photo and tool or gun randomly mixed. Thus, Payne randomly mixed what each participant saw instead of randomly assigning the participants. In a second experiment, everything was the same except that Payne added pressure. If participants failed to respond within 500 milliseconds after the second photo, they saw a dramatic red warning and had 1 second to respond. In the first experiment, the participants showed no differences in accuracy. In the second experiment, with time pressure, the error rate was much higher. Many of the participants who first saw the black man's face mistook a hand tool for a gun. However, their errors did not increase after seeing the white man's face. Interestingly, participants who made the most errors of mistaking a tool for a gun were those who, according to their answers to the survey at the start of the study, had the greatest acceptance of negative stereotypes about African Americans.

independent variable is different "priming" that the experimenter created by showing participants either a white man or black man's face.

Professional researchers strive to create realistic conditions to produce specific reactions and feelings within experimental participants. For the independent variable, a researcher often manipulates what different participants see or think is happening. He or she may give them different instructions, show them different situations using visual images or elaborate equipment, use different physical settings, or stage different contrived social situations.

Researchers measure dependent variables in many ways, including response times, percent accurate scores, social behaviors, attitudes, feelings, and beliefs. In the experiment on student stereotypes that opened this chapter, the dependent variable was a student's acceptance of African American stereotypes after reading the news item. In the experiment described in Example Study Box 1, the dependent variable was participant accuracy about whether a second photo showed a gun or a tool. You can measure dependent variables by paper-and-pencil indicators, such as a questionnaire that asks about stereotypes, by interviews, by observing behaviors (making a choice or response time), or by physiological responses (e.g., heartbeat or sweating palms). In many experimental designs, you measure the dependent variable more than once. You measure it before you introduce the independent variable, in a **pretest**, and then again after introducing it, in a **posttest**. In the study about stereotypes that opened this chapter, the researchers measured stereotypes before participants read news stories, and then again after they had read them.

When introducing an independent variable, researchers can use two or more groups that experience different situations or a single participant group that experiences varied situations. If they have two or more groups, they are using an **independent group design**. In the study that opened this chapter, the independent variable was introduced by having one group read a made-up story whereas the other did not. The group that read the made-up story was the **experimental group**; the **control group** did not. When the independent variable has several different values, you may have more than one experimental group, called comparison groups, one for each level of the independent variable. At other times, experimenters use a **repeated measures design**. They have only one group but have the same participants experience multiple situations over time. This was the case in the study about seeing a gun or a tool in Example Study Box 1: Was It a Gun or a Tool?.

To plan an experiment, you must decide on a specific experimental design (to be discussed later) and plan what participants will experience from beginning to end. Planning includes decisions about the number of groups, how and when to create independent variable conditions, and how often to measure the dependent variable. You also develop measures of the dependent variable and pilot test the experiment (see Summary Review: Steps in Conducting an Experiment).

pretest a measure of the dependent variable prior to introducing the independent variable in an experiment.

posttest a measure of the dependent variable after independent variable has been introduced in an experiment.

independent group design experimental designs in which you use two or more groups and each gets a different level of the independent variable.

experimental group in an experiment with multiple groups, a group of participants that receives the independent variable or a high level of it.

control group in an experiment with multiple groups, a group of participants that does not receive the independent variable or receives a very low level of it.

repeated measures design an experimental design with a single participant group that receives different levels of the independent variable.

Summary Review Steps in Conducting an Experiment

1. Begin with a straightforward hypothesis that is appropriate for experimental research.
2. Decide on an experimental design that will test the hypothesis within practical limitations.
3. Decide how to introduce the independent variable or create situations to induce it.
4. Develop a valid and reliable measure of the dependent variable.
5. Set up an experimental setting and conduct a pilot test of the variables.
6. Locate appropriate participants.
7. Randomly assign participants to groups and give careful instructions.
8. Gather data for the pretest measure of the dependent variable for all groups.
9. Introduce the independent variable to the experimental group only (or to relevant groups if there are multiple experimental groups) and monitor all groups.
10. Gather data for posttest measure of the dependent variable.
11. Debrief the participants. Ask participants what they thought was occurring and reveal the true purpose and situation you deceived them about in any aspect of the experiment.
12. Examine data collected and make comparisons between different groups using statistics and graphs to determine whether the data support the hypothesis.

Managing Experiments

Careful management is crucial in experimental research. The logic of experimental research requires that you carefully manage all aspects of the experimental setting. You want to isolate the effects of the independent variable and eliminate alternative explanations. Any aspects of an experimental situation that you do not control might become an alternative explanation for changes in the dependent variable. Alternative explanations weaken your ability to show a causal connection between the independent and dependent variables (see the discussion of internal validity later in this chapter).

In the study that opened this chapter, experimenters falsely told participants they were part of a communication study to evaluate news reports on public opinions. They used deception to manipulate how the participants defined the situation. Experimenters often use deception to prevent participants from altering their behavior or opinions to fit the researcher's hypothesis. By focusing attention on a false topic, the unaware participants acted more "natural" with regard to the variables of interest. Experimenters have deceived participants by intentionally misleading them with written or verbal instructions, by using the actions of helpers or **confederates**, or by arranging a setting. Experimenters also invent false dependent variable measures to keep the true ones hidden. Obviously, using deception raises ethical concerns (to be discussed later).

Types of Experimental Design

To plan an experiment, you combine the parts of an experiment (e.g., pretests, control groups, etc.) into an **experimental design**. Experimental designs vary in their components: Some do not use random assignment, some lack pretests, some do not have control groups, and others have several experimental groups. In research reports, researchers name widely used designs. You will be better able to understand an experiment's design if you learn the standard designs. They also illustrate various ways to combine the parts of an experiment.

We can illustrate the standard experimental designs by looking at variations on this simple example: You want to test whether servers (waiters and waitresses) receive bigger tips if they introduce themselves by first name before taking an order and return 8 to 10 minutes after delivering food to ask, "Is everything fine?" The independent variable is server behavior. The dependent variable is the size of the tip received.

We can divide standard designs into three groups: true experimental, preexperimental, and quasi-experimental designs. We will start with the "gold standard" of the true experimental designs, the classical experimental design. All other designs are variations on it.

True Experimental Designs

Classical Experimental Design. **Classical experimental design** has random assignment, a pretest and a posttest, an experimental group, and a control group.

> **EXAMPLE.** You give 40 newly hired servers a training session and instruct them to follow a script. They are not to introduce themselves by first name or return during the meal to check on the customers. You randomly divide the participants into two equal groups of 20. You record the average weekly tips for all participants for one month (pretest score). Next, you retrain one group of 20 participants (the experimental group). You instruct them henceforth to introduce themselves to customers by first name when taking an order and to check on the customers 10 minutes after delivering food. They are to smile and ask, "Is everything fine?" You instruct the other participants (control group) to continue without an introduction or checking. Over a second month, you record average weekly tips for both groups (posttest score). See Figure 7.2.

confederates people who work for an experimenter and mislead participants by pretending to be another participant or an uninvolved bystander.

experimental design how parts of an experiment are arranged, often in one of the standard configurations.

classical experimental design an experimental design that has all key elements that strengthen its internal validity: random assignment, control and experimental groups, and pretest and posttest.

■ **Figure 7.2**   Example Using Classical Experimental Design

	Month 1			Month 2	
Randomly assign participants to training sessions	Group 1 **Serve food without introduction or checking**	Pretest (amount of tips)	Independent Variable Present **Self-introduction and return to check on customer**		Posttest (amount of tips)
	Group 2 **Serve food without introduction or checking**	Pretest (amount of tips)	Independent Variable Absent **Serve food without introduction or checking**		Posttest (amount of tips)

Two-Group Posttest-Only Design. This design has all the parts of the classical design except a pretest. It is similar to the static group comparison (discussed below), except that you use random assignment. Random assignment improves the chance that the groups are equivalent, but without a pretest you cannot be as certain that the groups really began equal on the dependent variable.

EXAMPLE. You randomly divide 40 newly hired servers into two groups and give all training. You instruct one group not to introduce themselves by first name or to return during the meal to check on the customers. You instruct participants in the other group to introduce themselves to customers by first name and to check on the customers 10 minutes after delivering food. You record average weekly tips for both groups (posttest score). See Figure 7.3.

Jupiter Images Royalty Free/Brand X/AP Images

Solomon Four-Group Design. It is possible that your pretest measure sensitizes participants to your dependent variable or improves their posttest score. This can create a problem (see the discussion of testing effect later in this chapter). Richard Solomon developed a design to address this issue by combining the classical experimental design with the two-group posttest-only design and randomly assigning participants to one of four groups.

EXAMPLE. You randomly divide 80 newly hired servers into four groups and give them training. You instruct participants in groups 1, 2, and 4 not to introduce themselves or to return during the meal to check on the customers. You instruct participants in group 3 (experimental group 2) to introduce themselves and to return during the meal to check on the customers. During the first month, you count average weekly tips for groups 1 and 2 only (pretest). After the first month, you "retrain" group 1 participants (experimental group 1) henceforth to introduce themselves to customers by first name and to return during the meal to check on the customers 10 minutes after delivering food. All other groups continue as first instructed. During the second month, you record average weekly tips for all groups (posttest). As shown in Figure 7.4, groups 2 and 4 are identical, except that group 2 has the pretest. Groups 1

■ **Figure 7.3**   Example with Two-Group Posttest-Only Experimental Design

	Month 1		Month 2	
Randomly assign participants to training sessions	Group 1 **Serve food without introduction or checking**	Independent Variable Present **Self-introduction and return to check on customer**		Posttest (amount of tips)
	Group 2 **Serve food without introduction or checking**	Independent Variable Absent **Continue to serve food without introduction or checking**		Posttest (amount of tips)

■ Figure 7.4   Example with Solomon Four-Group Experimental Design

	Month 1		Month 2	
Randomly assign participants to training sessions	Group 1 **Serve food without introduction or checking**	Pretest (amount of tips)	Independent Variable Present **Self-introduction and return to check on customer**	Posttest (amount of tips)
	Group 2 **Serve food without introduction or checking**	Pretest (amount of tips)	Independent Variable Absent **Continue to serve food without introduction or checking**	Posttest (amount of tips)
	Group 3 **Serve food with introduction and checking**		Independent Variable Present **Continue self-introduction and return to check on customer**	Posttest (amount of tips)
	Group 4 **Serve food without introduction and checking**		Independent Variable Absent **Continue to serve food without introduction or checking**	Posttest (amount of tips)

and 3 are also the same. Both use a self-introduction and checking on customers.

Latin Square Designs. This design is used when you are interested in how several treatments in different sequences affect a dependent variable. The Latin square design is just like the classical experimental design, but it has multiple comparison groups. You have two or more levels or types of independent variables. All participants get all the levels or types of independent variables but in different sequences. You determine whether the time order matters.

EXAMPLE. You randomly divide 40 newly hired servers into two groups and give all training. You instruct one group to introduce themselves by first name when they first arrive at a table to take an order, and then return 10 minutes after serving the meal to ask whether everything is OK. They return after customers finish eating to ask whether the customers would like dessert or are ready for the bill. You instruct participants in the other group not to introduce themselves when they first arrive to take an order, but to return 10 minutes after serving the meal to ask whether everything is OK. They return after a customer finishes eating and only then introduce themselves. They also ask whether the customers would like dessert or are ready for the bill. You compare the size of tips for the two groups. In Figure 7.5, notice that everything is the same, except that the server's self-introduction comes before checking on customers for group 1 and after checking on customers for group 2. The only difference between the two situations is the timing of the self-introduction; it is not whether there is a self-introduction.

Factorial Designs. The previous designs all assumed you only looked at one independent and one dependent variable. However, the world is complex, and sometimes two or more independent variables may operate together to influence a dependent variable. Some research questions suggest that you look at the simultaneous effects of multiple independent variables. Perhaps a server's behavior is not the only factor affecting the size of tips. Maybe gender also plays a role, so you want to consider both server behavior and gender together. Do male and female servers who introduce themselves and those who do not receive the same tips irrespective of server's gender? In a **factorial design**, you use two or more independent variables in combination. You look at every combination of the variable categories (called *factors*). For two categories for two variables (server checking back and not checking back, and male or female), you need four groups. When each variable contains more than two categories, the number of combinations grows very quickly. In this kind of design, the independent variable becomes each combination of the vari-

factorial design an experimental design in which you examine the impact of combinations of two or more independent variable conditions.

■ **Figure 7.5** Example with Latin Square Experimental Design

		Customer Arrives	10 minutes After food	After Customer Finishes Meal	Posttest
Randomly assign participants to training sessions	Group 1	**Self-introduction** and take order	Check on Customer	Offer dessert or bill	Amount of tips
	Group 2	Take order	Check on customer	**Self-introduction** and offer dessert or bill	Amount of tips

ables and categories, such as the mix of gender and server behavior. At times, the independent variables combine a pre-existing variable situation, such as gender, with one that the researcher manipulates, such as training for a type of service.

EXAMPLE. Perhaps from previous studies you know that servers who self-introduces and checks back earns 10 percent higher tips than those who do not (a courteous service effect). You wonder whether there is also a gender effect or whether gender makes no difference. You can repeat the classical experimental design (Figure 7.2), only now do both with all-male server groups and all-female server groups (Figure 7.6).

Factorial designs can influence the dependent variable with two types of effects: main effects and interaction effects. **Main effects** are present in one-factor or single-treatment designs. They are how one variable alone affects the dependent variable (courtesy or gender alone). In a factorial design, combinations of independent variable categories can also have an effect. These **interaction effects** occur when specific combinations of variables and categories interact to produce an effect beyond that of each variable alone.

EXAMPLE. You discover that servers who self-introduce and check back get 10 percent higher tips than those who do not (a courteous service effect). You notice that female servers receive 6 percent higher tips than male servers (a gender effect). All servers work the same hours with the same number of customers. Let us say that a male server who does not self-introduce averages $1000 in tips in a month. If only main effects operated, a female who did not self-introduce and checked back averages $1060 in tips (a gender effect of 6 percent), a male who self-introduced and checked back averages $1100 in tips (a courtesy effect of 10 percent), and a female who self-introduced and checked back averages $1160 in tips (a courtesy plus a gender effect). Interaction

main effects the effect of a single independent variable on a dependent variable.

interaction effects the effect of two or more independent variables in combination on a dependent variable that is beyond or different from the effect that each has alone.

■ **Figure 7.6** Example with Factorial Experimental Design

		Month 1		Month 2	
Randomly assign participants to training sessions	All Female Group 1 **Serve food without introduction or checking**	Pretest (amount of tips)	Independent Variable Present **RETRAIN Self-introduction and return to check on customer**	Posttest (amount of tips)	
	All Female Group 2 **Serve food without introduction or checking**	Pretest (amount of tips)	Independent Variable Absent **Serve food without introduction or checking**	Posttest (amount of tips)	
	All Male Group 3 **Serve food without introduction or checking**	Pretest (amount of tips)	Independent Variable Present **RETRAIN Self-introduction and return to check on customer**	Posttest (amount of tips)	
	All Male Group 4 **Serve food without introduction and checking**	Pretest (amount of tips)	Independent Variable Absent **Serve food without introduction or checking**	Posttest (amount of tips)	

effects are like an extra boost beyond each separate effect alone. Perhaps females who self-introduce and check back have an extra boost. The interaction is extra over and above what we expect from gender and courteous service effects alone. If the courteous female servers got 9 percent extra due to interaction effects, they would receive $1250 in tips (10 percent courtesy, 6 percent gender plus the interaction effect of 9 percent).

Because factorial designs can be very complex, researchers created a shorthand way to talk about them. A "two by three factorial design," written 2 × 3, means there are two independent variables. The first has two categories and the other has three categories. A 2 × 3 × 3 design means that a study has three independent variables. The first variable has two categories, and two other variables each have three categories.

pre-experimental designs
experimental designs that lack
one or more parts of the classicial
experimental design.

Pre-Experimental Designs. Some designs lack random assignment and use compromises or shortcuts. Researchers use **pre-experimental designs** in situations where

 Example Study Box 2 Power and Sex Schemes

Sometimes the interaction effects in two-factor designs do not combine to boost the dependent variable in the same direction but work in other ways. Ong and Ward (1999) conducted a study of 128 female undergraduates at the National University of Singapore. They measured which of two ways participants understood the crime of rape (first independent variable, preexisting). Some women understood it as sex and due to the male sex drive (sex schema); others understood it as primarily an act of male power and domination over a woman (power schema). The researchers asked the participants to read a realistic scenario about the rape of a college student at their university. One randomly selected group of participants read a scenario in which the victim tried to fight off the rapist. In the other set, she passively submitted (second independent variable, manipulated by researchers). The researchers next asked the participants to evaluate the degree to which the rape victim was at blame or responsible for the rape (dependent variable).

Results showed that the women who held the sex schema (and who tended to embrace traditionalist gender role beliefs) more strongly blamed the victim when she resisted. Blame decreased if she submitted. The women who held a power schema (and who tended to hold less traditional gender role beliefs) were less likely to blame the victim if she fought. They blamed her more if she passively submitted. Thus, responses to the victim's act of resisting an attack varied by, or interacted with, how participants understood the crime of rape. The researchers found that two rape schemas caused participants to interpret victim resistance in opposite ways as they assigned responsibility for the crime. We can see the interaction effects illustrated in Figure 7.7.

■ Figure 7.7   Blame, Resistance, and Schema: Interaction Effect

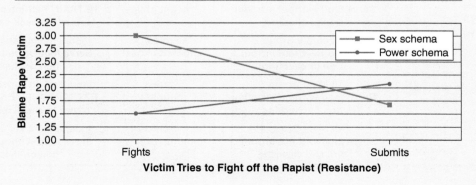

it is difficult to use the full classical design. Pre-experimental designs have weaknesses that make it more difficult to infer a causal relationship (see the discussion of internal validity later in this chapter).

One-Shot Case Study Design.   (Also called the one-group posttest-only design.) This design has only one group, a treatment, and a posttest. Since there is just one group, there is no random assignment. The design's logic has an implicit, unexamined assumption that dependent variable change is due to the independent variable. Although the design is very weak, we use it in daily life, such as classroom instruction. A teacher gives instruction (independent variable) and we assume that the instruction causes student learning (dependent variable).

> **EXAMPLE.**   You take a group of 40 newly hired servers and train all of them. You instruct them to introduce themselves to customers by first name and to check on the customers, asking, "Is everything fine?" 10 minutes after delivering the food (independent variable). You record the average weekly tips for all servers for one month (posttest score). You assume that the courteous service causes the tipping.

One-Group Pretest-Posttest Design.   This design has one group, a pretest, a treatment, and a posttest. It lacks a control group and random assignment. It allows you to measure change over time, but you lack a comparison group. Again, despite its weakness, we often use it in daily activities. A teacher might use this design if she measures what her students know on the first day of class and again measures how much they know after instruction.

> **EXAMPLE.**   You take a group of 40 newly hired servers and train all of them. You instruct them to follow a script in which they are not to introduce themselves by first name or return during the meal to check on the customers. All begin employment. You record average weekly tips for one month (pretest score). Next, you retrain all 40 servers and instruct them henceforth to introduce themselves to customers by first name and to check on the customers 10 minutes after delivering the food (independent variable). You record average weekly tips for the second month.

The one-group pretest-posttest design is a big improvement over the one-shot case study because you measure the dependent variable before and after introducing the independent variable. However, without a control group you cannot know whether something other than the independent variable is causing change in the dependent variable. Perhaps a teacher measured not only how much her class knew at the start of a term and how much other students knew who were not in her class. If she measured gain in knowledge in both groups at the end of the semester, she might discover that students not in her class gained just as much knowledge on their own. Unless she had the comparison group, she cannot be certain that her instruction caused her students to gain knowledge.

Static Group Comparison.   (Also called the posttest-only nonequivalent group design.) This design has two groups, a posttest, and treatment. It lacks random assignment and a pretest. Its weakness is that you cannot know whether group differences prior to the experiment caused differences in a posttest outcome rather than the independent variable.

> **EXAMPLE.**   You give 40 newly hired servers a training session and instruct them to follow a script in which they are not to introduce themselves by first name or check on the customers. After one month, you retrain 20 randomly picked participants (experimental group). You instruct them henceforth to introduce themselves to customers by first name and to check on the customers 10 minutes after delivering the food (independent variable). You instruct the rest of participants to continue without an introduction or checking. Over the second month, you record the amount of tips for both groups (posttest score).

Quasi-Experimental Designs. Quasi-experimental designs allow you to test for causal relationships in situations where a true experimental design is difficult or inappropriate. *Quasi* means "as if" in Latin. In general, you have less control with quasi-experimental designs than in true experimental designs. Many are repeated measure designs.

Interrupted Time Series. In an *interrupted time series* design, you only have one group. In this design, you make multiple measures of the dependent variable both before and after the treatment.

> **EXAMPLE.** You get a commitment from 20 newly hired servers for a six-month experiment. You instruct them to follow a script in which they do not introduce themselves or return during the meal to check on customers. You record their average weekly tips for three months. Next, you retrain all servers and instruct them henceforth to introduce themselves to customers by first name and to check on the customers 10 minutes after delivering the food. You record their average weekly tips for three months.

Equivalent Time Series. An *equivalent time series* is another one-group design that extends over time. It is similar to the interrupted time series, but instead of one treatment it has a pretest, then a treatment and posttest, then treatment and posttest, then treatment and posttest, and so on.

> **EXAMPLE.** You get a commitment from 20 newly hired servers for a six-month experiment. You instruct them to follow a script in which they are not to introduce themselves by first name or to return during the meal to check on customers. You record the amount in tips for month 1. Next, you retrain all 20 servers and instruct them henceforth to introduce themselves to customers by first name and to check on the customers 10 minutes after delivering the food. You record average weekly tips for month 2. Next, you retrain all

quasi-experimental designs
experimental designs that approximate the strengths of the classical experimental design but do not contain all its parts.

Summary Review   A Comparison of Experimental Designs

Design	Random Assignment	Pretest	Posttest	Control Group	Experimental Group
PRE-EXPERIMENTAL					
One-Shot Case Study	No	No	Yes	No	Yes
One-Group Pretest Posttest	No	Yes	Yes	No	Yes
Static Group Comparison	No	No	Yes	Yes	Yes
TRUE EXPERIMENTAL					
Classical	Yes	Yes	Yes	Yes	Yes
Two-Group Posttest Only	No	Yes	Yes	Yes	Yes
Solomon Four Group	Yes	Yes	Yes	Yes	Yes
Latin Square	Yes	Yes	Yes	Yes	Yes
Factorial	Yes	Yes	Yes	Yes	Yes
QUASI-EXPERIMENTAL					
Two-Group Posttest Only	Yes	No	Yes	Yes	Yes
Time Series Designs	No	Yes	Yes	No	Yes

20 servers and instruct them to stop introducing themselves to customers and checking back on customers. You record average weekly tips for month 3. Next, you retrain all 20 servers and instruct them again to introduce themselves to customers by first name and to check on the customers 10 minutes after delivering the food. You record average weekly tips for month 4. Next, you retrain all 20 servers and instruct them to stop introducing themselves to customers and not to return after delivering the food. You record average weekly tips for month 5. Next, you retrain all 20 servers and instruct them to introduce themselves to customers and to check on the customers 10 minutes after delivering the food. You record average weekly tips for month 6.

Design Notation

As you have seen, you can arrange the parts of an experiment to create many designs. Researchers have a shorthand symbol system to express the parts of a design. Once you learn **design notation**, you will find it easier to manipulate and compare designs. The system lets you express a complex, paragraph-long description in five or six symbols arranged in two lines. The symbols are as follows:

O = observation of dependent variable
X = independent variable
R = random assignment

The Os are often numbered with subscripts from left to right based on time order. Pretests are O_1, posttests O_2. When the independent variable has more than two levels, the Xs are numbered with subscripts. Place symbols in time order from left to right. The R is first, followed by the pretest, the independent variable, and then the posttest. Arrange symbols, with each row representing a group of participants. Figure 7.8 gives the notation for many standard experimental designs.

design notation a symbol system to express the parts of an experimental design with X, O, and R.

■ **Figure 7.8** **Summary of Experimental Designs with Notation**

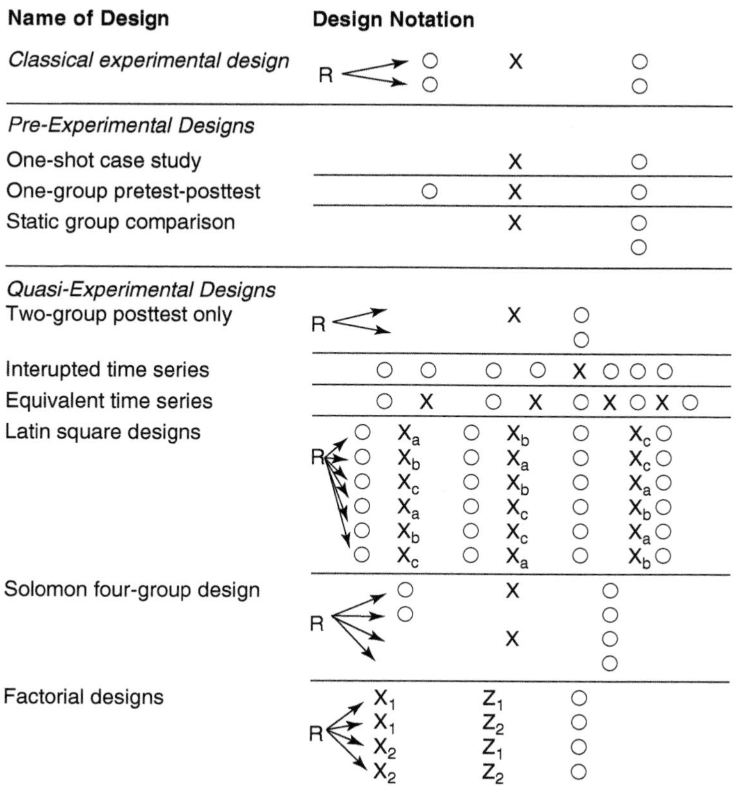

Example Study Box 3 Antimarijuana Television Ads

Alex Milan Tracy/Demotix/Corbis

Palmgreen et al (2001) conducted a two-part applied research experiment that combined interrupted and equivalent time series designs to test the impact of antimarijuana television ads on teenage drug use. Past studies told them that teenagers vary in "sensation seeking." High sensation seekers have a stronger need for novelty, fast-pasted drama, risk, and emotional impact than low sensation seekers. The experimenters focused on high sensation seekers because they were at greater risk to become habitual drug users. In two similar counties, they randomly selected 100 teenagers from local schools, grades 7 to 10. In both counties, students completed monthly surveys each month for 32 months. The surveys measured level of sensation seeking, television watching habits, specific television ads seen, attitudes about drugs, and drug use. Researchers found that the two groups were similar and that their rates of illegal drug use were close to national estimates for teens. Their dependent vari-

able was a report of marijuana use in the past 30 days. Their independent variable was a set of ads with antimarijuana messages targeted at high-sensation-seeking teens and aired during programs that teens tend to watch. Most students saw three of the ads per week during a campaign.

In Knox County, Tennessee (around the city of Knoxville), researchers used an interrupted time series design. Starting in March 1996, students completed the surveys each month. The ad campaign ran for four months, from January to April 1998. Students continued to complete surveys through December 1998. Prior to the campaign, marijuana use among high-sensation students had grown steadily, from 17 to 33 percent. Usage declined as soon as the campaign began. It continued to decline steadily, from May to December 1998, dropping to about 20 percent. Drug usage was much lower among low-sensation students, and it changed only a little.

The researchers used an equivalent time series design, with two independent variables (ad campaigns), in Fayette County, Kentucky (around the city of Lexington). Here, too, students completed monthly surveys starting in March 1996. One ad campaign ran from January to April 1997, and then it stopped. It ran again from January to April 1998, the same time as the one in Knox County, Tennessee. Prior to the first campaign, marijuana use among high-sensation students had steadily grown from about 20 to 37 percent. Usage declined as soon as the campaign began. It continued to decline, from May to November 1997, to about 27 percent, and then it slowly increased again. The increase continued for about two months into the second ad campaign (January to April 1998), and then use declined. It continued to decline after the campaign, to about 27 percent by December 1998.

Group	March–Dec 1996	Jan–April 1997	May–Dec 1997	Jan–April 1998	May–Dec 1998
Knox County TN	OOOOOOOOOO	OOOO TV ads	OOOOOOOO	OOOO TV ads	OOOOOOOO
Fayette County KY	OOOOOOOOOO	OOOO	OOOOOOOO	OOOO TV ads	OOOOOOOO

O = Dependent variable measure = a monthly survey of teen pot-smoking behavior.

EXPERIMENTAL VALIDITY INSIDE AND OUT

Looking at an Experiment's Internal Validity

The internal logic of an experiment should be tight and make the causal connection between the independent variable and the dependent variable very clear. For example, you want to make certain that it is the self-introduction and courtesy check on customers, not other factors (e.g., changes in the menu, features of the servers), that causes differences in tipping. You want to eliminate potential alternative explanations for change in the dependent variable. Anything other than the independent variable that influences the dependent variable is a potential threat to your study's **internal validity**. Internal validity allows you to rule out potential alternative causes by controlling experimental conditions and by experimental designs. Next, we examine threats to internal validity.

Threats to Internal Validity.   Researchers uncovered many potential threats to internal validity, here we consider seven common ones.

1. *Selection bias.* This occurs when participants do not start the same. For example, in an experiment on physical aggressiveness, all the participants put in the experimental group happen to be football, rugby, wrestling, and hockey players whereas all control group participants are classical musicians, chess players, dancers, and painters. Selection bias is often an issue in designs lacking random assignment. You can detect selection bias by looking at pretest scores, because all groups should begin the same on the dependent variable.

2. *History.* This is the possibility that an unexpected event unrelated to the independent variable occurs during the experiment and influences the dependent variable. History effects are more likely in experiments that continue over a long time. For example, halfway through a two-week experiment to evaluate participants' attitudes toward space travel, a spacecraft explodes on the launch pad, killing the astronauts.

3. *Maturation.* This is the threat that a biological, psychological, or emotional process within the participants that is not part of the independent variable induces a change in the dependent variable. Like the history effect, maturation effects are more common in experiments over a long time. For example, during an experiment on reasoning ability that lasts six hours without a break, participants become hungry and tired. As a result, they score lower. Designs with a pretest and control group help you to detect whether maturation or history effects might be present. You may suspect such effects if you see similar changes in both experimental and control groups.

4. *Testing.* Sometimes the act of measuring the dependent variable with a pretest itself affects an experiment. This threatens internal validity because measuring in addition to the independent variable alone has an impact on the dependent variable. The Solomon four-group design helps you to detect testing effects. For example, several years ago I wanted to experiment with a new teaching technique (independent variable) to raise student learning (dependent variable). Students were randomly assigned to two sections of the same course that I was teaching. On the first day of class, I gave students in both sections the final examination (pretest). During the academic term, I used the new teaching technique in one section (experimental group) but not the other (control group). On the last day of class, all students got the same final exam as on the first day of class (posttest). Perhaps students remembered the exam questions from the pretest and this affected what they learned (i.e., paid attention to) or how they answered questions on the posttest? If that had occurred, then a testing effect was present.

5. *Experimental mortality.* This effect arises when some participants do not continue throughout the experiment. Although mortality does not mean that participants died, if some participants leave partway through an experiment, you cannot know whether the results would be different had all stayed. For example, you begin a six-week weight-loss program with 50 participants. At the end of the program, 30 remain. All who remained to the end lost 15 pounds and reported no side effects. You do not know whether the 20 who left differed from the 30 who stayed. Maybe the program was highly effective for those who left, and they withdrew after losing 25 pounds. Perhaps they saw no results and quit in disgust. Or maybe the program made them sick so they quit. To detect this threat, you must report the number of participants in each group from the start to the end and in the pretests and posttests.

internal validity the ability to state that the independent variable was the one sure cause that produced a change in the dependent variable.

6. *Contamination or diffusion of treatment.* This is the threat that participants in different groups communicate with each other and learn about how the other group is being treated. You can reduce it by isolating groups or having participants promise not to reveal anything to others. For example, you place participants in a daylong experiment on a new way to memorize words. During a lunch break, participants from the experimental group tell those in the control group about the exciting new way to memorize what they just learned. The control group participants then start to use the technique. This threat is difficult to detect. To discover it, you need outside information such as debriefing interviews or monitoring participants at all times.

7. *Experimenter expectancy.* An experimenter's behavior, too, can threaten causal logic. We are not talking about purposeful, unethical behavior but indirectly communicating expectations. Many researchers are highly committed to the hypothesis. They accidentally and indirectly communicate desired findings to participants. For example, you study the effects of memorization training on learning. You believe that students with higher grades will do better at the training and will score higher. You learn participants' grades. Through eye contact, tone of voice, pauses, and other nonverbal communication, you unconsciously encourage and train the students with higher grades more intensely. Your unintended nonverbal behavior is the opposite for students with lower grades.

The way to detect experimenter expectancy is by hiring assistants who are the only ones who have contact with participants. You might give assistants fake transcripts and records showing that the participants in one group are honor students and those in the other group are on academic probation and failing. In reality, all the participants have equal academic records. Should the fake honor students, as a group, do much better in the learning study than the fake failing students, you uncovered experimenter expectancy as a problem.

Researchers control experimenter expectancy by using the **double-blind experiment**. In it, people who have direct contact with participants do not know some details about the study. It is *double* blind because the participants and the assistant in contact with them are blind to experimental details (see Figure 7.9). For example, a researcher wants to see if a new drug is effective. Using three colors of pills—green, yellow, and pink—the researcher puts the new drug in the yellow pill, puts an old drug in the pink one, and makes the green pill a **placebo**, a false independent variable that appears real (e.g., a sugar pill without any physical effects). Assistants who give the pills and record the effects do not know which color pill has the new drug. Only another person who does not deal with participants directly knows which colored pill contains the drug and examines the results.

External Validity and Field Experiments

Even if you successfully eliminate all threats to internal validity, you still want to generalize findings to beyond the study to a larger context or for it to have **external validity**. If a study's findings hold true only in experiments, making them useless to the real world and applied situations, then we say it lacks external validity.

Four threats might weaken external validity:

- *Participants are not representative.* Participants in the study may not fully represent characteristics such as age, gender, education level, race-ethnicity, and so forth of the population to which you want to generalize results.
- *Artificial setting.* You may conduct the experiments in a very "unnatural" setting, such as a campus laboratory, that limits generalizing to more chaotic and uncontrolled natural settings, such as a retail store, a street corner, a playground, a working office, or an informal public social setting.

double-blind experiment an experimental design to control experimenter expectancy in which the researcher does not have direct contact with participants. All contact is through assistants from whom some details are withheld.

placebo a false or noneffective independent variable given to mislead participants.

external validity an ability to generalize experimental findings to events and settings beyond the experimental setting itself.

■ **Figure 7.9**   An Illustration of Single-Blind, or Ordinary, and Double-Blind Experiments

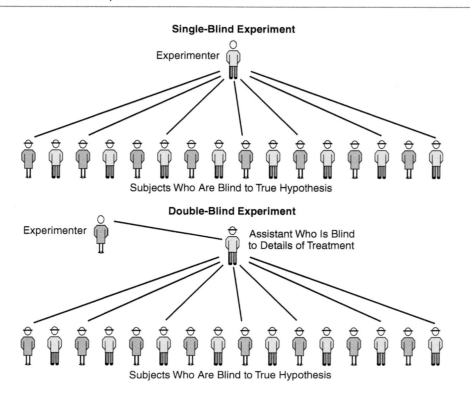

Single-Blind Experiment

Experimenter

Subjects Who Are Blind to True Hypothesis

Double-Blind Experiment

Experimenter   Assistant Who Is Blind
                      to Details of Treatment

Subjects Who Are Blind to True Hypothesis

- *Artificial treatment.* You may create a treatment, such as showing a photograph of a person's face to create a reaction to people of a race, or have participants memorize nonsense words to see how well they learn. Such treatments may not be realistic enough to allow generalizing to daily life experiences.
- **Reactivity.** Research participants respond differently than they would in real life to situations because they are aware that they part of a study (see Learning from History: The Hawthorne Effect).

Field Experiments. Thus far, we have focused on experiments conducted under controlled laboratory conditions. You can also conduct experiments in real-life or field settings. The amount of control you have varies on a continuum. At one end is the highly controlled laboratory experiment that takes place in a specialized setting or laboratory. At the opposite end is the **field experiment**, which takes place in the "field"— in natural settings such as a person's home or a public sidewalk. Participants in a

reactivity a threat to external validity due to participants modifying their behavior because they are aware that they are in a study.

field experiment an experiment that takes place in a natural setting and over which experimenters have limited control.

Hawthorne effect a type of experimental reactivity in which participants change due to their awareness of being in a study and the attention they receive from researcher.

Learning from History **The Hawthorne Effect**

Elton Mayo discovered a specific kind of reactivity in a series of experiments at the Hawthorne, Illinois, plant of Westinghouse Electric during the 1920s and 1930s. Researchers experimented by modifying many aspects of working conditions (e.g., lighting, time for breaks, heating, etc.) and then measured worker productivity. They discovered that productivity rose after each modification, no matter what it was. Thus, improved lighting and reduced lighting, greater heat and reduced heat, and so forth all had the same effect. This curious result occurred because the workers were not responding to the independent variable. They responded to the additional attention they got from being part of the experiment and knowing that researchers were closely watching them. The results were so surprising that the effect was named after the study, the **Hawthorne effect**.

Summary Review Threats to Internal and External Validity

Seven Threats to INTERNAL VALIDITY	Four Threats to EXTERNAL VALIDITY
1. Selection	1. Participants not representative
2. History	2. Artificial setting
3. Maturation	3. Artificial treatment
4. Testing	4. Reactivity
5. Experimental Mortality	
6. Contamination	
7. Experimenter Expectancy	

laboratory experiment usually know they are in a study. Those in field experiments may be unaware that they are part of an experiment and react in a natural way.

An experimenter's degree of control over an experimental setting directly affects internal and external validity. In general, laboratory experiments allow for more internal validity but less external validity. They can be logically tighter and better controlled but may be less generalizable. Field experiments allow greater external validity but less internal validity. They are more generalizable but permit less experimenter control. Examples of studies on restaurant tipping, the study on marijuana and TV antimar-

Example Study Box 4 Drinking Age Enforcement

A natural experiment about laws on underage drinking took place in New Orleans. Until the mid-1990s, liquor law enforcement was a low priority in New Orleans. State and local governments assigned three enforcement officers to monitor 5000 alcohol outlets. They barely enforced laws against selling liquor to underage customers. If caught, an offending liquor retailer met privately with the liquor commission and paid a small fine. Then in early 1996, public officials shifted enforcement priorities. Scribner and Cohen (2001) conducted an evaluation research study with a natural experiment to examine the impact of the enforcement campaign. Police had several people who clearly looked under 18 years old attempt to purchase alcoholic beverages illegally (the law required being at least 21 years of age) at 143 randomly selected liquor outlets from November 1995 through January 1996 (Time 0). The percentage who bought liquor illegally was a pretest measure. After assessing the rate of illegal sales, the dependent variable, the police issued citations to 51 of the sales outlets. A citation was the primary independent variable. About the same time, officials initiated a media campaign that urged better law compliance. The experimenters checked 143 outlets from March to April 1996 (Time 1) and again from November 1996 to January 1997 (Time 2). These are posttest measures.

The experimenters compared rates of illegal selling activity before and after citations/media campaign (pretest and posttest measures) and compared outlets that directly received citations (experimental group) with those that did not receive citations (control group). By making comparisons, they found that the citations and media campaign did not stop the illegal activity but had some effect. The impact was greater on outlets that received fines. Their law compliance rose from 6.7 to 51 percent. Compliance rose from 13.3 to 35 percent for outlets in the control group. From a later follow-up (Time 2), they saw that the impact slowly decayed over time.

Making It Practical **Tricks of the Trade**

Experienced researchers use practical techniques to carry out effective experiments. Three are discussed here.

1. *Planning and pilot tests.* During the planning phase, think of alternative explanations or threats to internal validity and how to avoid them. Also, develop a neat and well-organized system for recording data. You will want to devote serious effort to pilot testing any apparatus (e.g., computers, video cameras, tape recorders, etc.) that you will use and prepare a backup. If you use confederates, train and pilot test them as well. After the pilot tests, interview the pilot participants to uncover any aspects of the experiment that need refinement.

2. *Instructions to participants.* In most experiments, you give instructions to set the stage. Word your instructions

carefully and closely follow a prepared script each time so that all participants hear the same thing. This ensures reliability. The instructions are also important in creating a realistic cover story if you use deception.

3. *Postexperiment interview.* You should interview participants at the end of the study for three reasons. First, if you used deception, you must **debrief** the participants and reveal the true purpose of the experiment. Second, you can learn what the participants thought and how their definitions of the situation affected their behavior. Finally, you can explain the importance of not revealing the true nature of the experiment to other potential participants.

ijuana ads, and the experiment on drinking age law enforcement in New Orleans (see Example Study Box 4: Drinking Age Enforcement) are highly generalizable. All took place in real-life settings.

The introductory study about reading a fake news report about student opinions, the study about mistaking a gun for a tool, and student reactions to rape are less generalizable.

Natural Experiments. Thus far, we have considered intentional, planned experiments. **Natural experiments**, also called ex *post facto* (after the fact) control group comparisons, are field experiments that people did not intentionally plan as an experiment but had an arrangement of events that had features of an experiment. After the fact, researchers can gather data, apply experimental logic, and make comparisons to test causal relations.

Internal validity is often an issue in natural experiment because there is limited control. In the New Orleans study, the outlets that received the independent variable had higher rates of illegal behavior than others did. This was a source of possible selection bias. The media campaign had effects on all outlets. It made the true independent variable a citation combined with the media campaign. The authors had hoped to compare the New Orleans area with another area that did not have a media or citation campaign but were unable to do so. They lacked a control group. Outlets that did not receive a citation for law violation learned about it from others in the same business. This was a form of diffusion of the treatment. The study began with 155 outlets, but only 143 were in the study. Also, 12 outlets went out of business during the study, suggesting experimental mortality. The experimenters do not mention any external events in New Orleans that happened during the time of the study (e.g., a publicized event such as an underage drinker dying of alcohol poisoning from overdrinking). If nothing occurred, the history effects are not a problem.

MAKING COMPARISONS AND LOOKING AT EXPERIMENTAL RESULTS

Comparison is critical in all forms of research. By examining the results of experimental research, you can see whether the independent variable affected the dependent variable. You can also learn a great deal about threats to internal validity. For

debrief an interview or talk with participants after an experiment ends in which you remove deception if used and try to learn how they understood the experimental situation.

natural experiments events that were not initially planned to be experiments but permitted measures and comparisions that allowed the use of an experimental logic.

■ Figure 7.10 Comparisons of Results, Classical Experimental Design, Weight-Loss Experiments

| | **Enrique's Slim Clinic** | | | **Natalie's Nutrition Center** | |
	Pretest	*Posttest*		*Pretest*	*Posttest*
Experimental	190 (30)	140 (29)	Experimental	190 (30)	188 (29)
Control group	189 (30)	189 (30)	Control group	192 (29)	190 (28)
	Susan's Scientific Diet Plan			**Pauline's Pounds Off**	
	Pretest	*Posttest*		*Pretest*	*Posttest*
Experimental	190 (30)	141 (19)	Experimental	190 (30)	158 (30)
Control group	189 (30)	189 (28)	Control group	191 (29)	159 (28)
	Carl's Calorie Counters				
	Pretest	*Posttest*			
Experimental	160 (30)	152 (29)			
Control group	191 (29)	189 (29)			

example, in the chapter opening study on racial stereotypes, the researchers compared differences in stereotype acceptance for experimental and control groups. In the study on presenting photos of black versus white male faces and guns or tools, researchers compared mistakes made in identifying a photo as a gun or tool. In the study on television ads and teen marijuana smoking in two counties, researchers compared rates of smoking marijuana among teens over time—before, during, and after the television ad campaign.

Figure 7.10 presents the results of a series of five weight-loss experiments. All use the classical experimental design. Look carefully and compare the data. You can see potential threats to internal validity and the independent variable's impact. In the example, the 30 participants in the experimental group at Enrique's Slim Clinic lost an average of 50 pounds, whereas the 30 in the control group did not lose a

Tips for the Wise Consumer Examining How an Experiment was Conducted

When you read an experimental research study, you should closely examine several of its features:

- How many participants? Experiments that have very small numbers of participants in each group (10 or fewer) are not as strong as those with at least 30 participants per group.
- Who participated? Experiments with participants who are all undergraduate volunteers from a single course are weaker than those with participants diverse by age, experience, and social background. Likewise, experiments highly unbalanced by gender (such as 75 percent of one gender) are not as strong as those that have close to a 50/50 gender balance.
- Was randomization used? Multigroup experiments that use random assignment of participants are stronger than those that do not.

- How many groups? Experiments that involve at least one control and one experimental group are stronger than those that lack a control group.
- How was the dependent variable measured? Does it have high reliability and validity (see Chapter 5)?
- What was the independent variable? The treatment should be highly realistic and tightly controlled. Many experimenters use "manipulation checks" in which they evaluate their independent variable.
- Is internal validity strong? Consider all the internal validity concerns discussed in this chapter, such as selection bias or experimental mortality, and see whether they are potential issues.

single pound. Only one person dropped out during the experiment. Enrique's clinic appears to be effective. Susan's Scientific Diet Plan had equally dramatic results, but 11 participants in her experimental group dropped out. This suggests a threat from experimental mortality. Participants in the experimental group at Carl's Calorie Counters lost 8 pounds, compared to 2 pounds for the control group. You may notice that the control group and the experimental group began with an average of 31 pounds difference in weight. This suggests a threat from selection bias. Natalie's Nutrition Center had no experimental mortality or selection bias problems. Yet participants in the experimental group lost no more weight than those in the control group. Natalie's independent variable appears to be ineffective. Pauline's Pounds Off also avoided selection bias and experimental mortality problems. Her experimental group participants lost 32 pounds, but so did those in the control group. This suggests that the maturation, history, or diffusion of treatment effects may have occurred. Thus, Enrique's Slim Clinic appears to offer the most effective treatment without clear internal validity problems.

HOW TO BE ETHICAL IN CONDUCTING EXPERIMENTS

Ethical considerations can be a significant issue because many experiments are intrusive (i.e., interfere with participant activity). The independent variable may involve placing people in contrived social settings and manipulating their feelings or behaviors. Ethical standards limit the amount and type of intrusion. Researchers use extra care and consult closely with the IRB if they ever place participants in physical distress or in embarrassing or anxiety-inducing situations. They must painstakingly monitor events and control what occurs.

Some researchers use deception. They mislead or lie to participants. Dishonesty is never condoned; however, deception may be acceptable under imited conditions. It may be accepted if it is the only way to achieve a clear research goal impossible to achieve otherwise. Even for a worthy goal, it is used with restrictions. The amount and type of deception should never go beyond what is minimally necessary to achieve the effect for a clear research purpose. In addition, you must always debrief participants as soon as possible and explain the true situation.

WHAT HAVE YOU LEARNED?

In this chapter, you learned about random assignment and experimental research. Comparison is critical in experimental research, and random assignment is a highly effective way to create two (or more) groups that you treat as equivalent and compare. Experimental research can provide you with precise evidence for a causal relationship. It produces quantitative results that you can analyze with statistics, and it is often used in evaluation research.

In this chapter, you also learned about the parts of an experiment and how to combine them to produce different experimental designs. In addition to the classical experimental design, you learned about pre-experimental and quasi-experimental designs. You also learned how to express various designs using the sym-

bol system of design notation. You learned how the logic of experiments, or an experiment's internal validity, is a way to reduce alternative explanations. Threats to internal validity are sources of possible alternative explanations to a study's independent variable. You also learned about external validity and how field experiments can maximize external validity.

The greatest strength of experimental research is its ablity to control alternative explanations and its logical rigor to establish evidence for causality. Experiments are easier to replicate, less expensive, and less time consuming than the other research techniques. Experimental research also has limitations. First, you cannot use it to address some questions because control and experimental manipulation are impossible. Also, you can usually test one or two hypotheses at a time with experiments, which fragments the growth of knowledge. External validity is another potential problem. Too often researchers use social experiments with small, nonrandom samples of college students and then try generalize to the entire population. You saw how a careful examination and comparison of results can alert you to potential problems. Finally, you learned about practical and ethical issues with experiments.

In the next chapters, you will examine other research techniques. The basic logic of nonexperimental research differs from that of experiments. Most experimenters focus narrowly on a few hypotheses, have one or two independent variables, a single dependent variable, and few participants. By contrast, researchers using nonexperimental methods often test many hypotheses at once, measure numerous variables, and gather data on a large numbers of participants.

KEY TERMS

APPLYING WHAT YOU'VE LEARNED

Activity 1

A good way to learn about experimental designs is to practice diagraming experimental studies using design notation. Diagram the study by Deaux and others (2007), "Becoming American: Sterotype Threat Effects in Afro-Caribbean Immigrant Groups" excerpted in Appendix C (and available in full on My Sockit), and answer these questions: How many participants in total were involved? How was the dependent variable measured? What is the treatment?

Activity 2

A very important aspect of experimental research are the threats to internal validity. Read the following experiment along with its results and determine which threats, if any, might be operating in each of four experimental conditions.

Dr. Wacko wanted to see whether sex, drugs, or rock and roll improved student self-esteem more than

traditional counseling or no treatment at all over a six-week period. He randomly assigned four groups of 30 students to two groups. In all four groups the control group received no special treatment.

In Experimental Group A, he gave the students favorable information about illegal drug use, supplied them with quantities of several types of illegal drugs free of charge, and encouraged them to try the drugs.

In Experimental Group B, he told the students about the history of rock and roll and gave them MP3 players with a large quantity of rock and roll music. He also encouraged them to listen to the music at least six hours per day.

In Experimental Group C, he told the students the benefits of premarital sex and encouraged them to experiment with sexual behavior. He introduced them to attractive members of the opposite sex who had very liberal sexual attitudes. He also supplied them with contraceptives and private rooms.

In Experimental Group D, he placed the students in traditional counseling to improve self-esteem.

Note: He measured self-esteem with a questionnaire in which self-esteem went from 0 = very negative to 100 = very positive. Here are his results; the number in parentheses () is the number of participants.

Self-Esteem Score and (Number of Students)

	Pretest	Posttest
A. Experimental	65 (15)	63 (13)
Control	60 (15)	66 (14)
B. Experimental	65 (15)	89 (14)
Control	45 (15)	79 (14)
C. Experimental	66 (15)	90 (6)
Control	65 (15)	67 (14)
D. Experimental	64 (15)	88 (14)
Control	63 (15)	66 (15)

Activity 3

Here is a simple field experiment you can replicate, although you may need to get prior approval from your college IRB (discussed in Chapter 3). The study looked at the "Lady Macbeth effect." If you ever read or saw Shapespeare's play *Macbeth*, you may remember Lady Macbeth's famous line, "Out, damned spot! Out, I say!" when the guilt of a bloody murder overcomes her. The researchers hypothesized that people who feel greater guilt or shame are more likely to be desire cleanliness. They randomly divided students into two groups. One group was asked to recall an unethical act from their past, such as betraying a friend, telling a lie, and so forth. They were to think about it and write it down. The other group was told to reflect on a positive ethical deed they had done, such as returning lost money. Afterward, the students were given their choice of one of two gifts for their participation: either a pencil or an antiseptic wipe. The researchers hypothesized that participants who had reflected on a shameful act would be more likely to take the wipe. To see what they found, refer to the article by Chen-Bo Zhong and Katie Liljenquist. "Washing Away Your Sins," *Science*, September 8, 2006, vol. 313, no. 5792, pp. 1451–1452. Did you find the same thing as the researchers found?

REFERENCES

Ong, Andy S. J., and Colleen A. Ward. 1999. "The Effects of Sex and Power Schemas, Attitudes toward Women, and Victim Resistance on Rape Attributions." *Journal of Applied Social Psychology* 29:362–376.

Palmgreen, Philip, Lewis Donohew, Elizabeth Pugzles Lorch, Rick Hoyle, and Michael Stephenson. 2001. "Television Campaigns and Adolescent Marijuana Use." *American Journal of Public Health* 91:293–296.

Payne, B. Keith. 2001. "Prejudice and Perception." *Journal of Personality and Social Psychology* 81:181–192.

Rummel, Nikol, Joel Levin, and Michelle Woodward. 2003. "Do Pictorial Mnemonic Text-Learning Aids Give Students Something Worth Writing About?" *Journal of Experimenal Psychology* 95:327–334.

Scribner, Richard, and Deborah Cohen. 2001. "The Effect of Enforcement on Merchant Compliance with the Minimum Legal Drinking Age Law." *Journal of Drug Issues* 31:857–867.

Tan, Alexis, et al. 2001. "Changing Negative Racial Stereotypes: The Influence of Normative Peer Information." *Howard Journal of Communication* 12:171–180.

Zhong, Chen-Bo, and Katie Liljenquist. 2006. "Washing Away Your Sins." *Science* [September 8, 2006] 313(5792):1451–1452.

Research with Nonreactive Measures

BWAC Images/Alamy

What do you throw away? Have you ever gone through your trash to find something accidentally thrown away? Thieves, private detectives, and police investigators comb through trash to gather information. Researchers also study trash to learn about social behavior. Just as archaeologists study bits of broken pottery to learn about ancient cultures and reconstruct social life from long ago, you can learn about people and their behavior by studying what they discard. I sometimes look through trashcans in my classroom and notice many soft drink and beverage containers. Over the years, I have seen changes in the popularity of beverages among my students. Urban anthropologists have studied the contents of garbage dumps to learn about lifestyles based on what people throw away (e.g., liquor bottles indicate alcohol consumption). They found, based on garbage, that people underreport their liquor consumption by 40 to 60 percent (Rathje and Murphy 1992:71). Examine my family's trash and that of our neighbor, and you will discover differences in our respective eating habits, lifestyles, and recreation habits. My neighbor's family eats a lot of carryout fast food and delivered pizza. Their primary form of recreation is to watch television, especially professional sports. They drink a lot of soft drinks and beer. They subscribe to a weekly television guide and a sports magazine. My family eats a lot fresh fruits and vegetables and drinks bottled water and wine. We cook from scratch and almost never eat fast food or drink sodas. Our recreation is to go to the theater and to read books and newspapers. We subscribe to two newspapers, and to one news and one arts magazine. Trash is physical evidence that can become data to inform us about human behavior. It is a form of nonreactive data, the topic of this chapter.

Most quantitative social research, such as experiments and survey research, are reactive. The people who are studied know that they are part of a research study. As you read in the previous chapter, reactive research can be problematic. People sometimes modify their words or actions because they are aware that they are in a study. The example of studying trash is a type of **nonreactive research**. The people being studied are not aware of being studied in nonreactive research, but the nature of the data rather than covert or secret data collection and spying makes such research nonreactive. In this chapter, you will learn about four *nonreactive* quantitative research techniques:

Physical evidence analysis
Content analysis
Existing statistics analysis
Secondary data analysis

Quantitative nonreactive research techniques have two advantages: first, people do not act differently because you study them, or because they are aware that data about them is part of a research study. Second, it is often faster and easier to collect data. Quantitative nonreactive research has some disadvantages. With several nonreactive techniques you have limited control over how the data are collected. Also, you often must infer the meaning of data indirectly. You follow the quantitative measurement process to create a nonreactive measure: (1) Conceptualize a construct and create a theoretical definition, (2) develop an operational definition of a variable, and (3) collect empirical evidence.

ANALYZING PHYSICAL EVIDENCE FOR CLUES ABOUT SOCIAL LIFE

As shown in the study on trash that opened this chapter, you can learn about social life by looking creatively at various types of physical evidence. It begins when you notice evidence that indicates a variable of interest. Discarded beverage containers indicate beverage availability and people's taste preferences. The critical thing about nonreactive or **unobtrusive measures** (i.e., measures that are not obtrusive or intrusive) is that people who generate it are not aware of its use in a research study.

Over the years, social researchers used many kinds of physical evidence to create nonreactive measures of variables. They have

- looked at family portraits in different historical eras to see how seating patterns reflected gender relations within the family;
- measured public interest in exhibits by noting worn floor tiles in different parts of a museum;
- compared graffiti in male versus female high school restrooms to examine gendered themes; and
- examined high school yearbooks to compare the high school activities of people who later had psychological problems with those who did not.

Nonreactive data can confirm or reveal different things from direct, reactive data. This happened with the alcohol consumption measure based on the study of trash. We know that people's answers to a survey question do not always match their behavior. Perhaps my favorite music is heavy metal rock. In a survey question, I say my favorite music is classical because I want to appear refined and sophisticated. In an experiment, if given a choice to listen to heavy metal or classical, I pick classical music to present myself as sophisticated and educated. However, you might follow how some researchers studied the listening habits of drivers. They checked the radio stations that drivers had tuned to when cars were taken in for service. If you checked my car radio, you might find that it is never tuned to classical, only to heavy metal rock. Going through my trash for lists of purchases, you see no classical music, only heavy metal rock. At times, nonreactive data can give a more accurate measure of music preference than direct reactive measures.

nonreactive research a collection of research techniques in which the people in the study are unaware that someone is gathering information or using it for research purposes.

unobtrusive measures most nonreactive research measures do not intrude or disturb a person, so the person is unaware of them.

To conduct a study with physical evidence, you need to do the following:

- Identify a physical evidence measure of a behavior or viewpoint of interest.
- Systematically count and record the physical evidence.
- Identify and measure other variables of your hypothesis.
- Consider alternative explanations for the physical data and rule them out.
- Compare the two variables of your hypothesis using quantitative data analysis.

Limitations of Physical Evidence

Physical evidence measures are indirect. This means you must infer or make a cautious "educated guess" from the evidence to people's behavior or attitudes. For example, you infer that leaving a radio station in my car to a station that plays heavy metal indicates my music preference. You do not know whether I set the radio to that station because it has the best weather forecasts or a favorite announcer. You do not know whether someone else who also drives the car likes heavy metal and I never listen to the radio when driving. Perhaps a different person takes the car in for service and changes the radio settings. For these reasons, you need to confirm inferences from nonreactive data with reactive evidence. When you must infer indirectly from data, looking for patterns in a very large sample makes it less likely to be misled by a few unusual situations.

You want to confirm the meaning of a physical evidence measure to rule out alternative explanations. For example, you can measure walking traffic by customers in a store by the amount of dirt and wear on floor tiles. To use this measure, you first must clarify what the customer traffic really means (e.g., Is the floor a path to another department? Does it indicate a good location for a visual display?). Next, you systematically measure dirt or wear on the tiles and record results on a regular basis (e.g., every month). Next, you compare the wear and dirt in one area to wear in other locations. Finally, you rule out alternative reasons for the data (e.g., the floor tile is of lower quality and wears faster, or the location is near an outside entrance).

Example Study Box 1   Data in the Graveyard

Bob Daemmrich/PhotoEdit Inc.

Have you ever walked through an old cemetery and read what was on the tombstones? You can learn a lot. Writing on tombstones provides data about conditions in the past. In addition to official written records, which may be incomplete or destroyed over time, we can look at the physical evidence on tombstones. Foster and colleagues (1998) examined the tombstones in 10 cemeteries in an area of Illinois for the period from 1830 to 1989. From the tombstones, they retrieved data on birth and death dates and gender. In total, they gathered information from over 2000 of the 2028 burials in the 10 cemeteries. They learned how the area differed from national trends. For example, they found that conceptions had two peaks (spring and winter), and females aged 10 to 64 had a higher death rate than males. Younger people tended to die in late summer but older people in late winter. Cemeteries can also reveal information about family size and relations (e.g., a married adult woman is buried with her parents and not her husband).

Another limitation of nonreactive data is possible privacy violation. You could be violating a person's privacy by noting the stations on a car radio or detailing what is put in his or her trash. The potential for privacy violation means that you must take extra care in collecting data to protect anonymity and confidentiality. For example, you record the make and year of a car and the radio stations, not the owner's name. You observe whether two types of garbage occur together (pizza boxes and beer cans) but not other information in the same trash (a name and address on discarded junk mail).

Creativity is an important aspect of nonreactive research using physical measures. A researcher needs to think creatively about what observations might indicate. Perhaps you notice that people driving bright red or yellow cars seem to speed more than people who drive black or gray ones. You might hypothesize that people who are attracted to bright colors and want to be noticed feel less constrained by rules or laws. If you obtained a radar gun to measure car speed and record car color, you could see whether color and speed are related. You need to be aware of alternative explanations and be cautious in drawing conclusions. Perhaps younger people like brightly colored cars and are also more likely to speed. Age and not the desire to have a bright car could be the real causal factor.

REVEALING THE CONTENT BURIED WITHIN COMMUNICATION MESSAGES

Content analysis is a nonreactive technique that lets you explore both hidden and visible content in communication messages. The *content* can be words, meanings, pictures, symbols, ideas, themes, or any message that the **text** communicates, directly or indirectly. Text appears in all communication media, including books, newspaper or magazine articles, advertisements, speeches, official documents, films or DVDs, musical lyrics, photographs, articles of clothing, and works of art. Professionals in many fields use content analysis, including marketing, communication, education, politics, and public health. Researchers have used content analysis to study the following:

- themes in popular songs and religious symbols in hymns
- trends in the topics that newspapers cover
- the ideological tone of newspaper editorials
- sex-role stereotypes in textbooks or feature films
- how often people of different races appear in television commercials and programs
- answers to open-ended survey questions
- enemy propaganda during wartime.
- the covers of popular magazines
- personality characteristics evident from suicide notes
- social class and identity themes in advertising messages
- gender differences in conversations

You use objective, systematic counting and recording procedures to carry out an analysis of the content in text. This produces quantitative data on the symbolic content that is present in the text. There are also qualitative versions of content analysis that emphasize interpreting symbolic meaning. Here, we focus on quantitative data about a text's content.

Content analysis is nonreactive because words, images, or symbols of text are produced without the creator or author of a communication message being aware that someone someday might study it. Content analysis allows you to uncover aspects of the content (i.e., messages, meanings, bias, etc.) in the text of a communication medium (i.e., a book, article, movie, song, etc.) differently from what you learn in ordinary reading, listening, or watching. With content analysis, you can compare content across many texts and analyze it with quantitative techniques (e.g., charts and

content analysis a nonreactive technique for studying communication messages.

text in content analysis, it means anything written, visual, or spoken in a communication medium.

tables). In addition, you can reveal difficult-to-see aspects of the text's content. For example, you might watch television commercials and feel that nonwhites rarely appear in commercials for expensive consumer goods (e.g., luxury cars, furs, jewelry, perfume, etc.). By using content analysis, you can document—in objective, quantitative terms—whether your vague feelings from nonsystematic observation are true.

You use coding to create repeatable, precise data about the text of a communication medium. With coding, you turn aspects of text content into quantitative variables. After you have gathered the quantitative data, you use statistics to examine variables in the same way that an experimenter or survey researcher would.

Content analysis is useful for three research issues:

- *Large volumes of text.* With careful sampling and measurement, you can analyze what appears in all television programs of a certain type on five major channels over a five-year period.
- *Topics studied "at a distance".* You can study the writings of someone who has died, or you can study broadcasts in a distant hostile foreign country.
- *Content difficult to see with casual observation.* You can note themes or bias about which a text's creator and people who read it are not aware (e.g., preschool picture book authors who portray children in traditionally stereotyped gender roles).

How to Measure and Code in Content Analysis

In content analysis, you convert a large mass of text information (words or images) into precise, quantitative data. To do this, you carefully design and document procedures in a manner that makes replication possible. It should be possible for someone else to repeat what you have done. To operationalize variables in content analysis, you create a **coding system**. By using a coding system, you observe in a systematic, careful way by consistently following written rules. The rules explain how to categorize and classify observations. As with other kinds of measurement, you want mutually exclusive and exhaustive categories. The written rules make replication possible and improve reliability.

You must tailor the coding system to the specific type of text or communication medium you are examining, such as television dramas, novels, photos in magazine advertisements, and so forth. You must also tailor it to your unit of analysis (you learned about units of analysis in Chapter 2). The unit of analysis varies widely in content analysis. It can be a television commercial, a phrase, a book's plot, a newspaper article, a film character, and so forth. For this reason, decide on the unit of analysis before you develop measures or record any of the data. If your unit is a full-length film, a television commercial, or a newspaper editorial, you adjust the coding to that type of unit (see Example Study Box 2: Film and Gender Roles).

What Do You Measure? You begin with a preliminary coding system that has rules you can use to conduct a pilot study on a small amount of data. You use pilot study results to refine the coding rules for the full study. As you develop rules, you can measure five characteristics of variables in the text content you will code:

- *Direction.* Note the positive/support or negative/oppose direction of messages in the text relative to an issue, trait, or question. For example, you devise a list of ways an elderly television character can act. Some are positive (e.g., friendly, wise, considerate) and some are negative (e.g., nasty, dull, selfish).
- *Frequency.* Count whether something occurs in the text and how often. For example, how many elderly people appear on a television program within a week? What percentage of all characters are they, or in what percentage of programs do they appear? How frequently do they have speaking parts?
- *Intensity.* Measure the strength of a variable. For example, the characteristic of forgetfulness can be minor (e.g., not remembering to take your keys when leaving home) or major (e.g., not remembering your name, not recognizing your children).

coding system in content analysis, a set of instructions or rules stating how text was systematically measured and converted into variables.

Example Study Box 2 Film and Gender Roles

Lauzen and Dozier (2005) studied gender stereotypes in the most popular U.S. films in 2002. They developed a coding system based on prior studies of prime-time television shows and film. They began with a list of the 100 most popular U.S. films of 2002 and employed three graduate students to work as coders. Their unit of analysis was the film. During an initial training period, Lauzen and Dozier created a coding system and variable definitions. Next, they had the coders practice by coding several films independently of one another. They compared results and discussed the practice coding. Two coders independently coded 10 percent of all the films. This allowed the researchers to calculate intercoder reliability measures (discussed later in this chapter). The intercoder measure for the gender of the major character in the film was 0.99, for occupation of the characters it was 0.91, and for the age of characters it was 0.88. This told the researchers that different coders were coding in a highly consistent way.

- *Space.* Measure the size, volume, and amount of time or physical space. One way to measure space in written text is to count words, sentences, paragraphs, or physical space on a page (e.g., square inches). For video or audio text, you can measure the duration of time. For example, a TV character may be present for a few seconds or continuously in every scene of a two-hour program.
- *Prominence.* Prominence is related to space—is it located in a time or physical location to get a lot of attention? A television show aired in "prime time" versus 3 A.M. has greater prominence. An article on the front page of a newspaper has greater prominence than one buried inside.

Coding, Validity, and Reliability. There are two major types of coding in content analysis, manifest and latent.

Manifest Coding. With **manifest coding**, you count the number of times a phrase or word appears in written text, or whether a specific action (e.g., a kiss, a slap) or object (e.g., a gun, a dog) is in a photograph or video scene. The coding system is a list of terms or actions for you to locate in text. For written text, you may be able to use a computer program to search for words or phrases. To do this, you must first develop a comprehensive list of relevant words or phrases, and then put the text into a form that computers can read. Manifest coding is highly reliable because a word, object, or action is either present or not. A weakness of manifest coding is that it cannot take into account the specific meaning, context, and connotations of the words, phrases, objects, or actions. A word, object, or action has multiple meanings, and this weakens the measurement validity of manifest coding.

For example, I read a book with a *red* cover that is a real *red* herring. Unfortunately, its publisher drowned in *red* ink because the editor could not deal with the *red* tape that occurs when a book is *red* hot. The book has a story about a *red* fire truck that stops at *red* lights only after the leaves turn *red*. There is also a group of *Reds* who carry *red* flags to the little *red* schoolhouse. They are opposed by *red*-blooded *red*necks who eat *red* meat and honor the *red*, white, and blue. The main character is a *red*-nosed matador who fights *red* foxes, not bulls, with his *red* cape. *Red*-lipped little *Red* Riding Hood is also in the book. She develops *red* eyes and becomes *red*-faced after eating many *red* peppers in the *red* light district. Her angry mother, a *red*head, gives her a *red* backside.

Latent Coding. In **latent coding**, you read an entire paragraph or book or view an entire film and then decide whether it contains certain themes (e.g., danger, erotic)

manifest coding content analysis coding in which you record information about the visible, surface content in a text.

latent coding coding in content analysis in which you look for the underlying, implicit meaning in the content of a text.

or a mood (e.g., threatening, romantic). Instead of lists of words or actions, a latent coding system has general rules that guide how you interpret text and determine whether themes or moods are present. Compared to manifest coding, latent coding tends to be less reliable because it relies on a coder's in-depth knowledge of language, subtle clues, and social meaning. Training, practice, and clear written rules can improve reliability, especially if several people do the coding. However, even with training and practice, it is difficult to identify themes, moods, and so forth consistently. On the other hand, latent coding can have greater measurement validity. This is because we communicate meaning in many indirect and implicit ways that depend on the context, not just on specific words or actions. Latent coding captures the direct and indirect meanings that may be embedded in a specific text context.

It is very time consuming, but the ideal is to use both manifest and latent coding. If they agree, you can have confidence in the results. If they disagree, you may want to reexamine the operational and theoretical definitions.

Intercoder Reliability. In most situations, you will code text from a very large number of units. You may code the content in dozens of books, hundreds of hours of television programming, or thousands of newspaper articles. In addition to coding personally, you may have assistants to help. You must instruct the assistants on the coding system and train them. The coder-assistants need to understand the variables, carefully follow the coding system, and ask you about ambiguities. As the coding progresses, you must document every decision about how to treat a new coding situation so you will be consistent and have a written record.

If you use assistants as coders, *always* check for consistency across them. To do this, ask several coders to code the same text independent of one another. If you have three assistants coding television commercials, have the three coders independently code the same 15 commercials. Check for consistency across the coders and determine whether they coded the 15 commercials the same. With **intercoder reliability**, you measure the degree of consistency with a statistical coefficient. *Always* report the coefficient along with the results.

There are several intercoder reliability measures. All range from 0 to 1. Perfect agreement among coders is 1.0. Most researchers treat a coefficient of 0.80 or higher as very good and 0.70 as acceptable. When the coding process stretches over a considerable time span (e.g., over three months), you should check coding reliability over time by having each coder independently code samples of text that were previously coded. For example, the assistants code six hours of television episodes in April and recode the same six hours in August without looking at their original decisions. A deviation in coding between the two times means retraining coders and recoding text.

Content Analysis with Visual Material. Using content analysis to study visual "text," such as photographs, paintings, statues, buildings, clothing, and videos and film, is more difficult than doing so for written text. Visual material communicates messages or emotional content indirectly through symbols and metaphors. Moreover, visual images often contain mixed messages and operate at multiple levels of meaning. Learning to "read" visual media takes substantial effort and skill. You need to be aware of multiple symbolic meanings and references.

To conduct a content analysis of visual text, you "read" the meaning(s) within visual text (i.e., you interpret signs or symbols and the meanings they convey). Reading visual text is not mechanical (i.e., image *X* always means *G*) but depends on cultural context. We attach cultural meanings to symbolic images (see Learning from History: Visual Text Is Cultural Bound).

Most people in one culture share a common meaning for its major cultural symbols. However, visual text is often multilayered with several meanings. Different people can read the same symbol differently. For example, one person "reads" graffiti as vandalism that defaces a building, another reads it as a work of art, and a third

intercoder reliability a measure of measurement consistency in content analysis when you have multiple coders.

Learning from History Visual Text Is Cultural Bound

Ingo Jezierski/Photodisc/
Getty Images Royalty Free

Many people associate the swastika with the Nazi government in Germany or extreme racist groups. This is because they first saw the image in history books, films, and news reports. However, the origin of the image goes back over 2000 years. The swastika is on religious buildings across Asia as a good luck symbol, and it is used in decorative art and clothing. People were using the symbol for over a thousand years before the Nazi movement adopted it. Many people use the image without any awareness of the Nazis. This shows how a symbol's meaning depends on when and where it appears. (See Quinn 1994.)

A second example is the smile. We treat a smile as a reflex indicating a positive feeling, and it is nearly a cultural universal. However, it is not always a friendly sign. Its meaning varies by how and when it appears. In some cultures, a smile can signal deceit, insincerity, or frivolity. Smiling depends on the social situation as well as the culture. Smiling at a funeral is appropriate in some cultures but highly disrespectful in others. A smile's meaning can also change over time. Perhaps you noticed that in very old photographs, the people never smiled. This was not because they were always unhappy but because smiling as a social convention when being photographed only developed later (in the 1920s in the United States). (Also see Rashotte 2002)

Bettmann/Corbis

reads it as a mark of a street gang's territory. To conduct a content analysis of images, you need to be aware of possible divergent readings of images or symbols.

Symbol use can be a source of conflict. Sociopolitical groups invent or construct new symbols and attach meanings to them. For example, the Nazis originally used a pink triangle in concentration camps to mark homosexuals who were condemned

Example Study Box 3 Magazine Covers and Cultural Messages

Chavez (2001) conducted a content analysis of the covers of major magazines that dealt with the issue of immigration into the United States. Looking at the covers of 10 magazines from the mid-1970s to the mid-1990s, he classified them into sending one of the following messages: affirmative, alarmist, or neutral and balanced. He also examined the mix of people (i.e., race, gender, age, and dress) in the photographs and whether major symbols, such as the Statute of Liberty or the U.S. flag, appeared. Chavez argued that magazine covers are a cultural site. They are a place where media create and communicate cultural meanings to the public. Visual magazine covers carry multiple levels of meaning. When people see a cover and apply their cultural knowledge, they construct specific meanings. Collectively, the covers convey a worldview and express messages about a nation and its people. For example, we usually see the icon of the Statute of Liberty as strong and full of compassion. Its usual message is, Welcome immigrants. However, when a magazine cover altered this icon to give it Asian facial features, its message shifted to become, Asian immigrants are distorting the U.S. national culture and altering the nation's racial make-up. When a magazine showed this icon holding a large stop sign, its message became, Go away immigrants—we do not want you. The symbolic messages sent by visual images can have a powerful emotional effect on people that is sometimes stronger than written text.

to extermination along with Jews, and other "undesirables." The pink triangle later came to mean gay pride. Competing sociopolitical groups often wrestle to control the meaning of symbols. Thus, some people want to assign a Christian religious meaning to the Christmas tree; others say it represents a celebration of tradition and family values without religious content; others see its origins as an anti-Christian pagan symbol; and still others see it as a profit-oriented commercial symbol. Because a symbol has complex, multilayered meanings, you must make qualitative judgments about how to code images.

How to Conduct Content Analysis Research

STEP 1. Formulate a research question. Start with a topic and research question. When your research question involves variables that are messages or symbols, content analysis may be appropriate. Conceptualize each variable. Let us say you want to study newspaper coverage of a political campaign. Your must refine the idea of "coverage"—do you mean the amount of coverage, prominence of the coverage, or direction of coverage? You must decide how to examine newspaper coverage. You could survey people about what they think of newspaper coverage or examine the newspapers directly using content analysis. Your research question will guide you to the variables to measure. You might have a research question such as, Does the newspaper give more coverage to one presidential candidate over the other as the date of the election gets closer? This suggests the variables of amount of coverage for each candidate and dates of coverage relative to the election.

STEP 2. Identify the text to analyze. Find the communication medium that best matches your research question. Your research question and decision about type of text are usually a single process—candidate coverage and the newspaper as a type of text (versus television, radio, or other media). You still must identify the specific text (such as which newspapers) and its scope (which dates).

STEP 3. Decide on units of analysis. This is a major early decision in content analysis. There are many possible units in content analysis—the page, the episode, the character, and so forth. The unit of analysis determines the amount of text to which you assign a code. For example, for a political campaign, you may code what each newspaper article reports (excluding editorials, letters to the editor, and advertising). In this case, the article is your unit of analysis. You still need to determine how to identify "campaign-related" articles from others (such as by scanning the headlines).

STEP 4. Draw a sample. Random sampling works well for most content analysis studies because you often have a huge collection of units to which you want to generalize (such as all newspaper articles) but only have time to code a small proportion of the units. The steps are as follows:

- Define the population (e.g., all articles, all sentences).
- Select the sampling element (your unit of analysis).
- Create a sampling frame.
- Use a random selection process.

STEP 5. Create a coding system. Once you decide on variables to measure, operationalize them by creating a coding system. To create a coding system, carefully conceptualize each variable and decide whether you will use a manifest or latent coding method or both. For each variable, you decide what it is you wish to measure (a variable's direction, frequency, intensity, space or prominence, or all of them).

STEP 6. Construct and refine coding categories. The coding category is a critical aspect of the coding system. It determines the number and types of distinctions you make within a variable and how you distinguish among them. Let us say you are measuring the variable "violence." You must decide, Do you want high, medium, and low levels of intensity, or are there more levels? How do you distinguish a low

Making It Practical Sampling in Content Analysis

Suppose your research question is, How do U.S. weekly newsmagazines portray women and minorities? Your unit of analysis is the article. Your population is all articles published in *Time, Newsweek,* and *U.S. News and World Report* between 1997 and 2007. You will need to define precisely the unit of analysis, the article. Do film reviews count as articles? Does a letter to the editor count? Does an article have a minimum size (two sentences)? Will you count a multipart article as one or two articles?

Next, you examine issues of the three magazines. You need to find out how many articles are in the average issue of the magazine. You might look at two issues of each magazine in the first (1997), middle (2002) and last year (2007). This gives you (3 magazines × 2 issues × 3 time periods = 18) 18 issues to look at and count articles. If each issue contains 45 articles and the magazines publish an issue each week or 52 weeks per year within 10 years, your population of articles has (3 magazines × 45 articles × 52 issues × 10 years = 70,200) 70,200 articles. Your sampling frame is a list of all the articles.

Next, decide on the sample size and design. After looking at your budget and time, you may decide to sample 1404 articles. Your sampling ratio is 2 percent (70,200 × 0.02 = 1404). You must choose a sampling design. Avoid

systematic sampling because magazine issues are published cyclically according to the calendar (e.g., an interval of every 52nd issue results in the same week each year). Because issues from each magazine are important, you probably want to use stratified sampling. You stratify by magazine, sampling 1404/3 = 468 articles from each magazine. If you want to ensure that articles represent each of the 10 years, you can also stratify by year. With rounding, this results in (468/10 = 46.8) 47 articles per magazine per year. To simplify matters, you may use cluster sampling, in which the issue of a magazine in a year is the cluster. Since each magazine has 52 issues in a year, you may wish to randomly sample 8 issues of each magazine for each year. You then only have to count all articles in those 8 issues for a year and then draw a random sample of 47. For example, in 2002 you use a random sampling computer program to get 8 numbers from 1 to 52. These are your sample of 8 issues of *Time* magazine from the 52 that were published. Next, you count the total number of articles in all 8 issues and number them. If there are 380 total articles, you create a list of articles from 1 to 380. Now use a random number table or random sampling computer program to select your sample of 47 articles from those 380. You are now ready to apply your coding system to these 47 articles.

Making It Practical Coding Systems and Categories

Suppose your research question is, Has the appearance of people of different races-ethnicities or genders shown in significant leadership roles in U.S. newsmagazines changed over a 10-year period? You must define "significant leadership role" in operational terms. This means creating written rules for classifying people named in an article. For example, if an article discusses the achievements of someone who is now dead, does the dead person have a significant role? What is a significant role—a local Girl Scout leader or a corporate president? You need to record information on the race-ethnicity and gender of people in significant leadership roles. What do you do if the race and sex are not evident in the text or accompanying photographs? How do you decide on the person's race and sex? Are you interested in both positive and negative leadership roles? You can measure this using either latent or manifest coding. With manifest coding, you must create a list of adjectives and phrases. If a sampled article re-

ferred to someone using one of the adjectives, then the direction is decided. For example, the terms *brilliant* and *top performer* are positive, whereas *average* and *uninspired* are negative. For latent coding, you must create rules to guide coding judgments. For example, you classify stories about a diplomat resolving a difficult world crisis, a business executive unable to make a firm profitable, or a lawyer winning a case into positive or negative terms.

When planning a research project, you should calculate the time required to complete the research. For example, during a pilot test, you may learn that it takes an average of 15 minutes to read and code one article. This does not include sampling or locating magazine articles. If you have approximately 1400 articles, it means 350 hours of coding—not counting time to verify the accuracy of coding. Because 350 hours is about nine weeks of nonstop work at 40 hours a week, you may consider hiring assistants as coders or making other adjustments.

from a medium level? Do you want to consider different types of violence (e.g., physical, emotional, sexual) and look at the intensity of each?

STEP 7. Code the data onto recording sheets. Once you decide the variables, type of coding, and coding categories, you should construct a sheet (paper- or computer-based) on which to record information. Typically, you will have one recording sheet (piece of paper or word processing page) for each unit or case. If you planned to code 1000 television commercials and the commercial was your unit of analysis, you would have 1000 sheets, one for each. Put general information about the study (title, who does the coding) on each sheet. Also have space for basic information about the unit (the date and time) and space for each variable and its categories. You then code the text by filling in the information on each unit. Place them into spaces on the recording sheet.

STEP 8. Data analysis. Content data analysis is like other quantitative data analysis. You must transfer the data from the recording sheets into a machine readable form that computer programs use. Typically, this is a grid or spreadsheet. Each row

---

Making It Practical Recording Data in Content Analysis

EXAMPLE OF BLANK RECORDING SHEET

Professor Neuman, Sociology-Anthropology Department   Coder:_____

Minority/Majority Group Representation in Newsmagazines Project

ARTICLE #_____   MAGAZINE:_____   DATE:_____   SIZE:_____ col. in.

Total number of people named_____   Number of photos_____

No. people with significant roles:_____   Article topic:_____

Person_____:	Race:_____	Gender:_____	Leader?:_____	Field?_____	Rating:_____
Person_____:	Race:_____	Gender:_____	Leader?:_____	Field?_____	Rating:_____
Person_____:	Race:_____	Gender:_____	Leader?:_____	Field?_____	Rating:_____
Person_____:	Race:_____	Gender:_____	Leader?:_____	Field?_____	Rating:_____
Person_____:	Race:_____	Gender:_____	Leader?:_____	Field?_____	Rating:_____
Person_____:	Race:_____	Gender:_____	Leader?:_____	Field?_____	Rating:_____
Person_____:	Race:_____	Gender:_____	Leader?:_____	Field?_____	Rating:_____
Person_____:	Race:_____	Gender:_____	Leader?:_____	Field?_____	Rating:_____

EXAMPLE OF COMPLETED RECORDING SHEET FOR ONE ARTICLE

Professor Neuman, Sociology Department   Coder: <u>Susan J.</u>

Minority/Majority Group Representation in Newsmagazines Project

ARTICLE # <u>0454</u>   MAGAZINE: <u>Time</u>   DATE: <u>March 1–7, 1998</u>   SIZE: <u>14</u> col. in.

Total number of people named <u>5</u>   Number of photos <u>0</u>

No. people with significant roles: <u>4</u>   Article topic: <u>Foreign Affairs</u>

Person <u>1</u>:	Race: <u>White</u>	Gender: <u>M</u>	Leader?: <u>Y</u>	Field? <u>Banking</u>	Rating: <u>5</u>
Person <u>2</u>:	Race: <u>White</u>	Gender: <u>M</u>	Leader?: <u>N</u>	Field? <u>Government</u>	Rating: <u>NA</u>
Person <u>3</u>:	Race: <u>Black</u>	Gender: <u>F</u>	Leader?: <u>Y</u>	Field? <u>Civil Rights</u>	Rating: <u>2</u>
Person <u>4</u>:	Race: <u>White</u>	Gender: <u>F</u>	Leader?: <u>Y</u>	Field? <u>Government</u>	Rating: <u>0</u>
Person _____:	Race: _____	Gender: _____	Leader?: _____	Field? _____	Rating: ___
Person _____:	Race: _____	Gender: _____	Leader?: _____	Field? _____	Rating: ___
Person _____:	Race: _____	Gender: _____	Leader?: _____	Field? _____	Rating: ___
Person _____:	Race: _____	Gender: _____	Leader?: _____	Field? _____	Rating: ___

is a unit or case, and the columns represent variables. You can then use standard analysis techniques for quantitative data.

Limitations of Content Analysis

Generalizations in content analysis are limited to the cultural communication itself. Unfortunately, by itself content analysis cannot do any of the following:

- Determine the truthfulness of an assertion
- Evaluate the aesthetic qualities of literature or visual text
- Interpret the content's significance
- Reveal the intentions of the organizations or people who created the text
- Determine the influence of a message on its receivers

Content analysis can only describe what is in the text and reveal patterns in it. With content analysis, you can say that a certain type of message appears regularly on television, but you cannot say how that message influences the thinking of viewers who receive it. You can build on the content analysis using other research to understand fully the process of how messages influence people's beliefs and behaviors. If you wish to talk about the appearance of a message and its influence, combine content analysis with other types of studies, such as experiments. You can then see both how widespread a message appears and how it affects message receivers. For example, your content analysis shows that children's books contain sex stereotypes. Alone, that does not mean that such stereotypes influence children's beliefs or behaviors. You next conduct a separate research study on how what children read influences their beliefs and behaviors. Putting the two types of research together can give you a complete picture.

MINING EXISTING STATISTICAL SOURCES TO ANSWER NEW QUESTIONS

Thus far, we have discussed research techniques, such as the survey, experiment, or content analysis, in which you create a design and collect data. You are lucky to have mountains of information about the social world already collected and available. Some of it is in statistical documents (books, reports, etc.). Other information is in computerized records. In either case, you can search through collections of information with variables and a research question in mind and then statistically analyze the information to address the research question.

Existing statistics research involves analyzing previously collected public data to answer new research questions. It differs from most other research techniques in that you must learn what data are available before you develop a research question and hypothesis. Recall that in other quantitative research, the process was to (1) begin with ideas or concepts, (2) conceptualize them into variables with definitions, (3) operationalize variables into specific measures, (4) gather data, and (5) analyze the data. For the other research techniques, you start with a research question or hypothesis. Now you must start by learning what is available. The process goes as follows:

1. Search and scan existing statistical information or data.
2. Conceptualize the data you found into variables.
3. Identify variables that have the same unit of analysis and verify the accuracy of the data.
4. Organize hypotheses with independent and dependent variables from the variables you found.
5. Test the hypotheses using statistical data analysis.

An experiment is best for topics in which you can control a situation and manipulate an independent variable. Survey research is best for topics in which you can ask questions and learn about reported attitudes or behavior. Content analysis is best for topics in which you look at the content in a communication medium. The best topics for existing statistics research are ones on which large bureaucratic organizations routinely collect and report quantitative information; many measures in such reports are **social indicators**

During the 1960s, many social scientists were dissatisfied with the information available to decision makers. Information was limited to a few economic measures. The dissatisfied scientists spawned the "social indicators movement" and developed many new measures, or indicators, of social conditions or well-being. Their goal was to combine data on social conditions with economic indicators (e.g., gross national product, income) to create a more complete picture of social-economic life that could better inform policy-making officials. Social indicators measure negative aspects of social life (the death rate of infants during the first year of life, crime rate, divorce rate, alcoholism) or positive aspects (job satisfaction, volunteering activity, park land, homeownership, housing with indoor plumbing) (see Table 8.1). Organizations also regularly report measures of the physical environment (air pollution) and psychological conditions (reports of stress, mental health visits).

Hundreds of public or private organizations have ongoing data collection and reporting activities for internal policy decisions or as a public service. They rarely collect data to address one specific research question. Existing statistics research is appropriate when you have an issue or question about the various social, economic, and political conditions on which organizations gather and report information. Often organizations collect the data over time or across wide geographic areas. The information is often free or nearly free. For example, free, public existing statistics allow you to determine whether unemployment and crime rates are associated in 150 cities across a 20-year period.

Some of the initial data collection may have been reactive. For example, a measure of the unemployment rate comes from a survey that asks people whether they are looking for work. Other data collection is without reactive effects, such as recording how many people voted in an election or the number of students who received high school diplomas. Organizations collect the data as part of their routine bureaucratic planning and monitoring activities, not for research. Your use of the data to answer research questions is nonreactive. People on whom the information is gathered are unaware of its research use.

You will face three challenges in doing existing statistics research: searching and locating data sources, verifying data quality, and being creative in thinking about how to turn the data into variables that can answer research questions.

social indicator any measure of social conditions or well-being that can be used in policy decisions.

■ **Table 8.1**   Examples of Publicly Available Social Indicators

---

Turnout to vote in elections

Number of hours that people volunteer per year

Percent of the population that is literate

Percent of the population that lacks health care coverage

Number of child abuse cases

Average length of time people commute to work

Number and size of parks and recreation areas

Number of crimes reported to police

Example Study Box 4 **Pollution, Race, and Housing Choice in Detroit**

Downey (2005) conducted an existing statistics study on the topic of black-white racial inequality and living near a toxic pollution site in Detroit. He wanted to test the hypothesis that blacks more than whites lived near toxic waste sites. He used public census data that have years of information on population and housing (including home ownership and race of owner) and on manufacturing facilities (location of factories, where most employees lived). Downey identified the location of polluting factories using the Environmental Protection Agency's (EPA's) inventory of toxic chemicals. His unit of analysis was the census tract (a geographic unit created by the U.S. Census Bureau). So he had information about all his variables from each census tract and combined it with other public information. Downey tested three models of environmental inequality:

1. *Racist site location policy.* Companies and officials placed the toxic sites near existing black residential areas.
2. *Economic inequality.* Low-income people who are disproportionately black moved into areas near toxic sites because that is where the low-cost housing was located.
3. *Residential segregation.* Whites moved into desirable areas and tried to keep out nonwhites. The nonwhites were forced to live in remaining open areas that are near toxic sites.

Downey's data showed greatest support for the residential segregation model. However, his findings differed from his original hypothesis. He discovered that although whites tried to maintain all-white neighborhoods, they also wanted to live close to where they worked. Many whites worked at factories that produced toxic pollution and stored it on site. Paradoxically, this meant whites more than blacks lived close to the toxic pollution sites. The whites had kept blacks from moving into their neighborhoods; neighborhoods that were close to polluting factories.

Locating Data

Governments, international agencies, private companies, and nonprofit organizations gather an enormous volume and variety of quantitative information. The quantity is overwhelming and specifics are difficult to pinpoint. If you plan to conduct an existing statistics research study, discuss your interests with an information professional—in this case, a reference librarian, who can point you in the direction of possible sources. Many existing sources are "free"—that is, publicly available at libraries or over the Internet. Nonetheless, it can take a huge amount of time and effort to search for specific information. There is a paradox: You do not know what information you will find until you look for it, and you do not know what to look for until you begin to search. Professional researchers can spend many hours searching in libraries, searching on the Internet, or contacting specific organizations with requests for information. Once you locate information, you need to record it. Some information is already available in a computer readable format. For example, instead of recording voting data from published books, it is already in a format that computers read (e.g., spreadsheets, statistics programs).

There are so many diverse sources that it is a full-time job for professionals to keep track of it. The single most valuable source of statistical information about the United States is the *Statistical Abstract of the United States* (see Figure 8.1). The U.S. government has published it annually since 1878. It is available in all libraries and on the Internet. The *Statistical Abstract* contains 1400 charts, tables, and statistical

Percentage of Adults Engaging in Leisure-Time, Transportation-Related and Household-Related Physical Activity: 2003

[In percent. Covers persons 18 years old and over. Based on responses to questions about physical activity in prior month from the Behavioral Risk Factor Surveillance System. Estimates are age-adjusted to the year 2000 standard population. Based on a survey sample of approximately 257,000 persons in 50 states and the District of Columbia in 2003]

Characteristic	Persons who meet recommended activity[1]	Persons not meeting recommended activity[2]	Persons who are physically inactive[3]	Characteristic	Persons who meet recommended activity[1]	Persons not meeting recommended activity[2]	Persons who are physically inactive[3]
Total	**46.0**	**54.0**	**24.3**	45 to 64 years old	42.6	57.4	26.7
Male	48.2	51.8	22.0	65 to 74 years old	37.1	62.9	31.2
Female	44.0	56.0	26.3	75 years old and over	27.6	72.4	42.0
White, non-Hispanic	49.0	51.0	20.9	School years completed:			
Black, non-Hispanic	36.3	63.7	32.7	Less than 12 years	33.8	66.2	45.7
Hispanic	37.5	62.5	36.0	12 years	43.1	56.9	30.5
Other	43.5	56.5	25.2	Some college (13 to 15 years)	47.5	52.5	21.0
Males:				College (16 or more years)	51.9	48.1	13.1
18 to 29 years old	57.8	42.2	17.1	Household income:			
30 to 44 years old	48.7	51.3	20.7	Less than $10,000	34.7	65.3	42.2
45 to 64 years old	43.2	56.8	24.4	$10,000 to $19,999	37.0	63.0	38.9
65 to 74 years old	45.7	54.3	24.9	$20,000 to $34,999	43.6	56.4	29.4
75 years old and over	36.7	63.3	31.0	$35,000 to $49,999	47.3	52.7	21.9
Females:				$50,000 and over	53.6	46.4	13.6
18 to 29 years old	50.1	49.9	21.9				
30 to 44 years old	47.7	52.3	23.4				

[1]Recommended activity is physical activity at least 5 times/week × 30 minutes/time or vigorous physical activity for 20 minutes at a time at least 3 times/week. [2]Persons whose reported physical activity does not meet recommended level or report no leisure-time, transportation-related, or household-related physical activity. [3]Persons with no reported physical activity.

Source: U.S. National Center for Chronic Disease Prevention and Health Promotion, "Nutrition and Physical Activity"; and unpublished data: <http://www.cdc.gov/needphp/dnpa>.

Households and Persons Having Problems With Access to Food: 2000 to 2003

[**106,043 represents 106,043,000**. Food secure means that a household had access at all times to enough food for an active healthy life for all household members, with no need for recourse to socially unacceptable food sources or extraordinary coping behaviors to meet their basic food needs. Food insecure households had limited or uncertain ability to acquire acceptable foods in socially acceptable ways. Food insecure households with hunger were those with one or more household members who were hungry at least sometime during the period due to inadequate resources for food. The omission of homeless persons may be a cause of underreporting. The severity of food insecurity and hunger in households is measured through a series of questions about experiences and behaviors known to characterize households that are having difficulty meeting basic food needs. These experiences and behaviors generally occur in an ordered sequence as the severity of food insecurity increases. As resources become more constrained, adults in typical households first worry about having enough food, then they stretch household resources and juggle other necessities, then decrease the quality and variety of household members' diets, then decrease the frequency and quantity of adults' food intake, and finally decrease the frequency and quantity of children's food intake. All questions refer to the previous 12 months and include a qualifying phrase reminding respondents to report only those occurrences that resulted from inadequate financial resources. Restrictions to food intake due to dieting or busy schedules are excluded. Data are from the Food Security Supplement to the Current Population Survey (CPS); for details about the CPS, see text, Section 1 and Appendix III]

Household food security level	Number (1,000)				Percent distribution			
	2000	2001	2002	2003	2000	2001	2002	2003
Households, total	**106,043**	**107,824**	**108,601**	**112,214**	**100.0**	**100.0**	**100.0**	**100.0**
Food secure	94,942	96,303	96,543	99,631	89.5	89.3	88.9	88.8
Food insecure	11,101	11,521	12,058	12,583	10.5	10.7	11.1	11.2
Without hunger	7,785	8,010	8,259	8,663	7.3	7.4	7.6	7.7
With hunger	3,315	3,511	3,799	3,920	3.1	3.3	3.5	3.5
With hunger among children[1]	255	211	265	207	0.7	0.6	0.7	0.5
Adult members	**201,922**	**204,340**	**206,493**	**213,441**	**100.0**	**100.0**	**100.0**	**100.0**
In food secure households	181,586	183,398	184,718	190,451	89.9	89.8	89.5	89.2
In food insecure households	20,336	20,942	21,775	22,990	10.1	10.2	10.5	10.8
Without hunger	14,763	14,879	15,486	16,358	7.3	7.3	7.5	7.7
With hunger[2]	5,573	6,063	6,289	6,632	2.8	3.0	3.0	3.1
Child members	**71,763**	**72,321**	**72,542**	**72,969**	**100.0**	**100.0**	**100.0**	**100.0**
In food secure households	58,868	59,620	59,415	59,704	82.0	82.4	81.9	81.8
In food insecure households	12,895	12,701	13,127	13,265	18.0	17.6	18.1	18.2
Without hunger	12,334	12,234	12,560	12,845	17.2	16.9	17.3	17.6
With hunger among children[1]	562	467	567	420	0.8	0.6	0.8	0.6

[1]One or more children in these households was hungry at some time during the year because of the household's food insecurity. Percent distribution of households with hunger among children excludes households with no child from the denominator. [2]One or more adults in these households was hungry at some time during the year because of the household's food insecurity.

Source: U.S. Department of Agriculture, Economic Research Service, *Household Food Security in the United States, 2003, Food Assistance and Nutrition Research Report No. 42*; October 2004; <http://www.org.usda.gov/briefing/foodsecurity/>.

lists. It is a selected compilation of thousands of more detailed reports from hundreds of government and private agencies. At times, you will want to examine the more specific government documents. It is hard to grasp all that the *Statistical Abstract* contains until you skim through it. Most information is by state or county as the unit of analysis, and often it goes back many years.

Most national and state governments publish similar statistical yearbooks. If the country is your unit of analysis, the United Nations and international agencies (the World Bank, Organization for Economic Cooperation and Development) have their own statistical publications with information on countries (e.g., literacy rates, percentage of the labor force in agriculture, birth rates).

Verifying Data Quality

Despite its low cost and ease of access, six issues can limit your research when using existing statistics:

- Missing data
- Reliability
- Validity
- Topic knowledge
- Fallacy of misplaced concreteness
- Ecological fallacy

1. *Missing data.* Missing data can be a major limitation with existing statistics and documents. Sometimes the data were collected but have been lost. More frequently, no one collected the data. Officials in government agencies decide whether to collect official information, and their political beliefs and values can influence what data are gathered. Government agencies can start or stop collecting information for political, budgetary, or other reasons. For example, the U.S. federal government stopped the collection of several types of information that social researchers had found highly valuable. The official reason was cost cutting, but later some officials revealed it had to do with promoting a political agenda. If the government stopped gathering or publishing information that could document certain inequalities or health risks, critics would find it difficult to make claims of discrimination or unsafe conditions. Missing information is especially a problem when you want to cover a long time period.

A related type of missing data is data collected with less refined categories than you want. Perhaps you are interested in racial-ethnic groups. You want to compare some aspect of whites, blacks, Asians, and Latinos in the United States, but the official data only offer you white and nonwhite as variable categories. The data are not available at the level of refinement needed for your research question.

2. *Reliability.* Reliability problems plague many existing statistics sources. Reliability problems develop when official definitions or methods of collecting information vary over time. For example, the official definitions of *work injury*, *disability*, *unemployment*, and the like have changed several times. Even if you learn of the changes, consistent measurement may be impossible. For example, during the early 1980s, the U.S. government changed how it calculated the U.S. unemployment rate. Until then, government agencies calculated it as the number of unemployed people divided by the total number of people in the civilian work force. The new method divided the number of unemployed by the civilian work force, plus all people in the military. A similar complication happens when police departments computerize their records. The number of crimes reported increases not because actual crime increases but due to improved recordkeeping.

3. *Validity.* You can encounter three kinds of measurement validity problems in existing statistics research. First, the agency or organization that collects informa-

tion uses a different conceptual definition from yours. For example, you define a *work injury* as including minor cuts, bruises, and sprains that occur while working on a job. The official definition includes major injuries that required a visit to a physician or hospital. Many injuries you define as work injuries would not be in the official statistics. Another example is that you define a person as being *unemployed* if he or she would work if a job for which he or she is trained is available, if the person is forced to work part time but wants to work full-time, or if after a year of trying the person has given up looking for work. The official definition includes only people now actively seeking any full- or part-time work at any job. Excluded are people who stopped looking, who work only 15 hours a week because they cannot find more hours, or who are not looking because there are no jobs for someone with their special training (e.g., a dentist can only find a job driving a taxi). To add complications, different countries or states often use different official definitions. (See Making It Practical: Official Unemployment Rates versus the Nonemployed.)

A second validity problem arises when official statistics are a proxy for a variable of interest. The official statistics do not really measure what you want, but they are all you have so you use them. Let us say you want to know how many people were robbed in a city last year. You use police statistics on robbery arrests as a proxy. However, many robberies go unreported. If half of robberies are not reported to the police, by using official statistics you are not really measuring the number of people robbed. You have only part of what happened, the number of robberies known to police. Such reporting bias can affect hypotheses testing. Let us say young people are less likely to report a robbery to police than old people. Using official data, you find that most robbery victims are older. In fact, this may not be true but it is due to the reporting bias in official statistics.

Making It Practical **Official Unemployment Rates versus the Nonemployed**

In most countries, the official unemployment rate measures the unemployed as a percent of all working people. It excludes two related categories of not-fully-employed people: involuntary part-time workers and discouraged workers. In some countries (e.g., Sweden and the United States), the unemployment rate would double if these people were included. Most official statistics exclude other nonworking people such as transitional self-employed and the underemployed. Different definitions treat the situation of unemployment differently. An economic policy or labor market perspective sees the unemployment rate as measuring people ready to enter the labor market immediately. It sees nonworking people as a supply of labor that is available to employers, or as an input to the economy. A social policy or human resource perspective sees the unemployment rate as measuring people not currently working to their full potential. The rate tells us who cannot fully utilize their talents, skills, or time. Nonworking people viewed individuals who are unable to be productive, contributing members of society. Thus, a nation's official statistics will include a definition that reflects a particular value perspective or theory of what unemployment means for society. Consider the following list of all nonemployed people:

Categories of Nonemployed/Fully Utilized
- *Officially unemployed.* People who meet three conditions: (1) lack a paid job outside the home, (2) are actively engaged in looking for work, and (3) can begin work immediately if it is offered.
- *Involuntary employed.* People with a job, but who work irregularly or many fewer hours than they are able or willing to, or who are working part time but desire and are able to work full time.
- *Discouraged workers.* People able to work and who had actively sought work for some time, but being unable to find work have stopped looking.
- *Other nonworking.* People not working because they are retired, on vacation, temporarily laid off, semidisabled, homemakers, full-time students, or in the process of moving.
- *Transitional workers.* Self-employed people who are not working full time because they are just starting a business or are going through bankruptcy of a failed business.
- *Underemployed people.* Persons with a temporary full-time job for which they are seriously overqualified. They seek a permanent job in which they can fully apply their skills and experience.

Source: Adapted from *The Economist,* July 22, 1995, p. 74.

A third validity problem arises because you must depend on official agencies that collected the information. Information collecting may have systematic errors (e.g., census people who avoid poor neighborhoods and make up information, or people who put a false age on a driver's license). Or people in an agency may make errors in organizing and reporting the information (e.g., a police department that is sloppy about filing crime reports and loses some). Some errors occur in publishing information (e.g., a typographical error in a table).

An example of such errors in official statistics is illustrated by data on the number of people permanently laid off from their jobs. Official U.S. Bureau of Labor Statistics data on permanent job losses come from a survey of 50,000 randomly selected people. The agency counted percent saying they were laid off based on the number of questionnaires sent out and failed to adjust the data for people who did not respond. Here is an example of what happened. The agency sent 50,000 people questionnaires. In 1993, 8000 returned the questionnaire reporting that they had been laid off. This is 16 percent of the total and is reported as the laid-off rate. In 1996, 4500 returned the questionnaire saying that they had been laid off of work. This is 9 percent of the total. The agency reports a 7 percent decline in laid-off people between 1993 and 1996. However, in 1993, 40,000 people returned their questionnaires. This makes the true rate 20 percent (8000/40,000). In 1996, only 22,500 people returned the questionnaire. This is also 20 percent (4500/22,500). Instead of a 7 percent decline in laid-off people between 1993 and 1996, as officially reported, there was no change. Only a university researcher's careful detective work uncovered the error (see Stevenson 1996).

4. *Topic knowledge.* Because existing statistical data are easily accessible, you may be able to get a lot of data on an issue that you know little about. This can lead to erroneous assumptions or false interpretations of results. Before using any data, you should become informed about the topic. For example, perhaps you are interested in the percent of the U.S. population covered by some form of health insurance. The *Statistical Abstract of the United States* (2006, Table 142) shows that this was 15.6 percent in 2003. However, it is easy to make errors in interpreting results because there are many forms of health insurance coverage. Some are government provided, some are purchased privately, and some are employer provided; some only cover the bare basics and only after a person has paid a great amount personally, whereas others cover all health care visits plus medicine at no cost to a person; some are open and available to anyone, whereas others have very restrictive entry requirements. You may have a statistic, but do you know what it really means? This issue is far greater when using international statistics because the definitions and situations in different countries can vary widely.

5. *Fallacy of misplaced concreteness.* The **fallacy of misplaced concreteness** occurs when you quote statistics in excessive detail to give an impression of scientific rigor and precision. For example, an existing statistics report says that Australia has a population of 19,179,083. It is better to say that it is about 19.2 million, because the exact number is not that precise. The counting of people could easily be higher or lower by a few thousand people. If you calculated the percentage of divorced people in a town as 15.655951, only report it to one decimal place, or 15.7 percent.

6. *Ecological fallacy.* The **ecological fallacy** happens when your research question is about a lower-small unit of analysis (such as individual behavior) but you only have data on a higher-larger unit of analysis (an entire state). Published data are often available on a higher or larger unit of analysis. If you are interested in variables on a much lower level than your data, you may be seriously misled. For example, data may be available on the state level (such as unemployment rate by state), but you are interested in individuals (characteristics of individuals who become unemployed). From existing statistics, you find that states with high unemployed rates also have a high percentage of cigarette smokers. It is an ecological

fallacy of misplaced concreteness when statistical information is reported in a way that gives a false impression of its precision.

ecological fallacy mistaken interpretations that occur when you use data for a higher or bigger unit of analysis to examine a relationship among units at a lower or small unit of analysis.

Tips for the Wise Consumer   Using Data from Existing Statistical Sources

When you use data from existing statistical documents, do the following:

1. Be certain that the definition and measure of a variable truly fit the variable of interest to you.
2. Watch out for missing data or variable categories that combine distinctions of interest to you.

3. Be aware of the units of analysis used in measures and avoid the ecological fallacy.
4. Know about a topic area that applies to the data you are using.
5. Read statistical tables very carefully, including the details in footnotes and other explanations, so you know exactly what the table offers.

fallacy to say that unemployed people are more likely to smoke. Data for the state as a unit of analysis do not show which individuals smoke. Simply because more smokers are in a state that also has a high unemployment rate does not make the unemployed people more likely to smoke than employed people. If you want to know whether unemployed individuals are likely to smoke, you need data for which the individual is the unit of analysis. Official statistics may not have the data to match your research question, so you must change your question or switch to a different research technique, such as the social survey. You can ask individuals, Do you smoke? What is your employment status? Then see whether the two variables are associated among those individuals.

Creative Thinking About Variables of Interest

When you use existing statistical data, someone else already collected data that represent conceptual variables. At times, the data does not match the exact variable of most interest to you. When using existing data sources, you frequently must be creative to identify a surrogate or proxy for your conceptual variable. To do this, you first search through existing statistical sources looking for data measures that most closely match your concept. Perhaps you are interested in measuring "upper class neighborhood" but no existing data source has such a measure. You nonetheless find data on various social characteristics by city block. If you are careful and creative, you can build a close substitute measure of "upper class neighborhood." Let us say you believe that upper class people tend to own their own house that has a high value (over one million dollars), completed a college degree or more schooling, send their children to expensive private schools, and belong to exclusive country clubs. You find data by city block on percent of owner-occupied houses of a high value and percent of residents with a college degree or more schooling. You also obtain address lists of student at expensive private schools and for members of exclusive private clubs, then match the addresses to city block. You find a dozen city blocks in which most houses are owner-occupied and worth over 1 million dollars, almost all residents have at least a college degree, and that contain addresses of at least ten children attending expensive private schools and at least ten members of an exclusive private club. By merging the existing statistics data measures, you can create your own indicator of an "upper class neighborhood."

Standardization of Data

You have heard of crime rates (e.g., 11 murders per 10,000), birth rates (e.g., 5 births per 1000 women), or the unemployment rate (e.g., 4 percent). Many measures are expressed as rates or percentages. Percentage is a kind of rate, a rate per 100. The rates standardize the value of a variable to allow for valid comparisons. A lot of existing statistics information is standardized. At times, you must standardize it before you can use the information. Without standardization, it is difficult or impossible to compare and very easy to misinterpret the information.

Let us say you are interested in citizen participation in elections in various states. The *Statistical Abstract of the United States* shows that 12,421,000 people in California and 741,000 people in Maine voted in the 2004 presidential election. Does the bigger number mean Californians are more politically active than people in Maine? You might realize that California has more people (population was 35.8 million in 2004) than Maine (1.3 million people in 2004), so California should have more voters. To compare the voting rate or percentage of voters in the two states, you must first standardize the data.

Standardization involves selecting a base and dividing a raw measure by it. The base is simply a number or characteristic that influences how you interpret raw measures. Population size is an example. It is relevant to the number of people who vote. If California and Maine had the exact same number of people, you would not need to standardize. Standardization lets you compare on a common base by adjusting or removing the effect of relevant but different characteristics. It makes important differences visible. You can remove the size difference in the two states to make true differences in voting rates visible. The percentage is a common form of standardization; it standardizes on base 100. We can divide the number of voters in each state by the state's population size. If 12.4 million out of 36.8 million voted in California, about 33.7 percent voted. If 741,000 out of 1.3 million people in Maine voted, then 57 percent voted. Of course, California's population size means it had a bigger impact on the national election's outcome, but if your interest is in active participation in elections, then you need to remove the effect of different state population sizes.

You might say wait, not everyone can vote! Recent immigrants, noncitizens, and people under the age of 18 cannot vote but are in the population. The entire state population is not the best base to use. A critical question in standardization is deciding what base to use. The choice is not always obvious. It depends on the variable, and you need to think about it. To get an accurate measure of the percent who voted, we need to divide number of voters by the number eligible voters. In 2004, California had 26.3 million people eligible to vote. If 12.4 million showed up to vote, then California's voter turnout rate in the 2004 presidential election was 47 percent. Maine had 1.04 million eligible voters in 2004. Since 741,000 voted, Maine had a much higher voter turnout rate, 71.6 percent.

Different bases can produce different rates, and the base is influenced by how you define a variable. For example, some define the unemployment rate as the number of people in the work force who are out of work. The overall unemployment rate is given by the following fraction:

$$\text{Unemployment rate} = \frac{\text{Number of unemployed people}}{\text{Total number of people working}}$$

You can also divide the total population into subgroups to get rates for subgroups in the population, such as white males, African American females, African American males between the ages of 18 and 28, or people with college degrees. Rates for subgroups are often relevant to a research question. Perhaps you conceptualize unemployment as an experience that affects an entire household. You can change the base to households, not individuals. The formula for an unemployment rate will look like this:

$$\text{Household unemployment rate} = \frac{\text{Number of households with at least one unemployed person}}{\text{Total number of households}}$$

How you conceptualize a variable suggests different ways to standardize, but failing to standardize can produce distorted results. A few years ago, a student announced to me that based on the *Statistical Abstract of the United States*, New York had a terrible child abuse record with over 74,000 child victims, whereas her home

standardization adjusting a measure by dividing it by a common base to make comparisons possible.

state of Utah had only about 13,500. She failed to standardize on population size. Once she adjusted for the number of children in each state, New York had 16.3 victims of child abuse per 1000 children whereas Utah had 18.3 per 1000. Thus, the situation looked worse for Utah. Of course, the detection and follow-up of abuse cases may not be the same across the states, but the importance of standardizing data was clear.

Secondary Sources

Secondary data analysis is similar to existing statistics research in that you analyze data that someone else collected. The difference is that organizations often release official statistical information in aggregate form; or for large, macro units of analysis; or they publish it in descriptive tables that do not have all variables on all units. For example, from official statistics you learn the percent of doctors in a state affiliated with hospitals and the percent of hospitals with certain medical technology (e.g., an MRI [magnetic resonance imaging] machine). You cannot find out the number of doctors affiliated with each separate hospital and what equipment each hospital has. If you are interested in whether the number of doctors at a hospital is associated with it having certain medical equipment, you need data in which the unit of analysis is the hospital, but this may not be in any of the official statistics available to the public.

As opposed to primary data research (e.g., experiments, surveys, and content analysis), you do not focus on collecting data in secondary data analysis. Rather, the focus is on statistically analyzing data. Secondary data analysis facilitates replication and permits asking research questions that the original researchers did not consider. In a way, it is similar to entering the research process after the data collection phase has been completed. Collecting data on a large scale (such as nationally) is very expensive and difficult. A major national survey with rigorous technical support can cost tens of thousands of dollars. Fortunately, several organizations gather, preserve, and share survey data or other types of data. They make their data available for others to analyze. The most widely used source of survey data in the United States is the **General Social Survey (GSS)**. The U.S. government pays for the social survey, and the National Opinion Research Center at the University of Chicago has conducted it nearly annually for over 30 years. Data from it are made available to the public for secondary analysis. In recent years, many other industrialized nations have started similar surveys (see Making It Practical: The General Social Survey and Secondary Data Analysis).

General Social Survey a large-scale survey with many questions of a large national sample of adult Americans conducted almost every year. Data from it are made available to researchers at low or no cost.

Making It Practical   The General Social Survey and Secondary Data Analysis

The General Social Survey (GSS) is the best-known source of survey data for secondary analysis in the United States. It is available in computer-readable formats. Neither the datasets nor codebooks are copyrighted. Users can copy or disseminate them without obtaining permission. Results using the GSS appear in over 2,000 research articles and books. The National Opinion Research Center (NORC) has conducted the GSS almost every year since 1972. Data comes from face-to-face interviews of a random sample of 1,500 to 4,000 adult U.S. residents. The NORC staff carefully selects and trains its interviewers. The interviews are typically 90 minutes long and contain about 500 questions. The response rate has been 71 to 79 percent. Each year a team of researchers selects questions for inclusion.

They repeat some questions and topics each year, include others on a four- to six-year cycle, and add other topics in specific years. You can learn more about the GSS by visiting the NORC web site. You can order a copy of the GSS data or analyze it online. Online analysis of the data is available through several sources, such as Survey Data and Analysis (SDA) at the Computer-assisted Survey Methods Program of the University of California–Berkeley. You will want to begin with a list of survey questions or variables that are available at several online sites. To analyze data in detail you will need statistical analysis software and a raw data file. Several sources sell the data file at low cost, and they pre-format it for major statistics software packages.

Limitations of Secondary Data Sources

Using data collected by others is not trouble free. As with existing statistics research, you first must locate a data source and see what variables it contains. The most common limitation is that secondary data lack the variables you want for a research question. For example, in the GSS you are dependent on other researchers including survey questions on topics that you find interesting. Even when the data are available on variables of interest, the researchers who designed a study and collected the data may have conceptualized them differently. Before you proceed with secondary data analysis, you need to consider units in the data (e.g., types of people, organizations), the time and place of data collection, the sampling methods used, and the specific issues or topics covered in the data. For example, you may want to examine race/ethnic tensions between Latinos and Anglos in the Southwestern and Pacific regions of the United States. However, you find secondary data that include only the Pacific Northwest and New England states. You will have to reconsider the research question or use other data if they exist.

Secondary data analysis seems easier because the data are provided and you only need to know how to use and interpret statistical software programs. However, the other limitations common for existing statistics research, such as validity and topic knowledge, also apply in secondary data analysis. As with existing statistics research, you first need to examine the data and then develop hypotheses and a research question. Let us say you obtain a copy of the GSS. You may discover three limitations to its use:

1. Data are on all adults across the United States and not on specific types of individuals and geographic locations that you need for a research question. Perhaps you are interested in how 18- to 22-year-olds in your state feel about an issue, but the GSS does not allow you to examine this topic.
2. GSS survey questions are not on issues in your research question. Perhaps you are interested in a specific issue, such as whether a person engaged in sexual activity with his or her spouse before marriage, but the GSS did not include such questions.
3. GSS questions are worded differently than you wish or have different answer choices. For example, a long-used GSS question about prayer in public schools asks about whether respondents agree with a U.S. Supreme Court decision banning it. You cannot really learn people's opinions about favoring or opposing specific types of prayer or religious activities in a school. If the GSS offers a two-choice answer, support/oppose abortion under certain conditions, but you want a wide range of choices (strongly support to strongly oppose), you will be restricted.

 Summary Review Strengths and Limitations of Four Kinds of Nonreactive Research

Nonreactive Research	Major Strengths	Major Limitations
Physical Evidence	Indirect and unobtrusive evidence	Must infer to people's intentions
Content Analysis	Reveal hidden content in communication	Patterns in text, not its effects on people
Existing Statistics	Quantitative data of wide scope, low cost	Measurement reliability and validity
Secondary Analysis	Large-scale survey data, low cost	Limited variables are available

CONDUCTING ETHICAL NONREACTIVE RESEARCH

Ethical concerns are not at the forefront of most nonreactive research because the people who you study are not directly involved. In secondary analysis and content analysis, few ethical concerns arise. The primary ethical concern of physical evidence analysis is to protect people's privacy and the confidentiality of data.

The use of official existing statistics raises other issues. They are social and political products. Implicit theories and value assumptions guide which information researchers collect and how they collect it. Measures or statistics that agencies define as being official and collected regularly can be involved in political disputes. If measuring something one way is official and another way is not, measuring in the official way may benefit certain political positions over others. What information is gathered and made public also shapes public policy decisions. For example, political activity pressured government agencies to collect information on certain social conditions (e.g., the number of patients who died while in public mental hospitals). Government officials previously did not think the condition was sufficiently important to warrant public attention, or preferred to keep it quiet and hidden. Likewise, information on the percentage of nonwhite students enrolled in U.S. schools at various ages only became available in 1953. Nonwhite students attended schools before 1953, but court decisions and public interest in racial discrimination caused government agencies to begin to collect the data. Just as organized concern about an issue stimulates the collection of new official statistics, the collection of official statistics on an issue can stimulate public attention. For example, drunk driving became more of a public issue after government agencies began to collect and publish statistics on the number of automobile accidents and on whether alcohol was a factor in the accidents.

Most official statistics are collected for top-down bureaucratic or administrative planning, not for a researcher's purposes or for people who strongly oppose the bureaucratic decision makers. A government agency may gather data on the number of tons of steel produced, miles of highway paved, and average number of people in a household. It decides not to gather information on drinking-water quality, contamination at food processing plants, or stress-related job illness. Some officials see the gross national product (GNP) as a critical measure of societal progress. However, the GNP omits noneconomic aspects of social life (e.g., time spent playing with one's children) and ignores some types of work (e.g., housework). To a large degree, official statistics reflect the outcome of political debates about what we need to know and the values of officials who head government agencies. It is your ethical-moral decision to question or closely examine the values and decisions that guide which official statistics are collected and made public. It is important to recognize that people in positions of power are making decisions about what information to collect and make public. By not collecting and making public certain information, they may be protecting their position or advancing a social-political value position.

WHAT HAVE YOU LEARNED?

In this chapter, you learned about several types of non-reactive research techniques. You can use these techniques to measure or observe aspects of social life without affecting the people who you study. The techniques can produce numerical information that you can analyze to address research questions. You can use the techniques with other types of quantitative or qualitative social research to address a large number of issues.

As with other quantitative data, you need to be concerned with data quality and measurement. It is easy to take available information from a previously conducted survey or government document, but this does not mean that it is the best measure of what really interests you. Another limitation of nonreactive research stems from the availability of existing information. Existing statistics and secondary data analysis are low-cost research techniques. However, you lack control over or detailed knowledge of the data collection process. This can be a potential source of mistakes and errors, and you must be especially vigilant and cautious.

In the next chapter, we move beyond designing research projects and collecting data to analyzing data. The analysis techniques apply to quantitative data. Thus far, you have seen how to move from a topic, to a research design and measures, to collecting data. Next, you will learn how to look at data and see what they can tell you about a hypothesis or research question.

KEY TERMS

coding system *209*
content analysis *208*
ecological fallacy *222*
fallacy of misplaced concreteness *222*
General Social Survey (GSS) *225*
intercoder reliability *211*
latent coding *210*

manifest coding *210*
nonreactive research *206*
social indicator *217*
standardization *224*
text *208*
unobtrusive measures *206*

APPLYING WHAT YOU'VE LEARNED

Activity 1

Locate eight trashcans in public places (such as a classroom, student lounge, or waiting room). Obtain permission from a person in charge of the area and take the content of the trashcan and catalog the types of items you find for each of 10 days, five weekdays in a row, for two weeks. This gives you 10 observations from eight locations. Are there patterns in what you find, either by location or day?

Activity 2

Content analyze television commercials (not including ones for upcoming TV shows or public service advertisements) by first developing a recording sheet. The sheet should have the (1) television network (2) day of week, (3) time of day, and (4) estimated price of prod-

uct: (a) under $10, (b) $10–$100, (c) $101–$500, (d) $501–$10,000, (e) over $10,000. Pick two TV networks, and four days—two weekdays and both weekend days. Divide the time of day into four parts: morning (8 A.M. to noon), afternoon (noon to 5 P.M.), early evening (5 P.M. to 9 P.M.), and late evening (9 P.M. to midnight). Now observe each network each day for each time slot (you may enlist a friend to help). After you gather the data, do you find patterns by the price of products based on time of day or by day of the week? Are the two networks the same or different?

Activity 3

Go online to the *Statistical Abstract of the United States* (http://www.census.gov/compendia/statab/). Once there, click on Print Version to see many sections (chapters) with the topics they cover. Can you locate the following five pieces of information and the table in which it appears in the *Statistical Abstract*?

a. What percentage of U.S. households reported that they owned a dog as a pet?
b. What percentage of rapes/sexual assaults occurred in the victim's home or place of lodging?
c. What percentage of all youth, aged 12 to 17, engaged in "binge drinking"?
d. In terms of per capita (i.e., per person) consumption, which of the following was the highest (in terms of total pounds eaten)—beef, chicken, fish/shellfish, or pork?
e. For the entire U.S. population (all ages, races, genders), what percent say they have serious limitations in activity caused by chronic health conditions because of a serious physical, mental, or emotional problem?

Activity 4

Go online to the NORC Web site (http://www.norc.org/ GSS+Website/). Click on Browse GSS variables, then Subject Index (be sure to look past the blank space in the upper half of the screen). Click on the letter D and find the survey question on the Military Draft. Look at the question Return to the Draft. Click on Trends at the bottom to see the years this question was in the GSS and overall support. What exactly did the GSS ask in this question? During what years did this question appear in the GSS? See if you can find out who is more in favor of the military draft, men or women.

REFERENCES

Chavez, Leo. 2001. *Covering Immigration*. Berkeley: University of California Press.

Downey, Liam. 2005. "The Unintended Significance of Race: Environmental Racial Inequality in Detroit." *Social Forces* 83:971–1007.

Foster, Gary, Richard Hummel, and Donald Adamchak. 1998. "Patterns of conception, Natality and Morality from Midwestern Cemeteries." *Sociological Quarterly* 39:473–490.

Lauzen, Martha, and David Dozier. 2005. "Maintaining the Double Standard: Portrayals of Age and Gender in Popular Films." *Sex Roles* 52:437–446.

Quinn, Malcolm. 1994. *The Swastika: Constructing the Symbol*. New York: Routledge.

Rashotte, Lisa Slattery. 2002. "What Does That Smile Mean? The Meaning of Nonverbal Behaviors in Social Interaction" *Social Psychology Quarterly* 65(1): 92–102.

Rathje, William, and Cullen Murphy.1992. *Rubbish: The Archaeology of Garbage*. New York: Vintage.

Stevenson, Richard W. (Oct. 16, 1996). U.S. to revise its estimate of layoffs. *New York Times*.

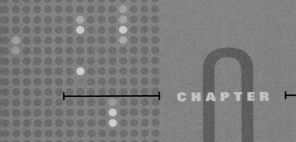

Making Sense of the Numbers

Image Source Royalty
Free/AP Images

n 2005, about half of U.S. households were comprised of married couples, 26 percent individuals living alone, 18 percent single adults with children, and about 5 percent unmarried couples living together. About 87 percent of the unmarried couples living together as a household were mixed sex, and 13 percent same sex. Today, few Americans object to a man and a woman living together before marriage. About one in three couples who marry first lived together. Living together increased 10-fold between 1970 and 2000. Almost half (41 percent) of all women aged 15–44 cohabited at some time. Higher-income couples and those who are white are most likely to move from cohabitation to marriage (see Figure 9.1). As more people live together, they are delaying the age of marriage. The median age of a first marriage rose from 20.8 in 1970 to 26 in 2004 for women and 23.2 to 27 for men. An unmarried, opposite-sex couple lives together for a mean duration of two years. Eventually about half of these couples marry, about 40 percent split up, and the rest continue to live together. Several states (Florida, Michigan, Mississippi, North Carolina, North Dakota, Virginia, and West Virginia) have (unenforced) laws that say male-female cohabitation is illegal. Living together is popular in many but not all countries. In some countries, over 75 percent of people are cohabiting (such as Sweden), but in others under 4 percent live together (e.g., Japan). As this brief look at cohabitation shows, numbers and statistics can help you to see the trends in intimate social relationships.

■ Figure 9.1   Bar Graph of Chances of a Cohabitating Couple Making the Transition to Marriage

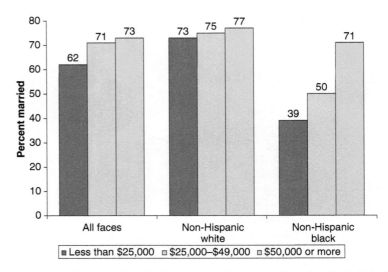

Less than $25,000 $25,000–$49,000 $50,000 or more

Source: From *Vital Health Statistics, Cohabitation, Marriage, Divorce and Remarriage in the United States* (July 2002), Series 23, Number 22 U.S. Department of Health and Human Services.

Most research reports with quantitative data use charts, graphs, and tables. Before you skip over this part of a report, remind yourself that their purpose is to give you, the reader, a condensed visual image of the data. Graphs and tables can tell a vivid story. You just need to learn their language.

Data collected using the techniques discussed in previous chapters are in the form of numbers. The numbers represent values of variables that measure characteristics of subjects, respondents, or other cases. Initially the numbers are in a raw form, on questionnaires, note pads, recording sheets, or paper. They are the start of a process. Before you can discuss and analyze these numbers, you must reorganize them into a form compatible with computer programs. You use computer programs to create charts or graphs that summarize the features of the data. You must then interpret or give substantive and theoretical meaning to the computer results (see Figure 9.2).

■ Figure 9.2   A Flow Chart of Data in the Form of Numbers

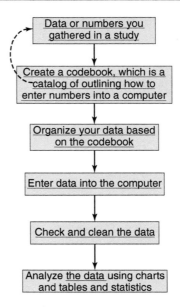

WHAT TO DO ONCE YOU HAVE THE NUMBERS

If you do secondary data analysis, the data often arrive in a computer-readable format and you can skip over data preparation. When you gather your own data, on the other hand, you first need to convert the raw numbers into a computer-friendly format or engage in **data coding**. As with coding in content analysis, you must create and consistently apply clear rules to transfer information from one form to another. Computers organize numerical information as variables and **data records**. As you code data, you might have each data record on a separate file card or computer document. Often it is a row of information in a spreadsheet or grid. Each data record has information on all variables for one person, unit, or case, and you have as many data records as cases or units. If you had survey data on 100 people, you would have 100 data records, one for each person. You need to assign numbers to variable attributes or categories in each variable. You use numbers because the information will go into a computer, and numbers are far easier to use with computers than letters or words. Some of the numbers reflect quantitative information (ratio or interval-level measurement). Others are arbitrary and assigned to qualitative (nominal or ordinal-level) differences.

Let us say you gathered information on five variables (age, gender, amount of schooling, and two attitudes). You will code, or assign numbers, for each variable category or level. Age is easy, since we already think of age as number of years. For gender, you might code males as 1 and females as 2. The numbers for male and female are arbitrary and could just as easily be 5 and 7. Amount of schooling is the number of years in school. If you have a five-point Likert scale for the attitude measures, you might assign numbers as follows:

1 Strong agree
2 Agree
3 Disagree
4 Strong disagree
9 Did not answer question

As you assign numeric codes to each category of a variable, and even items of missing information, it is essential to keep a written record of coding rules in a **codebook**. As you code data, you create a well-organized, detailed codebook and make multiple copies of it. If you fail to write down the details of the coding procedure, or if you misplace the codebook, you have lost the key to the data and may have to start all over again.

Once you have assigned numeric codes and organized all the data records, you can transfer the information into a computer-readable form. The dozens of computer programs that analyze quantitative data require information in the form of numbers and in a grid format. In the grid, each row is a data record (that is, a respondent, subject, or case) and each column is a variable. Computer programs also let

data coding the process of putting the raw quantitative information into a computer-readable format.

data record information on one person, unit, case, or your unit of analysis in a computer-friendly format.

codebook a document that describes the coding procedure and the location of data for variables in a format that computers can use.

Making It Practical Precoding Saves Time

You should begin to think about coding before you collect any data. It is best to anticipate what is coming later in the process. Experimenters need to decide how to code dependent variable measures before starting the experiment. Survey researchers often precode a questionnaire before collecting data. *Precoding* is placing the code categories (e.g., 1 for male, 2 for female) on the questionnaire itself. If you do not precode, the first step after collecting data will be to create codes. Precoding speeds and simplifies the process. In addition to precoding, you want to assign each case or unit an identification number to keep track of them. Each is the data record for a single case. Identification numbers make it possible to go back to the original source of data (such as a questionnaire) if problems arise later in the process.

you enter the codebook information so that they can display results in a clearly labeled form (e.g., 1 = "Strongly Agree" for a survey question answer).

Figure 9.3 shows the steps from a survey questionnaire, to a codebook, to putting the data in a computer-readable format. Your task is to transfer information from the questionnaire—what humans can read—into an organized set of num-

■ **Figure 9.3**   Coded Data for Three Cases and Codebook

Exerpt from Survey Questionnaire (precoded)

Respondent ID_____

1. Note the Respondent's Gender: _____ Male (1) _____ Female (2)

2. How old are you? _____

3. How many years of schooling have you completed?_____

4. The first question is about the President of the United States. Do you Strongly Agree, Agree, Disagree, or Have No Opinion about the following statement: The President of the United States is doing great job.
_____ Strong Agree (1)_____ Agree (2)_____ Disagree (3)_____ Strong Disagree (4)_____ No Opinion (9)

5. What are your overally feelings about the future, the next 2–3 years specifically?
_____ Very positive (1)
_____ Somewhat positive (2)
_____ Neither positive or negative (3)
_____ Somewhat negative (4)
_____ Very negative (5)
_____ No idea/no opinion/refused (9)

Exerpt from Codebook

Column	Variable Name	Description
1–3	ID	Respondent identification number (001 to 250)
4	Gender	Interviewer report of respondent's gender 1=Male, 2=Female
5–6	Age	Two digit respondent's age in years
7–8	Schooling	Respondent's years of schooling 01 to highest years.
9	Presjob	The president of the United State is doing a great job.
		1 = Strongly Agree
		2 = Agree
		4 = Disagree
		5 = Strongly Disagree
10	Future	Respondent's feelings about the future
		1 = Very positive
		2 = Positive
		3 = Neither

Data on first three respondents, as you put the data into the computer

Case Number	Age	Gender	Years of Schooling	Presjob Answer	Future Answer
001	20	1	14	1	3
002	19	2	15	5	1
003	21	1	16	2	4

Exerpt of data records in the computer, first three data records

```
0012011413 42736302 182738274 10239 18.82 3947461 ... etc.
0021921551 23334821 124988154 21242 18.21 3984123 ... etc.
0032111624 0123982 1137272631 2345 17.36 1487645 ... etc.
etc.
```

bers—what computers read. Humans cannot easily read information in a computer-readable format. Without the codebook, such information is meaningless. The computer format condenses the information from survey questions for three respondents into three rows of numbers. Raw data often look like a block of numbers. For example, a 15-minute telephone survey of 250 students yields a grid of 250 rows, with each row being a data record. If you asked 25 survey questions, the grid will have at least 25 columns plus space for identification number. It becomes a block of numbers with 250 rows by over 25 columns. Often the first three numbers are identification numbers. Example data in Figure 9.3 show information for the first (001), second (002), and third (003) respondents. Notice that zeros are placeholders to reduce confusion. Eventually you will have 001 through 250.

A codebook lets you can work backward to decode information. Look at the data record for the computer with the codebook. Case 1 is data on a 20-year-old male with 14 years of education. He answered Strongly Agree to the Presjob question and Neither to the Future question. Case 2 is data for a 19-year-old female with 15 years of schooling. She answered Strongly Disagree to the Prejob question and Very Positive to the Future question. Case 3 has information on a 21-year-old male who completed 16 years of schooling. He answered Agree to the Presjob question and Somewhat Negative to the Future question.

CLEANING UP THE NUMBERS

Data coding must be highly accurate. You can have a perfect sample, perfectly valid measures, and no errors in gathering data, but if you make errors coding or entering data into a computer, your entire research project can be ruined. After coding data, you need to check and "clean" the data. To do this, recode a 10 percent random sample of the data a second time. If you find no coding errors, proceed with confidence; if you find many errors, recheck all coding. You can also verify coding after the data are in a computer by checking variables for impossible codes. For example, respondent gender is coded 1 = Male, 2 = Female. Review all numbers for gender; if you discover the number 4 for the gender variable in a data record, you have a coding error.

HOW TO DESCRIBE QUANTITATIVE RESULTS

Statistics refers both to a set of collected numbers such as existing statistics in the *Statistical Abstract of the United States* and a branch of applied mathematics. As applied mathematics, statistics tell us how to manipulate and summarize the numbers. Descriptive statistics is a major branch of statistics (later you will learn about the other branch, inferential statistics) that describe and communicate numerical information. We can organize descriptive statistics by the number of variables you consider at one time: one, two, or three and more. Univariate statistics describe one variable (*uni-* refers to one; *-variate* refers to variable), Bivariate statistics describe two variables, and multivariate statistics describe three or more variables.

Looking at Results with One Variable

How Many Are in Each Variable Category?   The easiest way to describe numerical data on one variable is with a **frequency distribution** You can present the same information in a visually dramatic or graphic form, such with the pie chart, bar chart, or histogram. You probably are familiar with the pie chart from elementary school math. It divides the total into slices. The bar chart is used for discrete variables and has a vertical or horizontal orientation with a small space between the bars. The

frequency distribution a simple table showing how many, or what percent, of the cases fall into each variable category.

■ **Figure 9.4**   Univariate Statistics, Opinion about Premarital Sex

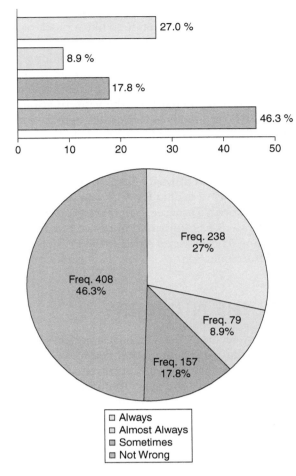

Data from GSS, 2004.

terminology is not exact, but histograms are usually upright bar graphs for interval or ratio data. As you can see in Figure 9.4, in 2004 almost one-half of American adults said that sexual relations before marriage is not wrong. The frequency distribution gives exact percents. The pie chart can distort information, and people usually find it easier to see information on a variable in a bar chart. The bar chart shows that the always wrong and "not wrong" answer choices, the two extremes, are most common.

Where Is the Middle?   You may want something simpler than showing cases for all variable categories, especially for ratio or interval data. You can summarize information into a single number, or a kind of average. You can use **measures of central tendency** in descriptive statistics. Three main measures of central tendency are the mean, median, and mode. All are called *averages*, which is a less precise and less clear way to say the same thing. Most of us learned about these long ago, but you may have forgotten specificis about them.

The **mode** is the easiest to compute but the least useful measure of central tendency. It is simply the most common or frequently occurring number. For example, the mode is 5 in the following list of eight childrens ages who are waiting at a bus stop: 6, 5, 7, 10, 9, 5, 3, 5. A distribution can have more than one mode. For example, the mode of the following list is both 5 and 7: 5, 6, 1, 2, 5, 7, 4, 7. If the list gets long, just look for the most frequent score. There is always at least one case that has a score that is exactly equal to the mode. If you were selling ice cream and could only

measure of central tendency one number that summarizes the center or main tendency in a set of numbers.

mode measure of central tendency that is the most common value.

stock one flavor, you would want to know the flavor that is the mode to make the most sales.

The **median** is the middle point and the 50th percentile. Half the cases are above it and half below it. You may be able to spot it or can compute it with a two-step process. First, organize the scores from highest to lowest. Next, count to the middle. If you have an odd number of scores, this is simple. For example, seven people are waiting for a bus; their ages are 12, 17, 20, 27, 30, 55, 80. Count in four people from either end. The median age is 27. Note that the median does not change easily. If the 55-year-old and the 80-year-old both got on one bus and the two 31-year-olds joined the remaining people, the median would be the same. What if there is an even number of scores? For example, six people at a bus stop have the following ages: 17, 20, 26, 30, 50, 70. If you count from either end, you see that the median is somewhere between 26 and 30. To compute the median, add the two middle scores and divide by 2, or 26 + 30 = 56/2 = 28. The median age is 28. Notice that no one is 28 years old. This list of six ages has no mode because each person is a different age.

SW Productions/Brand X/Corbis Royalty Free

The **mean**, or arithmetic average, is the most widely used measure of central tendency. Many advanced statistical measures use it. You compute it by adding up all scores and then dividing the total by the number of scores. The mean age in the previous example is 17 + 20 + 26 + 30 + 50 + 70 = 213; 213/6 = 35.5. Notice that no one in the list is 35.5 years old and that the mean does not equal the median. Changes in extreme values (very low or very high) can strongly influence the mean. If the 50-year-old and 70-year-old left and were replaced with two 31-year-olds, we have the following distribution: 17, 20, 26, 30, 31, 31. The median is unchanged at 28. The mean is 17 + 20 + 26 + 30 + 31 + 31 = 155; 155/6 = 25.8. It dropped almost 10 years, from 35.5 to 25.8. Thus, the mean dropped a great deal when we removed a few extreme values.

It is often useful to plot a frequency distribution. The bottom line has values of a variable (from lowest to highest), and a vertical line on the left indicates the number of cases. As you plot each case, cases appear to pile up over each other. The plot of cases can form many shapes. One widely used one is a bell-shaped curve. Many naturally occurring phenomena fit this form if plotted (e.g., tree diameter, people's height, weight, IQ) so it is called a normal distribution. The curve is tall in the center and smoothly falls off to the right and left sides as they approach the extreme highest and lowest scores. The curve looks like a bell and is symmetrical. You could cut it in half and each side could fold over on the other side precisely. When your data forms a bell-shaped curve, the three measures of central tendency will equal each other. Let us say 15 people of the following ages are waiting for a bus: 2, 4, 5, 6, 8, 8, 10, 10, 10, 12, 12, 14, 15, 16, 18. This forms a symmetrical, bell-shaped curve. The mode, median and mean are all 10 years old.

Not all curves form a nice bell shape; some form a **skewed distribution**. A skew is an imbalance with more cases in the extreme upper or lower scores. When this occurs, the three measures of central tendency are not equal. If most cases have low scores and few are high scores, then the mean will be the highest, the median in the middle, and the mode the lowest. If most cases have higher scores with a few

median measure of central tendency where one half are above and one-half are below, that is, the mid-point.

mean the measure of central tending that is the arithmetic average.

skewed distribution a distribution of cases that is not bell shaped or normal but instead has many cases at one of the extreme values (very high or very low) of a variable.

Summary Review   Three Measures of Central Tendency

```
        1  2  3  4  5  5  6  7  8  9
```
5 Mode = most common in the list above, because there are two number 5s.

5 Median = midpoint in the list above, because it is the middle: 1, 2, 3, 4, 5, 5, 6, 7, 8, 9

5 Mean = arithmetic average of the list above, because 1 + 2 + 3 + 4 + 5 + 5 + 6 + 7 + 8 + 9 = 50; 50/10 = 5

■ **Figure 9.5**   Measures of Central Tendency in Normal and Skewed Distributions

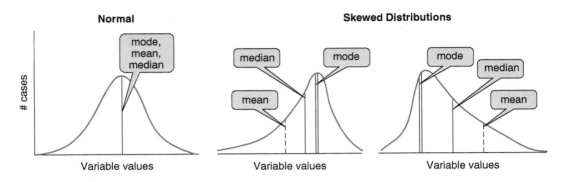

extreme low scores, the mean will be the lowest, the median in the middle, and the mode the highest. In general, the median is the best measure of central tendency to use for a skewed distribution (see Figure 9.5).

The discussion on cohabitation that opened this chapter gave the median age of marriage and the mean number of years that unmarried people lived together. The median is best for a skewed distribution, such as ages of first marriage. Many people marry in their twenties, but by the time people are in their fifties or sixties, very few marry for the first time. You can use the mean when a distribution is normal, such as how long most people live together.

What Is the Spread? Measures of central tendency give you one number, the *center*. Another important characteristic of a distribution is its spread around the center. Two distributions can have identical measures of central tendency but differ greatly in their spread about the center. For example, seven people are at a bus stop in front of a bar. Their ages are 25, 26, 27, 30, 33, 34, 35. Both the median and the mean are 30. At a bus stop in front of an ice cream store, seven people have the identical median and mean, but their ages are 5 10 20 30 40 50 55. Ages of people in front of the ice cream store are spread farther from the center, or the distribution has more variability. Of course, you might have 70 people rather than seven (see Figure 9.6), but the principle is the same.

You can measure variation in three ways: range, percentile, and standard deviation.
Range is the simplest. It consists of the largest and smallest scores. The range for the bus stop in front of the bar is from 25 to 35, or 35 − 25 = 10 years. If the 35-year-old

range the highest and lowest ends of a set of numbers.

Making It Practical **Mean Salary Data**

50 clerks   5 supervisors    1 general manager   1 CEO

Why avoid the mean for a skewed distribution? Consider the example of salary levels. Joe owns a chain of five coffee shops and has a total 56 employees. Here are their salaries:

- 50 clerks make $15,000 a year.
- 5 supervisors make $30,000 a year.
- 1 general manager makes $100,000 a year.
- Joe, the owner and CEO, takes home $450,000 a year.

Calculate the mean salary (50 × $15,000 = $750,000) + (5 × 30,000 = $150,000) + $100,000 + $450,000 = $1,450,000/56 = $25,893. The mean is deceptive as an average, because 50 of the 56 people earn $10,000 less than it. The only people close to it are the five supervisors, who earn $4,107 over the mean.

■ **Figure 9.6**   Spread of a Distribution

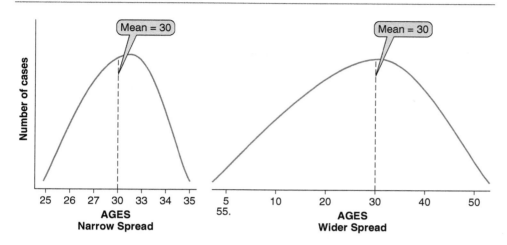

got onto a bus and a 60-year-old joined the line, the range would change to 60 − 25 = 45 years. Range has limitations. For example, here are two groups of six numbers that both have a range of 35 years: 30 30 30 30 30 65 and 20 45 46 48 50 55.

Percentiles tell us the score at a specific place within the distribution. You already learned about the 50th percentile, also called the median. Some researchers use the 25th and 75th percentiles or the 10th and 90th percentiles to describe a distribution. For example, the 25th percentile is the score at which 25 percent of the cases are at that score or lower. You compute a percentile similar to the median. Let us say you want to know the 25th percentile of 100 people. Rank the scores and count up from the bottom until you reach number 25. If the total is not 100, you simply adjust the distribution to a percentage basis. Many standardized tests for admission to college or graduate schools, as well as IQ tests, are reported using percentiles. If you did average on one of these tests, you would be at or near the 50th percentile. If you scored very low on the test compared to others who took it, you might be at the 20th percentile. This means that 80 percent of people who took the same test did better on it. If you scored very high, such as the 95th percentile, you scored better than 95 percent of others, and no more than 5 percent equaled or exceeded your score.

Standard deviation is the most comprehensive and widely used measure of variability. It uses the mean and gives you a kind of "average distance" between all scores and the mean (see Figure 9.7). By itself, it is difficult to see the value of the standard deviation. When you use it to compare populations, it becomes very useful.

Let us use the standard deviation to compare populations. The standard deviation of parents' level of schooling for class A at local elementary school is 3.317 years; for class B, it is 0.812; and for class C, it is 6.239. Comparing the standard deviations, you quickly see that the parents of children in class B are very similar, whereas those for class C are very different. In fact, in class B, the schooling of an

percentile a score at a specific place in a set of numbers, such that a particular percent of scores is below that place.

standard deviation a widely used measure of the variability of a variable that indicates the average distance of cases from the mean value.

Making It Practical   Income Spreads in Evanstown and Newville

Variability has important social implications. For example, in Evanstown, a city of 100,000, the median and mean family income is $39,600, and it has zero variation. *Zero variation* means that every family has an income of exactly $39,600. Forty miles away is another city of 100,000, Newville. It has the same mean family income of $39,600,

but 95 percent of its families are at the poverty line with incomes of $12,000 per year, and 5 percent have incomes of $300,000 per year. Evanstown has perfect income equality, whereas Newville shows great inequality. If you do not know about the variability of income in the two cities, you will miss very important information.

■ **Figure 9.7**   The Standard Deviation

Example of Computing the Standard Deviation
[8 respondents, variable = years of schooling]

Score	Score − Mean	Squared (Score − Mean)
15	15 − 12.5 = 2.5	6.25
12	12 − 12.5 = −0.5	.25
12	12 − 12.5 = −0.5	.25
10	10 − 12.5 = −2.5	6.25
16	16 − 12.5 = 3.5	12.25
18	18 − 12.5 = 5.5	30.25
8	8 − 12.5 = 4.5	20.25
9	9 − 12.5 = −3.5	12.25

Mean = 15 + 12 + 12 + 10 + 16 + 18 + 8 + 9 = 100, 100/8 = 12.5
Sum of squares = 6.25 + .25 + .25 + 6.25 + 12.25 + 30.25 + 20.25 + 12.25 = 88
Variance = Sum of squares/Number of cases = 88/8 = 11
Standard deviation = Square root of variance = $\sqrt{11}$ = 3.317 years.
Here is the standard deviation in the form of a formula with symbols.

Symbols:
X = SCORE of case Σ = Sigma (Greek letter) for sum, add together
$\bar{X}$ = MEAN n = Number of cases
S = *standard deviation*

$$S = \sqrt{\frac{\sum(x - \bar{x})^2}{n - 1}}$$

There is a slight difference in the formula depending on whether you are using data for the entire population or a sample to estimate the population parameter. If you have a sample, divide by $n - 1$ as shown in the formula; if you have the entire population, just use n.

Learning from History **Teen Pregnancy**

Knowing the mean plus the standard deviation is useful when making comparisons. The National Center for Health Statistics reported that in 1990 a mean of 12.24 percent of all births in U.S. states were to a woman under 19 years old (the median was 11.95 percent) and the standard deviation was 3.429 percent. This information is more useful if compared to other countries or times. Twelve years later, in 2002, the mean of teen births dropped to 10.646 percent (median was 10.60 percent) and standard deviation 2.644 percent. The lower mean and median tells us that the teen birth rate declined. A smaller standard deviation shows us the rate across the states became more alike. Teen childbearing in the United States has fallen since the late 1950s. It reached a high of 96 births per 1000 women aged 15–19 in 1957. It dropped to roughly one-half that level by 2000.

Birth rates fell throughout the 1960s and 1970s, were steady in the early 1980s, rose sharply between 1988 and 1991, then declined again. The downward trend was among teens of all ages and races. Teen birth rates have declined in all advanced nations, but the U.S. rate dropped less than other countries. The United States has higher teen birth rates than all other advanced countries. Rates of teen sexual behavior do not differ among countries. Due to its moral-religious views on teen sex education and contraception, the United States has adolescent pregnancy rates that are nearly double that in Canada and Great Britain and four times higher than in France and Sweden. Americans also seem to be the most obsessed and moralize most over teen pregnancy. Moreover, they treat it as a cause rather than an effect of poverty (Luker 1997).

■ **Figure 9.8** Calculating Z-Scores

Personally, I do not like the formula for z-scores, which is:

Z-score = (Score − Mean)/Standard Deviation,

or, in symbols, $z = X - \bar{X}/\text{sd}$

where X = score, $\bar{X}$ = mean, sd = standard deviation

I usually rely on a simple diagram that does the same thing and that shows what z-scores really do. Consider data on the ages of schoolchildren with a mean of 7 years and a standard deviation of 2 years. How do I compute the z-score of 5-year-old Miguel, or what if I know that Yashohda's z-score is a +2 and I need to know her age in years? First, I draw a little chart from −3 to +3 with zero in the middle. I will put the mean value at zero, because a z-score of zero is the mean and z-scores measure distance above or below it. I stop at 3 because virtually all cases fall within 3 standard deviations of the mean in most situations. The chart looks like this:

(a)

Now, I label the values of the mean and add or subtract standard deviations from it. One standard deviation above the mean (+1) when the mean is 7 and standard deviation is 2 years is just 7 + 2, or 9 years. For a −2 z–score, I put 3 years. This is because it is 2 standard deviations, or 2 years each (or 4 years), lower than the Mean of 7. My diagram now looks like this:

(b)

It is easy to see that Miguel, who is 5 years old, has a z-score of −1, whereas Yashohda's z-score of +2 corresponds to 11 years old. I can read from z-score to age, or age to z-score. For fractions, such as a z-score of −1.5, I just apply the same fraction to age to get 4 years. Likewise, an age of 12 is a z-score of +2.5.

"average" parent is less than a year above or below than the mean for all parents. In short, the parents are very homogeneous. In class C, the "average" parent is more than six years above or below the mean. The parents are very heterogeneous in their level of schooling.

Making it Practical *Z-Scores and GPAs*

Z-scores are easy to calculate if you have the mean and standard deviation. For example, an employer interviews students from Kings College and Queens College. Suzette is from Kings College and has a grade-point average of 3.62. Jorge is from Queens College and has a grade-point average of 3.64. Both students took similar courses. The colleges both grade on a 4.0 scale. However, the mean grade-point average for students at Kings College is 2.62 with a standard deviation of .50, whereas the mean grade-point average at Queens College is 3.24 with a standard deviation of .40. The employer suspects that professors at Queens College are easy graders, and the grades at Queens College are inflated. To adjust the grades of the two students for the grading practices of the two colleges (i.e., create standardized scores), the employer converts the GPA

for each student into z-scores. She does this by subtracting each student's score from the mean, then dividing by the standard deviation. Suzette's z-score is 3.62 − 2.62 = 1.00/.50 = 2, whereas Jorge's z-score is 3.64 − 3.24. = .40/.40 = 1. After this adjustment, the employer sees that Suzette is two standard deviations above the mean GPA in her college. By contrast, Jorge is only one standard deviation above the mean GPA for his college. Suzette's absolute grade-point average is a little lower but relative to all the students in each of college her grades are much higher than Jorge's. Z-scores help the employer see that Suzette's grades are well above the average student at her college, but Jorge's grades are close to those of an average student at his college.

■ Figure 9.9   Map of U.S. Teen Birth Rates

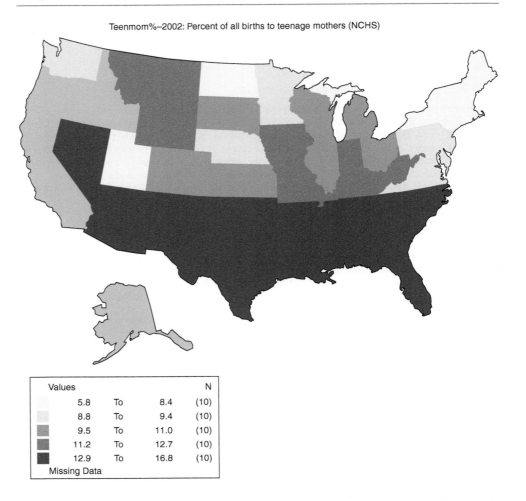

Teenmom%–2002: Percent of all births to teenage mothers (NCHS)

Values			N
5.8	To	8.4	(10)
8.8	To	9.4	(10)
9.5	To	11.0	(10)
11.2	To	12.7	(10)
12.9	To	16.8	(10)
Missing Data			

The standard deviation is not easy to interpret. Its smallest value is always zero, indicating that there is no variation at all and all the cases are identical, but its largest value can vary depending on a variable's scores. A variable with higher mean or median scores will have a bigger standard deviation. To deal with this issue and provide more information, researchers developed a standardized measure, **Z-scores**, which take into account a variable's standard deviation and the value of its scores. A Z-score expresses points or scores on a frequency distribution in terms of a number of standard deviations from the mean. Z-scores adjust for specific distributions. This is very useful whenever the means and standard deviations are different and you want to compare the same variable in two populations (see Figure 9.8). Z-scores are also used in other statistical measures, such as calculating correlation coefficients.

Displaying Information on a Map.   If you have information by geographic location, you can display data on a map. Compared to a table or chart, a map is a little more complex. In addition to showing different levels of the variable, you can show its spatial form, or how it spreads across a geographic area. The National Center for Health Statistics provides information on the percent of all births that are to women under the age of 19. Its range is from 5.8 to 16.8 percent in 2002. The mean is 10.646 and median 10.646 and they form a normal distribution. We can look at the information by U.S. states (see Figure 9.9).

Z-score a standardized measure that allows comparisons of groups that differ in their means and standard deviations.

■ **Figure 9.10**   Teen Birth Rates in the United States, 1940–2004

Sources: Ventura, S. J., Mathews, T. J., & Hamilton, B. E. (2001). Births to Teenagers in the United States, 1940–2000. *National Vital Statistics Reports, 49*(10).; Hamilton, B. E., Sutton, P. D., & Ventura, S. J. (2003). Revised Birth and Fertility Rates for the 1990s and New Rates for Hispanic Populations, 2000 and 2001: United States. *National Vital Statistics Reports 51(12);* Martin, J. A., Hamilton, B. E., Sutton, P. D., Ventura, S. J., Menacker, F., & Munson, M. L. (2005). Births: Final Data for 2003. *National Vital Statistics Reports 54 (2).* Martin, J. A., Hamilton, B. E., Sutton, P. D., Ventura, S. J., Menacker, F., & Kirmeyer, S. (2006). Births: Final Data for 2004 *National Vital Statistics Reports 55(1).*

The map shows us that the states with a higher percent of teen births are located in the South. All six states in the highest category are in the South, and all other Southern states are in the second highest category. By displaying a variable with geographic information, we can learn more about it.

Information along a Time Line.   If you have data that vary by time, you can display data about a variable along a time line. Compared to a table or chart, a time line is more complex. In addition to showing different variable levels, you can show how the variable changes across time. Suppose you are interested in teen birth rates over time. Information is available over a 64-year period (1940–2004). Knowing the mean or median is useful, but being able to plot the divorce rates by year is more informative. We quickly see that the rates began low and grew in the 1950s, then declined (see Figure 9.10). When we compare this to divorce rates for the same period (see Figure 9.11), we notice that periods when divorce rates were low were the same ones when teen births were high.

■ **Figure 9.11**   U.S. Divorce Rates, 1950–2004

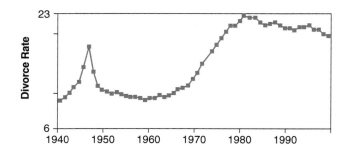

Results with Two Variables

A Bivariate Relationship. You can describe the number of cases in a variable's category by looking at a single variable in a table or graph or calculating its central tendency or variation. Placing it in a map or along a time line adds complexity and lets you consider how it fits with space or time. Geographic space or time can provide you with greater insight into the variable. However, spatial location and the passage of time are not variables in a causal explanation. To examine a causal explanation, you need to examine at the relationship of two variables, one the cause (independent variable) and one the effect (dependent variable). For example, you cannot say time passed and therefore teen pregnancy went up as a causal explanation. You can say social customs and morals about the value of premarital chastity weakened and this caused more sexual relations among teens, but because knowledge and access to birth control was limited, teen pregnancy rates increased.

With bivariate statistics, you can look at two variables together simultaneously and evaluate the statistical relationship between variables—that is, whether and how the variables operate together. Bivariate statistical relationships are based on two ideas: covariation and statistical independence.

Covariation means to vary together. If two variables covary, the cases with certain values on one variable tend to have certain values on the other one. For example, people with higher values on the income variable tend to have higher values on the life expectancy variable. Likewise, people with lower incomes have lower life expectancy. We can say this in a shorthand way—income and life expectancy are related to each other, or they covary. If we know income levels, we know probable life expectancy. Life expectancy depends on income level (the independent variable). **Statistical independence** is the opposite of covariation. For example, Rita wants to know whether number of siblings is related to life expectancy. If the variables have statistical independence, then people who have many brothers and sisters have the same life expectancy as those who are only children. In other words, knowing the number of siblings tells Rita nothing about the person's life expectancy. Life expectancy does not depend on number of siblings.

A first task in the statistical analysis of two variables is to find out whether a relationship exists, or whether there is statistical independence between the variables. Three techniques will help you to decide whether there is a relationship between two variables:

1. A scattergram, or a graph or plot of the bivariate relationship;
2. Cross-tabulation, or a percentaged table; and
3. Measures of association, or statistical measures that express the amount of covariation by a single number (e.g., correlation coefficient).

Seeing the Relationship: Scattergrams. The purpose of putting numeric information into charts, graphs, and tables is to communicate what is in the data to other people. If you do not know how read data patterns in a chart, graph, or table and see variable relationships in them, you will not be able to set up charts, graphs, and tables that communicate this to other people.

What Is a Scattergram (or Scatterplot)? A **scattergram**, or scatterplot, is a graph that allows you to see bivariate relationships. Usually the independent variable (often symbolized by the letter X) goes on the horizontal axis and the dependent variable (often symbolized by Y) on the vertical axis. In the graph, you want to place the lowest value for each in the lower left corner and the highest value at the top or to the right. Scattergrams are ideal for interval- or ratio-level data and do not work with nominal data. For ordinal-level data, you should have many levels or categories (10 or more). Scattergrams do not work well with few cases (under 15) but are ideal with many cases (100 or more).

covariation when two variables go together or are associated with one another.

statistical independence the absence of an association or covariation between two variables.

scattergram a graph on which you plot the value of each case or observation. Each axis of the graph represents the values of one variable, and the graph can reveal bivarate relations.

Cohabitation and Divorce Vary by Context

Past studies found that people who cohabitate prior to marriage may be more likely to divorce, but this is not the same across all countries. Liefbroer and Dourleijn (2006) looked at the impact of cohabitation on marriage across 16 European countries. They found that what happens with regard to cohabitors depends on what everyone else in a society is doing. If hardly anyone cohabits, the rate of marriage dissolution among former cohabitors is more than twice as high as that for those who did not cohabit prior to marriage. The cohabitor/noncohabitor difference becomes smaller as cohabitation becomes more widespread. If the number of cohabitors roughly equals the number of noncohabitors, differences in marriage stability between the groups disappear. In other words, cohabitation itself is not what influenced divorce, rather the social setting in which cohabitation occurs. As Graph 9.1 shows, the divorce rate varies by country between people who marry straightaway and those who cohabited. In Austria, Norway, both Germanys, and Latvia, it is about the same. In Spain, Italy, and Poland, it is much higher for people who cohabitated. In the other countries, it is a little higher for those who cohabitated. In general, if about 50 percent of the population cohabits, then married women who formerly cohabited have the same dissolution risk as those who did not cohabit.

■ **Graph 9.1**   **Relative Risk of Union Dissolution for Women in Different Types of Union, by Country**

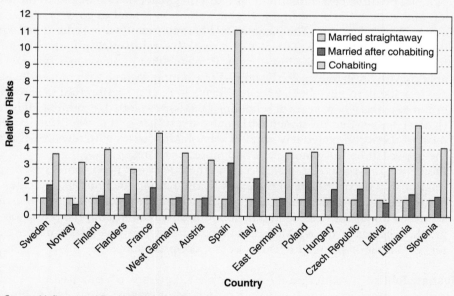

Source: Liefbroer and Dourleijn (2006, Figure 1)

How to Construct a Scattergram

STEP 1. Note the highest and lowest values (the range) of the two variables. Mark each axis with the name of the variable it will display and divide each axis into appropriate number ranges (graph paper is helpful).

STEP 2. For each case, find the value of each variable and mark the graph where the two values intersect. For example, you can make a scattergram of years of schooling by number of children. Look at the first case to see years of schooling (e.g., 12) and at the number of children (e.g., 3). Now go to the place on the graph where 12 for the "schooling" variable and 3 for the "number of children" variable intersect and put a dot for the case.

STEP 3. Continue until you have plotted all cases on the graph.

What Can You Learn from Scattergrams? A scattergram reveals three aspects of a bivariate relationship: form, direction, and precision.

- *Form.* Relationships between two variables can be independent, linear, or curvilinear. *Independence* or no relationship on a scattergram looks like a random scatter with no pattern. It can also be a straight line exactly parallel to the horizontal or vertical axis. A linear relationship shows up as a straight line that can be visualized in the middle of a clump of cases running from one corner to another. A curvilinear relationship (also called nonlinear) does not follow a line. On a scattergram, it may look as if a maze of cases forms a U curve, right side up or upside down, or an S curve.
- *Direction.* Linear relationships can have a positive or negative direction. The plot of a **positive relationship** looks like a diagonal line that begins in the lower left and goes to the upper right. Higher values on *X* tend to go with higher values on *Y,* and vice versa. The income and life expectancy example described a positive linear relationship. The plot of a **negative relationship** looks like a line from the upper left to the lower right. It means that higher values on one variable go with lower values on the other. For example, people with more education are less likely to have been arrested. If we look at a scattergram of data on a group of males where years of schooling (*X* axis) are plotted by number of arrests (*Y* axis), we see that most men with many arrests are in the lower right because most of them completed few years of school. Most cases with few arrests are in the upper left because most have had more schooling.
- *Precision.* Bivariate relationships vary in their degree of precision. A very precise relationship occurs when all the cases fit right along the line that indicates the relationship and direction. A relationship with little precision shows the cases scattered about the line. Thus, the amount of spread among the points on the graph indicates *precision*. Measures of association (discussed later in this chapter) get larger or stronger when there is more precision.

Bivariate Tables. A scattergram (see Figure 9.12) gives you a picture of a relationship if your data are at the interval or ratio level of measurement, but many variables are at the nominal or ordinal level with a few categories. Perhaps you are interested in colors of cars or trucks and their owners. Who drives bright red cars? You go to a large parking lot and you notice that about 13 percent of the 320 vehicles parked there are bright red. Car color, your dependent variable, is at the nominal level of measurement. In the United States, you find out that about 22 percent of the adult population is single, never married. If there is no relationship between the two variables, color of car and marital status (that is to say, they are independent), you would expect to find 22 percent of red car owners to be single. Of all single people, about 13 percent own red cars. This means there is nothing special about the color of a car and marital status. What if there is a statistical relationship between these two nominal-level variables? What if single people are more likely to own

positive relationship a connection between two variables such that as one increases the other variable also increases, and vice versa.

negative relationship a connection between two variables such that as one rises the other variable falls, and vice versa.

■ **Figure 9.12   Scattergram Examples**

Not Wrong   Almost Always   Sometimes

Forms of a Scattergram: Linear versus Non-Linear

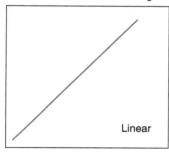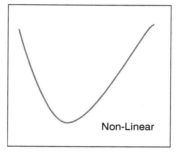

Linear   Non-Linear

Direction of Scattergram: Positive versus Negative

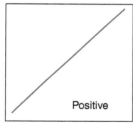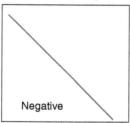

Positive   Negative

Precision of Scattergram: Precise Versus Imprecise

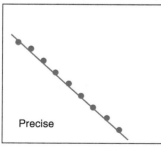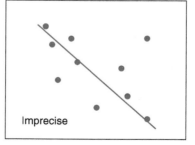

Precise   Imprecise

red cars? To test this hypothesis, you might go to a large parking lot and note the license plates of the cars and then see whether marital status is on official ownership records. Alternatively, you could survey people about their martial status and what color their vehicle is (if they own one).

Let say you had a small survey of 188 adults and found that 26 percent were single (close to but slightly higher than the national average) and about 15 percent of

Monty Rakusen/Digital Vision/Getty
Images Royalty Free

them owned red cars (close to what I found checking several times in three large parking lots). To see if there is a relationship, create a bivariate table.

What Is a Bivariate Table? Bivariate tables are are widely used. A bivariate contingency table presents the same information as a scattergram but in a more condensed form. Scattergrams are useful when your variables are ratio or interval or have many categories. Bivariate tables work with variables that have a few categories (two to five) and data at the nominal or ordinal level of measurement. If your data are at the interval or ratio level of measurement, you must first group the data into a few categories before putting them into a bivariate table.

To create a bivariate table, you use the process of **cross-tabulation** to create a **contingency table**. To do this, you organize cases in the table with two variables at the same time. The table is "contingent" because the cases in each category of one variable are distributed by, and contingent upon, categories of a second variable. As the table distributes cases into the categories of two or more variables it reveals how the cases, by category of one variable, depend upon the value of categories of other variables. Contingency tables can be expressed in terms of the count or raw frequency or percentages.

Table 9.1 is a raw count table of car color by martial status. Its cells contain a count of the cases. It is easy to make such a table, but interpreting a raw count table is difficult because the rows or columns can have different totals. You cannot easily discern the proportions. What is of real interest is the relative size of cells compared to other cells. This is why you nearly always convert the raw count table into a percentage table. Without a percentage table, you can be easily misled if the rows or columns have unequal numbers of cases. By using percentages, you adjust for unequal totals and standardize information. For example, if the numbers in two cells of the table indicate that counts of red car ownership among singles and nonsingles are 16 and 14, respectively, you cannot compare them because the number of single and nonsingle people is unequal. You must first standardize the information based on the total. This makes comparison possible. The easiest way to do this is to use percentages.

You can percentage a contingency table in three ways: by row, by column, and for the total. The first two are often used and show relationships. The last way is almost never used and almost impossible to interpret. Which is best? Percentaging by row or column can be appropriate; it depends on the question you want to answer with the table. It also depends on placement of your independent and dependent variables in a table. Always remember, columns go across the top, and rows are along the side.

The mechanics of how to percentage tables are as follows: To calculate column percentages, compute the percentage for cases in each cell (small box in the center part of a table) based on the column total (located at the bottom of the column). The first column total is 50 (there are 50 single people), and the first cell of that column is 16 (there are 16 red car owners who are single). The percentage is 16/56 = 0.32 or 32.0 percent. Now let look at 14 red car owners who are not single. There are 138

cross-tabulation placing two variables in a table at the same time allows you to see how cases that have values on one variable align with values on a second variable for those same cases.

contingency table a table with two or more variables that have been cross-tabulated.

■ Table 9.1   Red Car Ownership and Martial Status, Raw Count Table

Color of Car	Single	Not Single	Total
Red	16	14	30
Other	34	124	158
Total	50	138	188

■ Table 9.2   Red Car Ownership and Martial Status, Column Percent Table

Color of Car	Single (%)	Not Single (%)	Total (%)
Red	32.0	10.1	16.0
Other	68.0	189.9	84
Total (*N*)	100 (50)	100 (138)	100 (188)

nonsingle people. The red car owners are 14/138 or 10.1 percent. By comparing the two percentages, you see that 32 percent is almost three times larger than 10.1 percent. This tells you that single people are more likely to own a red car than a non-single people (see Table 9.2).

Computing row percentages is a similar process (see Table 9.3). To compute the percentage of each cell, take the number of cases in the cell as a percentage of the row total (total is on the right side). Using the same cell with 16 in it (single and own a red car), you want to know what percentage it is of the row total of 30 (red car owners). It is 16/30 = 0.533 = 53.3 percent. This tells you that a little over one-half the people who own red cars are single. Percentaging by row or column gives different percentages for a cell unless the row totals are the same.

Reading a Percentaged Table. Once you understand how to make a table, reading it and figuring out what it tells you are easier. To read a table, first look at the title, the variable labels, and any background information. Next, look at the direction in which percentages have been computed—in rows or columns. Notice that Tables 9.1 through 9.3 share much the same title because the same variables are used. Many titles do not indicate the direction of percentages. Some researchers use abbreviated tables that omit the 100 percent total. This can create confusion. It is best to include all the parts of a table with clear labels.

The row or column percentages allow you to address different questions. The column percentage table answers the question, Among single people, what percentage own a red car? In Table 9.2 you saw that nearly 1 in 3 single people own a red car. The row percentage table addresses the question, Among red car owners, what percentage of them are single? In Table 9.3 you saw that just over one-half of all red car owners are single. The first question is about car colors among people of different martial status. The second question is about the martial status of the owners of red cars. These are similar but different questions. Keeping them straight is important. Each question that a table can answer has practical uses. Knowing that about 1 in 3 single people drive red cars is useful to a car salesperson; it tells the salesperson that there is about a 1 in 3 chance that a single customer will be attracted to a red car. Knowing that over half of all red car drivers are single is helpful to a company selling car finish protection products. The company can market a red car finish products to singles, since over half of the potential customers would be single.

Your hypothesis guides you to look at row or column percentages. At first, you might want to calculate percentages both ways and practice interpreting what each says. If your hypothesis is "a person's marital status influences his or her choice of car color," place marital status as the column variable, then percent by column. You want to percentage in the same direction as your independent variable. When you

■ Table 9.3   Red Car Ownership and Martial Status, Row Percent Table

Color of Car	Single (%)	Not Single (%)	Total (*N*)
Red	53.3	46.7	100 (30)
Other	21.5	78.5	100 (158)
Total	26.6	73.4	100 (188)

put the independent variable in the column, then calculate percent by column. There is no "industry standard" for putting independent and dependent variables as row or column. Most researchers place the independent variable as the column and percentage by column, but a large minority put the independent variable as the row and percentage by row.

To read a percentage table and make comparisons, you make the comparisons in the opposite direction from that in which percentages are computed. This sounds complex, but it means the following: Compare across the rows if a table has column percents, and compare up and down in columns if the table has row percentages. For example, in the table with row percentages (Table 9.3), compare columns or martial status groups. In the table with column percentages (Table 9.2), compare across rows. About one-half of red car owners are single, and about 1 in 5 people who own a nonred cars is single. For example, one-third of single people own red cars and 10 percent of nonsingle people own red cars.

With a little practice, you will quickly be able to spot a statistical relationship in a percentage table. If there is no relationship among variables in a table, the cell percentages look equal across all rows or columns. You can only determine the direction of a relationship (positive/negative) if the data are ordinal or if the data are interval/ratio and have been grouped to make them ordinal. Normal data have no direction. If both variables are ordinal, a table can reveal a linear relationship and determine its direction. A linear relationship among variables looks like larger percentages in the diagonal cells. If it is a curvilinear relationship, the largest percentages form a curve pattern across cells. For example, the largest cells might be the upper right, the bottom middle, and the upper left. It is easiest to see a relationship in a moderate-sized table (9 to 16 cells), where most cells have some cases (at least five cases are recommended) and the relationship is strong and precise.

You can use scattergram reading principles to see a relationship in a percentage table. Imagine a scattergram divided into 12 equal-sized sections. The cases in each section correspond to the number of cases in the cells of a table superimposed onto the scattergram. The table is a condensed form of the scattergram. The bivariate relationship line in a scattergram corresponds to the diagonal cells in a percentaged table. A easy and simple way to see strong relationships in percentage tables is to circle the biggest percentage in each row (for row-percentaged tables) or column (for column-percentaged tables). Does a diagonal line appear?

Look at a Table 9.4, which examines education level and TV watching. Table 9.4 shows that highly educated people watch TV fewer hours per day than less educated people. Among those who did not finish high school, 18.9 percent watch TV eight hours or more; none of those with graduate degrees watch that much TV. The relationship is negative and linear. To see this relationship, try circling the biggest per-

■ **Table 9.4**   General Social Survey 2004, Hours of TV Watching per Day by Educational Degree

| Daily TV Watching | Amount of Education | | | | | |
	Less than High School (%)	High School (%)	Some College (%)	4-yr College Degree (%)	Graduate Degree (%)	Total (%)
8+ hours	18.9	7.8	3.8	4.3	0	7.5
5–7 hours	12.6	7.6	7.6	4.3	4.3	7.3
3–4 hours	36.0	30.0	26.6	20.6	18.5	27.8
1–2 hours	29.7	49.4	59.5	58.9	66.3	51.1
None	2.7	5.3	2.5	12.1	10.9	6.3
Total	100	100	100	100	100	100
(*N*)	(111)	(476)	79	141	(92)	(899)

■ Table 9.5   General Social Survey 2004, Hours of TV Watching per Day by Age

| Daily TV Watching | Age | | | | | |
	Under 30 (%)	30–40 (%)	41–50 (%)	51–65 (%)	66+ (%)	Total (%)
8+ hours	6.7	7.1	2.9	7.9	(13.5)	7.4
5–7 hours	9.6	4.7	5.3	6.9	(12.0)	7.4
3–4 hours	24.7	24.2	26.5	28.1	(39.1)	27.8
1–2 hours	51.7	53.6	(58.8)	(54.2)	32.3	51.3
None	(7.3)	(10.4)	6.5	3.0	3.0	6.3
Total	100	100	100	100	100	100
(N)	(178)	(211)	(170)	(203)	(133)	(895)

centage in each row. If the difference is small (under 6 percent), circle the two biggest cells. To see a positive relationship, look at hours of TV watching by age (Table 9.5).

Measures of Association. A measure of association condenses information about a bivariate relations into a single number. It expresses the strength, and often the direction, of a relationship. There are many measures of association (see Figure 9.13). The correct one depends on the level of measurement in your data. Many are called by letters of the Greek alphabet: lambda, gamma, tau, chi (squared), and rho. The emphasis here is on interpreting the measures, not on their calculation. To understand them fully, you should complete a beginning statistics course.

If a measure of association is zero, it indicates statistical independence. If it is a large nonzero number, it indicates a relationship. A very strong relationship between two variables means you would make few errors predicting a dependent variable based on knowing the independent variable. In short, knowing the independent variable causes a big reduction in prediction errors. Figure 9.13 describes six commonly used bivariate measures of association. Most range from −1 to +1, with negative numbers indicating a negative relationship and positive numbers a positive relationship. A measure of 1.0 means a 100 percent reduction in errors, or perfect prediction (see Figure 9.14).

The measures of association give you more precise information about the strength of relationships than you get by just looking at percentage tables. The two tables of TV watching categories with educational degree and age looked similar. Comparing the two gammas, you see that the negative relationship of education degree by TV watching has a stronger gamma (−0.384) than the positive relationship of TV watching with age (0.163).

■ Figure 9.13   Six Measures of Association

Measure	Greek Symbol	Type of Data	Highest Association	Independence
Cramer's V		Nominal	1.0	0
Lambda	λ	Nominal	1.0	0
Gamma	γ	Ordinal	+1.0, −1.0	0
Tau (Kendall's)	τ	Ordinal	+1.0, −1.0	0
Rho	ρ	Interval, ratio	+1.0, −1.0	0
Chi-square	χ^2	Nominal, ordinal	Infinity	0

■ **Figure 9.14** Strength of Measures of Association

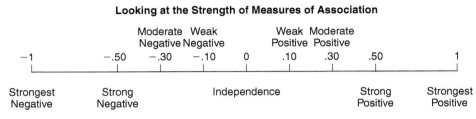

Looking at the Strength of Measures of Association

Here are measures of association for data you have seen in this chapter:

• The table with marital status and car color has two nominal-level variables. Cramer's V = .264

• The scattergram of education years by TV watching hours has two ratio-level variables. Rho = −.293

• The table of education degree by TV watching categories has two ordinal-level variables. Gamma = .384

• The table of age by TV watching categories has two ordinal-level variables. Gamma = +.163

Results with More than Two Variables

Statistical Control. Showing an association between two variables is helpful, but it is not sufficient to say that an independent variable *causes* a dependent variable. Recall that to say "cause" in addition to temporal order and association, you must eliminate alternative explanations—explanations that can make the hypothesized relationship spurious (see the definition of *spurious* in Chapter 2). Experimental researchers control for possible alternatives by choosing a research design that physically reduces problems that threaten internal validity (discussed in Chapter 7).

Recall from Chapter 2 that spurious results occur when a third variable (for an alternative explanation) is the true cause. Failure to consider such a variable means that what appears to be a bivariate relationship could be a mirage or false. Experimenters control for alternative explanations by improving internal validity. Nonexperimental researchers use control variables and statistical techniques. To use the statistical techniques, they anticipate and measure possible alternative explanations. If they fail to consider and measure the alternative explanations with **control variables**, they cannot test whether a relationship they discover is likely to be real or spurious.

To find out whether a bivariate relationship is spurious, you examine control variables using multivariate tables and statistics. Another reason for using multivariate statistics is to see the relative impact of several independent variables simultaneously on a dependent variable. Sometimes two independent variables both influence the same dependent variable, and you want to find out which of them is has a bigger impact.

Let us return to the example of single people and red cars. Single, never married people are usually younger than married or previously married people. In fact, the mean age of single people is 33.1 years old whereas for nonsingle people the mean is 45.57 years old. Younger people like red cars (see Table 9.6). Over one-third of

control variables variables measured in nonexperimental research studies that represent alternative explanations for a causal relationship.

■ **Table 9.6** Color of Car by Age (percentaged by column)

Color of Car	Under 30 Years (%)	30 to 60 Years Old (%)	Over 60 Years Old (%)	Total (%)
Red car	34.6	10.5	3.2	16.0
Other color	65.4	89.5	96.8	84.9
Total (N)	100 (52)	100 (105)	100 (31)	100 (188)

Tips for the Wise Consumer Noticing Statistical Significance

Do not let a maze of numbers, tables, charts, and statistics intimidate you when you look at the results section in a quantitative research report. Remember, even if the author is using advanced statistics that are beyond what you have learned, he or she is only documenting what is in the data. Most advanced statistical techniques use a form of statistical significance that tells you which variables or parts of the results are most important. This is how researchers identify which of many variables are most powerful. Many authors use superscripts or asterisks to indicate level of statistical significance, such as one * for .05 level, ** for .01

level, and *** for .001 level. You can see them described in a key or footnote. Other times they use the symbol p for probability. They may give you something such as $p > .05$. This indicates that p is greater than the .05 level of statistical significance. When you see a list of variables and some of the variables have a symbol or asterisks, you can interpret those as the most influential ones (i.e., ones with the biggest impact on the dependent variable). Many researchers try to explain the meaning of their results in simple language, but this not always easy to do because the results often include advanced statistical ideas and terms.

young people own a red car, versus 10 percent of the middle-aged and about 3 percent of older people.

Does age or being single have a stronger impact on wanting a red colored car? We can compare the two Cramer's V numbers, for color of car by age $V = .323$, for marital status by color of car $V = .264$. These are relatively close. Another way to check is to use age as a control variable. To use it as a control variable, we can create three tables, one for each age group. This lets us look at the relationship of marital status on car color among the people in each age group. If it is equally strong within each age group, then age group is not important. If it does not appear any longer, then age must be the most important factor. (See Tables 9.7a through 9.7c.)

■ Table 9.7a   People under Age 30 Only

Car Color	Single (%)	Not Single (%)	Total (%)
Red car	77.8	44.1	55.8
Other color	22.2	55.9	44.2
Total (N)	100 (18)	100 (34)	100 (52)

Cramer's $V = .322$

■ Table 9.7b   People Age 30–60

Car Color	Single (%)	Not Single (%)	Total (%)
Red car	18.25	13.85	14.35
Other color	81.85	86.25	85.75
Total (N)	100 (11)	100 (94)	100 (105)

Cramer's $V = .038$

■ Table 9.7c   People over Age 60

Car Color	Single (%)	Not Single (%)	Total (%)
Red car	0	20.0	19.4
Other color	100	80.0	80.6
Total (N)	100 (1)	100 (30)	100 (31)

Cramers $V = .089$

A red car is more popular for people under 30 years old than older people, and the impact of being single on wanting a red car is strong for people under 30 years old. Over three-fourths of single people under 30 own a red car. Being single makes little difference in red car ownership among people over 30. This suggests that of the two factors, age and marital status are working together, with age being more important. Had we seen no relationship in the under 30 table as for the other two age groups, this would suggest that the relationship between marital status and car color was spurious. If the martial status–car color relationship were nonspurious, it would persist even after we considered control variables. Three-variable percentage tables can reveal a lot, but looking at many of them can become complex, and it is difficult to go much beyond looking at three variables at once.

Multiple Regression Analysis. One of the most widely used statistical techniques for nonexperimental data analysis in professional research reports is multiple regression. It is a powerful technique that takes the idea of statistical control to a higher level. The calculation of multiple regression is beyond the level of this book, but its results are not difficult to read or interpret. It is only for interval- and ratio-level data. Many statistics computer programs produce multiple regression results. The power of multiple regression is an ability to control for many variables simultaneously.

Multiple regression results tell you two things:

1. R-squared (R^2) or the percentage of prediction accuracy. It indicates reduced errors when predicting the dependent variable based on information from the independent variables. With several independent variables, you might account for, or explain, a large percentage of variation in a dependent variable. For example, an R^2 of .50 means that knowing the independent and control variables improves the accuracy of predicting the dependent variable by 50 percent. In short, you would make half as many errors as you would without knowing the independent variables. An R^2 of .20 is considered very good in professional social science. It means that independent variables explain 20 percent of change in the dependent variable. The R^2 size may not seem impressive, but we judge its size not based on 100 percent perfect prediction, rather on improvement over zero.

2. Multiple regression results tell you the direction and numerical size of each independent variable's impact on a dependent variable. Multiple regression analysis may indicate how five independent variables simultaneously affect a dependent variable, with all variables controlling for the effects of one another. This is especially valuable for testing theories that state that multiple independent variables cause one dependent variable. Effects on a dependent variable are measured indicated by a standardized regression coefficient, symbolized by the Greek letter beta (β). The interpretation of β is similar to a correlation coefficient, r. In fact, for a multiple regression with only two variables, the beta coefficient equals the r correlation coefficient. A beta coefficient tells you the size and direction of effects.

Perhaps you have a dependent variable, family income (ratio level), and four independent variables: age, years of schooling, hours worked, and hours of TV watched each day. Which one is most important for predicting income? You may say schooling, but what about the other variables? Multiple regression results show that schooling, age, and hours worked each have large positive effects. Watching TV has a small and negative effect. Combined, all the independent variables together are 21.5 percent accurate in predicting a person's family income (see Table 9.8). Another way to say this is that for U.S. adults, only knowing four facts about them allows you to predict their family income level and be correct 1 in 5 times. One in five is a lot better than zero.

■ Table 9.8 Multiple Regression of Family Income (Dependent Variable) with Education Level, Age, Hours Worked per Week, and Hours of TV Watching per Day for Adults Age 18–65

Independent Variable	Beta Coefficient
Years of schooling	.306
Age	.242
Hours worked	.169
Daily hours watch TV	−.064

(Based on GSS 2004 data)

GOING BEYOND DESCRIPTION: INFERENTIAL STATISTICS

In most studies, you want to move beyond just describing the data to test hypotheses and say whether results from sample data hold true in a population. You also need to decide whether differences in results (e.g., between the mean scores of two groups) really indicate that a strong relationship among variables exists. Inferential statistics uses probability theory to allow you to test hypotheses, permit inferences from a sample to the population, and to evaluate the strength of relationships among variables. In Chapter 4 you encountered probability sampling. Inferential statistics assumes you have a random sample and are a precise way to talk about how confident you can be when inferring from sample results to the population.

You may have heard about "statistical significance" or results "significant at the .05 level." These are aspects of inferential statistics. They are a precise way to decide whether to accept or to reject a null hypothesis (you encountered the null hypothesis in Chapter 2). There are many statistical "tests" such as a t test or F tests. These "tests" use statistical significance to help you decide whether a hypothesis is likely to be true or false, or supported by the data with a lot of confidence or not.

Statistical Significance

Statistical significance indicates the probability of finding a relationship in sample data when there is none in the population. Probability samples involve a random process, so it is possible that sample results differ from a population parameter. You can estimate the odds that sample results are due to chance factors of random sampling. Statistical significance uses probability theory and specific statistical tests to tell you whether random error could produce the results (e.g., an association,

statistical significance a way to determine how likely sample results could be due to random processes.

■ Figure 9.15 Looking at Statistical Significance

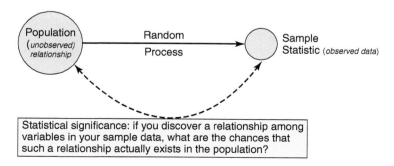

Statistical significance: if you discover a relationship among variables in your sample data, what are the chances that such a relationship actually exists in the population?

regression coefficients). If a random process did not produce the results, you can be more confident that the results reflect a real relationship in the population.

Statistical significance can only tell you what is likely. It cannot prove anything with absolute certainty. It builds on probability theory and tells that particular outcomes are more or less probable. Statistical significance is *not* the same as practical, substantive, or theoretical significance. To determine practical, substantive, or theoretical significance you use other criteria in addition to statistical processes. A relationship can have statistical significance but be theoretically meaningless or trivial. For example, two variables may have a statistically significant association with no logical connection between them (e.g., length of fingernails and ability to speak French). The mathematics and calculations of statistical significance is beyond the level of this book, but reading and interpreting statistical significance is not difficult.

Levels of Significance

Computer programs quickly calculate statistical significance and produce a probability estimates. These tell you whether a relationship among variables is likely to be due to chance alone. If it is not likely to be due to chance, then a real relationship is likely in the population. If a relationship has a 5 percent or higher chance of being due to a random process, we say it is not statistically significant. In other words, only if the odds are 5 percent or smaller that it is due to chance do we call a relationship statistically significant.

Computer programs produce specific probabilities, and researchers express statistical significance in terms of a few levels (e.g., a test is statistically significant at a specific level) rather than giving the specific probability. The **level of statistical significance** tells you likelihood that results are due to chance factors—that is, that a relationship appears in the sample when there is none in the population. If results are statistically significant, it is at one of three levels:

.05 level
.01 level
.001 level

To say that results are significant at the 0.05 level means the following:

- Results like these are due to chance factors only 5 in 100 times.
- There is a 95 percent chance that the sample results are not due to chance factors alone but reflect the population accurately.
- The odds of such results based on chance alone are .05, or 5 percent.
- One can be 95 percent confident that the results are due to a real relationship in the population, not chance factors.

These all say the same thing in different ways. They may sound like a discussion of sampling distributions. This is no accident. Both use probability theory. In both, you link sample data to a population. Probability theory lets us predict what is likely to happen in the long run over many events. It does not predict for a specific situation. We cannot know for certain that a relationship we find in a particular sample is what occurs in the population. However, we can state it in probability terms—how likely it is that the sample shows one thing whereas something else is true in the population.

You may ask, Why use the .05 level? It means a 5 percent chance that randomness could cause the results. Why not use a more certain standard—for example, 1 in 1000? This gives a smaller chance that randomness versus a true relationship caused the results. The simple answer is that the scientific community has informally agreed to use .05 as a "rule of thumb" for most purposes. Being 95 percent confident of results is the accepted standard for explaining the social world. In short, it is "good enough" to take seriously. However, in some cases you may want to be even more sure that results are not due to chance.

level of statistical significance
a simplified way to indicate the statistical significance of a relationship.

Making It Practical **Is There a Significant Difference by Gender?**

Let us say you have sample data showing that college men and women differ in how many hours they study. Men study an average of 14.5 hours a week and women 15.9 hours per week. Is the result due to an unusual sample? If we had the entire sample, would we see that men and women really do not differ, or does the result reflect a true difference in the population? We can conduct a statistical test of differences between two means (called a *t*-test) and check its statistical significance. If the difference between means (based on sample size, degree of variability, as well as the size of the difference) is statistically significant at the .05 level or higher, we can say that there is a real gender difference in the population. Remember the age and red car preference? We can use statistical significance to see how likely it is that the gamma between age and red car ownership is due to chance. The gamma is statistically significant at the .001 level. In other words, assuming random sample, you can say

with 99.9 percent confidence that based on your data there is a real age difference in red car owners in the population.

Rhoda Sidney/The Image Works

There is a logical dilemma about trying to be as accurate as possible. If you demand a very high standard, such as 1 in 1000, you will only be wrong 1 in 1000 times in saying a relationship exists in the population when, in reality, there is none. However, you are increasing the chances that you are making the opposite type of mistake—saying there is no relationship in the population when in reality one exists. In other words, there are two types of mistakes or errors: false positives and false negatives. A false positive is saying something is true or present when in reality it is not. A false negative is saying something is false or not there when in reality it is. Ideally, you do not want to make either type of mistake. The dilemma is that as you reduce the odds of avoiding a false positive, you increase the odds of a false negative. In other words, there is a trade-off.

This dilemma with false positives and false negative appears outside research settings. In fact, the term *false positive* comes from medical settings. If you go in for a cancer test, it can be accurate, a false positive, or a false negative. A false positive is a mistake saying you have cancer when you really do not. A false negative means a test says you are cancer free but you really have cancer. Another example is a jury trial. A jury can err by deciding that an accused person is guilty when in fact he or she is innocent (false positive), or err by deciding that a person is innocent when in fact he or she is guilty (false negative). The jury does not want to make either error. It does not want to jail the innocent or to free the guilty.

We can combine the ideas of statistical significance and the two types of error (false positive or false negative). If you are overly cautious and set a high level of significance (.0001), you are likely to make a false negative error—you are likely to say no relationship exists but there is really one. You may falsely accept the null hypothesis when there is a relationship in the population. The formal name for this is a **Type II error.** By contrast, you may be a risk-taker and set a low level of significance, such as .10. You say there is a relationship even if two events could occur by chance 1 in 10 times. You are likely to make a false negative error; that is, say that a causal relationship exists when in fact random factors (e.g., random sampling error) is the reason. You may falsely reject the null hypothesis when

Type II error The error of falsely accepting a null hypotheses.

■ Table 9.9   Type I and Type II Errors

What You Say Is Happening Based on Your Sample Data	What Is Actually Happening in the Population	
	No Relationship	A Relationship Exists
No Relationship	No Error	Type II Error (false negative)
A Relationship Exists	Type I Error (false positive)	No Error

there is actually no relationship. The formal name for this is a **Type I error**. The rule of thumb of a .05 level is a compromise between Type I and Type II errors (see Table 9.9).

Inferential statistics let you say, with specific degrees of certainty, that sample results are likely to be true in a population. If a relationship is statistically significant at the .05 level, you can say that the sample results are probably not due to chance factors. Indeed, there is a 95 percent chance that a true relationship is in the population (or the social world to which you want to generalize). Remember, to use inferential statistics, your data must be from a random sample. Another limitation is that nonsampling errors (e.g., a poor sampling frame or a poorly designed measure) are not considered. Do not be fooled into thinking that statistical tests offer simple, final answers. Many computer programs produce inferential and descriptive statistics (see Making It Practical: Statistical Programs on Computers: User Beware).

Type I error the error of falsely rejecting a null hypotheses.

Making It Practical   **Statistical Programs on Computers: User Beware**

Almost every social researcher calculates statistics using a computer program. Statistics are even produced by basic spreadsheet programs, such as Microsoft Excel®. Unfortunately, spreadsheets were designed for accounting and bookkeeping functions. Their statistics tend to be clumsy and limited. Dozens of computer programs have been designed for calculating statistics for researchers. The marketplace can be confusing to a beginner, for products evolve rapidly with changing computer technology. In recent years, the software has become less demanding for users. The most popular programs in the social sciences are *Minitab*®, Microcase®, and SPSS® (Statistical Package for the Social Sciences). Others include SAS® (Statistical Analysis System), STATISTICA® by StratSoft, and Strata®. Many began as simple, low-cost programs for research purposes.

The most widely used computer program for statistics in the social sciences is SPSS. Its advantages are that social researchers used it extensively for almost four

decades, it includes many ways to manipulate quantitative data, and it contains most statistical measures. A disadvantage is that it can take a long time to learn because of its many options and complex statistics. Also, it can be expensive to purchase unless the user gets an inexpensive, "stripped down" student version included with a textbook or workbook.

As computer technology makes using a statistics program easier and programs quickly produce a variety of statistics, there is an increased danger that people might use the programs without understanding the statistical results. If someone does not really understand the statistics, he or she might violate basic assumptions required by a statistical procedure, use the statistics improperly, and produce results that are total nonsense but that look very technically sophisticated. To avoid such mistakes, you need to have one or more courses in statistics or have someone who knows the statistics review the statistical results that the computer program produces.

WHAT HAVE YOU LEARNED?

In this chapter, you learned about organizing quantitative data for analysis. You also learned how to organize data into charts or tables or summarize them with statistical measures. You can describe results, test hypotheses, and answer research questions with univariate or bivariate statistics. You can test hypotheses with bivariate analysis, but because bivariate relationships might be spurious, you may wish to use control variables and multivariate analysis. You also learned some basics about inferential statistics.

Beginning researchers sometimes feel their results must support a hypothesis. Keep in mind that *there is nothing wrong with rejecting a hypothesis*. The goal of scientific research is to produce knowledge that truly reflects the social world, not to defend an idea or hypothesis. Hypotheses are predictions about relationships based on limited knowledge, so we need to test them. Excellent-quality research can find that a hypothesis is wrong, and poor-quality research can support a hypothesis. Good research depends on high-quality methodology, not on supporting a specific hypothesis.

As you do research, you want to avoid making errors about inferences from data to the social world. Errors can enter into the research process and affect results at many places: research design, measurement, data collection, coding, calculating statistics and constructing tables, or interpreting results. Even if you design, measure, collect, code, and calculate without error, you must properly interpret the tables, charts, and statistics. Finally, you need to answer the question, What does it all mean? The only way to assign meaning to facts, charts, tables, and statistics is to use some type of theory. You cannot answer research questions with data, tables, or computer output alone. The facts cannot speak for themselves. As a researcher, you must return to theory, concepts, relationships, assumptions, and theoretical definitions to give the data results substantive meaning.

Before we leave our discussion of quantitative research, there is one last issue. Journalists, politicians, and others increasingly use statistical results to make a point or bolster an argument. This has not produced greater accuracy and information in public debate. More often, it has increased confusion and made it more important to know what statistics can and cannot do. The cliché that you can prove anything with statistics is false; however, people can and do *misuse* statistics. Through ignorance or conscious deceit, some people use statistics to manipulate others. The best way to protect yourself from being misled by statistics is not to ignore them but to understand the research process and statistics, think about what you hear, and ask questions.

We turn next to qualitative research. The logic and purpose of qualitative research differ from those of the quantitative approach of the past chapters. Qualitative research is less concerned with numbers, hypotheses, and causality and more concerned with words, norms and values, and meaning.

KEY TERMS

APPLYING WHAT YOU'VE LEARNED

Activity 1

Quantitative data analysis builds on the arithmetic that you learned in elementary school and continued to learn about in later mathematics classes. People who love numbers tend to like this aspect of social research; those who have a phobia of numbers try to avoid this aspect of research. Today, computers do the "grunt work" of calculations. This makes our lives easier but means we can quickly lose touch of what is happening to the numbers. Let us explore calculations the old-fashioned way that everyone can appreciate. As you learned in this chapter, variation (or spread or dispersion of values/scores) is a critical aspect in quantitative data. The standard deviation is the common way to measure it, but the formula for it looks frightening at first. This is especially true when statisticians use Greek letters to symbolize its parts. This might have made sense back when most high school and college students knew some Greek, it seems strange today unless you are from Greece. Also, some people get "freaked out" by square roots. What the formula says in words is, The standard deviation = the square root of the "variance" in a set of scores. You get the variance by subtracting each score from the mean and then squaring that result. You must add together all the squared results and divide the total by the number of cases you have to get the variance. Recall that the mean is the total divided by the number of scores. All the steps sound complex as words. This is why we usually write it out as a formula with symbols (see Figure 9.7 for the square root formula). Now try to calculate the square root of the following four sets of scores. Each is size of eight pieces of fruit. For simplicity, use a hand calculator for taking square roots.

Apples: 5 6 4 7 8 10 7 5
Bananas: 9 10 11 8 13 12 11 9
Cherries: 7 2 4 3 2 6 3 3
Dates: 2 3 2 1 2 4 5 4

What is the mean and variance for each fruit? What is the standard deviation of each? Which fruit has the greatest and the least amount of variation or dispersion?

Activity 2

Data analysis means looking for patterns in a set of numbers. The numbers represent some aspect of the social world. You can put them into a visual representation (pie charts, histograms, scattergrams) or percent tables to see such patterns. Look at the following table on supporting/opposing a law that would forbid abortions.

Antiabortion Law	MEN (%)	WOMEN (%)
Support	44	33
Mixed	22	36
Oppose	<u>34</u>	<u>31</u>
TOTAL	100	100

Answer the following questions:

a. Which gender shows strongest support for a law against abortion?
b. Which gender shows strongest opposition to a law against abortion?
c. Is the male:female percent difference, or gender gap, greater in support or opposition?
d. What is the more prominent position for the women?

Acitivity 3

You usually want to compare results with something else. Let's look at one chart in one study. First, locate the following article: "Race and Environmental Voting in the U.S, Congress," Paul Mohai and David Kershner, *Social Science Quarterly* (2002), vol. 83, pp. 167–189. Look at the histogram on page 181 (Figure 4). You see eight bars or lines of different lengths, and the bars come in two shades. A note at the bottom says, "medium dark bar = Liberal Score and very dark bar = Environmental Score." Along the left side, it says Percentage Support. The higher the bar, the greater the support—support is the votes by representatives in the U.S. Congress. At the bottom each bar has a label: South or Outside the South, indicating geographic location of states in the United States, and CBC or Non-CBC (CBC = Congressional Black Caucus). All African Americans are members of the CBC, and only African Americans belong, so this is an indicator of race. You are shown two dependent variables: percent support for liberal social issues, and percent support for environmental issues, and two independent variables: being a member of the CBC or not, and being from a Southern or non-Southern state. In sum, you have information about four variables in just few bars of different lengths. Now answer these questions about the results:

a. Which geographic and racial group showed the most support for environmental issues?
b. Which geographic and racial group showed the least support for environmental issues?

c. Did the same people with most support on liberal social issues also show most support environmental issues?

Activity 4

Z-scores frighten many people at first, but once you understand them, you will find them useful and easy to calculate. They are useful in many situations. Read the following, and calculate z-scores for the women in the two companies. Then answer the question.

Samatha has been working at Company X for 10 years as the Human Resources manager. She went to school with Yilin, who has had the same position job at Company Y for the same amount of time. The companies are a similar size and are located in different cities, but the cities have a similar cost of living. Samantha and Yilin got together at a class reunion, and Samantha said she made $65,000 and was satisfied with that salary. Yilin said she also made $65,000 but complained and felt underpaid. The mean manager salary at Company X is $70,000 with a standard deviation of $5,000. At Company Y, the mean manager salary is $72,000 and the standard deviation is $1000. What would Yilin be earning if she made a comparable amount (that is, she had the same z-score) as Samantha?

REFERENCES

Liefbroer, Aart C., and Edith Dourleijn. 2006. "Unmarried Cohabitation and Union Stability: Testing the Role of Diffusion Using Data From 16 European Countries." *Demography* 43:203–221.

Luker, Kristin. 1997. *Dubious Conceptions: The Politics of Teenage Pregnancy*. Cambridge, MA: Harvard University Press.

Observing People in Natural Settings

Digital Vision/Alamy Royalty Free

Many occupations involve "emotion work." The "work" is labor or effort you expend, usually in return for pay. The "emotion" refers to your feelings, or at least a public display of inner feelings. In emotion work, you are required or expected to show certain feelings as part of a job. Your job is to display certain emotions, and you may have to deny, suppress, or hide your own true feelings. In the travel, hospitality, and entertainment industries; in nursing, social service, and counseling fields; in grief counseling and funeral services; and in many sales jobs a large part of "doing a good job" is to display emotions; emotions help other people to experience certain feelings. Typically, jobs require you to be cheerful, friendly, positive, upbeat, empathetic, or concerned and caring. An employer may have written rules about your emotion work, and supervisors may monitor and enforce proper emotional displays/attitudes. Of course, we may do a kind of emotion work when we negotiate with friends or intimate partners, get along with coworkers, or go take part in daily events. There is a difference when emotion work is not something you decide to do on your own but is required as part of a job. In the *Managed Heart,* Arlie Hochschild (1983) outlined emotional labor and described how she went about studying it among airline attendants. She and others learned that employees put forth serious effort to display a friendly smile and cheerful manner. They did this even when they felt tired or depressed or were thinking about a serious personal, family, or work problem. Emotion work drains people physically and emotionally. Acting pleasant, warm, and comforting toward demanding clients or customers can extract a high personal toll, especially when the customers or clients are hostile, rude, or obnoxious. Some businesses, such as Disneyland, carefully plan, manage, and coordinate staff members' emotion work as a central part of creating a total customer experience (Van Maanan 1991). To study emotion work, researchers gathered first-hand qualitative information by directly participating and observing in natural work settings (i.e., they performed field work). They got a job that required them to do emotion work themselves. They spent many hours in daily contact, both closely observing and talking with people whose jobs involved a lot of emotion work. The field research method is especially well suited for studying emotion work.

WHAT IS FIELD RESEARCH?

Unlike the quantitative research discussed in previous chapters, field research produces qualitative data and involves a different approach to doing research. Field researchers directly observe and participate in a natural social setting. Actually, there are several kinds of field research, including ethnography, participant-observation research, informal "depth" interviews, and focus groups.

If you have heard about field research, it may sound like you simply hang out with a group of people who are unlike you. Maybe it sounds easy. In field research, there are no statistics or abstract deductive hypotheses. You observe a setting and may chat informally with the people you are studying. Unlike quantitative research, you personally engage in direct, face-to-face social interaction with "real people" in a natural setting. Professional researchers may devote months or years to studying people in a setting. They learn about the daily activities, life histories, hobbies and interests, habits, hopes, fears, and dreams of the people they study. Meeting new people and discovering new social worlds can be fun. It can also be tedious, time consuming, emotionally draining, and sometimes physically dangerous.

Field research is ideal for examining the micro-level social world and everyday interactions of ordinary people "up close." It is best suited for studying issues (e.g., classroom behavior, street gangs) that are difficult to study using other methods (e.g., surveys, experiments). In field research, you can get a close-up look and develop insights that may be impossible with other methods. Many areas use field research, such as anthropology, education, health care, marketing, hospitality-tourism, human service delivery, recreation, and criminal justice. Field researchers have explored a wide range of social settings, subcultures, and aspects of social life (see Figure 10.1). Students in my classes conducted successful short-term, small-scale field research studies in a barbershop, beauty parlor, daycare center, bakery, bingo parlor, bowling alley, church, coffee shop, laundromat, police dispatch office, fast food restaurant, elementary school classroom, nursing home, tattoo parlor, gay bar, bridal shop, hospital waiting room, and athletic weight room, among other places.

Ethnography

A major type of field research, ethnography, comes from cultural anthropology. *Ethno* means "people" or "folk," and *graphy* means "to describe something." The purpose of **ethnography** is to provide a detailed description and up-close understanding of a way of life from the standpoint of its natives/members/insiders. Ethnography builds on the idea that humans live in cultures, from micro-cultures (a single family or small friendship group) to macro-cultures (entire societies or world regions). We continuously learn, use, and modify cultural knowledge. Cultural knowledge has two parts: explicit and tacit. Explicit knowledge is what we easily see and directly know. We often talk about it. Tacit knowledge is what remains unseen or unstated. We rarely acknowledge it and are often only indirectly aware of it. Cultural knowledge includes assumptions, symbols, songs, sayings, facts, ways of behaving, and objects (e.g., telephones, newspapers, etc.). People learn it by reading, watching television, listening to parents, observing others, and the like. *Tacit knowledge* includes the unspoken cultural norms. It requires making inferences (i.e., going beyond what someone explicitly does or says to what he or she means or implies). Most etiquette and polite behavior rely on tacit knowledge.

Ethnography is a study of how people activate and display culture—what they think, ponder, value, or believe to be true. They do this by what they say and do in

ethnography a detailed description of insider meanings and cultural knowledge of living cultures in natural settings.

■ **Figure 10.1**   Examples of Field Research Sites/Topics

Small-Scale Settings

Passengers in an airplane

Battered women's shelters

Camera clubs

Laundromats

Social movement organizations

Social welfare offices

Television stations

Homeless shelters

Waiting rooms

Occupations

Airline attendants

Artists

Cocktail waitresses

Dog catchers

Door-to-door salespersons

Factory workers

Gamblers

Medical students

Female strippers

Police officers

Restaurant chefs

Social workers

Taxi drivers

Social Deviance and Criminal Activity

Body/genital piercing and branding

Cults

Drug dealers and addicts

Hippies

Nude beaches

Occult groups

Prostitutes

Street gangs, motorcycle gangs

Street people, homeless shelters

Community Settings

Retirement communities

Small towns

Urban ethnic communities

Working-class neighborhoods

Children's Activities

Children's playgrounds

Little League baseball

Youth in schools

Junior high girl groups

Medical Settings and Medical Events

Death

Emergency rooms

Intensive care units

Pregnancy and abortion

Support groups for Alzheimer's caregivers

Leisure Industry

Bowling alleys

Hotel lobbies

Restaurants and bars

Resorts

---

specific natural settings. To figure out or infer the meaning of people's actions, you need to become very familiar with the cultural and social context. You shift from what you actually hear or observe to what an action means in a situation. For example, an adult brother and sister are sitting next to one another at a family Thanksgiving meal. During the entire event, they never exchange a single word. You might infer cool social relations between them.

Often people only become aware of tacit knowledge, such as the proper distance to stand from others, when it is not followed. A violation of social custom or practice can cause unease or discomfort, but people may find it difficult to pinpoint the source of unease. A good ethnographer will describe explicit and tacit cultural knowledge by offering highly detailed descriptions. He or she also analyzes social situations by taking them apart and reassembling them. Recognizing explicit and tacit levels

Making It Practical   Seeing Culture in the American Thanksgiving

Ethnographers study social gatherings and socio-cultural events, like the U.S. Thanksgiving holiday. Thanksgiving is part of *explicit knowledge*. It is on a Thursday in late November. Most businesses and all schools close on the day. It has some visible symbols and traditions. People say it is a celebration of abundance and dates back to the early settlers. The central focus of this holiday is people joining with family members or close friends to share a large feast that usually includes eating roast turkey. Related activities include parades with floats in some large cities, football games on television, the arrival of Santa Claus for children, and the beginning of Christmas holiday shopping. At the Thanksgiving meal, tacit knowledge says to use forks and knives when eating turkey meat, wait until finishing other parts of the meal before starting dessert, eat with others and not off alone in a corner, and engage in conversation with others who are at the meal. Eating large quantities or overeating is expected behavior. The timing of the main feast varies by family tradition, but it is rarely very early in the morning, as a breakfast, or extremely late at night. Most people eat Thanksgiving dinner between noon and 7 P.M. It is not the same as ordinary dinner. In addition to the

turkey, other foods rarely seen on other occasions may be served. Pumpkin pie is the most common dessert. The common color scheme is orange and brown. A few seasonal decorations (e.g., autumn leaves, pilgrims) may be seen but they are usually minor. Gift exchanges are rare. In some parts of the United States, people hunt deer or other wild animals on or around Thanksgiving Day.

Blend Images/Alamy Royalty Free

of knowledge, describing in detail, and analyzing events of a social setting are key ethnographic techniques. Often an ethnographer pays great attention to specific details and considers events in silence or by engaging in ordinary social interaction.

An ethnographer notes how people construct social meanings as ongoing processes in specific daily settings. He or she looks for unwritten scripts or routines. Since social activities and events unfold in real time, they are not always pre-

Example Study Box 1   Ethnographic Inference in a Hotel

Thinkstock/Corbis Royalty Free

Rachel Sherman (2006) did field research on luxury hotels (room rates in the range of $500 and up per night). She studied emotion work, workplace relations, and service provided by hotel employees to the wealthy hotel guests. Two luxury hotels in New York were her field sites. She interviewed, observed, and got a job working at the hotels. In the study, she noticed many hundreds of tacit and subtle exchanges among hotel guests and workers. For example, she noticed a service code for employees to provide "unlimited labor" to hotel guests. The employee was supposed to perform the labor in a way that made it appear to be a voluntary favor that he or she wanted to do. A tacit rule was that workers should display emotions of being sincere and truly caring about a guest's needs or desires. She gave an example (2006, p. 42) of when she worked as a housekeeper. Hotel guests asked her to wrap up a large bouquet of flowers for them to take home. She quickly smiled and responded to the request, "I'll deal with it." The guest repeated the phrase "deal with it." She instantly realized that she made a mistake. She should have expressed her joy at the task. The words *deal with it* implied that it might be undesired work. A proper response would have been to smile and say, "I'd be happy to wrap the flowers for you right away, sir."

dictable. Not everyone in a setting sees everything identically. The ethnographer will try to grasp multiple perspectives of people in a social setting. The ethnographer constantly switches perspectives and looks at activities from several points of view simultaneously. This is not easy to do at first, but with practice, it is a skill than can be learned and improved upon.

STUDYING PEOPLE IN THE FIELD

Field research is as much an orientation toward doing research as a set of techniques to apply. Field researchers use a wide variety of techniques in the field to gain information. A principle guiding field research is **naturalism**. Unlike quantitative research in safe settings such as an office, laboratory, or classroom, field research requires you to personally go into the "real world" and become directly involved. You become a part of the social world you study. If you are a beginning field researcher, you will want to start with a relatively small group (20 or fewer people) who regularly interact with each other in a stable setting (e.g., a street corner, church, barroom, beauty parlor, baseball field, etc.). Most field research is by one person alone, although sometimes small teams of two or three have been effective.

Direct, personal involvement in the field can have an emotional impact. Field research can be fun and exciting, but it may disrupt your personal life, unsettle your physical security, or strain your sense of well-being. More than other kinds of social research, field research can reshape your friendships, family life, self-identity, and personal outlook. Direct, personal involvement carries both risks and rewards.

Flexibility is another principle of field research. Field research is less structured than quantitative research. Field researchers recognize and seize opportunities, "play it by ear," and rapidly adjust to fluid, changing situations. Instead of starting with a hypothesis and then following a sequence of steps, you choose techniques based on their value for acquiring information in a specific setting and change direction to follow interesting new leads as they appear.

Flexibility has a down side. Without fixed steps, it is easy to become sidetracked and drift directionless and without focus. Beginning field researchers feel they have little control over events, need focus, and feel that data collection is unmanageable and the task is overwhelming. You may feel that you are collecting too little, too much, or the wrong data. Feelings of emotional turmoil, isolation, and confusion are common. This makes it essential for you to be organized and prepared. After you learn about a setting, you can slowly develop a specific focus for the inquiry. As you develop a focus, your focus will guide you to the qualitative data you need.

In this section, we will examine eight stages of doing a field research study:

1. Preparing for a field study
2. Starting the research project
3. Being in the field
4. Developing strategies for success in the field
5. Observing and taking field notes
6. Conducting field interviews
7. Leaving the field
8. Writing the field research report

1. Preparing for a Field Study

We can divide the early preparation for doing a field study into the following three parts:

- Increasing self-awareness
- Conducting background investigation
- Practice observing and writing

naturalism the principle that we learn best by observing ordinary events in a natural setting, not in a contrived, invented, or researcher-created setting.

Brand X/SuperStock Royalty Free

 Example Study Box 2 College Students Selling Door-to-Door

Schweingruber and Berns (2005) studied emotion work among college students who got jobs as door-to-door salespeople over the course of a year. They were directly and personally involved. Both worked for the company in several roles as salespeople. They observed recruitment interviews and went through the training programs themselves. During the summer, they accompanied college-student salespeople across five states on their long, 15-hour days, and during the time-off periods. In addition to working and living with the salespeople to understand their perspective, the researchers also analyzed company documents, engaged in field interviews, and conducted focus groups to "discover social meanings inductively" (Schweingruber and Berns 2005: 687).

Self-Awareness. Human and personal factors have a role in all social research projects, but they are crucial in field research. Direct, personal involvement with other people means your emotional make-up, personal biography, and cultural experiences are highly relevant. There is no room for self-deception. Your personal characteristics (including your physical appearance, gender, age, racial-ethnic background) are often relevant in the research process. You need to be candid and have a solid understanding of who you are. You are directly in the middle of the real, ongoing events, not safely hidden away in a laboratory, office, or computer room.

A good field researcher has a well-developed sense of self but is not self-absorbed. You must have an ability to notice details around you and have empathy for other people. You must also be aware of your own personal concerns, commitments, and inner conflicts. Expect anxiety, self-doubt, frustration, and uncertainty in the field, especially in the beginning. You may feel doubly marginal: an outsider in the field setting, and increasingly distant from friends, family, and other researchers.

Background Investigation. As with all research, reading the scholarly literature helps you learn useful concepts, potential pitfalls, data collection techniques, and strategies. Field researchers also use films, novels, or journalistic accounts about the type of field site or topic. They read autobiographies or diaries of people similar to those in the field site to gain familiarity and prepare themselves emotionally. More than a standard literature review, field researchers conduct a wide-ranging background investigation.

Practice Observing and Writing. Field research depends on skills of careful observing and listening, short-term memory, and writing. A good field researcher is observant and notices many details. He or she can also "pull back" to see the whole and grasp what occurs "between the lines." Much of what a field researcher does is to notice ordinary details of situations and to write them down. Attention to subtle details and short-term memory can improve with practice. Before you enter a field site, practice and refine your observation skills. Many people find that keeping a daily diary is good practice for writing field notes. Beyond personal strength and strong social skills, a field researcher needs to be a compulsive, organized note taker.

2. Starting the Research Project

We can divide the process of starting the research project into the following four parts:

- Getting organized
- Selecting a field site
- Gaining access
- Entering the field

Getting Organized. You need to adjust your mind-set and attitude as part of field research preparation. To begin, you want to defocus (i.e., be very open minded and clear your mind of preconceptions). Do not begin with set ideas, stereotypes, or notions about the topic, members, or field site. Be open to what you actually learn in the field, and do not impose preconceptions. You need to maintain a balance between being attentive and informed yet open to new experiences or ideas. You begin the field research process with a general topic, not with a narrow question or specific hypotheses. Avoid locking yourself into a narrow focus quickly, but do not become entirely directionless. Finding the research questions that fit a field situation takes time in the field. You develop the questions only after you know more about a site or situation. Patience is another valuable field research skill.

Selecting a Field Site. Field projects often begin with a chance occurrence or personal interest. Many studies began with a researcher's experiences, such as working at a job, having a hobby, or being a patient or an activist. The term *field setting* or **field site** can be misleading. It is more than a single, fixed physical location. It is a socially defined territory with fluid and shifting boundaries because social groups can interact across several physical sites. For example, a college football team may interact on the playing field, in the locker room, in a dormitory, at a training camp, or at a local hangout. The field site to study a football team includes all five physical locations. You need to recognize the interdependence that may exist among the physical site, the topic, the interacting members, and you, the researcher.

Selecting a field site is a major decision. Researchers often try several sites before settling on one and take notes on the site selection processes. Four factors affect your choice of a field research site: containment, richness of data, unfamiliarity, and suitability.

- **Containment.** It is easier to study field sites in which small groups engage in sustained social interaction within a bounded space. Field research in large, open public spaces where many strangers pass through with little social interaction (such as a shopping mall, large discount store, large outdoor park or parking lot) is much more difficult.
- **Richness.** More interesting data come from sites that have overlapping webs of social relations among people with a constant flow of activities and diverse events.
- **Unfamiliarity.** Despite some initial unease, you can more quickly see cultural events and relations in a setting that is new to you (see "Acquiring an Attitude of Strangeness" later in this chapter).
- **Suitability.** Consider practical issues, such as your personal characteristics and feelings. Also important are your time and skills, your physical safety, ethical protections, conflicts on the site, and your ability to gain access.

Gaining Access. Personal characteristics, such as age, gender, and race, can facilitate or limit access. You may find that you are unwelcome or not allowed on a site, or that you face legal and political barriers to entry. We can array field sites on a continuum. At one end are open access public areas (e.g., public restaurants, check-in airport waiting areas). At the other end are closed, private, or semiprivate settings (e.g., exclusive clubs, activities in a person's home). Laws and regulations in institutions (e.g., public schools, hospitals, prisons) can restrict access. In addition, institutional review boards (see Chapter 3) may limit field research on ethical grounds.

Almost all field sites have a **gatekeeper**. The gatekeeper can be the thug on the corner, an administrator of a hospital, a manager of a restaurant, or the owner of a beauty parlor. Informal public areas (e.g., sidewalks, airport waiting areas) often have gatekeepers. Formal organizations have authorities from whom you must obtain explicit permission. Whether or not it is required, it is good practice to identify and ask permission of gatekeepers.

field site any location or set of locations in which field research takes place. It usually has ongoing social interaction and a shared culture.

gatekeeper someone with the formal or informal authority to control access to a field site.

Example Study Box 3 Negotiating with Gatekeepers

In her study of luxury hotels, Rachel Sherman (2006) described gaining access to two five-star hotels. At one hotel, she received permission from the general manager and human resources manager. When she was assigned to be an intern at that hotel, she had to work with other gatekeepers who were managers or supervisors in various areas (such as guest services, "doorman" and parking, front desk). She found that gaining access from a gatekeeper at one level or area did not automatically transfer to other levels or areas. In addition to formal gatekeepers, she had to negotiate with informal gatekeeper-workers as she worked with the hotel employees. At another hotel, the human resource manager was the primary gatekeeper and there was less negotiation with each area. The internal arrangements and authority within each hotel altered access issues.

Expect to negotiate with gatekeepers and bargain for access. In addition to being flexible, a field researcher sets nonnegotiable limits to protect research integrity. For example, a gatekeeper who demands you only say positive things or insists on reading and censoring field notes makes research at a site impossible. If there are many restrictions initially, often you can reopen negotiations later. Gatekeepers may forget their initial demands as trust develops. Dealing with gatekeepers is a recurrent issue as you enter new levels or areas of the social setting.

Entering the Field. When entering a field site, adopt a flexible plan of action. Each site is different, and the way you enter a site depends on your prior experience, contacts, commonsense judgment, and social skills. Three issues to consider are presentation of self, amount of disclosure, and social role.

Presentation of Self. When you begin any new social relationship, including entering a field site as a researcher, you display the type of person you are or would like to be. Consciously or not, you do this through physical appearance, through what you say, by tone and mannerisms, and in how you act. The message may be, "I'm a serious, hard-working student," "I'm a warm and caring person," "I'm a cool jock," or "I'm a rebel and party animal." You can show more than one self, and the self you present can differ by the occasion.

You should be aware of self-presentation processes in the field. Your demeanor—your manner of speaking, the way you walk or sit, your facial expressions and eye contact, your hairstyle and your clothing—"speaks" for you. Be aware of what they are saying to members in the field. For example, how should you dress in the field? The best guide is to respect both yourself and the people you are studying. A professor who studies street people does not have to dress or act like one; to dress and act informally is sufficient. Likewise, if you study corporate or school officials, formal dress and a professional demeanor are expected. You need to be conscious of how self-presentation affects field relations. You want to fit in, but it is difficult to present a very deceptive front or to present a self that deviates sharply from your ordinary self. Your discomfort and awkwardness will show through and can impede developing smooth relations in the field.

Disclosure. A field researcher decides how much to disclose about self and the research to gatekeepers and members in the field. Revealing details of your personal life, such as hobbies, interests, and background, can build trust and help to create intimate relationships with people in the field. It also can result in a loss of privacy. We can think of disclosure on a continuum. At one end is covert research, in which no one in the field is aware that research is taking place. At the opposite end is fully open research, in which everyone becomes familiar with the researcher and is aware of the research project. The degree and timing of disclosure depend on your judgment and the particulars of a setting. Disclosure may unfold over time, as you feel more secure.

Social Roles. You play many social roles in daily life—daughter/son, student, customer, sports fan, friend, and so forth. You can switch roles, play multiple roles, or play a role in a particular way. You choose some roles, and others are prestructured for you. Few of us have a choice but to play the role of son or daughter, although you have some control over *how* you play the role. Some social roles are formal (e.g., bank teller, police chief), others are informal (e.g., flirt, elder states person, buddy).

Field researchers assume and play social roles in the field. At times, they adopt an existing role, such as the role of housekeeper that Rachel Sherman adopted in her study of hotels. Some existing roles provide greater access to all areas of the site. They let you observe and interact with all members and give you freedom to move around the site. Other roles are more restrictive. For example, the role of bartender when studying a tavern permits access to all areas, but it may limit freedom because it requires providing service, protecting the business, and collecting money. At other times, researchers create a new role or modify an existing one. For example, Fine (1987) created a role of the "adult friend" and performed it with little adult authority when studying preadolescent boys. He was able to observe parts of the boys' culture and behavior that were otherwise inaccessible to adults. It may take time to adopt some roles, and you may adopt several different field roles over time.

Your skills, time, and personal features—such as age, race, gender, and attractiveness—influence the roles open to you. You can only control some of these. Such factors can influence gaining access or can restrict available roles. Since many roles are sex typed, your gender is an important consideration. Female researchers have encountered difficulties in a dangerous setting where males are in control (e.g., police work, firefighting). They may be shunned or pushed into limiting gender stereotypes (e.g., "sweet kid," "mascot," "loud mouth," "hard bitch"). For example, Gurney (1985) reported that being a female in a male-dominated setting required extra negotiations and "hassles." Nevertheless, her gender also provided insights and created situations that would have been absent with a male researcher. Race and age can have a similar impact on role selection.

3. Being in the Field

Once you have selected a site, gained access, and assumed a social role, you need to settle in. We can divide ongoing observation and research in the field site into five parts:

- Learning the ropes
- Normalizing
- Building rapport
- Negotiating continuously
- Deciding on a degree of involvement

Learning the Ropes. New researchers often face embarrassment, experience discomfort, and become overwhelmed by the details in the field. Maintaining a "marginal" status is stressful. It is difficult to be an outsider who is not fully involved, especially when studying settings full of intense feelings (e.g., political campaigns, religious conversions). Do not be surprised if you feel awkward until you "learn the ropes" (i.e., acquire an understanding of micro-level norms, rules, and customs of a local field site). As you learn the ropes and fit in, you learn how to cope with stress and how to **normalize** the social research.

normalize how a field researcher helps field site members redefine social research from unknown and potentially threatening to something normal, comfortable, and familiar.

Normalizing Social Research. A field researcher not only observes and investigates members in the field, but he or she is also being observed and investigated. Frequently, members are initially uncomfortable with the presence of a researcher. Many may be unfamiliar with field research and confuse sociologists, psychologists, counselors, and social workers. They may see you as an outside critic or spy, or as a savior or all-knowing expert. You need to normalize. To help members adjust to the research process, you may present your own biography, explain field research a little at a time, appear nonthreatening, and accept or ignore minor rule violations in the setting. For example, the clerks at a work setting you are observing sometimes leave 20 minutes early when they should not. You do not report them to a supervisor. Soon, they begin to accept you as less threatening and like one of them.

Building Rapport and Trust. As you overcome your initial bewilderment to an unusual way of talking or system of meaning, you can slowly build relations of trust and establish rapport. This takes time and repeated positive social interactions. To do this you need to "get along with" members in the field. This may require listening sympathetically to complaints, sharing experiences, swapping stories, and laughing or crying with field site members.

Many factors influence building trust and rapport—how you present yourself; your role in the field; and the events that facilitate, limit, or destroy trust. Gaining rapport and trust is a developmental process that builds up through many social nuances (e.g., sharing of personal experiences, story telling, gestures, hints, facial expressions). Trust and rapport are easier to lose once established than to gain in the first place. Maintaining good rapport requires repeated social engagements with almost daily reinforcement. For example, if you establish rapport with a group of people and then disappear for three months, do not expect the same level of rapport instantly when you return. Creating trust often requires taking risks or passing mini social "tests." It also requires continuous reaffirmation, and you re-create it anew as you enter new topics, issues, physical locations, or social groups. Perry (2001) explains how she presented herself and gained rapport in her study of two high schools (see Appendix C).

> Although I looked somewhat younger than my age (thirty-eight when the research began), I made concerted efforts to minimize the effects of age difference on how students related to me. I did not associate with other adults on campus. I dressed casually in attire that I was comfortable in, which happened to be similar to the attire students were comfortable in: blue jeans, sandals or athletic shoes, T-shirt or sweatshirt, no jewelry except four tiny hoop earrings—one in one ear, three in the other. I had students call me by my first name, and I did not talk down to them, judge them, or otherwise present myself as an authority figure. To the contrary, I saw the students as the authorities, and they seemed to appreciate that regard. Those efforts, on top of having developed some popular-cultural frames of reference with the students, contributed to my developing some very close relationships with several of the students and fairly wide access to different peer groups and cliques on campus. (Perry 2001:63)

Rapport and trust may be very difficult to achieve in some field sites. Some sites may be filled with fear, tension, and conflict. The local members may be unpleasant, untrustworthy, or untruthful. They may do things that disturb or disgust you. Experienced researchers are prepared for a range of events and relationships. However, it is sometimes impossible to penetrate a setting or get really close to members. Settings in which cooperation, sympathy, and collaboration are impossible may require different techniques.

Building rapport and trust is a step toward obtaining an understanding of the social life of a field site. Rapport helps you to understand the members. The understanding is a precondition for gaining greater access to a deeper level—a member's inner worldview and perspective. The step after seeing an event from a member's point of view is getting inside and grasping how the member thinks, feels, and reacts. You move beyond understanding toward empathy (i.e., seeing, feeling, and experiencing events in the field site as a member does). Empathy is not the same as sympathy, agreement, or approval. It means to see, feel, and think as another person does. Rapport helps to create understanding and ultimately empathy. At the same time, empathy facilitates greater rapport.

Negotiating Continuously. Most field sites have multiple levels or areas. Entry can be an issue for each. Entry is more analogous to peeling the layers of an onion than to opening a door. Moreover, bargains or promises made at entry may not be permanent. You should have fallback plans and expect renegotiation. Perhaps you got permission from the principal and parents to observe young children. After you arrive at the school, you find that two teachers control the children's time closely. They block your access and give you no chance to observe the children playing or interacting spontaneously. Your fallback plan may be to shift to study and spend more time with the two teachers. You try to see the world from their viewpoint. Once you better understand them and win their trust, you might be able to renegotiate with them to observe the children more.

Frequently, the specific focus of a field research study only emerges late in the research process, and it can change. This means you must negotiate for access to new areas as your research focus develops. Also, as you encounter new people in the field site, you may have to negotiate over social relations again with each new person until a stable relationship develops or has to be renewed. Expect to negotiate and explain what you are doing repeatedly. Although you may feel it, try not to express your irritation or impatience with the repetition.

Deciding on a Degree of Involvement. In addition to a social role in the field, you adopt a researcher role. This kind of role is on a continuum by the degree of direct involvement with members in the field and their activities. At one extreme is a detached and remote outsider. You only observe events from the distance and do not directly interact with people. At the opposite extreme is an intimately involved and engaged participant. You fully engage and begin to become just like another member in the field site (see Figure 10.2).

The outsider is faster, easier, and necessary at the start of observation. At the outsider end of the continuum, you need less time for acceptance, and overinvolvement is less likely. At times, people find it easier open up to someone seen as a detached outsider visitor. This role also protects your self-identity. However, you may feel marginal and unable to grasp an insider's experience. You are also more likely to misinterpret events. To understand local social meaning fully, you must participate in the setting with other people.

Roles at the insider end of the continuum facilitate empathy, sharing of a member's experience, and fully experiencing the intimate social world of field site members. However, with little social distance and too much sympathy for members, overinvolvement is possible. Intimate contact can make serious data gathering difficult, and you may lose the distance needed for research analysis. Feelings of loneliness and isolation in the field may combine with a desire for rapport and empathy to create overinvolvement or **going native**. This can destroy a research study because

going native when a field researcher drops a professional researcher role and loses all detachment to become fully involved as a full field site member.

■ **Figure 10.2**   Researcher Role by Degree of Involvement in the Field Site

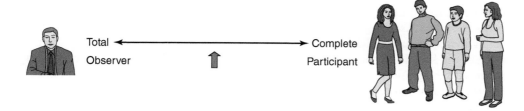

Total ←——————————→ Complete
Observer   Participant

being like the others in the field takes priority over doing careful research, observation, or analysis. Maintaining a high degree of involvement without being overly involved is difficult.

4. Strategies for Success in the Field

All field researchers have strategies that they tailor to the specifics of a field site and their own background. In this section, we look at six of the strategies that many field researchers have used:

- Building relationships
- Performing small favors
- Appearing interested and exercising selective inattention
- Being an earnest novice
- Avoiding conflict
- Adopting an attitude of strangeness

Building Relationships. Over time, you develop social relationships with people in the field site (see Learning from History: Taxis, Customers, and Tips). This requires putting in time, remembering personal details about members, and making "small talk" (such as saying good morning, commenting on the weather). Members who are cool at first may warm up later. Alternatively, they may put on a front of initial friendliness, with fears and suspicions surfacing later. You are in a delicate position because early in a study, when you know little about a field site, you may resist forming a close relationship with particular people because you are unfamiliar with the social scene. If you quickly develop one or two close friends, they can become allies and valuable sources of information. They can explain events to you, introduce you to others, defend your presence, and help you to gain access. However, depending on who the first friends are, they can also block you from having access to some parts of the field site or inhibit creating social relations with others in the setting.

You need to notice quickly the social cliques, friendship ties, disputes or tensions, and power relations in a social setting. For example, after two days in a field site you recognize that Samantha and Judy seem to avoid one another and do not get along. George and Roberto appear to be close friends. Minsook looks quiet, shy, and uncertain of herself and has few friends. April appears to be outgoing and confident and seems to be in charge.

As you acquire awareness of the social "lay of the land," you also need to monitor how your own actions or appearance affect others. For example, a physically attractive researcher who interacts with members of the opposite sex often encounters crushes, flirting, and jealousy. You need to be aware of these field relations and manage them. You must maintain some level professional detachment and discipline but not hurt feelings, harm rapport, or close off access. At times, you need to be able to break off relations or withdraw from them. You may discover that to forge social ties with some people, you must break off close social ties with others. As with the end of any friendly relationship, social withdrawal can cause emotional discomfort or pain for both you and the other person. As a field researcher, you must constantly balance social sensitivity with your research goals.

Performing Small Favors. You have probably noticed that social life is full of exchange relationships. You do something for someone else and he or she usually returns the favor. Exchange relationships also develop in a field site. People exchange small favors, including deference and respect. A research strategy for gaining acceptance in the field is to help in small ways but not expect anything in return. As you repeatedly help and perform "small acts of kindness," people in the field incur an informal social obligation. They may feel they should reciprocate by offering you help in the field.

Learning from History Taxis, Customers, and Tips

In a famous article, Fred Davis (1959) analyzed what he learned from field research when he worked as a taxi driver for six months in 1948 in Chicago. He focused on the social relationship between the driver and passenger or fare. He observed that drivers have limited control over the job. They have little choice of passengers and only a few regular clients-customers. Mobile and without a fixed business location, the low-status cabdriver devoted long hours to short-term encounters with many diverse individuals. The encounters were highly variable and contained risk (such as fare jumpers, women in labor, robbers). Customers often ignored the driver or acted as if he or she was not there. Davis noticed that taxis drivers, like others in similar low-status service jobs, "sized-up" and quickly classified their customers. Customer categories were a large part of the taxi driver's daily social world. Using a customer category system added a small degree of control and predictability in a highly uncertain job. It also helped when evaluating risk. Drivers also used it to gain some control and estimate the likelihood of tips. The driver had little discretion over how to perform a service. Beyond careful driving, opening doors, or speedy delivery, using a customer classification let the driver to assert some control and engage in strategic emotion work—smile, make small talk, display kindness—to improve tips.

Appearing Interested and Exercising Selective Inattention. At times, you may feel bored or distracted in the field site. Looking bored is a nearly certain way to break off or weaken a developing social relationship. You should learn to "act" and maintain an **appearance of interest**. Appearing interested in the people and events of a field site with your words and actions (e.g., facial expression, going for coffee, going to a party, listening to jokes), even if you are not truly interested, is an important strategy.

Putting on a temporary front of involvement to be sociable is a common small deception of daily life. It is a part of being polite. Of course, selective inattention (i.e., not staring or appearing not to notice) is also part of acting polite. If someone makes a social mistake (e.g., accidentally uses an incorrect word, passes gas), the polite thing to do is to ignore it. Selective inattention in fieldwork gives an alert researcher an opportunity to learn by casually eavesdropping on conversations or observing events not meant to be public.

Being an Earnest Novice. When you are new to a setting and first forming relationships, you may be curious and ask many questions. One field strategy is to extend this mode of operating for some time. Being the "expert" or "know-it-all" is *not* how you learn about a field site or win friends. As the outsider, your primary mission in the field is to observe, listen, and learn about other people. It is not to brag, talk a lot, promote your opinions, or correct others' mistakes. If anything, you should act slightly less informed and knowledgeable than you really are. This is a good way to learn from people in the field. Being humble and adopting a learner role pays research dividends. You learn more by listening and asking questions. Treating local members as experts encourages them to share confidences with you. You do not want to appear unnecessarily stupid or naive, but you want to ask for explanations rather than assume that you already know what is happening or why things are done in certain ways. By adopting a novice role as someone who wants to learn, you both learn more and help members to feel respected and valuable.

Avoiding Conflicts. Fights, conflict, and disagreements can erupt in the field. You may study people with opposing positions. In such situations, you may feel pressure to take sides. People may test you to see if you can be trusted or are on the enemy's side. In such occasions, it is usually best to stay on the neutral sidelines and try to walk a tightrope between opposing sides. Once you align closely with one side, you will be cut off from access to the other side. In addition, you will only see the situation from one point of view and may get a distorted picture of events.

appearance of interest a micro strategy to build or maintain relationships in a field setting in which a researcher acts interested even when he or she is actually bored and uninterested.

Adopting an Attitude of Strangeness. Life is filled with thousands of details. If you paid attention to everything all the time, you would suffer from severe information overload. We manage life by ignoring much of what is around us and by engaging in habitual thinking. We overlook what is very familiar and assume that other people experience reality the same as we do. We treat our way of living as being natural or normal. We rarely recognize what we take for granted. For example, someone hands you a wrapped gift. You probably say "thank you," open the gift, and then praise it. Yet gift-giving customs vary by culture. In some cultures, people barely acknowledge the gift and quickly put it aside unwrapped. In others, people expect the gift receiver to complain that the gift is inadequate. Habitual thinking and not noticing what is familiar makes doing field research in a familiar setting very difficult. Field researchers adopt an **attitude of strangeness**. With the stranger's perspective, the unspoken, tacit culture of a setting becomes more visible. When you first go to a new, unfamiliar place as a stranger, you are extra sensitive to the physical and social surroundings. You do not know what will happen. By adopting an attitude of strangeness, you retain such an extra-sensitive perspective and use it to look at field events in a new way.

If you visit a very different culture, you will encounter different assumptions about what is important and how to do things. This confrontation of cultures, or culture shock, makes it easier for you to see cultural elements and facilitates self-discovery. By acquiring the attitude of strangeness, you notice more details. You find that reflection and introspection are easier and more intense. As a field researcher, you want to adopt both a stranger's and an insider's point of view. Your understanding will expand if you learn to see the ordinary both from an outsider-stranger's perspective and as an insider-member does. Switching back and forth is key to good field research.

5. Observing and Collecting Data

In this section, we look at ways to get good qualitative field data. Field data are what a researcher experiences, remembers, records in field notes, and makes available for systematic analysis.

The Researcher Is a Data Collection Instrument. The good field researcher is a resourceful, talented individual with ingenuity and an ability to think quickly on his or her feet while in the field. In quantitative research, you may use various instruments (e.g., questionnaire, response reaction measures in a computer) to acquire data. In field research, you are the instrument for acquiring field data. This has two implications. First, you must be alert and sensitive to what happens in the field and disciplined about recording data. Second, your social relationships and personal feelings and personal, subjective experiences are field data. They are valuable in themselves and for interpreting events in the field. Instead of trying to be objective and eliminate personal reactions as in quantitative studies, you reflect on your reactions and feelings and then record them as an important data source. For example, a field researcher visits a pornography shop to study what happens inside. He notices an increase in personal unease and anxiety (rapid heartbeat, sweaty palms). He reflects on sources of the unease—is it a fear of discovery, is it excitement from transgressing a moral line, is it uncertainty over someone approaching him in the store to solicit for sex? The researcher's inner anxiety and feelings that have accompanied his observing of customers and clerks at the shop are legitimate field data. He should notice and record them, as Karp (1973) did in his study of porn shops.

What to Observe. In the field site, you must pay very close attention, watch all that is happening, and listen carefully (see Example Study Box 3: Negotiating with Gatekeepers, p. 270). You use all your senses. Notice what you see, hear, smell, taste, and touch to absorb all sources of information.

attitude of strangeness a perspective in which the field researcher questions and notices ordinary details by looking at the ordinary through the eyes of a stranger.

Example Study Box 4 Noticing Details

In one of the luxury hotels she studied, Rachel Sherman (2006) noticed that management sent contradictory messages to workers: (1) You are part of a family or community and have free choice; (2) you are under surveillance and required to perform your job. How did she arrive at this conclusion? She noticed many details in the employee handbook, at training sessions, in worker-manager interactions, and many little things in general. For example, she saw a sign posted for an upcoming employee meeting. It said, "come enjoy the refreshments," and under this message it said "attendance is mandatory" (2006, p. 75). Through her careful attention to details that she recorded and on which she later reflected, she could build a picture of the corporate culture sustained in each luxury hotel.

The Physical Setting. In the beginning, you want to scrutinize the physical setting and capture its atmosphere. What is the color of the floor, walls, ceiling? How large is the room? Where are the windows and doors? How is the furniture arranged and what is its condition (e.g., new or old and worn, dirty or clean)? What type of lighting is there? Are there signs, paintings, or plants? What are all the sounds or smells?

Why bother with such details? Stores and restaurants often plan lighting, colors, and piped-in music to create a certain atmosphere. Used-car salespeople spray a new-car scent into cars. Shopping malls and stores intentionally send out the odor of freshly made cookies because it attracts customers. To sell a house, people often add a fresh coat of paint. These subtle, unconscious signals influence human behavior. As a field researcher, you want to notice, capture, and record anything in the surroundings that could influence social relations and create "atmosphere."

You may find that field observing is detailed, tedious work, but motivation is based on a deep curiosity about the details. A good field researcher is intrigued with details. The mass of ordinary details can reveal "what's going on here." The mass of ongoing mundane, trivial, and daily minutiae can communicate very important aspects of social life. This is what people often overlook but what field researchers notice and from which they learn.

People and Their Behavior. In addition to physical surroundings, you observe people in the field. Notice each person's observable physical characteristics: age, sex, race, and stature. Why? People socially interact differently depending on whether someone is 18, 40, or 80 years old; male or female; white or nonwhite; short, thin, and frail or tall, heavyset, and muscular. For example, an attitude of strangeness can heighten your sensitivity to a group's racial composition. A white researcher in a multiracial society who does not notice that everyone in a group in a field setting is also white is racially insensitive and missing a feature of the setting that could be important for understanding it. The 20-year-old researcher observing a crowded restaurant who notices nothing unusual until an elderly couple walks in is suddenly aware that all people in the restaurant are under 30 years old. The youthfulness of the staff and customers is actually a major feature of the restaurant setting. In her study of luxury hotels, Sherman (2006) noticed a "stark" racial/ethnic division of labor in one hotel—"front office workers, many of whom were European, were white; the only nonwhite worker at the desk was Inga, a young Swede of Asian descent. Three of the four doormen were white. . . . A striking and important feature of the front office workers . . . was their youth. Annie, Jackie, Betsy and, Ginger, white front desk/concierge workers, were all under twenty-three" (pp. 86–97).

You record all the details because something of significance *might* be revealed. You may not become aware of a detail's relevance until later. You want to err by including everything rather than missing potentially significant details. Highly specific, descriptive details capture the setting and events. For example, "a tall, white, muscular 19-year-old male in jeans sprinted into the brightly lit room just as the short, slight black woman in her sixties and a tailored blue dress eased into a battered plastic chair" says more than "one person entered, another sat down."

Physical appearance—such as makeup, neatness, clothing, or hairstyle—sends messages that can influence social interactions. Some people devote a lot of time and money to selecting clothes, styling and combing their hair, putting on makeup, shaving, ironing clothes, and using deodorant or perfumes. This is part of their self-presentation. People who do not groom, shave, or wear deodorant are also presenting themselves and sending messages. No one dresses or looks "normal." Such a statement suggests that you are not seeing the social world through the eyes of a stranger or are insensitive to social signals.

Beyond appearance, people's actions can be significant. Notice where people sit or stand, the pace at which they walk, and their nonverbal communication. People express social information, feelings, and attitudes through nonverbal communication, including gestures, facial expressions, and how they stand or sit (standing stiffly, sitting in a slouched position, etc.). People express relationships by where they position themselves in a group and through eye contact. You want to read social communication by quickly noticing who is standing close together, having a relaxed posture, and making eye contact and who is not.

You also need to notice the context in which events occur: Who was present? Who just arrived or left the scene? Was the room hot and stuffy? Was it late or early in the day? Such details help you assign meaning and learn why events occur. If you fail to notice such details, they are lost. Also lost is a full understanding of the event. In their study of timeshare sales presentations, Katovich and Diamond (1986) documented how sales staff carefully deployed situational details, such as timing, phrasing, and the staging of events, to influence sales.

Lastly, you need to notice exactly what people say, their specific words and phrases. Also note how it is said—the loudness, tone of voice, accent, and so forth. Intense listening is tiring and difficult in a noisy room with many conservations or distracting sounds. If you are not part of a private conversation, listening to what people say is eavesdropping and considered very impolite. Yet a stranger who overhears a loud conversation is not being rude. Eavesdropping is intentionally listening to something meant to be private, but overhearing is unintentionally hearing when speakers show little concern for privacy. Field researchers engage in both, but they exercise care and discretion.

As you hear phrases, accents, and grammar, listen to what is said, how it is said, and what it implies. For example, people often use ambiguous phrases such as "you know" or "of course" or "et cetera." A field researcher tries to discover meaning behind such phrases. If someone fails to complete a sentence but ends with "you know," what does she mean? You hear a 14-year-old boy say, "We all went to the mall and hung out until 2, you know." The phase "you know" may be a sloppy speaking habit. It could mean he expects you to be aware of what 14-year-old boys do with their friends hanging out at a shopping mall for two hours in the middle of the day. Or the phrase could be deflecting attention since he engaged in forbidden behaviors and does not want to tell you.

When "Nothing" Happens. Inexperienced field researchers complain that they observed in a field site but "nothing happened." They get frustrated with the amount of "wasted" time waiting for something to occur. They have not yet learned the importance of serendipity in field research. You do not know the relevance of what you observe until later. Keen observations are useful at all times, even when it appears that "nothing happens." Although "nothing happened" from your perspective, what about from that of members in the field? As a field researcher, you need to operate on other people's schedules and observe events as they occur within their flow of time. You may be impatient to get in, get the research over, and get on with your "real life." For people in the field site, this *is* their real life. You may need to subordinate your personal wants to the flow and demands of the field site.

Field researchers appreciate "wait time." Waiting is a necessary part of fieldwork that can be valuable. Wait time can indicate inactivity and a slow pace, a delay because of scheduling problems, a stalemate in a conflict, or power relations in which unimportant people are expected to wait. Wait time reveals the pace and rhythm of a setting. Also, wait time is not always wasted time. You can use wait time for reflecting, for observing details, for developing social relations, for building rapport, and for becoming a familiar sight to people in the field setting. Wait time also displays that you are committed and serious; perseverance is a significant trait. Like the appearance of interest, it signals to people in the field that you are earnest and committed. It shows them that you believe what occurs in the field site is valuable and important.

Sampling. Field research sampling differs from that of survey research. Field researchers do not use random sampling. They sample by taking selective observations from all possible times, locations, people, situations, types of events, or contexts of interest. You might sample time by observing a setting at different times of the day. For example, in studying a bowling alley you observe at three times of the day, on weekdays and weekends, to get a sense of what remains the same and what changes. It is often best to overlap sampling times (e.g., 9:00 to 11:00 A.M., 10:30 A.M. to noon, 11:30 A.M. to 1:00 P.M.). You may want to sample locations because sitting or standing in different locations provides a better sense of the whole site. Let us say you are studying the emotion work of a waitress. You want to observe interactions in the front area (with customers), in a back area (with cooks, etc.), and in a back break room with coworkers. You would sample all shifts and meal times, both the slow and very busy times. Observations from multiple locations and times will give you a much richer picture of the entire social setting.

You can sample people by focusing attention on different kinds of people (old-timers and newcomers, old and young, males and females, leaders and followers). As you identify all the types of people, or people with various outlooks in a field site, you want to interact with and learn about all of them.

You can also sample three types of field site events: routine, special, and unanticipated.

- **Routine.** Events that occur over and over again the same way (e.g., opening up a store for business every day). Do not be mistaken and think they are unimportant simply because they are routine.
- **Special.** Events announced and planned in advance (e.g., annual office party). These events focus member attention and can reveal aspects of social life not otherwise visible.
- **Unanticipated.** Events that just happen while you are present (e.g., how unsupervised workers act when the manager gets sick and cannot oversee them for a day). In this case, you may see something unusual, unplanned, or rare. Such events might reveal new aspects of a setting, such as how much the workers really respect the manager and follow her rules even when she is not around to observe them.

Becoming a Skillful Note-Taker. Field research data are your memories of observations and experiences and your field notes. Field notes are the permanent record of observations and experiences. Producing good field notes is essential for a high-quality ethnography or field research study. Do not plan to take notes while in the field site. After spending some time in the field, plan to sit down in a quiet place and write from memory. Especially in the beginning, you leave the field to write notes after only one or two hours of observation. Expect to spend nearly as much time writing as you did observing in the field site. If you observed for two hours, you may be writing for two hours.

Types of Notes.   Any notes taken directly in the field site differ from full field notes. A common mistake of new field researchers is to try to take the full field notes while still in the field site (see Making it Practical: Recommendations for Taking Field Notes). Only take **jotted notes** in the field site, not full field notes. If you take jotted notes, write them on a small scrap of paper inconspicuously or in private (such as in a bathroom). You use them to get down one or two critical key words or phrases that can stimulate your memory later.

Immediately after you leave the field site, sit down in a quiet place to write notes. Writing field notes requires self-discipline and can be boring, tedious work. You need to make writing notes a compulsion. Your notes should contain extensive descriptive detail drawn from short-term memory. New field researchers find they can recall more details with some effort. Generally, the quality and quantity of notes improve over time. Be sure to keep field notes neat and organized. You will return to them over and again. Always put the date and time of the observation at the top of the first page for a session in the field. Once written, the notes are private and valuable; treat them with care and protect their confidentiality. Sometimes hostile parties, blackmailers, or legal officials will want to read them. Some professional field researchers write their field notes in code. Your mood, state of mind, attention level, and conditions in the field can affect note-taking.

Supplements.   Beyond detailed descriptions, your full field notes can contain maps, diagrams, photographs, interviews, tape recordings, videotapes, memos, objects from the field, and jotted notes taken in the field. For a field project of a few weeks, you might fill several notebooks or the equivalent in computer memory. Some professional researchers have produced 40 single-spaced pages of notes from three hours of observation. With practice, even a new field researcher can soon produce four or five pages of notes for each hour in the field.

jotted notes optional, very short notes of a few words written inconspicuously in the field site that are used only to trigger memory later.

 Making It Practical **Recommendations for Taking Field Notes**

1. Record notes immediately after being in the field. Avoid talking with others until you record observations.
2. Begin the record of each field visit with a new page. Enter the date and start and ending times.
3. Use only the optional jotted notes as a temporary memory aid, with one or two key words or terms.
4. Use wide margins so you can add to your notes at any time. Go back and add things you remember later.
5. Plan to type notes and keep the note levels (to be discussed later) separate so you can easily return to them.
6. Record events in the order in which they occurred. Note their length (e.g., a 15-minute wait, a one-hour ride).
7. Be as specific, concrete, complete, and comprehensible as possible. You can always throw away extra details.
8. Try to recall exact phrases. Use double quotes for exact phases and single quotes for paraphrasing.
9. Record small talk or routines that do not appear to be significant at the time; they may become important later.

10. "Let your feelings flow," and write quickly without worrying about spelling or "wild ideas."
11. Never substitute tape or video recordings completely for written field notes.
12. Include diagrams or maps of the setting. Outline your own movements along with those of other people during observation.
13. Include your own words and behavior in the notes. Also, record your emotional feelings and private thoughts.
14. Avoid evaluative generalizing or summarizing words. For example, rather than writing "The sink looked disgusting," it would be much better to write, "The sink was rust-stained and looked as if it had not been cleaned in a long time. Pieces of food and dirty dishes looked as if they had been piled in it for several days."
15. Reread your notes periodically and record any ideas generated by the rereading.
16. Always make backup copies of your notes and store the copies in different places in case of fire or other disaster.

How to Take Notes. There is more than one way to take field notes. The recommen-dations here (also see Making It Practical on page 280 and below) are only sugges-tions. With experience, you may develop your own system. Full field notes have several levels. Keep all the notes for an observation period together, but distinguish the levels of notes by starting each level on a new page or use a new color or font for each level. You will not produce the same amount of notes for each level. If you observe for six hours, you might have a tiny scrap paper of jotted notes, 40 pages of direct observation, 5 pages of researcher inference, and 2 pages in total for the methodological, theoretical, and personal level notes.

Maps and Diagrams. Many field researchers make maps and draw diagrams or pictures. Maps and diagrams help the researcher organize ideas and events in the field, and it helps when conveying life in a field site to other people. For example, you observe a lunch counter with 15 stools. You may draw and number 15 circles to simplify recording (e.g., "Yosuke came in and sat on stool 12; Phoebe was al-ready on stool 10"). Field researchers create three types of maps: spatial, social, and temporal (see Figure 10.3).

- A spatial map orients the data in space or physical location.
- A social map shows connections among people and follows the flow of interac-tions indicating power, influence, friendship, division of labor, and so on.
- A temporal map shows time starts, endings, and durations for people, goods, services, and communications.

Making It Practical Five Levels of Field Notes

Jotted notes. Short, temporary memory triggers such as words, phrases, or drawings taken inconspicuously, often scribbled on any convenient item (e.g., napkin, matchbook). You will incorporate them into direct ob-servation notes. They are never substitutes for full notes.

Direct observation notes. These are the core of your field data and are written immediately after leaving the field site. Order them chronologically, with the date, time, and place on each entry. They are a detailed description of everything you heard and saw in very concrete, spe-cific terms. To the extent possible, they are an exact recording of the particular words, phrases, or actions, never summaries or generalizations.

Researcher inference notes. You need to look and listen without inferring or imposing an interpretation. Obser-vations without inferences go into direct observation notes. *You record inferences in a separate section that is keyed to direct observations.* Keep inferred meanings separate from direct observation because the meaning of actions is not always self-evident. For example, a couple registers at a motel as Mr. and Mrs. Smith. You record what actually happened in the direct observa-tion level but put your inference that they are not mar-ried in the inference level. A great deal of social behav-ior is ambiguous and has multiple possible meanings. Your own feelings, interpretations, and reactions are part of data in the field and should be in the notes, but separated.

Analytic notes. Keep methodological ideas in analytic notes to record plans, tactics, ethical and procedural de-cisions, and self-critiques. You may have educated hunches or emerging theoretical ideas during data col-lection, and you should put them in the notes. Analytic notes are a running account of your attempts to give meaning to field events. You can "think out loud" in your analytic notes by suggesting links between ideas, proposing conjectures, and developing new concepts. Your analytical notes can include ethical concerns that you encounter and strategies you invent.

Personal notes. Personal notes serve three functions: They are an outlet for you and a way to cope with stress; they are a source of data about personal reac-tions; and they are a way to evaluate direct observation or inference notes later when you reread notes. For ex-ample, if you were in a good mood during observations, your mood might color what you observed or how you felt about events.

Recordings to Supplement Memory. The novice field researcher could mistakenly think audio or video recorders make field note-taking unnecessary. Professional researchers sometimes use them as supplements in field research but not as substitutes. Recorders provide a close approximation to what occurred and are a permanent record that can help you to recall events. However, machines are never a total substitute for written field notes or your presence in the field. Recording devices have many limitations, including the following:

- You cannot introduce them into all field sites for practical reasons (large area with noise) or legal reasons.
- People in the field will see them as a threat; recording devices frequently create a disruption and raise awareness of surveillance. You can only use them after you have developed rapport and trust.
- Recorders frequently miss action or are out of range, they break down or fail, or they may require your attention and reduce direct personal involvement with what is happening in the field site.
- Recorders rarely save time. You can expect to spend two to three times longer reviewing and transcribing recorded material than the time of the recoding. You may have three hours of recording, but it could take you an additional eight hours to review and transcribe what you recorded.

6. Interviewing in Field Research

Field researchers use unstructured, nondirective, in-depth interviews. These differ from formal survey research interviews in many ways (see Making It Practical: Survey Interviews versus Field Research Interviews, p. 284). In a field research interview, you ask questions, listen, express interest, and record. The field interview is a joint production between you and a field site member or informant (see the discussion of informants on page 283). People you interview are active participants in the discussion process, and their insights, feelings, and cooperation reveal their perspectives and subjective meanings.

You interview in the field or a convenient location and are informal and nondirective. It is acceptable for you to share your background to build trust and encourage the informant to open up. Do not force answers or use leading questions. You want to encourage and guide in a process of mutual discovery.

In field interviews, field members express themselves in their habitual way of speaking, thinking, and organizing reality. You want to retain their expressions, jokes, and narrative stories in a natural form without repackaging them into a standardized format. You want to stay close to the field member's experience. This means you ask questions in terms of concrete examples or situations—for example, "Could you tell me things that led up to your quitting in June?" instead of "Why did you quit your job?"

Field interviews can occur in a series over time. You first build rapport and avoid probing inner feelings until intimacy is established. After several meetings, you may be able to probe more deeply into sensitive issues and seek clarification of less sensitive issues. In later interviews, you can return to topics and check past answers by restating them in a nonjudgmental tone and asking for verification—for example, "The last time we talked, you said that you started taking things from the store after they reduced your pay. Is that right?" The field research interview is a "speech event," closer to a friendly conversation than the stimulus/response model used in a survey research interview. It differs from a friendly conversation in that it has an explicit purpose—to learn about the informant and setting. You may include explanations or requests that diverge from friendly conversations. You may say, "I'd like to ask you about," or "Could you look at this and see if I've written it down right?" The field interview is less balanced than a conversation. You ask more of the questions and may express more ignorance and interest than an ordinary conversation. Repetition is common. You may ask a field site member to elaborate on unclear abbreviations. You do not have to ask every person you interviewed the same questions, but tailor questions to specific individuals and situations.

Types of Questions in Field Interviews.   Field researchers ask three types of field interview questions: descriptive, structural, and contrast questions. You can ask all concurrently, but each type is more frequent at a different stage in the research process. When you first enter the field site, you will primarily ask descriptive questions. You can gradually add structural questions until, in the middle stage after analysis has begun, most of the questions are structural. Contrast questions begin in the middle of a study and increase until, by the end, you ask more of them than any other type.

Descriptive Questions.   You ask descriptive questions to learn about the setting and members. Descriptive questions can be about time and space—for example, "Where is the bathroom?" "When does the delivery truck arrive?" "What happened Monday night?" They can be about people and activities: "Who is sitting by the window?" "What is your uncle like?" They can be about events or activities: "What happens during the initiation ceremony?" They can be about objects: "When do you use a saber saw?" Questions asking for examples or experiences are descriptive questions: "Could you give me an example of a great date?" "What happens in a perfect game?" You can ask about hypothetical situations: To the new teacher—"If a student opened her book during the exam, how would you deal with it?"

Structural Questions.   You use a structural question after spending time in the field and after you started a preliminary analysis of your data. You ask structural questions after you have organized specific field events, situations, and conversations into preliminary conceptual categories and started to figure out how things are organized. You ask them for clarification and confirmation. For example, you observe a highway truck-stop restaurant. Over time, you see that the employees informally classify customers patronizing the truck stop. Based on a preliminary analysis, you think there are five types of customers. Using structural questions, you seek verification of the five types and their features. You might ask whether a category includes features beyond those you already identified—for example, "Are there any types of customers other than regulars, greasers, pit stoppers, road rangers, and long haulers?" You ask for confirmation: "Is a greaser a type of customer you serve early in the morning?" "Would you consider Johnny Jensen to be a long hauler?"

Contrast Questions.   After you have verified major categories, processes, or aspects of life in the field with structural questions, you can begin asking contrast questions. Contrast questions focus on the similarities or differences among the categories, processes, or aspects. You ask questions to verify similarities and differences that you believe to exist among categories. You may ask, "You seem to have a number of different kinds of customers come in here. Two types just stop to use the restroom without buying anything—entire families and a lone male driver. Do you call both of them pit stoppers?"

Informants.   The term **informant** has a specific meaning in field research. It is someone with whom you develop a relationship and who informs you about life in the field. The ideal informant is a person currently in the field site, completely familiar with its culture, and in position to have witnessed and participated in its significant events. The informant should not be too busy to spend some time talking with you. The ideal informant is nonanalytic. He or she uses ordinary native folk theory or pragmatic commonsense thinking. People who are highly educated and try to analyze the field site by imposing ideas or categories taken from the media or academic work are not good informants. In a long field study, you might interview various types of informants, such as rookies and old-timers, people who recently changed status (e.g., through promotion), and those who are static. You seek out in-

informant a member in a field site with whom a researcher develops a relationship and who tells the researcher many details about life in the field site.

Making It Practical Survey Interviews versus Field Research Interviews

TYPICAL SURVEY INTERVIEW

1. It has a clear beginning and end.
2. You ask the same standard questions of all respondents in the same sequence.
3. You appear neutral at all times.
4. You as the interviewer ask all questions, and the respondent only answers.
5. The interview is with one respondent alone.
6. You maintain a professional tone and businesslike focus; you suppress or ignore diversions.
7. Closed-ended questions are common, and probes are rare.
8. You as the interviewer alone control the pace and direction of the interview.
9. You ignore the social context in which the interview occurs.
10. You mold the communication pattern into a standard framework.

TYPICAL FIELD INTERVIEW

1. The beginning and end are not clear. The interview can stop and be resumed later.
2. You tailor the questions you ask and the order in which you ask them to specific people and situations.
3. You show interest in specific answers/responses and encourage elaboration.
4. The typical field interview is somewhat like a friendly conversational exchange, but with more interviewer questions.
5. Field interviews can occur in a group setting or with others in the area.
6. The interview can be interspersed with jokes, asides, stories, diversions, and anecdotes, and you record them.
7. Open-ended questions are common, and probes are frequent.
8. You and the field site member jointly control the pace and direction of the interview.
9. You note the social context of the interview and treat it as important for interpreting the meaning of responses.
10. You adjust to the member's norms and language usage.

formants who are frustrated or needy as well as those who are happy and secure, people at the center of the action and those on the fringes, and the leaders as well as followers. You can expect mixed messages when you interview a range of informants, but this is not a problem. It reflects the multiple points of view that can coexist in a field site.

Most people only reveal highly intimate, confidential information in private settings. Likewise, the field interview varies by its context. You generally want to conduct field interviews in the field member's home environment to increase the comfort level. Context and past interactions between you and an informant can shape what is said and how, so you want to note those things as well as what the informant actually says. You also want to note nonverbal communication in the interview that can add meaning, such as a shrug or a gesture (see Making It Practical: Survey Interviews versus Field Research Interviews).

7. Leaving the Field

A professional field researcher may be in a field site from a few weeks to a dozen years. At some point, work in the field ends. It may end naturally—when learning new things diminishes and theory building reaches a closure. Alternatively, it could go on without end, and you must decide to cut off relations and exit. At times, external factors force an ending (e.g., a job ends, gatekeepers order you to leave, a project deadline arrives).

You should plan for and anticipate the disengaging and exiting process. Depending on the intensity of involvement and the length of time in the field, exiting can be disruptive or emotionally painful. You may feel guilty and depressed immediately before and after leaving. You may find it difficult to let go because of personal and emotional ties. Professionals with a long, intense involvement in a field site sometimes need a month or more of adjustment time after exiting before they feel at home with their original cultural surroundings.

The exit process depends on specifics of the field setting and relationships developed. You have to decide length and form of disengagement. You can leave quickly (simply not return one day) or slowly reduce your involvement over several weeks. You also need to decide how to tell members and how much advance warning to give. If you spend a lot of time in a field site and have intense involvement with members, you should give some warning of the exit. Try to fulfill any bargains or commitments you built up in the field so you can leave with a clean slate. Often a small ritual, such as a going-away party or thanking and shaking hands with everyone, helps to signal the social break.

Anticipate the effect exiting may have on members. Some members may feel hurt or rejected because a close social relationship is ending. They may try to pull you back into the field. Over time, as warm social relations develop and many experiences are shared, members may have forgotten that you were an outsider there for research purposes. Bringing the research aspect of your relationship to the forefront may cause members to grow cold and distant or to become angry and resentful. Some researchers continue to maintain social relations with people they got to know in a field site after the study ends. For example, in her study of luxury hotels, Rachel Sherman (2006) reported that a few years after she left the field site, she continued to get together socially several times a year with workers who she got to know during the research.

8. Writing the Field Research Report

This section provides a brief overview of the field research report. More details on writing research reports are presented in Chapter 12. Field researchers start to think about what will appear in a report while they are still gathering data. More than in other types of social research, the researcher may use first person in the study report and recount his or her personal observations and experiences. More than in other reports, a field research report depends on the researcher's writing skill to fully convey a feeling of the field site, to describe individual people in the field, and to recount events in great depth. Unlike quantitative research reports, field research reports do not follow a fixed pattern. Many field research reports are book-length or are long, descriptive articles. Tables with numbers, graphs, or charts are very rare. In the report, the researcher provides supporting data in the form of photos

Tips for the Wise Consumer

You look for different things in a report on a field research study or ethnography than in a quantitative research study. Here are some things to look for:

- Exactly who conducted the study? Was it one person or several? What are the background or other characteristics of the person who conducted the study?
- What is the field site? Exactly when and where was the study conducted?
- Who constitute the members in the field site?

- How did the researcher gain access to the field site? Was it easy or difficult to gain access?
- How long did the researcher spend in the field conducting observations?
- Did the researcher supplement field observations with other types of evidence or documentation?
- What social role and what researcher role did the researcher use?
- Did the researcher conduct interviews for this study?
- How did the author use data to back up statements about themes, concepts, or processes in the field site?

Summary Review **The Process of Doing Field Research**

1. Preparing for a field research study
    Self-awareness
    Background investigation
    Practice observing and writing
2. Starting the research project
    Getting organized
    Selecting a site
    Gaining access
    Entering the field
        Presentation of self
        Amount of disclosure
        Selecting a social role
3. Being in the field
    Learning the ropes
    Building rapport
    Negotiating continuously
    Deciding on a degree of involvement
4. Developing strategies for success in the field
    Building relationships

Performing small favors
Being inept but accepted
Avoiding conflict
Adopting an attitude of strangeness
5. Observing and taking field notes
    The researcher as instrument
    What to observe
        Physical setting
        People
        Routines, events, and activities
        Learning to listen
    What if nothing happens?
    Sampling
    Becoming a skillful notetaker
        Types of notes
        Supplements
6. Conducting field interviews
7. Leaving the field
8. Writing the field research report

and quotes or short selections of concrete situations taken from the observations in field notes. The researchers use the quotes both to document and illustrate the concepts or themes that are part of the analysis.

ETHICS AND THE FIELD RESEARCHER

Several ethical issues are introduced by your direct, personal involvement in the social lives of others when doing field research. Often you are alone in the field and must make a quick ethical decision about situations that appear unexpectedly in the field. Privacy is the most common ethical issue. As you gain intimate knowledge in a field site and people give you information in confidence, you incur an ethical obligation to uphold the confidentiality of data. You must keep it confidential from other people in the field as well as from the public. You may want to disguise real names in field notes and in a report for the public.

New field researchers often ask about deception. When do you not fully and honestly disclose your role as a researcher and true purpose for being at a site? Professional researchers debate over covert versus overt field research. Everyone agrees that covert research is not preferred. Some say it is never acceptable. Others see covert research as acceptable and necessary for entering into and gaining knowledge about certain areas of social life, such as a secret society or ring of illegal drug dealers. In general, you should be honest and openly disclose why you are in a site whenever possible. This is especially true if you are a beginning researcher. Covert research raises ethical and sometimes legal issues. It is more difficult to maintain a false front and to be in a constant anxiety over being caught.

Professional researchers who conduct field research on people who engage in illegal behavior face additional ethical issues as well as personal risk. They may know of and are sometimes indirectly involved in illegal activity. Such knowledge is of interest both to law enforcement officials and to other criminals. The researcher faces an extra challenge in building trust and rapport but not becoming so involved as to violate personal moral standards or endanger other people. In such situations, professional researchers often make an explicit arrangement with the members—such as, I will leave when certain serious illegal behavior occurs. Field research with criminals is for experienced researchers who have extra training and a knowledge of the risks involved.

FOCUS GROUPS

What do you think about a male elementary school teacher? Most elementary school teachers are women. A traditional female gender role includes close physical contact with young children and nurturing emotional relationships that are necessary for successful elementary school teaching. By contrast, the traditional male gender role is to be emotionally remote, engage in coarse or rough behavior, and avoid intimate physical contact, such as hugging and touching. A male elementary school teacher may have his masculinity questioned. People may see him as being weak and not ambitious. They may suspect he is a homosexual or a dangerous pedophile. Beyond the gender role issue, males may avoid the job because of its low pay and low status. It is socially defined as "women's work" not appropriate for a "real man."

Many observers note that highly gender stratified elementary schools perpetuate and reinforce traditional gender roles. Young boys and girls learn a traditional adult male model, one that they also see daily in the mass media and among many adults. They learn that a male is supposed to be emotionally cool and aggressive. They are indirectly "taught" that adult men are not emotionally expressive and caring. Having male elementary teachers promotes social equality and gives young children a positive male role model. Young children learn gender roles in which it is acceptable for an adult male to express emotional intimacy and be nurturing. Having male elementary school teachers also enables males who enjoy working with active young children and who do not repress the caring, emotionally warm side of their self to have a rewarding professional career.

The **focus group** is a special qualitative research technique that differs from traditional ethnography. It does not require an extended period of detailed observation in a field site. It is similar in that you acquire qualitative data from a small number of selected people participating in a naturalistic open group conversation.

Christina Kennedy/Photo Edit Inc.

Focus group research has rapidly grown over the last 20 years. In it, you informally interview people in a group-discussion setting. It can take place in a natural field setting (e.g., restaurant, break room of work site) or a special setting (e.g., classroom, conference room). To create the group you gather together 4 to 12 people in a room with a trained moderator to discuss a few issues. The group members should be homogeneous but not include close friends or relatives. Most focus group sessions are 45 to 90 minutes long. The moderator must be nondirective and facilitate free, open discussion among all group members. The moderator offers open-ended questions and does not let one person dominate the discussion. In a typical study, you might create four to six separate focus groups. All would discuss the same questions or focus on the same topic.

focus group a qualitative research technique that involves informal group interviews about a topic.

To understand why men become elementary level teachers and how they feel about the reactions of others, Cushman (2005) conducted a focus group study with male elementary teachers.

Cushman (2005) contacted 17 practicing elementary teachers to participate in 90-minute focus group discussions. Three or four teachers were together in each group with a moderator. The semistructured discussion centered on several questions, such as the following:

- What aspects of elementary school teaching initially attracted you to this career?
- What sort of reaction did you get when you told family and friends?
- Did you go straight from school or try other career options first?
- Was the salary or status of an elementary teacher a concern to you?
- Do you face any challenges being part of a school staff in which males are a minority?
- To what extent does having physical contact with young children concern you?

Cushman found that all the teachers overwhelmingly chose the career because of the intrinsic joy they got from working with children. They found the play aspect of teaching young children to be most rewarding. Many also liked the strong service aspect of teaching. They tended to value intrinsic over extrinsic rewards (e.g., job satisfaction versus salary). Reactions by others to their decision varied but were often negative. Fathers were the most negative about the career choice. Positive reactions were most common when the men had teachers in their fami-

 Summary Review **Advantages and Limitations of Focus Groups**

ADVANTAGES

- They are fast, easy to do, and inexpensive.
- They occur in a more natural setting that helps to increase external validity.
- They provide exploratory researchers with new insights and give survey researchers ideas for questions and answer categories.
- They give quantitative researchers a window into how people naturally discuss topics and aid in the interpretation of quantitative results.
- They allow research participants to query one another and explain their answers to each other.
- They encourage open expression among members of marginalized social groups who may not otherwise speak.
- They help people to feel empowered by a group setting, especially in action-oriented research projects.

LIMITATIONS

- You cannot generalize the discussion outcomes to a large, diverse population.
- They create a "polarization effect" such that attitudes become more extreme after group discussion.
- They are limited to discussing one or a few topics in a session.
- A moderator may unknowingly limit full, open, and free expression by all group members.
- Focus group participants tend to produce fewer ideas than in individual interviews.
- A large quantity of open-discussion results can be difficult to analyze.
- Reports on focus groups rarely report all the details of study design/procedure.
- Researchers find it difficult to reconcile differences that arise between responses given by an individual-only interview and those from a focus group.

Making It Practical Using Focus Groups to Learn Why Students Picked a Private High School

Several years ago, I used focus groups as part of an applied study on why parents and students chose a private high school. I formed six focus groups. Each group had 8 to 10 student volunteers from the high school. A trained college-student moderator asked questions, elicited comments from group members, and made sure that no one person dominated the discussions. The six groups contained male and female members from either one grade level or two adjacent grades (e.g., freshmen and sophomores). For 45 minutes, students discussed their reasons for attending the high school. They were asked about the importance of specific factors in the decision. These included parent pressure, participating in school sports, academic reputation,

cost of the school, being with their friends, siblings or parents who went to the same school, school size, and the school's religious orientation. We tape-recorded the discussions and then analyzed the tapes to understand what the students saw as most important to their decisions. In addition, the data helped us to interpret survey data on the same topic. We used the results to design three survey questionnaires. One questionnaire was for all high school students, another for a sample of parents, and a third for students at junior high schools that often sent students to the high school. Results were part of a written report and presented at an open meeting of the parents and the school's administration.

lies. Many men came to elementary teaching after having tried other career options and only after developing a strong sense of self and their major life priorities. All were aware that homophobic communities made false accusations against male teachers. They knew that false accusations could have tragic consequences for a teacher.

Researchers have examined many topics using the focus group technique. Topics include issue attitudes (e.g., race relations, workplace equality), personal behaviors and relations (e.g., how to live with a child who has disabilities), a new product (e.g., breakfast cereal), or a political candidate. The focus group procedure has its own strengths and weaknesses (see Summary Review: Advantages and Limitations of Focus Groups, p. 288).

WHAT HAVE YOU LEARNED?

In this chapter, you learned about the field research process, including its logic, choosing a site and gaining access, developing relations in the field, observing and collecting data, and conducting a field interview. You saw how field research differs from quantitative research; field researchers begin data analysis and theorizing as they collect data. In field research, you as the researcher are directly involved with the people you study. You become immersed in the social life of a natural setting to learn about it. More than quantitative research, doing field research can have a large impact on your emotions, personal life, and sense of self. Field research is a way to study parts of the social world that you otherwise could not study.

To do good field research requires a combination of skills. You need a strong sense of self, an excellent abil-

ity to listen and absorb details, tremendous patience, sensitivity and empathy for other people, superb social skills, a talent to think very quickly on your feet, the ability to see subtle interconnections among people/events, and an ability to express yourself in writing. Field research is especially valuable for studying micro-level social life and face-to-face interactions among small groups of people who interact with one another. It is less effective when the concern is macro-level processes and social structures, such as events that occurred in the distant past or that stretch across decades. Historical-comparative research, discussed in the next chapter, is better suited to investigating these types of concerns.

KEY TERMS

analytic notes *281*
appearance of interest *275*
attitude of strangeness *276*
ethnography *264*
field site *269*
focus group *287*

gatekeeper *269*
going native *273*
informant *283*
jotted notes *280*
naturalism *267*
normalize social research *271*

APPLYING WHAT YOU'VE LEARNED

Activity 1

A good way to learn about ethnography and field research is to read studies that use them. Locate three field research studies on different settings or topics. Many studies are book-length, but two journal sources are the *Journal of Contemporary Ethnography* and *Qualitative Sociology*. You can also try a keyword search of scholarly articles using the terms *ethnography*, *participant observation*, or *field research*. Look for the features outlined in Tips for the Wise Consumer box of this chapter.

Activity 2

Doing detailed field research observation takes practice. Find a public social location that meets the criteria of a good field site and assume a total observer role for 30 minutes. Return to the same location 24 to 48 hours later for a second 30-minute observation period. During your first visit, notice everything about the physical setting using all your senses. After you leave the site, try to write down everything you can recall. During your second visit, (1) notice what you missed about the physical setting the first time that helps produce its atmosphere; and (2) notice the people—their number, age, gender, ethnicity—and entry/exit location. After you leave the site, try to write down everything you can recall. Two days later, reread your notes for both observations and add any other details you recall.

Activity 3

You can learn to see social settings in a new light by drawing three types of field site maps: temporal, social, and spatial. Find a social location that meets the criteria of a good field site and assume a total observer role for 20 minutes. Return to the same site five times. Pick different days of the week and times of the day. After leaving the site, try to create each type of map. The spatial is usually the easiest, the temporal and social more difficult. Can you begin to see how the three types of maps capture and together begin to present a picture of life in the field site?

Activity 4

Conduct an informal, open-ended interview for about 15 minutes with someone who works full time as a waiter or waitress at a sit-down restaurant about "emotion work." Do not use that term. Instead ask about specifics—do they have to "act nice," "say pleasant things," "smile when dealing with people who are difficult or rude," and so forth? Try to get a sense of how they deal with unpleasant customers, the pressure on them from management, or tips to be nice and friendly. Have them recount specific instances or tell stories. Ask whether there is a gap between how they really feel and how they must act on the job. Do they hide their true emotions and feelings as part of the job? Have they ever let their true feelings show when they should not have?

REFERENCES

Cushman, Penni. 2005. "It's Just Not a Real Bloke's Job: Male Teachers in Primary Schools." *Asia-Pacific Journal of Teacher Education* 33:321–338.

Davis, Fred. 1959. "The Cabdriver and His Fare: Facets of a Fleeting Relationship." *The American Journal of Sociology* 65:158–165.

Fine, Gary Alan. 1987. *With the Boys: Little League Baseball and Preadolescent Culture*. Chicago: University of Chicago Press.

Gurney, Joan Neff. 1985. "Not one of the guys: The female researcher in a male-dominated setting." *Qualitative Sociology* 8(1): 42–62.

Hochschild, Arlie. 1983. *The Managed Heart: Commercialization of Human Feeling*. Berkeley: University of California Press.

Katovich, Michael A., and Ron L. Diamond 1986. "Selling Time: Situated Transactions in a Noninstitutional Environment." *Sociological Quarterly* 27(2): 253–271.

Perry, Pamela. 2001. "White Means Never Having to Say You're Ethnic: White Youth and the Construction of "Cultureless" Identities." *Journal of Contemporary Ethnography* 30(1): 56–91.

Schweingruber, David, and Nancy Berns. 2005. "Shaping the Selves of Young Salespeople through Emotion Management." *Journal of Contemporary Ethnography* 34:679–706.

Sherman, Rachel. 2006. *Classic Acts: Service and Inequality in Luxury Hotels*. Berkeley: University of California Press.

Van Maanen, John. 1991. "The Smile Factory: Work at Disneyland." in P. Frost, L. Moore, M. Luis, C. Lundberg, and J. Martin (eds.), *Reframing Organizational Culture* (pp. 58–76). Thousand Oaks, CA: Sage.

Looking at the Past and Across Cultures

The Granger Collection, New York

Do people who immigrate form attachment to their new country or stay connected across international borders? McKeown (2001) asked this question and studied Chinese migrant networks in Peru, Chicago, and Hawaii early in the twentieth century. As part of his study, he examined events taking place over 100 years of history and in three nations. He looked at major international events, national laws, and individual family biographies. Although his study was historical and qualitative, he also examined quantitative data. He provided us with graphs, charts, and tables of statistics. The data included geographic maps, photographs, quotes from 100-year-old telegrams, official government documents, original newspaper reports, and personal letters in three languages. By comparing Chinese migrants over a long period in different social-cultural settings, he traced the formation and operation of transnational communities and social identities. He learned that people had formed social networks that linked back to villages in China and crossed several national borders. These networks helped people to sustain a vibrant, interactive social community. Ties in the village of origin, clan and family, business transactions, and a shared language and customs held the social network together. People in the network helped each another with legal and financial issues. They consulted on major social events or concerns. Their children often intermarried. McKeown discovered an ethnic-immigrant network that mixed local customs and language with those of the country of origin to sustain long-term family and other social relationships across international borders for several generations. People in the network mixed languages and customs. They created business and family relationships that operated across countries. McKeown concluded that if we only see people as individuals inside a nation or treat people as a single ethnic group, we fail to see that they may also be part of a large transnational social community that is a hybrid of several cultures.

WHAT IS HISTORICAL-COMPARATIVE RESEARCH?

You will learn about historical-comparative (H-C) research in this chapter. It is the most relevant research method for explaining and understanding macro-level events—a terrorist attack, a nation going to war, sources of racism, large-scale immigration, violence based on religious hate, or urban decay. The major nineteenth-century founders of the social sciences, such as Emile Durkheim, Karl Marx, and Max Weber, used this method. Researchers used it to study issues in many macro-level topic areas—such as social change, political sociology, social movements, and social inequality—and in other areas—such as health care, criminology, gender relations, race relations, and family. H-C has become increasingly popular. Researchers probably conducted more H-C studies in the past 10 years than in the previous 30 years combined.

H-C studies are ideal when you want to address "big questions," but people question their practical value. True, most H-C research studies address basic rather than applied research questions (see Chapter 1 on basic and applied research). In addition, H-C studies can take a long time to complete. It typically requires over a year to complete an H-C study. In contrast, field research studies often take about a year, and many experiments, surveys, or existing statistics research studies are finished within a few months. On the other hand, often there is no better way to answer important questions than H-C research.

H-C research provides answers to questions such as, Why are there has two types of physicians with different medical degrees and different approaches medicine in the United States? Most people are familiar with medical doctors (MDs) but few know about osteopathic physicians (DOs). About 55,000 DOs practice medicine in the United States, representing about 6 percent of all physicians. A DO practices medicine based more on a broad mixture of medical and health remedies and is more holistic than the MD who tends to use laboratory-based pharmaceuticals and surgery. This fast-growing type of medical professional is trained in separate medical schools, licensed in all 50 states, and can practice in all medical specialties.

H-C studies also provide innovative ideas in fields such as education, business, law enforcement, and medical care. Long forgotten practices or practices used in other cultures can stimulate exciting new ways to approach current issues and solve problems. In addition, the methodological issues of H-C research have wider implications in comparison to other research techniques, and being aware of them will build your general research skills.

You use a blend of research techniques in H-C research. Some are like traditional history, some are like field research, and others extend quantitative research such as surveys or existing statistics research. In this chapter, we focus on H-C research that places historical time and/or cross-cultural variation at the center. It is best to use H-C research when your research question involves the flow of history and/or two or more sociocultural contexts. H-C researchers look at how a specific mix of diverse factors have come together in time and place to generate a specific outcome (e.g., civil war). They compare entire societies to see what they share and do not share. They also examine the same social process across several cultural or historical settings (see Example Study Box 1: Women's Right to Vote, p. 295).

Many people enjoy reading H-C studies because they learn about distant places or the past. However, the studies can be difficult to follow if you lack background knowledge about history or other cultures. H-C studies assume that readers have a minimal level historical-geographic literacy and cultural knowledge. Most people acquire a background in high school or general education college classes. H-C studies extend and build on the existing background knowledge. To appreciate H-C studies and conduct H-C research, you need an awareness of geography, history, and cross-cultural differences (see Example Study Box 2: Race Relations in Different Countries, p. 296 and Learning from History: Conditions in Medieval Western Europe, p. 297).

Example Study Box 1 Women's Right to Vote

Underwood & Underwood/Corbis

Both Switzerland and the United States have strong democratic traditions and highly individualistic cultures. Both have similar federalist forms of national government and local governments that allow direct democracy (also called public referendums or local ballot initiatives) (see Kriesi and Wisler 1999). In 1920, the United States joined other proactive nations in allowing women to vote in nationwide elections. However, Swiss women did not win the right to vote until 1990. Switzerland was among the last nations to extend the right to vote to women. Banaszak (1996) examined the 70-year difference on this basic issue in countries with numerous political and cultural similarities. In her study, she looked at published studies, official records and documents on women's movements, government, and social-political conditions in each society across a century. She discovered that the United States suffrage movement was very different from the one in Switzerland. The Swiss women's movement favored consensus politics, supported local autonomy, and worked closely with the major political parties. A more confrontational grass-roots suffrage movement emerged in the United States. It worked outside the major political parties and purposely disrupted the established system to win voting rights for women. Thus, the two nations' women's movements differed dramatically in orientation even though their political institutions were alike.

Most H-C researchers use a variety of data to examine a central issue and place it in a context with background knowledge. They generally gather qualitative data and focus on issues of culture. Like field researchers, they want to see things through the eyes of the people they are studying. They examine specific individuals or groups and are sensitive to specific historical or cultural contexts. As with field research and unlike quantitative research, most H-C researchers only make limited generalizations.

How Are Field Research and H-C Research Alike?

First, we consider similarities between H-C research and field research. In the next section, we examine the unique features of historical-comparative research. Field and H-C research have five similarities:

- They incorporate an individual researcher's point of view as part of the research process.
- They examine a great diversity of data types (diaries, maps, official statistics, newspapers, novels).
- They focus on processes, time passage, and sequence.
- They use grounded theory.
- They make limited generalizations.

An individual researcher's characteristics, place in history, and geographic-cultural situation may influence the research process. The time, place, and culture

Example Study Box 2 Race Relations in Different Countries

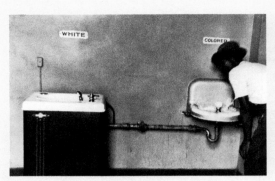

Elliott Erwitt/Magnum Photos Inc.

What are the origins of racism and why did it take very different forms in multiracial countries? Anthony Marx (1998) compared racial relations in Brazil, South Africa and the United States. Each country had black-white racism, but it took different forms based on specific historical conditions and politics in each country. Marx assumed his readers knew basic geography and something about U.S. racial conditions, and he provided background information, such as that Brazil and the United States are geographically large countries with mixed-race populations. Both had large-scale European immigration and slaves taken from Africa from the 1700s to the mid-1800s. By contrast, South Africa had a small European-immigrant population since the 1700s and a large majority native African population. Marx provided many historical and comparative details to build on this foundation of knowledge. To conduct his study, he devoted years to reading hundreds of historical books and articles and examining statistical records and official reports. He traveled to each country and conducted interviews. From the data collected, he shows us how each country developed a different pattern of race relations over time. Brazil developed moderately integrated black-white relations, whereas the Southern U.S. and South Africa both developed highly segregated racial patterns. Marx explains why these differences occurred. In the United States and South Africa, but not in Brazil, social-political elites emphasized racial superiority to unify a white population characterized by internal divisions of social class and other issues (religion, nation of origin). To do this they enforced long-term, legally enforced systems of official racial segregation.

in which you live may affect your data collection and interpretation. Both H-C and field research recognize this feature. In both, you may see specific biographic details of the person who conducted the research included somewhere in the study.

In both types of research, you immerse yourself fully in a huge amount of qualitative data. The goal is to understand in depth the lives, language, and perspective of the people you are studying so you can acquire an empathic understanding of them. You try to capture their subjective feelings and details of their daily lives. Only after an immersion in the data do you narrow the focus to specific areas for analysis. As you acquire an up-close understanding of the people studied, you "translate" from events their worldview for readers of your research report.

In field and H-C research, you devote attention to processes, time passage, and sequence, and you never treat people or social life as being static or unchanging. You treat the passage of time (micro-level clock time as well as long-term historical time) as an essential aspect of the data.

All researchers begin with concepts and ideas, but in H-C and field research you often create new concepts based on the data. The ideas emerge during data collection and analysis in a process of grounded theory (you read about grounded theory in Chapter 2). As you gain greater knowledge about a particular place and time, it may be difficult to make broad generalizations that apply to all places or times. Typically, field and H-C research offer more limited generalization than quantitative research.

Learning from History Conditions in Medieval Western Europe

You need background information to read H-C studies and put them in context. Perhaps you read about Western Europe in the 1500s. You may already have learned that roughly one-third of the population (75 million people) died in the Black Death and about 90 to 95 percent of the population in that era could not read or write. However, you know that using the number zero was considered the devil's work, using Arabic numbers (the ones we use today) instead of Roman numerals was forbidden, and only a handful of math experts could do simple multiplication or division (what you learned in third or fourth grade). This lack of math skills profoundly affected business, accounting, and engineering. Basic banking—lending or counting money for buying and selling goods—was so primitive that it slowed the growth of trade. Most people considered loaning money for interest or making profits slightly immoral or possibly illegal. This example shows the importance of background knowledge. If you look at some past situation and ask, "Why didn't people do things differently?" you often discover the answer in the many differences from the present. For example, you may it unusual that people looked up to a local 29-year-old scribe as

if he was a respected wise man when his scribe skills equaled those of a bright sixth-grader today. This makes sense in a social world where only 5 percent of adults had basic literacy skills (versus 95 percent today) and life expectancy was about 40 years old (versus nearly 80 years old today).

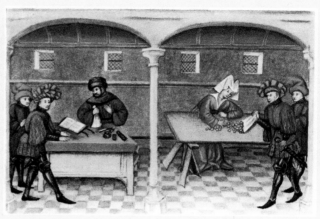

Bettmann/Corbis

What Is Unique about H-C Research?

Despite its many similarities to field research, H-C research has important differences. In H-C research, how you conduct research on the historical past and another culture differs from doing field research in the present in your home culture. The H-C researcher learns to do each of the following things:

1. Work with limited evidence.
2. Interpret evidence with minimum distortion.
3. Integrate the micro and macro levels.
4. Use specific as well as transcultural, transhistorical concepts.

1. Build on Limited and Indirect Evidence. In all studies, you construct an understanding of social life based on the empirical evidence you gathered. Historical evidence depends on data that have survived from the past. Even if you have many excellent historical documents (e.g., letters and newspapers), you are limited to what has not been destroyed and what has left a trace or other evidence behind. You cannot directly observe or be involved in the past. In comparative research, only a native member of two cultures can grasp all the similarities and differences. You may learn another language, study a new culture, and spend time in that culture, but unless you grew up in and fully absorbed the other culture, your understanding will always be that of an outsider. To see and feel like a native in both cultures, you must be truly bicultural.

2. Interpret the Meaning of Events in Context. Data in H-C studies are rarely simple and unambiguous. The data usually contain multiple messages from which you extract meaning. Do not expect to get a full understanding based on a quick first glance of the evidence. Immerse yourself in it, absorb its complexity, and place it in context. Only after you reflect on the evidence and consider its many meanings can you interpret what it means.

Perhaps you want to conduct a study on family relations of 120 years ago or in a distant country. To start, you need to learn the social context (e.g., the nature of daily work, forms of communication, transportation technology). You may want to study maps and events of that time and place. You want to be aware of local laws, the nature of health and medical care, types of foods eaten, daily household tasks, and common social practices. You may have data for a simple event, "the visit of a family member." Kinship customs and obligations of the time shape the event. To put the event in context, you need to realize that the roads are made of dirt and mud, traveling is by foot, no one can call ahead of time, and there are few places to stop and rest. Without a full immersion in the evidence, you cannot grasp the meaning of "visit of a family member." As you learn the context, you need to guard against three common types of distortion:

- Supracontext awareness
- Coherence imposition
- Capacity overestimation

Supracontext Awareness.   You are aware of events beyond the immediate people or setting that your are studying, such as events that occurred later in time or elsewhere. This knowledge could distort your understanding because you know things that the people you are studying could not know. For example, you study people living in colonial America in 1760. You know that there will soon be a war of independence from Britain and the colonialists will win. However, the people you are studying did not know that. Do not to judge their actions based on what you know happened later. From their perspective, things may have looked different. You must see situations as they saw them. In a comparative study, you may become familiar with another culture but study people who know only their own culture. For example, you notice that there is a food spoilage problem, people spend lots of time storing food, putting it in jars in dark rooms, and people often get sick from spoiled food. You may think, Why don't they store food by wrapping it up as the people of my home culture do? It takes less time than other methods, and the food rarely spoils. It is unfair to evaluate life in one culture based on your awareness of a life in different culture that most people know little or nothing about.

Coherence Imposition.   We like consistency and order. If you impose the expectation that people engage in predicable behavior and hold stable beliefs, you may introduce distortion. Prepare to study events or people that are contradictory or have "loose ends" that do not neatly come together. Try not to impose your own sense of order to make people's beliefs or actions coherent, noncontradictory, and consistent more than they actually are. For example, you study people having a birthday party. You expect a clear beginning and ending, with the person having a birthday at the center of attention. You see people wandering in or out, one by one, without signaling that they are leaving, and you cannot even tell whose birthday it is. From an outsider perspective, you may want to organize and impose boundaries around the event, but the people you are studying do not see or experience that way. Instead of interjecting your desire for order, accurately describe how they see/experience the world.

Capacity Overestimation.   People learn, make decisions, change direction, and act on (or fail to act on) what they learn. However, people have a limited capacity to learn, make decisions, and modify the course of events. It is easy to overestimate the ability of people to act. Recognize that people may not quickly take actions. For example, you think, Those parents could have met with the teacher about their child's problem. However, from the parents' life situation and point of view, that may not be an easy or realistic option. Do not become frustrated and say, "They could have done X; why did they not act?" Try to grasp their point of view and recognize the constraints they feel.

3. Integrate the Micro and Macro Levels. H-C researchers often examine and integrate data from both the micro (small-scale, face-to-face interaction) and macro (large-scale social structures) levels. For example, you read diaries or letters to get a feel for the everyday lives of individuals who lived in the distant past. You learn about the food they ate, their recreational pursuits, clothing, sicknesses, relations with friends, and so on. You link this micro-level view to macro-level, societal-wide processes (increased immigration, mechanization of production, tightened labor markets, and the like). Perhaps you want to compare schooling in two cultures. You visit and spend time in classrooms, talk to students and teachers, and devote hours to learning the daily routines and micro-culture of schools. In addition, you study the overall structure of education in each culture, such as requirements, graduation rates, numbers and types of schools, the books and tests used in schools, official curriculum guides, teacher training requirements, and so forth. You then integrate the micro-level or face-to-face life in classrooms with the macro-level structure of the national education system in each culture.

4. Use Specific and Transcultural, Transhistorical Concepts. We use many concepts to study and think about the social world. Imagine them on a continuum. At one end are universal concepts. They apply across social settings, historical time, and cultures. They are transcultural or transhistorical. You can use the same idea to exam-

Summary Review A Comparison of Approaches to Research

TOPIC	BOTH FIELD AND H-C RESEARCH	QUANTITATIVE RESEARCH
Researcher's perspective	Include the researcher as an integral part of the research process.	Remove the researcher influence from the research process.
Approach to data	Become immersed in many details to acquire an empathetic understanding.	Precisely operationalize variables.
Theory and data	Use grounded theory, create a dialogue between data and concepts.	Compare deductive abstract theory with empirical data.
Present findings	Translate a meaning system to others.	Test specific hypotheses.
Action/structure	People construct meaning but do so within social structures.	Social forces shape people's behavior whether or not they are aware of them.
Laws/generalization	Make limited generalizations that depend on context.	Discover universal, context-free general laws.

Features of a Distinct H-C Approach to Doing Research

TOPIC	THE HISTORICAL COMPARATIVE RESEARCHER
Evidence	Reconstructs from many fragments and incomplete evidence
Distortion	Guards against using own awareness of factors outside the social or historical context
Human role	Includes the consciousness of people in a context and uses their motives as causal factors
Causes	Sees cause as contingent on conditions, hidden beneath the surface, and due to a specific combination of factors
Micro/macro	Links the micro to macro levels or layers of social reality
Cross-contexts	Moves between concrete specifics in a context and across contexts for more abstract comparisons

ine all times and all cultures. At the opposite end are concepts that apply only to particular social settings, cultures, or historical eras. Of course, many concepts fall between these extremes.

A universal concept, such as fear, exists in all societies in all eras. Specific concepts may be found in one historical era or culture but few if any in others. Perhaps a culture has as an event marking a girl's fourteenth birthday as a major signal of the end of childhood and her being ready for marriage and childbearing. H-C researchers use both types of concepts. Sometimes an event, activity, or social situation is unique in time or place, you grasp this, and you explain and apply it as appropriate. At other times, you can use universal concepts that let you make comparisons across time and culture and build broader explanations. Quantitative studies usually use transcultural, transhistorical concepts; however, they are frequently assumed and rarely examined to see whether they actually apply in different cultures or historical eras.

HOW TO DO A HISTORICAL-COMPARATIVE RESEARCH STUDY

In this section, we discuss how to do H-C research. Like field research, H-C research does not require you to follow a fixed set of steps; nonetheless, it involves several processes that usually occur in order:

- Acquire the necessary background.
- Conceptualize the issue.
- Locate and evaluate the evidence.
- Organize the evidence.
- Synthesize and develop concepts.
- Write the report.

Acquire the Necessary Background

As a preliminary step, learn about the basics of the setting (i.e., historical period and/or cultures). If you are not already familiar with the historical era or culture of your study area, engage in orientation reading (i.e., read several general books on the setting).

Conceptualize the Issue

Early in the process, think through the topic and develop ideas about it with clear definitions. You can begin with a general topic and a few ideas, but after you have background knowledge and start to gather data, start focusing on a specific issue. The focused issue will direct you to relevant evidence but remain flexible. It is impossible to begin research without some assumptions, concepts, and theory. Allow concepts and evidence to interact and stimulate the research direction. As in field research, you can change direction based on what you learn from the data. Start with some preliminary, provisional concepts to "package" evidence and guide you. As you acquire a strong grasp of the details of a specific setting, adjust or refine the concepts. Create new organizing concepts, subdivide the main issue, and develop lists of questions to ask. Often you find that the data do not fit neatly with the original concepts, and you must revise them. For example, you study a restaurant in the distant past or another culture. You begin with a few concepts such as dining pleasure, consumer choice, price competition, and so forth. You quickly discover that the restaurant does not wash dishes in clean water, all of the customers are neighbors who live within a 10-minute walk from the restaurant, there is no written menu, and no one mentions prices. You may rethink what is happening and develop new ideas to make sense of the situation.

Locate and Evaluate the Evidence

You will need to do a lot of bibliographic work, especially for historical research. Historical research requires using indexes, catalogs, and special reference works that list what libraries or other sources contain. Professional researchers may spend months searching for sources in libraries, travel to different specialized research libraries, and read dozens (if not hundreds) of books and articles. For comparative research, this means you must focus on one or more specific nations or areas. Comparative research often requires learning a foreign language and/or travel to another country and then establishing contacts with local people. Once you find evidence, you need to evaluate its accuracy (see the following discussion of primary historical evidence). As you gather evidence, try to keep two questions in mind:

- How relevant is the evidence to emerging research questions and evolving concepts?
- How accurate and strong is the evidence?

Your research focus often shifts. As this happens, evidence that was once relevant becomes less relevant and previously ignored evidence may become highly relevant. Also, you want to constantly evaluate alternative interpretations of the evidence and look for "silences." Silences are situations in which the evidence fails to address an event, topic, or issue. For example, you study a group of leading male merchants in the 1890s. You find a lot of evidence and documents about them and their business dealings. However, there is no evidence about their wives and many servants—who are invisible in the data. To assess the whole situation, you want to notice both what is clearly documented and what has "disappeared."

Organize the Evidence

As you gather and locate sources, you also organize the data. Obviously, it is unwise to take notes madly and let them pile up haphazardly; instead you sort, label, and categorize. Begin with a preliminary analysis by noting themes in the mass of details. As you sort and label, reflect and develop insights that can stimulate new ways to organize data and new questions for your study. Let data and theory interact and influence one another. Evaluate the evidence based on emerging ideas or theory. Your thinking on an issue advances as you reexamine and reorganize evidence. This occurs because you use newly created ideas to look at old data in new ways and the new ideas will guide your search for additional data.

Synthesize and Develop Concepts

Once most of the evidence is in, move toward creating an overall picture or general explanation. You want to synthesize and pull the parts together into one story. As you read and reread your notes and you sort and resort them based on various organizing schemes, look for new connections. Try to see the evidence in different ways. By looking for patterns, you can draw out similarities and differences to accompany your analogies. You might organize events into sequences and group them into a step-by-step process. You can synthesize by connecting a body of evidence with an abstract concept or causal mechanism. Many researchers find metaphors useful. For example, you note that relations between a foreman and workers are "like an emotional roller coaster drop" in which things seemed to be getting better and moving higher and higher, and then there is a sudden letdown after expectations have risen very fast. You can use metaphors as organizing and sensitizing devices.

Write the Report

Assembling evidence, arguments, and conclusions into a written report is a crucial step in all research. If anything, this step is more important for H-C than for quantitative research. A carefully crafted, well-written report often "makes or breaks" the success of H-C research. You must distill mountains of evidence into clear exposition, document numerous sources with extensive footnotes, and weave the evidence and arguments together in a manner that communicates a coherent, convincing picture. You gathered mountains of specific details in the study but can only include a few critical examples of the raw evidence. These illustrate and give credence to your larger story. Achieving a good balance between generalization and documented specific details can be difficult, but you want do this as you tell readers a dramatic, compelling story (writing a research report is discussed in more depth in the next chapter).

RESEARCHING THE PAST

In this section, we look at research into past events or people. Of course, the past begins five minutes ago, but something usually is at least 10 years in the past before we call it history. After about 10 years, direct experience has faded and our perspective shifts. The word *history* is confusing because of its several meanings:

- Actual events that occurred in the past (e.g., it is *history* that the French withdrew troops from Vietnam)
- A documented record of the past (e.g., a *history* of French involvement in Vietnam)
- An academic field in which specialists study the past (e.g., a course in the department of *history*)

Specialists in the field of history, or historians, devote most of their time and efforts to gathering and analyzing historical data. They often use specialized techniques. Nonhistorian social researchers rarely "do history," but they too examine historical data—that is, evidence about actual past events, including documented records. Compared to a professional historian, social researchers often consider a wider scope of historical evidence and have different goals in mind. Let us look at the contrast in goals and activities between the historian and the H-C social researcher. The historian usually

- sees collecting highly accurate historical evidence as a central goal in itself;
- interprets the data's significance in light of other historical events; and
- is not overly concerned about developing a theory to explain social relations or processes.

By contrast, the H-C social researcher

- treats gathering carefully documented, extremely accurate, and highly detailed descriptions of specific past events as important but secondary;
- wants to extend or build a theory or apply social concepts to new situations;
- uses historical evidence as a means to an end (e.g., to explain and understand social relations).

Types of Historical Evidence

Social researchers and historians both draw on four types of historical evidence:

- Primary sources
- Running records
- Recollections
- Secondary sources

The historian's main goal is to locate, collect, validate, and analyze the first one on the list—primary sources (to be discussed shortly). By contrast, a social researcher will look more at secondary sources or running records. Both use recollections. In the study about Chinese immigrants that opened this chapter, McKeown (2001) used all the sources except recollections.

Primary Sources. The letters, diaries, newspapers, magazines, speeches, movies, novels, articles of clothing, photographs, business records, and so forth from people in the past that have survived into the present are called **primary sources**. You can find them in official archives (a place where documents are stored), in private collections, in family closets, or in museums. Today's documents and objects (letters, television programs, menus, commercials, clothing, toys, and automobiles) will become primary sources for future historians. A widely used primary source is a published or unpublished written document. Documents may be in their original form or in preserved form on microfiche or film. They are often the only surviving record we have of the words, thoughts, deeds, and feelings of people in the past. A classic primary source is a bundle of yellowed letters that a traveling businessman wrote to his wife and that the historian discovers in an attic 75 years after both the husband and wife have died.

A limitation of written sources is that elites or people in official organizations write most of the documents. It is easy to overlook the views of the illiterate, the poor, or people outside official institutions. For example, during early nineteenth century, in the United States it was illegal for slaves to read or write. You will find it difficult to locate written sources on how a slave actually experienced slavery. By contrast, most slave owners could read and write. Written documents from the slave era tend to give a slave owner's rather than the slave's point of view.

primary sources sources created in the past and that survived to the present.

Making It Practical   **Old Newspaper Articles as Sources**

A widely used and easily accessible primary source is the newspaper. The "official" national newspaper of the United States is the *New York Times*. Luckily, you can search old copies of it electronically through online services such as Proquest™. For example, you are interested in articles on the topic of immigration between 1900 and 1910. You quickly find 3711 articles, so you narrow the topic. Let us say you want to find out about immigration from one country, Japan. You discover 224 articles discussing the topic in the *New York Times* during those 10 years (see Figure 11.1). As you read, you find one 1902 article about how the Japanese government wanted to protect from discrimination its citizens who came to the United States and distinguish Japanese laborers from Chinese coolies. Japan's government said it would limit who it allowed to immigrate irrespective of U.S. immigration laws. The article says that fewer than 14,000 Japanese live in the United States, excluding Hawaii (at that time a U.S. territory but not a state). To study this topic more fully, you want to read secondary sources and newspapers from the Pacific coast, where the topic was hotly debated. You need background knowledge, such an awareness of hostility toward Asians and rioting against Chinese in Pacific states in the 1880s. This turmoil led to the 1882 Chinese Exclusion Act, which ended most immigration from China. A look at the

Statistical Abstract of the United States for 1900 (which is available online) shows you that immigration from all of Asia was very low—fewer than 4400 entered in 1890—less than from the tiny country of the Netherlands in the same year. However, between 1890 and 1900, immigration from Asia increased to 17,000. If you had background knowledge of the time, you might suspect that the increase around 1900 may be people from Philippines. This is because the United States had made the Philippines a colony in 1899. The *Statistical Abstract* is not very useful. It divided immigration information on Asia into China and the rest of Asia. You notice that the number from China dropped between 1890 to 1900. A look at more detailed U.S. Census records will show that 55 Japanese lived in the United States in 1870 (excluding Hawaii). This number rose to 2000 by 1890. If you pursue the topic and search libraries for secondary literature and books on the topic, you will find about 10 books written on pre-1920s immigration from Japan. So by starting with a general topic and a 10-year time period, you found a 1902 newspaper article. Fom that article you could develop a more focused search and move toward a research question, Why and how did Japan control which of its people immigrated to the United States? Did other countries try to control who came to the United States or this unique to Japan?

A big concern of primary sources is that only a fraction of what existed in the past has survived into the present. Moreover, what survived is a not a representative sample of what once existed.

As you read primary sources, avoid the distortion of supracontext awareness. You want to "bracket," or hold back, knowledge of subsequent events and modern values. For example, you read a source written in 1840 by a Southern slave owner. Moralizing against the owner based on the evils of slavery or faulting him for not seeing that slavery would soon end is not worthwhile. Instead, withhold judgment and try to see things from the perspective of the person who lived in the past. Researchers who study primary sources try to avoid a specific form of supercontext awareness distortion, **presentism**. Presentism has a parallel distortion in comparative studies, **ethnocentricism**. In both fallacies, you treat your culture and time in history as being "normal" or "the best." You use it as a standard to evaluate other times or places instead of seeing things from another's point of view.

Locating primary documents can be very time-consuming. You must search through specialized indexes and may have to travel to archives or specialized libraries. Once you arrive, you may discover that sources, such as newspapers, diaries, letters, memos, and other records, are stored in a dusty and rarely visited room filled with stacked boxes that contain fading documents. The documents may be incomplete, disorganized, and in various stages of decay. After you locate documents or other primary sources, you must evaluate them with external and internal criticism (see Figure 11.2).

- **External criticism.** You want to be certain that a source is not a fake or a forgery. Relevant questions to ask are, When was the document really created? Where was it really created? Did the person claiming to be the source's author actually produce it? Why was the source created and why did it survive into the present? For example, you find a letter written on a typewriter, but the letter's date is 10 years before the first typewriter was invented. You know that the letter is not authentic.
- **Internal criticism.** After you have determined that a primary source is not a fake, you want to be certain it accurately reflects events, people, and situations. Relevant questions to ask are, Did the source's author directly witness what it contains or is it secondhand information? Is information in the source consistent with other accounts at that time? What conditions (e.g., wartime censorship, an author's desire to appear moral or important) might have influenced what was included in or omitted from a source? You want to place a source in context and examine both explicit (literal, visible) and implicit (subtle connotations, implications) meanings in it. For example, you locate a pile of letters and notes by a women about her dead husband. As you read the material, you notice no references to the husband's alcoholism. The alcoholism is in sources from neighbors and relatives, in arrest records of the husband for public intoxication, and in a large bill of daily charges by the husband at a nearby tavern. You question the credibility of the wife's report on the husband as a complete, accurate picture and wonder whether she was trying to make him appear more respectable in the source documents.

Running Records. Luckily, many organizations maintain files or records for their own purposes that you can use. For example, a country church has records of every marriage, baptism, and funeral from 1880 to the present. By looking at the church's running records in combination with other historical evidence, you can trace the social life of a village for over a century. Two limitations of running records are as follows: (1) Organizations do not always maintain them; and (2) organizations do not record information consistently over time. Changing policy or other events may cause an organization to stop keeping records, or new administrators, clerks, policies, or events may cause changes in the way records are kept and what they record.

presentism the fallacy of looking at past events from the point of view of today and failing to adjust for a very different context at the time.

ethnocenticism as applied in comparative research, the fallacy of looking at the behaviors, customs, and practices of people in other cultures narrowly from your culture's point of view.

external criticism evaluating the authenticity of primary source materials.

internal criticism evaluating the credibility of information in primary source materials.

running records ongoing files or statistical documents that an organization, such as a school, business, hospital, or government agency, maintains over time.

■ Figure 11.1   *New York Times* Article on Emigration

JAPAN TO STOP EMIGRATION.

Mikado's Government Will Restrict Movement of Coolies to America.

WASHINGTON, April 23.—Information has reached Washington that the Japanese Government itself, without waiting a request from the United States, is about to take steps to restrict the emigration of Japanese coolies to the United States.

It is asserted that the figures relative to this emigration have been magnified, and that, as a matter of fact, there are not more than about 15,000 ot 16,000 Japanese within the limits of the United States, outside of Hawaii. It is said that such emigration as has lately occurred has resulted entirely from the competition of the two great Japanese emigration societies; that the laborers have been practically brought here under the delusion that there were untold opportunities for work at great wages. The Japanese Government is interested in protecting its people from the hardships resulting from impositions and that, it is said, is the reason it intends to establish restrictions on the outward flow.

It is said, however, that the Government would never contemplate with equanimity legislation by the United States directed exclusively against Japanese immigration, for, though perfectly willing to abide by the results of any legislation on the subject of immigration that affects all outside nations alike, discriminations against Japan would certainly have most disastrous effects upon trade. The position of the Japanese Government upon that point is that the Japanese emigrant is not for a moment to be classed with the Chinese coolie.

Source: New York Times (1857–Current file); Apr. 24, 1900; ProQuest Historical Newspapers The New York Times (1851–2003) pg. 10

Before the use of electronic telecommunications, computers, cell phones, and video technology, people usually communicated and kept records in writing. You can examine letters, memos, diaries, ledgers, or newspapers to learn about past communication or ideas. Many of today's communication forms do not leave a permanent physical record (e.g., telephone conversations, e-mails, radio broadcasts) unless they are electronically archived. This could make the work of future historians and H-C researchers more difficult.

■ Figure 11.2   Internal and External Criticism

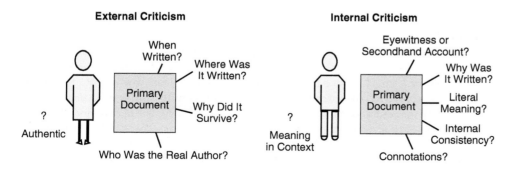

Recollections. People's memories of the past and their experiences originated in the past like primary sources, but they are not a primary source. **Recollections**, such as a written memoir or autobiography, are created afterward from memory. A special type of recollection, the **oral history**, is especially valuable for people who do not keep detailed written diaries and for the illiterate (see Example Study Box 3). Because memory is imperfect, recollections and oral histories can be a distorted picture of the past in ways that primary sources are not. They may not be perfectly accurate, but often they are our only window into the how people living in the past experienced events.

recollections a person's words or writings about past experiences created by the person some time after the experiences took place.

oral history interviews with a person about his or her life and experiences in the past.

Secondary Sources. The strength of primary sources is their authenticity, but they have practical limitations. It can take a huge amount of time to locate, verify, and read primary sources. You may discover thousands of pages of primary source documents to sort and read. In addition, primary sources may cover a short period of

Example Study Box 3 Women of the KKK

Bettmann/Corbis

Blee (1991) was interested in right-wing extremist groups and conducted a historical study on the Ku Klux Klan in the Midwest. Her six years of research illustrates great ingenuity. She focused on the state of Indiana, where 32 percent of the white Protestant population belonged to the Klan at its peak in the 1920s. In addition to reviewing studies on the Klan, she investigated newspapers, pamphlets, and unpublished reports. She conducted library research on primary and secondary materials at over half a dozen college, government, and historical libraries. She provides readers with historical photographs, sketches, and maps to create a feel for the topic and its context.

Bee also conducted oral histories with women about being in the Ku Klux Klan. She noted that, prior to her research, no one had studied the estimated 500,000 women in the largest racist, right-wing movement in the United States. Many people had assumed that women were apolitical and passive. The Klan was a secret society, no membership lists survived, and finding information was difficult. To locate survivors 60 years after the Klan was active, Blee had to be persistent and inventive. She identified Klan women by piecing together a few surviving rosters, locating old newspaper obituaries that identified women as Klan members, and looking for names by scrutinizing historical documents that were public notices or anti-Klan documents. She mailed a notice about her research to every local newspaper, church bulletin, advertising supplement, historical society, and public library in Indiana. Most of her informants were over age 80. They recalled the Klan as an important part of their lives. Blee verified parts of their memories through newspaper and other documentary evidence.

Membership in the Klan remained controversial. In the interviews, Blee did not reveal her opinions about the Klan. She was tested, but Blee remained neutral and did not denounce the Klan. She stated, "My own background in Indiana (where I lived from primary school through college) and white skin led informants to assume—lacking spoken evidence to the contrary—that I shared their worldview" (p. 5). She did not find Klan women to be brutal, ignorant, and full of hatred. When she asked why the women had joined the Klan, most women were puzzled by the question. To them it needed no explanation—it was just "a way of growing up" and "to get together and enjoy."

time or one very specific location. Perhaps they may let you document events in one tiny village for a two-year period, but many research questions are about a longer time and a wider range of locations. H-C researchers rely on secondary sources when they want to address broader questions.

Secondary sources are the dozens of books and articles specialist historians wrote on specific people, places, or events. You can use these sources as information about a broader topic. Historians may have produced over one thousand books and articles on numerous specific, narrow topics about a broad topic that interests you. Secondary sources have a maze of details and interpretations. You must transform the numerous separate studies into an intelligible picture organized around your research question. You need to evaluate the sources and exercise care when using them.

Secondary sources have limitations. Despite producing many studies, historians have not studied every aspect of all topics from the past. There may be holes or gaps in the historical record and few studies on your topic. Other limitations include the issue of inaccurate historical accounts and the historian's interpretation of data. Even if there are many studies on your topic and you locate and read them all, history books contain more than theory-free, objective "facts." Historians frame and organize their primary source data with concepts, ideas, and assumptions. The historian's concepts originate in journalism, the language of past people, ideologies or philosophy, today's language, and theory. Historians do not always define their concepts or apply them consistently. For example, you read a book in which a historian calls 10 families in a nineteenth-century town "upper class." However, the historian never defines "upper class" or ties it to any studies of social class. This makes it difficult for you to know what "upper class" means in the history book.

The historical study does not reveal everything the historian saw in primary sources. The historian might read 10,000 pages of newspapers, letters, and diaries and then reduce those data to summaries and selected quotes in a 180-page history book. You locate the 180-page book and must rely on the historian's judgments about the primary source data. The historian's judgments about what to include contain selection criteria and biases. You rarely know what they were. Perhaps the historian omitted information relevant for your research question.

When organizing their data, many historians use a *narrative history* format, which organizes the evidence chronologically around a single coherent "story." They connect each part of the story to other parts by its place in the time order of events. Together, all the parts form a unity or whole. The story often makes interesting reading. However, the historian will emphasize or downplay information based on how it fits into the story. You might read a history book (such as Blee looking for information about information on the Klan in Indiana in the 1920s), but the historian downplayed information relevant to your question (women's activism in the Klan) because it was not central to the historian's story (how financial corruption and infighting weakened the Klan). Also, historians add events in the narrative to enrich the background or to add color. They note what a particular person has done or said but may not analyze unseen influencing factors. Just because a fact is in the history narrative, it may have little theoretical significance. For example, a historian discusses family relations among a group of settlers in seventeenth-century America. The historian focuses on intrafamily gender dynamics but downplays factors such as problems with securing a stable food supply. This does not mean that lack of food was unimportant for your research topic (decisions by settlers to give up and return home). It only means that the historian decided to downplay such factors in his or her narrative. While you read the historian's narrative, you can learn a lot but need to look for details relevant to your own research question even if they are not central to the narrative.

The writing of historians is influenced by the era in which they live and by their outlook or school of historical scholarship. In certain historical periods, various interpretations or themes are popular. You will find similar themes in most historical books written in that period (e.g., an emphasis on immigration, labor-management

secondary sources specific studies conducted by specialist historians who may have spent many years studying a narrow topic. Other researchers use these secondary data as sources.

Making It Practial   A Life History Interview

The life history interview is a special kind of recollection in which you interview a middle-aged or elderly person about his or her entire life. You ask many open-ended questions in a sympathetic, nonjudgmental manner to help the person open up and elaborate on specific details of his or her life. You usually begin by asking about events when the person was a child. Be flexible, and do not structure the interview too much. You want to encourage the person to open up and reveal many specific details. You can prepare a long list of possible topics to ask about (family, schooling, work, travel, friendships, and so forth) but also rely on other things you already learned earlier in the interview for new questions. For example, you ask, "Do you remember any details about the year you were six years old? Was that the year your younger brother Jonathan got very sick and almost died?" Anything the person recalls is relevant. You want to capture details, relationships, and events from the point of view of the person you interview. Many people never had an opportunity to sit down and reflect about all the past events in detail. Life history interviews can be therapeutic for some people. Approach the interview with care and consideration. People may block out certain events, and recalling some events may generate great sorrow, anger, or anxiety, even many years later. You can ask about events taking place around the person (major political events, world events, and so forth) to get the person's own perspective on them. Most researchers tape record life history interviews. Depending on the person, you may have six or more hours of interviewing. People tire of a very long interview, so plan to break the interviewing into three or more two-hour interview sessions that are spaced across several days. This not only lets the interviewed person rest but also lets you review the early interviews and return to major turning points or life events to ask for additional details or clarification.

conflicts, or gender issues). Historians tend to follow a school of historical scholarship when they conduct a study, such as diplomatic, demographic, ecological, psychological, Marxist, intellectual, and so forth. Each school has its own priorities about data and key questions. If you use secondary sources, you need to be aware of major themes popular when the historian wrote and the outlook he or she adopted.

RESEARCH THAT COMPARES ACROSS CULTURES

Comparative research is as much an orientation toward research issues as it is a separate research technique. Doing a comparative study is not doing anything dramatically different from other social research; however, many of the issues or problems in social research are greatly magnified in a comparative study. In a sense, a comparative perspective exposes potential weaknesses that can exist in all social research. This awareness of possible concerns can help improve the quality of all social research.

Some comparative research takes place to demonstrate that basic social processes (e.g., psychological orientations, family relations) hold across countries; other research examines differences. The focus is to examine similarities and differences between units of comparison (cultures, nations). In comparative research, you see what is shared across units and what is specific to one unit alone.

The comparative orientation improves measurement and conceptualization. One reason is that when we develop concepts based on comparative research, the concepts are less likely to be restricted to a specific culture. We can develop a concept for a familiar or home culture but be unaware of hidden biases, assumptions, and values until we try to apply it to different cultures. For example, you develop a concept of reverse discrimination based on the U.S. experience. You think it is a general idea, but until you try to apply the concept in many other cultural settings, you do not know whether it is applicable or limited to the U.S. context. By using a concept in a range of cultures, you see whether it applies in diverse settings. Comparative research also reveals important but unrecognized factors. If all the studies of a topic are in one culture, you may not realize that something in the culture but not elsewhere is a cause. For example, gun ownership is 100 times greater in the United States than in other advanced nations. If you only look within the United States, you may not find gun ownership connected with another factor, but if you compare the United States and other nations, the gun ownership rate of the United States may stand out as a key factor.

It is important to look across cultures to see a wider range or variation in a variable. For example, two researchers, Hsi-Ping and Abdul, look at the relationship between the age at which a child is weaned and the onset of emotional problems. Hsi-Ping looks only at U.S. data. They show a range from 5 to 15 months at weaning and indicate that emotional problems increase steadily as age of weaning increases. She concludes that late weaning causes emotional problems. Abdul

Example Study Box 4   Abortion Politics in the United States and Germany

Alex Wong/Getty Images

Ferre, Gamson, Gerhards, and Rucht (2002) conducted a comparative study of abortion politics in the United States and Germany. They specifically looked at public discussions about abortion in the two countries. In both countries, abortion was made legal and became a heated and widely debated moral-political issue. The authors examined four types of data: (1) secondary historical evidence, (2) a content analysis, (3) a survey of leaders in organizations, and (4) open-ended interviews. The secondary evidence came from books about the history, organized movements, court rulings, and public debates about abortion. The authors examined articles in the two major newspapers of both countries for the period 1970–1994, looking for all articles that mentioned the abortion issue in any way. They selected articles meeting certain criteria (such as longer than three paragraphs, not book reviews, no letters to the editor) and found 1243 articles in the United States and 1425 in Germany. They then content analyzed the articles. The authors also sent a questionnaire to 150 abortion-issue organizations. The questionnaire asked about organizational goals, activities, media relations, internal resources, and alliances with other organizations. The authors also interviewed leaders or media directors of 20 U.S. and 23 German abortion-issue organizations and several leading journalists in each country who regularly wrote on the abortion issue. The study produced many findings. One major finding was that people discussed the same issue very differently in the two countries. In Germany, there is less open conflict over the issue, and people discussed abortion in terms of fetal rights and protecting women. In the United States, there was great conflict associated with activism by advocacy organizations outside government or political parties. The issue was framed in terms of individual rights or freedom from government interference, or as a religious-moral issue. Religious and women's organizations related to the issue very differently by country. In the end, the authors identified specific features of the culture, advocacy organizations, mass media, and political institutions in each country that influenced the abortion debate. They found that a country's government structure, media system, legal system, and so forth had a large influence on how people thought about and debated the exact same public issue.

looks at data from 10 cultures. He discovers a range from 5 to 36 months at weaning. He finds that the rate of emotional problems rises with age of weaning until 18 months; it then peaks and falls to a lower level. Abdul has a more complete picture. Emotional problems are likely for weaning between the ages of 6 and 24 months. Weaning either earlier or later reduces the chances of emotional problems. Hsi-Ping reached false conclusions because of the narrow range of weaning age in the United States.

Comparative research is more difficult, costly, and time consuming than research that is not comparative. You may be limited in the types of data that you can collect and have problems with equivalence (see the following discussion). In comparative research, you cannot randomly sample cultures. Sufficient information is not available for all world cultures and is unavailable for a nonrandom subset (poor countries, nondemocratic countries, etc.). In addition, cultures or nations are not equal units. Some have over a billion people and others only 100,000.

Can You Really Compare?

For convenience, most comparative researchers use the nation-state as their unit of analysis. Most people see the globe as divided in terms of nation-state (or country), and this is how official statistics are collected. The nation-state is a socially and politically defined unit. In it, one government has sovereignty (i.e., military control, political authority) over a populated territory. People living in the territory may share a common language, culture, and customs, but the nation-state is not the only possible unit for comparative research.

If you want to compare something clearly within nation-state boundaries, such as legal system, voting and government, or economic relations, then it makes sense to compare nation-states. However, for comparative research, the relevant unit is often the culture. Culture is more difficult to define. It refers to a shared identity, social relations, beliefs, and technology. Cultural differences in language, custom, traditions, and norms often follow nation-state borders, but national borders do not always match cultural boundaries. A single culture may be divided among several governments, or one nation-state may be multicultural with several cultures. If you want to compare cultures, then the nation-state may not be the best unit. For example, the people of one region may have a distinct ethnic background, language, customs, religion, social institutions, and identity, such as Quebec in Canada, Wales in the United Kingdom, and Flanders in Belgium.

Over the centuries, wars and conquests carved new political units onto territory and in the process destroyed, rearranged, or diffused boundaries between cultures. In many world regions, Western empires imposed arbitrary boundaries on distinct cultural groups and made them into colonies. Later the colonies became independent nations. At other times, one nation-state expanded and absorbed the territory of people who had a distinct culture. For example, the U.S. government took over American Indian lands and the islands of Hawaii and Puerto Rico. Likewise, new immigrants or ethnic minorities did not always assimilate into the dominant culture. Such intranational cultures can create tension or regional conflict, since ethnic and cultural identities are the basis for nationalism. In his Presidential speech to the Canadian political science association, McRoberts (2001) argued that Canada is more than multicultural—it is multinational. Multiple nations (British, French, aboriginal) exist within one political structure. This implies that we should treat Canada as three units, not one.

You need to ask, What is the appropriate comparative unit for my research question—the nation, the culture, a region, or a subculture? For example, your research question is, Are income level and divorce related? Your hypothesis is that higher-income people are less likely to divorce. Perhaps income and divorce are related among the people of one culture. However, elsewhere in the same nation-state where

Making It Practical   **Which Units Should You Use?**

How do you decide on the appropriate units of analysis for comparative research? If you want to study two different national cultures, such as the United States and Kenya, is the nation or a smaller unit such as the state, region, or tribe best? The answer hinges on whether a nation-state has a single homogenous culture. You need to be cautious if a country has regional divisions in which people of different regions do not share the same religion, customs, or language. You must to learn about the internal divisions and minority groups within a nation before conducting a study. In some nations, such as Belgium, formal political and geographic divisions separate the country by distinct

cultures. In such situations, subnational units may be best. In other countries, such as the United States, the cultural dividing lines are not as sharp and are not in distinct geographic regions.

The appropriate units to study vary by your research question. For example, you are interested in marriage customs and childrearing practices. If there is one homogenous culture, you can study it anywhere in a nation. If the nation has several different cultures and marriage practices might vary by culture, it might be best to limit your study to one or two cultural groups within the nation rather than use the nation as a whole.

a different culture prevails, income and divorce are not related. If you use the nation-state as the unit and mix everyone together, your findings will be unclear and show a weak correlation. If you instead use two separate regions, you will find a strong correlation among the variables in one culture and no correlation in the other. Thus, it is best to ask what is appropriate rather than assume that every nation-state has only one culture. Some cultures do not fit into one geographic region and are scattered. This weakens a distinct culture and makes cultural comparison more complex. The Latino or Chinese-American or African-American are ethno-religious cultures scattered geographically across the U.S. territory. Should we study them as distinct cultures or as ethnic/racial groups?

Learning from History   **The Galton-Tylor Discovery**

The Granger Collection, New York

Sir Edward B. Tylor (1832–1917), founder of British social anthropology, presented a paper, "On a Method of Investigating the Development of Institutions, Applied to Laws of Marriage and Descent," at the Royal Anthropological Institute in 1889. Taylor had information on marriage and descent for 350 cultures and found correlations between marriage/descent forms and measures of social complexity. He interpreted the results in terms of an evolutionary sequence. Over time, as societies became more complex, they changed from a maternal to a paternal descent line. Francis

Galton, a statistical genius also at the Institute, raised objections. He pointed out that the correlation could be a mirage because the cultures may not be totally distinct and separate. Marriage forms could diffuse, cultures could borrow forms, or a marriage form could have a common origin in a different culture that crossed into other cultures. Galton maintained that before we can say that evolving social complexity and marriage forms are correlated, we must first rule out diffusion across different cultures and a common origin. Tylor agreed with Galton, and this sparked an innovation in comparative research called Galton's problem.

Bettmann/Corbis

Galton's Problem

To make a valid comparison, the units must be distinct and non-overlapping. If two units are actually subparts of a single larger unit, relationships you find in both of them may have a common origin. Here is an extreme example to illustrate the idea. Let us say you are interested in the association of two traits: the language people speak and what they use as money. Your research question is, Does the language people use affect what they use as money? Your units are territories in five nations (prefectures in Japan, the states in the United States, Lander in Germany, provinces in Argentina, and governorates [*muhafazat*] in Egypt). You add 47 prefectures, 50 states, 16 Lander, 23 provinces, and 26 governorates for a total of 162 units. You discover a perfect correlation between language and money for your 162 units. Where people speak English, they use the dollar, when they speak Japanese, they use the yen; when they speak Spanish, they use the peso; when they speak German, they use the euro; and when they speak Egyptian, they use the pound as currency. The association between language and currency is not because language and currency are actually related to one another; rather, your units of analysis (i.e., the states, provinces, etc.) are actually subparts of a larger unit (i.e., nations). The larger unit is the common source of both traits. Before you examine the association of two variables/traits, look closely at your units. Galton's problem is important because the boundaries between cultures are unclear or changing (see Figure 11.3). It may be hard to say where one culture ends and another begins. You can think of Galton's problem as a special case of the spurious relationship that you learned about in Chapter 2.

Gathering Comparative Data

Comparative researchers use several types of data and combine types together in one study:

- Comparative field research
- Existing qualitative data
- Cross-national survey data
- Existing cross-national quantitative data

Galton's problem a possible mistake when comparing variables/features of units of analysis, in which an association among variables or features of two units may be due to them both actually being part of one large unit.

■ **Figure 11.3**   Galton's Problem.

Galton's problem occurs when a researcher observes the same social relationship (represented by X) in different settings or societies (represented as A, B, and C) and falsely concludes that the social relationship arose independently in these different places. The researcher may believe he or she has discovered a relationship in three separate cases. But the actual reason for the occurrence of the social relation may be a shared or common origin that has diffused from one setting to others. This is a problem because the researcher who finds a relationship (e.g., a marriage pattern) in distinct settings or units of analysis (e.g., societies) may believe it arose independently in different units. This belief suggests that the relationship is a human universal. The researcher may be unaware that in fact it exists because people have shared the relationship across units.

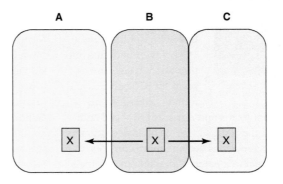

Comparative Field Research. Comparative researchers use field research in cultures other than their own. The training of social-cultural anthropologists prepares them for this type of research. The overlap of research techniques between anthropological and field research suggests modest differences between doing field research in your home culture and in a different culture. Conducting field research in another culture is usually more difficult and places more requirements on a study than doing research in your home culture. You first must immerse yourself in and learn the other culture in depth. This takes time and requires many adjustments, but can it yield new insights and personal as well as professional gains.

Existing Qualitative Data. Comparative researchers use qualitative primary and secondary sources. For example, you want to conduct a comparative study of the Canadian, Chilean, and Chinese school systems. Ideally, you visit each country to learn about each first-hand. Before visiting or if you cannot visit, locate existing qualitative data, such as videos, photos, music, novels, and essays about or by the country's schools, their teachers, and students. Read historical and field-research studies that describe the education systems in the three nations. You can use the descriptive details you learned from these sources as part the evidence for a study.

Cross-National Survey Research. You can conduct a survey in several different countries, but survey research in multiple cultures is more complex and creates additional methodological issues. In principle, the issues also exist in a survey conducted in your home culture, but they differ in magnitude and severity. A survey in a different culture requires knowing the language, norms, practices, and customs. Without such knowledge, you can easily make serious errors in procedure and interpretation. Knowing a language is not enough; cultural expectations and practices are essentials. It is best to work in close cooperation with people who are natives of the other culture.

Substantive (e.g., theory, research question) and practical factors are relevant when choosing cultures for a cross-national survey. You must adjust each step of the survey process (question wording, data collection, sampling, interviewing, etc.) to the culture. People in all cultures do not approach survey research the same. In some cultures, people might see survey interviewing as a strange, frightening experience, somewhat analogous to a police interrogation. You want to check local conditions and learn how people in the culture view surveys.

Cultural context also influences sampling. In addition to concerns about an accurate sampling frame, there are issues such as records privacy, quality of mail or telephone service, and transportation to remote rural areas. You need to be know how often people move, the types of dwellings in which people live, the number of people in a dwelling, the telephone coverage, and typical rates of refusal (i.e., refusal to participate in the survey).

The difficulties of writing a good survey question for your home culture are greatly magnified when you study a different culture. The cultural context affects question wording, questionnaire length, introductions, and the topics you include. You need to learn the local norms and topics that are highly sensitive in a culture. Questions about political beliefs, alcohol use, religion, or sexuality that you might ask in your home culture might be taboo in a different culture. In addition to these cultural issues, translation and language equivalency often pose problems (see the later discussion of lexicon equivalence). It is best to use bilingual people, but it may be impossible to ask the exact same question in a different language/culture.

Cross-cultural interviewing can be difficult. The selection and training of interviewers depends on the education, norms, and etiquette of the culture. An interview situation introduces issues such as norms of privacy, ways to gain trust, beliefs about confidentiality, and differences in dialect. In some cultures, you must spend a day in informal socializing before you achieve the rapport needed for a short interview. In other places, you must get prior approval from an official, headman, or local elder. Elsewhere, a male cannot interview a female without her elder brother, husband, or father being present.

Survey research across nations/cultures can be a challenge, but it can be highly rewarding and produce information not otherwise attainable. More than anything else, you need to be culturally aware at each step. You must evaluate whether you can do the same as in your home or need to make adjustments. This careful, step-by-step evaluation in itself raises your awareness of how to conduct good survey research.

▶▶ **Example Study Box 5** **Prisons and Unemployment across Nations**

Dennis MacDonald/PhotoEdit Inc.

Sutton (2004) conducted a quantitative cross-national study looking at data on 15 nations between 1960 and 1990. For a long time, researchers knew that changes in the crime rate do not predict imprisonment rates. They asked, What does predict them? About 70 years ago, researchers Rusche and Kirchheimer (1939) offered a thesis that unemployment rates cause a rise in imprisonment rates. They argued that prisons are a government social control mechanism. If there are many unemployed young males in a population, they can become unruly and threaten the social order. For this reason, governments adjust policies when many men are unemployed to make it easy to fill prisons with out-of-work males. The government maintains social order by keeping a surplus population of unemployed males in prison. When the economy is booming and jobs go unfilled, national policies shift and the prisons begin to empty out. Sutton tested the Rusche and Kirchheimer thesis by gathering data from government statistical yearbooks, international organizations such as the World Health Organization, and studies on unionization patterns, political party structure, and so forth. He found limited support for the thesis as originally put forth. However, he learned that the association between unemployment and imprisonment was spurious (you learned about spurious relationships in Chapter 2). Sutton discovered that political-organizational factors in a nation influence both its unemployment and imprisonment rates. In some nations, low-income workers are politically weak compared to the upper middle class and corporation owners. In those nations, both unemployment and imprisonment rates tend to be high. In other nations, low-income workers acquire political power and have strong political influence. In those nations, both the unemployment and imprisonment rates are low. Thus, Sutton found that the political strength of low-income working people is the true causal factor that explains both unemployment and imprisonment rates (see Figure 11.4).

■ **Figure 11.4** What Sutton Learned About Unemployment Rates and Prison Populations

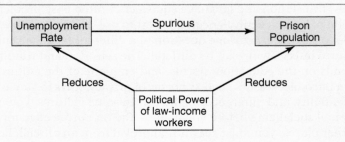

Existing Cross National Quantitative Data. Organizations gather and publish data on numerous features for many nations. A wide variety of data are available in major national data archives in a computer-readable format. This makes it easy to conduct secondary analysis on international existing statistics data. As with existing statistics for a single nation, existing cross-national data have limitations. These limitations are of greater magnitude than is the case for existing statistics on a single nation. The definitions of variables and the reliability of data collection can vary dramatically across nations. Perhaps you want to study statistics on crime in various nations. However, nations vary by what constitutes a crime and by legal system. What is criminal behavior in one nation might be acceptable and legal in another. What one nation treats as a breach of etiquette another nation may see as a serious crime that requires harsh punishment. The standards of legal evidence and law enforcement may also vary widely. Missing information is a common problem in cross-national existing statistics. Intentional misinformation in the official data from some governments is also a problem. Another limitation is the nations for which data is collected. For example, during a 35-year period, new nations come into existence, others change their names or form of governments, and some have different territorial borders.

The Issue of Equivalence

You have probably heard the expression, Compare apples to apples, not apples to oranges. The expression is not about fruit; it is about comparison. You cannot examine the similarities among things that are completely different; what you compare must be equivalent in some way. Equivalence is a critical concern in all types of social research. It is the issue of whether you can compare across divergent social contexts. You cannot easily compare family relations, crime rates, and business patterns for people or societies that are radically different—for example, an advanced urban industrial nation of 300 million with a tiny hunting and gathering tribal society of 1000 people. The technology, material conditions, and social environment differ radically. The units must have some basic similarity in order to make a valid comparison.

The issue of equivalence exists in all social research, but it is especially important for doing H-C research. Without basic equivalence, you cannot apply ideas or measures across different cultures or historical periods. You will misinterpret events in a different era or culture, or there may be no equivalent feature for you to compare. There are several forms of equivalence. They are closely related, but we can subdivide them into four types:

- Lexicon
- Conceptual
- Context
- Measurement

Summary Review **Data in H-C Research**

Thus far, we have considered four types of historical evidence and four types of comparative data.

4 Types of Historical Evidence	4 Types of Comparative Data
Primary evidence	Comparative field
Recollections	Existing qualitative
Running records	Cross-national survey
Secondary evidence	Existing cross-national quantitative

Lexicon Equivalence. **Lexicon equivalence** is easiest to see across two languages. For example, in many languages you use one form of address and pronouns for private settings, intimates (e.g., close friends and family members), and subordinates (e.g., younger persons, lower-status people) and another for address in public settings, with strangers, or for persons of higher social status. Modern English usage lacks this feature, although it once had something similar (the pronouns *thou*, *thee*, *thine*, and *thy*). In cultures where age is an important status, many status-based words exist that are absent in English. You cannot say, "my brother" without indicating whether you are talking about an older or younger brother because "my younger brother" or "my older brother" are different words. The meaning of words also varies across historical eras. For example, today the English word *weed* refers to unwanted plants or to marijuana. In Shakespeare's era, *weeds* meant clothing. Linguists study whether what you can express in one language (or the same language long ago) has a precise meaning in another language.

If your study goes into the distant past or involves different languages or dialects, lexicon equivalence can be an issue. Do not assume that a word or expression used in a different cultural or historical context has the same or a simple and comparable meaning. Lexicon equivalence is relevant in four situations of H-C research:

- When you are reading a document from the distant past or written in a different language
- When you are writing a survey questionnaire or talking to people who use or think in a different language
- When you are describing events, activities, or social relations from a different culture or historical era that you have studied to people today, in your home culture
- When you are theorizing and analyzing data or conditions across different cultures or historical eras

Conceptual Equivalence. Every day you use many concepts—such as friendship, loyalty, trust, family, parent, employee, and self-esteem—to discuss and examine social life. In a study, you use concepts from the research literature, personal experiences, and background knowledge to analyze and discuss the data or to test and build theory. The concepts you use are from a specific culture and historical era. People discuss concepts in the research literature live in specific cultural and historical settings, but they try to stretch beyond one time and one culture. The issue of conceptual equivalence is whether a concept developed and used in one historical era and culture applies to a very different time or place. The question is whether an idea (e.g., sibling conflict, customer service, blood honor) that may be best for understanding and organizing data in one historical era or culture can be applied in a very different era or culture wherein the idea may be inappropriate and incomprehensible. Conceptual equivalence is part of the broader issue of using universal (transcultural, transhistorical) concepts versus culturally and historically specific ones. Let us say you want to discuss "income." In pre-money bartering societies in which most people grow their own food, make their own furniture and clothing, barter goods, and rarely use money, income means something very different from today's advanced societies. The same concept of "income" may not fit both settings. Likewise, if you study people who believe that spirit forces cause certain diseases or health conditions, you may not have a concept that easily and fully captures the concept of "spirit forces" for comparison with a society that uses concepts such as bacteria, germs, DNA, and so forth. The concept of "attending college" has a different meaning today than in a historical context in which only the richest 1 percent of the population attended college, most colleges had fewer than 300 students, all were private all-male institutions, and the college curriculum consisted of learning classical languages and receiving moral training. The event or idea "attending college" has a different meaning from today.

lexicon equivalence being able to say the same thing with the same meaning across languages or dialects in different cultures or historical eras.

conceptual equivalence being able to apply the same concept across different cultures or historical eras.

At one time we automatically treated the beliefs and ideas of other cultures or eras as inferior or as "superstition" and treated those of own era and culture as "real" or "true." Nowadays, we try to avoid ethnocentrism and presentism. This is an improvement, but it does not provide is a simple, easy solution when doing research.

Cultural anthropologists and historians create new concepts that can capture what they study in a different culture or past era. To compare and discuss similarities and differences, sensitivity to whether a concept fits a setting is essential. You must ask whether a concept you are using really applies to both settings. If it does not, you may have to use different ones for each part of the comparison.

Contextual Equivalence. Our conversations, actions, events, and activities always take place in a social context. The same action (singing, telling a joke) may be acceptable in one social setting but not another. The context helps give meaning to the action. It might be acceptable to sing loudly at a lively party, but it is not acceptable for a physician to sing while carrying out a medical procedure on a patient. How a context shapes an action, event, or activity may vary across cultures and historical times. Perhaps in the historical past or in a different culture, singing during a medical procedure was not only acceptable but expected behavior. You need to evaluate not just what someone does or says, but how it fits into a context, and the influence of a context can vary by historical era or culture. **Contextual equivalence** means you should recognize how a specific context can shape the meaning of an event or activity. The specific context is within a broader culture or historical era. For example, you study a culture in which everyone has to pay a small amount of cash before a government official will do a task (e.g., stamp an official document, approve a driver's license). In your home culture, this may be considered a bribe and clearly inappropriate or illegal. Perhaps in one culture if you want a driver's license application approved, you must slip a five-dollar bill to the clerk with your application. If you do not slip the money, the clerk puts your application in a huge pile that might be processed next year. In the local context, the payment is acceptable as a kind of small service fee. The larger culture shapes the local context. In the larger culture, small amounts are paid regularly to help out the extremely underpaid government officials who work with impossible-to-implement bureaucratic rules. In a different context, paying a fee for a government service (having your passport stamped at the local airport) may be unacceptable. In a local context, government officials want to appear "modern" and impress foreign visitors that one set of rules applies, but when they provide a service to local people, another set of rules applies. To understand what is occurring, you need to be sensitive to the local context and the larger culture. How do you compare this government service event to that occurring in a different culture where handing a cash payment to a government employee would be seen as an unacceptable bribe? In a study, you may only be able to remark on the differences based on the context. The key point is, do not assume that the same activity has the same meaning across different contexts.

Measurement Equivalence. You may identify a concept, event, or activity for your study and adjust for the context and the broader cultural or historical setting. A question remains: Do you measure in the same way if you want to compare it to a different cultural or historical setting? **Measurement equivalence** recognizes that you cannot always use the same measure (such as survey questionnaire or official records such as birth certificates) in different historical or cultural settings. Let us say you are studying two cultures. In one culture, the local police keep a careful record of each household, including each person in a dwelling unit, their kinship or relations to each another, and where each person works or attends school. You want to compare this to another culture, where there is no police record of who lives where, except for the name of the legal owner, and no other information about the people. You cannot use

contextual equivalence seeing the same event or activity in context across different cultures or historical eras.

measurement equivalence using very different ways of measuring across different cultures or historical eras. The measurement method may influence outcomes.

the same measure of household size—looking at official police records in both countries. In one culture, you have to conduct a survey and ask about household size. In the other culture, you use official police records. The issue is whether the two different methods give identical answers if you had used them in the other culture (i.e., use a survey in the culture where police keep records). Perhaps you adjusted the way you measure a concept, event, or activity for a culture or historical setting so that it differs from how you measure it in a different setting. Did the measurement method affect what you learned in each setting, or can you treat the information as the same? There is no simple solution to this issue. You may have to measure differently in various settings and then compare results across settings, and you cannot be certain whether the different measurement methods influenced what you found.

BEING AN ETHICAL H-C RESEARCHER

Ethical concerns in H-C research are similar to those of nonreactive research techniques, especially when using secondary sources or existing cross-national quantitative data. Primary historical sources can introduce special ethical issues. The ethical researcher needs to carefully document where and how primary sources were obtained, make explicit the selection criteria for including some sources and not others, and apply external criticism and internal criticism to the source materials. At times, protecting privacy may interfere with gathering evidence. A person's descendants may want to destroy or hide private papers or evidence of scandalous behavior. We know that political figures (e.g., U.S. presidents) have tried to destroy or hide embarrassing official records.

Comparative researchers want to be sensitive to issues of cross-cultural interaction. Ethical behavior means respecting moral values and beliefs. You should learn what a culture considers to be acceptable or offensive and show respect for the traditions, customs, and meanings of privacy in the host culture. Actions that may be acceptable in your home culture may be unacceptable in a different culture, and vice versa. Be aware of and check your assumptions about what is appropriate behavior. Perhaps in your home culture you can enter a religious building and take photos when there is no service in progress. In another culture, taking a photo of religious buildings, even from the street, may be offensive and unacceptable. If this is the case, is it ethical to take the photo in the other culture? Perhaps you study a culture in which a father invites a male researcher to have sexual relations with his teenage daughter as a friendly gift to a visitor after completing an interview. In your home country, such behavior would be highly unethical and perhaps illegal. Is it unethical in both situations?

If you visit another culture to do research, establish good relations with the host country's government and do not take data out of the country without giving something (e.g., results) in return. At times, the military or political interests of the researcher's home culture or the researcher's personal values may conflict with official policy in the host nation. This introduces complexity. People in the other culture may distrust you and suspect you of being a spy, or your home culture's government may pressure you to gather covert information. In the past, these issues have created serious difficulties for social researchers.

At times, a researcher's presence or findings create diplomatic problems among governments. For example, a researcher examines health care practices in a different culture and then declares that official government policy is ignoring a serious illness and not providing medical care. This may create a major controversy. Likewise, a researcher may be sympathetic to the cause of people who oppose the government. Sometimes even talking to and working with such a group might cause a researcher to be threatened with imprisonment or deported. Anyone who conducts comparative research needs to be aware of such issues and the potential consequences of their actions.

WHAT HAVE YOU LEARNED?

In this chapter, you learned about historical and comparative research. The H-C approach is especially appropriate when you want to ask "big questions" about macro-level change, or when you want to understand social processes operating across historical eras or across cultures. Historical-comparative research involves a different orientation toward research that goes beyond applying specialized techniques. There are several ways to do H-C research, but a distinctly qualitative H-C approach is similar to field research in many respects. H-C has some specialized techniques, such as the external criticism of primary documents. Nevertheless, the most vital feature is how you approach a question, probe data, and move toward explanations.

Historical-comparative research is usually more difficult to conduct than other types of research. The same complexities or difficulties are often present to a lesser degree than in other research. For example, issues of equivalence are present to some degree in all social research. Such issues cannot be treated as secondary concerns in H-C research but are at the forefront of how you do research and seek answers to research questions.

In the next and final chapter, we return to some issues you encountered at the beginning of this book: what to do once you have finished a study and need to put all the parts together into a research report.

KEY TERMS

conceptual equivalence *316*
contextual equivalence *317*
ethnocentrism *304*
external criticism *304*
Galton's problem *312*
internal criticism *304*
lexicon equivalence *316*

measurement equivalence *317*
oral history *306*
presentism *304*
primary sources *303*
recollections *306*
running records *304*
secondary sources *307*

APPLYING WHAT YOU'VE LEARNED

Activity 1

Locate a family member or neighbor who is elderly, ideally 40–50 years older than you. Ask the person if you can have two 90-minute interviews with him or her. Schedule the open-ended interviews on different days and use a tape recorder. Ask the person to tell you about his or her life, starting when he or she was no more than six years old. Just ask a few guiding questions and let the person talk, following a chronological order if possible. Pay close attention to major life events, such as marriages, deaths, new jobs, and moving to a new town. Ask the person to explain how these events felt at the time. Ask the person to comment on major historical events that occurred during his or her lifetime (e.g., wars, major political events). Allow the person to repeat stories or tell about the same event more than once, and ask

for clarification if there is something you do not understand. After you have 2–3 hours of taped interviews, transcribe the interviews onto paper. You now have a record of the person's life, which he or she may read if desired.

Activity 2

Locating newspaper articles that are over 100 years old can be fun and fascinating. You may have to ask your local reference librarian how to get them most quickly from your specific location. Once you access the newspaper articles, identify a topic and narrow it down (as I did with immigration in Making It Practical: Old Newspaper Articles as Sources, p. 303). Read all the articles for a five-year period about that topic. Write an essay on what they learned.

Activity 3

Pick a country with a population of 5 to 50 million and about which you know very little. First, develop some background knowledge by finding out about the country's history, conflicts, internal social divisions, economy, family traditions, culture, form of government, religious beliefs, holidays, and so forth. An online source to check is the *CIA World Factbook*. After you have a basic understanding of the country, pick one feature about it (e.g., marriage practices, school system) and make comparison with your home culture. Develop a list of at least 10 similarities and/or differences. Draw on at least five different sources to develop your comparison list. If you were to visit the country and conduct a study of the feature, what would you want to observe and learn about it?

Activity 4

Two free online sources that have primary historical materials on the United States are: (1) *American Memory* at http://memory.loc.gov/ammem/index.html (Library of Congress), which contains photographs, maps, manuscripts, and sheet music; and (2) *Historical Census Browser* at http://fisher.lib.virginia.edu/collections/stats/histcensus/ (University of Virginia Library), which contains data from the U.S. Census of Population and Housing volumes and provides statistics for each decade from 1790 to 1960. Go to the *American Memory* Web site and then select Culture/folklife, then select Slave Narratives (audio interview 1932–1975) or Slave narratives (federal writer's project 1932–1938). Read what the ex-slaves said in the interviews and identify five people to follow. Go the *Historical Census Browser* Web site. Find the number of slaves in the same state and country at 1850 as each of those five people (first select 1850, then scroll down to slave population). Select the state, and at the bottom of the list of states and territories, select Retrieve County level data. Find out as much as you can about that county in 1850 and write a short essay about the five people's life conditions when they were young children.

Activity 5

Go online to locate international existing statistics about many countries. A free online source with lots of information is *Nationmaster* (http://www.nationmaster.com/index.php) and the *World Bank* (http://web.worldbank.org/WBSITE/EXTERNAL/DATASTATISTICS/0,,contentMDK:20535285~menuPK:1192694~pagePK:64133150~piPK:64133175~theSitePK:239419,00.html). Two other online sources are the *Statistical Abstract of the United States* and the *CIA Factbook*. Using these sources, identify a set of 15 countries and 15 variables that are available for all 15 countries (such as infant mortality rate, per capita GDP, and birth rate). Create a 15 × 15 chart. List the countries along the side and put letters A–O in the columns across the top. At the bottom, create a key for the letters with the name of each variable. Using this chart, what patterns do you see?

URLs

World Bank

http://web.worldbank.org/WBSITE/EXTERNAL/DATASTATISTICS/0,,contentMDK:20535285~menuPK:1192694~pagePK:64133150~piPK:64133175~theSitePK:239419,00.html

NATIONMASTER

http://www.nationmaster.com/index.php

CIA Fact Book

https://www.cia.gov/library/publications/the-world-factbook/

Statistical Abstract of the United States

http://www.census.gov/compendia/statab/past_years.html

REFERENCES

Banaszak, Lee Ann. 1998. "Use of the Initiative Process by Women Suffrage Movements." Pp. 99–114 in *Social Movements and American Political Institutions*, (Ed.) A. Costain and A. McFarland. Lanham MD: Rowman and Littlefield.

Blee, Kathleen. 1991. *Women of the Klan*. Berkeley: University of California Press.

Ferree, Myra Marx, William Gamson, Jurgen Gerhards, and Dieter Rucht. 2002. *Shaping Abortion Discourse*. New York: Cambridge University Press.

Kriesi, Hanspeter and Dominique Wisler. 1999. "The Impact of Social Movements on Political Institutions" Pp. 42–65 in *How Social Movements Matter*, (Ed.) M. Giugni, D. McAdam, and C. Tilly. Minneapolis MN: University of Minnesota Press.

Marx, Anthony W. 1998. *Making Race and Nation*. New York: Cambridge University Press.

McKeown, Adam. 2001. *Chinese Migrant Networks and Cultural Change*. Chicago: University of Chicago Press.

McRoberts, Kenneth. 2001. "Canada and the Multinational State." *Canadian Journal of Political Science / Revue Canadienne de Science Politique* 34:683–713.

Rusche, Georg and Otto Kirchheimer. 1939. *Punishment and Social Structure* New York: Russell and Russell.

Sutton, John. 2004. "The Political Economy of Imprisonment in Affluent Western Democracies, 1960–1990." *American Sociological Review* 69:170–189.

CHAPTER 12

Writing a Research Report

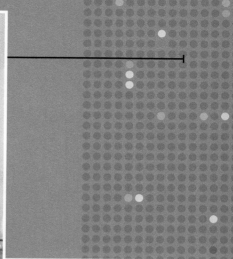

Stephan Hoeck/Stock
4B/Getty Images

A crucial phase in the research process takes place *after* you have gathered and analyzed the data. You must communicate what you learned to others. Whether your study was in chemistry, criminology, education, engineering, marketing, nursing, psychology, public policy, or another field, you need to communicate how you conducted it and its findings. Your communication can be oral but should also be in a written form. As with all written communication, you want to maximize readability. Readability indicates how accessible the writing is, and how effectively it will reach a given reading audience. An audience's ability to read and understand your writing will depend on their knowledge and reading skills. These vary widely. Medical doctors differ from teens. Whatever your audience, try to make your writing both highly accurate and easy to understand. Do this by using precise wording, a clear organizational structure, and a logical flow of ideas.

In previous chapters, you learned how to design studies, gather data, and analyze the data. Yet research is not complete until you share results with other people. Communicating how you conducted a study and its results with others is a critical stage of the research process. It is usually in the form of a written report. In this chapter, you will learn how to write a report on research.

Example Study Box 1 Who Writes How

Hartley, Pennebaker, and Fox (2003) examined the readability of research reports. They noted that past studies suggested that men and women wrote differently, and that individuals writing alone differ from people who write together. To see whether this happened in research reports, they looked at reports in the *Journal of Educational Psychology* for 1997–2001. They found 21 articles that individual men wrote, 21 by individual women, and 19 written by pairs of men and 19 by pairs of women. They examined each article's abstract, and most of its Introduction and Discussion sections. They measured readability with two computer-based writing style programs. They did not find gender differences or group versus individual author differences. However, they did find differences among article sections that replicated findings from past studies. The Introduction sections were harder to read than Discussion sections. In addition, Introduction sections had more specific quotations from other authors than the Discussion sections.

WHY WRITE A REPORT?

After you complete a study or a significant phase of a large project, you need to communicate to others what you learned through a research report. You can learn a lot about writing a research report by reading many reports or taking a course in scientific and technical writing. A **research report** is organized in a particular way. It requires writing that differs from other types, such as news stories, personal autobiography, and creative fiction. The report communicates the methods and findings in a straightforward and serious manner. More than a quick summary, it is a full, complete, and detailed record of the entire research process.

Do not wait until you finish all research activities to begin thinking about the report. Instead, begin to think ahead while early in the research process. The report is one reason to keep careful records while you are conducting research. In addition to the findings, the report includes the reasons for initiating a study, a description of the research procedures, a presentation of evidence, and a discussion of how the evidence relates to the research question. It has a reference section of the literature that you cited in the report. The references provide background on the research question and show how your study fits within past research.

The purpose of a report is to tell others what you did, how you did it, and what you discovered. People write research reports for many reasons: to fulfill a course, academic degree, or job assignment; to meet an obligation to an organization that paid for the research; to persuade a professional group about specific aspects of a problem; or to tell the general public about findings. Telling the public what you learned is a second stage of disseminating findings. The first stage is to communicate with people who are knowledgeable about the study topic and the research process. They can seriously evaluate the research in the report; they are also in the best position to understand what you did in the study and why.

Assume that people who will read the report are scientifically literate. Hurd (1998) suggested that a scientifically literate person can

- distinguish experts from uninformed people, theory from dogma, data from myth, empirical evidence from propaganda, facts from fiction, and knowledge from opinion;
- understand that the research process is cumulative, tentative, and skeptical; as well as understand the limitations of scientific inquiry and causal explanations;

research report a written document that summarizes the way a study was conducted and its major findings, and is a complete report on the research process.

the need to gather sufficient evidence to support or reject claims; and the influence of society on research; and

- analyze and process data, and be aware that problems often have more than one accepted answer and that many issues are multidisciplinary with political, judicial, ethical, and moral dimensions.

THE WRITING PROCESS

There are many good books on how to write a research report. My favorite is by Howard S. Becker and is titled *Writing for Social Scientists: How to Start and Finish Your Thesis, Book, or Article* (University of Chicago Press, 2007). It has many tips and tricks, as well as a general philosophy of writing, social relationships, and doing research. Many other books focus more on step-by-step mechanics. In this section we discuss the general consensus on writing research reports.

Know Your Audience

Professional writers tell us, Always know for whom you are writing. This is because communication is most effective when you tailor it to a specific audience. You should write a research report differently depending on whether the primary audience is an instructor, students, professional social scientists, practitioners, or the lay

---

Making It Practical Tailoring a Report to the Audience

- *Writing for instructors.* An instructor assigns a research report for different reasons and may place requirements on how you are to prepare it. In general, instructors want to see good writing and an organization that reflects clear, logical thinking. They want to see a report that demonstrates a solid grasp of substantive and methodological concepts. They want to see you only using technical terms explicitly *when appropriate*, and not used excessively or incorrectly. Often instructors are concerned more with how the report demonstrates your thought process, specific details about research steps, and use of the correct format than with your findings.

- *Writing for other students.* You want to define all technical terms and clearly label each part of a report. Your discussion section should proceed in a very logical, step-by-step manner. You should offer many specific examples. You will want to use less formal language to explain how and why you conducted the various steps of the research project. One strategy is to begin with the research question, then structure the rest of the report as an answer to that question.

- *Writing for expert professionals and scholars.* You do not need to define technical terms or explain why you used research standard procedures (e.g., random sampling). Professionals are interested in how the research links to theory or past findings in the literature. They want to see a compact but detailed description of the research

process. They will pay close attention to how you measured variables and gathered data. They like a condensed, tightly written, but extensive section on data analysis, with a precise and meticulous discussion of the results.

- *Writing for practitioners, managers, and policy makers.* Provide a short summary of how you conducted the study, and present the main results in a few simple charts and graphs that are easy to read and understand. Practitioners like to see an outline of alternative paths of action implied by results with the practical outcomes of pursuing each path. Practitioners focus on the main findings, but you may have to caution practitioners not to overgeneralize from the results of one study. For practitioner reports, you want to place the details of research design and the long version of the results in an appendix.

- *Writing for the public.* You need to use simple language, provide concrete examples, and focus on the practical implications of findings for specific issues or problems. You do not have to include many details of research design or of results. You need to be very careful not to make unsupported claims when writing for the public, because people can easily misinterpret findings. Informing the public is an important service. It helps nonspecialists make better judgments about public issues.

public. In all cases, the writing should be clear, accurate, and organized. This usually takes hard work and practice.

Pick a Style and Tone

Write reports of research studies in a narrow range of styles with a distinct tone. They have one primary purpose—to communicate clearly the research method and findings.

Style refers to the type of words, length and form of sentences, and pattern of paragraphs. In the report, avoid a poetic or flowery style with many extra colorful adjectives and illusions. Also avoid a highly formal, dense, and turgid style that is common in government and bureaucratic documents. Such documents use passive voice and are full of long, complex sentences and unnecessary technical jargon (see Making It Practical: Suggestions for Rewriting later in this chapter). Research reports have a formal and succinct style (they say a lot in few words).

Tone is the attitude or relation toward the subject matter that you express as a writer. For example, an informal, conversational way of writing (e.g., colloquial words, idioms, clichés, and incomplete sentences) with a personal tone (e.g., these are my personal feelings) is appropriate if you are writing a letter or e-mail to a close friend. You may use comedy or a whimsical tone to express humor. This is inappropriate for research reports. The tone in a research report expresses some distance from the subject matter. It is professional, semidetached, and serious. Field researchers sometimes use an informal style and a more personal tone, but this is the exception. Also, avoid moralizing and "preaching" a specific point of view. Your goal is to inform, not to advocate a position or to entertain. You persuade through systematic empirical evidence and using accepted research techniques.

Your research report should be accurate and clear. You must check and recheck details (e.g., page references in citations) and fully disclose how you conducted the research project. If readers detect carelessness in your report, they may question the research itself. The details of a research study can be complex. This complexity makes confusion possible. It also makes clear thinking and plain writing essential. To achieve these goals, think and rethink your research question and study design. You should explicitly define major terms, write in short declarative sentences, and limit the conclusions to what you can support with empirical evidence.

Organize Your Thoughts

Writing is serious, time-consuming work. It does not happen magically or simply flow automatically when you put pen to paper (or fingers to keyboard). Think of writing as a process. It has a sequence of steps and activities that result in a final product. Writing a research report is not radically different from other types of writing. The steps may differ and the level of complexity may be greater, but what a good writer does to write a long letter, a poem, a set of instructions, or a short story also applies to writing a research report.

Go Back to the Library

Few researchers totally finish the literature review before they complete the study. You should be familiar with the literature before you start, but expect to return to the literature after completing data collection and analysis. The following are three reasons for doing this:

- Time has passed between the beginning and the end of a research project, and new studies may have been published.
- After completing a research project, you will know better what is or is not central to the study and may have new questions in mind as you reread studies in the literature.

1. *Have something about which to write.* The "something" in the research report includes the topic, research question, design and measures, data collection techniques, results, and implications.

2. *Get organized.* When you have many parts to write about, organization is essential. The most basic tool for organizing writing is the outline. Outlines help you ensure that all ideas are included and that the relationship among them is clear. Outlines have topics (words or phrases) or sentences. Most of us are familiar with the basic form of an outline (see Tips for the Wise Researcher: Outlining and Figure 12.1).

3. *Avoid procrastination and writer's block* Some people become afflicted with a strange ailment when they sit down to compose writing—the mind goes blank, the fingers freeze, and panic sets in. **Writer's block** also occurs when procrastination becomes writing constipation! After many delays, you cannot get the writing process moving. You stall without ideas or motivation. Many people delay writing until the last possible moment and then, under great pressure or panic, force themselves to write. This is not a successful strategy for professional writing. The pressure of a deadline might be motivation, but frantic, rapid writing is only useful as a prewriting activity (discussed later), not as a final draft. Writers from beginners through experts occasionally experience writer's block. If you experience it, calm down

and work on overcoming it. There are many tricks to overcome it (e.g., taking a walk, getting a back rub, organizing files, sharpening pencils). A common technique is to identify small parts of a larger task that you can easily accomplish and do them first. Set a reasonable schedule for such parts. After you finish a part, give yourself a small reward (e.g., have a special dessert). The best way to avoid writer's block is by writing, at least a little, all the time. Set aside a small amount of time to write every day. If you are always writing something, even if you later throw it away, you are less likely to be blocked.

Somos Images/Corbis Royalty Free

4. *Engage in prewriting activities.* Writing is an ongoing process, not a one-time event. Sometimes it helps to build up momentum. Writing starts with prewriting activities—creating self-imposed deadlines and a schedule, arranging your notes, preparing lists of ideas, drafting rough outlines, making certain that bibliographic references are complete, and reviewing the data analysis. Of course, there is a danger that you will get distracted and sidetracked by such activities. Self-discipline is central to the writing process.

• As you write the report, you may find that your notes are not complete enough or a detail is missing in the citation of a reference source. The visit to the library after data collection is less extensive and more selective or focused than that conducted at the beginning of research, but it may be necessary to fill in missing details.

When writing a research report, you will probably discard some of the notes and sources that you gathered. This does not mean that your initial library work and literature review were a waste of time and effort. Researchers expect that some of the notes (e.g., 25–30 percent) taken before completing the study will become irrelevant as the study gains greater focus. Do not include notes or references in a report that are no longer relevant. They will distract from the flow of ideas and reduce the report's clarity.

You return to the library to verify and to complete references. Going back to the library also helps you avoid plagiarism (discussed in Chapter 3), a very serious form of cheating. Take careful notes and identify the exact source of phrases or ideas to avoid unintentional plagiarism. Cite the sources of what you directly quote and of ideas that you paraphrase. For direct quotes, always include the specific location of the quote with page numbers in the citation. Using another person's words and failing to give credit is always clearly wrong. **Paraphrasing** is not using another's exact words; rather, you restate someone else's ideas in your own words. Researchers regularly paraphrase and cite the source. To paraphrase, you need a solid

writer's block a temporary inability to write that some people experience when they have a writing task to complete.

paraphrasing restating another person's ideas in your own words, condensing at the same time.

Tips for the Wise Researcher Outlining

Outlines can help you as a writer. However, they can also become a barrier if you use them improperly. An outline is a tool that helps you organize ideas. With it you do three things:

1. Put ideas in a sequence (e.g., what will be said first, second, and third);
2. Group related ideas together (e.g., these are similar to each other, but differ from those); and
3. Separate the more general, or higher-level, ideas from more specific ideas, and the specific ideas from very specific details.

Some students feel they must have a complete outline before they can start to write, and that once they prepare an outline, they cannot deviate from it. Few professional writers begin with a complete, detailed outline and stick to it rigidly. Your initial outline can be sketchy, because until you write everything down, it is impossible to put all ideas in a sequence, group them together, and separate the general from the specific. For most writers, new ideas develop or become clearer in the process of writing itself.

Your beginning outline may differ from the final outline by more than its degree of completeness. The process of writing not only reveals and clarifies ideas, it also stimulates new ideas, new connections among ideas, a new sequence of parts, or new relations between the general and the specific. In addition, the writing process may stimulate you to reanalyze or reexamine the literature or findings. This does not mean beginning all over again. Rather, it means you need to maintain an open mind to new insights and be candid about reporting how you conducted the research.

■ **Figure 12.1 Outline Form**

I. First major topic	High level of importance
A. Subtopic of topic I	Second level of importance
1. Subtopic of A	Third level of importance
a. Subtopic of 1	Fourth level of importance
b. Subtopic of 1	"
(1) Subtopic of b	Fifth level of importance
(2) Subtopic of b	"
(a) Subtopic of (2)	Sixth level of importance
(b) Subtopic of (2)	"
i. Subtopic of (b)	Seventh level of importance
ii. Subtopic of (b)	"
2. Subtopic of A	Third level of importance
B. Subtopic of topic I	Second level of importance
II. Second major topic	High level of importance

understanding of what you paraphrase. It is more than replacing another's words with synonyms; you condense statements to the core ideas and give credit to the source.

Engage in Prewriting Activities

Many people find that getting started is difficult. Beginning writers often jump to the second step and go from there. This often results in poor-quality writing. **Prewriting** means that you begin with a file folder full of notes, outlines, and lists. You spend thinking time to consider the form of the report and audience. Thinking time often occurs in spurts over time before the bulk of composing begins.

Many writers begin to compose by **freewriting**. Freewriting creates a link between a rapid flow of ideas in the mind and writing. As you freewrite, do not stop to reread what you wrote, do not ponder the best word, do not worry about correct grammar, spelling, or punctuation—just get your ideas on paper (or on screen) as quickly as possible to get and keep the creative juices or ideas flowing. You can later clean up what you wrote.

Writing and thinking are intertwined. It is impossible to know where one ends and the other begins. If you plan to sit and stare at the wall, the computer output, the sky, or whatever until your thoughts are totally developed and clear before you begin to write, you probably will not get anything written. Writing itself ignites the thinking process, which, in turn, feeds further writing.

prewriting activities that prepare you for a serious writing process.

freewriting a way to begin serious writing in which you write down everything you think of as quickly as it enters your mind, not worrying about correct grammar or spelling.

Rewrite Your Report

Perhaps one in a million writers is a creative genius who can produce a first draft that communicates with astounding accuracy and clarity. For everyone else, writing means that rewriting—and rewriting again—is necessary. For example, Ernest Hemingway is reported to have rewritten the end of *A Farewell to Arms* 39 times. Professional researchers may rewrite a report a dozen times. If rewriting sounds daunting to you, do not become discouraged. If anything, rewriting reduces the pressure; it means you can start writing and just produce a rough draft that you will polish later. Plan to rewrite a draft at least three or four times. A draft is a complete report, from beginning to end, not a few rough notes or an outline.

Making it Practical **Suggestions for Rewriting**

1. *Mechanics*. Check grammar, spelling, punctuation, verb agreement, verb tense, and verb/subject separation with each rewrite. Remember that each time you add new text, new errors can creep in. Many mistakes are distracting, and they weaken the confidence readers place in the ideas you express.

2. *Usage*. Reexamine terms, especially key terms. When you rewrite, check to see whether you are using a word that best expresses your intended meaning. Do not use technical terms or long words unnecessarily. Use the plain word that best expresses a clear meaning. Get a thesaurus and use it. A thesaurus is an essential reference tool, like a dictionary. It has words of similar meaning and can help you locate the exact word for a meaning you want to express. Precise thinking and expression requires precise language. Do not say *average* if you intend to use *mean*. Do not say *mankind* or *policeman* when you intend *people* or *police officer* (i.e., strive for gender neutrality in your writing). See Pitt (1994) or url: http://www.jeanweber.com/newsite/?page_id=55 for advice on gender neutral writing. Do not use *principal* for *principle*, *there* for *their*, or *than* for *then*. Also avoid unnecessary qualifying language, such as *seems to* or *appears to*.

3. *Voice*. Some writers make the mistake of using the passive voice in a research report instead of the active voice. It may appear to be authoritative, but the passive voice obscures the actor or subject of action. Compare the voice in these two examples: PASSIVE: "The relationship between grade in school and more definite career plans was confirmed by the data." ACTIVE: "The data confirm the relationship between grade in school and more definite career plans." PASSIVE: "Respondent attitude toward abortion was recorded by an interviewer." ACTIVE: "An interviewer recorded respondent attitude toward abortion."

4. *Coherence*. Make the sequence of ideas logically tight. Include transitions between ideas. Try reading the entire report one paragraph at a time. Does each paragraph con-

tain a unified idea? Does it have a topic sentence? Did you include transitions between the topics and paragraphs within the report?

5. *Repetition*. Remove repeated ideas, wordiness, and unnecessary phrases. It is best to state ideas once, forcefully, rather than repeatedly in an unclear way. When revising, eliminate deadwood (words that add nothing) and circumlocution (the use of several words when one precise word will do). Directness is preferable to wordiness. Here is an example: WORDY: "To summarize the above, it is our conclusion in light of the data that *x* has a positive effect of considerable magnitude on the occurrence of *y*, notwithstanding the fact that *y* occurs only on rare occasions." LESS WORDY: "In sum, the effect of *x* on *y* is large and positive but occurs infrequently."

6. *Structure*. Make the organization of your research report transparent. Move sections around as necessary to fit the organization. It is wise to use headings and subheadings. A reader should be able to follow a report's logical structure with great ease.

7. *Abstraction*. A good research report mixes abstract ideas with concrete examples. A long string of abstractions without specifics is difficult to read. Likewise, a mass of specific concrete details without a periodic generalization to summarize the main point can also lose readers.

8. *Metaphors*. Many writers use metaphors to express ideas. They use phrases such as "the cutting edge," "the bottom line," and "penetrating to the heart" to express their ideas. Metaphors can be an effective method of communication if you use them sparingly and with care. A few well-chosen, consistently used, fresh metaphors can communicate ideas quickly and effectively; however, excessively using metaphors, especially overused metaphors (e.g., the bottom line), is a sloppy, unimaginative method of expression.

Rewriting helps you to express yourself with a greater clarity, smoothness, precision, and economy of words. When rewriting, focus on clear communication; do not use unnecessary pompous or complicated language. When rewriting, you slowly read what you have already written. Some people read what they wrote out loud to see whether it sounds right. It is always wise to share your writing with others. Professional writers have others read and criticize their writing. New writers quickly learn that friendly, constructive criticism is very valuable. Sharing your writing with others may be difficult at first. It means exposing your written thoughts and encouraging criticism. Yet the purpose of the criticism is to clarify the writing. A good critic is doing you a favor.

Rewriting involves two processes: revising and editing. **Revising** is inserting new ideas, adding supporting evidence, deleting or changing ideas, moving sentences around to clarify meaning, and strengthening transitions and links between ideas. **Editing** is cleaning and tightening up the mechanical aspects of writing, such as spelling, grammar, usage, verb tense, sentence length, and paragraph organization. As you rewrite, go over a draft and revise it brutally to improve it. You will find this is easier to do if you allow some time to pass between writing a draft and rewriting. Phrases that seemed satisfactory in a draft may look fuzzy or poorly connected a week later.

Even if you have not acquired typing or keyboarding skills, it is a good idea to type and print out at least one draft before the final draft. It is easier to see errors and organization problems in a clean, typed draft. Freely cut and paste, cross out words, and move phrases on the printed copy. Serious professionals find that the time they invest in building keyboard skills and learning to use a word processor pays huge dividends later. Word processors make editing much easier. They also check spelling, offer synonyms, and check grammar. Do not rely on the computer program to do all the work; the computer can miss errors (e.g., if you have used *their* when you should have used *there*), but it makes writing easier.

One last suggestion: Write the introduction and title after you finish a draft of the report. This ensures that they will accurately reflect what you have said. Make titles short and descriptive. They should communicate the topic and the major variables. They can describe the type of research (e.g., "An experiment on") but should not have unnecessary words or phrases (e.g., "An investigation into the"). Look at the following the titles of the example studies in Appendix C: "Racially Biased Policing: Determinants of Citizen Perceptions," "White Means Never Having to Say You're Ethnic: White Youth and the Construction of 'Cultureless' Identities." The first title tells you the topic "Racial Bias" and research question, "What determines citizen's

revising part of the rewriting process in which you move ideas around or add and subtract ideas or evidence.

editing part of the rewriting process in which you focus on improving the mechanical aspects of writing, such as spelling or sentence structure.

  Summary Review **Steps in the Writing Process**

The way to learn to write is by writing. Writing takes time and effort and improves with practice. There is no single correct way to write, but some ways are better than others are. The writing process has three steps:

1. *Prewriting.* Prepare to write by arranging notes on the literature, making lists of ideas, outlining, completing bibliographic citations, and organizing comments on data analysis.

2. *Composing.* Get your ideas onto paper as a first draft by freewriting, drawing up the bibliography and footnotes, preparing data for presentation, and writing a draft introduction and conclusion.

3. *Rewriting.* Evaluate and polish the report by improving coherence, proofreading for mechanical errors, checking citations, and reviewing voice and usage.

perceptions of police being racially biased?" but not about the data or research method. The second tells you the study is about racial-ethnic relations, identity, and youth.

SHOW CAUSE-EFFECT RELATIONS

In many research studies, you want to demonstrate cause-effect relations. You want to see whether one or more factors, conditions, or variables cause another factor or variable. You saw this earlier in Chapters 2, 4, and 9, with an independent (cause) and dependent variable (effect) in a simple hypothesis. Although most common in quantitative data research, causal relations can appear in all types of studies. If you wish to show a cause-effect relationship in a study, you need to think about how you will write about and explain it to readers.

As you saw in Chapter 7, experimental researchers can demonstrate cause-effect relations most clearly. Experiments best meet the three conditions required to show causality: temporal order, association, and control over alternative causes. Hard-core experimenters tend to think that only an experiment can show cause-effect relations, and they question it in other types of research. You show cause-effect in an experiment by introducing the independent variable at a specific time, looking for an association in data on dependent variable measures, and creating an experimental design to control for factors that could influence the outcome (internal validity). Of course, the experimental approach has limitations, including a lack of random samples, difficulties with generalizing (external validity), the need to examine a single variable at a time, and an emphasis on micro-level relationships. If you conduct an experiment, you can talk about causal relations in a report by showing a strong association between the independent and dependent variable in results and a high degree of internal validity in the experimental design.

Researchers who use survey or existing statistical methods also want to show cause-effect relations. Of the three conditions for causality, they can best demonstrate an association among variables. However, as you already learned, an association or correlation alone is not enough for causality. Demonstrating time order in survey or existing statistics data requires extra effort. For example, a respondent may answer all survey questions at one point in time. If some questions ask about past events (e.g., what did you do in high school, or how much education did you parents receive?) whereas others are about present events or attitudes, you can establish time order by carefully looking at the time of a variable in a survey question or variable. This is how a survey or existing statistics researcher argues for temporal order. Survey and existing statistics researchers also control for alternative explanations. They cannot exercise physical control through experimental design as experimenters do. Instead, they measure any variables that might indicate an alternative explanation. These are control variables (you read about control variables in Chapter 9). Advanced statistical methods allow researchers to add control variables along with the main causal variables and check whether the main variables are still association, net of the control variables. If you conduct survey or existing statistics research, you can talk about causal relations by showing a strong association among variables, by noting the temporal ordering of variables, and by ruling out alternative explanations by using control variables. By using control variables and logically arguing that alternatives are unlikely, you can say that an association among variables supports a causal relationship and is not spurious.

Many field researchers and historical-comparative researchers also want to show cause-effect relations. They observe events over time, so meeting the temporal order condition is usually easy. Showing an association is more difficult. To do this, they carefully note the co-occurrence of events in the qualitative data. For example, a researcher studying a small work setting notices that employees become upset and make a lot of complaints about work conditions and superiors for a week or two several times during a year of field observation. The researcher notes when this occurred and what occurred before, during, and after the employee dissatisfaction peaks. Each peak of complaints occurred shortly after employees returned from a holiday or vacation. During weeks before a holiday or vacation, employees appeared happy and satisfied, but during the week or two following they complained. Listening to the informal talk among employees, the researcher learned that employees often spent vacation or holiday time with adult friends, family members, and neighbors who worked in other jobs. In postholiday informal conversations, the employees talked about how their friends, family members, or neighbors had nice, rewarding jobs. The researcher observed an association between (1) expressions of dissatisfaction and (2) the opportunity the employees had to compare their work situations to the jobs held by other people.

Eliminating alternative explanations is the most difficult condition to satisfy. Researchers do this by becoming intimately familiar with a setting and providing in-depth details and specifics about a particular context. They think about alternatives while conducting the research and try to look for evidence of possible alternative explanations. For example, is it having time away from work on a vacation or holiday and not comparing jobs with friends, family, and neighbors that increased dissatisfaction? If you conduct a field or H-C study, you can talk finding a causal relationship in a report if you show a sequence of events and can document events that occurred earlier or at the same time. To eliminate alternative explanations, be familiar with the literature on the topic and note whether anyone suggested or found evidence for alternative explanations. You can also suggest potential alternatives along with any evidence you found for them with your judgment of whether they might be present.

THE QUANTITATIVE RESEARCH REPORT

The principles of good writing apply to all types of reports, but the parts of a report differ depending on whether your study used quantitative or qualitative data. It is always wise to read many reports on the same kind of research for models and ideas. We begin by looking at the quantitative research report. The sections of the report roughly follow the sequence of steps of a research project.

Abstract or Executive Summary

Quantitative research reports begin with a short summary or abstract (you read about the abstract of a study in Chapter 2). The size of an abstract varies; it can be as few as 50 words (this paragraph has 82 words) or as long as a full page. Most scholarly journal articles have abstracts on the first page of the article. The abstract has information on the topic, the research problem, the basic findings, and any unusual research design or data collection features.

Applied research reports for practitioners substitute a long summary, the **executive summary**, for an abstract. The executive summary has more detail than an article abstract and is longer (often three to five pages). It has most major findings, the implications of findings, and major recommendations. The executive summary has more in it because many practitioners and policy makers only read the executive summary and then just skim parts of the full report.

Abstracts and executive summaries tell a reader what is in a report. They help the reader looking for specific information to screen many reports and decide whether to read the entire report. An abstract also gives serious readers who intend to read the full report a quick overview of it. This makes reading the report easier and faster. Although the abstract or executive summary are the first thing someone reads, you should write them last. Write them after you have finished the rest of report so you know what the report contains.

executive summary a summary of a research report that is longer than an abstract and used in applied research studies for practitioners.

Presentation of the Problem

The first section of a report is very important because in it you introduce readers to the main topic, research question, and overall tone of the report. Your goal is to present the research question, define major concepts, and begin to guide a reader through your report. The introductory section has several possible headings, such as "Introduction," "Problem Definition," "Literature Review," "Hypotheses," or "Background Assumptions." Although the headings vary, the contents include a statement of the research problem/question and a rationale for its importance. Here, you explain the significance of and provide background on the research question. Explain the significance of your study by showing how different solutions to the problem lead to different applications or theoretical conclusions. This section is where you place the literature review and link the specific question of your study to past studies. You also define key concepts and present the main hypotheses in general, conceptual terms.

Description of the Method

The next section of the report describes how you designed the study and collected the data. It goes by several names (e.g., "Methods," "Research Design," or "Data") and may be subdivided into other parts (e.g., "Measures," "Sampling," or "Manipulations"). It is the most important section for the professional when he or she is evaluating the quality of research methodology. This section answers several questions for the reader:

1. What type of study (e.g., experiment, survey) did you conduct?
2. Exactly how did you collect the data (e.g., study design, type of survey, time and location of data collection, experimental design used)?
3. How did you measure/introduce each variable? Are the measures reliable and valid?
4. Did you sample? How many participants are in the study? Exactly how did you select them? What are their characteristics (age, gender, race-ethnicity, and so forth)?
5. Did any ethical issues or specific design concerns arise, and, if so, how did you deal with them?

Results and Tables

After you described how you sampled, collected data, and measured variables, you present the data. In this section you present—not discuss, analyze, or interpret—the data. Researchers often combine the "Results" section with the next section, called "Discussion" or "Findings," but many keep the sections separate. You have a few choices in how to present the data. When you analyzed the data, you looked at dozens of univariate, bivariate, and multivariate tables and statistics to get a feel for the data. Do not put every statistic and table you looked at in a final report. Rather, select the minimum number of charts or tables that fully informs a reader. Charts or tables should summarize the data and show any tests of hypotheses (e.g., frequency distributions, tables with means and standard deviations, correlations, and other statistics). Your goal is to give readers a complete picture of the data without overwhelming them—not to provide data in excessive detail or present irrelevant data. Readers can make their own interpretations by examining the data. Detailed summary statistics and very technical explanations belong in appendixes.

Discussion

In the discussion section, give the reader a concise, unambiguous interpretation of the data's meaning. The discussion is not a selective emphasis or partisan interpretation. You candidly discuss what is in the results section. You separate the discussion section from the data results section to allow a reader to examine the

Making It Practical **Writing the Discussion Section of a Report on Quantitative Research**

Many beginning researchers find it difficult to organize a discussion section. Reading many research reports can help you see how to do it. One approach is to organize the discussion according to hypotheses. You can discuss how the data relate to each hypothesis. In addition to reporting how data relate to your hypotheses, you should discuss unanticipated findings that look interesting. Also, give pos-

sible alternative explanations of results. Your may also note the weaknesses or limitations of your study. Many beginning researchers find it unusual to point out limitations. Remember that a major principle of the research process is to be fully open and candid, not to hide or defend a particular outcome. Readers will have more confidence in your report if you openly disclose its limitations.

data and arrive at his or her own interpretations. Organize your discussion to make it easy for a reader to follow. One way to do this is to repeat hypotheses and describe how the findings specifically support, modify, or reject each hypothesis. After reading the discussion section, a reader should leave with a clear picture of the findings.

Conclusions

In the conclusion or summary section, you restate the research question and summarize major findings. This is a place to highlight limitations of the study and possible implications for the future. The only sections after the conclusion are notes, references, and appendixes (if any). You should only include sources you referred to in the references section. If you have an appendix, place additional detailed information on methods of data collection (e.g., questionnaire wording) or specialized results in it. Use footnotes or endnotes sparingly to expand or elaborate on information in the text. Put secondary information (information that clarifies your in-text statements) in notes to avoid distracting readers from the flow of your text.

Making It Practical **Looking at the Parts of a Published Quantitative Data Study**

Look at the quantitative data study by Weitzer and Tuch (2005) in Appendix C. From the abstract, a reader learns the following five things:

1. The topic of this study is racial bias by police, specifically racial profiling in the United States.
2. The study is important because the extent of police racial bias and public perceptions of it are not well known.
3. Data for this study are a national survey on citizens' views of and experiences with police bias.
4. Findings of the study are that three factors shape a person's views on the issue: race, prior experiences with police discrimination, and exposure to news media.
5. The study finds support for a group-position theory of race relations.

The authors divided the introduction section into a short introductory paragraph that outlines the topic and

research question, a section with the literature review, and the hypotheses they test. The researchers present three hypotheses; each has two parts. The authors also outline alternative explanations or theories that they will consider. The next section, Methods and Data, is divided into several parts: Sampling, Panel Representation (repeated measures of the same people over time), Independent, Dependent, and Control Variables. In the methods section, the authors also present readers with basic descriptive statistics for each variable in a table. The Results section combines results and discussion. There are many tables with numbers in this section. The authors organized the discussion of results by each hypothesis. The Conclusion section is three pages long. In it, the authors discuss the significance of their study, repeat their major findings, and point to directions for future research. After the conclusion are endnotes and references.

THE QUALITATIVE RESEARCH REPORT

Compared to a quantitative data research report, most people find writing a report on qualitative research to be more difficult. It has fewer rules and is less structured. Nevertheless, all reports have the same the purpose: to communicate how you conducted a study, what data you collected, and what you learned from a through examination of the data.

In a quantitative research report, you present hypotheses and evidence in a logically tight and condensed style. By contrast, a report on a qualitative study can be longer and less compact. In fact, book-length reports on qualitative research are common. Reports on qualitative research are longer for several reasons:

- It is difficult to condense data that are in the form of words, pictures, or sentences.
- Providing evidence often means offering readers specific quotes and extended examples.
- You want to create a subjective sense of empathy and understanding of real people, events, and settings. It takes more words to give highly detailed descriptions of specific settings and situations.
- In qualitative data studies, you use less standardized techniques for gathering data, creating analytic categories, and organizing evidence. You may create new the techniques for a particular setting. This means you must explain in depth exactly what you did in the study and why rather than simply referring to a well-known standard technique.
- Many qualitative data studies construct new concepts or theories. It takes more words to develop new concepts and explain the relationships among them than to use existing concepts. Because theory flows from the evidence, you need to show readers how the concept is linked to the evidence.
- Many writers use a variety of writing styles in a qualitative data report. This freedom to depart from a precise, standard style tends to increase overall length. You may employ literary devices to tell a story or recount a colorful tale.

Report on Field Research

Reports on field research rarely follow a fixed format with standard sections. You can use a less objective and formal tone when writing about field research. You can write a report on field research in first person (i.e., using the pronoun *I*) because you, as an individual person, were directly involved in the setting and interacted face-to-face with the people studied. Your decisions or indecisions, feelings, reactions, and personal experiences are legitimate parts of the field research process.

In the report, you do not separate theoretical ideas from data into distinct sections. Instead, you intertwine generalizations with the empirical evidence. This takes the form of detailed description with frequent quotes. You must balance the presentation of data and analysis. Too much data without analysis and too much analysis with supporting data are both problems to avoid.

Data reduction is a major issue in field research. Field research data are in the form of a huge volume of field notes, but you can only share a very small percent of observations or recorded conversations with the readers.

Field researchers organize reports in several ways. Two major ways are by chronological natural history and by themes. When you use natural history organization, you present the sequence of ideas and data in the same time order as you discovered or came across them. When you use a thematic organization, you present a theme and then provide data that illustrate or support it. You can choose between using abstract analytic themes from the scholarly literature or your own thinking, and using themes that are used by the people you studied. Both have advantages. The former makes it easier to connect your study with other studies or more abstract theory. The latter gives readers a vivid description of the setting and lets you display

Learning from History *Boys In White*

The book *Boys In White* (Becker et al. 1961) describes the pioneering study by Howard Becker and his colleagues into how medical students become doctors. It is a classic ethnographic study that details the lives of young men at the University of Kansas—their schedules, efforts to find out what professors wanted from them, "latent culture," and assimilation of medical values. It also describes how they learned to negotiate a hospital or clinic in all its complexity as well as develop a perspective on their futures.

The clarity and thoughtfulness of the method used and its write-up are equally important as the findings. The authors started with about 5000 pages of single-spaced field notes. Of these, they put less than 5 percent in the book-length report as quotations. The remaining 95 percent were not wasted. The field notes are a rich, deep reservoir of empirical evidence from which the authors created the report. As you prepare a report, carefully select quotes and indirectly convey the rest of the data to readers.

the language, concepts, categories, and beliefs of the people you studied. You can use a mix of both types of themes.

In a field research report, you discuss the methods used in the report, but its location and form vary. One technique is to interweave a description of the setting, the means of gaining access, the role of the researcher, and the subject/researcher relationship into the discussion of evidence and analysis. A chronological or theme-based organization allows you to put the data collection method near the beginning or the end. In book-length reports, most authors put a discussion of methodological issues in a separate appendix at the end.

Field research reports can contain transcriptions of tape recordings, maps, photographs, and charts illustrating analytic categories. They supplement the discussion and are placed near the discussion they complement. Qualitative field research can use creative formats that differ from the usual written text with examples from field notes. The photographs give a visual inventory of the settings described in the text and present the meanings of settings in terms of those being studied. For example, field research articles have appeared in the form of all photographs, a script for a play, or a documentary film.

Direct, personal involvement in the intimate details of a social setting heightens ethical concerns. Researchers write in a manner that protects the privacy of people they study. They usually change the names of members and exact locations in field reports. Personal involvement in field research leads researchers to include a short autobiography. For example, in the appendix to *Street Corner Society*, the author, William Foote Whyte (1955), gave a detailed account of the occupations of his father and grandfather, his hobbies and interests, the jobs he held, how he ended up going to graduate school, and how his research was affected by his getting married.

Making it Practical **Organization of a Report on Field Research**

1. Introduction
   a. Most general aspects of situation
   b. Main contours of the general situation
   c. How you collected materials
   d. Details about the setting
   e. How the report is organized

2. The situation
   a. Analytic categories
   b. Contrast between situation and other situations
   c. Development of situation over time

3. Strategies

4. Summary and implications

Making It Practical **Looking at the Parts of a Published Qualitative Data Study**

Look at the qualitative data study by Perry (2001) in Appendix C. From the abstract, a reader learns the following five things:

1. The topic is the processes by which people construct white racial identities.
2. The study examined white youth in two high schools: one predominantly white, the other multiracial.
3. The researcher used ethnographic techniques and in-depth interviews.
4. A main idea is that racial superiority is based on whites having no culture, because their culture is the norm.
5. The study has implications for "critical white studies," sociology of education, and racial identity formation.

The report begins with an open-end question that Perry asked a participant and a quote of the participant's response. The introduction section has a description of the field sites (two high schools) and major organizing concepts (white culture, naturalization, a claim to be culture-less, and rationalization). The next section is the literature review. After reviewing the literature and elaborating on the study topic, Perry provides the reader with a method and reflections section. In it she describes her own study of existing statistics and other sources to acquire a background on setting and topic, describes the two field sites in greater depth, and explains in detail how she did the study, such as spending two and one-half years observing and interviewing, as well as her specific activities in the field sites. She tells her age and how she dressed and techniques she used to gain rapport with field participants. She also describes types of participants she interviewed, where she conducted the interviews, and for what length of time (about two hours). Her results are not in a section by that name, but she presents results for each of the two field sites, one after the other, mixed with conceptual categories. The results include description and analysis intermixed with frequent quotes from field notes or interviews. The conclusion section summarizes major findings and concepts and outlines implications of the study. It is followed by endnotes and references.

Report on Historical-Comparative Research

There is no single best way to write a report on historical-comparative research. Most frequently, researchers "tell a story" and describe details in general analytic categories. They go beyond description to include some limited generalizations. Thus, a major feature is to connect abstract concepts with specific empirical details.

Researchers rarely describe their methods in any detail in a report on historical-comparative research. The methods may have involved visiting many specialized libraries or obtaining documents, but beyond listing sources, other details are not necessary. You will rarely see an explicit section of a report or an appendix describing the methods used. Occasionally, a book-length report contains a bibliographic essay that discusses major sources used. More often, you see numerous detailed footnotes or endnotes. For example, a 20-page report on quantitative or field research typically has 5 to 15 notes or sources. A report on historical research of equal length may have over 60 notes or sources.

Historical-comparative reports often have photographs, maps, diagrams, charts, or tables of statistics. You see them throughout the report sections that discuss evidence that relates to them. The charts, tables, and so forth are less the "make or break" evidence of a quantitative research report. Instead, they are part of a slow build-up of a large quantity of diverse evidence. You put them in the report to give readers a more complete picture and better feel for the places and people in the study. You use them in conjunction other evidence, as part of creating a broad web of meaning with many descriptive details. Skill at organizing the large amounts of qualitative evidence is itself a way to convey interpretations and generalizations to a reader.

You can organize a report of historical-comparative research in two major ways: by topic and chronologically. Most writers mix the two types. For example, you can organize information chronologically within topics, or organize by topic within chronological periods. If the report is truly comparative, you have additional options, such as making comparisons within topics. Some historical-comparative researchers mimic the quantitative research report and use quantitative research techniques. Their reports follow the model of a quantitative research report.

Many researchers use a narrative style of report writing, in which they "tell a story." If you use a narrative style, you organize the data chronologically and try to "tell a story" around specific individuals and events.

THE RESEARCH PROPOSAL

In Chapter 2 you learned about research proposals. You write a proposal for a supervised project submitted to instructors as part of an educational degree (e.g., a honor's or master's thesis or a Ph.D. dissertation) or for a funding source. The proposal's purpose is to convince reviewers that you, the researcher, are capable of successfully conducting the proposed research. Reviewers will have confidence that you can successfully complete the study if your proposal is well written and organized and if you demonstrate careful planning. A proposal is similar to a research report, but you write it before the research begins. A proposal describes the research problem and its importance and gives a detailed account of the methods that you will use and why they are appropriate. See Appendix A for example proposals.

Proposals for Research Grants

The purpose of a research grant is to provide the resources needed to help complete a worthy project. Researchers whose primary goal is to use funding for personal benefit or prestige, to escape from other activities, or to build an "empire" are less successful. The strategies of writing proposals and "winning" grants are separate skills in themselves.

There are many sources of funding for research proposals. Colleges, private foundations, and government agencies have programs that award grant funds to researchers (see Figure 12.2). You may use the money for purchasing equipment, for paying salaries, for research supplies, for travel to collect data, or for help with the publication of results. The degree of competition for a grant varies a great deal depending on the source. Some sources fund more than three out of four proposals they receive; others fund fewer than one in twenty.

Tips for the Wise Researcher Quantitative and Qualitative Research Proposals

A proposal for quantitative research has most of the parts of a research report: a title, an abstract, a problem statement, a literature review, a methods or design section, and references. It lacks results, discussion, and conclusion sections. It is a plan for data collection and analysis (e.g., types of statistics) and frequently includes a schedule of the steps to be undertaken and an estimate of the time required for each step.

A proposal for qualitative research is more difficult to write. This is because the research process itself is less structured and preplanned. You prepare a problem statement, literature review, and references. You can demon-strate an ability to complete a proposed qualitative project in two ways:

1. Your proposal is well written, with an extensive discussion of the literature, significance of the problem, and sources. This shows reviewers your familiarity with qualitative research and the appropriateness of the method for studying the problem.
2. Your proposal describes a qualitative pilot study. This demonstrates motivation, familiarity with research techniques, and ability to complete a report about unstructured research.

■ **Figure 12.2**   Examples of Announcements to Fund Research.

Spencer Foundation
Eligibility: Principal Investigators applying for a Research Grant must be affiliated with a school district, a college or university, a research facility, or a cultural institution. The Foundation accepts proposals from institutions and/or researchers from the U.S. and internationally. Researchers must also have an earned doctorate in an academic discipline or professional field or appropriate experience in an education-related profession. Budget Restrictions: Indirect costs may not be charged to proposed budgets with less than $50,000 in direct costs. Proposals exceeding $500,000 in direct costs require particularly close scrutiny and are generally developed in close consultation with Spencer staff prior to submitting a proposal.

Determine whether your project fits within one or more of the Foundation's current areas of interest:

- The Relation between Education and Social Opportunity;
- Organizational Learning in Schools, School Systems, and Higher Education Institutions;
- Teaching, Learning, and Instructional Resources; and
- Purposes and Values of Education.

In addition to proposals in these defined areas, the Foundation will continue to accept proposals that do not fit one of these areas.

Deadlines: There are no deadlines for preliminary proposals. They are welcome at any time.

If invited, full proposals in the Major Research Grants Program are considered four times per year.

Blue Cross Foundation Announces Letter of Inquiry Deadlines for Minnesota Projects
Grants up to $150,000 will be provided to Minnesota nonprofits and government organizations for programs focusing on the health/well-being of immigrants or children. . . .

Deadline: Various

Komen for the Cure Seeks Applications for Washington, D.C. Area Community Grants
Grants of up to $700,000 will be awarded to nonprofits, government agencies, and educational institutions working to reduce breast cancer disparities in Washington, D.C., and seven surrounding counties. . . .

Deadline: August 20, 2007

You need to investigate funding sources so you can direct your proposal to the funding source with which it has the greatest chance of success. Ask questions:

- What types of projects get funded—applied versus basic research, specific topics or research techniques?
- What are the deadlines and proposal format requirements (page length, font size)?
- What kind of proposal is necessary (e.g., short letter, detailed plan)?
- How large have most previous grants been?
- What parts of doing the research (e.g., equipment, personnel, travel) are or are not funded?

There are many sources of information on funding sources. Librarians or officials responsible for research grants at a college are good resource people.

Many funding agencies periodically issue **requests for proposals (RFPs).** These ask for proposals to conduct research on a specific issue (see Figure 12.3). In evaluating proposals, funding agencies look for a record of past success. The researcher in charge of a study is the **principal investigator (PI)** or project director. Proposals usually include a curriculum vitae or academic resumé, letters of support from other researchers, and a record of accomplishments. The reviewers of proposals feel safer investing funds in a project headed by someone who already has research experience than in a novice. You can build a record with small research projects or by assisting an experienced researcher before you seek funding as a principal investigator.

requests for proposals (RFPs) an announcement by a founding source that it seeks research proposals to fund.

principal investigator (PI) the main researcher who conducts a study that is funded by a grant.

■ **Figure 12.3**   Example RFP

ANNOUNCEMENT OF AVAILABILITY OF FUNDS, TRAINING, AND TECHNICAL ASSISTANCE IN JUVENILE JUSTICE AND DELINQUENCY PREVENTION

> KEEP THIS ANNOUNCEMENT TO REFER TO
> WHILE COMPLETING THE APPLICATION FORM.

A. **ISSUING OFFICE.**   This announcement of availability of federal funds, training, and technical assistance is issued for the State of Colorado by the Colorado Department of Public Safety, Division of Criminal Justice (DCJ), in conjunction with the Juvenile Justice and Delinquency Prevention (JJDP) Act of 1974 (42 U.S.C. 5601), as amended. DCJ is the sole point of contact concerning this Announcement. All communications must be done through the Division of Criminal Justice.

B. **APPLICATION PROCESS AND INQUIRIES.**   An application and application instructions may be obtained by mailing or faxing the attached "Intent to Apply" form to the address/fax number listed on that form, or e-mailing the same information to the e-mail address on the form.

C. **ELIGIBLE APPLICANTS.**   **General:** Eligible applicants are public and private state-level agencies or local agencies, including local law enforcement, courts, probation offices, district attorneys' offices, schools, school districts, BOCES, and community-based not-for-profit organizations. Applicants may propose to subcontract any or all of the required activities but are not required to do so. Subcontractors can be other public state or local agencies or private not-for-profit organizations as identified under Section 501(c)(3) of the federal tax code. The applicant agency must certify that all participating agencies/organizations have collaborated in the design of the project and agree that the identified lead agency is appropriate.

Specific: For **Program 1, Juvenile-Focused Community Policing Programs,** eligible applicants are local law enforcement agencies or local public/private community-based agencies collaborating with law enforcement. Applications must include Memoranda of Understanding signed by all project participants, which delineate the role(s) of the community partners in the support and implementation of the project. The applicant agency must certify that all participating agencies/organizations have collaborated in the design of the project and agree that the identified lead agency is appropriate. Applicants that are not law enforcement agencies must provide written endorsement of the proposal from the primary law enforcement agency for the area and demonstrate the project's relationship to community policing programs/philosophy. Likewise, applications submitted by law enforcement agencies must provide written endorsement from the community organization(s) that is/are collaborating in the problem-solving effort.

For **training and technical assistance for comprehensive delinquency prevention planning,** requests must come from units of local government, including departments such as law enforcement and social services, and from advisory groups associated with the local government.

D. **BACKGROUND AND AVAILABLE FUNDS.**   These federal funds are available under Title II Formula and Challenge Grant Programs of the Juvenile Justice and Delinquency Prevention (JJDP) Act. The Colorado Juvenile Justice and Delinquency Prevention (JJDP) Council oversees these grant programs and has prioritized and budgeted funds for the following four areas:
   1. the expansion of both the restorative justice philosophy in programs that focus on juvenile accountability and juvenile-focused community policing programs ($150,000)
   2. the implementation of interventions to address the over representation of minority youth in the juvenile justice system ($200,000)
   3. the provision of quality female-specific services in the juvenile justice system ($150,000)
   4. an in-depth look, through a pilot site, at the quality of and access to counsel for juveniles ($70,000)

The purposes and principles identified for each area are described below under Item E. Awards will be made, on a competitive basis, for twelve-month periods (unless otherwise stated), beginning October 1, 2001. Individual award amounts (minimum of $5,000) will be determined by the number and quality of eligible applicants, and funds available. These funds cannot be used to supplant (replace) existing dollars from other sources; however, they may enhance or expand an existing program.

The Colorado Juvenile Justice and Delinquency Prevention Council will judge the merits of the proposals received in accordance with the evaluation factors listed in this announcement. Failure of the applicant to provide any information requested in this announcement and the application form may result in disqualification of the application. The responsibility is that of the applicant. The plan of the Council will be to fund those applicants whose proposals are most responsive to the specifications in this announcement, within the available funds.

Source: Logo Courtesy of the Colorado Department of Public Safety

■ Figure 12.3   *Continued*

E. **PURPOSES, PRINCIPLES, AND GUIDELINES FOR FUNDED PROGRAMS.**   It is the intent of the Council and DCJ to allow applicants to design their projects to meet local needs. However, there are several primary principles which must be included in the application problem statement, project description, goals and objectives, and evaluation plan. These are listed by program area below.

1. **Juvenile-Focused Community Policing and Restorative Justice.** ($150,000)
   Juvenile-Focused Community Policing These funds are intended for projects that use community policing principles to foster positive relationships with the community, involve the community in the quest for better delinquency control and prevention, and pool resources with those of the community to address the most urgent needs of community members regarding youth crime.

   OJJDP has defined community policing as "a policing philosophy that promotes and supports organizational strategies to address the cause and reduce the fear of crime and social disorder through problem-solving tactics and community-police partnerships." It should empower law enforcement and the community to implement specific problem-solving strategies that address the underlying causes of the youth-focused problematic issues.

Example of the Community Policing Problem-Solving Approach:

Problem Statement/Identification: Repeat calls for service for juvenile loitering activity in the community. Large number of kids, ages 12–14 years, are without recreational activity. Youths in the neighborhood need recreational activities. Current facilities close early and are outside the area.

Action Plan: To provide recreational activities at the local baseball field and elementary schools to develop art programs and team sports of baseball, basketball and volleyball.

Risk/Protective Factor Addressed: Provide access to resources, provide supportive networks and social bonds to community.

Anticipated Results: Reduced youth-related police calls for service, increased involvement of residents in youth activities and increased neighborhood participation in the neighborhood association.

Evaluation: Are calls for juvenile loitering reduced in the area during programmed activities? Are the youth involved in the program seeking alternative activities once the program is compete?

Under the community policing model, the citizen is asked to assume a greater responsibility and contribute individually and collectively to public safety. By relying on expertise and resources which already exist in communities, police can perform their duties more effectively and will give the members of the larger community a key role in problem solving.

Project dollars must be for the specific purpose of development, enhancement, implementation, or evaluation of *youth-focused*, neighborhood-based community policing programs. The geographic boundaries of the neighborhood or community must be clearly defined. The problem identification process must be documented: How did the community verify *what* is occurring; *who* is it affecting; *when* is it occurring; *where* is it occurring; and *how* is it impacting the community? Memoranda of Understanding, delineating the roles and responsibilities of the law enforcement and community partners, must be included.

*Please do not staple your proposal pages.

Reviewers who evaluate a proposal first ask whether the proposal project is appropriate to the funding source's goals. For example, programs that fund basic research have the advancement of knowledge as a goal. Programs to fund applied research often have improvements in the delivery of services as a goal. Instructions specify page length, number of copies, deadlines, and the like. Follow all instructions exactly.

Your proposal should be neat and professional looking. The instructions for proposals may ask for a detailed plan for the use of time, services, and personnel. State them clearly and be realistic. Excessively high or low estimates, unnecessary add-ons, and omitted essentials will result in a less favorable evaluation. Creating a budget for a proposed research project can be complicated and requires technical assistance. There are official pay rates, fringe benefit rates, and so on. It is best to

Simon Battensby/Photographer's
Choice/Getty Images

consult a grants officer at a college or an experienced proposal writer. In addition, endorsements or clearances of regulations are often necessary (e.g., IRB approval). The proposal should also include specific plans for disseminating results (e.g., publications, presentations before professional groups) and a plan to evaluate whether the project met its objectives.

The proposal is a type of contract between the researcher and the funding source. Funding agencies often require a final report. It includes details on how funds were spent, the findings, and an evaluation of whether the project met its objectives. A failure to spend funds properly, complete the project as described in the proposal, or file a final report has serious consequences. The funding agency may sue for a recovery of funds or a researcher might be banned from receiving future funding. A serious misuse of funds may result fines, jail terms, or the penalties for the institution (school, hospital, research institute) where the research was to occur.

The process of reviewing proposals after they are submitted takes from a few weeks to almost a year. In most cases, reviewers rank a large group of proposals, and only highly ranked proposals receive funding. Most government agencies or research centers use a peer review process. Private foundations may have a mix of non-researcher lay people and professional researchers review proposals. Instructions on preparing a proposal indicate whether you are to write for professional specialists or for an educated general audience. As with writing a research report, it is always a good idea to have others read it and give you comments and to revise as necessary before you submit your proposal.

If your proposal is funded, celebrate, but only for a short time. If your proposal is rejected, do not despair. Given the competition, funding sources reject a majority of proposals the first or second time they are submitted. Many funding sources provide you with written reviewer evaluations of the proposal. You should always request evaluations if they are available. Sometimes a courteous talk on the telephone with a person at the funding source will reveal the reasons for rejection. You should strengthen and resubmit a proposal based on the reviewer comments. Most funding sources accept repeated resubmissions of revised proposals. Propos-

Making It Practical **A Successful Research Grant Proposal**

Before you submit a grant proposal, be certain that the funding agency is looking for proposals on your topic or research question. If you are uncertain, check with the funding agency officials first. If you submit a proposal to an appropriate funding source, reviewers are more likely to rate it higher when the following are present:

1. For basic research: Your proposal addresses an important research question, clearly builds on past studies, and represents a substantial advance in knowledge. For applied research: Your proposal carefully documents a major social problem, shows an awareness of all alternatives, and offers solutions.
2. You have followed all instructions in detail.
3. You submitted the proposal well within the deadline. Funding agencies automatically reject late proposals.
4. The proposal is written clearly and has easy-to-follow objectives. Many proposals provide charts or dia-

grams that make it easy for a reader to following all details.
5. You completely described your research procedures and used high standards of research methodology. The research techniques you describe are the most appropriate ones for your specific research question.
6. You included specific plans for how you will disseminate the results and evaluate all project objectives.
7. You provided a study design that shows serious planning and realistic budgets and schedules.
8. You have the experience or background required to complete the study successfully and/or include other researchers with technical background and experience as consultants.
9. You include letters of support from knowledgeable people or involved organizations.

Making It Practical **Select Undergraduate Research Sources**

Council on Undergraduate Research
   Council on Undergraduate Research
   734 15th St. N.W. Suite 550 Washington, DC 2005
   PHONE: (202) 783-4810 WEB SITE: http://www.cur.org/
National Conference on Undergraduate Research
http://www.ncur.org/
National Science Foundation: Research Experiences
   for Undergraduates
http://128.150.4.107/pubs/2005/nsf05592/nsf05592.htm
Undergraduate Research Community for the Human
   Sciences
http://www.kon.org/urc/undergrad_research.html

Stewart Cohen/Blend Images/Corbis Royalty Free

als that have been revised based on past reviews tend to be stronger in subsequent competitions.

UNDERGRADUATE RESEARCH

Many people engage in social research—high school students, undergraduates, graduate students working on master's or doctoral degrees, and professionals in many fields. Learning to do research has long been an essential part of earning advanced degrees. Learning research skills often begins while a student is an undergraduate. The Council on Undergraduate Research (CUR), founded in 1978, promotes research by all undergraduates. The CUR has grown to include 900 colleges and universities. The CUR hosts an undergraduate research conference, produces a scholarly journal, and provides special Institutes on undergraduate research for students and faculty. In addition to CUR, other national organizations and many colleges and universities actively promote undergraduate research as a highly engaging and effective form of learning and professional growth. They offer small grant programs or summer research opportunities to assist students in conducting research.

WHAT HAVE YOU LEARNED?

In this chapter you learned about the research report and the process of writing such a report. You saw how features of a research study, such as qualitative versus quantitative data, affect the organization and content of a report. You also learned about the process of preparing a research proposal and seeking funding for research, as well as the fast growing area of programs and support for undergraduate research.

Clearly communicating results is a vital part of the research process, as are the ethics and politics of social research. I urge you, as a consumer of social research or a new social researcher, to be self-aware. Be aware of the place of research in society and of the societal context in which social research can thrive. Social researchers bring a unique perspective to the larger society.

KEY TERMS

editing *330*
executive summary *332*
freewriting *328*
paraphrasing *327*
prewriting *328*

principal investigator (PI) *339*
request for proposals (RFPs) *339*
research report *324*
revising *330*
writer's block *327*

APPLYING WHAT YOU'VE LEARNED

Activity 1

Practice preparing an outline for a research report. To do this, first identify five scholarly journal articles that report on the same type of research on one topic. Develop of an outline of each research report. Notice what is similar and what is different about each. After outlining each and conducting a comparison, develop an outline of your own in two stages. First, develop general categories with major headings and no more than one secondary level in the outline. You should have four or five major headings and two or three subcategories under each. Second, refine your outline by developing two levels of greater detail, so that you have major headings, first-level headings, second-level headings, and one more level of subheadings. There should be two or more items at each level.

Activity 2

Locate five RFPs for a topic of interest. You can find a few with a general search on the Internet, but many are only available in specialized publications or databases. A good one to check is the U.S. government's *Federal*

Register. It is available in most college libraries and online, and it has an overwhelming amount of information. It is often easier to locate specific private foundations or government agencies at the national, state, or city level. For example, specific agencies such as Big Brothers or Big Sisters to might ask for RFPs for applied research, or a state Department of Education might seek RFPs to evaluate its bilingual education programs. The RPF may be active or have already had a deadline that passed. Once you found five RFPs, answer the following six questions about each:

1. What is the name of the funding source?
2. From whom are applications sought, or who is eligible to apply for funding?
3. What topics or research questions does the funding source want to be examined?
4. How much money is provided either in total or as the maximum for a proposal?
5. What is the submission deadline for a proposal, and are there specifications for how the proposal should be delivered?
6. Are there specifications for the format of the proposal (e.g., page length, specific sections)?

Activity 3

Go onto the Internet and conduct a search using Google. Enter the term *Undergraduate Research*. Create three lists. In list 1, include colleges and universities that have a program for undergraduate research. In list 2, place government or private agencies that provide financial support for undergraduate research. In list 3, put all scholarships, summer institutes, and research grant support for undergraduates. Note whether the funding is for a specific academic field (e.g., chemistry) or is open to all fields.

REFERENCES

Becker, Howard S. et al. 1961. *Boys in White: Student Culture in Medical School.* Chicago: University of Chicago Press.

Hartley, James, James Pennebaker, and Claire Fox. 2003. "Using New Technology to Assess the Academic Writing Styles of Male and Female Pairs and Individuals." *Journal of Technical Writing and Communication* 33(3):243–261.

Hurd, P. D. 1998. "Scientific Literacy: New Minds for a Changing World." *Science Education* 82:407–416.

Perry, Pamela. 2001. "White Means Never Having to Say You're Ethnic: White Youth and the Construction of 'Cultureless' Identities." *Journal of Contemporary Ethnography* 30(1):56–91.

Pitt, M. J. 1994. "A Practical Guide to Gender Neutral Language" *Management Decision* 32(6):41–44.

Weitzer, Ronald and Steven Tuch. 2005. "Racially Biased Policing Determinants of Citizen Perceptions." *Social Forces* 83(3):1009–1030.

Whyte, William Foote. 1955. *Street Corner Society: The Social Structure of an Italian Slum.* Chicago: University of Chicago Press.

Appendix A　Sample Research Proposals

EXAMPLE RESEARCH PROPOSAL, QUALITATIVE EXPLORATORY STUDY OF ANIME FANS IN THE UNITED STATES

INTRODUCTION AND RESEARCH TOPIC

Anime, or Japanese-origin animation, has become widely popular among some teens and young adults. Enthusiasts watch many hours of the films, collect the films, read magazines about characters and films, attend fan conventions, create Internet sites with fan information, and dress up as their favorite characters. While the public might be familiar with a few box-office hits, such as *Spirited Away* or children's cartoons, there is an entire world of fans in their teens through twenties who avidly follow anime.

A few studies have been conducted on the cinematic form and industry of Japanese animation and its spill-over to Japanese popular culture products, but almost nothing is written about the anime fan subculture in America. It appears to have arisen in 1990s and greatly expanded during the early 2000s. Casual observation suggests it is about equally among popular both genders and all ethnic-racial groups. It primarily attracts young people from the pre-adolescence and early teens (11–15) through early adulthood (25–28). Apparently, children discover the Japanese-style cartoons, and some become attracted to more sophisticated animation forms as well as video game spin offs.

The scant journalistic commentary on anime fans implies that many are "social misfits" or "geeks." They do not cause trouble or break laws, but they do not fit in with mainstream peers. Many U.S. fans have self-adopted the Japanese term *otaku* (which translates as an obsessed misfit/geek and has negative connotations) as a badge of honor. Some apparently excel at academics, but few appear seriously involved in sports or other social activities common for their age group. There is speculation is that these young people are bright and pulled into a fantasy world that offers rapid action escape, adventure, morality tales, and intrigue. Somewhat socially separated from peers, they apparently seek out others with the same interest. While most appear socially adjusted and operate in daily life without serious difficulties, a few withdraw and devote more time in the fantasy world of animation than in reality. Reactions by parents and other adults who work with young people (teachers, librarians) are not known.

There are many forms of anime. Most genres have an adventure-fantasy theme, but some offer elaborate alternative worlds, and others are very violent or graphically pornographic. With little formal adult or institutional support, the fans seek one another out to form clubs at schools, libraries, or community centers at which they watch and discuss their favorite characters and tales. They organize conventions at the state, regional, or national level. The role of the anime production and distribution industry in these is unknown. At the conventions, they discuss and analyze the animation stories and also engage in dress-up or "cosplay" (a Japanese term for costume play). It appears that many young people dress as their favorite characters then admire one another's costumes and interact in ways that mimic the character. There are many products (posters, clothing, trinkets) sold to fans but little is known about the people who produce and sell these products.

RESEARCH OBJECTIVE AND PROCEDURE

1. Research Objective

This is an exploratory, qualitative study, in which we seek to describe the anime fan culture. Our goal is to gather preliminary information that can be used for a future study.

2. Research Participants

The principal investigator and/or trained assistant will locate anime fans at clubs, anime conventions, and through referrals. The exact number is not clear since this is an exploratory and uncharted area. Additional fans will be located using purposive and snowball (referral) sampling. We hope to locate a least 30 fans for interviews. The age, race, gender make-up is unknown but will probably involve an equal mix of gender, all racial-ethnic groups, and persons aged 13 to 30 years. Persons under the age of 13 will be excluded.

3. Research Procedure

The principal investigator and/or trained adult college student assistants will personally observe fans in public places using participant observation techniques, conduct informal small talk-conversations, and make arrangements to interview participants at a later time. We may take a few brief notes (such as a person's name and address or phone number) in the field setting, but take extensive notes of the club activities and convention events after the observation.

While at meetings and conventions, we will gather names for future interviews or conduct interviews after club meetings or during conventions. The interviews will be open-ended and tape-recorded. See Appendix for questions/topics in the interviews. Prior to interviewing or tape-recording, we will explain the purpose of the study to participants and tell them that their involvement is voluntary. We will collect the names of participants but hold them in confidence. Personal identifiers (age, gender, etc.) will be released to the public in a way that protects the identity of participants. Because some anime fans may be under the age of 18, we will obtain parental permission prior to interviews.

We expect interviews to vary in length (ten minutes to an hour) and may take place on more than one occasion in a semi-private location (e.g., room alcove, table or booth in a restaurant). Interview questions will not be fixed prior to interviewing but will follow a general list of topics (see below). We may ask different participants different questions based on their early responses. We will listen to tape recordings and take notes, but not transcribe the interviews. We may take photos, with permission, of conventions and participants, and will collect artifacts (e.g., announcements, brochures on conventions, etc.). We will document the types of products (shirts, posters, etc.) sold to fans at the conventions to identify patterns and trends.

4. Anticipated Results

As an exploratory study into a relatively unknown area, we can only speculate about possible results. We will describe anime fan activities (clubs, conventions, etc.) and characteristics of the fans we interview. We will identity repeated themes and patterns within the clubs/conventions and examine themes in anime fan conversations, and about fan social activities. We will use the results to develop a more systematic study into the anime subculture.

5. Schedule and Budget

Schedule

Months 1–2   Locate fan clubs and conventions and scan Internet sites.
Months 3–4   Visit clubs and conventions, interview fans.
Months 5–6   Assemble and organize collected materials and field notes to analyze them.

Budget

Supplies
  notebooks
  tape recorder and supplies (batteries)
Travel
  To clubs and conventions

APPENDIX

Questions in the interviews will include the following topics:

- What is your age? If in college, what is your major and GPA?
- Do you have a part-time job, what is it?
- What are your career goals and aspirations for the future?
- What is your favorite anime film/character? Has this changed over time?
- At what age did you first develop an interest in anime? Explain, please.
- What got you interested in anime?
- Have your interests/favorites changed over time?
- About how many hours per week do you watch anime?
- How many anime films do you personally own?
- How often do you get together with friends to discuss anime?
- Of all those who you consider close friends, how many follow anime?
- Do you engage in cosplay or other anime social activities?
- What other hobbies or interests do you have besides anime?
- If you have social activities, what proportion are centered on anime?
- About how much money do you spend on anime per month?
- Do you have any other Japan-related interests other than anime?
- Do you have friends who were once interested in anime but dropped out?
- What do you and your anime friends talk about?
- What interests you in anime, how does it make you feel?
- Do you ever get very angry or upset watching anime?
- What types of anime do you like? Dislike?
- What types do you feel excited by or bored by?
- What do you think about people who do not like anime?
- Do you watch/play video games related to anime?
- In general, what type of student are you?
- In what ways, if any, does anime relate to your school work?
- Do you have any other hobbies or interests based on your anime interest?
- Do you think you will always love anime? Why or why not?
- Do you encourage people younger than yourself to learn about anime?
- How would you describe your relations with your parents?
- Does anime relate to your sexuality and interest in sex in any way?

QUESTION TOPICS FOR ADULT PARTICIPANTS (18 AND OLDER) ONLY

- Do you currently consume alcohol or recreational drugs while viewing anime?
- Did you consume alcohol or recreational drugs while viewing anime when you were younger, under 18?
- Of your sexual partners, do many share your interest in anime?
- Do you get sexually aroused when you watch anime?

EXAMPLE RESEARCH PROPOSAL A QUANTITATIVE STUDY OF ANIME ENTHUSIASTS IN THE UNITED STATES

INTRODUCTION AND THEORY

We all "consume" many popular cultural products, such as media forms (e.g., video or music), food dishes, electronic devices, and so forth. Most achieve a mass distribution, but some are specialized. Specialized products can attract a small number of people who become enthusiasts. At times, the enthusiasts develop social relations with one another, exchange information, and discuss product details. More than being casual consumers, their interest includes studying, collecting, and becoming experts on the products. By communicating and interacting, they might develop a distinct subculture around the products. A cultural product subculture is likely to develop when the cultural product is unusual or obscure, requires special knowledge, or has devotees in a geographic region or specific age group.

Early in subculture formation, the devotees may meet to exchange information, create publications, or form clubs. Fans set themselves apart from "outsiders" unfamiliar or not yet entranced by the product. Their skill and expertise with the product helps them develop self-esteem and gain respect from their like-minded peers. Even more than other cultural products, media forms change "fashion" very quickly. Young people tend to be more interested in new media that appeared in the late 20th and early 21st centuries. With fewer family or job responsibilities and a disposable income, young people are the primary consumers of popular media and may develop a "fan" following around specific products, artists, musicians, or a genre. With globalization, some cultural productions, and particularly new media, are shared across international borders and marketed to people in many countries. The cultural products are part of a developing international youth culture.

RESEARCH QUESTION

This study examines the U.S. fans of the cultural media product Japanese animation, or anime. Artists, writers, and producers in Japan create anime. It has a "different" foreign or exotic look compared to most American-created animated media. Compared to traditional U.S. animation, Japanese anime is more diverse, has more complicated plots and developed characters, and appeals to a wider age range. Anime takes some themes from Japan and builds on Japanese settings or situations that are not widely known in the United States. This study looks at several questions about anime:

1. Does anime with its "foreignness" attract people who feel somewhat outside the U.S. cultural mainstream?

2. Are males and females attracted to different aspects or themes in anime that relate to emerging gender issues?
3. Over time do anime fans develop an interest in the country or culture of its origin, Japan?

Each research question has broader implications. With globalization, more products from other countries for people are available. It could be that some people that are not part of a somewhat homogenized mainstream culture find foreign products more attractive and a way to express their feelings of difference or individuality. One aspect of a foreign cultural product is that they might offer an alternative set of social relations or cultural viewpoint, even it if is not realistic or easy to act upon. When a cultural product of foreign origin includes some elements of the foreign culture or country, avid consumers of the product may develop an interest in the foreign country or culture as an ancillary effect of their devotion and interest in the cultural product.

LITERATURE REVIEW

Several studies of anime productions have documented the themes and situations borrowed from Japanese culture in the stories, characters, and situations (see references). Anime films fall into a set of categories (fantasy, adventure, and so forth) and is somewhat differentiated by age and gender. Both male and female characters are often shown with superpowers, and changing or ambiguous gender of characters is present in several anime series (reference). Other studies of the anime industry emphasize its rapid growth and connection to other media, Japanese-style comics and video games (reference). A few theorists emphasized anime as part of an transnational youth culture (reference).

Only two studies (see reference) have looked at anime fans. One unpublished study found that college student anime fans were first attracted to anime but knew very little about Japan or had little interest in Japan. Another study that was a doctoral dissertation found that while many anime fans fit a "geek" or "nerd" stereotype, this was not universal. All did share a strong interest in media (watching film) and related media product (video games), and most began at a young age.

HYPOTHESES

HY 1: Persons with fewer "mainstream" hobbies or interests, and with fewer "mainstream" close friends are likely to be stronger anime fans.
HY 2: Female anime fans identify more with androgynous/ambiguous gendered characters than male fans.
HY 3: Intense and committed anime fans are the most likely to want to learn about Japanese culture, learn the Japanese language, and/or wish to visit the country of Japan.

METHOD

1. Sample

The *population* is self-identified anime fans between the ages of 13 and 26. A fan is defined as someone who attends club meetings or a convention that is focused on anime, or who describes his or her main hobby as watching anime films, dressing and acting as anime characters, and/or talking with others anime enthusiasts about anime films.

We will draw a stratified random sample of 200 fans from university, school, and community anime clubs in the area and conventions. First, we will identify ten anime clubs or conventions and attend multiple meetings to obtain lists of members or attendees. Next, we will create a *sampling frame* that has the names, ages, addresses, phone numbers, and e-mails of the members, attendees, and self-described fans at the clubs or conventions. Next, we will divide the sampling frame into two age groups: (1) fans aged 13–18, and (2) those aged 19–26. Finally, we will draw a random sample of 100 names from each age group.

We will contact each sampled person to set up an interview. For persons under 18 years of age, we will use a two-stage process. First, we will contact the sampled person and request the name, address, and phone number of a parent or legal guardian. Before scheduling an interview, we will mail the parent or legal guardian an informed consent form that explains the study and asks permission to interview the legal minor along with a stamped return envelope. We will telephone parents who fail to respond in seven days to make an oral request and offer a second informed consent form.

If we cannot contact or obtain permission to interview a sampled name after six tries using phone, regular mail, and e-mail, we will randomly draw a replacement name from the same age-stratified sampling frame until we have 200 people who agree to be interviewed.

2. Data Collection Procedure

We will conduct face-to-face or telephone interviews with each respondent. We estimate that about one-half will be face-to-face and one-half by telephone, depending on logistics and scheduling. We will ask permission to tape record all telephone interviews. After obtaining permission to record, we will read an informed consent statement prior to interviewing. For face-to-face interviews, we will ask each respondent to sign an informed consent form. Informed consent will be obtained for persons under 18 in addition to a parent or guardian consent form.

We will conduct the face-to-face interviews in any public place (school grounds, shopping mall, or restaurant) but without another person participating and no one listening in. After completing a questionnaire, we will offer to send a copy of the report to a respondent and provide contact information should he or she have further questions. We will number and store the questionnaires and begin to enter data from each questionnaire into a statistical computer program after the first twenty are completed.

We anticipate spending 10 minutes per interview locating and arranging for the interview, and the interview itself to take about 15 minutes to complete. We estimate about 20 minutes to travel to and meet with people for each face-to-face interview and 20 minutes to transcribe each of the telephone interviews. To complete the 200 interviews it will take about 33 hours for locating and scheduling, 50 hours for actual interviewing, and 67 hours for traveling and transcribing.

3. Variable Measurement

We will create three general measures by combining multiple survey questions to measure: (1) being a "nerd" or "geek" or being outside the mainstream of U.S. culture, (2) being a committed anime fan based on years of watching anime, spending time with anime and other fans, and expressing a strong interest in anime, and (3) having an interest in learning about Japan and Japanese culture. We anticipate the questionnaire will have about 40 items. Examples of some preliminary questions to be in the final questionnaire are listed below.

Variable Name	Questionnaire Item
1. Gender	Are you, _____ Male _____ Female _____ GBLT
2. Age	How old are you now? _____
3. School	Do you now attend school? If No Next, If Yes, what school/grade _____
4. Start	At what age did you first start watching anime regularly? _____
5. Games	Do you play video games? If No skip to #8, If Yes, how often? _____ daily _____ 2–3 times a week _____ weekly _____ less often
6. Games 1	What are your favorite two games (1)_____
7. Games 2	(2)_____
8. Own	How many anime DVDs do you personally own? _____
9. Often	How often do you watch anime? _____ every day _____ 3–5 times a week _____ about once a week _____ several times a month _____ less than once a month
10. Where	Where do you usually watch anime films? _____
11. Friends	Of your five best friends, how many are anime fans? _____
12. Alone	Think back to the last 10 times you watched an anime film. How many of those 10 times were you watching it alone? _____
13. Favorite1	Name your four favorite anime films of all time, (1) _____
14. Favorite2	(2) _____
15. Favorite3	(3) _____
16. Favorite4	(4) _____
17. Character1	Name your two favorite anime characters of all time, (1) _____
18. Character2	(2) _____
19. Products	Do you own any anime-related products, such as posters, clothing, stuffed animals, etc.? If No skip to #21,
20. Type	If Yes, what products do you own, type and number? _____
21. Cosplay	Do you ever dress up in a costume as an anime character? _____ Yes _____ No
22. Japan1	Have you ever read a book about Japanese history or society?
23. Japan2	Have you ever traveled to Japan? If Yes #25, If No,
24. Japan3	How interested are you in traveling to Japan? _____ Extremely _____ Very _____ Somewhat _____ A little _____ Not at All
25. Club	Do you belong to an Anime Club, No _____ Yes _____
26. Conven1	Have you ever attended an anime convention? If No skip to #28, If Yes,
27. Conven2	How many conventions have you attended in the past three years? _____
28. FriendG	Of your five closest friends, how many are your same gender? _____
29. Internet	How often do you go to anime related sites on the Internet? _____ Never _____ once a month _____ several x a month _____ Weekly _____ Daily or more
30. Magazine	Do you subscribe to an anime magazine? _____ Yes _____ No

Time Schedule

Month 1	Obtain IRB approval, continue literature review, prepare draft of complete questionnaire, develop list of anime clubs and conventions
Months 2–3	Visit anime clubs and conventions to collect names and create sampling frame, pilot test questionnaire
Month 4	Draw a random sample of names and contact under 18 sample for parental permissions, revise questionnaire, begin to schedule interviews
Months 5–7	Contact and arrange for all interviews, begin interviewing
Month 8	Complete last interviews, and start to code data into computer program
Month 9	Finish coding, and analyze data using statistics program
Month 10	Write up results as a report and present findings

Budget Extimate

Supply and Service Expenses
    Printing and postage
    Tape recorder and supplies
    Telephone
Travel Expenses
    To go to anime clubs and conventions
    To go to interviews
    To go to professional meeting to present final report
Labor Expenses
    General clerical help
    Interviewing help
    Tape transcription help
    Data entry help
    Statistical analysis

Appendix B Data and Literature Research

SOURCES OF ONLINE STATISTICS

It is important that research be supported by up-to-date information. There are many online databases that will provide the latest statistics on many topics of interest. Some examples are as follows:

Albany.edu/sourcebook: The Sourcebook of Criminal Justice Statistics has over 600 tables, covering diverse aspects of criminal justice in the United States.

CDC.gov: The Centers for Disease Control and Prevention provides health statistics, and is an excellent source for birth and mortality data.

Census.gov: The U.S. Census Bureau provides extensive population statistics, including online access to the *Statistical Abstract*.

FedStats.gov: This site provides data and information from over 100 federal government agencies. FedStats also has links to many other helpful resources.

Gallup.com: The Gallup Poll is an excellent source of public opinion statistics. Some of this information is free online, and some polls require a subscription.

ICPSR.umich.edu: The Inter-University Consortium for Political and Social Research is the world's largest archive of social science statistical data. The site houses data sets that can be analyzed with statistical software, but also provides publications based on the data collected.

NCES.ed.gov: The National Center for Education Statistics analyzes and provides data collected from U.S. schools.

Thearda.com: The American Religion Data Archive has demographic, church membership, and religious practice information for the United States.

LITERATURE SEARCH DATABASES

Literature databases can help you navigate the seemingly limitless amounts of professional journals and research articles that are available electronically. College libraries have subscriptions to some databases, allowing students to download full-text articles, in many cases. Examples of literature databases include the following:

EBSCO: College libraries have free access to *EBSCOhost*, a database that allows users to search an extensive collection of popular and scholarly publications.

ERIC: Free via the Internet, the *ERIC* database provides abstracts to over one million unpublished documents and published articles on educational research and practice.

Ingentaconnect: The Ingenta database allows the user to search an extensive collection of abstracts by most major journal publishers. Ingenta is an excellent source for browsing journals by academic discipline.

JSTOR: JSTOR has digitally preserved hundreds of scholarly journals, including historical documents. Through this database, researchers can access back runs of journal articles, spanning over 40 disciplines.

MEDLINE: MEDLINE has over 10 million searchable records of life science and biomedical information.

PsycARTICLES: PsychARTICLES is a database of full-text articles from the more than 50 journals published by the American Psychological Association.

SELECTED PEER REVIEWED JOURNALS, BY DISCIPLINE

Anthropology and Archaeology

American Anthropologist
American Antiquity
American Ethnologist
American Journal of Archaeology
Annual Review of Anthropology
Ethos
Folklore
Man

Criminology and Legal Studies

Aggressive and Violent Behavior
Crime and Delinquency
Criminal Justice and Behavior
Criminology
Journal of Criminal Justice
Journal of Criminal Law and Criminology
Journal of Interpersonal Violence
Journal of Quantitative Criminology
Journal of Research in Crime and Delinquency
Justice Quarterly
Law and Society Review
Victimology

Education

American Educational Research Journal
Computers and Education
Contemporary Educational Psychology
Early Childhood Research Quarterly
Educational Leadership
Educational Psychology
Educational Researcher
International Journal of Educational Research
Journal of Education Policy
Journal of Special Education
Learning and Instruction
Literacy
Review of Educational Research
Review of Research in Education
Teaching and Teacher Education
Teaching Exceptional Children

General Business and Consumer Behavior

Administrative Science Quarterly
Advances in Consumer Research
Business and Society Review
Consumption, Markets and Culture
Harvard Business Review
Journal of Consumer Behavior
Journal of Consumer Culture
Journal of Consumer Marketing
Journal of Consumer Research
Journal of Marketing

Human Development, Family Studies, Gerontology

Child Development
Developmental Psychology
Families in Society
Family Relations
The Gerontologist
Human Development
Infant Behavior and Development
Journal of Adolescence
Journal of Gerontology
Journal of Human Development
Journal of Marriage and Family
The Journal of Sex Research

Human Resource Management

Academy of Management Journal
Academy of Management Review
Human Resource Management
Industrial and Labor Relations Review
International Journal of Human Resource Management
Journal of Human Resources
Journal of Organizational Behavior
Organizational Behavior and Human Decision Processes
Personnel Psychology
Work and Occupations

Political Science

American Journal of Political Science
The American Political Science Review
Comparative Politics
International Studies Quarterly
The Journal of Conflict Resolution
The Journal of Politics
Political Behavior
Political Science Quarterly
Politics and Society
The Public Opinion Quarterly
Social Science Quarterly
World Politics

Psychology

American Journal of Psychology
American Psychologist
Journal of Abnormal Psychology
Journal of Applied Social Psychology
Journal of Personality and Social Psychology
Psychological Bulletin
Psychological Methods
Psychological Review
Psychological Science
Social Psychology Quarterly

Sociology

American Journal of Sociology
American Sociological Review
Annual Review of Sociology
Comparative Studies in Society and History
Current Sociology
Demography
Gender and Society
Journal of Health and Human Behavior
Journal of Marriage and the Family
Social Forces
Social Problems
Sociological Quarterly

Social Work

Affilia: Journal of Women and Social Work
Child Abuse and Neglect
Child Welfare
Health and Social Work
Journal of Social Service Research
Journal of Social Work Education
Research on Social Work Practice
Social Service Review
Social Work
Social Work Research

The following three articles are examples of research articles published in professional journals. By the time research comes to be published in a journal of this type, the researcher has often spent years on his or her project, following the many processes described in this text. These particular articles result from research conducted through the following methods: (a) field research, (b) survey research, and (c) experimental research, consecutively. The articles, as presented here, are abbreviated versions of the full articles, for the purpose of illustration. The full articles can be viewed at www.myresearchkit.com/.

White Means Never Having To Say You're Ethnic: White Youth and the Construction of "Cultureless" Identities

ABSTRACT: This article examines the processes by which white identities are constructed as "cultureless" among white youth in two high schools: one predominantly white, the other multiracial. The author proposes that whites assert racial superiority by claiming they have no culture. This is because to be cultureless implies that one is either the "norm" (the standard by which others are judged) or "rational" (developmentally advanced). Drawing on ethnographic research and in-depth interviews, the author argues that in the majority-white school, white students use naturalization practices about feels "normal" and feelings of cultural absence. (Pamela Perry, *Journal of Contemporary Ethnography*, February 2001, Vol. 30(1), pp. 56–91)

How would you describe white American culture?" I ask Laurie, a white, middle-class senior at Valley Groves High, a predominantly white, suburban public school near the Pacific Coast of northern California. She pauses, her face looking visibly perplexed as if she did not understand the question or her mind was drawing a blank. I awkwardly reiterate, "Like, you know, what would you say white American culture is like?" "I wouldn't be able to tell you. I don't know." She pauses again and laughs nervously. "When you think about it, it's like—[a longer pause] I don't know!" Twenty miles away from Valley Groves is the postindustrial city of Clavey. Clavey High School has a brilliant mosaic of students from different ethnic and racial groups, about 12 percent of whom are white. In an interview with Murray, a white, Jewish, middleclass senior, he and I talked a great deal about the consequences of race in the United States and what privileges come with being a white person. When I probed into his identification with being white or Jewish, he said, [Cultural pride] doesn't make sense to me. To me it doesn't. I mean, what difference does it make what my great, great grandfather was or his whole generation. That's not affecting my life. . . . I'm still here now. I've got to make what's best for me in the future. I can't harp on what the past has brought.

Laurie and Murray express what the racial category "white" means to each of them. Although their responses differ markedly, they share something fundamental; they perceive white raciality as cultureless. For Laurie, whiteness is not culturally defined. She lives within it but cannot name it. It is taken for granted. For Murray, to be cultural means having emotional attachment to tradition and history. He eschews culture, in this regard, and lives in the present, looking forward.

These excerpts are from qualitative research I carried out in 1994–97 at Valley Groves, a predominantly white, suburban high school, and Clavey, a multiracial, urban high school. The research focused on what differences, if any, the two demographically distinct contexts made on the ways white youth constructed white identities. I found that it made a large difference: white students at Valley Groves did not reflect on or define white identity as a culture and social location to the extent that the white youth at Clavey did. Moreover, white identities at Clavey tended to be more variable and contradictory.

In what follows, I present and interpret ethnographic and interview data to argue that at Valley Groves, the tendency for youth to explicitly define themselves and other whites as people without culture came about through processes of naturalization—cultural practices in that which is taken for granted and seems "normal" and natural. This study advances theories on racial-ethnic identity formation by vividly illustrating the social construction of white identities and culture in schooling. [The literature review is omitted.]

METHOD AND REFLECTIONS

In choosing my research sites, I looked for two schools: one predominantly white and located in a predominantly white town or city; the other multiracial, minority white and located in a minority white town or city. It also concerned me that the schools be in the same geographical region, of similar size and academic standing, and with student bodies of similar socioeconomic backgrounds to keep those factors as "constant" as possible. I studied census data and school statistics for different towns and cities across the United States before I decided on Valley Groves, which was 83 percent white, and Clavey, which was 12 percent white. Although Clavey was located in a city and Valley Groves a suburb, Clavey was very similar to Valley Groves in all respects besides racial composition. White students at Clavey were primarily middle class, which allowed me to focus on middle-class whites in both schools.

I spent two and a half years in the schools doing participant observation and in-depth interviewing. Daily practices included sitting in on classrooms with students, hanging out with them during breaks and lunch, attending school club meetings, and participating in student-administrator advisory committees; I also observed or helped out with after-school programs and events, such as school plays, major rallies, games, and the junior and senior balls of each school. To familiarize myself with the music and leisure activities the students were involved in, after hours I listened to the local rap, R & B, punk, alternative, and classic rock radio stations; bought CDs of the most popular musical artists; went to live underground punk and alternative concerts; read fanzines and other youth magazines; watched MTV; studied music that students dubbed for me; and attended a large rave produced by some Clavey students.

Although I looked somewhat younger than my age (38 when the research began), I made concerted efforts to minimize the effects of age difference on how students related to me. I did not associate with other adults on campus. I dressed casually in attire that I was comfortable in, which happened to be similar to the attire students were comfortable in: blue jeans, sandals or athletic shoes, T-shirt or sweatshirt, no jewelry except four tiny hoop earrings—one in one ear, three in the other. I had students call me by my first name, and I did not talk down to them, judge them, or otherwise present myself as an authority figure. To the contrary, I saw the students as the authorities, and they seemed to appreciate that regard. Those efforts, on top of having developed some popular-cultural frames of reference with the students, contributed to my developing some very close relationships with several of the students and fairly wide access to different peer groups and cliques on campus. Having stood in the middle of secret hideouts, food fights, fist fights, tongue lashings, and over-the-top fits of goofiness, I can say that in most cases, I seemed to have little impact on students' behaviors.

My other most apparent traits—race, gender, and middle-class/intellectual appearance—had both positive and negative effects. I connected most readily and easily with girls. At Clavey, however, I did make a few close relationships with boys that helped balance my findings at that school. Similarly, my class background made crossing class differences awkward at times for me and for some participants, particularly working-class males. However, since I was focusing on middle-class white students, my own middle-class whiteness seemed to work mostly on my behalf. With respect to students of color, of which I interviewed quite a few, my race limited my ability to hang out with them in groups at school. Because my focus was on white students, I do not feel this limitation compromises my argument, but deeper perspectives from students of color would certainly have improved it. I formally interviewed more than 60 students at Valley Groves and Clavey. They included, at Valley Groves, fourteen white youth, one Filipino female, and a group of ten African-American students. At Clavey, I interviewed 21 white youth, ten African American youth, two Chinese American, one Filipino, and two Latino youth. A little more than half of my interviewees were female. Most were middle class, but six were working class. I did not randomly sample interview participants because I had specific desires regarding to whom I wanted to speak: liberals and conservatives; whites, blacks, Asians, and Latinos; punks, hippies, homies, alternatives, rappers, and such; high achievers and low achievers; girls and boys; middle class and working class.

I sought out interviewees through multiple methods. Mostly, I directly approached students I observed in classrooms or in their cliques. I also went to club meetings and asked for volunteers and, for the hard to find students, sought recommendations or introductions from youth. Interviews took place on campus, in coffee shops, and in students' homes and generally lasted two hours. Students and their parents signed consent forms that explained that I was examining racial identities and race relations in the two demographically distinct contexts. In the interviews, I explored youth's experiences at school, their experiences of racial difference, how they thought of themselves racially, how they thought of racial-ethnic others, their cultural interests and other significant identities, and what types of meanings they gave to their interests and identities. Interviews and informal discussions were also a time for me to discuss with youth my interpretations of school practices, youth cultures, and other events around campus. Students spoke candidly and openly; they seemed eager to talk to an adult who would listen to and treat them respectfully.

The interviews were tape-recorded and transcribed. They and my field notes were manually coded and analyzed along the way to illuminate processes, practices, terms, and conceptions calling for deeper investigation or changes in focus. Along the way, also, I read widely, looking for existing studies and theories that might shed analytical light on my observations. My final coding and analysis were carried out without the aid of software—only colored markers, a Xerox machine, and lots of post-its.

VALLEY GROVES SCHOOL

Whiteness saturated Valley Groves school life not only demographically but culturally as well. The dominant culture at Valley Groves that oriented the social organization of students, and expected behaviors—fit tightly with the dominant culture outside of the campus, namely, a white European American culture. By "white European American culture," I refer to the dominant culture in the United States that is composed of the different cultures of the peoples that populate the United States, its core characteristics are of European origin. These include the values and practices derived from the European Enlightenment, Anglican Protestantism, and Western colonialism, such as rationalism, individualism, personal responsibility, a strong work ethnic, self-effacement, and mastery over nature. I also include material cultures such as hamburgers, spaghetti, cupcakes, parades, and line dancing. By being numerically and politically dominant, whites tend to share certain dispositions, worldviews, and identities. A race-neutral or "color-blind" worldview and sense of oneself as normal are examples of that. At Valley Groves, student cliques and social categories revolved around a "norm" versus "other" dichotomy. "Normal" meant that one conformed to the dominant culture and expectations placed on them, and "other" meant one did not. For example, when I asked Billy how he would describe his group of friends he said, "Normal. We don't smoke or drink or anything and [we] wear clothes we would call normal." "And what is that?" I asked. "Not oversized, baggy clothes like the skaters were, or, obviously, we don't wear cowboy hats or boots."

The normal clothes Billy referred to were the styles one might find at mainstream department stores like The Gap: loose, not overly baggy blue jeans; cotton T-shirts and blouses; sundresses; khaki shorts. The kids who did not dress or act normal served to define the boundaries of what was and was not normal. For instance, skaters wore excessively baggy pants and overall filthy clothes; "hicks" wore ten-gallon cowboy hats, tooled-leather boots, and tight jeans with big brassy pants buckles; and druggies flagrantly carried and consumed illicit drugs. (Flagrant is the key word here since, as a popular girl told me, "Popular kids do drugs. They just don't want anyone to know it.") Carli, a white girl who considered herself "hippie," referred to the nonmainstream kids as "rebels." She said, "I call them rebels 'cause they know the system sucks."

This norm–other dichotomy was race neutral. Maria, a popular senior of Mexican-American descent on her mother's side, told me that the "first cut of students starts with who is popular" and who fits in with the other cliques on campus. Anyone, regardless of racial-ethnic ascription, could be popular, a skater, a druggie—even a "homie," which, as groups went at Valley Groves, was the most nonwhite. Price of admission was conformity to the styles and demeanor of the group. Hence, black kids who were skaters were not "black skaters," nor were white kids who were homies "white homies"; they were simply "skaters" and "homies," respectively. A white skater I spoke to pointed to an African American boy in his crowd and said, "That doesn't matter. We all love to skate together, hang out together." And when I asked black students if the white kids who were homies were considered "wanna-be black," they looked flatly at me and said, "No." Ron, who was a homie himself, said, "One of the guys who hangs out with us is white. He's not a racist and we've known each other for years." "These are all good kids," is what administrators, teachers, and ground supervisors would say to me nearly every time I spoke with them.

At schoolwide rallies and events, collective consensus, reinforcement, and approval of white American norms came from a wider span of individuals: school adults, other students, and the outside community. Such events suggested a consensus of what is true, right, and white but always indirectly, never by saying and, thus, never sayable. For example, homecoming—a high school tradition that celebrates the school football team—was a time to raise school spirit. It was, for me, an excellent time to observe shared assumptions and normative expectations of students and observe the rewards and sanctions applied to different types of behaviors. One day during homecoming week, students held rallies in the gym for the entire student body. To the thunder of heavy-metal music, rivers of white students flowed into the gym and took seats in different quadrants of the auditorium. Just before the official ceremony began, two big, husky white males (appearing to be seniors) dragged into the center of the auditorium a small boy (appearing to be a freshman) whose feet and legs were bound with silver duct tape. The crowd laughed and applauded. The two husky guys pumped their fists in the air to encourage the crowd then dragged the boy off center stage. After a brief greeting, members of the student leadership committee introduced the junior varsity and varsity football players. The players came out in succession and formed a line across the middle of the gym floor. The boys were all white except for three black players on the junior varsity team and, on the varsity team, two boys with Hispanic surnames. As his name was called, each player stepped forward to acknowledge the applause. Most did so with an air of shyness or humility, their heads bowed, cheeks blushing, shoulders pulled up to their ears. Two boldly strutted out, trying to play up the roar of the crowd, but their efforts fell flat. Then, the varsity cheerleaders bolted to center stage, leaping energetically before getting into formation for their choreographed performance. The girls were all thin, some overly so, and wore uniforms with close-fitted bodices that made them look all the smaller. But their body size betrayed their strength. Their routine, driven by the firm beat of a heavy-metal tune, was rigorously gymnastic, with lots of cartwheels, flips, and pyramid constructions that were punctuated by the top girls falling trustingly into the arms of their comrades. Long, silky blonde hair parachuted out with each acrobatic stunt. Through the performance, the audience remained silent and attentive, with an occasional collective gasp at the girls' athleticism, until the show was over. At that time, the cheerleaders received roaring, vocal applause.

On the day after the rally was the homecoming parade. The parade took off from the basketball field and wound its way onto a residential side street. Four adult males, two of whom appeared to be Mexican American, led the parade mounted on prancing horses and wearing Mexican serapes and sombreros. The front two carried large replicas of the California and American flags. Following the horsemen were two convertibles, one of which was a white Corvette carrying the (white) city mayor, who waved ceremoniously to the onlookers on the sidewalks. The music of the marching band, which followed closely behind the mayor, announced the arrival of the parade along its path. A group of eight white and one African American female dancers led the band, tossing and spinning colored flags in sync with the beat of the band's percussion section. The fifty musicians in the band, most of whom appeared white with five or six exceptions, marched militarily in tight formation and played their instruments with competence and finesse. Following the band was a procession of American-built pickup trucks carrying, first, the varsity and junior varsity football players, then the "royalty"—the senior "king" and "queen" and underclass "princes" and "princesses"—and finally, an open-bed truck loaded with seniors, hooting and cheering as if their graduation day had already arrived.

The parade made its way through blocks of residences before returning to the main street and slowly back to the school. Proud parents perched on the sidewalks with their cameras in hand. Community residents stepped onto their front landings to wave and cheer as the parade passed their homes. Others peered out through large pane windows with cats in arms and dogs at heel. The homecoming rally and parade were packed with assumptions, values, behaviors, and origin stories that privileged white European American perspectives. The homecoming parade, with its display of the national and state flags, American cars, marching band, and school royalty, was a stunning coproduction of whiteness, Americanness, citizenship, and gendered codes of conduct. Included was even an origin story of white American colonial victory over Mexico. And, by virtue of who was there and who was not, the themes of mastery, domination, nationhood, and industry with whiteness was seamless. Other cultures in the school and community were not represented in the parade. There were no Filipino dancers, Asian martial artists, or African-American rappers. The event was performed by whites and for whites. In sum, at Valley Groves High, white people and white European American culture saturated school life.

Given this sociocultural milieu, white youth could say nothing when I asked them to describe white culture; they had no words to describe that which comes naturally. Laurie, whom I quoted at the beginning of this article, struggled to describe white culture and finally succumbed to "I don't know!" Billy, a popular white senior, had a similar response. I asked him what he thought was culturally specific about white American culture. After a long pause in which he said only, "hmmm," he asked, "Like, what's American culture?" "Uh-huh," I replied. "Hmmm. [Another long pause]—I don't really know, 'cause it's like [pause]—just [pause]—I'm not sure! I don't know!" However, Valley Groves white students were not always speechless about white identity. When my questions probed into the youth's social experiences and identities as whites and not their cultures, they could find something to say. Not too surprisingly, most told me that being white meant you had no cultural ties. Students I spoke to would explain that they had mixed European roots that held no significance to them; therefore they were "just white."

CLAVEY HIGH SCHOOL: WHEN WHITE IS NOT THE NORM

Clavey High School stands like a fortress overlooking a dense urban landscape. The schools magnet academies draw in youth from all over the city, bringing in a mosaic of students from different racial and ethnic groups. Whites comprised 12 percent of the two thousand students at Clavey. African Americans were the majority, making up 54 percent of the school. They were followed by Asian Americans (23 percent), then Hispanics (8 percent), Filipinos (2 percent), and a few Pacific Islanders and Native Americans. At any given moment during lunch break, one could tour the campus and hear students speaking in standard English, black English ("ebonics"), Eritrean, Cantonese, Mandarin, Korean, Spanish, Spanglish, Tagalog, Samoan, Russian, and Vietnamese, among others. The racial composition of the administrative and teaching staff at Clavey was also quite diverse. The principal of Clavey was a white male, but the other top administrators, two assistant principals and the dean, were African American. Of all the administrators and their staff, 50 percent were African American, 25 percent were Asian, and 25 percent were white. Clavey teachers were 53 percent white, 30 percent African American, 8 percent Asian American, 6 percent Hispanic, and 3 percent Pacific Islander.

Life at Clavey High was very different from that at Valley Groves. White youth at Clavey were in daily, up-close association with marked racial and cultural difference to whiteness. Race was the primary means of sorting out who was who and where one belonged in the social organization of the school. Clavey's tracking structure was racially segregated, with whites and Asians disproportionally represented in the high-tracked (honors, advanced) classes and African Americans and Latinos overrepresented in the low-tracked classes. As well, certain areas on the campus were "where the white kids hang out"; others were "where the black (or Asian American or Latino) kids hang out." And student cliques and subcultures were racially marked such that "straights" (who were like "normal" kids at Valley Groves), alternatives, hippies, and punks were all "white people's groups"; rappers, athletes, gangsters, and "fashion hounds" were "black people's groups"; housers, natives, newly arrived, and martial artists were "Asian people's groups"; and so forth. This meant that the styles, slangs, vernaculars, and demeanors that marked identification with a certain clique or subculture simultaneously inferred racial identification. In a word, peer group activities racialized youth.

Speaking to this fact and the sanctions that came with crossing racialized boundaries in styles or leisure activities, Gloria, an immigrant from El Salvador, said to me, "For my race, if you start wearing a lot of gold, you're trying to be black. If you're trying to braid your hair, you'll be accused of trying to be black. I'm scared to do things 'cause they might say, 'that's black!' Or if you're Latino and you listen to that, you know, Green Day-that [alternative rock] kinda thing. If you listen to that, then you wanna be white. . . . 'Oh my god, why you listening to that music?'

they'd say, . . . Aren't you proud of who you are?" Also different from Valley Groves was the dominant school culture. Overall at Clavey, African American youth claimed the majority of open, public spaces, and black popular cultural forms and practices shaped the normative culture of the school. By "black popular culture," I refer to the music, styles, and other meaningful practices that have risen out of black communities. Unlike at Valley Groves, where the dress code did not diverge much from white adult mainstream style, at Clavey, basic elements of black hip-hop style were generalized into the normative styles for all youth. One informant called it the "leveler" style because it made all who wore it "the same." This basic style included clean, oversized, and sagging denim pants or sweatpants; large and long untucked T-shirts or hooded sweatshirts; large, bulky parkas; and sparkling-clean athletic shoes. The look was particularly common for boys, but girls' styles were also influenced by it. Only if and when students wanted to mark a distinctive style and/or racial identification did they embellish on this basic, baggy theme. Duncan, a middle-class, white male skater and "raver" (someone who frequents rave parties) told me, "We all wear baggy pants, right? So parents think! But you find that ravers have cut-off bottoms to their [sagging] jeans, they wear bigger t-shirts they have hanging out of their pants, they carry packs that's full of crap that they take everywhere."

What Duncan specified as "raver" style, other students specified as "white," particularly the cut-off bottoms to large pants. Other markers of white kids' styles were Van shoes, instead of Nike or Fila brands (which marked black style), and macrame or silver-chain neck chokers. Informal and formal activities on campus were also shaped by black popular culture. During breaks or at lunchtime, the ambient din of casual conversation was composed of the sounds, words, and inflections of black English and the most recent innovation in "street" slang. Lunchtime events, school rallies, and dances were enlivened with rap and R & B music, predominantly, with an occasional reggae tune or specially requested techno or alternative song. Often, students performed raps on the steps in front of the cafeteria or graced an audience with a spontaneous hip-hop dance performance.

Homecoming week at Clavey, like at Valley Groves, was a time to unite the school and raise the collective spirit. Leadership students attempted to appeal to the breadth of diverse interests and cultures of the school with "fashion shows" of traditional or native garments and a variety of games designed to mix students. At lunch, they played a range of music, from R & B to techno and alternative rock, but songs by African-American and Afro-Carribean artists were predominant. The main events—the rally and game—were attended by and played predominantly to a majority-black audience. The rally took place during lunch on the day of the "big game." Students, of which all but a few were black, crammed into the auditorium to the pulse of a rap song. The rally opened with a greeting from the student body president and a soulful a cappella song performed by three African-American students. Then the cheerleaders, composed of one white and ten black girls, sprung out onto the gym floor. Their choreographed routine was fluid, rhythmic, and dancelike, with movements drawn from traditional and contemporary African and African American dance forms. To the infectious beat of an upbeat R & B song, the girls playfully flirted with their appreciative audience with beckoning hand and eye gestures. Several boys succumbed to the urge to dance in dialogue with the girls and leapt down to the floor to join them. Others, boys and girls alike, stood up and swayed or danced in place until the performance was over. Then, the varsity football players were called to line up in the center of the auditorium. The players were African American with the exception of two white boys and one Latino. When each name was announced, the football player leapt forward a few steps and embraced the cheers from the crowd. Each took his moment in the limelight proudly, with his fist in the air or maybe a little dance to augment the roar of his audience.

At Clavey, there was no homecoming parade that extended into the community. At the game, a small procession of vehicles featuring the elected school "emperor" and "empress" circled the football field during half time. There was no marching band, either, but the award-winning school gospel choir sang several lively songs at halftime. In short, school life at Clavey was heavily infused with styles, music, and activities that marked the identities and cultures of the majority black students. This had a few important implications for the experiences and identities of the white students. First, white was not the norm, either numerically or culturally. Barry, a middle-class, "straight" white male, told me, "School is like a foreign country to me. I come here to this foreign place, then go home where things are normal again." When I asked white students why they did not attend the rallies and dances, they said things like, "I don't enjoy the people," "They don't play my kind of music," and "I can't dance to that music." All in all, the message was that they could not relate to the dominant school culture. No white student I spoke to at Clavey was completely unable to describe something about white culture. All had reflected on it to some extent, even if only to ruminate on how difficult it was to define. And some youth could say a lot about white culture. One white, middle-class senior girl, Jessie, elaborated extensively on differences in attitudes toward food consumption that she noticed between her white, Filipino, and Chinese American friends, and she commented on how much more visible white culture is to her in places outside of California. She said, "Minnesota, Denver and . . . places like that. It seems like . . . you know, you've got the whole thing going on—beer bread, polka, parades, apple pie and things like that." Most stunning to me about the white students at Clavey was not what they said explicitly about white culture but what they said implicitly. In our discussions about the types of music they liked and why. White students would tell me that they liked rock or punk or alternative music and not rap or R & B because "their" music spoke more to their "interests" or experiences as whites. For example, Kirsten and Cindi were good friends. They both were from middle-class homes, were juniors at the time, and liked alternative rock. Kirsten was white, European American, and Cindi was part white and part Chinese, although she admittedly "looked white" and hung out solely with other white youth. I asked them why they thought students tended to self-segregate on campus: Cindi: I think there is . . . the factor that some people feel like they may not have very much in common with someone from a different race, which in some ways is true. Because you have, like, different music tastes, different styles of clothes. Also, like what your friends think. Kirsten: Or like different things you do on weekends. Cindi: Yeah, so I think that's something that separates the races. Kirsten: It's kind of interesting because my musical interests have changed. . . . It seems like [in junior high school] everyone, regardless of if they were black or white or Asian, . . . listened to the [local rap and R & B station.] But then I think when you are little you don't really . . . have too much of an identity of yourself. As you get older and mature more you, like, discover what your "true being" is. So then people's musical tastes change. [Later in the conversation.] I think punk is more of a "I don't get along with my parents" kind of music and rap is more of "lets go kill someone" music. Cindi: Punk . . . expresses a simpler anger. It's just kind of like "Oh, I broke up with my girlfriend" . . . something like that. Usually rap has more to do with killing and gangs—stuff that doesn't really relate to me.

In this discussion, Kirsten and Cindi defined white identity and culture in terms of interests and tastes in leisure culture. This was the language of choice among all students for articulating racial-ethnic differences. Behind it was the belief that different life experiences accounted for different tastes. Sometimes, white youth named explicit experiences they believed were common to or defining of whites. Class experience, expressed by Kirsten and Cindi in terms of the type of neighborhood one lived in, was often evoke by youth. Other times, white youth spoke in terms of intangible but presumably race-based, emotional, aesthetic, and ethical sensibilities they felt when they listened to, say, punk or alternative music but not when they listened to rap.

ANALYSIS

Ironically, even as Clavey whites demarcated white culture and identity boundaries through their popular-cultural tastes and leisure activities, they also imagined whiteness as cultureless, as postcultural. This was not as explicit as it was at Valley Groves. It would show its face when white students referred to people of color as people with "race" or "ethnicity," as though whites had neither. Tina, a working-class junior who had always been a racial minority in school and had many close black and Latino friends, told me that she "had a lot of ethnicity in [her] family . . . Hispanic, Korean. We all get along." By this she meant that white relatives had married "out" of whiteness and into culture, ethnicity. Common also was the explicit and implicit definition of white as empty, meaningless, bland, and without tradition. Eric touches on all of those: I think it's more difficult [to define white culture] for Americans because the culture of America is more just consumption. In America, we buy stuff, and that's the basis of our culture. If you talk to people who want to come to America?— They want things. TV is a very American thing. We don't have lengthy traditions. . . . A lot has been lost because of the good ol' melting pot. I heard a cool one about a salad bowl—that's what America is, and along comes the dressing and turns everything into dressing flavor. Vegetables all got that white American spin on it. Note, too, that Eric equates "white" with "American" until his last line, when he specifies "white American." That is a faux pas that whites often fall into because of the dominant construction of white as the "unhyphenated" American standard. Finally, several Clavey white students told me that they did not like to think about themselves as "white" but as "human." These students expressed an explicitly rationalist construction of whiteness. It denied the significance of a past orientation and exalted an individualistic and present- or future-oriented construction of the self. White, middle-class boys expressed this most boldly, which might be expected given that they are triply constructed as the most rational by race, class, and gender.

CONCLUSION

Scholars of race and whiteness have understood that the construction of white culture as the invisible norm is one of the most constructions of whiteness in the post–civil rights era. However, very few have examined the everyday social processes by which white people come to think of themselves as normal and culturally empty. My research suggests that, at Valley Groves, a predominantly white high school, white identity seemed cultureless because white cultural practices were taken for granted, naturalized, and, thus, not reflected on and defined. At Clavey, a multiracial school, white culture was not taken for granted-white youth thought about and defined it to an extent, particularly through their tastes in popular culture. However, in part, whites reflected on their sociocultural location through the lens of European American rational authority, which school structures and practices helped construct and reinforce. Whiteness appeared good, controlled, rational, and cultureless. Otherness appeared bad, out of control, irrational, and cultural. This argument has implications several areas including theories in racial-ethnic identity formation. The argument proposes that the concept of culture denotes more than, simply, a way of life organized around sets of symbolic practices. It connotes a relationship of power between those who "have" culture (and are, thus, irrational and inferior) and those who claim not to (and are, thus, rational and superior). More research and thought needs to go into examining the ways postcultural whiteness is inculcated in daily practice and into the profits whites gain by denying that they have a culture.

The full article can be viewed at www.myresearchkit.com.

Racially Biased Policing: Determinants of Citizen Perceptions

By Ronald Weitzer and Steven A. Tuch

ABSTRACT: Current controversy surrounding racial profiling in America has focused attention on the issue of racial bias by the police. Yet little is known about the extent of police racial bias and less about public perceptions of the problem. This article analyzes national survey data on citizens' views of, and reported personal experiences with, several forms of police bias. We find that attitudes toward the prevalence and acceptability of these practices are largely shaped by citizens' race, personal experiences with police discrimination, and exposure to news media reporting on incidents of police misconduct. The findings lend support to the group-position theory of race relations. (© The University of North Carolina Press Social Forces, March 2005, 83(3): 1009–1030)

Race is one of the most consistent predictors of attitudes toward the police. African Americans are more likely than whites to hold negative views of the police, but very little is known about Hispanics' views. Do Hispanics tend to take a "minority group" perspective similar to that of African Americans; do they take an intermediate position in a white–Hispanic–black "racial hierarchy" pattern; or are their views more closely aligned with those of whites? The literature is insufficient to address these questions. A larger deficiency in the empirical literature concerns why racial differences exist in citizens' relations with the police. We argue that part of the explanation rests in the group-position thesis, a variant of conflict theory. The group-position thesis focuses on intergroup competition over material rewards, status, and power. Racial attitudes reflect a collective "sense of group position" vis-à-vis other racial groups, including (1) perceived threats: dominant group members fear that their group will lose privileges or resources to competing racial groups, and (2) perceived advantages: minority group members believe that their group interests will be enhanced if they challeng the prevailing racial order. If the dominant group believes that it is entitled to valuable resources, it follows that the group will have an affinity with the institutions that serve their interests. One such institution is the criminal justice system. Dominant racial groups typically see the police as allies, especially in divided societies where the police are or were a key institutional pillar, and where the dominant racial or ethnic group views the police as way to suppress subordinate groups. Our extension of group-position theory predicts that whites tend to be dubious or dismissive of allegations of police misconduct. African Americans and Hispanics, on the other hand, should be more inclined to view the police as engaged in frequent abuse of minority citizens and, thus, as a "visible sign of majority domination." The group-position thesis stresses perceived (not necessarily real) threats to dominant group interests.

Our data do allow us to test the key predictions of group-position theory—namely, white defense of the police against charges of racial discrimination and minority belief that police racial bias is a serious problem. We test the following hypotheses:

Hypothesis 1: Blacks and Hispanics more than whites believe that racially biased policing exists. Also, racial differences persist net of the influences of experiential, media, and control variables.

Hypothesis 2: Exposure to media reports of police misconduct increases perceptions of police bias among all groups; The effect is stronger for blacks and Hispanics than for whites.

Hypothesis 3: Personal experience with police bias increases perceptions of bias among all groups; the effect, however, is stronger for blacks and Hispanics than for whites.

DATA AND METHODS

Data come from a 2002 national survey of 1,792 white, African American, and Hispanic adult residents of U.S. metropolitan areas with at least 100,000 population. The sample is representative of adults living in households with telephones in urban and suburban areas. Knowledge Networks, a Webbased survey research firm conducted the survey; it combines probability sampling with the Internet to yield representative samples. Knowledge Networks uses list-assisted random-digit dialing sampling on a sample frame consisting of the entire telephone populations.

Independent Variables

Race   "Race" broadly includes both racial and ethnic groups based on self-identification.

Experiences with Police Discrimination   We measured personal and vicarious experiences with discriminatory police behavior with the following questions: "Have you ever felt that you were treated unfairly by the police specifically because of your race in [your city/your own neighborhood]?" "Have you ever felt that you were stopped by the police just because of your race or ethnic background?" Parallel questions tapped vicarious experience, with reference to whether this had happened to anyone else in the respondent's household. We combined responses to form an index of reported personal experience with police bias.

Media Exposure   The following question indicated exposure to media accounts of police misconduct: "How often do you hear or read about (on the radio, television, or in the newspapers) incidents of police misconduct (such as police use of excessive force, verbal abuse, and corruption) that occur somewhere in the nation?" Response options were "never," "rarely," "sometimes," and "often" on a 4-point scale coded so that higher scores indicate more frequent exposure.

Control Variables

Age, in years; gender; place of residence city versus suburb; region south versus nonsouth; education, measured on a 9-point scale; and household income, measured on a 17-step scale. Three items measure respondents' assessment of neighborhood crime conditions: "Overall, how safe do you feel being alone outside in your neighborhood [during the day/at night]—very safe, somewhat safe, somewhat unsafe, or very unsafe?" "How serious a problem is crime in your neighborhood—very serious, somewhat serious, not serious, or not a problem at all?" Responses to these questions are coded so that higher scores reflect less safety and more perceived neighborhood crime.

Dependent Variables

Four sets of questions indicates of police racial bias with four sets of questions, with each set of items combined into a scale: (1) Racial bias against individuals: "Do you think the police in your [city/neighborhood] treat whites and blacks equally, do they treat whites worse than blacks, or blacks worse than whites?" A parallel question asked respondents to compare whites and Hispanics. (2) Racial bias against neighborhoods: "In general in the U.S., do you think that police services in white neighborhoods are better, worse, or about the same as in black neighborhoods?" A parallel question asked for a comparison between white and Hispanic neighborhoods. (3) Police prejudice: "How common do you think racial or ethnic prejudice is among police officers [throughout the U.S./in your city/in your neighborhood]?"

(4) Racial profiling: "Since many drivers engage in minor traffic violations like speeding, it is sometimes hard to tell why some drivers get stopped by the police while others do not. Do you think that black drivers are more likely to be stopped by the police than white drivers for the same types of violations?" A parallel question compared Hispanic and white drivers. Approval of profiling, we replicated a 1999 Gallup poll question: "There have been reports that some police officers stop drivers from certain racial groups because they think members of these groups are more likely to commit crimes. This is known as 'racial profiling.' Do you approve or disapprove of the use of this practice?"

RESULTS

The discussion of results and statistics are omitted from this short version of the article.

CONCLUSION

Race structures citizen views of police racial bias, as it does other aspects of policing. In all four models, blacks and Hispanics are more likely than whites to believe that police bias is a problem. Blacks, however, are more likely to perceive such bias than Hispanics. This finding addresses an unanswered question in the literature on police–minority relations—whether blacks and Hispanics share a minority-group perspective or whether perceptionstake the form of a white–Hispanic–black racial hierarchy. Consistent with the racial-hierarchy pattern, blacks and Hispanics differ significantly. On some questions, Hispanics are much less likely to perceive bias than are blacks. Blacks are more likely to perceive police discrimination against Hispanics than Hispanics themselves. Blacks may be more vulnerable than Hispanics to traffic stops by police because their skin color heightens their visibility. But further research is needed to account more fully for black–Hispanic differences in relations with police.

Americans are overwhelmingly opposed in principle to racially biased law enforcement. But support for the principle of equal justice does not necessarily mean that one believes the system dispenses unequal justice. Our data indicate that many whites believe that the system operates impartially. Over three-quarters of whites think that police treat individual blacks and Hispanics the same as whites; a substantial majority of whites take the same view of minority and white neighborhoods. Only one-third of whites believe that police engage in racial profiling of minority drivers—stopping them more frequently than whites for the same kinds of traffic violations. That many whites are skeptical with regard to police discrimination, or see it as isolated. Blacks and Hispanics are more likely than whites to report that they have personally been discriminated against by the police and that this has happened to another member of their household.

Personal and vicarious experience of racially biased policing shapes perceptions of police bias, net of other factors. Repeated exposure to media reports on police abuse (i.e., excessive force, verbal abuse, corruption) is a strong predictor of the belief that police bias exists, is widespread, and is unacceptable. Media effects operate for all three racial groups. People who frequently hear or read about incidents of police misconduct, as transmitted by the media, are inclined to conclude that the police engage in racial profiling, are prejudiced, and discriminate against minority individuals and neighborhoods. Though it is usually overlooked by researchers who study public perceptions of the police, the mass media appears to be an important determinant of those perceptions.

Our extension of the group-position thesis holds that views of social institutions are influenced by group interests and perceived threats. Dominant groups should perceive the police as an institution allied with their interests, whereas minorities should be more inclined to view the police as contributing to their subordination. These predictions are generally supported by our findings. Whites tend to minimize or discount the existence of racialized policing and perhaps view charges of police racism as a threat to a revered institution. Blacks are inclined to believe that police bias is common, and many Hispanics share this view.

Becoming American: Stereotype Threat Effects in Afro-Caribbean Immigrant Groups

Kay Deaux, Nida Bikmen, Alwyn Gilkes, Ana Ventuneac, Yvanne Joseph, Yasser A. Payne and Claude M. Steele

ABSTRACT: Educational and occupational data suggest that second-generation West Indian immigrants have less favorable outcomes than their first-generation counterparts, who typically outperform comparison groups of African Americans. We explore the social psychological process of stereotype threat as it affects the performance of first- and second-generation West Indian students. An initial questionnaire study of 270 West Indian students provided data on perceived favorability of African American and West Indian stereotypes, ethnic identification, and perceptions of discrimination. An experimental study of stereotype threat showed a significant interaction between generation and stereotype threat condition: first- and second- generation West Indian students performed equally in neutral conditions, but differed significantly when stereotype threat was present. While first generation students increased their performance in the threat condition, second-generation students showed the performance decrements characteristic of African American students. (Social Psychology Quarterly, 2007, vol. 70, no. 4, pp. 384–404)

Black immigration to the United States has increased markedly since the post-1965 changes in immigration policy. As of the 2000 census, foreign-born blacks constituted 12% of all first-generation immigrants in the United States and accounted for approximately 6% of the total U.S. black population. Although there is some immigration from Africa, the primary source of black immigration to the United States is from the Caribbean nations. Among Afro-Caribbean immigrants, West Indians (defined as those countries originally colonized by the British) have been of particular interest to social scientists because of two competing factors. On the one hand, they are an immigrant group whose first language is English, thus giving them some advantage over other immigrants who must learn a new language before having ready access to educational and occupational opportunities in the United States. On the other hand, because the majority of these immigrants are black, they enter a country in which their skin color becomes the basis for discriminatory treatment. To the extent that the first of these factors—facility with English—is dominant, one would predict that West Indian immigrants would do well in educational and occupational domains, making progress more rapidly than immigrants from non-Anglophone countries. On the other hand, to the extent that West Indian immigrants are subject to color-based discrimination, they should be impeded relative to white immigrants. Indeed, one might expect that being subjected to some of the same discriminatory conditions that confront native-born African Americans, West Indians would become similar to these groups in a variety of psychological ways. Of particular interest here is the degree to which West Indian immigrants are susceptible to the effects of stereotype threat, in which an awareness of negative group stereotypes about the capability of African Americans results in performance decrements for members of this group.

BACKGROUND AND THEORY

Occupational and Educational Outcomes of West Indian Immigrants Despite the potential for negative treatment, West Indian immigrants have fared well by traditional educational and occupational markers. Typically these assessments are made in comparison to native-born African Americans. Although there continues to be debate as to whether West Indians have an earnings advantage over native-born African Americans, the employment and occupational advantage of first-genera-tion West Indians is reliable. Whereas first-generation West Indian immigrants sys-tematically outperform native born African Americans, their advantage is not as clear in the second generation. Indeed, analyses of immigrant pathways from first to second generation (often referred to as models of segmented assimilation) point to downward assimilation as one possible outcome, most likely to be experienced by groups who are most subject to societal discrimination

The Potential Role of Stereotype Threat Work on stereotype threat shows that when negative stereotypes about a group's abilities and potential are "in the air," they can undermine the performance of members of that group. When a stereotype is be-lieved to be relevant, it poses the threat that the person will be judged or treated in terms of the stereotype. Particularly relevant to the present work are studies that con-sider the performance of African American students. Data show that when the neg-ative stereotype of black intellectual ability is made salient, African American students perform more poorly on achievement tasks than do whites. In contrast, when ethnicity is not salient, the two groups perform at equivalent levels (after ad-justing for SAT scores). These experimental data are important in arguing against explanations that rely primarily on assumed differences in cultural dispositions. African Americans and whites can differ in their academic performance, but whether they do or do not in this particular task setting depends on characteristics of the sit-uation, not to inherent differences in their capabilities or to the cultural context and social structure that frame their lives.

Differential stereotypes in the culture at large does not establish that West Indi-ans themselves are aware of these stereotypes. However, data suggest that stereo-types about black Americans are both known and endorsed by West Indians. To the extent that West Indian immigrants believe that there is a meaningful distinction between their group and the general black American group, we might also antici-pate that they could show enhanced performance under conditions of stereotype threat. This stereotype lift effect refers to a boost in performance. It is shown by members of groups (e.g., whites, males) who are not negatively stereotyped them-selves but are aware of the negative stereotypes associated with comparison groups. In the present case, a stereotype lift effect would be more likely if West Indians as-sumed that their ethnic group was more favorably regarded than African Americans and wanted to distinguish themselves from that group.

Ethnic Identification in West Indians Earlier investigators typically assumed that a person's ethnic identification was coterminous with the categorical definition, that is, if you were born of Italian parents, then your ethnic identification was as an Ital-ian. Recently social psychologists recognized that ethnic identification is a subjec-tive state as well as. This can be more important than an objective characterization. Like other forms of social identification, it is essential to consider what people call themselves. Ethnic identification is a personal choice, both in terms of which ethnic identity to claim and whether to self describe in terms of ethnicity at all.

Hypotheses

We hypothesized that the differences between first- and second-generation West Indian immigrants are associated with differential susceptibility to stereotype threat effects. Specifically, we predicted that first-generation West Indian immigrants are protected from or insensitive to stereotype threat, and thus will not show a performance decrement when stereotypes are salient. In contrast, we predicted that second-generation West Indian immigrants will show the same pattern of stereotype threat effects evidenced in African American respondents, that is, decrements in performance when a test is labeled diagnostic as opposed to non-diagnostic. Thus, we predicted a significant interaction between stereotype threat condition and generation. The purpose of the experimental study is to test the hypothesis that second-generation West Indian immigrants are more susceptible to stereotype threat than are first-generation immigrants. In addition, we consider the extent to which possible moderators, such as ethnic identification, might influence reactions to stereotype threat of the hypothesis.

QUESTIONNAIRE STUDY

In this study, a total of 270 West Indian students who were currently enrolled at one of the 4-year undergraduate colleges within the City University of New York system completed the initial questionnaire. Students identified through university records as being of West Indian heritage were contacted by letters; additionally, the researchers made direct contact with students at three selected colleges within the system that have a high percentage of enrolled West Indian students. All students who agreed to complete the questionnaire were paid $10 for their participation.

Questionnaire. The questionnaire was designed to assess a number of concepts pertinent to the hypotheses of the study, as well as relevant background material on the participants. Key concepts in terms of the theoretical framework that we are using were stereotype knowledge and ethnic identification. Additional measures collected to explore possible differences between groups included sensitivity to race-based rejection and demographic material, including immigration history.

EXPERIMENTAL STUDY

Method: To assess the effect of stereotype threat on the performance of West Indian immigrants, we conducted an experimental study in which first- and second-generation students were randomly assigned to conditions that would or would not activate stereotype threat. The goal was to determine whether, within this specific sample, performance would vary as a function of the particular experimental condition. A $2 \times 2 \times 2$ design was used, crossing generation of student (first vs. second), diagnosticity of the test (diagnostic vs. non-diagnostic of ability) and race of experimenter (black vs. white).

Participants: From the sample of students who completed the questionnaire, 75 students (41 women and 34 men) were recruited to participate in the experimental study of stereotype threat. First- and second-generation students were recruited in approximately equal numbers (N = 41 and 34, respectively). Because self-ascribed ethnic identification was correlated with generation, and because the distribution of ethnic identification scores was heavily skewed toward identification as West Indian, it was not possible to select participants on the basis of their identification, independent of generational status. However, we did attempt to recruit as many students as possible from that group who identified themselves as more African American or at least equally West Indian and African American to balance out the more numerous West Indian identified participants.

Procedures: Participants were tested in small rooms at the colleges, in groups ranging in size from one to six. Typically two experimenters were present at a session, and we kept teams "color consistent," thus allowing us to systematically consider possible experimenter effects. Race of experimenter team was randomly assigned across experimental conditions. Both first and second-generation students were mixed within a typical session, and the experimenters were not aware of the generational status of the participants in their sessions.

Manipulation of stereotype threat: One experimenter read the instructions aloud to participants, and participants could read along with the same text, printed on the first page of their booklet. The manipulation of stereotype threat was contained within these instructions, using a task description that has proved to be effective in establishing different levels of stereotype threat. In the Diagnostic (Stereotype Threat) Condition, the instructions stressed that the test was an assessment of the student's verbal abilities and limitations. In the Non-diagnostic condition, the test was described as an exercise in test development, evaluating the test itself rather than individual ability.

Participants were then given 25 minutes to answer as many questions as they could, on a 27-item exam. Items were taken from a GRE preparation text and were selected to be reasonably difficult for the study sample. The average performance was 9.8 out of a possible score of 27, thus verifying the anticipated difficulty of the test. At the end of the allotted time period, the experimenters collected the performance material and participants were given a postexperimental questionnaire to complete, assessing their views of the test, their performance, and the testing conditions. Participants were then debriefed, providing them a full explanation of the ways in which instructions affect performance and of the normative difficulty of the test. The participants were asked not todiscuss the findings with others at their college until the end of the term.

Results

The principal test of our hypothesis is based on analysis of variance, appropriate to the experimental design that we used and consistent with other studies of stereotype threat. The three dichotomous categories were generation (first vs. second), diagnostic condition (threat vs. no threat), and race of experimenter (black or white), with performance as the dependent variable.

Tests of Generational Hypotheses

Analysis of variance results are presented showed no main effects of diagnostic condition, generation, or experimenter team on the measure of percentage of problems solved correctly. The predicted two-way interaction between generation and diagnostic condition on performance was significant, as shown in Figure 1. Tests of simple effects within each diagnostic condition showed that the difference between first- and second-generation participants was not significant when the test was presumed to be non-diagnostic. This lack of a difference is theoretically important, as it counters claims that first- and second-generation immigrants possess intrinsic differences in motivation, ability, or cultural characteristics that might account for differential outcomes. Instead, we find that when conditions are psychologically neutral, there is virtually no difference in capability on a difficult academic test. In contrast, the performance of first- and second-generation students differed significantly when the instructions stressed the diagnosticity of the test.

To further explore the significant interaction between generation and diagnostic condition, a number of statistical analyses were performed. First, we considered the possible role of length of time in the United States as a factor. Because second-generation students have spent more time in the United States, it is likely that they have had greater exposure to its norms and culture, including the negative stereotypes about African Americans. However, time in the United States had relatively little impact on the finding. We also examined the correlation between time in the United States and the various measures of performance within the first

■ **Figure 1**   Performance (Percentage Correct) of First- and Second-Generation Students
in Diagnostic and Non-Diagnostic Conditions.

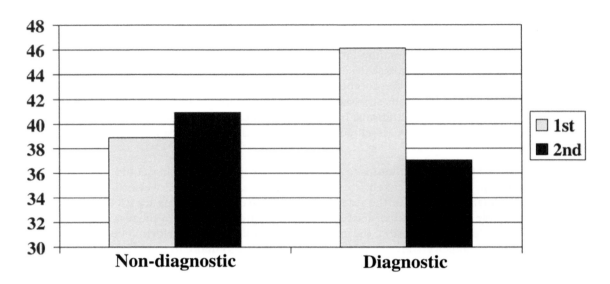

generation only (and separately for diagnostic and non-diagnostic conditions). No
significant relationships were found, suggesting that time in the United States,
though a frequently-used demographic index, is not a reliable gauge for psychological processes. Additionally, an examination of gender differences showed that men
and women performed equally in both diagnostic and non-diagnostic conditions.
Thus differences between the generations in the two experimental conditions appear quite robust.

Discussion

Macro-level differences between first- and second generation West Indian immigrants (e.g., educational and occupational achievement) have a parallel at a psychological level. Although the difference in the time that first and second-generation
students have spent in the United States is only 11.5 years, their performance under
conditions of stereotype threat differs significantly. Both groups are affected by the
instructions, but in opposite directions. Second-generation students perform similar to that reported previously for African American students. Specifically, when
stereotype threat is present, their performance drops in comparison to the first-
generation comparison group and to their own performance when the test is non-
diagnostic. When conditions do not make stereotype threat salient, first- and
second-generation students perform equivalently.

This equivalence of first- and second-generation students in the non-diagnostic
condition rules out alternative explanations based on assumed differences between
the two groups in terms of competency or general test taking ability. The difference
between the groups is not in their capability to perform on the test (or their academic
preparation and motivation to perform), but in the specifics of the testing condition
that bring other influences to bear. Further, although not testable here, the results
also give us some reason to question the utility of those explanations of differences
between West Indians and African Americans that rely on dispositional factors,
such as migration selectivity and differential ability or motivation. First-generation
immigrants show a quite different reaction to stereotype threat conditions. Not only
do they not show a decrement, but in fact their performance increases, relative to
the non-threat condition. The seeming immunity of first-generation West Indian
immigrants to stereotype threat effects cannot be explained either by a lack of aware-

ness of the prevailing images of African Americans, nor by the absence of experience with race based discrimination. Indeed, despite their relatively short time in the United States, first generation immigrants do not differ in either respect from their second-generation counterparts who were born in the United States. Both are equally likely to expect discrimination and to anticipate anxiety in the variety of social situations

Both see a difference in the images that society has of African Americans in contrast to West Indians. The difference between the two generations may be explained in part by the positivity of their meta-stereotype of West Indians. First-generation students are more positive in their appraisal, believing that others view West Indians more favorably than do the second generation students. Accordingly, first-generation students appear able to turn to a positive image of their group in the face of diagnostic pressure and to distance themselves more effectively from the negative stereotypes associated with black performance in the United States. This distancing strategy appears to have limited utility for the second generation, however, who are more aware of and immersed in the prejudicial views against blacks that persist in the United States. The first-generation pattern of increased performance in the face of possible threat is also suggestive of the stereotype lift effect. The consequence is a significant increase in performance, as compared to a non-threat control condition.

Ethnic Identification   Generational effects in performance are paralleled by differences in ethnic identification. Second-generation West Indian immigrants are significantly less likely to identify as West Indian. It is important to note, however, that even second-generation students in this sample were more identified as West Indian than as African American. This makes a strong test of the ethnic identification and stereotype threat hypothesis difficult, in that those who might be most strongly identified as African American are not well represented in the sample. Nonetheless, the fact that we found a clear trend in the predicted direction, in the face of relatively weak differences in ethnic identification, suggests that the influence of identification is a real phenomenon.

This study was with undergraduate students at a public university in New York City, a context whose particular features need to be kept in mind. Accordingly, we can not generalize to the population of West Indian immigrants at large. At the same time, the general composition both of the immediate university setting and the larger community could well be influential. Stereotype lift effects might be more common, for example, when there is a viable West Indian community with which one can identify. Although we talk in a language of contrasts convenient to experimental design, that is, a contrast between identification as West Indian or African American, it is evident to us that ethnic identification in immigrant communities is resistant to such simple dichotomies. Open-ended responses to a question asking for ethnic identification frequently elicit multiple terms that include references to both race and ethnicity. Both the labels themselves and the meanings associated with the categories differ among first- and second-generation Afro Caribbean immigrants.

Experimenter Effects

We had anticipated a possible three-way interaction when race of experimenter was included in the analysis, such that the predicted two-way interaction between generation and diagnostic condition would be more likely to occur with white experimenters and less likely, or even absent, in the presence of black experimenters. This three-way interaction did not emerge. However, race of experimenter clearly influenced the performance of our participants, as shown in the two significant two way interactions between experimenter and both diagnostic condition and generation. White experimenters elicited better performance when the test was diagnostic and when the participants were first-generation; black experimenters elicited better performance when the test was non-diagnostic and when the participants were second-generation. The finding that second-generation students do better with a black experimenter is consistent with other studies that a context with a higher percentage of minority faculty was more favorable for black and Latino students. The difference between first- and second-generation students in these different experimenter conditions is perhaps more easily understood if we consider the differing meta-stereotypes of first- and second-generation students. First-generation immigrants believe that their group is regarded more favorably by society in general, which we can assume would be defined largely in terms of the white majority. Accordingly, a white experimenter may act as a proxy for that larger reference group and lead participants to want to live up to that perceived standard and distinguish themselves from the African American image that they view as significantly less favorable. Second-generation students, in contrast, have a diminished view of the meta-stereotype of West Indians and are at the same time more likely to see themselves as defined by the stereotype of African Americans.

Future Directions

A key question for future research concerns the possible mediators of the generation performance relationship. Although identification is clearly related to generation, as well as to stereotype threat, it alone can not account for the differences between first- and second generation respondents. As is the case for stereotype threat research in general, the search for mediating mechanisms continues. One possibility is that differences in motivational states or self-regulatory focus may be related to the generational patterns. It might be that first-generation West Indians are more characterized by a promotion focus, in which the emphasis of achievement is on the approach to a desired goal. Second-generation West Indians, in contrast, because of more experiences with race-based discrimination in the United States, might be more motivated by a prevention strategy, in which achievement is seen as the avoidance of possible negative events.

The findings reported here contribute to the burgeoning literature on stereotype threat effects, adding immigration status to the categories of persons potentially subject to performance decrements under threat conditions. More importantly, however, the results speak to the dynamic relationship between person and context. West Indian immigrants do not automatically become subject to stereotype threat because they are black; rather they learn to experience stereotype threat as a result of their socialization into U.S. society where being categorized as black has negative contingencies. Because these connections are learned, one has to allow the possibility that, given optimal interventions, they can be overcome as well.

The generality of these findings for other immigrant populations is also of considerable interest. Immigrants from Mexico, for example, are often burdened with negative stereotypes of intellectual capability as well. They could be subject to the same kind of stereotype threat effects as we observed here among West Indians. In the case of Mexicans, however, it is not certain whether first-generation immigrants would be impervious to stereotype threat effects, given the negative stereotypes that often characterize both Mexican nationals and Mexican immigrants. Thus, first-generation Mexican immigrants might show equal or even greater stereotype threat effects than would later generations. In contrast, we might think about a group such as Asian immigrants, for whom the stereotype of a high-performing "model minority" is frequently invoked. Would stereotype lift effects be more evident in this group when the group stereotype was made salient? These questions speak to the complexity of the immigrant experience and the need for careful consideration of specific stereotypes and contexts.

These results also speak to the importance of understanding social psychological processes inherent to the immigration experience. Sociologists and demographers have generated a wealth of data on the fortunes and adaptations of immigrants, including occupational status, educational outcomes, and intermarriage patterns. Underlying these group level analyses are a wealth of psychological processes that need to be unpacked and articulated. We suggest here that stereotype threat is one of the psychological processes that may be at work. We of course recognize that our data are based exclusively on college students, considering the ways in which a form of academic performance can be affected by stereotype threat. Whether this process could also be detected in more complex settings remains to be established. More than simply an account of the numbers of people entering a country, immigration is a dynamic process of interplay between people and their social and cultural environment. Further analysis of the psychological processes will allow us to determine what factors either enhance or impede the participation of immigrants in their new culture.

Credits

Figure 1.1 & 1.2 From Thomas N. Robinson, MD, MPH, Dina L. G. Borzekowski, EdD, Donna M. Matheson, PhD and Helena C. Kraemer, PhD, 2007, "Effects of Fast Food Branding on Young Children's Taste Preferences," *Archives of Pediatrics & Adolescent Medicine*, 161(8): 792–797. Reprinted by permission of American Medical Association.

Figure 1.4 Source: Guttmacher Institute, Community health centers and family planning, *In Brief*, New York: Guttmacher, 2001, <http://www.guttmacher.org/pubs/ib_6-01.html>, accessed March 10, 2008.

Figure 2.2 From "Learning English in a Midwestern urban high school: A case study of an ELL Vietnamese student by Yanan Fan, PhD as appeared in *Dissertation Abstracts*. Reprinted by permission of the author.

Figure 2.4a From Tawnya J. Adkins Covert and Philo C. Wasburn, 2007, "Measuring Media Bias: A Content Analysis of *Time* and *Newsweek* Coverage of Domestic Social Issues, 1975–2000," *Social Science Quarterly*, Vol. 88(3), pp. 690–706. Reprinted by permission of Blackwell Publishing Ltd.

Figure 2.4b From Juliette C. Rederstorff, Nicole T. Buchanan, Isis H. Settles, 2007, "The Moderating Roles of Race And Gender-Role Attitudes In The Relationship Between Sexual Harrassment and Psychological Well-Being," *Psychology of Women Quarterly*, Vol. 31 (1), pp. 50–61. Reprinted by permission of Blackwell Publishing Ltd.

Figure 2.5 © EBSCO Publishing, Inc., 2007. All rights reserved. Reprinted by permission.

Figure 3.3 "Learner Demands to be Shocked" from *Obedience to Authority: An Experimental Review* by Stanley Milgram. Copyright © 1974 by Stanley Milgram. Reprinted by permission of HarperCollins Publishers and Pinter & Martin, Ltd.

Figure 3.5 Reprinted with permission from the American Association for Public Opinion Research.

Figure 6.1 From NPR - Swing Districts Frequency Questionnaire. Reprinted by permission of Greenberg Quinlan Rosner Research.

Chapter 6 Table From General Social Survey, 2004. Reprinted by permission of National Opinion Research Center.

Chapter 9 Graph 1 & Figure 9.11 From Aart C. Liefbroer and Edith Dourleijn, 2006, "Unmarried Cohabitation and Union Stability: Testing the Role of Diffusion Using Data From 16 European Countries," *Demography*, 43(2): p. 203–221. Reprinted by permission of Demography.

Figure 9.4 From General Social Survey, 2004. Reprinted by permission of National Opinion Research Center.

Chapter 10 Table 4 & 5 From General Social Survey, 2004. Reprinted by permission of National Opinion Research Center.

Figure 12.2 Reprinted by permission of The Spencer Foundation.

Abstract & Article: From Ronald Weitzer and Steven A. Tuch, 2005, "Racially Biased Policing: Determinants of Citizen Perceptions," *Social Forces*, Volume 83, no. 3. Copyright © 2005 by the University of North Carolina Press. Used by permission of the publisher. www.uncpress.unc.edu.

Abstract & Article: From Pamela Perry, 2001, "White Means Never Having to Say You're Ethnic: White Youth and the Construction of 'Cultureless' Identities," *Journal of Contemporary Ethnography*, Vol. 30(1), pp. 56–91. Copyright 2001 by Sage Publications Inc. Journals. Reproduced with permission of Sage Publications Inc. Journals in the format Other book via Copyright Clearance Center.

Abstract & Article: From Kay Deaux, Nida Bikmen, Alwyn Gilkes, Ana Ventuneac, Yvanne Joseph, Yasser A. Payne and Claude M. Steele, 2007, "Becoming American: Stereotype Threat Effects in Afro-Caribbean Immigrant Groups," *Social Psychology Quarterly*, Vol. 70, No. 4, pp. 384–404. Reprinted by permission of American Sociological Association and Kay Deaux.

Name Index

Atkinson, M., 26

Babbie, E., 126
Bell, S., 124
Borgadus, E., 118
Brewer, P., 144
Brown, J., 23

Caplan, J., 59
Chavez, L., 212
Cherlin, A., 14
Connor, S., 87, 94
Crozat, M., 138
Cushman, P., 288

Davis, D., 173
Davis, F., 275
DeMello, M. 59
DeRango, K., 131
Downey, L., 218
Draus, Pl, 74, 104
Duncan, O., 131

Fine, G., 271
Fischer, J., 59
Foddy, W., 166
Foster, G., 207

Gantz, W.,1
Gee, G., 117
Glassner, B., 5
Gallup, G., 90
Gordon, P., 135
Gurney, J., 271
Guttmacher Institute, 23

Harris Interactive, 25
Hawkes, D., 25, 136
Heise, D., 135
Hochschild, A., 263
Horne, J., 59
Humphreys, L., 67, 72
Hurwitz, J., 166

Kane, R., 81
Kang, M., 59
Katovich, M. 278
Kleg, M., 140

Lauzen, M., 210
Liefbroer, A., 245
Luker, K., 240

Mathematica Policy Research, Inc., 20
Milgram, S., 69
Mohai, P., 290
Mooney, C., 82

Ong, A., 190

Palmgreen, P., 194
Payne, B., 184
Perry, P., 121, 272
Pew Research Center, 6
Presser, S., 166
Piliavin, I., 67

Quinn, M., 212

Rashotte, L., 212
Rathje, W., 206
Robinson, T, 1-2
Rosenberg, M., 134
Rummel, N., 202

Savelsberg, J., 82
Scarce, R., 75
Schuman, H., 169
Scribner, R., 198
Schweingruber, 268
Sherman, R., 266, 270-271, 277
Smith, D., 113
Smith, T., 166
Stack, S., 13
Stevenson, R., 222

Tan, A., 179
Taylor, S., 68
Tobler, N, 23

Valquera, E., 102
Van Laar, C., 140
Van Maanen, J., 68, 263
Vidich, A., 73

Weitzer, R., 119, 120
Whyte, W., 18
Wysong, E., 23

Zagumny, M. 23
Zhong, C., 203
Zimbardo, P., 70

Subject Index